A COMPREHENSIVE HISTORY OF THE LONDON CHURCH AND PARISH OF ST. MARY, THE VIRGIN, ALDERMANBURY

The Phoenix of Aldermanbury

The Wren fabric of the Church of St. Mary, Aldermanbury. (Courtesy of The Churchill Memorial Archive)

A COMPREHENSIVE HISTORY OF THE LONDON CHURCH AND PARISH OF ST. MARY, THE VIRGIN, ALDERMANBURY

The Phoenix of Aldermanbury

Christian E. Hauer, Jr.
and
William A. Young

The Edwin Mellen Press
Lewiston/Queenston/Lampeter

Library of Congress Cataloging-in-Publication Data

Hauer, Christian E. (Christian Ewing), 1930-
    A comprehensive history of the London church and parish of St.
Mary, the Virgin, Aldermanbury : the phoenix of Aldermanbury /
Christian E. Hauer, Jr., and William A. Young.
        p.   cm.
    Includes bibliographical references.
    ISBN 0-7734-9390-5
    1. St. Mary, the Virgin, Aldermanbury (Church : London, England)-
-History. 2. Winston Churchill Memorial and Library--History.
3. Westminster College (Fulton, Mo.)--History. 4. London (England)-
-Church history. 5. England--Church history. 6. Fulton (Mo.)-
-Church history. 7. Missouri--Church history. 8. Churches-
-England--Conservation and restoration. 9. Wren, Christopher, Sir,
1632-1723. I. Young, William A., 1945-   . II. Title.
BX5195.L6677H38   1993
283'.4212--dc20   93-36433
                                                                                                                             CIP

A CIP catalog record for this book
is available from the British Library.

Copyright © 1994 Christian E. Hauer, Jr. and William A. Young

All rights reserved. For information contact

The Edwin Mellen Press	The Edwin Mellen Press
Box 450	Box 67
Lewiston, New York	Queenston, Ontario
USA 14092-0450	CANADA L0S 1L0

The Edwin Mellen Press, Ltd.
Lampeter, Dyfed, Wales
UNITED KINGDOM SA48 7DY

Printed in the United States of America

*This book is dedicated
to*

Dr. Robert L.D.Davidson, OBE

and

Dr. Noel P. Mander, MBE, FSA

"In appreciation of their friendship, and of their work to restore the Church of St Mary, Aldermanbury, to the glorious state that Wren envisioned"

TABLE OF CONTENTS

List of Illustrations	ix
Preface	xxi

CHAPTER ONE: FOUNDATIONS—THE CITY, THE NEIGHBORHOOD, THE CHURCH (ca. 50- 1200 C.E.) — 1

Introduction	1
The City During Roman Times	1
The Aldermanbury-Cripplegate Neighborhood during Romano-British Times	4
London During Saxon Times	6
The Saxon Palace in Aldermanbury and its Successor	8
The Name "Aldermanbury"	10
The Foundation of the Church of St. Mary, Aldermanbury	12
Conclusion	15
Bibliography	16

CHAPTER TWO: A MEDIEVAL PARISH CHURCH (ca. 1200-1485) — 19

Introduction	19
A Native Son's Praise	20
London and the Norman Conquest	20
Institutions	23
The Parish	23
Sokes and Hagas (Haws)	27
Wards	28
Guilds	30
The Parish Church and Medieval Economics	32
The Church and Parish of St. Mary,	35

Aldermanbury during the Middle Ages
Conclusion 44
Bibliography 44

CHAPTER THREE: ST. MARY'S DURING THE 49
ENGLISH REFORMATION (1485-1639)
Introduction 49
The Coming of the Renaissance 49
The Tudor Dynasty 51
   Henry VII (1485-1509) 51
   Henry VIII (1509-1547) 52
      Aldermanbury during the Reign of Henry VIII 55
   Edward VI (1547-1553) 56
      Aldermanbury during the Reign of Edward VI 59
   Mary I (1553-1558) 60
   Elizabeth I (1558-1603) 62
      Excursus: The Puritan Movement 64
      Aldermanbury during the reign of Elizabeth I 66
      Excursus: William Shakespeare's 76
        Aldermanbury Connection
         John Heminges (ca. 1556-1630) 77
         Henry Condell (?-1627) 78
         The First Folio 79
         Conclusion 81
The Stuarts 81
   James I/VI (1603-1625) 81
      Aldermanbury during the Reign of James I/VI 86
Conclusion 93
Bibliography 94

CHAPTER FOUR: A PRESBYTERIAN PARISH 99
DURING TUMULTUOUS TIMES: THE
EDMUND CALAMY ERA (1639-1662)

Introduction	99
Edmund Calamy's Background before coming to St. Mary's (1600-1639)	100
The Stuarts (continued)	101
<u>Charles I (1625-1649): Prior to the Civil War (1625-1642)</u>	102
<u>Excursus: The City Polity</u>	105
Calamy's Early Years at St. Mary, Aldermanbury (1639-1642)	110
<u>*Excursus: Calamy's Patron—Robert Rich, Earl of Warwick*</u>	112
Calamy's Early Years (continued)	113
<u>Charles I: The Civil War and the Westminster Assembly (1642-1649)</u>	119
Calamy and Aldermanbury during the Civil War	123
The Commonwealth and the Protectorate	133
<u>The Cromwells (1649-1659)</u>	133
Calamy and Aldermanbury during the Commonwealth and Protectorate	135
<u>*Excursus: Allen and Margaret Robinett*</u>	137
Calamy and Aldermanbury during the Commonwealth and Protectorate (continued)	138
<u>*Excursus: John Milton's Association with Aldermanbury*</u>	141
Calamy and Aldermanbury during the Commonwealth and Protectorate (continued)	143
The Restoration and early Reign of Charles II	145
<u>General George Monck and the Restoration (1659-1660)</u>	145
Calamy's Role in the Restoration	146
<u>The Early Reign of Charles II (1660-1666)</u>	148
Calamy's Final Years	150
Conclusion	159
Bibliography	159

CHAPTER FIVE: THE PHOENIX OF ALDERMANBURY: THE PLAGUE, THE GREAT FIRE, AND THE REBUILDING BY SIR CHRISTOPHER WREN (1665-1677)   167

Introduction   167
The Stuarts (continued)   168
    The Later Years of Charles II (1666-1685)   168
       Finding a Successor for Edmund Calamy   170
    The Plague And Great Fire Of London (1665-1666)   171
       The Effects of the Fire on Aldermanbury   174
       The Parish after the Great Fire   176
    The Rebuilding Of The London Churches   178
       Excursus: Sir Christopher Wren and Robert Hooke   178
       Wren and Hooke's Rebuilding of the Church of St. Mary (1670-1677)   183
Conclusion   193
Bibliography   194

CHAPTER SIX: A PROSPEROUS PARISH (1677-1790)   199

Introduction   199
The Stuarts (continued)   200
    James II (1685-1688)   200
       Monmouth's Rebellion   200
       The Policies of James   201
       The Glorious Revolution   204
          Aldermanbury during The Last Years of Charles II (1677-1685) and the Reign of James II   207
          The Benjamin Calamy Era (1677-1683)   207
             Excursus: Sir George Jeffreys (1648-1689)   208

The Benjamin Calamy Era (continued)	213
The Nicolaus Stratford Era (1683-1689)	216
William III (1689-1702) and Mary II (1689-1694)	219
Anne (1702-1714)	221
Aldermanbury during the Reigns of William and Mary and Anne	227
The Short Incumbency of Ezekiel Hopkins (1689-1690)	227
The Lilley Butler Era (1690-1717)	227
The Early Hanoverians (1714-1760)	232
Aldermanbury during the Early Hanoverians	238
The Joshua Smith Era (1717-1731)	238
The William Sandford Era (1731-1754)	242
Conclusion	247
Bibliography	247
CHAPTER SEVEN: EXPANSION AND DECLINE DURING THE INDUSTRIAL REVOLUTION (1760-1887)	253
Introduction	253
The Later Hanoverians (1760-1837)	254
Aldermanbury under the Later Hanoverians	264
The John Lawrence Era (1755-1790)	264
The Charles Smith Era (1791-1802)	267
The James Salisbury Era (1802-1843)	270
Victoria and her Great Ministers (1837-1894)	279
Victorian London	286
Aldermanbury during the Victorian Age	292
The John Bean Era (1843-1854)	292
The Charles Collins Era (1854-1917)	295
Plans to Merge St. Mary, Aldermanbury with St. Michael, Bassishaw (1861-1872)	299
Conflict with the Charities Commission (1874-1887)	306

Conclusion	311
Bibliography	312
CHAPTER EIGHT: THE STRUGGLE FOR SURVIVAL (1887-1940)	315
Introduction	315
The End of Eras (1887-1914)	315
Aldermanbury during the End of Eras	319
<u>The Charles Collins Era (1854-1917) (continued)</u>	319
More Plans to Merge St. Mary, Aldermanbury with other parishes (1887-1907)	319
The Great War and its Aftermath (1914-1920)	327
Union with St. Alphage, London Wall (1908-1917)	333
The Great Depression and the "Gathering Storm" (1920-1939)	337
<u>The H. A. Mason Era (1917-1940)</u>	341
Excursus: The Inns of Aldermanbury	346
<u>The H. A. Mason Era (continued)</u>	349
World War II (1939-1945)	350
St. Mary, Aldermanbury, and the Second Great Fire of London (29 December, 1940)	353
Conclusion	355
Bibliography	356
CHAPTER NINE: FROM THE ASHES AGAIN (1941-)	359
Introduction	359
War Goes On	360
After the War	365
<u>Austerity</u>	366
<u>The World Outside</u>	366
<u>Domestic Politics</u>	368

London	368
The Post-War Fate of the Church of St. Mary, Aldermanbury in London (1941-1961)	369
The Selection and Securing of the Church of St. Mary as The Winston Churchill Memorial (1961-1964)	374
The Reconstruction of the Church of St. Mary on the Westminster College Campus (1964-1969)	380
St. Mary Aldermanbury as the Churchill Memorial (1969-	386
Conclusion: St. Mary's "Westminster" Connection	389
Bibliography	390
CHAPTER TEN: THE TREASURES OF ST. MARY ALDERMANBURY	393
Introduction	393
Before the Great Fire	393
Wren's Rebuilding	394
After the Union with St. Alphage, London Wall	394
After the Restoration on the Campus of Westminster College	396
Conclusion	405
APPENDIX: THE CLERGY OF ST. MARY ALDERMANBURY	407
GENERAL BIBLIOGRAPHY	411
INDEX	431

Illustrations

Frontispiece

The Wren fabric of the Church of St. Mary, Aldermanbury. (Courtesy of The Churchill Memorial Archive)

Figure 1.1

Cripplegate Fort in relation to the Aldermanbury parish. This map portrays the northwest corner of the City of London within the walls, including the locations of the Church of St. Mary, Aldermanbury and its parish (hatched), the Aldermanbury tenement, and Guildhall, as well as the layout of the earlier Roman fort ("Cripplegate fort"). The deviation of Aldermanbury to the west and Basinghall Street to the east would be explained by the location of the Roman amphitheater in the Guildhall area. (Courtesy of Mr. Tony Dyson, FSA)

Figure 1.2

Overview of the site of St. Mary, Aldermanbury, during the excavation directed by Prof. W.F. Grimes. After the removal of the Wren fabric of the Church, Prof. Grimes conducted an archaeological excavation of the site. Note the Shakespeare monument in the south Churchyard. (Courtesy of Guildhall Library, Corporation of London)

Figure 1.3

The 1181 Inquisition of London Churches. Dean Ralph DeDiceto (the "good dean" of St. Paul's Cathedral) ordered an inquisition (inventory) of churches in the diocese in 1181. This document includes the earliest known written reference to the Church of St. Mary, Aldermanbury. St. Mary's was by this time a flourishing parish Church and so must have had some history already behind it. (Courtesy of Guildhall Library, Corporation of London Guildhall Library MS 25.504, FO84R [Modern 87R])

Figure 2.1

A reconstruction of the 1437 Church of St. Mary. Mr. Bryce Gordon executed this conjectural drawing of the 1437 Perpendicular Gothic Church of St. Mary, Aldermanbury, utilizing information collected by Prof. Hauer (the Copper Plate Map, the description in the Wren family work (Parentalia), the 1929 report of the Royal Commission on Historical Monuments, and Prof. Grimes' archaeological excavation). The precise sort of stone and the size of the blocks used in the structure is not known. (Courtesy of The Churchill Memorial Archive)

Figure 2.2

The tower stairs from the medieval Church of St. Mary, Aldermanbury, as incorporated into the present reconstruction. Information from Christopher Wren, Jr., in the Wren family volume Parentalia, the 1929 report of the Royal Commission on Historical Monuments, and Prof. Grimes' investigations combine to suggest that this spiral staircase, originally in the lower course of the tower, was part of the 1437 Gothic St. Mary's. It now rises from the gallery level in the tower of the reconstructed Wren Church. (Courtesy of The Churchill Memorial Archive)

Figure 2.3

The foundations of the Church of St. Mary, Aldermanbury. This small relief in the permanent exhibit of the Churchill Memorial Museum shows the foundations of the successive St. Mary Aldermanbury buildings, from the early rectangular Church (later enhanced with side chapels) through the 1437 Gothic foundation reused by Wren. Note that Wren also used a wall of the earliest building to support one row of his columns. The relief is based on Prof. Grimes' site plan. (Courtesy of Mr. Bruce Hackmann)

Figure 3.1

The Copper Plate Map (1553). The "Moorgate Plate" of the Copper Plate Map (1553) supplies the earliest known view of the Church of St. Mary, Aldermanbury. It exaggerates the size of the tower in relationship to the nave of the Church, a convention typical of 16th/17th century view maps. (Courtesy of the Museum of London)

Figure 3.2

A Portrait of William Shakespeare from the First Folio of Shakespeare's Plays (1623). John Heminges and Henry Condell were Aldermanbury residents and officers in the Church of St. Mary, Aldermanbury, who were close friends of William Shakespeare and actors in many of his plays. In order to preserve and protect the authenticity of their friend's plays, they edited the plays and published this First Folio edition after his death. Theirs was the first publication of such plays as "Macbeth," "Julius Caesar," and "As You Like It." This portrait of Shakespeare, by Martin Droeshout, is one of two images of the dramatist considered authentic. (Courtesy of Folger Shakespeare Library, Washington, D.C.)

Figure 3.3

The Shakespeare monument in the Aldermanbury Churchyard. This monument, erected by Mr. C. C. Walker in 1895, stands in tribute to the work of John Heminges and Henry Condell in preserving the plays of William Shakespeare. It was left in place after the removal of the Wren fabric and can be seen today in the park created on the site of the Church in London. (Courtesy of The Churchill Memorial Archive)

Figure 4.1

Edmund Calalmy. Dr. Edmund Calamy was perpetual curate of St. Mary, Aldermanbury, from 1639 until 1662, and a leader of the Presbyterian wing of the Puritan movement in the Church of England. (Courtesy of The Churchill Memorial Archive)

Figure 4.2

The Robinett Wedding. The 29 September, 1653 wedding of Allen and Margaret Robinett is recorded in the Parish Register in the Church of St. Mary, Aldermanbury. During a service of worship at a biennial meeting of the Robbinett Family Association at the Churchill Memorial, the wedding was re-enacted in the Church of St. Mary, Aldermanbury, with Dr. William Young playing the role of minister Edmund Calamy, and two teenage descendants of Allen and Margaret Robinett representing their ancestors. (Courtesy of The Churchill Memorial Archive)

Figure 4.3

King Charles II. The dedication plate of William Morgan's map and panorama, "London &c Actually Survey'd" (1682), shows Morgan's step-grandfather and professional mentor, John Ogilby, presenting the subscription book for his own

xii

survey to King Charles II and Queen Catherine of Braganza. Dr. Edmund Calamy (see Figure 4.1) was active in the Restoration of the monarchy, which brought Charles II to the throne. (Courtesy of The Museum of London)

Figure 4.4

The Second Wedding of John Milton. This page from the Aldermanbury parish register records the wedding of famous author John Milton and Katherine Woodcock, a resident of the Aldermanbury parish, which took place on 12, November 1656. (Courtesy of Guildhall Library, Corporation of London, Guildhall Library MS 53, 572, Voc 1)

Figure 5.1

Sir Christopher Wren (the Pierce Bust). The original of this bust of Sir Christopher Wren (1673), by sculptor Edward Pierce, stands in the Ashmolean Museum, Oxford. This reproduction is in the Wren section of the Churchill Memorial Museum. (Courtesy of The Churchill Memorial Archive)

Figures 5.2 and 5.3

The Wren City Church Account Books. Two pages from the Account Books for the Reconstruction of the London City Churches, show charges for the rebuilding of the Church of St. Mary, Aldermanbury, according to the plan of Sir Christopher Wren. Figure 5.2 shows charges paid to the famous mason Joshua Marshall, and 5.3 shows the mark of Grace Smith, one of the craftswomen who participated in the reconstruction of the City churches. It is the only signed receipt in the St. Mary, Aldermanbury, account books. (Courtesy of Guildhall Library, Corporation of London, Guildhall Library MS 25.539, Vol 1)

Figure 5.4

Sir Christopher Wren (Royal Society Portrait). Wren was a founder of the Royal Society and served as president, 1681- 1683. His "presidential portrait" is attributed to Closterman. (Courtesy of the Royal Society)

Figure 5.5

Morgan Panorama. The Morgan map and panorama (1682) furnish the earliest

xiii

views of the Wren fabric of St. Mary, Aldermanbury. They show the building before the lead lantern was installed atop the stone tower. This detail from the panorama shows the tower (shaded). (Courtesy of The Museum of London)

Figure 6.1

Judge George Jeffreys. Baron George Jeffreys became known as the "Hanging Judge" because of his role in the "Bloody Assizes" after Monmouth's Rebellion in 1685. Jeffreys took up residence in the Aldermanbury parish in 1671 and was an active member of the Church of St. Mary. Although he moved from the parish in 1685, he was buried in a vault beneath the chancel in 1698, a decade after his death in the Tower of London. This portrait, by an unknown artist, is in the National Portrait Gallery. (Courtesy of the National Portrait Gallery)

Figure 6.2

Judge George Jeffreys' house in Aldermanbury. In 1671, when he became Common Sergeant of the City of London, Judge Jeffreys received title to a tenement located behind Nos. 18 and 19 Aldermanbury. He remained in the house until he moved to Westminster in 1685. (Courtesy of the Corporation of London Records Office)

Figure 6.3

Swan with Two Necks Inn. This prominent coaching inn was located on the southern boundary of the Aldermanbury parish. (Courtesy of Guildhall Library, Corporation of London)

Figure 6.4

A Table of Fare for coaches leaving from the Swan with Two Necks Inn. (Courtesy of Guildhall Library, Corporation of London)

Figure 7.1

An 1886 map of the Aldermanbury parish. (Courtesy of Guildhall Library, Corporation of London)

xiv

Figure 7.2

Aldermanbury Business Card. A card from one of the many businesses in Aldermanbury illustrates the 19th century commercialization of the parish. (Courtesy of Guildhall Library, Corporation of London)

Figure 7.3

The Church of St. Mary, Aldermanbury (1814). This is the best rendering of the Wren fabric of the Church, prior to the Victorian "improvements." The impression was prepared for a publication on London Churches which appeared in 1830, but the originals were engraved in 1814. (Courtesy of TheChurchill Memorial Archive)

Figure 7.4

Grave Robbers. An early nineteenth century engraving shows grave robbers stealing a lead coffin from St. Mary, Aldermanbury. (Courtesy of Guildhall Library, Corporation of London)

Figure 7.5

A 19th century warehouse in Aldermanbury. (Courtesy of Guildhall Library, Corporation of London)

Figure 8.1

The east end of the nave of St. Mary, Aldermanbury. This sketch was drawn following the Victorian refurbishment of the church, described by the Wren Society as "a most unfortunate restoration." The pulpit, altar and reredoes were of stone. They were removed to make way for oak furnishings from St. Alphage, London Wall, after the amalgamation of the two parishes early in the 20th century. (Courtesy of The Churchill Memorial Archive)

Figure 8.2

The interior of St. Mary Aldermanbury (early 20th Century). This widely published photograph was taken following the installation of the oak pulpit, reredoes, altar and pews from St. Alphage, London Wall. The organ occupied the easternmost bay of the north aisle, the Lady Chapel two bays at the east end of the south aisle. The wooden chancel furnishings were less alien to the Wren ambience than their stone predecessors, but the two latter innovations represent departures from the Wren style. (Churchill Memorial Archive)

Figure 8.3

St. Mary, Aldermanbury (1930). This photograph was taken from a point near Gresham Street, looking north on Aldermanbury. (Courtesy of The Churchill Memorial Archive)

Figure 8.4

1934 Programme. Before it was bombed in 1940, the Church of St. Mary, Aldermanbury was open on workdays to provide shelter for workers who came into the City on the cheaper early hour fares and needed a place to stay until their places of employment opened. There was also a program of weekly concerts and services on weekdays rather than Sundays. These efforts to offer a relevant ministry to a changing parish were quite successful. (Courtesy of The Churchill Memorial Archive)

Figure 9.1

Sir Winston Churchill on the Westminster Campus. Sir Winston Churchill approaches Washington West House, then the home of the President of Westminster College, on March 5, 1946, for a luncheon, with President Harry S Truman on the left and Westminster President Franc L. McCluer on the right. The menu included Callaway County country ham, about which Sir Winston remarked: "The pig has reached the highest state of evolution." (Courtesy of The Churchill Memorial Archive)

Figure 9.2

The "Iron Curtain" Speech. Sir Winston S. Churchill stands at the podium in the gymnasium of Westminster College on March 5, 1946, delivering his Green Foundation lecture, "The Sinews of Peace," better known as the "Iron Curtain" speech. The podium, once a pulpit in the College's Swope Chapel, is on permanent display in the Churchill Memorial Museum and was used by other prominent speakers, including former Soviet president Mikhail Gorbachev on May 6, 1992. (Courtesy of TheChurchill Memorial Archive)

xvi

Figure 9.3

Westminster College President R. L. D. Davidson and reconstruction architect Marshall Sisson, conferring in the ruins of the Church in London. (Courtesy of The Churchill Memorial Archive)

Figure 9.4

The fabric of the Church showing the devastation caused by the bombing raid of 29 December, 1940. (Courtesy of The Churchill Memorial Archive)

Figure 9.5

The park created on the site of the Church, after removal of the Wren fabric to Westminster College. (Courtesy of The Churchill Memorial Archive)

Figure 9.6

The plaque placed by Westminster College in the park created at the site of St. Mary, Aldermanbury in London, after the removal of the fabric of the Church. (Courtesy of The Churchill Memorial Archive)

Figure 9.7

President Harry S Truman turning the symbolic first shovel for the Churchill Memorial on 19 April, 1964. The ceremony was held at the historic Westminster Columns, since the site on campus for the Memorial had not been finally settled. Mr. Truman cheerfully turned spadeful after spadeful as photographers called out, "One more, Mr. President!" (Courtesy of The Churchill Memorial Archive)

Figure 9.8

Master stonemason Eris Lytle. Mr. Lytle of the John Epple Construction Company, was responsible for laying the stones of the reconstructed Church of St. Mary, Aldermanbury, which had been transported from London. He proved himself a worthy successor to the great master masons who worked with Sir Christopher Wren. Lytle's recorded memories of the project are held in the Churchill Memorial. (Courtesy of The Churchill Memorial Archive)

xvii

Figure 9.9

The "greatest jigsaw puzzle in the history of architecture." The stones of the Church of St. Mary, Aldermanbury, are laid out on the campus of Westminster College in preparation for the reconstruction. (Courtesy of The Churchill Memorial Archive)

Figure 9.10

Westminster College President R. L. D. Davidson; College Board of Trustees Member and Project Chairman, Neal Wood; British Reconstruction architect Marshall Sisson; and American architect Frederick Sternberg announcing the Churchill Memorial project. (Courtesy of The Churchill Memorial Archive)

Figure 9.11

The Church of St. Mary, Aldermanbury, reconstructed according to the design of Sir Christopher Wren. This view of the Church from the southwest, shows the statue of Sir Winston Churchill by sculptor Franta Belsky. (Courtesy of The Churchill Memorial Archive)

Figure 9.12

Lord Mountbatten of Burma, Churchill's daughter Lady Mary Soames, Gen. Mark Clark, official representative for President Richard Nixon, and R.L.D. Davidson, Westminster College president at the rehallowing of the church and the dedication of the Churchill Memorial on 7 May, 1969. (Courtesy of The Churchill Memorial Archive)

Figure 9.13

The Breakthrough Sculpture. This sculpture, made from panels of the Berlin Wall, was designed and executed by Churchill's granddaughter, Edwina Sandys. It symbolizes the end of the era of the Iron Curtain. It was dedicated on 9 November, 1990, by former U. S. President Ronald Reagan, one year after the Berlin Wall "came down". (Courtesy of The Churchill Memorial Archive)

Figure 9.14

Former President of the U.S.S.R. Mikhail Gorbachev speaking before the xviii

Breakthrough Sculpture. On May 6, 1992, President Gorbachev came to Westminster College and spoke before a crowd of 20,000. As Sir Winston Churchill had done in 1946, Mr. Gorbachev delivered a Green Foundation lecture in which he called for international cooperation in facing the common enemies of humanity. History had come full circle! (Courtesy of TheChurchill Memorial Archive)

Figure 10.1

The altar of the reconstructed Church of St. Mary, Aldermanbury. The reredoes above the altar was designed by reconstruction architect Marshall Sisson, with carvings by Arthur Ayres, in the style of Grinling Gibbons, the master woodcarver who worked with Sir Christopher Wren in the rebuilding of St. Paul's Cathedral and at least a few of the City churches. The communion silver on the altar is the 17th century set from the Church of St. Anne and St. Agnes. The Ten Commandments above the altar were a typical feature of 17th century churches in England. (Courtesy of The Churchill Memorial Archive)

Figure 10.2

The Mander tracker organ. This organ, built under the direction of Noel P. Mander at St. Peter's Organworks, London, is one of the finest Baroque organs in North America. The central part of the case dates to the 18th century and is from the parish church in Woolwich, Kent. Two flute pipes by George England, who built St. Mary's first organ, are incorporated into the instrument. The crown and bishops' mitres atop the organ, symbolizing the Restoration of 1660, are from the London City Church of St. Michael Paternoster Royal. (Courtesy of Mr. Bruce Hackmann)

Figure 10.3

A 17th century cherub from one of the vestry screens. This carving, from Wren's St. Dionis Backchurch, was incorporated into the reconstructed Church of St. Mary, Aldermanbury. Perhaps from the shop of Grinling Gibbons, this cherub and the surrounding adornments served as the basic motifs for Arthur Ayres' 20th century reproduction carvings on the reredoes gallery and pulpit. (Courtesy of The Churchill Memorial Archive)

Figure 10.4

Pulpit carving in the reconstructed Church. A 20th century cherub, by artist Arthur Ayres, adorns the pulpit of St. Mary, Aldermanbury. (Courtesy of The Churchill Memorial Archive)

Figure 10.5

Victorian Communion Silver. This communion silver was in the St. Mary, Aldermanbury safe on the night of 29 December, 1940. It still bears the scars of the Blitz. The 18th century bust of the Virgin Mary, which once again caps the Churchwarden's staff, can be seen in the right rear. (Courtesy of The Churchill Memorial Archive)

Figure 10.6

Candlesticks from Westminster Cathedral. The Roman Catholic Westminster Cathedral was the source of St. Mary's handsome candlesticks. They were a gift to the Church of St. Mary, Aldermanbury, from the Cathedral. The communion silver is the St. Anne and St. Agnes plate, a memorial to Canon C. B. Mortlock. Some of the pieces were originally from St. John Zachary, a Church not rebuilt after the Great Fire of 1666. (Courtesy of Dr. Christian Hauer, FSA, FRSA)

Figure 10.7

Lord Mayor's Sword and Stand. As a London city church, St. Mary, Aldermanbury, required a sword stand for the Lord Mayor's ceremonial sword during official visits. The St. Mary's stand bears the arms of the Worshipful Company of Haberdashers and is a replica of a 17th century stand in Haberdashers Hall. St. Mary's was the guild Church of the Haberdashers; they and a company of other British donors catalogued in chapter 10 made the gift of the stand. The restored 18th century sword was presented by the Corporation of the City of London. (Courtesy of Dr. Christian Hauer, FSA, FRSA)

Figure 10.8

Dr. Noel P. Mander, MBE, FSA. Dr. Mander, organbuilder for St. Mary Aldermanbury, Christ Church, Canterbury, and St. Paul's Cathedral, is official representative of the Churchill Memorial in the United Kingdom. He was an early advocate of the project to bring the Church to Westminster College and is responsible for many of the furnishings and adornments which enhance the beauty of the Church. (Courtesy of N. P. Mander, Ltd.)

Preface

The Phoenix of Aldermanbury is a labor of love, not an exercise in specialized scholarship. Our scholarly credentials are in the study of the world of antiquity and ancient texts, not ecclesiastical history or the history of Britain. In these fields we are, like many of the readers of this book, amateurs and laypersons. Although the methods of our own disciplines have enabled us to make what we hope are informed judgments, we do not pretend to an expertise beyond our areas of specialization. Rather, we have tried to write a book for laypersons by laypersons, with the hope that even experts in the fields it transgresses will not take offense, but find something of interest and value in what we have to say.

We have tried to do our homework. Even the confessed amateur owes that to readers. Professor Hauer has a longstanding avocational interest in the history and antiquities of Britain. Professor Young has a concern for the dynamics of life within local religious communities. We have attempted to draw upon the primary sources—documentary, archaeological, and topographic. We have consulted the most reliable secondary sources we could find. We have walked the streets of Aldermanbury parish and much of the City of London, trying to visualize them as they were in times past. Above all, we have been instructed by experts who have graciously shared with us their unpublished as well as published research which bears on our project.

Our primary inspiration for writing this book has been the restored Christopher Wren fabric of the Church of St. Mary the Virgin, Aldermanbury. As most of our readers are aware, the stones of St. Mary, Aldermanbury, were brought to Westminster College in Fulton, Missouri, from London to crown the Winston S. Churchill Churchill Memorial and Library in the U.S. We salute the vision and hard work that realized the remarkable achievement of St. Mary's rebirth, the Phoenix of Aldermanbury's most recent rise from her ashes. We have been associated with the Church of St. Mary, Aldermanbury, for a combined total of forty years. It is a privilege to enjoy the beauty and symbolism of the Church and to worship in it. It is a particular honor for us to be able to lead worship, to preach, and to celebrate the sacraments and ordinances of the Church in a setting where inspired human art bears such tangible witness to the glory of God. And the appreciation grows when one delves into the past to encounter the great cloud of witnesses associated with its history—people of faith, energy and vision, but also with human foibles rather like our own. Our admiration for the people of Aldermanbury, some famous and most quite ordinary, whose lives weave the fabric of the story we are about to tell, will, we hope, be evident on the pages of this book.

Early in this project we decided <u>not</u> to write a typical parish history, full of sometimes trivial information about the church but unconnected to the outside world. Rather, we committed ourselves to the task of placing the nearly thousand year history of one London parish, St. Mary, Aldermanbury, in its social, economic, and political as well as ecclesiastical contexts. We have related the history of the parish to the history of the City of London and Britain, and even, on occasion, Europe and the wider world. We have not attempted radically new interpretations of the larger history, but have tried to follow what seemed to us a moderate path guided by established historical perspectives.

Our work <u>does</u> have a point of view, which we readily acknowledge. It is generally pro-British and favorably disposed toward the principles of liberty and democracy. From the 16th through the 18th centuries that means also viewing positively the Protestant cause, as did the majority of parishoners in Aldermanbury parish whose views have survived. Sometimes the connection between events in the larger worlds and events in the parish is obvious, as when the moderate Presbyterian stance of the clergy and leading laity of Aldermanbury put them first at odds with Charles I and the Cavaliers, then at odds with the regicides and radical Roundheads, and finally at the heart of the scheme to restore the Stuart monarchy. At other times one is left wondering. Did the vestry sell its South Sea bonds before the "Bubble" burst, or did the parish endowments suffer the consequences of the collapse? But we believe that, even when a direct connection between events in the parish and events outside does not even lend itself to speculation, we understand things better by having the larger picture ready to hand. Professional historians and serious history buffs carry that picture in their heads. Although some of our readers will fall into those categories, many others will, we hope, appreciate having the backdrop to our central story provided as part of the narrative.

There have been few histories of St. Mary, Aldermanbury, and its parish. The only major piece of critical scholarship on the complete history is a long article by Charles F. W. Goss, "A History of the Parish of St-Mary-the-Virgin, Aldermanbury" (1944). A devoted churchwarden, Mr. Pierson Cathrick Carter published a useful and interesting compendium entitled <u>History of the Parish of St Mary the Virgin,</u>

Aldermanbury (1913). Fortunately, there is good primary documentation on the Church and parish from 1567, when the keeping of Church records was officially ordained. Guildhall Library, London, preserves the vestry minutes, parish registers, churchwardens' account books and a host of other parish documents. Grants from Mr. and Mrs. Whitney R. Harris and the Library Committee of the Churchill Memorial enabled the microfilming of some of these records so that they might be available to scholars at the Memorial Library. Dr. Noel Mander located a copy of the Harleian Society Publication of the Parish Registers, which is also in the Memorial collection. The Guildhall Library also has wills, charters, and deeds which give a fleeting glimpse of the medieval history of the parish. The Bishop of London's Visitation Returns (most from the 19th century) provide insight into the recent history of the parish. The files of the Church Commissioners of the Church of England contain material on the amalgamation of St. Mary, Aldermanbury, with St. Alphage, London Wall, and the securing of permission to remove the fabric of St. Mary's to Westminster College. The archives of the Churchill Memorial document the story of the reconstruction of the Church on the Westminster campus. Other institutions consulted include the Museum of London and its archaeological service, the Royal Commission on Historical Monuments, the Sir John Soanes Museum, the British Library, the Codrington Library (All Souls College, Oxford), Cambridge University Library, the Royal Society, the Royal College of Surgeons Library, and the Royal Institute of British Architects. We are well aware that more material in various libraries and institutions in the United Kingdom and elsewhere remain to be consulted in order for the complete story of Aldermanbury to be told. Therefore, this study must be considered only a first step in a longer process of research on the parish.

We would like to express our gratitude to the above institutions, for granting us access to their holdings. In particular, we are indebted to the following staff members: Mr. Ralph Hyde, FSA, Keeper of Prints and Maps at the Guildhall Library (and his assistants Mr. Jeremy Smith and Mr. John Fisher); Mr. C. R. H. Cooper and Mr. Stephen Freeth, Keepers of Manuscripts at Guildhall Library (and Mrs. Clare Clubb, former Deputy Keeper of Manuscripts); Mr. E. G. W. Bill, Lambeth Palace Librarian; and Mr. David Armstrong, Records Officer for the Church Commissioners (Church of England).

We express our particular thanks to Mr. Tony Dyson, FSA, and Mr. John Schofield, FSA, of the Museum of London Archaeological Service (formerly the

Department of Urban Archaeology) who graciously shared their research on Aldermanbury with us. Mr. Dyson reviewed the manuscript of Ch. 1 and 2 and saved us from some embarrassing errors. The late W. F. Grimes, excavator of the site of St. Mary, Aldermanbury, and director of much of the early post-War archaeological investigation in the City of London, granted us two interviews which enhanced our understanding of the early history of the parish. We pay tribute to his memory and his outstanding contributions to scholarship.

We are also grateful for the support provided by Westminster College. Sabbatical leaves, Bushman travel grants, and small research awards were fundamental to our work on this book. Mrs. Elizabeth Hauer and Mrs. Barabara Ault of Reeves Library, Westminster College, were responsible for the interlibrary loans and for the copies of hard-to-find journal articles which were the sources of much information. Former President Dr. J. Harvey Saunders and Mr. Jack Marshall, Vice-President for Development and current Interim President, have been very supportive throughout the project. Mrs. Jane Flink, retired Director of the Churchill Memorial; Ms. Judith Pugh, the present Director; and Memorial staff members Mr. Randy Hendrix, Mr. Warren Hollrah, and Mr. Kevin Mathis have all been quick to respond to our requests for access to information in the Memorial files and archives. Mr. Bruce Hackmann, Director of Public Relations for Westminster College, provided assistance with illustrations. We are particularly grateful to Ms. Pugh for her preparation of the camera ready copy. Dr. John Charmley, Robertson Visiting Professor of British History at Westminster College and Lecturer in British History at the University of East Anglia, graciously read and commented on the entire manuscript.

Two individuals deserve final mention and the expression of our deepest gratitude. Dr. Robert L. D. Davidson, President Emeritus of Westminster College, was (as readers will learn in Ch. 9) one of the principal participants in the conception and execution of the project which brought St. Mary Aldermanbury to the College. He read and offered suggestions on the manuscript. Dr. Davidson has been a strong supporter of our work. Dr. Noel Mander, MBE, FSA, St. Mary's organ builder and United Kingdom representative of the Churchill Memorial, who is responsible for many of the treasures of the Church (see Ch. 10), shared with us his considerable knowledge of and love for the City of London and the Wren churches. He read and commented on the entire manuscript, providing many helpful suggestions. To Drs. Davidson and Mander this work is dedicated.

While we are grateful to the above scholars and others unnamed, who have provided us with information and direction, we assume full responsibility for the selection and organization of material and the interpretations expressed in this book.

Our wives and families have been patient and supportive during the long and winding road to completion of this work. They have been partly compensated by the opportunity to travel in the United Kingdom while we pursued research, but their willingness to endure our commitment to a seemingly unending project has exceeded even that reward.

The Phoenix of Aldermanbury is our second major literary collaboration. Our previous enterprise, <u>An Introduction to the Bible: A Journey into Three Worlds</u> (Prentice-Hall, Inc) is now in its second edition (1990). We offer this book, as we did our first, in the hope that readers will find it both enjoyable and informative. We each thank our coauthor for the diligence, hard work, and good humor which made writing this work a pleasant and exhilarating adventure in learning. As in the past, we both express our willingness to let the coauthor assume full responsibility for all mistakes!

Like our first work, the present book is organized as a journey. In the pages which follow the reader will travel through the history of London and Great Britain from the vantage point of the people of the parish of St. Mary, Aldermanbury. The story will be told as follows:

Chapter One: The establishment of the Roman City of Londinium and the Saxon City of London, and how these affected the birth of a Church named St. Mary's at the corner of Aldermanbury and Love Lanes.

Chapter Two: The founding of the parish system in London and the emergence of St. Mary, Aldermanbury, during the Middle Ages as a parish church.

Chapter Three: The English Reformation and its impact on Aldermanbury during the Tudor Period and the early Stuart monarchy, with special attention to the relationship of William Shakespeare to the parish.

Chapter Four: The prominent role played by the Aldermanbury parish and its most famous minister, Edmund Calamy, as a center of the Presbyterian wing of the Puritan movement during the turbulent period of the English Civil War, Commonwealth, Protectorate, and Restoration of the Stuart monarchy. This chapter includes brief accounts of the relationship of the poet John Milton to the parish as well as several persons who tie St. Mary Aldermanbury to the British colonies in North America: Puritan patron Sir Robert Rich, Earl of Warwick, and a young couple named Allen and Margaret Robinett.

Chapter Five: The horrendous plague and Great Fire of London of 1666, their effects on Aldermanbury, and the reconstruction of the Church of St. Mary as part of the rebuilding of parish churches and St. Paul's Cathedral by the greatest English architect, Sir Christopher Wren.

Chapter Six: The growth of the parish in a prosperous London during the later Stuart and early Hanover dynasties, including an account of the most infamous Aldermanbury parishoner, the illustrious "Hanging Judge," George Jeffreys.

Chapter Seven: The explosion of the Industrial Revolution in England, focusing on its effects on London and the Aldermanbury parish during the later Hanoverian and Victorian periods. The changes in the life of the Aldermanbury parish as the historic City of London becomes a thriving, but lightly populated, center of industry, finance and commerce.

Chapter Eight: The struggle to save the Church of St. Mary and its building while World War I, the Great Depression, and World War II rage. Then, abruptly, on the night of 29 December, 1940, the seeming end to the illustrious history of St. Mary, Aldermanbury.

Chapter Nine: Like the mythological phonenix, St. Mary, Aldermanbury, arising once more from the ashes. The fascinating story of how St. Mary, Aldermanbury, came to be the home of the Winston S. Churchill Memorial and Library in the United States, and a description of the role of St. Mary's in the life of Westminter College.

Chapter Ten: An account of the many treasures of the Church of St. Mary, Aldermanbury, some of which are lost, but many of which can be seen in the Church and Undercroft museum today.

If you have half as much fun reading *The Phoenix of Aldermanbury* as we have had researching and writing it, you are in for a fascinating journey!

Christian E. Hauer, Jr.
William A. Young

Feast of the Assumption of the Virgin Mary
15 August, 1992

CHAPTER ONE: FOUNDATIONS
THE CITY, THE NEIGHBORHOOD,
THE CHURCH (ca. 50- 1200 C.E.)

Introduction

Although the Church of St. Mary, Aldermanbury, was not founded until the medieval period, we must begin our story a thousand years earlier, with the Roman city of Londinium. We shall see that the layout of the Roman city played a role in the location of the Church. To set the stage for the story of St. Mary's we must also examine London during the subsequent Saxon and Norman periods, with special attention to the link between the Aldermanbury neighborhood and the Saxon palace. The name "Aldermanbury" derives from these eras as does the first Church of St. Mary, Aldermanbury.

The City During Roman Times

London, or "Londinium" as the Romans called it, was founded by the Romans. Sir Christopher Wren, about whom we shall hear much more later in our story, was the first to establish this fact on the basis of excavation. During his extensive digging in the course of his reconstruction of London after the Great Fire of 1666, Wren found not a shred of evidence to support medieval legends about a pre-Roman city (Hobley 1986:2). Modern archaeological research has confirmed Wren's conclusion. Humans inhabited the site of the city as early as the stone age, but until the Romans came there were never more than hunting camps and small agrarian villages. It is natural that earlier, larger settlements would have been up stream at the fords on the Thames. There was an early Roman installation on Thorney Isle, the defensible land between the two mouths of the Tyburn stream, which later became the site of King Edward's Westminster Abbey.

The Romans brought with them a complex, state level society, with centralized authority. They also brought the developed technology which they had inherited from their predecessors and which they had honed to new levels of achievement. The Greeks had tended toward philosophy and science. The Romans were more inclined toward such practical arts as engineering and administration. Indeed, they were probably the best engineers the western world had yet seen, or would see for quite a time to come. Roman engineering recognized in the future site of London an ideal location for a city. It marked the upper limit of the tidal estuary of the Thames, and thus the head of deep water navigation on that remarkable river with its self-dredging tendencies, despite its limited flow of fresh water. It also marked the furthest downstream point that the Thames could safely be bridged with the technology then available.

The bridge across the Thames probably predates the town. Both London, to the north of the Thames, and Southwark, on the other side, were products of the bridge. They served as the northern and southern foci of road networks converging on the span. Londinium, on its high, dry banks offered a more favorable site for urban development and reaped the benefits of the location for a deep water port.

The tidal pool of the Thames apparently terminated at the bridge in the first century C.E. Later Roman, Saxon, Medieval and modern filling would narrow the Thames substantially. In the first century the Thames at high tide was 1,000 meters wide (Hobley 1986:6). The modern channel at London is only 200 meters. During Roman times the tidal pool encroached upstream so that flow between the arches of the medieval bridge constituted a serious hazard. The Roman and medieval span(s) stood a city block east of their modern successor. Medieval records show that the Church of St. Magnus the Martyr stood hard by the landward terminus of the bridge, and excavations by the Department of Urban Archaeology of the Museum of London in 1981 revealed the Roman bridgehead and established that the Roman bridge street ran along the same line. It was Fish Street Hill (called "Bridge Street" in the Middle Ages and "New Fyshe Streate" on the Agas map of 1580).

The establishment of London is most likely related to the invasion of the Roman armies under the emperor Claudius in 43 C.E. Although Roman troops first reached Britain in 55-54 B.C.E., under the command of Julius Caesar, they came more as raiders than invaders. The most likely date for the foundation of Londinium is around 50 C.E. (Marsden 1986).

About a decade later a native uprising under Boudicca ravaged Londinium. Scorched destruction layers at Camulodunum (Colchester), Verulamium (St. Alban's), and Londinium, dated by pottery to around 60 C.E., witness to the vengeance and brief ascendancy of the native tribes. The Roman governor, Suetonius Paulinus, took swift and vicious revenge. His recall and replacement suggest that imperial authority was more eager for reconciliation with native populations, realizing it would pay higher dividends than suppression.

Boudicca's rebellion may have led to the first significant building activity in what would one day become the Aldermanbury neighborhood. A Roman fort was constructed on the well-drained gravel bank northwest of the main part of the civilian settlement toward the end of the first century C.E. The precise location of the fort was unknown before its discovery by Prof. W. F. Grimes during his post-World War II excavation of blitzed areas in the City of London. He dubbed it "Cripplegate Fort," for its north gate became Cripplegate, one of the main northern gates of medieval London (see Figure 1.1). Troops quartered in the fort would be able to provide protection for Londinium. The fact that it was built may suggest that Londinium had gained a new political and administrative importance. Perhaps it had already become, as archaeological data clearly shows it later was, the seat of the Roman governor of Brittania. Grimes' excavations showed that Cripplegate Fort was of the standard Roman type. It had the rectangular "playing card" shape, with gates at the cardinal points and main streets bisecting the fort into quadrants, each leading to one of the main gates of the fort.

The Church of St. Mary, Aldermanbury, would one day rise within what had been the walls of Cripplegate Fort, just south of the eastern gate. This datum will play a significant role in our understanding of the early history of the Church of St. Mary. However, roughly a thousand years would pass before the founding of the church.

The entire city of Londinium was walled on the landward side in ca. 200 C.E. in response to the tumults of the age. In the mid-3rd century the wall was extended along the Thames. The riverside wall collapsed during the early middle ages, but archaeological evidence confirms its existence. Parts of the landward wall are still visible, some several blocks from the site of the Aldermanbury church (near what is now "London Wall Street"), others near the Tower of London. The wall was an example of excessively ambitious urban planning. At no time did Roman Londinium fill all the territory fortified by its enceinte. However, from a military point of view, the configuration of the wall was a logical response to the topography of the city. The wall had to enclose the Forum and Basilica and the principal civilian settlement on Cornhill, the fort on the northwest, and the governor's place to the south. Archaeological data are incomplete, but from the lay of the land we can assume that once significant installations had been established west of the Walbrook, the fortification line must have run from Newgate to Ludgate and thence south on high ground above the Fleet to the Thames.

The fort was originally built with a two-course wall, fronted by a fosse. When the city wall, four courses thick, was built, the northern and western walls of the fort were incorporated into it. Two additional courses of masonry were added to them in the process (Grimes 1968). It is not known how long the eastern and southern walls of the fort, now encompassed by the enceinte, remained standing. Historical data, which we will consider below, suggests that they were still in place when the Saxon nobility established itself within the city.

Londinium had been a flourishing commercial center during the late first and early second centuries, but such activity slowed soon thereafter. From the time of the fire during Hadrian's reign (117-138), archaeological evidence points toward a city with a declining economy. By the late third century Londinium's role had changed from a commercial center to that of administrative and official hub of the province.

The Aldermanbury-Cripplegate Neighborhood during Romano-British Times

Before 1987 we knew little about the Romano-British use of the Aldermanbury-Cripplegate neighborhood. The northern gate of the fort did become one of the gates of the City, Cripplegate, and remained so as long as London was walled. (On the derivation of the name Cripplegate and the development of Cripplegate Ward, see below.) The western gate was blocked when the third century wall was constructed, with Aldersgate providing access from a different angle on the west. But whether the fort area continued as a military installation is not clear. We can assume, however, that with its existing officers' quarters, barracks, warehouses, etc. it continued to serve whatever garrison was posted to Londinium. Since Londinium was the seat of the provincial governor, there was likely a respectable guard.

In 1987 the Department of Urban Archaeology made a remarkable discovery, just across the street from the later site of the Aldermanbury church. The demolition of the Art Gallery at the southeast corner of London's Guildhall (the site of the Guildhall Chapel, which had been destroyed in the Great Fire of 1666), in order to make room for new development of the area, created the opportunity for archaeological investigation. The result was one of the most dramatic finds in London archaeology, the remains of the eastern end of the Roman amphitheater. As large as any known Roman amphitheater in Britain, and one of the few stone-built, its location fills a significant gap in knowledge of Roman London. Only the inner arc of the structure was unearthed. The rest of the eastern end lies under a building slated for future demolition. The northern and southern sides of the amphitheater are concealed under the Guildhall and the Church of St. Lawrence, Jewry, and the western end under the new Guildhall Library building, all places where excavation is out of the question. The location of the Guildhall, where the state box would have been in the amphitheater, and St. Lawrence, where a shrine would have stood, are enigmas giving rise to heated speculation, especially since the tradition of St. Lawrence places his martyrdom in an arena, albeit in Spain rather than London! However, enigmas they must remain until concrete evidence of cultural continuity at London is forthcoming.

Archaeologists believe that the amphitheater served as a drill and exercise ground for troops posted to the fort as well as for various sorts of public spectacles. Like the sturdy gatehouse of Cripplegate Fort, the great mass of the amphitheater's wall and fill continued to influence London topography long after the collapse of Roman power. Aldermanbury and Basinghall Streets began their paths south from the wall parallel and in close proximity until they approached the amphitheater site. There the medieval streets arced apart, tracing the curved outline of the amphitheater wall. The curve, still observable in Aldermanbury Street, was also influenced by the east gate of the fort. It is an important datum to which we shall return.

The internal street plan of the fort was also replicated in the medieval city, another matter which will receive later consideration. The Aldermanbury-Guildhall neighborhood thus provides several examples of a rare phenomenon: a cityscape which reflects internal topographic continuity from the Roman through the Saxon and medieval periods, to some extent right down to modern times. This was doubtlessly due to the formidable nature of the structures, or the ruins they left behind.

In other British cities the gates in the city walls were the only aspects of Roman topography respected in the Saxon reoccupation. Minor streets were usually laid out in a quite different pattern in the late Saxon period. If we recognize that the bridge was a very special sort of gate, the gates were the main Roman influence on the topography of London as well, though a few later lanes and property lines seem to reflect Roman street alignments and Roman masonry walling.

London During Saxon Times

At London the gap between the devolution of Roman culture (ca. 410 C.E.) and large scale Saxon occupation of the walled city (ca. 886 C.E.) was quite a long one. After Roman decline Britain reverted to a tribal agrarian society. The Saxons, who became the dominant element in southeastern Britain, were themselves village-tribal agrarians who had no use or need for cities. As historical anthropology reveals, cities are a phenomenon of state level cultures. The Saxon "Heptarchy," when it arose, was more an aggregation of competing chiefdoms than the array of kingdoms envisioned by anachronistic tradition.

Alfredan Wessex (886-899), mustered in response to Danish pressure, was one of the first real Saxon kingdoms. From the age of Alfred we have our earliest evidence of extensive Saxon activity within the walled city of London.

Recent archaeological research reveals that Lundenwic, the Saxon "emporium," as Bede called it, was located west of the walled city, along the Strand, perhaps from the Fleet all the way to Westminster. Aldwych ("old market") near St. Clement, Danes, probably preserves its memory. Remains of this major Saxon trading center have been found as far north as Covent Garden and as far west as Trafalgar Square (at the National Gallery). The sloping river banks along the future Strand were better suited to the shallow draft Saxon ships. They were more readily beached than moored as the old Roman quays would require. Lundenwic in the Middle Saxon period was a significant trading center, the equal of many along the northern shores of the continent.

Wheeler (1936) conjectured that when the Saxons settled in London, they established themselves around the Ludgate Hill, the neighborhood of St. Paul's Cathedral, the high ground between the Walbrook and the Fleet, because a Romano-British community still occupied Cornhill, the high ground east of the Walbrook, the area of the Roman Forum, and around the bridgehead. This was a daring speculation, but evidence for a major occupation, whether Romano-British or Saxon, is simply lacking prior to Alfredan times. Archaeological findings suggest that the City of

London itself was relatively depopulated while Lundenwic flourished. However, we need to remember that there was one feature of the northwestern section of Roman Londinium that might attract warrior chiefdoms, Saxon or otherwise, to settle there: Cripplegate Fort. If its internal (southern and eastern) walls still stood, it offered a relatively compact and inviting fortified refuge. The unusual circumstance of the internal street plan of the fort being preserved in the streets of medieval London suggests that the eastern and southern gates of the fort and a fair number of its buildings still stood when the City established its basic internal pattern. Wood Street even today runs almost perfectly along the alignment of the north-south street of the fort. And Silver and Addle Streets, while they survived in their medieval form, followed the east-west street, but for an interesting deviation to which we will return below.

Two documents, one medieval and one from the Tudor era, declare unequivocally that the Saxon "royal" palace (at first simply the stronghold of the chief) was located in Aldermanbury. Matthew of Paris, chronicler of St. Alban's Abbey, wrote in the 13th Century that the Church of St. Alban, Wood Street, a very short distance down Love Lane from the site of the Aldermanbury Church, had its origins as the chapel royal of Offa of Mercia, whose palace adjoined the church (cited in Goss 1944: 116). A chapter building account of St. Paul's Cathedral, dated to 1532, says that the palace of Ethelbert of Kent stood in Aldermanbury. Indeed, it was the victim of a demolition project noted in the narrative (Guildhall Ms. A54-34). Both of these traditions are late, and could be dismissed were not a substantial body of evidence consistent with their allegations. That evidence and related matters will occupy us more fully in our next section.

For the moment, let us note that the Saxon trading settlement outside the Roman walls of London, and the royal settlement within the walls, made for a sort of "kremlin" situation (also evidenced at Winchester). A ruling warrior class and their ecclesiastical retainers with their cathedral (and perhaps a few other churches), and possibly a market in Cheapside near St. Paul's, were inside the walls. A merchant settlement was outside the walls, to the west. The nobility apparently did not want merchants and traders of dubious loyalty within their secure hold. To be sure, important parts of the road network still passed through the city. If the bridge was in a working state, the traffic would be heavier. But passage is one thing, residence another. The result would match archaeological findings: a relatively unpopulated area within the walls and a substantial settlement to the west. Increasing harassment by Scandinavian raiders and pirates and the development of deeper draft shipping contributed in all likelihood to the changes which took place. The rulers benefitted from the fruits of commerce and the traders appreciated the benefits of greater security.

When Alfred the Great occupied London in 886 and expelled Danish interlopers, the situation changed (Hobley 1986:18). Merchants returned to the City proper in numbers for the first time since the demise of Roman authority, and once there they remained, outlasting the warriors and princes. And once London became Saxon, it stayed in a significant sense Saxon through the middle ages and beyond.

The Saxon Palace In Aldermanbury And Its Successor

As we have noted above, there is documentary evidence for locating the Saxon palace in Aldermanbury. A formal hypothesis to this effect was first developed systematically by Page (1923), even before archaeological investigation of the area. It has been refined in light of subsequent archaeological work by Dyson, in an as yet unpublished paper, and briefly summarized by Schofield and Dyson (1980), Dyson and Schofield (1984), and Schofield (1984). The account that follows is dependent on Dyson's work, which incorporates the results of Grimes' excavations (see Figure 1.2) and is undergirded by a formidable array of documentary evidence from the late Saxon period forward.

Dyson built his case for a Saxon palace in Aldermanbury on three classes of evidence: archaeological, topographic, and documentary. The two basic documents alleging the presence of a Saxon place in Aldermanbury have already been noted. Archaeology and topography provide a likely location for it. The eastern gate complex of the Roman fort stood just to the north of the site of St. Mary, Aldermanbury. Medieval property lines preserved into modern times produced a jog, or "kink" as Dyson called it, in Aldermanbury just north of the Church, with the result that the street widens dramatically at the east end of the Church even as it swung westward (presumably around the mass of the ruined amphitheater). This jog, or kink, coincides with the location of the eastern fort gate. It then narrows again opposite the location of the fort gate, the depth of the gatehouses accounting for the difference. Further, Addle Street, the successor to the eastern street of the fort, deviated northward from the path of its predecessor to enter Aldermanbury one hundred feet north of the gate complex. The gate complex must have been put to some important use to justify such a diversion. The diversion represents an adaptation which would only have been required following civil resettlement of the neighborhood. While the city retained its "kremlin" status, it would not be required. By then the eastern wall might be gone, just as its southern part had to be removed for Aldermanbury to pursue its curving path toward Gresham Street.

Precedents for Roman gatehouses being reused as royal or episcopal residences exist at Exeter, York, and Trier among other sites. One would expect the basic Roman structure was built onto and enlarged, and later documents suggest that such was in fact the case. So it appears that the three classes of evidence converge to establish the location of the royal palace of Aldermanbury in the precinct of the eastern gate of the old Roman Cripplegate Fort. It is likely that the fully developed palace complex ultimately extended south and west along Addle Street, possibly to Wood Street, since Matthew of Paris' reference associated St. Alban's, Wood Street, with the whole.

Documents postdating the 11th Century Norman conquest refer to an important structure in Aldermanbury, the great Aldermanbury tenement, or capital messuage, a "great house" (cited in Goss 1944: 119). This tenement was the center of a soke, an area of private jurisdiction. The soke was a "bundle of rights" (Brooke and Kerr 1975) or "urban manor" (Dyson n.d.). It was an adaptation of the medieval land-holding and jurisdictional customs to the urban setting. History records a number of sokes in medieval London, but none seems to have enjoyed the status of the Aldermanbury soke, which was on occasion equated with a city ward. (Cripplegate Ward, within which Aldermanbury lies, may have originally been called "Aldermanesgarde." [Dyson, n.d.:18]). Whether the geographic area of the soke was lesser, greater, or the same as the parish of St. Mary cannot be ascertained, but the unique liberties associated with its great house are quite clear. A charter of Henry III in 1247 confirmed to the holder of the property privileges which put it beyond the reaches of City jurisdiction, and confirmed to him the advowson (right of nominating the priest) of St. Mary, Aldermanbury, and two other nearby churches (Goss 1944: 120). The liberties enjoyed by the Aldermanbury tenement are otherwise documented only for royal institutions and religious houses favored by the crown. There can be little doubt that the Aldermanbury tenement, standing immediately north of the Church of St. Mary, was the Saxon palace, reduced in status but not entirely deprived of its prerogatives.

The holdings and status of the Aldermanbury tenement declined through time. The soke was absorbed by the rising City of London government. The tenement was reduced but retained many of its liberties. Finally, in the mid-sixteenth century, the then dilapidated structure was finally demolished and replaced by five houses.

The Name "Aldermanbury"

> "...if we could tell the history of Aldermanbury, a great slice of London's past would be revealed to us.... But it is the name which lends Aldermanbury its fascination .... It is possible that Aldermanbury, the burh of the alderman, hides some part of this story." (Brooke and Kerr 1975:154-155)

"Aldermanbury" in modern London refers simply to a street which originally ran from Aldermanbury postern in the city wall (just east of the join with Cripplegate Fort's east wall while it stood) southward to Gresham Street. Like Bucklersbury and Lothbury, Aldermanbury preserved the memory of great houses of the medieval period (Ekwall 1975:194-195). Aldermanbury means the burh or burgh, the fortified residence, of the alderman or aldermen.

We have just explained the most likely background of burh in Aldermanbury, namely the Saxon palace and its medieval successor, the tenement. But whence the term "Aldermanbury?" During the late Saxon period, the Alderman (or Ealdorman) was the king's agent, charged with tending royal interests. (In the rural context the ealdorman was also the headman of a shire. Cf. Brooke and Kerr 1975:155.) Alfred the Great entrusted London to his son-in-law, the Alderman, Aethelred of Mercia, after recovering the city from the Danes in 886. Aethelred is the only royal alderman in London known to history by name. As the king's agent, his residence would have been in the palace complex, and there he would carry out many of his duties. According to Dyson, "the gatehouse was [most likely] made over as part of the palace, to the special use of the alderman, who (presumably) looked after the king's interests in London in his absence. That is, the gatehouse itself wouldn't have represented the palace." (Dyson 1991). Was it his residence that gave the name "Aldermanbury" to the palace and future tenement? Mr. Dyson has reminded the authors that the ship landing on the Thames known from the early 12th Century as "Queenhithe" was previously known as "Aethelredshythe." This landing lies on a straight line south from Aldermanbury and is thus the dock most convenient to it. These data may strengthen the case for an Alfredan origin of the name "Aldermanbury." (See also Gordon and Dewhurst 1985: 7).

But surely Aethelred had successors in the two centuries that remained to the Wessex dynasty as kings of England. The procession of aldermen who held sway whenever the king was not resident in London may be collectively responsible for the designation "Aldermanbury," especially since the king was probably resident in London very seldom. Most of the time the "Alderman" was the senior resident official.

History offers us yet another occasion when "Aldermanbury" may have been affixed to the palace. King Edward the Confessor reached the height of his power in 1051, driving the Saxon champion, Earl Godwine and his sons, into exile, despoiling their estates and deposing Saxon officeholders both secular and ecclesiastical in favor of Norman appointees. However, within the year Godwine returned at the head of an armed force and moved on London, gathering strength as he came. Upheavals in the pro-Saxon city apparently persuaded Edward to evacuate the palace in favor of the new royal residence he was constructing alongside Westminster Abbey. The monks would be less boisterous and dangerous as neighbors! This event could have resulted in the London palace being turned over to the royal Alderman on a full time basis, offering another opportunity for the palace to become "Aldermanbury."

Dyson offered yet a third possibility for the derivation of the name. John Stow in his Survey of London (1598) suggested that "Aldermanbury" meant "court of the aldermen," referring to a sort of proto-guildhall in the neighborhood. Stow's assertion could easily be dismissed as bad folk etymology, but Dyson was intrigued by the certainty with which Stow advanced this notion and with some vague and confusing traditions about the location of this court and of the first Guildhall. It was as if Stow was quite certain of the traditions but uncertain about how to reconcile them with the topography of London as he knew it. The first Guildhall built for that purpose probably dates from about 1127. Dyson argued that both the fabric of the crypt and surviving documents show that all of the purpose-built Guildhalls stood on the same location. Thus, Stow's apparently confused materials point in fact to a move of the Court of Aldermen from a previous venue on the west side of Aldermanbury (the former palace) to the new Guildhall, east of the street and somewhat to the south.

Documents of the early 12th century witness to the existence of numbers of

Aldermen as well as to a change in the office of those bearing the title. Now they were no longer the king's appointed agents, but officers of London's emerging system of city government, associated with both guilds and wards. The abandoned palace would certainly have been an appropriate place for the Court of Aldermen to sit and transact its business. The palace would have an audience chamber, a banquet hall, a council room, fitting to its needs. The move of the Court to the new Guildhall would clear the way for the palace to become simply a tenement, albeit a privileged one.

Is there ground for preferring one of these theories for the derivation of "Aldermanbury"? The evidence permits the highly probable conclusion that the Saxon palace complex centered on the site of the east gate of Cripplegate Fort and (at least originally) incorporated its remains. It permits the certain conclusion that the Aldermanbury tenement (once connected to the Churchyard by a postern) occupied the same site, and hence the palace and the tenement were very likely the same structure. But the middle term, the question of how the name "Aldermanbury" became attached, does not admit a certain conclusion. The three possibilities may not be mutually exclusive. This is especially true in the case of the third. The fact that the City Aldermen held the same title as the royal Aldermen may have gained them entre to Aldermanbury, if the great residence had already been so named. Or perhaps their title came from their use of the Alderman's residence. This much is clear. Brooke was correct. If we understood Aldermanbury more completely, we would also know more about London's history, almost certainly more about the evolution of London's polity!

The Foundation Of The Church Of St. Mary, Aldermanbury

In 1181 Ralph De Diceto, who was remembered as "the good dean" of St. Paul's Cathedral, ordered an "inquisition" (inquiry, inventory) of the Churches in the Diocese (see Figure 1.3). This Inquisition of London Churches provides the earliest known dated reference to the Church of St. Mary, Aldermanbury. It also shows that St. Mary, Aldermanbury, was a flourishing institution in 1181 and hence must have been in existence for some time.

If Dean Ralph's Inquisition provides for us the latest possible date for the foundation of St. Mary's, archaeology provides us with the earliest. Professor W. F. Grimes excavated the site of St. Mary's in 1967, after the removal of the Wren fabric of the Church to Westminster College. Declining health prevented Prof. Grimes from publishing the results of his work beyond a brief news note (Grimes 1969). However, he generously afforded the authors two lengthy interviews, at the site of the church in 1984 and at his home in Wales in 1988. He also allowed us to study and record his site plan. In his note Grimes pronounced the earliest stone foundation remains "not closely dateable." In both of our interviews with him he said that such ceramic evidence as he found in association with the earliest foundation line was consistent with "a medieval date" (i.e., Norman). In other words, archaeological data suggests that the first Church of St. Mary with stone foundations was built no earlier than the 11th century.

Grimes has pointed out that the early incarnations of Saxon churches were frequently built in wood, and that their traces were sometimes obliterated by later construction. However, in his excavation of St. Alban's, Wood Street, just down Love Lane from St. Mary, Aldermanbury, he did find Saxon evidence (Grimes 1968). It seems likely that if St. Mary, Aldermanbury, had a Saxon foundation some evidence of it would have turned up during the Grimes' excavation. Prof. Grimes' final observation on the founding date of St. Mary, Aldermanbury, was that archaeology had done what it could. The rest was up to the historians! (Note: The late Prof. Grimes' archives are now in the hands of literary executors, but there has been no official announcement of a publication schedule. Professional archaeologists and historians are aware that the interpretation of an orginal excavator is sometimes revised in the course of later reassessment and publication. We have utilized the best information currently available. We will endeavor to incorporate any new information that may appear into our account.)

Prof. Grimes found three different sets of foundations on the St. Mary's site. The earliest was a small rectangular church, covering roughly the area of the nave of the Wren building, without the aisles, and divided into a nave and a choir. The second phase consisted of the first Church, augmented by north and south side chapels. The third was the perpendicular Gothic Church of 1437, the structure destroyed in the Great Fire of 1666. Wren reused the 1437 foundation (and grounded the columns of his south aisle on the south foundation of the first building) for his reconstruction. The first of these foundations is the one of present interest.

The Church of St. Mary never had a crypt or undercroft while it stood in London though there had been the customary burials in the floor of the medieval building, and vaults under the chancel and outside the south door of the 1437/Wren foundation. It is important to note that the disturbance produced by the vaults did not destroy any of the foundations, and they did not extend under the entire church, which was built essentially on the ground level. Indeed, only the south wall of the earlier south chapel is really missing, devoured by the foundation line of the 1437 structure. Thus, if there was an earlier Church of stone or wooden construction, or any other Saxon use of the site, the evidence should not have been totally obliterated. A trench sunk in the relatively undisturbed soil within the earliest foundations revealed no Saxon deposits. Rather, the next occupational level was the Cripplegate Fort of Roman times, part of a barracks block and a street with some fragments of Roman pottery.

The archaeological and documentary data seem to converge in suggesting a foundation date for the Church of St. Mary, Aldermanbury, no earlier than the very late Saxon or Norman period. What contexts would make the establishment of a Church or a chapel associated with the great residence next door likely? So long as the great residence north of the future St. Mary's Churchyard remained part of the royal palace, no such Church-chapel was required. The palace had its own royal chapel, the future St. Alban's, Wood Street. The establishment of St. Mary's therefore seems to presuppose the royal evacuation of 1052, and we would suggest that there is no need to look earlier.

At least three situations subsequent to Edward the Confessor's move to Westminster offer likely settings for the foundation of St. Mary's. The first would be the occupation of part of the former palace by the royal alderman after 1052. The chapel royal, St. Alban's, was the king's Church. The alderman might have felt a need to avoid the appearance of usurpation, or to demonstrate his personal piety, by founding his own church. Such would have been less pressing at an earlier period when the alderman was only temporary master of the house. The second setting would have been when (or if) the great house became the seat of the City Aldermen. They, even less than a royal servant, could lay claim to St. Alban's, and thus would have felt obliged to establish a Church for their official purposes. If this is correct, St. Mary, Aldermanbury, was, in effect, the first Guildhall Chapel. Finally, when the great house became the capital messuage of Aldermanbury with its soke, it would have been expected that the lord of this "urban manor" establish a proprietary church. Many parish churches had their origin as private chapels. For example, in nearby Cheapside a 12th century sheriff, William, son of Aluf, established St. Mary Colechurch within his property (Keene 1985: 9). As we shall see in the next chapter, that is what St. Mary, Aldermanbury, became and remained for a while, whether or not that was its origin. The dedication to the Blessed Virgin is consistent with 11th-12th century piety.

In the case of the name, "Aldermanbury," as we have seen, it is impossible to confidently select among alternatives. Construction of the Fidelity Bank Building after World War II probably obliterated any archaeological remains on the site of the Saxon palace that escaped Grimes' team. A Department of Urban Archaeology watch team observed the destruction of the Fidelity Bank Building in 1987 and found no evidence. If there is any remaining archaeological evidence of the east gate of the Cripplegate Fort, the subsequent Palace, or tenement, it is now sealed under the pavement and sidewalks of Aldermanbury and unavailable to archaeologists.

Unless currently unexpected urban renewal makes further archaeological investigation possible or some new relevant document miraculously emerges, nothing more can be said about this earliest phase of the history of the Church of St. Mary, the Virgin, Aldermanbury.

Conclusion

In this chapter we have briefly surveyed the known history of the City of London from its Roman origins through the Saxon period, into the Norman phase. The location of the Church, south of what had been the east gate of the Romans' "Cripplegate Fort" has been demonstrated. We have also established a setting for the foundation of the Church of St. Mary, the Virgin, Aldermanbury which links the Church to key events in the early evolution of the government of the City. It seems most likely that the Aldermanbury Church came into existence next to the Saxon Palace of London (which had been built out of or on the site of the east gate of the Roman Fort), after the palace had become the fortified residence of the King's agent in the area, or still later when this great house had become the meeting place of the City Aldermen, or later yet when it became the home of the Lord of an urban manor. Regardless, the Church had a distinguished foundation sometime in the 11th or early 12th century. As we shall see in subsequent chapters, the association of the Church of St. Mary, Aldermanbury, with key historical events in the City of London and the nation, and the persons involved in them, did not end with its foundation.

Bibliography

Arnold, C. J.
    1984   Roman Britain to Saxon England. Bloomington, IN: Indiana University Press.

Barlow, Frank
    1970   Edward the Confessor. Berkeley: University of California Press.

Blair, Peter Hunter
    1977   An Introduction to Anglo-Saxon England. 2 vols. Cambridge: Cambridge University Press.

Brooke, Christopher N. L. and Gillian Kerr
    1975   History of London: London, 800-1216: The Shaping of a City. Berkeley, CA: University of California.

Dyson, Tony
    no date   "Aldermanbury," an unpublished paper.

    1991   Personal correspondence with the authors.

Dyson, Tony and John Schofield
    1984   "Saxon London," in Anglo-Saxon Times in Southern England, ed. Jeremy Haslam. Chichester: Phillimore, pp. 285-313.

Ekwall, Eilert
    1954   Street Names of London. Oxford: Oxford University Press.

Frere, Sheppard Sunderland
    1978   Britannia: A History of Roman Britain. London: Routledge Kegan Paul. (rev. ed.)

Gordon, Caroline and Wilfrid Dewhurst

1985   The Ward of Cripplegate in the City of London. Oxford: Oxford University Press.

Goss, Charles
   1944   "A History of The Parish of St. Mary the Virgin, Aldermanbury," Transactions of the London and Middlesex Archaeological Society. 9 (1944-47), 113-164.

Grimes, W. F.
   1968   The Excavation of Roman and Medieval London. London: Routledge and Kegan Paul.

   1969   "London: Church of St. Mary, Aldermanbury," Medieval Archaeology 13, 251.

   1984   Interview with Prof. William A. Young at the site of the Church of St. Mary, Aldermanbury. London. 18 July.

   1988   Interview with Prof. Christian E. Hauer, Jr. and Dr. Noel Mander at Prof. Grimes' home. Swansea, Wales.

Hobley, Brian
   1986   Roman and Saxon London: A Reappraisal. London: The Museum of London.

Keene, Derek
   1985   Cheapside Before the Great Fire. London: Economic and Research Council.

Marsden, Peter
   1980   Roman London. London: Thames and Hudson.

Merrifield, Ralph
   1978   A Handbook to Roman London. London: Museum of London.

Museum of London
    1981   <u>Londinium: A Descriptive Map and Guide to Roman London</u>.

Page, William
    1923   <u>London: Its Origin and Early Development</u>. Boston: Houghton-Mifflin Co.

Potter, T. W.
    1983   <u>Roman Britain</u>. London: The Trustees of the British Museum.

Salway, Peter
    1981   <u>Roman Britain</u>. Oxford: Oxford University Press.

Schofield, John
    1984   <u>The Building of London from the Conquest to the Great Fire</u>. London: Collonade, 1984.

Schofield, John and Tony Dyson
    1980   <u>The Archaeology of the City of London</u>. London: The Museum of London.

Thomas, Charles
    1981   <u>Christianity in Roman Britain to AD 500</u>. Berkeley, CA: The University of California Press.

Wheeler, R. E. M.
    1936   <u>Saxon London</u>. London: The London Museum.

CHAPTER TWO: A MEDIEVAL PARISH CHURCH (ca. 1200-1485)

Introduction

In the first chapter we established that the Church of St. Mary, Aldermanbury, was founded just south of what had been the eastern gate complex of the Roman "Cripplegate Fort." The gate complex had likely been transformed into an portion of the Saxon palace of London; it then became the fortified residence ("bury") of the king's representative, the Alderman (hence Aldermanbury). We noted also the possible associations between this "great house" and the first civic leaders of the City of London, the court of Aldermen, who eventually moved their gathering place across the street to the present location of the Guildhall. The Aldermanbury became the great house of the Lord of an urban manor in the area, and it may have been the Lord of Aldermanbury who established St. Mary's as a proprietary chapel. In any event, by the 12th century, before the implementation of the parish system in the city, St. Mary's was clearly such an institution.

In this chapter we will carry the story of St. Mary, Aldermanbury, into the medieval period, recounting its development into a parish church in the context of the evolving government and institutions of the City, concluding on the eve of the English Reformation. So much material is available on London that it is now possible to reconstruct the development of the City almost house to house from the 12th Century onwards (Keene 1985: 5). Such a microcosmic study of Aldermanbury may one day be completed. However, our intent is a more general overview, to give the reader a sense of the social, political, and economic setting in which the Church of St. Mary, Aldermanbury, developed and then to recount the story of the life of the Church and parish within that context.

A Native Son's Praise

Thomas Becket was the son of a London merchant who entered the Church, studied on the continent, rose high in the royal service and enjoyed the personal friendship of King Henry II. Then he became a very political Archbishop of Canterbury and in 1170, a martyred saint. London thought well of her martyred son. A chapel in his honor was built in the middle of London bridge, conveniently located for pilgrims bound to and from his shrine at Canterbury.

William FitzStephen, Becket's friend and fellow Londoner, wrote a life of Thomas a few years following the martyrdom that retains the respect of historians (Brooke and Kerr 1975: 112). William included a famous description of their native city in his narrative (cf. Douglas and Greenaway 1953: 956-962):

> Amid the noble cities of the world, the City of London, throne of
> the English kingdom, is one which has spread its fame far and wide,
> its wealth and merchandise to great distances, raised its head on
> high. It is blessed by a wholesome climate, blessed too in Christ's
> religion, in the strength of its fortifications, in the nature of its
> site, the repute of its citizens, the honour of its matrons; happy
> in its sports, prolific in its noble men.

On the whole, despite this fulsome introduction, historians seem to feel that FitzStephen was stretching the truth, perhaps, but not inventing out of whole cloth. For example, although at least one modern historian called William's claim of a Roman riverside wall "a fiction" (Brooke and Kerr 1975: 114-115), archaeologists have discovered just such a wall (Schofield and Dyson 1980: 17 and Dyson 1989). A bit further on William wrote, "Other cities have citizens, London's are called Barons" (cited in Brooke and Kerr 1975:115). Was he speaking of the Aldermen?

London And The Norman Conquest

We noted in the previous chapter that London was a city which strongly supported the Saxon cause and opposed the interests of the Normans. This support was evident during those climactic days of late summer and early autumn, 1066. After the Saxon army under King Harold was defeated by Duke William's Norman invaders at the Battle of Hastings on October 14th, some of the remnants of the dead king's army took refuge within London's walls.

William did not place London under siege, though a contemporary account says he made noisy preparations to do so. His army was simply too small for such a task, which in any case would have rendered him vulnerable to assault by Saxon forces from the north. But the northern earls continued the apathetic policy which insured William's success until, to their grief, it was too late. The island stronghold of Ely, sheltered amidst its fens, was the last Saxon center to fall. Meanwhile, London, its defense prepared by a wounded veteran of Hastings, did not wait to fall. Recognizing the inevitable London negotiated. William, the Conqueror, entered the open gates of the City. He was crowned William I at Westminster Abbey on Christmas Day, 1066, beginning the practice of designating English monarchs by Roman numeral. The Londoners were not passive, however. Even while William was being crowned Saxon and Norman troops were having at one another in street riots.

William's approach to the City was a combination of conciliation and intimidation. One of his first acts was to issue a charter to London (which still survives), confirming the local laws and customs of the Confessor's time. But of the officials addressed, the bishop was a French holdover from Edward's reign and the portreeve a new French appointee.

Three major fortifications were raised on the periphery of the City. The Tower of London stood astride the old Roman wall at Thameside on the east, and the still present White Tower was itself raised up before the end of William's reign. Baynard's Castle stood on high ground about the Thames and Fleet not far from Ludgate and St. Paul's, probably just south of the Church of St. Andrew by the Wardrobe. The location of the third stronghold, Montfichet's Tower, was north of Baynard's castle, perhaps on the further side of Ludgate. These two fortifications secured the western approaches to London, especially from the river, while the Tower secured the eastern. But they also dominated the City, just as the keeps raised by the Normans did in other cities such as York.

London, or more properly Westminster, was not yet a national capital. The early Norman rulers had no capital city as such. That would come as the royal administration grew and became less portable. When this development took place, it would bode well for London's prosperity. The great bishops and secular magnates established residences along the Strand, or like the Archbishop of Canterbury in Lambeth, across the river to be near the seat of power. Meanwhile, the removal of the royal palace from

Aldermanbury to Westminster, and the establishment of the tangible centers of Norman power closer to the Thames, probably enhanced the opportunity for London's civic polity to develop relatively unmolested in the northwestern section of the City, perhaps already known as Aldermanbury, and soon to become the home of the Guildhall.

Although not officially a political capital, London was clearly the economic capital of Norman England. It was a vigorous and growing city, clearly the richest in the realm. The Norman churchmen and secular officials brought to the city mingled in a rich ethnic mix of Germans, Flemings, Scandanavians, Jews and others who came to do business amidst the English majority.

More than the Saxon nobility had been, the Normans were monumental builders and endowers of religious institutions. This latter tendency accelerated monastic developments in London and elsewhere throughout England. The growth and prosperity of the City, its religious life and a variety of charitable services were enhanced by the arrival of the great religious orders in force: the Benedictines, Cluniac Cistercians, Augustinians, and in due course the Dominicans, Franciscans, and the Crusading Orders—the Templars, Knights of St. John and others. Their counterparts among women's orders also arrived with their convents. The Norman tendency to construct impressive buildings was seen in St. Paul's Cathedral, in the great religious houses, in a few large parish churches (like St. Mary le Bow, built by the Archbishop of Canterbury), and in the royal fortifications.

William clearly needed London for the wealth it generated and drew into his realm. But London also needed William to provide the security within which manufacture and commerce could flourish. And so began the uneasy alliance of Crown and City which would carry forward through many centuries. The Crown needed the city for its wealth, but resented its power and independence, while the City needed the Crown for protection, but resented its exactions. These tensions subsided with the constitutional monarchy and the supremacy of Parliament, but they are still symbolized by the City dragons and Westminster royal lions which confront one another in modern boundary markers. Even more significant is the ceremony which accompanies a state visit to the City by the sovereign. The Lord Mayor meets the queen or king at the boundary and hands over the ceremonial sword of the City in an act of fealty. Then the sovereign immediately returns the sword in a recognition of reality!

Institutions

The Folkmoot, the thrice-annual assembly of Freemen at Paul's Cross on the north side of St. Paul's yard, may be the oldest documented London institution. But by the time the Church of St. Mary, Aldermanbury, was on the scene it had been eclipsed by the Court of Husting. The name of this Court reflects Danish influence, and it may go back to the 10th century (Dyson nd:39, Brooke and Kerr 1975: 249-250). It met weekly and may have originally been concerned with weights and measures and coinage, but soon was the arena for all sorts of litigation. The sheriffs were probably the original presiding officers, displaced by the mayor when that office emerged, and the aldermen were involved in some capacity as well. If one supposes that Aldermanbury was a proto-Guildhall, Husting may be the court that met there.

We will return to the mayor, the aldermen, and their courts in proper turn, as we examine the London institutions most significant for understanding the Church of St. Mary, Aldermanbury and its parish. These intertwined institutions are the parishes, the wards, the guilds, and the overarching City polity itself.

The Parish

The parish with its church was the institution which most frequently and directly touched the lives of Londoners. Under canon law the parish was responsible for baptism, burial and the collection of tithes (assessments on the landholders in the parish used in support of the church and its activities). But Londoners could be buried wherever they pleased, and the computation of tithes was at best an obscure business during the Middle Ages. (A Vatican delegation once concluded that many London parishes weren't worth the trouble!) The legalities certainly did not exhaust the functions of the parish and its church, and did not even touch some of the most important ones.

London's system of parishes was a product of the 11th and 12th centuries. The development was all but complete by 1200 (Brooke and Kerr 1975: 122, 130). The number of churches in the city had swelled from only 13 recorded in 1066 to a high of 120 in 1250. Most of the churches were small. There were 104 parishes in medieval London (Brooke and Kerr 1975: 123-125), and they survived even when about half the churches associated with them were not rebuilt after the Great Fire of 1666. It was not until Parliament passed the Reorganization of Parishes Act of 1907 that the situation changed.

Why so many churches in the City of London? Brooke and Kerr have identified several factors, including finance and the manner in which the churches were founded. The late 11th and early 12th century was a golden age of offerings for church construction all across Europe (1975: 127-128). Following the Conquest, England, and especially London, was more a part of the wider world than before. Further, in London, churches were established in two main ways, both grounded on local initiative. Some began as proprietary churches of sokes and other major properties. Just as the lord of a rural manor would be expected to provide a parish church for his dependents, so the lords of city establishments would found a church with their property. Others seem to have been neighborhood churches founded by people in some bounded part of the City, or sharing some common interest (1975:131-135). That some priests claimed to own the churches they served and, on becoming monks, presented the church and its advowson to the monastic chapter, may lead to a variety of speculations. In a time before celibacy was universal among the secular clergy, the gift often provided that the son of the donor would succeed to the living.

In some continental cities the cathedral was the only fully functioning church, and the parish churches were more like chantry chapels. Londoners by contrast seemed to prefer to worship in more intimate surroundings with their friends and neighbors and not at far remove from the priest and altar. It would seem that whatever the reason for their establishment, the social and gregarious side of religious life ("the fellowship of the saints") was nourished in London's modest churches.

As we have already noted in the first chapter, the Church of St. Mary, Aldermanbury, almost certainly had its beginning as a proprietary Church of the Aldermanbury soke, whether the founder was the royal Alderman, the City aldermen, or some Lord of the house. The parish may preserve the outline of the soke, running mostly along Aldermanbury, but branching on Addle Street (the north boundary of the tenement proper) and from there up Phillips Lane (Schofield and Dyson 1980:42-43).

A time soon came when the private ownership of churches was no longer recognized. Proprietorship in those terms had been overtaken by the parish system as the development of wards was to overtake the sokes and other private jurisdictions. However, an advowson (the right to choose and present the minister of the church to the Bishop for appointment) could still be owned, and that of St. Mary's was held with the great house next door for some time.

The parishes also assumed what would today be regarded as "secular functions," particularly in regard to city government. The major parish churches and the halls of important livery companies were the only places capable of accomodating indoor public meetings in many parts of London, and the church was a public building. Parishes thus became functioning subunits of the wards in which they stood, and wardmoots (ward conventions) were held in the churches of their more influential parishes.

The parishes themselves were governed by councils of lay people known as vestries (named after the "vesting" or "robing" rooms of the church, in which they met) of which there were two sorts. The <u>general vestry</u> was made up of all the rate (tithe and tax) payers in the parish, including women in some parishes. A <u>select vestry</u> was smaller and might be constituted in more than one way, It might be elected by the general vestry. It might be appointed by neighborhood notables. Or it might be a self-ordained company on its own motion. Some parishes had only a general vestry. Some had both, as was clearly the case in the Church of St. Mary, Aldermanbury. In others only a select vestry was ever called except in emergency or under duress. Given the accumulation of property and legacies in a parish by the 15th century most vestries had become well-heeled bureaucracies, holding considerable temporal power. The priests of the parish were not considered members of the vestry and did not attend vestry meetings. This practice continued in the Aldermanbury church until the 19th century. Ostensibly, the vestries were subject to the control of the Bishop. The Archdeacon of London paid an annual visit, and every three years the Bishop of London made an official visit. In practice, however, the laity of the parish exercised considerable autonomy in governance of the church.

Vestries were, in effect, branches of local government. They directly appointed parish officers, such as scavengers to deal with the sanitary condition of the parish. A general or select vestry was likely to meet prior to the wardmoot to prepare docket items and select candidates for nomination to ward offices. Occasionally, a vestry might make all the decisions in advance and declare the business of the wardmoot done without consulting anyone else. As we shall see, the Vestry of St. Mary's was apparently capable of such behavior on occasion.

The Vestry appointed Churchwardens to carry out the actual day to day governance of the church. Theirs was not an easy job, especially as the vestry's responsibility for the care of the poor within the parish increased. Disputes between priests and churchwardens over the collection and expenditure of tithes and bequests, and the collection of fees for burials, baptisms, and marriages, were not uncommon.

Much of the charitable work in medieval Europe was done by the Church, especially by religious orders and by specially endowed institutions: hospitals, almshouses, orphanages, etc., often themselves connected with a religious order. One such institution, called Elsing Spytal, was on the boundary of the Aldermanbury parish and will be described in some detail below. With the dissolution of the monastic houses under Henry VIII (see Ch. 3) and the late Elizabethan "Poor Laws" (1601) most of the responsibility for care of the poor shifted to the parishes, as we shall see when we reach that point in our account. However, well before this time the parishes had begun to play a role in various sorts of charitable activity. Many parishes, St. Mary, Aldermanbury among them, held endowments earmarked for such use, as we will see when we turn to the specific events in the life of the parish during medieval times.

The fundamental purpose of the parish was to provide for the religious well-being of its inhabitants. The parish and its vestry might not have a lot to say about their ministry unless the resident priest was sensitive to the views of neighbors. One might suppose that a prominent City parish like St. Mary's would have escaped the worst of the medieval abuses of Church benefits, such as an absentee incumbent and his incompetent curate. The work of the parish, including payment of the clergy, was funded by tithes collected in the parish; by other gifts; and by endowments, generally originating in the parish. Tension sometimes developed between parish priests, whose income was dependent on the tithes and fees, and the chantry priests who received a stipend from the bequest establishing the chantry. The chantry priests often received more than the priest parish. It took a ruling of the Court of Husting to clarify that chantry priests were to be subordinate to the parish priests. Ill-defined parish boundaries could also lead to disputes.

Canon law made daily attendance at mass compulsory. Regular offenders were denounced from the pulpit on the first Thursday of Lent and given the 40 days of Lent to repent. Those who did not were excommunicated on Good Friday and became social pariahs.

The parish was thus a fundamental institution of emerging London polity, the first to achieve the basic shape it would exhibit across the centuries. We shall specify later the important role it played in the evolution of self-government among the English-speaking peoples.

Sokes and Hagas (Haws)

Eleventh century London must have been a chaotic place from the administrative viewpoint. We can only speculate on the meaning of the names preserved in various records. The "haga" or "haw," was apparently a concentration of families with common trading interests in particular areas. "Haga" orginally meant "hedge" and may have been a rough synonym for burh. The owner of a haw was required to maintain law and order within its boundaries. Just west of Aldermanbury was Staininghaga during the mid-11th century, a haw possibly revolving around the staining industry or perhaps referring to the Staines family in Middlesex. To the east was the "haw" of the Basing family, where the church of St. Michael Bassishaw was founded. The family apparently had a rural seat at Basingstoke, Hampshire.

A soke was "a private jurisdiction which could only really have been effective over a closely defined area." The Aldermanbury soke was a classic example, "represented physically by the parish in which the burh itself and its annexed church stood in the dead centre." (Dyson 1991). It was "perhaps the most important of those created in the city" (Goss 1944: 122). Goss speculated that it may have covered the area extending roughly from Cheapside in the south to the soke of St. Martins-le-Grand on the north, on the east beyond Basinghall Street and on the west to a line midway between Philip Lane and Wood Street. However, as noted above, this issue cannot be resolved given the available evidence.

The sokes continued in existence until the 13th century, but by then the effective government within the City was through the system of wards and their Aldermen. Despite the introduction of the feudal system as the basis for law and administration, the City of London continued to base its legal system on Saxon and old Roman customs. Hence the concept of self-governing Freemen, who administered their own affairs through sokemotes, then wardmotes (first weekly, later yearly), was well-established and continued until the modern period. Until the 19th century only Freemen could regularly trade within the city, with others granted short term licenses.

When the death of Henry I in 1135 led to a breakdown of order, London had to rely more and more on its own resources. The "republican attitude," for which London was to become famous, was developing. Under the leadership of the Aldermen, the City had become an "empire within the Kingdom." This attitude grew stronger towards the beginning of the 12th century. In the mid-12th century we find the first reference to London as a "commune," importing a term from France which meant an "independent city."

Before the creation of wards, the lowest court was the sokemote (meeting). Numerous areas of private jurisdiction (Hagas, burghs, sokes) stood outside the reach of local authority with their own courts, ultimately answerable only to the king. Accused persons in hagas might be subject to trial at the rural manor of which it was a branch. Brooke and Kerr (1975: 149) remind us that London is notoriously missing from the Domesday Book, perhaps skipped over as past unravelling.

Wards

The solution to this administrative chaos was at hand in the institution of the ward, some of which Brooke believed went back to the Saxon period. The wards, though more malleable than parishes, may have arrived at their basic shape even earlier, though some seem to have developed along with parishes. Brooke suggested that the original 24 where in place by 1167 (Brooke and Kerr 1975: 162-167).

London was not restricted within its walls. Its boundaries extended to the "bars" on the main roads out of town ("Temple Bar" on Fleet Street being the most famous). This gave rise to the extramural wards and liberties of the City, and the question of their extension, a contentious issue between leaders of the City (including some in the parish of Aldermanbury) and those at the periphery, at various times.

Parish boundaries tended to stop at the wall. Ward boundaries did not, for wards had the maintenance of the gates and walls and other matters of defense as well as police measures ("ward and watch"), the keep of streets, and judicial and administrative matters in their charge.

Study of the early history of the London wards is made no easier by the fact that some early documents call the ward after the name of its alderman, so the name of the ward changed each time the alderman did. Discussion of the wards therefore leads to a consideration of the Aldermen, the chief officers of the wards. We have seen that the title derived from that of a Saxon official, an agent of the king or a shire headman, later designated by the Danish term jarl or earl. But "alderman" might also designate the head of a guild as well. The redundancy may be minimal, though, considering the salient part the guilds played and would play in London's government. The Alderman apparently played the role in their wards that the earldorman had played in the shires.

As time passed the private jurisdictions eroded before the emerging City polity, and the aldermen, acting in concert with the Mayor (one of their number), became the principal force in London's government. One early document calls an alderman a senator (Brooke and Kerr 1975:155, nl). When the aldermen sat in council, with the mayor at their head, they were indeed acting as a reincarnated Roman senate, a governing council of patricians.

The sheriff was originally a royal appointee, the tax farmer, but his office attracted additional powers. The sheriff came to be locally elected at some point, perhaps as early as 1129-1130 (Dyson n.d.: 39). From 1190 there were two sheriffs and the custom arose that the office offered a one time term of one year. They were elected from among the aldermen.

The office of mayor can be dated roughly to 1189. From then on the mayor (later Lord Mayor) remained the chief officer of London's civic polity. The mayor took precedence over the sheriffs and soon had his own court which eclipsed Husting. The first mayor, Henry FitzAilwin, was elected to a life term. Tenures varied until the term of one year became the norm. Dick Whittington (1358-1423), London's most storied, not to say legendary, Lord Mayor served three terms. Traditionally, the senior Alderman who had not so served was elevated to the mayoralty.

London's militia, heralded by the first mayor, and the precursor of the Trained Bands (at times the best organized, trained, and equipped troops in Britain) was made up of men mustered by the wards. In times of emergency the ward levees, the armed and able bodied men of the city, would each assemble at its appointed place and follow its banner to its duty station. As we shall see, the parish churches were used to house the arms for the militia.

The parish of Aldermanbury is located in the Ward of Cripplegate Within (the City Walls). Cripplegate Within was in existence by 1130. Its name came from the city gate (formerly the northern gate of the Roman Fort), called "Cripple" perhaps because it was a place of gathering and charity toward handicapped persons. Its 66 acres made it the second largest ward in the city. Most of this area was part of the royal demesne. In the Ward, prior to their expulsion by Edward I, was a large community of Jews, who engaged principally in banking. In fact, of the twenty-two Jewish homes in the City, ten were in Cripplegate Within.

The southern boundary of Cripplegate Within was Chepe (now Cheapside). Wood Street formed the major north-south axis. Milk Street was parallel to Wood, joining Aldermanbury at Cateaton (later Gresham Street). Aldermanbury stretched to the Wall, which formed the northern boundary of the Ward. Lad Lane linked Cateaton St. and Maiden Lane, which joined Gutter Lane, running South to Cheap. Addle Street continued Silver Street, running to the East out of Wood Street. Muggle (later Monkwell) ran north of Silver Street to a gate at the Wall. Phillip Lane ran north to the Wall out of Addle Street at a later date. Love Lane ran between Wood St. and Aldermanbury. According to legend, the name "Love" derived from the fact that prostitutes practiced their trade along the lane from Roman times onward. However, there is no corraborating evidence supporting the legend.

In addition to these streets there would have been a maze of winding alleyways and small courts, a pattern still evident in London outside the areas damaged by the Fire of 1666 and the Blitz of 1940. Drainage would have been virtually non-existent, with a constant stench arising from the rotting food and dead animals cast into the narrow streets. Transportation was provided by pack horses, mules, carts or wains, with boats and barges accessible on the Rivers Walbrook and Fleet, to the West and East.

Guilds

The Saxon custom of organization into guilds (joining people of similar interests, usually with a focus in a particular church) was evident from an early period in London. According to some interpreters, the first guilds were the Frithgild and Cnightengild (Gordon and Dewhurst 1985: 13). The former arose to cope with an outbreak of robberies. The latter emerged to provide leaders (knights) for the trained bands formed in the 10th century to protect the city against Norse attacks. When Edward left for Westminster in 1051, the guilds perhaps became part of the *de facto* city government. It is possible that leaders of the guilds moved their "offices" into the empty palace, which, as we have established, may have been the first guildhall, just north of the Church of St. Mary, Aldermanbury.

Other interpreters argue that the very nature and function of the first guilds in London are at best obscure. Brooke has likened the generality of the term "guild" to that of the modern "committee" and noted that 11th and early 12th century texts were specific on only two points: a guild was "something you paid for, and something you drank" (1975:98).

Some guilds *were* militia organizations, but others were social clubs. Some were religious fraternities. Some were charitable groups or mutual aid societies. Some were organizations of merchants or craftsmen. The element of conviviality was so great in the guild movement as a whole that it was the subject of street jokes. In any case, among the guilds that survived, the social, charitable, and religious aspects became or remained very much a part of things. Our attention will center on the London guilds that survived across the centuries to become the ancestors of the great livery companies (so called after their uniform ritual costumes).

Historians have classified the surviving guilds in England and elsewhere in Europe into two categories: merchant guilds and craft guilds. Both operated under royal charters which defined their jurisdiction and for which they paid an appropriate fee. The merchant guilds promoted the interests of their towns and of their members against other towns and against outsiders. The craft guilds regulated the training of apprentices and the quality of products. Masters, journeymen and apprentices alike were part of the guild structure. The guild structure was also reflected in the emerging universities: the doctors and masters of the university=masters of the guilds, the bachelors=journeymen, the students=apprentices. The guilds thus controlled entry into business and crafts, the wages paid and the prices charged.

The dogmas of modern economics, whether free-enterprise or socialist, make it difficult to appreciate the contributions the guilds made to the medieval world. By insuring the quality of products and stabilizing both wages and prices, and by contributing to the growth and independence of towns and the vitality of trades, theirs was a significant role.

As in London, they were also important in the development of local autonomy and self-government, though hardly of egalitarian democracy. Their restrictive practices in the end were part of their undoing, as were changes in industrial technology and patterns of trade. After the Industrial Revolution, few retained their original craft or mercantile functions, though in England the Pewterers Company of London still has a national responsibility for the assay of metals. Even in modern times, new guilds have been created, such as the Worshipful Company of Scientific Instrument Makers. Many livery companies became custodians of substantial charitable endowments across the centuries and the administration of these trusts has become a demanding activity for members. For example, the Haberdasher's Company, of which we will have more to say below, took a special interest in education and supports several excellent schools.

From an early period the great companies had their company halls where they met for social purposes or to transact business. The halls were also rented for use by churches and other institutions. Following the Great Fire of 1666, the congregation of St. Mary, Aldermanbury, met in Brewers Hall (see Ch. 4). During the tumultuous 17th century, various non-conformist groups made use of the company halls to hold meetings. Large independent congregations used Brewers Hall and Plaisters Hall in the Aldermanbury parish (Gordon and Dewhurst 1985: 120). Company halls also preserve treasures from the past, handsome sets of plate, works of art and examples of craftsmanship such as ceremonial sword rests.

The London livery companies also adopted parish churches as their company church. There they could celebrate the day of their patron saint and other religious activities of the company. St. Mary, Aldermanbury, was to become the church of the Worshipful Company of Haberdashers (royal charter, 1487). As time passed the aldermen of the companies became Masters. One of the great 17th Century Masters of the Haberdashers, the philanthropist Robert Aske, lived close by the Church.

We have noted that London's civic polity emerged in the neighborhood of Aldermanbury, perhaps in Aldermanbury itself, and that Cripplegate Ward may have earlier been called Aldermanesgarde. It may be further noted that since 1127 the seat of the local government of the City has been in a building called "Guildhall." The coincidence of Aldermanbury and Guildhall may be simply a coincidence. But as we have already indicated, it may have been more. The name "Guildhall" is certainly no accident. The great aldermen (and hence the mayors) were also great guildmen.

The Parish Church And Medieval Economics

Ecclesiastical institutions were probably the most important economic players in medieval London. In nearby Cheapside, before the Reformation, 60% of the land was in ecclesiastical ownership (Keene 1985: 6). The connection between the local economy and the parish churches was even more direct than that already mentioned for the monastic establishments. The building and maintenance of the parish churches involved the purchase of material and the payment of labor. In the case of St. Mary's, this would have involved the initial building and the subsequent enlargement and expansive rebuilding of 1437 (see below and Figure 2.1). There would be constant disbursements for candles, oil, communion elements, etc. and occasional expenditures on more durable liturgical items. Because of chantry endowments there may have been more priests associated with the church than just the incumbent. How much payments to them impacted the local economy depended on whether the priests were members of the secular clergy or religious orders, though presumably even a monk spent money in the community. The commissioners of 1548 reported that the priest at St. Mary's received £18 a year (Kitching 1980: 25).

Ecclesiastical properties were in fact capital goods in the medieval economy, on a par with modern stock and bond certificates. Foremost among these was the advowson, the right to nominate the priest (who would then be appointed, usually as a matter of course, by the bishop). This often included the right to a percentage of the tithes collected from the parish. Closely related was the "living" itself, the annual stipend of the incumbent. In the case of a good living (and St. Mary's was always so regarded) the holder of the advowson might get a kickback or an annual payment or both from the beneficiary or his family. The dean and chapter of St. Paul's, who held the St. Mary's advowson in 1204, granted the living to one of their number, canon John de Sancte Loren, for the payment of one mark a year (Guildhall Ms. A16-269). A family owning a valuable living might confer it upon a relative, as Joan de Talworth, tenant of Aldermanbury tenement, may have done for Roger de Talworth, priest at St. Mary's, and then in 1437 leased to him parts of the tenement and the postern connecting it with the Church (Dyson n.d.: 9).

What was true of the advowson was to a lesser degree true of the chantry endowments, which paid a priest to say regular masses for the deceased beneficiary or someone otherwise designated. Sometimes these chantries involved a special altar or chapel in the church. An incumbent who also held several chantries would thus enhance his income, though there was no guarantee that the incumbent in the church would also hold its chantries.

Having established that these ecclesiastical properties were in fact capital products, income-producing properties, it is not hard to understand why they were treated very much as people today treat bonds and stocks. They were bought and sold. They were bequeathed to heirs. Pious souls might will them to charitable or religious institutions. The advowson of St. Mary's was at various times held by St. Mary Hospital (Elsyng Spital) and the dean and chapter of St. Paul's, among others. We have seen that the dean and chapter collected "dividends" as it were by "renting" the appointment for an annual fee. But suppose the chapter encountered a cash flow crisis? Then some of these advowsons and chantry appointments could be put on the market and their capital value realized.

The Hundred Years War (1337-1453) probably benefitted London's economy as armies were outfitted and equipped. London, like other towns in England, largely ducked the War of the Roses (1455-1485), allowing the rival noblemen to have at one another without taking sides, except to open the gates to whichever army was on hand in force, and in the case of London to offer its bridges for the display of the heads of the losers at various stages.

The Black Death (from 1348) was more of a disaster to London than the rural areas. The visitations of plague from this first catastrophe through the last in 1666 usually struck hardest amid the crowded and unsanitary conditions of life in the City. The labor shortages in town and country and the dislocations, especially in rural areas, following the plague, probably increased townward migration. By the 14th century serfdom was disappearing and the labor shortage produced by the plague hastened its end.

London could be a place of rebellion, spurred on by difficult economic circumstances. However, rebel leaders did not fare well. The Lord Mayor himself struck down Wat Tyler, one of the principal figures in the Peasant's Revolt of 1381. The sympathy of London liverymen could hardly be expected to lie with violent advocates of higher wages and other worker benefits, particularly since the rebel march on London was apparently prompted by hopes of support from the urban laborers.

English efforts to divert an increasing share of the trade in finished woolens from the 13th century onward had to be a benefit to London's economy despite the resentment of guildmen when Flemish weavers with their improved techniques were imported. Some historians hold that the Renaissance followed the finished woolen trade northward from Italy to Flanders and finally to England. This could indeed have been one of the sources of the discretionary wealth necessary to support the outpourings of scholarship and various artistic endeavors during the Renaissance.

The last medieval century (the 15th) must have been a prosperous one in London. A substantial amount was spent on private gifts to civic improvements in Aldermanbury (see below) and elsewhere in the City.

That the wealth of the City of London grew during the Middle Ages has been documented by London historian Derek Keene. London was already the largest and wealthiest of English towns by the tenth century. "Between about 1100 and 1700 it increased its pre-eminence to a remarkable degree" (Keene 1989: 99). The assessed wealth of London was five times as great as its nearest rival (Bristol) in 1334. By 1400 London was doing about 35% of the overseas trade in the country. By 1500 this had increased to 68%; by 1540 it was 85%. Although wealth and trade increased faster than the population of London, the city experienced a population boom during the Middle Ages, peaking in 1300 when about 80,000- 100,000 people lived in the City and its immediate environs. The population declined every 25 years from 1300 until 1550, because of a succession of plagues (Keene 1985: 19). In 1100 one in every eighty Englishmen lived in London; by 1500 one in fifty did. Two centuries later one in ten Englishmen resided in London.

Throughout the Middle Ages rich and poor lived side by side in London. Perhaps in the 15th century the practice of the wealthy merchants to set their houses back from the busy frontages began, allowing some seclusion from the clamor and filth of the streets. Artisans tended to live in small houses on frontages with little room for gardens. The poor lived in single rooms, generally in upper storeys. (Keene 1985: 16).

The Church and Parish of St. Mary, Aldermanbury during the Middle Ages

In this era before the keeping of Church and parish records, our portrait of the actual events must, by necessity, be sketchy. However, from various manuscript sources and the Grimes excavations we can catch a glimpse of the evolution of the church building and the parish, as well as bits of the sometimes intriguing, but often hazy, events which transpired there.

We are able to trace some of these ecclesiastical properties associated with St. Mary, Aldermanbury, through several owners and a couple of generations by means of documents in the Guildhall Library manuscript collection. For example, in the 32nd regnal year of the durable Edward III (who reigned 1327-1377) a consortium of buyers purchased the Inn of Aldermanbury and a chantry in St. Mary's (Al9-330). Sir Thomas Bedyk, one of the company, subsequently released his interest to John de Beauchamp and John de Bovendon (Al9-331). Finally, in Edward's 47th year, the dean and chapter of St. Paul's, who had benefitted from the will of Sir John (de) Beauchamp, granted the chantry in St. Mary's to Alexander, son of Sir Thomas Bedyk, perhaps as a term of Sir John's will (Al9-1475, 1477). Goss (1944:158-159) listed 15 chantry endowments in St. Mary's from 1251 by Adam de Basing, beneficiary of Henry III's grant, through 1446 by Alderman/Mayor William Estfield, a major benefactor of the Church and parish (see below), who appointed the Mercers Company patrons of the endowment. And Sir Henry de Bedyk endowed not one but two chantries.

One of St. Mary's more interesting endowments was a gift of land in the parish to pay the priest's wages and other expenses. There were several donors, but chief among them was one "late Alderman Bury of London" (Kitching 1980:25). Foundlings of the parish after the institution of the Poor Laws were frequently christened with the surname "Bury" or "Berry." This gift was not dated by the commissioners of 1548, but it obviously had been in hand more than a half century before the Poor Laws were enacted. Did the custom predate the law? Was this alderman a foundling of the parish who went on to a successful career and then provided it a fulfillment of the text, "Cast your bread upon the waters" (Ecclesiastes 11:1) as it is usually interpreted?

According to a 15th Century mayor of London, William Gregory, one of the more memorable events during this early period of parish life occurred in 1222 when "a man that fayned himself Cryste, he was crucified at Aldermanbery at London" (cited by Goss 1944:146).

According to one historian of London churches, in 1223 Gervase Aldermanbir, Lord of the Manor, alleged that his father Alan de Aldermanbir had presented William de Aldermanbir for the living, and William had died thirty-one years earlier leaving the church void. In response the Dean and Chapter of St. Paul's alleged that the Church was not void, but that Nicholas, son of Jocey, was parson under the institution of the parson and that since the death of William there had been four parsons: John de St. Laurence, Jordan de Gloucester, John de St. Peter, then Nicholas. (Hennessy 1898: 298).

The London Eyre records that in 1244 a Margery, daughter of Hugh Chamberlain, and Agnes, daughter of Robert son of Reginald, fled to the Church of St. Mary and there acknowledged some impropriety. The record curtly adds "they had no chattels" (Chew 1970:59).

Gervase de Aldermanbir's claim to the advowson apparently held up. On the 16th of February 1247, he granted to Alderman Adam de Basynges or Basing, all the "liberties and free customs" of the manor "together with the advowson of the Churches of St. Mary Aldermanbury, St. Mary Magdalene, Melk strete and of St. Michael (to be named Bassishagh), which were appurtenant to the manor" (Goss

1944:120). In the deal de Basing also acquired six shops (Williams 1963: 323-324). The three churches of the Aldermanbury soke, with a £40 rent, were to support successive generations of parish patricians—Basings, Eswys, and Bedycks, in turn (Williams 1963: 56).

Adam de Basing was a wealthy cloth merchant, King's tailor and financier, who served as Sheriff and, in 1251, Mayor of London. His father had been one of the knightly landowners of the minority. Adam married into the influential Viels and FitzAlulf families. He immersed himself in the Irish trade, handling corn and hides, but he made his fortune supplying costly fabrics and other luxury goods to the crown. In 1244 de Basing acquired the entire wool production of the huge bishopric of Westminster. By 1250 his annual income was about £250 (Williams 1963: 72-73). He was apparently a favorite of King Henry III who called him "our well beloved Adam de Basing" (Goss 1944:121).

He may have built a new house on the east side of Aldermanbury, to replace or in addition to the existing manor house on the west side, in the process blocking one of the major northwest highways in London, resulting in litigation (Williams 1963: 199). This may also explain why the Axe Inn, which presumably replaced the manor house, was located on the east side of Aldermanbury. In any event, the name Basinghall attached to the street which ran parallel to Aldermanbury, across from the manor house, to the east (Williams 1963: 324).

When Adam de Baysing died in 1262 his eight year old son, Thomas, became lord of the manor. Thomas continued the family woolen trade. However, the family business must have run into trouble, for the records show that he disposed of considerable property before his early death in 1275 (Goss 1944:121). Thomas did have apparent affection for the Church. In his will he provided for maintenance of the Chapel of St. Mary de Aldermanbury "one mark rent of a tenement in Smithefield" and for a lamp and chantry in the Church rents in Godrone Lane (from the "Rolls of the Court of Husting," cited by Carter 1913:10).

In the same year (1275) a William de Carelton left to his cook, Hervey, a tenement in the parish and rents from Bassihawe parish to support a Chantry in the Church (Carter 1913:10).

In 1273 a Walter de Kingestone left rents to provide for a chantry for three years; in 1280 Isabella Bokrel left a bequest for a lamp and ordained her heirs to provide a chantry in the Church; and in 1335 a total of four chantries were funded by bequests from Henry de Bydyll and Lawrence Botoner (Carter 1913:10). In 1353 Roger de Taleworth provided funds to be used to maintain the High Altar, and in 1357 Henry de Chadesdene left money to found a chantry. In 1367 William de Bristowe left money for the maintenance of a chantry. In 1386 John Tours left a tenement to the Rector for the maintenance of a beam light. In 1399 Simon de Wynchecambe, who wanted to be buried in the church, provided for a Chantry. In 1431 Dennis Towers gave all his tenements in the parish to fund a priest and an anniversary (annual prayers) (Goss 1944:159).

The advowson of the Church of St. Mary passed from Thomas de Basing to his descendants, then in 1306 to a Sir John de Drokenisford, along with the manor and the six shops. However, Sir John returned the grant (which perhaps had been security for a loan) and the advowson continued in the de Basing family. On 9 June, 1331 the Hospital of Elsing Spital (see below) procured the approbation and annexation of the rectory of St. Mary, Aldermanbury. Since the benefice was technically in the gift of the Dean and Chapter of St. Paul's, the warden of the priory, William de Elsing, had to obtain their consent for appointment. He agreed to find a fit priest to serve the church (Pearce 1913: 14 and Hennessy 1898: 298). From 1360 until 1374, as we have already mentioned, the advowson was held again by the Dean and Chapter of St. Paul's, who then granted it to an Alexander de Bedyk. It must have once again returned to the de Basing family. However, in 1417, the de Basing line ended and the manor, and presumably advowson, reverted to the King (Goss 1944:121). Without a Lord of the manor, it is likely that when the Crown took control the manor house was either demolished or refurbished to serve as an inn. By 1424 the one time mansion, inhabited by Lords of the soke for several hundred years, became a brewhouse and inn under the sign of "ye Ax yn Aldermanne bury" (Goss 1944:122). The Axe Inn continued as an inn, then a pub until the 1940's when the building in which it was located gave way to the Charter Insurance Institute. (On the Inns of Aldermanbury see Ch. 8.)

In 1329 an important institution was created in the parish. In that year William de Elsynge, Mercer, obtained a license "to alienate in mortmain houses in the parishes of St. Alphage and St. Mary the Virgin, Aldermanbury, to found a hospital for 100 blind people in honor of the Blessed Virgin Mary." (Cal. Pat. Rolls 1327-1330:360). The hospital was known as Elsynge (or Elsyng or Elsing) Spital. It had served as a nunnery before Elsynge obtained the license and was located on the West side of

Gayspur Lane, with an entrance from the Street, London Wall. (Goss 1944:162). The nunnery had apparently deteriorated by Elsynge's time and he converted it into a priory. The staff of the hospital or priory consisted originally of a warden (Elsynge) and four secular priests (Cal. of Wills in the Court of Husting, I:362). However, in 1340 Elsynge obtained a license from the Bishop of London to change the secular canons into canons of the order of St. Augustine. A fifth canon was added by the bishop. Elsynge worked hard to secure support for the hospital. In 1338 and 1339 a total of seven messuages were transferred to the "Warden and Chaplains of the Hospital of St. Mary Aldermanbury" (Calendar, 1323-2364, Roll As, Membr. 8b and 10:182 and 187). A reference to a quit claim between the prior of the hospital, Robert Draycote, and a John Cyfrewust, Knight, dated 14 November, 1386, refers to a convent associated with the hospital (Calendar, Roll A28, Membr. 2b:127).

Elsyng Spital continued as a priory until it was dissolved during the Reformation on 11 May, 1530 (Pearce 1913: 15). The priory became the property of Sir John Williams, Master and Treasurer of the King's Jewels. He converted the prior's quarters and hospital into a large dwelling house which burned down on Christmas Eve, 1541, leaving only the arches of the priory church (Goss 1944:162). The house was rebuilt by Williams' daughter Margery and her husband Henry Norris. They sold it to Sir Rowland Hayward, Alderman, and John Lacs, a clothworker, in 1562. Hayward's descendants sold it to Robert and Helen Parkhurst, who sold it to Dr. Thomas White, vicar of St. Dunstan's in the East (Pearce 1913: 15). In 1623 the Rev. Dr. White bequeathed £3,000 to build on the site Sion College for the use of London clergy, where they could meet socially, and almshouses for ten men and ten women. The college received a charter on 7 March, 1626. Another clergyman, the Rev. Dr. John Simpson, provided £2,000 for a library and governor's residence. The college was destroyed in the Great Fire of 1666, but was rebuilt and continued in the parish until 1884. The site of Elsyng Spital itself, however, became the location of the Church of St. Alphage, London Wall, which was merged with St. Mary, Aldermanbury as part of the Reorganization of Parishes in 1907. To be exact, the tower and porch of the priory church were incorporated into St. Alphage's. When St. Alphage's was torn down early in this century, the tower was left standing as a memorial to Elsyng Spital. It survived the Blitz and remains today, crowded next to London Wall Street to the south and a parking garage to the north, and enclosed on the north side above by the Barbican Highwalk. A plaque marks the site.

On 20 July, 1341, there was a disturbance in the parish which resulted in an inquest before the Mayor of London and the Sheriffs. According to the Calendar and Plea and Memoranda (1323-1364, Roll A3 Membr. 25) the inquest was held on Friday the Feast of St. Margaret in the 15th year of King Edward III. It concerned a disturbance in the parish of St. Mary, Aldermanbury, opposite the house of Sir Robert Parnyng, chief justice of the King's Bench, King's Treasurer, and Chancellor. The jury said that certain men to whom the King owed money for wages went to the Treasurer with Letters under the Privy Seal instructing him to pay the sum due. The Treasurer put them off "with smooth and false words" after which members of his household wounded them without reasonable cause. Sir Robert's side of the disturbance and the disposition of the case are not given.

The role of the Church as caretaker of London's poor was not formalized until the Elizabethan poor laws early in the 17th century, but the records show that already in the 13th and 14th centuries the Church of St. Mary was providing relief to the many impoverished in the parish. In 1260 the aforementioned Alderman Adam de Basing left certain rents in his will to the Church "for charity." In 1307 a Hugh de Glovernia designated rents of a tenement for the poor "in bread, clothes, shoes and money." In 1361 Richard Lacey made a gift for charity, and in 1374 a Simon de Bristowe left money in his will for the poor.

In the record of taxation of the clergy between 1375 and 1381, the rectory of the Church of St. Mary is shown to have been appropriated to the Hospital of Elsing Spital. Chaplains are listed as Reginald atte Halle, Nicholas deVandlee, Nicholas Smothe, and William Farnews (McHardy 1977:10).

In the Ecclesiastical Assessment of Property for 1392 there is evidence of a rent of £8 from a tenement of a Sir Nicholas in Farringdon Ward Within for a chantry and other assessments from tenements of a Gilbert Bonce and Adam Fraunceys (McHardy 1977:51 and 56).

By the 15th century the Church had apparently fallen into some decay, perhaps reflecting a decline in the wealth of Cripplegate Ward. However, in 1437 Alderman Sir William Estfield, who lived in the parish near the site of the present Guildhall Library, funded a rebuilding project (see Figures 2.1 and 2.2). The steeple was rebuilt at Estfield's expense and the five old bells were recast "into more tunable ones." The church itself was substantially enlarged on new foundations. The resulting structure was a good example of the English Perpendicular style. Estfield also gave £100 for other improvements in the Church. (Goss 1944:152 and Malcolm 1803:116, based on Stow 1598).

William Estfield was a leading citizen, not only of the parish, but of the City of London. He served as sheriff (1422) and Lord Mayor (1429 and 1437) (Carter 1913:92). He served in Parliament in 1431 and 1442. Sir William was apparently a very devout man. In 1428 he obtained permission to erect a chapel at the rear of his mansion. According to a document dated 6 August, 1428, the Mayor and Aldermen granted permission to construct the chapel towards the East, up to the end of the Guildhall (Goss 1944:129). The grant stipulated that Estfield would yearly render "a red rose fashioned upon a rod, to be carried according to ancient custom, before the Mayor, when he goes to St. Paul's Cathedral."

When W. F. Grimes excavated the site of the Church of St. Mary in 1967, after the removal of walls and columns to Westminster College, he traced the foundations of the medieval church (see Figure 2.3). As mentioned in Ch. 1, he discovered two major phases, first a chancel and a nave to which northwest and southeast chapels had been added in the 13th century, then an open church with a West Tower. This represents the 1437 church, the foundations of which were utilized by Christopher Wren (Grimes 1969:251). Tiles from the 13th century church, recovered by Grimes, are in the Museum of London and several have been loaned for exhibit in the undercroft of the contemporary Church of St. Mary, Aldermanbury. The tiles themselves have been dated by Museum of London authorities to the 14th century and hence witness to yet another enhancement of the Church.

During the Medieval period the church was enclosed by cloisters (Stow 1598:233) with a churchyard adjoining.

In the 14th century buildings sprang up in the area surrounding the Church, and commercial activity increased. It is likely that already during this period Cripplegate Ward Within began to become less attractive as a residential area, and the wealth of the Ward had begun to decrease somewhat. However, even as its Ward began to decline, Aldermanbury remained relatively prosperous because of the location of the Guildhall, which drew some of the more prominent citizens of London to the parish.

The parish of Aldermanbury was one of the first areas of London to be served by piped in water. In 1444 Sir William Estfield initiated at his own expense the project of building a "fayre conduit by Alderman beirie Church" connected by a series of wooden pipes to Tyburn brook to the North. The conduit was at the intersection of

Aldermanbury and Love lanes across from the entrance to Estfield's mansion. The conduit was for use in the trades now well established in the parish and for washing. The Worshipful Company of Brewers, whose first company hall was established in the parish in 1420, may have been among those who made use of the conduit.

In his will Estfield left money to continue the conduit project, which was completed in 1471. Fourteen years later a Warden was assigned by the Mayor and Alderman to watch over the conduit. It is clearly visible on the Copper Plate map of 1553 and the inferior but more complete cloned Ralph Agas woodcut map of 1580 (Carter 1913:2). The conduit deteriorated and was rebuilt several times (including, of course, after the 1666 Fire) until it was taken down in the 18th century. However, in 1890 a drinking fountain was erected against the retaining wall of the churchyard, near the location of the original conduit (Goss 1944:128-129). The fountain continues in use to the present day, with a metal cup attached by a chain for use by thirsty passers by.

The value of the conduit can best be appreciated by recognizing the contaminated nature of other water sources: the Thames, the Holburn/Fleet and the Walbrook and its tributaries, and private wells. Professor Grimes excavated one coopered (barrel-lined) medieval well in the southern extremity of Aldermanbury parish which was only a bit over three feet deep, terminating in the fill which levelled the Roman fort ditch. He wrote that stone-lined wells nearby were equally shallow. Grimes observed, "If their contents were used for domestic purposes to any great extent such wells must have constituted a serious risk to health" (Grimes 1968:162-163; pl. 72).

Goss (1944:124-125) gives the following picture of parish life during the 14th and 15th centuries:

> In the 14th century, the main street, which for two centuries past
> had become Aldermanbury, with its northern adjunct, then called
> "Gaysporelane" or "Gayspur lane," was a narrow, irregular and
> winding thoroughfare (between 15 and 20 feet wide, broadening
> out near the church to between 40 and 50 feet) of gabled
> timber-built houses, with over-sailing upper storeys which,
> in the narrowest part, nearly touched the houses that might
> perchance be facing them on the opposite side, thus contracting
> the air space between them and shutting out the broad expanse
> of blue sky and sunlight, while keeping the streets damp and muddy.

The streets were of the roughest description, consisting of large stones interspersed with smaller ones and a slight depression in the centre for drainage; no footpaths; dogs the principal scavengers and rain the only cleanser, for the "rakyers" (scavengers) had great difficulty in compelling householders to clear away filth deposited at their doors by neighbours. Plagues in those early centuries were very prevalent, no less than eight occurring between the years 1348-1499, causing extensive mortality, ... From the overhanging upper storeys, jutting out into the narrow roadway some poles about 7 feet long, may have been seen carrying a sign to indicate ownership or the trade of the occupant, for houses were not numbered until some three centuries later. The houses were rarely more than three storeys high, sometimes with access to the upper rooms by means of outside staircases or ladders leading from the roadway.

At night, the streets were dimly-lighted; but, by the first quarter of the 15th century, an organised system was introduced by which lanterns holding candles of a prescribed size and character ("12 to the pound weight"), every citizen was compelled to hang at his window or door at the hour of "vij of the bell at night." In later years, there were a few stately houses with fair patches of garden ground at the rear. There were still many open spaces reaching up to the medieval wall.

Many of the residents of the parish were probably engaged in a variety of small business enterprises. Women could own businesses and property. Upward mobility was possible. An enterprising man or woman could open a stall in a market, then move up to owning a shop behind the stalls, then open a warehouse with an office or "seld" and a small room for his or her family above. In the 14th century in Cripplegate Within the following businesses were found: goldbeaters, tailors, tylers and fasters (joiners and makers of woodwork for saddles), clothworkers, fruiterers, puchmakers, cordwainers, kissers (makers of thigh armor), poulters, girdlers, leathermakers, and general merchants. There were also moneyers and bankers as well as brewers, corn chandlers, and a flourishing wool trade. The decline in the wealth of the ward is associated with the movement of the banking industry to the east, where it is still centered. As we shall see, the economic development of the parish in subsequent centuries was more and more toward the wool and cloth trade, and after the industrial revolution, toward large warehouses. (Gordon and Dewhurst 1985: 54).

Information about the church in the early decades of the 16th century is sparse. One will, which dates to late 1527 or early 1528, mentions burial in the churchyard "by the crosse" and a bequest of 20d to the "hyghe aulter of the ... church where I was late parishoner, for my tythes and oblacions negligently forgotten" (Darlington 1967:101).

Another record names a rector and a chantry priest and their stipends and fines in the 14th year of Henry's reign (1505) (Malcolm 1803:118):

Sir Thomas Cobb, serving, 61.13.4; goods £9; fined 30s

Sir Thomas Betynson (chantry priest), serving, 71.16.8; goods £20; fined 54s.

Conclusion

Information about London parish churches is limited prior to the requirement that parish records be kept, which was instituted under Henry VIII. Such evidence as is available has been summarized here. However, we do know and have here recounted just how important this period was in establishing institutions like the parish, vestry, wards, and guilds. They had a tremendous impact not only on St. Mary's in subsequent centuries, but on the history of London as well as the common heritage of all English-speaking peoples. The relative stability enjoyed by London and St. Mary, Aldermanbury, during the medieval period was soon to end. The next two centuries in the life of the City and the parish were so eventful and tumultuous (not to mention well-documented) that we will devote several complete chapters to them.

Bibliography

Brooke, Christopher N. L. and Gillian Kerr
    1975   History of London: London, 800-1216: The Shaping of a City.
           Berkeley, CA: University of California.

Carter, Pierson Cathrick
    1913   History of the Church and Parish of St. Mary the Virgin, Aldermanbury.
           London: W. H. and L. Collinbridge.

Chew, Helena M. and Mertin Weinbaum, ed.

1970   The London Eyre of 1244. London: London Record Society.

Darlington, Ida, ed.
   1967   London Consistory Court Wills. London: London Record Society.

Douglas, David C. and G. W. Greenaway
   1953   English Historical Documents, Vol. II. New York: Oxford University Press. (William FitzStephen's "Description of London," 956-962).

Dyson, Tony
   no date   "Aldermanbury," an unpublished paper.

   1989   Documents and Archaeology: The Medieval London Waterfront (The Annual Archaeology Lecture, 1987). London: The Museum of London.

   1991   Personal correspondence with the authors.

Ekwall, Eilert
   1954   Street Names of London. Oxford: Oxford University Press.

Gordon, Caroline and Wilfrid Dewhurst
   1985   The Ward of Cripplegate in the City of London. Oxford: University Press.

Goss, Charles
   1944   "A History of The Parish of St. Mary the Virgin, Aldermanbury," Transactions of the London and Middlesex Archaeological Society. 9 (1944-47), 113-164.

Grimes, W. F.
   1968   The Excavation of Roman and Medieval London. London: Routledge and Kegan Paul.

   1969   "London: Church of St. Mary, Aldermanbury," Medieval Archaeology

13, 251.

Hennessy, George
    1898   Novum Repertorium. London: Swan Sonneschein.

Honeybourne, Marjorie B.
    1960   A Sketch Map of London under Richard II. London: London Topographical Society (publication no. 93).

Keene, Derek.
    1985   Cheapside Before the Great Fire. London: Economic and Research Council.

    1989   "Medieval London and Its Region," The London Journal: A Review of Metropolitan Society Past and Present. 14, 99-111.

Kitching, C. J., ed.
    1980   London and Middlesex Chantry Certificates, 1648. London Record Society Publications XVI. London: The London Record Society.

McHardy, A. K.
    1987   The Churches in London, 1375-1392. London: London Record Society.

Malcolm, J. Peller
    1803   Londinium Redivivum: An Ancient History and Modern Description. London: John Nichols and Son.

Meyers, A. R.
    1972   London in the Age of Chaucer. Norman, OK: University of Oklahoma Press.

Pearce, E. H.

1913   Sion College and Library. Cambridge: University Press.

Pendrill, Charles
    1925   London Life in the 14th Century. New York: Adelphi.

    1937   Old Parish Life in London. London: Oxford University.

Pooley, Sir Ernest
    1947   The Guilds of London. London: Collins.

Schofield, John and Tony Dyson
    1980   The Archaeology of the City of London. London: The Museum of London.

Stow, John.
    1598   A Survay of London by John Stow, Citizen of London. London: John Windet (1603).

Thomas, A. H. and Philip Jones, ed.
    1926-61   Calendar of Pleas and Memoranda Rolls (1323-1482). Cambridge: University Press.

Williams, Gwyn A.
    1963   Medieval London: From Commune to Capital. London: The Athelone Press.

CHAPTER THREE: ST. MARY'S DURING THE PROTESTANT REFORMATION (1435-1639)

Introduction

Like almost every other Christian parish in northern Europe and England, St. Mary, Aldermanbury, was caught up in the sweeping changes brought by the Protestant Reformation. In this chapter we will first set the stage by describing the web of forces which brought reformation to the Church of England, beginning with the Renaissance and tracing economic, political, and religious developments in the reigns of successive monarchs. We will need to devote special attention to the Puritan movement in England, because of its impact on St. Mary, Aldermanbury.

After establishing the context, we will see St. Mary, Aldermanbury, as a parish church in transition. The extant records of the Church date to this period, so we will be able to use finer brush strokes in painting our picture of parish life. Evidence will be presented which shows that before the 17th century Aldermanbury had become a center of the Puritan movement in London. During this period two of Aldermanbury's more famous parishoners, Henry Condell and John Heminges, friends of and fellow actors with William Shakespeare, lived in the parish and held offices in the church. In an excursus we will examine Heminges and Condell's relationship with Shakespeare and the question of Shakespeare's connection to Aldermanbury. The chapter will conclude with England on the brink of Civil War and Aldermanbury about to enter center stage in the history of London and the nation.

The Coming of the Renaissance

During the late 14th and 15th centuries certain cultural, political, and economic developments swept out of northern Italy, southward to Rome and northward across Europe, reaching Britain. Even though these developments did not represent a break with the past as such, they were a departure from the immediate past, the medieval past, in the minds of many who participated in them. And although some contemporary revisionist historians question whether there ever was a Renaissance, or, if there was, whether it started before 1350, we can hardly question momentous changes wrought when intellectuals looked back over the middle ages for inspiration from the classical past. There was no new philosophy to replace the Greek masters and no new science to replace the astronomy of Ptolemy and Aristotle, the physics of Aristotle and Archimedes. (Vesalius in the 16th century undercut the anatomy of Galen). It was not until the 17th century that thoughtful scholars began to seek new grounds for both philosophy and science.

The Renaissance came late to northern Europe and latest of all to England. Inigo Jones (1573-1652), who served James I and Charles I, was the first "surveyor" (architect) in England to follow the example of the Italian Palladio, who had canonized the architectural conventions of the classical past. Through the Tudor period half timber houses and Gothic churches continued to be built in England.

When the Renaissance did spread to northern Europe it exhibited profoundly religious overtones that had been less obvious in Italy. Indeed, it has been argued that the Protestant Reformation was the northern expression of the Renaissance. Certainly, the humanistic scholarship that was one of the principal features of the Renaissance was a major factor in the rise of the reform movement. All the great leaders of the Reformation (such as Zwingli, Luther, Melancthon, Calvin, Butzer, and Bullinger) and fellow-travelers like Erasmus were scholars in the humanistic tradition. Some Renaissance humanists were secularist in outlook. Others, like the Englishman, Sir Thomas More, exhibited the intense piety of which martyrs are made. The Renaissance humanists were especially interested in the study of ancient texts in the original languages, at first classical Greek and Latin, then Hebrew, allowing for study of the Biblical texts in the original languages. Humanistic scholars tended to emphasize the plain meaning of Biblical texts, over against the allegorical reading of medieval interpreters. They were also skeptical of superstitious beliefs and practices.

Undergirded by disgust at Church abuses and fueled by the rise of nationalism and the middle class, it seemed that humanism and Reform marched hand in hand across northern Europe, except where they were suppressed by force and violence.

The Tudor Dynasty

Henry VII (1485-1509)

Popular tradition has it that the English middle ages died on Bosworth Field with Richard III in 1485. This did not mean that the Renaissance or modernity arrived on British shores when Henry Tudor, Earl of Richmond, donned the battered crown, legendarily found hanging in a bush, to become King Henry VII. Historians rather emphasize continuity between Edward IV and Henry VII. But Henry did put an end to the Wars of the Roses and to the great barons playing power politics within their own country. This was part of the more general trend toward centralization and heightening of the sense of nationalism.

Henry also brought England belatedly into the business of exploration. Tradition has it that Henry was ready to sponsor the first voyages of Christopher Columbus, but the Italian had already found sponsors. Henry did send out John Cabot, whose voyage in 1497 gave England a claim to the mainland of North America. Henry also built up the Royal Navy, the basis for England's future strength and prosperity.

When Henry took the crown the royal treasury was empty. At his death it contained a surplus of £1,500,000. Two significant economic developments of Henry's times had particularly substantial consequences. The enclosure of former agricultural land to pasture sheep accelerated. The landowners learned from the Cistercian monks that sheep keeping required less labor and returned higher profits than farming. The enclosures forced many peasants off the land and left them impoverished. Many sought work in the cities, including London, only to find themselves even more destitute. More sheep meant more wool, and the innovative "domestic system" of manufacture was able to find a use for it. Under the scheme, an entreprenurial merchant would buy and distribute wool to spinners and weavers, most working out of their own homes, promising to buy the finished product back at an agreed price. The merchant was then free to sell the product at the going price, usually at a large profit. The system would work in other than woolens, and damaged the interests of some of the old craft guilds. But it also increased London's, and Britain's, trade.

Henry VII's policies generally prospered the landholding gentry and the city middle class while hurting the higher nobility and the peasantry. The gentry were growing in power and influence in the shires and in the House of Commons, and the middle class likewise was becoming more powerful in the Commons. Both of these classes supported Henry for the law and order which he established and maintained, a necessary condition for their prosperity. It has been said that Parliament would give Henry anything he wanted—except money. He seldom asked for it because he seldom needed it, and only rarely called Parliament during his reign.

Henry discovered "popular absolutism," a practice skillfully followed by his Tudor successors, Henry VIII and Elizabeth I. It had two main features, respect for ancient forms and divining what the people wanted and helping them get it or at least seeming to do so.

London had come through the Wars of the Roses relatively unscathed. The City emerged from the age of Henry VII more vigorous and prosperous, and even better times were to come. Henry VII died in 1509, leaving a country in sound condition, poised on the brink of changes more dramatic than any could imagine.

Henry VIII (1509-1547)

The birth of the Renaissance in England is frequently associated with the work of John Colet, dean of St. Paul's Cathedral, the establishment of St. Paul's School (1509-1512), and his teaching there. Colet was a Christian humanist, acquainted with many of Europe's great scholars, and a harbinger of Church reform. St. Paul's School offered a non-clerical humanistic education.

Prince Henry, from 1509 King Henry VIII, was an accomplished humanistic scholar himself. The fact that such great English humanists as Colet and Sir Thomas More came of age in the reign of Henry VII and Erasmus paid his first visit to England in the late 15th Century, shows that the seeds had long been sown. Nonetheless, it is not inaccurate to say the Renaissance flowered in England during the reign of Henry VIII, even as the Protestant Reformation erupted in Germany and spread to England in those years.

Renaissance came first and through the early years of his reign Henry VIII remained loyal to Rome. He even penned a tract (although it may have been ghosted by a court humanist like Sir Thomas More) against Luther's views of the sacraments. The pope rewarded Henry's fidelity with the title "Defender of the Faith."

However, reform was in the air. In a sense it had been since the days of John Wycliffe (ca. 1320-1384), who had enlisted royal support in his efforts to reform the church. There is evidence that Wycliffe's followers, who became known as Lollards, were active in the Aldermanbury parish, as we shall see below. Henry was in the dying prayer of William Tyndale (1492?-1536), who was burned at the stake as a heretic after translating the Bible into English. Tyndale's translation, banned by bishops concerned about the danger of lay people interpreting Scripture for themselves, was to become the basis for the famed and still popular Authorized ("King James") Version (1611).

It must be suspected that Protestant notions found a sympathetic reception in staunchly bourgeois London. A bourgeois calculus was surely at work when English Protestants figured out that the bounty the bishops were offering on a single copy of Tyndale's English translation of the New Testament was adequate to purchase several replacements, resulting in many being turned in to authorities.

As a great seaport, London benefitted from the "balance of power" strategy developed under Henry. Whenever one continental power became dominant, England would go into alliance with the second power, preventing the first from dominating Europe. This diplomatic strategy became the norm for British diplomacy across the centuries. As a part of this strategy the British navy and international trade were strengthened, and with them the centrality of London.

Henry's first wife, Catherine of Aragon, his brother's widow, bore him five children, but only one lived—Mary (later Queen Mary). Henry diverted himself to a maid of honor at the court, Anne Boleyn. Thomas Cardinal Wolsey, Henry's crafty chancellor, sought to convince Pope Clement VII that Henry should be allowed to have an annulment of his marriage with Catherine, but the pope refused, and Henry dismissed Wolsey in 1529.

Determined to have a divorce and a son to succeed him, Henry denied that the pope had any authority over England and secretly wed Anne Boleyn in 1533. Henry's new Archbishop of Canterbury, Thomas Cranmer (author of the highly regarded first Book of Common Prayer), declared that Henry and Catherine's marriage was null and void, and Anne was crowned queen.

At Henry's urging, Parliament passed two acts in support of the break with Rome. The first declared that the pope had no authority in England. The other, the Act of Supremacy (1534), made the Church of England a separate institution with the King as its supreme head. Wolsey's successor as chancellor, Thomas More, refused to endorse the King's supremacy and was beheaded in 1535 for his conscientious stand.

It is inviting, but not correct, to say that Henry's own reformist zeal prompted the split with Rome. As early as 1351 Parliament had passed anti-papal legislation. The convocations of Canterbury and York had already recognized Henry as the head of the Church in 1530. Henry himself was certainly more motivated by economic and political reasons than doctrinal. The monastic properties were, as we shall see, a ripe fruit, which fell into royal hands as a result of the renunciation of papal authority. After the split the Church of England remained essentially medieval and Catholic in worship and doctrine. The Six Articles of 1539 were a reaffirmation of tradition except that now the King rather than the Pope was head of the Church, and the service book was in English.

When Henry VIII came to the throne, one sixth of the land in England was held by monastic establishments. Church income was estimated at £320,000 a year (£100,000 of this from monastic sources), more than the revenue of the government. Monks were popularly perceived as lazy, greedy and corrupt. Monastic lands, incomes and endowments represented capital that could be put to good use, but as hoarded wealth it was not helping England's economic growth. HRH, the Duke of Gloucester, a commissioner of English Heritage (which now cares for many of the monastic ruins), recently observed, " ... had the monks been able to adopt a more practical role in the community by providing education or medicine and health care, or even an effective support for the elderly and infirm, then they might have survived through popular pressure. But they did not develop a useful purpose ... ." (Gloucester 1991/92:55-57).

More's successor, Thomas Cromwell, was called "Vicar General of the Church" and was commissioned to bring down the monastic establishments. Between 1536 and 1538 all monastic establishments in England were "suppressed," with their wealth seized and their lands expropriated.

In London, the property of the monastic establishments became available for redevelopment, to the profit of London as well as the new proprietors. A tragedy for scholarship was the reckless dispersal and destruction of the monastic libraries.

On the positive side, it was under Cromwell's administration that parishes were first required to keep records of vital statistics in the parish and of the conduct of parish business. The surviving records of St. Mary, Aldermanbury date from the late 16th century (1569) and will provide some of the most valuable sources for our narrative.

In 1546 Parliament established a commission to look into the endowments held by parish churches, and to see if they were being properly administered. It was empowered to look, but not to act. Further reaching measures would be taken in the next reign.

Anne Boleyn gave Henry a daughter, Elizabeth (Queen Elizabeth I), but no son, and was beheaded for alleged infidelity in 1536. His third wife, Jane Seymour, died soon after giving birth to a son, Edward (Edward VI). Three more wives were to follow, with the last, Catherine Parr, surviving him.

The caricature of Henry as a diseased and bloated tyrant who grasped all power in his own hands, and as a fickle husband, is unfair to Henry as monarch, whatever his personal character. Henry was extravagant. He succeeded in spending his father's treasury surplus. His inflation of the currency created a precedent which did not bode well for the future. But he continued his father's policies of strengthening both the central government and the navy. His royal building projects, and especially his seizure of monastic properties, were a boost to the economy.

As far as London was concerned, rising Protestant sympathies meant London applauded the break with Rome but chafed under the religious conservatism of Henry's reign. And, of course, the London commercial class benefitted markedly from the infusion of new capital after suppression of the monasteries.

Aldermanbury during the Reign of Henry VIII

As mentioned above, the followers of the reformer John Wycliffe, the Lollards, were apparently active in the parish. The Lollards had many points of disagreement with the doctrine and practices of the Church, but principal among them was transubstantiation, the belief that the bread of the Lord's Supper actually becomes the body of Christ when the priest utters the prescribed words. In particular, the Lollards challenged the teaching that if a corrupt priest recited the proper liturgy, the sacrament was effective. In 1510 an Aldermanbury parishoner named Elizabeth Sampson proclaimed that "I will not give my dogs that bread some priests doth minister at the altar when they be not in clean life, and also said that thy self could make as good bread as that was and that it was not the body of Our Lord, for it is but bread, for God cannot be both in Heaven and on Earth." She also doubted the teaching of the general resurrection of all souls for final judgment, asserting that "more souls than is in

Heaven already shall never come to Heaven." (Brigden 1989: 91-92, citing Guildhall MS 9531/9, fo. 4ʳ).

Henry's reign marked a significant event in the Aldermanbury neighborhood. A minute book records "expens and charges in the clynsing of certyn old ruinous houses and grounds lying in Aldermanbury, sumtyme the palace of Sancte Aethelbert, Kyng" in Henry's 23rd regnal year (1532). The manuscript bearing this note was in the library of St. Paul's, then mislaid, until it came into the skillful care of the manuscript department of Guildhall Library, where scholars have ready access to it (Guildhall Ms A54-34). 58 through 62 Aldermanbury are probably the lots upon which the document notes further expense "in the settyng up and making fyve new Tenements." But 63 occupied the rear half of the lot fronting Aldermanbury as 62. 64 and 65 and the alleyway between them surely occupy part of the former Saxon palace property, but lie behind the Roman gatehouse. In terms of the present layout, 58-62 are the Aldermanbury front of the property on the "kink," north to Aldermanbury Square, now a new office block. The alleyway and 65 were on the Aldermanbury front of the narrow building now designated No. 1 Love Lane. (These designations are based on the 1677 plan of Olgivy and Morgan.)

One enigma may be noted. The Copper Plate Map (see Figure 3.1) shows a large structure next to St. Mary's that looks amazingly like the gatehouse of a Roman fort. But the Copper Plate was engraved about 1553, under Edward VI or Mary I, long after our documentary source says the structure was "clynsed."

Despite the evidence of the presence of early reformers in the parish, John Morris, curate of St. Mary Aldermanbury, defended the authority of priests to hear confessions, saying in 1540, "It is so determined by the King and his Council, therefore it is past argument of good Christian people" (Brigden 1989: 393). Other parishoners besides Elizabeth Sampson, however, objected to such traditional teachings. One, a man named Thomas Warbysshe, "refused to come to church 'until such times as certain abuses be taken away, for his conscience will not suffer him.'" (Brigden 1989: 564). During Henry's reign conventicles of reform-minded clergy were held in the parish (Brigden 1989: 407). On the basis of this admittedly slim evidence we can tentatively conclude that the tension building in the nation over reform was present in the Aldermanbury parish.

Edward VI (1547-1553)

Edward VI was only nine years old when he succeeded to the throne in 1547; he died of consumption before his sixteenth birthday. The council of regency that Henry had intended broke down before the willful policies of Edward's uncle, Edward Seymour, Duke of Somerset. Somerset ultimately went to the block, undercut by John Dudley, Duke of Northumberland, who induced the sickly boy king to sign a will naming the firstborn (and as yet unborn) son of Lady Jane Grey (Northumberland's daughter-in-law) his successor at the expense of the princesses Mary and Elizabeth. The duke then allegedly altered the will, making Lady Jane herself heir. The policies of Somerset and Northumberland were generally catastrophic for the nation as well as for themselves.

Edward's administration inherited late decrees from Henry, abolishing certain non-monastic church endowments, ending some of the main religious functions of the guilds, and confiscating some of their money and property. An act of 1548 (following on the Act of 1546 described above) established a commission with the power to expropriate "superstitious" endowments (i.e., chantry endowments). Endowments for educational and charitable purposes, and those of cathedrals and corporations were not molested (Kitching 1980:ix-x). We shall see below how the Aldermanbury vestry responded to these orders.

The monasteries had historically provided hospitality for travelers. Henry's abolition had created a social need that was filled by commercial taverns and inns, like the "Ax in Aldermanbury." The Edwardian actions also had social consequences. The guilds had provided charity for the poor, and those functions were reduced. A fair number of chantry priests maintained schools on the side, and while a few of these were replaced by "King Edward grammar schools," the replacement rate was low. The poor were again the net losers. Bad times produced social unrest and Somerset's perhaps well-intentioned attempts to legislate in their favor alienated the higher orders and hastened his fall. Somerset and Northumberland pushed currency debasement as the means to close the gap between revenue and expenses. The result was inflation and increasing financial distress.

In 1552 the Bishop of London, Nicholas Ridley, a prominent figure in the English Reformation, preached a sermon before King Edward VI on the despicable neglect of the poor in London. Although charity for the poor was practiced by parishes, as the bequests noted in Ch. 2 show, there was no systematic attention paid to their needs. After hearing Ridley's indictment, the King ordered the Lord Mayor to investigate.

He appointed a committee of twenty-four. On the basis of the committee's recommendation a tax was ordered in London (the "poor rate") to be collected and administered by parishes. The poor rate apparently began in London in 1556 and was mandatory by 1562. It became national policy under Queen Elizabeth, as we shall see. Thus began three centuries of London parish responsibility for setting and collecting the poor rate and using it to care for the poor of the parish. It continued until the Charities Commission was created in the 19th century to assume this responsibility.

London government was becoming a "multitude of overlapping courts and jurisdictions" (Pearl 1960: 15). The Court of the Lord Mayor and Aldermen was the highest authority, but there were also 79 guilds, numerous wards divided into as many as 242 precincts, and 111 parishes which were increasingly involved in local government because of the considerable amount of money spent for care of the poor.

Somerset fell in 1550 and was beheaded in 1552. He had pursued a moderate course of religious reform. Northumberland pushed a more radical course of reform. Cranmer's 1549 Book of Common Prayer ("First Edward VI") was less explicitly Protestant than the 1552 ("Second Edward VI") edition, which was issued with the Archbishop's "Forty Two Articles of Religion," a mildly Calvinistic creed reflecting Cranmer's own convictions. These documents would prove to be the most durable legacy of Edward's reign, the basis of the Anglican liturgy and indeed of Christian worship in the English language. A happy coincidence was Cranmer's use of the Tyndale- Coverdale translation with its many arresting turns of phrase for the Psalter and other Biblical portions of the liturgy. The Second Prayer Book of Edward VI, lightly edited, would become the Elizabethan Prayer Book and the Prayer Book of 1662, used in the Wren Church of St. Mary, Aldermanbury the entire time it stood in London, and for special services to this day.

Edward probably was sympathetic to Cranmer's blueprints for Church reform, but the pace of reform was too rapid for some. The mild Act of Uniformity of 1549, ordaining the new Prayer Book, was greeted by public disorders in the west country. But not all negative reaction was from the conservative side. Radical Protestants went on iconoclastic rampages, prophetic of events during the Civil War and Commonwealth a century later.

Religiously speaking a corner had been turned in England. Clerical marriage (forbidden by Henry's Six Articles) was now accepted, and Protestant ideas were taking root in the populace, deeply enough that many would accept martyrdom rather than recant in the next reign. A perceptive Venetian diplomat in the time of Mary remarked upon the fact that the most pious Catholics in England were middle aged or older, and that those who had recanted their Protestantism had hardly become good Catholics. If there were such a thing as a national temper or character, one might speculate that the British penchant for independence created a ready receptivity for Protestant ideas.

Aldermanbury, during the Reign of Edward VI

The Act of Supremacy of 1534 gave the Crown full control of the Church of England, including ownership of all parish churches and property. Henry VIII moved to expropriate Church property, but the process was a slow one. Edward VI, established a commission in 1552 to inventory the goods of each London parish church for the purpose of expropriation. The Commission required from each Church response to four articles:

1. Names of churchwardens in the first year of Edward's reign (1547-48).
2. Goods in possession of the Church in 1552.
3. A copy of an inventory made for the Bishop of London in 1548.
4. Goods sold between 1548 and 1552 with results of the sale.

The response from St. Mary's (Walters 1939:420-423) gives us a picture of the property of the Church in the mid-16th century. The Vestry gave Andrew Presse, deputy to the Churchwardens, the responsibility of responding to the articles. In response to the first article Presse named Silvester Edlyn and Thomas Wilkes as Churchwardens in 1547-1548.

In response to the second article Presse listed plate, altar and other cloth, vestments, bells and other ornaments. The plate consisted of "ij Cruettes A Crysmatorie j shipp ij candlestickes & a pase poiz. cxxij ounces Itm ij challiesses with ye patentes A communyon cupp with a dover gilt piz. lxxvj ounces It'm broken silver and a basin parcell gilt poyz. xl ounces." There was a total of lxiiij ounces di. of plate and broken silver, all in the custody of a Thomas Godfrey.

The list also included eight altar cloths ornamented with velvet and damsk of several colors, a desk cloth, two hearse cloths, and four velvet corpora cases.

The vestments were listed as eight suits of purple, gold, and red velvet and damask; a suit of black velvet for burials; various other vestments of velvet, damask, and satin; twenty copes for the suits, mostly velvet, some silk. In addition, two surplices for the curate, eight for men, six for children, three towels and nine additional altar cloths are mentioned.

Also listed were five bells in the Steeple (one bigger than another) and a little sanctus bell.

In response to the third article, Presse claimed to be able to find no record of any inventory of church goods prepared for the Bishop of London.

In response to the fourth article Presse lists a number of items sold between 1548 and 1552. These include a silver cross sold by Thomas Wilkes to a goldsmith, various items of silver (including a crucifix), old organ pipes, the organ case, a desk and all its possessions. Interestingly, all the "Churche bookes great and small" were sold to a "Thomas Turke Stacyoner." This may help explain why no church records prior to the late 16th Century survived.

Also sold were two silver clasps used for marking readings from Bibles given to the Church by the Lord Mayor in 1508. The clasps are now in the British Museum (2B.XII and XIII) (Walters 1939:34 and 543).

Presse then mentions a sum bestowed to the use of the Church "by appoyntment & consent of all the worshipfull of the paryshe." This included "sundry repairs" including two communion cups and the cost of "pulling down altars," presumably the numerous chantries in the Medieval church and the high altar.

A summary of the church finances concludes the document:

    money from church goods sold   107.10.11
    money bestowed for use of church   4.16.06
    money in the hands of the churchwardens   .10

The message was clear; if the Commission wished to secure the funds raised from the sale of the Church's property, the churchwardens were obviously not the ones to see!

A will dated 13 December 1544 speaks of a bequest of Thomas Cobbe "priest and chaplayn to the Company of the Brewers ... and of the parishe of Our Ladye Sainte Marye of Aldermanberye." He asked that his body be buried in the "lytll churcheyarde" and gives 12d to the "hey altare" of St. Mary's. The witness was "Sir John Webbe, curett." (Darlington 1967:202).

Mary I (1553-1558)

Mary I, sometimes characterized as the "most honest" and "most merciful" of the

Tudors, ascended the throne in 1553 to popular acclaim. That the nation was sincere in its acclaim was witnessed by the ease with which the 1554 risings against Mary were put down, even though the word of her unpopular marriage to Philip II of Spain was already out. Reassured by Mary, London shut its gates against Sir Thomas Wyatt and his followers. Had the rebels bided their time for a year or so, they might have succeeded, for Mary lacked the sensitivity to the popular will and the flair for public relations which characterized the two Henrys and Elizabeth I.

Mary earned the nickname "Bloody Mary" because of the more than 300 Protestants who were burned at the stake during her reign, among them Cranmer, Ridley, and Hugh Latimer. The fires of Smithfield (and elsewhere) which consumed Protestant martyrs were public events, not easily swept under the rug. Mary was a dedicated Roman Catholic, committed to the restoration of her faith in England and willing to use her power to achieve that end. Her marriage to the Catholic Philip was part of her strategy. Only a marriage to the pope or the Grand Inquisitor would have been less popular!

Parliament acquiesced in Mary's restoration of Roman Catholicism. However, it did not rehabilitate the monasteries or refund any confiscated wealth. The majority of the English people followed the easy course of returning to the Roman fold, though without enthusiasm. A minority resisted and paid with their lives. Many of Mary's victims were humble folk, but the "Oxford martyrs" named above, were well known, even beloved figures. According to legend, Latimer prophetically exclaimed from the stake, "We shall this day light such a candle, by God's grace, in England, as I trust shall never be put out."

The result of Mary's religious policy was the opposite of her intention. The English people came to identify Catholicism with tyranny, an identification reinforced by the Hapsburgs in Spain and, in due course, the Bourbons in France. Anticatholicism came to be identified with patriotism. Such was certainly to be the case in Aldermanbury.

Mary's short reign was, from the standpoint of national welfare, mercifully short. Her most important action for England's future was the fact that she spared the life of her younger sister.

Philip dragged England into a war with France, that served no good English purpose. Defeat brought humiliation to England and her queen. Calais, the last English stronghold in France, was lost. There had been celebrations when Mary became queen. Five years later news of her death was also greeted with bonfires and celebrations. Under the circumstances, the bonfires seemed particularly appropriate.

Elizabeth I (1558-1603)

When Elizabeth received the royal signet, she no doubt breathed a sigh of relief. During her sister's reign she had been once in the Tower of London and constantly in the shadow of the headsman's ax. She had persevered by remaining loyal to Mary and, like other English folk, nominally converting to Roman Catholicism (although in her case, the Roman restoration marked her as a bastard).

Elizabeth's reign has been described as a forty-five year flirtation with the English people. Most of her subjects were seduced by her charm. She had intelligence, cunning, an iron will, a flair for the appropriate word or gesture; in sum, all the talents required of a politician who would not be merely successful but great. She was a scholarly person. She knew the value of pageantry and of making herself visible to her people with frequent appearances in London and regular "progresses" through the country.

As imperious as her father, Elizabeth nevertheless had a fine sense of when to assert her royal authority and when to bide her time. Her views of royal authority may have been as extravagant as those of her Stuart successors. Unlike them, however, Elizabeth was too smart to say so.

Crucial to Elizabeth's success was her skill in trusting a few advisors and servants of superlative ability and unswerving loyalty. Among them were William Cecil and, in particular, Sir Francis Walsingham, who nipped every plot against the Queen with excellent intelligence/counterintelligence work. Sir Thomas Gresham turned the financial shambles Elizabeth inherited into a healthy treasury. Under Elizabeth the East India Company was chartered in 1600 and headquartered in London, increasingly a center of international trade. Things went less well when Elizabeth trusted her royal favorites, like the Earl of Essex.

Church historians frequently use the term "Elizabethan Settlement" to describe the set of compromises which set the Church of England on a middle course between Protestant and Catholic options. The term should be applied more broadly to the whole array of domestic policies of Elizabeth's reign. The Church settlement was broad enough to encompass all except zealots of either Protestant or Catholic persuasion. Similarly, in other matters, the notion was that all Englishmen and women had a place in Elizabeth's England if they were willing to live as peaceful, loyal subjects. Elizabeth was justifiably proud that Catholics and Protestants could live in peace, at a time when Protestant Huguenots in France were victims of the St. Bartholemew's Day massacre. Anti-Catholic sentiment did grow in response to Catholic involvement in plots against the Queen.

Elizabeth's reign was a much happier time for the (surviving) nobility, the shire gentry and the middle class than it was for the poor. The Poor Laws of 1601 did create four overseers of poor relief in each parish and gave them joint powers with the churchwardens to levy taxes (rates) for poor relief. The Law instructed them to relieve the old and impotent, train pauper children in a trade, and to provide the able-bodied umeployed with work (Rude 1971: 138). Hence the pattern was set for the English welfare system, and later developments in America.

Meanwhile, the years of peace under Elizabeth and relative domestic tranquility served the goals of trade and provided a context for accumulated wealth to be enjoyed. Great new houses arose, and it is indicative of the situation that many of the new residences were not fortified.

The Church of England under Elizabeth was avowedly Protestant. The Queen's claim to the throne depended on it, and a majority wanted it. The Elizabethan Act of Uniformity required all subjects to conform to the Church of England, but enforcement was not harsh except in times of emergency. The Elizabethan Book of Common Prayer was basically the Second Prayer Book of Edward VI and the Thirty-Nine Articles of Religion were an edited version of Cranmer's forty-two. The result was a Church independent of Rome with a mildly Catholic liturgy and a mildly Calvinist theology. It was a compromise which might have sustained peace in England had the successors to the Tudors, the Stuarts, been as capable as Elizabeth. Certainly, as we shall see, the Presbyterians who came to dominate the Aldermanbury parish could have lived with it.

During Elizabeth's reign sympathy ran high for embattled Continental Protestants, especially the Dutch rebels against Spain. Although not going so far as to declare war, Elizabeth did clandestinely support the raiding of Spanish shipping and bases by the "Sea Dogs," Drake, Hawkins and Frobisher being the most famous. Drake's heroic voyage around the world on the Golden Hind paid handsome dividends in Spanish treasures.

The execution of the Catholic Mary, Queen of Scots, and the onslaught of Spain's

Grand Armada are probably the two most remembered events of Elizabeth's reign. They are not unconnected. Mary was a guest/prisoner in England for two decades before her beheading in 1587, after repeated Catholic plots, all focusing on her, were thwarted. Mary's execution was the final weight in the balance and Philip of Spain decided on a holy crusade to return England to the Catholic fold by force. The Invincible Armada set sail in 1588, but English determination and North Sea weather combined to wreak havoc on the Spanish fleet.

Elizabeth's reign was a literary golden age. Many think it was the classical period of the English language. All sorts of literature, and especially the theater, flourished both in private venues (including the court) and in the commercial playhouses that arose, especially in Southwark, on the south bank of the Thames, opposite London. There Marlowe, Shakespeare, Jonson, and others plied their craft. As we shall soon see, the parish of St. Mary, Aldermanbury had a particularly strong connection with the most famous of these great playwrights, William Shakespeare.

Elizabeth was not eager to discuss the royal succession, for it implied her demise. She is said to have mentioned James VI of Scotland, son of Mary Stuart, on her death bed. James had his champions in the court, and within thirty hours of the queen's death a courier had brought the official summons of the Council to Edinburgh calling for the Scottish king to assume the English throne. If the members could have anticipated the anguish the house of Stuart would bring to England, they might have attended the credentials of other candidates more closely!

Excursus: The Puritan Movement

Because of its importance in the history of the Aldermanbury parish during the reign of Elizabeth and throughout the next century, we will give separate attention to the Puritan movement in England. The term "puritan" has come to refer simply to strictness in moral matters and in modern America is usually used pejoratively. Such usage is both unfair and unfortunate. It is unfair because Puritans were never as prudish as most people seem to think. For example, Puritans did not disapprove of the use of alcohol nor of dancing or, in general, enjoying life. It is unfortunate because of the contributions of the Puritans to some of the most basic and cherished values of English and American life.

The name "Puritan" appeared in England in the late 16th century to identify a growing movement within the Church of England. Puritans sought to continue the

Protestant reformation in England, "purifying" the Church from all Roman Catholic (usually called "papist") influences in doctrine and liturgy. Puritans sought to simplify worship, placing the emphasis on Bible reading and preaching rather than the sacramental drama and prescribed prayers. They also stressed personal piety, claiming that grace was received through individual self-examination and prayer rather than through the mediation of the clergy and sacraments. Puritans emphasized education of the clergy and laity, so that clergy could be enlightened teachers and so that everyone could read and interpret the Bible for himself or herself. The teachings of the Swiss reformer, John Calvin, influential on the English Protestants in general, were a particular source of inspiration for the Puritan movement.

The seeds of the Puritan movement can be found in the work of William Tyndale in the 1520's and 30's and the preaching of leaders like Hugh Latimer in the 1530's and 40's. Latimer, a onetime Roman Catholic priest, became Protestant bishop of Worcester, an outspoken critic of Queen Mary's attempt to restore Catholicism in England, and, as mentioned above, one of "Bloody Mary's" victims. Tyndale, Latimer, and others maintained that the Bible should be the sole source of authority for the governing of the Church of England.

By the late 1500's Puritans began to divide among themselves on the question of church polity. Some (the Presbyterian wing) reflected Calvin's teaching that the church should be governed by area councils of presbyters (elders) called "presbyteries," following what he believed to be the model of the New Testament church. It should be noted that Calvin did not oppose episcopacy itself, as long as bishops followed the Reformed faith. Others (the Independents) believed that each congregation was a complete church in itself, with its own covenant with God. Independents rejected both the episcopacy of the Church of England and the modified episcopacy of the Presbyterians. Among the Independents some became Separatists, calling for a complete break with the Church of England. Other Independents and virtually all Presbyterians sought to remain a part of the Church of England and "continue the reformation" from within.

The influence of the Puritans is hard to exaggerate. In England the Puritans gained power during the period of the Civil War and Commonwealth and left a lasting mark through the adoption of the principle of a limited, constitutional monarchy. After the restoration of the monarchy the more radical, democratic political ideals of Puritanism faded in England, but were later revived by the Whig Party. Religiously, beginning in the 18th century, Methodism kept alive Puritan religious principles in England.

However, the greatest impact of Puritanism was to be not on England but the English colonies in North America. Puritans seeking a place to establish the kind of Biblically-based society they envisioned came to America and founded settlements along the New England coast and in Virginia. A group of Separatists (known in American folklore simply as "the Pilgrims") landed at Plymouth Bay in 1620.

In four areas the Puritans have had a particularly profound impact on American life. The Puritan commitment to education led to the establishment of such distinguished schools as Harvard and Yale. And the Puritan view that government should be based on contracts with the governed contributed to the development of the U. S. Constitution in particular and American democratic values in general. Economically, the Puritan emphasis on hard work and self-discipline contributed to the development of the free-enterprise system. Religiously, the Puritan movement is kept alive in America in a number of large and influential denominations, including Baptists, Congregationalists, and Unitarians (heirs of the Independent wing); Presbyterians; and Methodists, to name the most prominent.

During the late Elizabethan era and into the 17th Century, different parishes within London sided with different parties within the Church of England. In 1569 Thomas Cartwright, a newly appointed Cambridge professor, publicly called for congregational election rather than episcopal appointment of ministers and for greater emphasis on the teaching role of the clergy and presbyterian nature of the apostolic church. This date is usually considered the time at which many Puritans turned decisively toward Presbyterianism. Aldermanbury was, as we shall see, a Puritan parish and became an important center of the Presbyterian wing of the Puritan movement during the turbulent days of the Civil War and the Commonwealth.

Aldermanbury during the Reign of Elizabeth I

The extant Vestry Minutes of St. Mary, Aldermanbury, begin in 1569 and the Churchwarden Accounts date to 1570. Thus, we have a fairly complete picture of church affairs from this date onward, upon which we will draw extensively in our narrative.

A note in the Vestry Minutes for St. Thomas Day, 1570 (Guildhall Ms. 3570a:1) indicates the role of the parishoners in selecting their curate. It names a new curate, a Mr. Rose or Rese, Master of Arts, who was given a stipend of £16 yearly "so long as the parishoners liking of him." The present curate had apparently been dismissed or resigned as the note mentions him "having warning the Feast of St. Michael next coming." At the Vestry meeting a year earlier there is a note about lease of a house for the curate (Ms. 3570a:1). Subsequent mention of lease of a house occurs on 24 December 1570, 1573 or 4, and 15 January, 1575.

Total receipts in 1570 were £69.12.10 with the tithe set at 2s9d on the pound. In the same year an organ was installed in the Church with 5d paid by the Churchwardens "for bread and drink" for the laborers for "drawing the organ into the loft" (Malcolm 1803:127).

A close look at the complete Churchwarden accounts for 1569-1570 reveals the following picture of parish affairs (Carter 1913:101-106).

The record begins with the note that the account is of Robert Davy, Churchwarden, by his deputy Andrew Preste (probably the same as Andrew Presse mentioned in 1552), for the year ending with the Feast of St. Michael, 1570. Davy had received 32.2.10 from the previous Churchwarden, Richard Fallowes. It was the practice that a Churchwarden personally receive and transfer church funds, and at the end of the year pass the balance to his successor or make up the shortfall.

The account then lists rents received by Davy for tenements belonging to the parish. Rents totalling 15.10.18 were collected from five renters and "from the rent of old time due upon the house wherein the curate dwelleth."

A total of 2.10 is listed as receipts from "divers parishoners for sondrie casualties," namely for "laystalls" (graves) in the cloister, the North Chapel and in the "middle of the church" as well as for tolling the "great bell."

The account also notes 8.5.2 collected quarterly from the parishoners for the parish clerk's wages. The assessments for Clerk's wages and tithes were entered on a long roll of parchment which in 1919 was still in the church safe. A rate of 2s9d on the pound was collected for "the Queens farmers of the parsonage" and brought in 24.16.4. Rents from other tenements in the parish belonging to the parsonage were collected.

The final form of receipt listed is the Easter Book. Each year at Easter lead tokens were distributed to all in attendance at Easter communion. Later the Churchwarden went house to house collecting the tokens. Failure to produce a token resulted in a small fine. The collection, called the Easter Book, netted 18s in 1569.

At the end of the Receipt section of the Accounts for 1569-1570 we find the note that "all other small profittes incident to the parsonage as for Christenings, Marriage and Burialle are granted to the curate in augmentation of his living."

In the Payment section of the Account £7.12 is listed as the wage for Nicholas Croft for serving as "clarke and Sexton and for keeping the alley." A sum of 20s was paid to Michael Shallow "underchamberlain of Powles [St. Paul's]" as a pension. The Archdeacon of London received 3s for a visitation "for procuracons." The Queen was paid £11 rent for the parsonage.

The curate's wages were divided between Christopher Bateman "late curate" and William Trevor. Each received £8. The rent for the curate's house was 16s. At total of 10s2d was reimbursed to the curate for communion wine and bread. The organ maker received 2s10d and the scavengers of the parish 16d.

A total of 25s5d was spent on minor repairs in the church such as putting four pairs of joints on doors for the women's pews, mending a lock on a cloister door, and putting pavement in front of the curate's house.

Miscellaneous expenses included washing two surplices on 22 December (4d), paying a messenger who brought a psalm of thanksgiving for the overthrow of the Rebellion in the North (6d), and candles to serve at morning prayers (11d). Before 1573 prayers were read between 5:00 and 6:00 a.m. (Malcolm 1803: 118).

Therefore, in 1569-1570 £65.5. was collected, with allowances of 40.10.2, leaving a remainder of 49.2.7. The Account notes that 19.0.3 was collected for the "relief of the poor." £3.10 went to Christ Hospital for the poor harbored there and 11.5.3 directly to impoverished in the parish.

In 1571 money was received for the sale of vestments in addition to regular sources and paid for new glazing "for the great window at the east end of the church" and candlesticks for the Lecture desk and for the pillars to be lighted during Morning Prayer. An hour glass was also purchased, perhaps to encourage the preacher to be more aware of time. A messenger was paid 12d for "a prayer that the Bishop sent for overthrow of Turks" (Carter 1913: 107).

In 1572 we find the first reference to the parish owning armor and weapons, as money was spent to clean the armor and to purchase a lock for the chest "where the Artillierie lyeth" (Carter 1913: 107). This apparently reflects the involvement of the parish in the London militia.

The next year we find the first reference to a dinner paid for out of parish funds for the curate, churchwardens and sidemen at an inn (Carter 1913: 70). In the same year there is the earliest mention in the Church's own records of communion vessels— 2 quart pots and a pint pot (Carter 1913:34). A Robert Carre was hired to preach on Sundays, Tuesdays, and Thursdays at a salary of £34 annually (Malcolm 1803:118).

In 1573 a lectureship was created at St. Mary, Aldermanbury, one of the first fifteen in London (Seaver 1970: 124). The lectureships were important instruments in the spreading of the Puritan cause in the City. There were thirty in London by 1581 and 100 by 1600. By 1630 ninety percent of the parishes had lecturers.

On 11 March 1575 Robert Bliethman was admitted as minister of the parish at a stipend of £16, with a house to inhabit (Carter 1913: 39). Several months later a Mr. Gilpin was hired at the same stipend but was made to promise to give at least a month's notice before departing. Apparently Rev. Bliethman had found a better offer and departed without notice. (Ms. 3570a:1).

A Charnal house (depository for bones) was added to the church or repaired in 1575. The accounts show 9s10d paid for work "done about the Charnell House." (Carter 1913: 107)

At the Vestry meeting on 17 February, 1576, it was agreed by the consent of the parish "that at the next Lady Day Christopher Blythman would become curate with the "same stipend as his brother had before him and that he shall not depart but upon one quarter's warning given to the parish." Blythman was also made to promise not to live outside the parish (Carter 1913: 39). The Vestry chose Michael Salford in 1576, either as lecturer or as an assistant to Mr. Blythman.

The Vestry did not miss an opportunity to earn money. An entry in the account book for 1577 shows 5s received "for the old torne Bible not fitte for use of the parish." (Carter 1913: 107). This also probably reflects the growing desire of lay people to read the Bible for themselves.

In 1578 a note in the Account book shows provision of a parish house for the curate with the rent waived. That same year 11s was spent to clean the armor, the swords, and purchase new leather for the "corslettes." A key for the loft over the porch, and "a dozen ballettes and bookes bought against New Year's Day concerning the Queen's Majestie were also purchased." (Carter 1913: 108).

In 1580 a small service book for the Minister, three psalm books and six books concerning the Queen's Majesty were purchased. 5s8d was paid to a Father Henshaw "in respect to his povertie." And 7s8d was authorized for a license for the curate to preach.

On 11 July, 1582 Churchwarden Michael Lenton came before the Vestry to seek guidance concerning a dispute he was having with Mr. Salford (Ms. 3570a:2). The issue was whether fees paid for breaking the ground in the chancel for burials, funeral hangings and altar covers were to go to the curate or be used by the parish in their care of the poor. According to Mr. Lenton "He [the curate] maketh claim for the offerings to be his duty which I take to be for the poor." The Vestry held that the curate had no claim to these funds for "the parson is the parish." This phrase, oft repeated in the Vestry minutes, shows how deeply ingrained was the attitude that the parishoners themselves, not any clerical authority, had the right to make decisions about the life of the church. We can appreciate Mr. Salford's desire to secure these fees. When Sir William Damsel was buried in the Church in 1583 the fees amounted to £11, almost the annual salary of the curate (Carter 1913: 109; Malcolm 1803: 118). The Account Book for 1587 suggests that this decision was changed, for we find 8s paid to the curate as "his fee for ye cloth that covered the communion table at Mr. Trapp his funeral."

At the same time the Vestry was showing concern to limit the fees paid to the curate, 9.17.3 was being spent to make a new pew for Mr. Alderman Woodcock and his wife, with wainscotting and carved lions to set upon them. 5s7d was spent to ring the Church bells on the day the Queen began her reign (Carter 1913: 108-109).

There are indications that the curate, Mr. Blythmann, was involved in the Puritan opposition. In 1585 Blythmann joined other London ministers in signing a very qualified subscription to Whitgift's Articles, and at the episcopal visitation of the same year it was noted that he was one of two London ministers who were lecturing without a license (Seaver 1976: 210, 213). However, by 1586 the visitation book noted that his license was in order.

The implementation of the mandate for parishes to collect a "poor rate" is witnessed in an entry in the Minute Book for 25 March, 1584. The "Vestry of parishoners" ordered the Churchwarden to make an annual survey of houses belonging to the parish and the land and state of repair and to impose a 10s levy to be used "for the care of the poor" for every default in bonds or covenants (Ms. 3570a:4). Several years later (9 July, 1587) the Vestry appointed three "viewers" to make this inspection and paid them 8s3d and their dinner on "view day" (Ms. 3570a:7-8).

Also in the account book for 1584 a Roger Phillips was hired at 20s "for warding for vagrant persons going about the parish" and 3s11d for a warding staff. (Carter 1913: 109). His job would have been to keep any new poor from taking up residence in the parish. In 1586 Phillip's wife was paid to carry a child around for four days to learn its mother. Mrs. Phillips was also paid 15d for nursing the child for a week and 3d for making supplications to have the child admitted to Christ's Hospital. The Beadles of the Hospital were paid 7s to continue the search for the child's mother for six days. (Carter 1913: 110). These are the first references in the church records to foundlings, infants left in doorways by impoverished mothers.

An entry for 1 May 1586 clarified the collection of fees for ringing the "great Bell" and digging the graves and hints at a dispute between the Sexton and Parish Clerk about keys. (Carter 1913: 73). On 5 September 1586 Alderman Woodcoke gave 20s for the poor and when he died the same year his wife paid 16s8d for burying her husband in the Chancel and "the knille with the great Bell" and 40s for other fees. (Carter 1913: 109- 110). The accounts for 1586 also speak of 3s2d spent for bread and drink on the 15th of August for the bell ringers "for joye at the apprehension of Babington and other traitors" (Carter 1913: 110).

On the 25th of September 6s8d was paid "by the appointment of the parish" to a Mr. Symmes for a sermon in the church (Carter 1913: 110). And a scrivener was hired to write down all the names of householders and apprentices in the parish.

Also in 1586 the growing Presbyterian influence in the parish can be documented. That year a Scot named Duncan Anderson preached at St. Mary Aldermanbury, among other parishes, and was charged by the Bishop with preaching without a license (Seaver 1976: 216).

On the 3rd of March, 1587, the Vestry agreed to grant pensions to two poor women of the parish. On 10 October, 1587 the Vestry ordered and the parishoners agreed to have "a Lecture wekely redde in the parish Church of this parish every Sondaye at IX of th clok in the fornoon and every Sundaye at five o'clock in ye afternoon and to begin at Michelmas next and to continue during ye pleasure of the parishoners so as the Bishop of London assent thereunto." A four member delegation was sent to secure the Bishop's permission (Carter 1913: 39-40). At the same Vestry the Churchwarden was ordered to remove the pulpit to the South Side of the Church by a pillar and to wash and whiten the church and have branches with candles installed for the lectures" (Ms. 3570aI:8). The Account Book shows purchase of a brass candle branch and a new hour glass.

An indication of a dispute with the bishop over the parish's right to hire preachers appears in the accounts for 1587. Money was authorized to pay for a boat hire and other charges "for getting libertie for Mr. Bonne to preach being inhibited by the Bishop" (Carter 1913:110).

The account books for 1588 contain a mysterious note about fees of 19s15d paid "in the Arches" when the "said Accomptant" was excommunicated. The entry says fees were paid to Doctor Stanhop on the 6th and 20th of July and to a Register (Carter 1913: 110). The excommunication may very well have related to an unusual incident which took place on the 29th of June, 1588, recorded in the Historical Manuscripts Commission 7th Report (p. 433). On that date a man named Daverson, a Scot, preached in the church "with a kerchief on his head, a velvet nightcap upon that, and a felt hat over that, and prayed a long prayer with all on." He then removed his hat and said, "Let us sing a psalm to the praise of God." (Goss 1944:156 and Pendrill 1937:88). Perhaps the "said Accomptant" had invited Daverson to preach!

The incident was part of the post-Reformation debate over vestments for the clergy, in this case, hats. It is also probably an indication of the growing Presbyterian influence in the parish. The Scotsman Daverson was undoubtedly a Presbyterian. His act of disdain for clerical vestments and prescribed prayers and his use of the psalms show that his was a calculated challenge to the established church.

It seems likely that "Daverson" was actually John Davidson, who had come to London in 1584, with several other Scot ministers, to press for Presbyterian reform (Collinson 1967: 277; Seaver 1976: 216). He was called "the thunderer" because of his forceful preaching style. In March, 1589, the High Commissioners banned Davidson and other "irregular preachers" from speaking in London pulpits.

Christopher Blythmann had died in 1588 (Seaver 1976: 210), so it is possible that Daverson/Davidson was being examined as a possible successor. In any event, Michael Salford was named curate and lecturer in 1588 (Seaver 1976: 167).

On 10 November, 1588, the Vestry agreed to pay 31s for the expenses of a delegation sent to Cambridge to pursue "the suit in law against Mr. Styll and Mr. Basfords" (Ms. 3570aI:8-9). The subject of the suit is not known.

On 27 April, 1589, 23.6.8 from the bequest of Sir William Damsell, received six years earlier, was set aside "to a yearly benefit for the poor of our parish" (Ms. 3570aI:9). On 29 June collectors for the poor were appointed (Ms. 3570aI:10), reflecting that Aldermanbury was in compliance with the 1601 Poor Laws before they were enacted. The account books during this year are full of references to money spent for the poor, for a pair of shoes or "carrying away a poor woman that laie sick at Sir William Damsell's gate" (Carter 1913:111). There is also a reference to bringing a bed to a woman in "the cage" (Carter 1913: 111). The cage was used to confine malefactors of the parish. There is a reference in 1621 to it being repaired (Goss 1944: 146). On 24 February 1589 the Vestry agreed to a pension of 60s a year for a family" in respect of their poverty." (Ms. 3570aI:12).

A minor dispute between the Vestry and Churchwarden arose in 1590 when the Churchwarden paid 4s6d for a dinner for the Surveyors of the property of the parish without authorization of the Vestry (Carter 1913: 111). The account entry includes the note "not to be allowed hereafter." Was this a result of puritan parsimony? It was indeed the first episode in a centuries long parish dispute about the custom of the church paying for dinners. Such disputes were not uncommon in parishes. The diversion of funds by the unpaid and overworked parish officers for banquets and carousals in pubs was frequent. The same year 12d was spent for "a soldier for conduct money to Dover being prest for Portugall" (Carter 1913:111).

Throughout this period there are frequent references to the Henshaw family as among the poor of the parish. For example, in 1586 the parish paid for a winding sheet for Father Henshaw. Apparently the patience of the Vestry wore thin, at least with the Widow Henshaw, as an entry dated 24 June 1590 shows (Ms. 3590aI:13). The Vestry agreed on a pension for Widow Henshaw of 6d a week "so long as she use herself well and quietly" and "so long as we have not case to cut if off again."

In 1590 six corsetts, two muskets, and three daggers were purchased "for the Queen's service" (Malcolm 1803:127). Two years later money was paid to a cutler for cleaning and repairing the "arming swordes" (Carter 1913:111). This is among the last entries in the Account books until 1630, the books for the years 1593- 1629 are missing.

On 19 December 1591 the Vestry received a letter, dated 15 December, from the Lord High Treasurer, naming Robert Harland curate and stipulating that he receive the same salary as the last curate, plus a sum for serving as lecturer (Malcolm 1803: 118 and Carter 1913: 40). The vestry acquiesced, saying that they were "greatly bound for his Lordship's sundry favors extended towards them." The Vestry at first balked at paying Harland £34 annually as lecturer, pointing out that the lecture was privately funded (Seaver 1976: 167). They did agree, but with the note that "it is not to be doubted but that upon Mr. Harland's well usage of himself and painestaking therein there will be collected a number of well-disposed persons that waie a competent yearelie income or his good contentment, ..." (Carter 1913: 40).

It was also agreed not to make Harland pay for "painted papers" in the study of the Curate's tenement which his predecessor Mr. Salford had installed, but only for "painted hangings in the hall and chamber above it ... " (Carter 1913: 40).

The parishoners were apparently satisfied with Mr. Harland as curate for he remained in office until his death in 1617. We owe him a debt of gratitude for collecting and binding the old registers of the church (Carter 1913: 41).

On the 21 January 1592 the Vestry ordered the Churchwarden to pay £11 for rent of a parsonage out of that belonging to the "late Priory of Elsing Spittal." On 5 November 1592 the Vestry granted the "humble request" of John Paynter for 10s and "fagots and coals" to be given at the Churchwarden's discretion. (Ms. 3570aI:16).

On 21 December 1594 the Vestry ordered the Churchwarden to sell the "Arms, Swords, and Daggers belonging to the pyshe ... to the most benefyt of ye pyshe."

On New Year's Day, 1595, the Vestry in open session met to discuss the fact that in recent years many in the parish had not been attending Easter Communion, but "the Duties of the Easter Booke have risen farre short to the Receivings of former tymes" despite the fact that the number of inhabitants in the parish had increased. To resolve this problem the "greatest number of the parishoners" agreed that all householders would have to pay the Easter duties owed by their families when they paid their tythes for Ladie daye (or Easter) quarter." The householders should deduct from wages and benefits the appropriate amount so that "the Parish ... be no loosers."

At a Vestry meeting on 11 January, 1595, William Levenson assumed responsibility for care of the poor from Richard Fox who had been the caretaker since the late 1580's. Levenson "consented and promised to relieve the poor of the parish with so much as he can conveniently profit thereby" (Ms. 3570aI:19-20).

On 29 August, 1595, a Thomas Diggs, reputed to be a distinguished mathematician and astrologer, was buried in the Church.

On 16 October 1597 Robert Hare, Schoolmaster, was given the Chamber in the Church previously used by Widow Gunard "as a school to teach such children in as shall be put to him by the parishoners or any others yielding unto the parish a load of the best fagots to be distributed unto the poor yearly." (Ms. 3570aI:20). This is an early indication of the Puritan practice of educating the poor, so that they might develop the ability to support themselves, and yet another piece of evidence that Aldermanbury was by this time a decidedly Puritan parish.

On 25 February and 11 March, 1598, the Vestry met to discuss a plan to buy the parsonage and a committee was appointed to raise the money. (Ms. 3570aI:25). It took 23 years for the parish to secure the parsonage, as we shall soon see.

On 22 May, 1598 the Vestry agreed to allow Fowlke Yerland to "lodge in the Chamber of the Church Porch until such time as he grow in strength that he be able to work or follow his trade ..." At the same meeting the Schoolmaster was directed to use the Church Vestry house for school with relief from rent.

In the late 16th century, parishoner participation in parish government was apparently high, for in October 1598 "a very great Vestry" appointed four viewers of the parish, undoubtedly as part of the building effort to secure ownership of the parsonage. (Ms. 3570aI:23).

It was in 1598 that the first edition of John Stow's survey of London was published. His description of the Church of St. Mary reads:

There is the parish Church with a churchyard, and cloister adjoining,
in the which cloyster is hanged and fastened a shankebone of a man
(as is said) very great, and larger by three inches and a halfe then
that which hangeth in S. Lawrence Church in the Jurie, for it is in
length 28 inches and a halfe of assise, but not so hard and feele
like as the other, for the same is light and somewhat porie and spongie.
This bone is said to bee found amongst the bones of men removed from
the charnell house of Paules ... (Stow 1598: 233).

He then lists 13 buried in the church, from 1391 through 1586.

On 3 June, 1599 "divers reparations for the Church" were authorized, to be supervised by the Churchwarden. At a meeting on 23 September 1599 the Committee appointed the previous year to buy the parsonage was ordered to try again because of a decrease in land values. A 29 May 1599 Crown Lease deeded to James Dalton and others the Rectory and Church for 21 years at £11 (Ms. 23,737A: 174).

In 1600 the dispute over the parish's attempt to buy the parsonage continued with the Lord High Treasurer asserting that "inhabitants [of the parish] were not men of reputation." The parishoners themselves could not agree on what course to follow. Finally, the Lord High Treasurer brought the dispute to a temporary, unspecified resolution. (Ms. 3570aI:27). On 20 February 1601/2 the rectory of the church was sold by Thomas Hayes and John Coomes to Richard Chamberlayne and Roger Bushe (Ms. 23,737A: 174). They sold various parish property to William Bourne and others on 2 March, 1602/3.

At a meeting on 30 January 1602 the Vestry threatened to cut off pensions to any of the poor who "receive inmates into their houses." The Vestry also appointed some of the poor to be "searchers of the dead that shall decease within this parish." A year later the Vestry made other such appointments, so apparently the practice was deemed successful.

At the same time the Vestry was concerned about the poor taking advantage of the parish, it also was attending to the concerns of wealthy members. On 11 March 1603, a pew was ordered constructed for Sir Thomas Hayes and his lady.

Excursus: William Shakespeare's Aldermanbury Connection

Sometime between 1598 and 1602 William Shakespeare (1564-1616), considered by many to be the greatest dramatist in the English language, went to live with a Huguenot wigmaker named Christopher Mountjoy at the corner of Silver and Monkwell Streets. It was "a quiet little enclave within the north-west angle of the City Wall" (Rowse 1988: 172). The house is visible on the Agas map, showing a twin-gabled structure and shop front. It was in the parish of St. Olave, Silver Street. However, within 200 yards (about one block) was Aldermanbury parish and the Aldermanbury homes of Shakespeare's close friends and fellow actors, John Heminges and Henry Condell. Shakespeare could have walked a block down Silver Street, across Wood Street. He would then enter the parish on Addle Street. If he proceeded another block he would have reached Aldermanbury. Across Aldermanbury was the Axe Inn, where his friends certainly would have gathered. Just south of the Inn and across the street was the Church of St. Mary, Aldermanbury.

Shakespeare maintained this as his London residence for 14 years, until he purchased a home in the Blackfriar's district. He was apparently close to the Mountjoy family, since he was called on to perform the betrothal of one of the daughters and testified in a suit involving the daughter's dowery. According to a record of the French Huguenot Church in London, Mountjoy lived a "licentious life." Perhaps, he was involved with Shakespeare in the theatre, which would have earned him the disdain of pious Huguenots.

The proximity of Shakespeare's residence to Aldermanbury for fifteen years, and his close association with two Aldermanbury residents—Heminges and Condell—raises the question of the playwright's association with the parish. Did William Shakespeare ever worship in the Church of St. Mary, Aldermanbury? Did he spend time in the parish? The best way to approach these questions is to determine how much we know about Heminges and Condell and Shakespeare's association with them. (For the following account we are dependent primarily on They Gave Us Shakespeare by Charles Connell and the Dictionary of National Biography.)

John Heminges (ca. 1556-1630)

According to his will, John Heminges (also spelled Hemings, Hemings, Hemmings, Hemminge, and Heming) was an Aldermanbury grocer. He was born near Stratford-on-Avon in about 1556. We cannot ascertain when he moved to London, or whether he knew and/or worked with Shakespeare in Stratford. He was married to Rebecca Knell, widow of an actor named William Knell, in the Church of St. Mary, Aldermanbury in 1587 (Carter 1913: 87). This suggests he was already involved in London's theatrical life for a while before 1587. The Aldermanbury registers record fourteen children born to John and Rebecca and baptised in the parish. After the marriage Heminges moved into a house on the west side of Aldermanbury south of the church, across Love Lane. He moved several doors south in 1596, then into a house on Addle Street by 1600. His service to the parish included election as a sidesman in 1602, and as churchwarden and trustee in 1608. He again served as a trustee in 1619 (with Henry Condell), the year his wife died. He then apparently moved from the parish, for when he was buried in the parish in 1630, he is called "a stranger."

A grocer by trade, Heminges was an actor by avocation and interest. At some point it is likely he turned the family business over to his wife or others and devoted himself entirely to the theater. He began his theatrical career as a member of Queen Elizabeth's company and in 1593 transferred to the troupe of Ferdinando, Lord Strange's Men. By 1597 or 1598, he was, along with his friends Henry Condell and William Shakespeare, a member of the King's Company, previously known as Lord Chamberlain's Company. In 1603 his name appears, along with Condell and Shakespeare and Richard Burbage, on the formal patent establishing the company.

Heminges' acting career included a number of roles. He performed in many of

Ben Jonson's plays, and was affectionately called by Jonson "Old Master Hemings" (Connell 1982: 9). In about 1594 he was listed (along with Condell) as actors in a performance of Shakespeare's "Titus Andronicus." Although we cannot be sure, because individual roles were not designated, he may have played Polonius and the Ghost in "Hamlet." He may also have been the original Falstaff, and played Caesar to Condell's Antony in "Julius Caesar." In any event, Heminges was frequently listed among the players at performances of Shakespeare's plays. Although he was still listed as a member of the King's Company in 1625, he had probably stopped acting some years earlier.

Early on Heminges became involved in the business side of the theater. In fact, he may have been more interested in theater management than performing. He is listed as having received on behalf of the company L30 for three plays performed before Queen Elizabeth in 1599. Similar entries continue in the royal journals until 1618. Also in 1599 Heminges became a shareholder, along with Shakespeare and others, in the Globe Theatre. He later became its principal proprietor. When the Globe burned in 1613 a ballad inspired by the tragedy included these lines:

> There with swolne eyes, like druncken Flemminges
> Distressed stood old stuttering Heminges.

In 1608 with Shakespeare and others he assumed control of the nearby Blackfriars Theatre. Apparently, Shakespeare and his friends performed in the Globe publically in the Summer and privately in the Blackfriar in the Winter (to thwart the growing Puritan opposition to theater as an inappropriate form of entertainment). In 1615 Heminges may have been among those who were called before the Privy Council with Richard Burbage to answer the charge of playing during Lent.

Henry Condell (?- 1627)

Not much is known of Henry Condell's (also spelled Condall, Cundell, Cundall, and Condye) early years. Whether, like Heminges and Shakespeare, he was from the Stratford-on-Avon area has not been established. Condell's name first appeared on the assessment roll of the Aldermanbury parish in 1600. He lived very near his friend John Heminges, on the west side of Aldermanbury, south of the Church. He probably had a business in the parish, but we do not know what it was. In 1607 he had been named a sidesman of the church. In 1615 he was appointed to the wardmote inquest. In 1618 he was elected Churchwarden of the parish. In 1619 he was chosen (along with Heminges) as a trustee for the parish lands. When the parish purchased the advowson in 1621 Condell's name appears on the deed. He held tenements both in Aldermanbury and St. Bride's, Fleet Street. He was married in 1599, and he and his wife, Elizabeth, had nine children.

Like Heminges, Condell acted in a number of Ben Jonson's plays, earning a reputation as one of Jonson's ten "principal comedians." In 1598 he appeared in Jonson's "Every Man in his Humour" and a year later "Every Man out of His Humour." He must have begun his acting career considerably earlier, because a newcomer would not have been given such roles. We do know that in 1590 he was a member (with Heminges) of Lord Strange's Men. Like Heminges, he appeared in a 1594 production of Shakespeare's "Titus Andronicus." In 1603 he was sixth on the list of the members of the King's Company, after having been (with Heminges and Shakespeare) in the Lord Chamberlain's Company. The same year he became a partner in the Globe Theatre. In 1604 he appeared in John Marston's play "The Malcontent." He then was cast in a series of Jonson's plays, with Heminges ("Sejanus," "Volpone," and "The Alchemist"). In 1613 Condell was among those listed as performers in Shakespeare's "All is True" (later "Henry VIII"). The following lines from a contemporary ballad, commemorate Condell's performance:

The riprobates, thoughe drunk on Monday,

Prayed for the foole and Henry Condye.

Like Heminges Condell was probably more interested in the business of theatre than acting!

In 1618-19, two year's after Shakespeare's death, Condell appeared third on the new patent for the King's Company, with only Richard Burbage and John Heminges before him. In Shakespeare's will, published on 5 March, 1616, both Heminges and Condell were left 26s8d "to buy ringes."

Condell retired from the stage in 1623, presumably to his country home in Fulham, where he had entertained fellow actors. He died in 1627 and was buried in St. Mary, Aldermanbury, on 29 December.

The First Folio (see Figure 3.2)

Several events encouraged Heminges and Condell to publish Shakespeare's plays in a folio edition. First, Ben Jonson's plays had been published in 1616. Second, Richard Burbage, who played the lead in many of Shakespeare's plays, died in 1619, taking Macbeth, Othello, Hamlet, and Lear with him. Third, and probably most important, was the publication, also in 1619, of an unauthorized and "indifferent" collection of Shakespeare's plays. In fact, between 1594 and 1619, twenty publishers had released editions of single plays. There was a need for an authentic collection to counter these often inferior editions. Indeed, in the preface to the first folio, Heminges and Condell specifically mention their concern that the public was being cheated by pirated texts of the plays, which had been altered and distorted.

Whether Shakespeare himself, before his death, had asked his friends to publish his plays in a posthumous, single edition we do not know. Like other playwrights of the time, he would not have wanted his plays published too widely before his death, lest this cut down on attendance at the performances. Certainly, no more appropriate editors could have been found. Heminges and Condell knew the plays intimately, as actors and producers. They had a great deal of loyalty to the author and undoubtedly wanted his actual words preserved.

Heminges and Condell had several sources to work from in producing the first folio. They had actors' prompt books, first and foremost their own. They also had quarto editions of the individual plays. They may have had their own copies of Shakespeare's actual manuscripts. Probably most importantly they had their own memory of what the Bard had written and what had actually been said on stage.

The first folio appeared in 1623, seven years after Shakespeare's death. In the preface Heminges and Condell wrote, "We have but collected [the plays] and done our office to the dead without ambition either of selfe profit or fame, onely to keep the memory of so worthy a friend and fellow alive as was our Shakespeare." The folio included all the plays now accepted as authentically Shakespearean, except "Pericles." Eighteen of the plays (including such famous dramas as "Julius Casesar," "As You Like It," "Macbeth," "The Taming of the Shrew," and "The Tempest") appeared originally in the first folio. Without it they might very well have been lost. The plays are grouped as comedies, histories, and tragedies. The actors listed, following Shakespeare, are next Richard Burbage and John Heminges, and eighth, Henry Condell.

Although Heminges and Condell have now largely been forgotten by students of Shakespeare, their contribution to the preservation of his works cannot be overestimated. Without their labor of love, his reputation as the greatest playwright in the English language may very well not have been secured. In 1895 a monument to

Heminges and Condell was erected in the Aldermanbury churchyard (see Ch. 7 and Figure 3.3). After the church fabric was moved to Westminster College, the monument was left standing in the Aldermanbury park garden as a tangible memorial to two of Aldermanbury's most famous and important parishoners.

Conclusion

We cannot say with certainty that William Shakespeare ever worshipped in the Church of St. Mary. His name does not appear in the records of the church. His church attendance anywhere was, at best, probably spotty. The fact that he left his permanent home in Stratford during his stay in London does suggest that without loyalty to a London parish, he may have gone to services on occasion with his friends, Heminges and Condell. As church officers and active parishoners they certainly attended. Shakespeare may have been present in the church for the christenings of their children. Perhaps the Bard attended with his two friends some of the periodic parish feasts and joined in the revelry. However, he almost certainly <u>did</u> spend time in the parish, probably eating many a meal at the homes of his fellow actors and business partners, or dining with them at the Axe Inn, near the church.

The Stuarts

James I/VI (1603-1625)

The story had all the elements of an adventure movie. A young rider dashed forth from the palace grounds in the dark of night and took the road northward from London. Fresh mounts awaited him at convenient points along the way. With courage, perseverance and derring do he broke all records for the ride between London and Edinburgh. Exhausted, he delivered his message. It was from Robert Cecil, most trusted and trustworthy servant of the Queen, to James VI, King of the Scots. The great Elizabeth was dead. He, James, was now also James I of England. The anticlimactic part is this. There were apparently no rival riders headed in other directions.

It was a French observer who gave James the label that probably suited him best, "the wisest fool in Christendom." He was an intelligent and learned person. But his stubborness and dogmatism, his lack of political acumen, his loud devotion to the doctrine of royal absolutism ("the divine right of kings"), perhaps above all his unwillingness to learn anything about the English people and English institutions, Parliament chief among them, promised difficulty. And unfortunately these flaws seemed endemic to the Stuart house.

Historians have noted that the great Tudors, the two Henrys and Elizabeth, probably entertained notions of royal prerogative at least as lofty as the Stuarts. But they had the wit not to go prating about it incessantly and the political acumen to get their way without resort to repression. Indeed, they generally succeeded in vesting royal policy with the appearance of the popular will. Nowhere was this more evident than in what we have called "the Elizabethan settlement" in state and society as well as in the Church, a centrist accomodation which may have worked best for the Queen and the higher orders, but which gave the majority of men and women in England the sense that they had a stake in England and in the prosperity of the crown.

When the center holds, discontent is a phenomenon of the fringes, of disaffected minorities which may be safely ignored or easily dealt with depending on the circumstances. Stuart absolutism, propelled by Stuart stubborness, was a direct assault on the center. And thus were unleashed all the social, political, religious, economic and ideological forces of modernity coming to be, and their counterparts in an old order ultimately doomed in England and in the rest of Europe. One may argue that England can thank the house of Stuart for precipitating the crisis, culminating only in 1688, which catapulted England in to the modern world a century ahead of the rest of Europe. (Actually, Holland got there first, but after their precocious performance in the 17th century the Dutch settled back into comfortable small power status.) But one may also argue that a couple of sovereigns as wise as Elizabeth might have led England into the new world with many fewer traumas.

James did pursue a consistent foreign policy, to avoid war at all costs. This policy was complicated with the outbreak of the Thirty Years War In Europe (1618-1648). There was strong sympathy for the Protestant side in Britain. But if a nation was to fight it had to have something to fight with, and James systematically neglected the military and naval establishments. Particularly galling to British sensibilities was the neglect of the fleet, Britain's pride since the defeat of the Armada. And soon the decay of the fleet led to genuine security risks. Foreign vessels treated British ships with contempt, fearing no reprisal. Barbary pirates raided along the coasts of England and Ireland, taking human booty to sell in slave markets of North Africa as well as material loot. Before it was over the British found themselves in the disgraceful position of being obliged to ransom their fellows from slavery in Muslim lands.

It might be supposed that James' pacifistic policies would result in substantial economies, but such was not the case. Following Gresham's brilliant work in the previous reign, the Elizabethan administration seems to have operated on a budget of £400,000 per annum. The Jacobean court expended half again as much, perhaps a quarter of it in deficit. The court was corrupt, self-indulgent and irresponsible. A considerable sum went to James' "favorites," his homosexual lovers, on whom he lavished wealth, titles, and high office. Most notorious were Robert Carr, created Earl of Somerset, and George Villiers, created Duke of Buckingham. Such was Buckingham's influence on events that we shall return presently to his achievements.

James' flamboyant sex life was a substantial source of embarassment to his son, the future Charles I, and probably to the unfortunate Prince Henry as well. But neither family chagrin nor the attempted rebuke of well-intentioned advisors swayed the king on the issue. Also disquieting was the status in the court of Count Godomar, the Spanish ambassador. Despite British animosity for Spain, James treated him almost as a crown minister. Had public opinion polls existed in the early 17th century, the rating of the Jacobean court would have been quite low!

James was served by two very able counselors, Robert Cecil (created Lord Salisbury) whom he inherited from Elizabeth and the brilliant lawyer-philosopher, Sir Francis Bacon. But Cecil died halfway through the reign, and Bacon's brilliance was little appreciated despite yeoman service as Lord Chancellor.

We shall reserve for the next chapter detailed discussion of developments in the polity of the nation, the City and the Church, because they were propelled even more rapidly with the deterioration of conditions under Charles I. Here let it suffice to note particular Jacobean problems with the courts and with Parliament.

The Common Law, a body of case precedent law (as opposed to legislation) had grown up over the centuries. It was preserved by learned judges and lawyers and was alleged to embody the fundamental rights of Englishmen. Detractors might point out that precedents were concocted at convenience by ingenious lawyers, but by the Elizabethan age a year's study in one of the Inns at Court was deemed a proper capstone to a university degree.

There were three great common law courts: King's Bench (criminal cases), Common Pleas (private civil cases), and Exchequer (government financial cases). James found himself at frequent cross-purposes with the courts. Ultimately, he deposed Lord Chief Justice Coke, who thereafter plagued his sovereign from a seat in the House of Commons. But even the undermining of judicial tenure did not bend the courts to James' will. However, the Stuart dynasty inherited also the so-called royal prerogative courts, Star Chamber and High Commission, where common law precedents were not binding. The abuses of these courts have made "Star Chamber" a synonym for judicial tyranny and they would be abolished by Parliament in the next reign.

Parliament itself wielded two powerful quasi-judicial weapons. One of these was the act of impeachment which could bring down an office holder. (Sir Francis Bacon was one of its victims.) The other was the old Tudor favorite, the bill of attainder, an act which (with royal assent) could sentence a person to death without the benefit of a trial.

The story of Parliament is from one standpoint the tale of the waxing of the Commons and the waning of the Lords, a process reinforced during the 17th century. The Commons was in Jacobean times largely a rural institution. The City, despite London's estimated population of about 90,000, held only four of the nearly 500 seats. Most seats at this time were filled by members of the gentry, the gentleman farmer class, largely men of some wealth and men of moderate, perhaps predominantly, Presbyterian sympathies. The members seem to have been mostly men of high purpose, not the opportunistic political adventurers of a later century. And they were, on the whole, not enamored with the lifestyle or the policies of the court. However, they did have many notions in common with the middle class merchants and tradesmen of London and Bristol.

James had been accustomed to the Scots Parliament, very much a pro forma body at the royal disposal. Many historians believe that one of James' chief considerations in taking the English crown was to escape the relative poverty of Scotland and gain access to the wealth of England. However, the members of the English parliament were not as docile as their Scottish counterparts. They had a deep sense of Parliament's historic prerogatives, rooted as firmly in the common law as those of the crown. Traditionally, when the crown required revenue beyond resources in hand, the sovereign called a Parliament. A national parliamentary election was held and the two houses, the hereditary Peers (Lords) and the newly elected Commons, met to act on crown requests and other legislative business. Once Parliament was in session and prior to the completion of its business, the crown had two legal ways of dealing with a troublesome assembly. The sovereign could "prorouge" (adjourn without dissolving) Parliament, or dissolve the body outright, requiring a new election before a Parliament could meet again. Four Parliaments were called under James, and but for the last (1624), all had a wretched relationship with the King. James tried to bully them, but to no avail. The 1624 Parliament gave James a little over a third of the revenue requested and endorsed the first of Buckingham's ill-fated military adventures.

With legal sources of revenue shut off, the government turned to irregular means for funding its activities. These included the sale of monopolies, coerced "loans" (with the City and its merchants and tradesmen favorite targets), increases in import duties, the collection of the wartime "ship tax" in peacetime, the sale of titles, and the sale of Church advowsons in the gift of the crown. The last of these was to play an important role in the history of Aldermanbury.

Several commercial and quasi-commercial ventures of Tudor and early Stuart times bore rich fruit for England and particularly for London and the other growing trading ports. The first to bring great rewards were the joint stock trading companies, the Muscovy Company (1553), the Levant Company (1581) and above all the East India Company (1600).

The establishment of colonies in North America and in the West Indies began haltingly under Elizabeth. But the unpleasant conditions of life generated by Stuart hostility to Puritans motivated a generation to seek their fortunes in New England. The prospect of escape from persecution also led English Catholics to Lord Baltimore's relatively benevolent proprietary colony of Maryland. Virginia settlement was probably prompted by opportunism or personal necessity (e.g., indentured servants and "social undesirables" swept up from the streets of London). Later, however, the victory of the Parliamentary side in the Civil War made Virginia attractive to Royalist sympathizers.

The Ulster Plantation was a settlement venture closer to home that would be fraught with tragic consequences right down to the present time. The policy of settling staunchly Protestant Scots in the northern part of Ireland as a means of pacifying the country was launched following the late Elizabethan suppression of the restive Irish. The policy continued under the Stuarts. The government of Charles I used stock in the Ulster adventure to secure a loan from the City. The burghers did not expect much in the way of returns from this particular investment, and they were not disappointed. The first major act of violence came late in Charles' reign in 1641, when the native Catholics massacred nearly 4,000 Protestants. Neither King nor Parliament would trust the other with an army, so the event went unavenged until Cromwell and the New Model Army retaliated a decade later.

An event of lasting religious significance took place early in James' reign. The Hampton Court Conference (1604) attempted to settle disputes between the High Church and Puritan parties in the Church. However, the three-day affair ended with James ranting at the Puritans, leaving them even more estranged from the crown. However, the conference did set in motion a new translation of the Bible, the Authorized Version of 1611, popularly known as the King James Version. The objective was not only to produce an accurate Bible translation for reading in the Church of England (hence "authorized"), but one without the inflammatory, partisan footnotes that were so much the rage in translations of the period. The AV would be a long time displacing the Geneva Bible (with its doctrinal Puritan footnotes) in popular affection. However, it was destined to become the most popular English version of the Bible ever produced, and take its place alongside the works of Shakespeare as the embodiment of "classical" English.

James I/VI was in a sorry state by his last year of life. Even his beloved Buckingham had strayed. He cast his lot with Charles, who thought he needed Buckingham's knowledge of palace intrigue and his skills in statecraft.

England paid a substantial price for the indiscretions of James and his son, Charles I, as we shall see when we continue the story of the Stuarts in the next chapter. One of Britain's great popular celebrations, Guy Fawkes Day (November 5), celebrates the failure of the Gunpowder Plot of 1605, in which a band of disgruntled Catholics attempted to blow up both the King and Parliament. Before the reign was over many may have felt that England would have been better off had the plotters gotten the king before they were apprehended.

Aldermanbury during the Reign of James I/VI

In March 1604 the Vestry continued its "crackdown" on pensioners, ordering that "all the Pensioners of this Parish [sit] in two of the last pews of the Church at the discretion of the Churchwarden." If they refused their pensions were to be revoked.

In 1606 the rectory, church, and diverse houses were granted by King James I to Robert Morgan and Thomas Butler, presumably as part of the king's efforts to raise funds to support his extravagant court. Letters patent for the grant were dated 18 August, 1606. A rent of £11 was reserved for the King, and the King agreed to discharge the grantees from all other payments except the minister or curate's salary, rent for a house for the minister, 20s to St. Paul's and 3s to the Archdeacon of London, charges for bread, wine, wax and other necessaries, and charges for "four ordinary Sermons" (Carter 1913: 7).

On 21 December 1607 the Vestry mandated that anyone who received money for the poor would have to put up a Surety from year to year. Apparently money assigned for the poor was being diverted by someone.

The squabbling between the parish and the crown over parish property continued as the following entry in the Vestry minutes, dated 1 May, 1608, shows: (Carter 1913: 11)

> At a Vestry holden this present daie upon a demand of certain quitrent
> by the King's Commissioners of fyve tenements there are appointed
> Mr. John Combe, Mr. Edward Rotheram, Mr. Daniell Pointell,
> Mr. Atkinson to advise with learned Councell and to shewe forth
> the evydens of the church lands, to be informed the parish whether
> the same be paid or not.

At the same Vestry new trustees of the parish estates were appointed to replace those who had died or left the parish. They included Sir Clement Skydymore, Knight; an Alderman, Mr. Harry Finch; Councell at Law, Mr. Daniell Pointell; Theopilas Brereton; John Heminges; and Thomas Kertone.

In 1611 Sir John Davye and others entered into a suit with Thomas Clarke and his wife Joan and others concerning ownership of the Rectory (Ms. 23,737A: 174).

On 10 May 1612 the Vestry voted to beautify the Church, since a distinguished parish resident, Sir John Swynerton, had been chosen to serve as Lord Mayor for the next year (Ms. 3570aI:38). John Swinarton (as he spelled his name) was a member of a family which had lived in the parish for at least 50 years. His father (also named John) had been Master of the Merchant Taylor's Company. He had been elected Alderman and Sheriff in 1602 and knighted in 1603. In his capacity as Sheriff and

Alderman he had led his fellow citizens to Stamford Hill to greet King James upon his arrival in London. When he was installed as mayor in 1612 a pageant planned by John Heminges and the poet Thomas Dekker was held. He was a founder of the East India company and the Irish Society. He died on 1616 and was buried next to his father in the Southeast corner of the church. (Carter 1913: 93).

Once again as the wealthy and prominent were being honored the needs of the less fortunate were not being ignored. At the same Vestry a pension was allocated to "the Widow Ireland."

At a meeting on 8 June, 1612 the Vestry responded favorably to a request of Sir Clement Scudamore, Alderman, for a piece of ground within the Church for a vault for "himself, his Ladie, and children and his posteritie." The entry goes on to say that Sir Clement "did (not being moved thereunto) liberallee and of his own free will give the sum of Ten Pounds currant English money" because of the parishoners' kindness" (Carter 1913: 73-74).

A deed entered into record on 17 April, 1613, is evidence of a lease of the rectory by Sir John Swynerton and others to Rowland Trewlove (Ms. 23,737A: 174).

On 2 April, 1615 the Vestry minutes record that a John Bride agreed to vacate the room over the Church door (which apparently was being used to house the homeless poor) and reserved its use for auditors of the Churchwarden accounts and "not for any more dwellers".

On 17 November, 1616, Sir John Swinerton (sic) and others leased the rectory to Robert Harland, clerk.

In 1617 Thomas Downing became curate (Carter 1913: 41). In the interim a John Davenport had been prosecuted by the Bishop for lecturing and officiating at St. Mary's without a proper license (Seaver 1976: 227). Two years later (7 June 1619) the Vestry agreed to allow Mr. Downing to have use of "the little house near the Church late in the possession of Mr. Harland" (Carter 1913: 41).

On 29 April, 1619 a moiety of the Rectory and Church was sold by Robert Morgan and Thomas Butler to Roger Rante and his son (Ms. 23,737A: 175). Another moiety was sold by the same pair to Thomas Clarke and others on 8 May (Ms. 23,737A: 175). A year later (1 May, 1620) the rectory and others premises were conveyed by Sir John Leman, Alderman, and Cornelius Fish, Chamberlain, to Edward Rotherman, Alderman, and other parishoners (Ms. 23,737A: 175). Sir John Davye and other parishoners purchased from Roger Rante and his son their moiety on 15 June, 1621.

At an assembly of the parishoners on 7 June, 1621 "it was confirmed ... and good allowance given for the purchasing of the parsonage and houses thereunto belonging which was heretofore bought to the use of the parish in ffee ffarme at price £440 beside charges for the assurance to be taken ... " (Carter 1913: 11-12). Thirty-one parishoners were elected to negotiate the purchase. At the same meeting the house in which Mr. Downing lived and another one were sold to Richard Bridges and Robert Eccleston for £234 with the agreement that the parish pay £10 a year rental for Mr. Downing's house. An "Indenture for Bargain and Sale" dated 15 June, 1621 (Ms. 23,737A:175) confirmed the sale. The property was conveyed to "Sir John Davy, Knight, and other parishoners" (Carter 1913: 7-8). To make matters perfectly clear, the current holders of the parsonage released to the parish their "right, title, and interest in the Rectory, Church and houses" on 15 November 1621 (Ms. 23,737A: 175). Thus did the parish, through its vestry, come to control the advowson. This insured that St. Mary's would be served by ministers with views congenial to the Puritan temper of the community.

On 22 July 1621 an assembly of the general parishoners agreed to pay the £100 outstanding for the parsonage houses through assessing each parishoner twice the yearly poor rate (Carter 1913: 12).

A study of the records ordered by the Vestry in 1885, when the parish was embroiled in a dispute with the City Parochial Charities Commission over ownership of parish properties (see Ch. 7), concluded that "the parishoners ... have exercised the right of presentation to the said church from the date of said purchase in 1621 to the present time" (Carter 1913: 8).

About this time a plague struck London, and Mr. Downing, now the first perpetual curate of St. Mary, Aldermanbury, and another paid clergyman, left the parish. Downing refused to return (Carter 1913: 42). The incumbent of St. Mary's came to be styled as the "perpetual curate," the parish itself being the minister.

A minute dated 5 November 1624 records that a "general meeting of the pishe" named a committee of 13 to work out how best "to settle the difference between Mr. Downinge and the pishe." The dispute was apparently over Downing's refusal to have an Independent lecturer (Seaver 1976: 135). The committee was to submit a plan to the general parish for final approval (Carter 1913: 42). At at meeting of the parish on 25 November the committee reported. On the advice of the diocesan chancellor, they recommended that Downing surrender the living in exchange for a life annuity of £20 per year. Some felt the committee had gone beyond the limits of its charge. "It was therefore putt to hands whether they would allowe of that wch was passed which they did ... "The assembly further directed the Committee to pursue legally whether the parish had the right to "place or displace their curate at their pleasure." Apparently Downing was refusing to acknowledge the right of the parish to dismiss him. Several days later another "ample assemblye" voted to put Downing out (Carter 1913: 42).

By the 10th of December Downing had accepted the suspension and "cast himself upon the good will of the pishe." The parish agreed to pay Downing the £20 annually for life. A committee was then appointed to see how to pay for both a new curate and Downing, but the point became moot shortly afterwards when Downing, his wife and three children all died of the plague.

As we have already noted in Ch. 2, Sion College for the London clergy was founded in 1623, on the northern boundary of the parish. Although every rector, vicar, licensed lecturer, and curate within the city was made a fellow of the college and governor of the associated almshouse, during its initial years Sion was likely a haven for puritan clerics, providing a place to meet and a place to reside for ministers arriving in London to take up cures within the city. The 35,000 volume library provided ministers with access to virtually every work in theology. Until 1836 every work published in England was gratuitously presented to the library. The four yearly dinners, with a Latin sermon at each, provided ministers an opportunity to hear their most respected colleagues give theological addresses. The almshouse provided ten rooms for ten poor men within the College and ten for poor women outside the college. To be eligible candidates had to be impoverished, single, and over fifty years of age.

On 17 December, 1624 Robert Harris was chosen curate in a "free election." When informed of his selection, Mr. Harris wanted some assurances about his job description and wages, so the Vestry on 16 January, 1625, agreed to pay Harris for a house, the charge of the lecturer (reader), £120 salary, £20 of this from weddings, christenings and burials (or the balance to be made up by the parish). Harris agreed to provide for three sermons weekly, two on Sunday by him and the third on a weekday by a lecturer appointed by him. During the Summer only two sermons weekly would be preached. Mr. Harris had been taken to the Bishop's ordinary and registered as Curate with a license to preach.

Concern was expressed in the parish that such a large salary was a bad precedent, so it was decided to record the special reasons for paying Harris so much. They were his "extraordinarye gifts" and "his great charge of familye." It was also stipulated that this was not to be seen as a precedent and that Mr. Harris' salary was to be raised from "the benevolence of the well disposed inhabitants whose harts the Lord hath thus enlarged for the bringing of a worthye man amongst them whereof for a long time they have had great want" (Carter 1913: 42-43). The background of this controversy is the shift in payment of ministers during the Puritan period from tithes to a stipend authorized by the vestry. Since payment of a stipend was a new practice, the vestry did not want to establish a precedent they would be unable to follow. £120 was one of the higher stipends paid to clergy in London.

Ironically, Harris was curate for only one year. He was one of 10,000 Londoners who died of the plague in 1625-1626. Harris died in January, 1626. He was apparently a minister of prominence, for he was asked to address the judges at the Oxford assizes. In 1628 two of his sermons were posthumously published.

On 22 January 1626 an "ample assemblye" voted to pay the new curate, Dr. Thomas Taylor, the same £120 annually, so the concern over establishing a precedent which was to benefit later curates was well-founded! Taylor was from a Puritan family in Richmond, Yorkshire, the son of the town recorder. He received a Cambridge B.D. (1628) and an Oxford D.D. (1630). Taylor had a reputation as an excellent preacher and theologian (Walzer 1966: 136). In 1601, when he was only 25, he preached a sermon before Queen Elizabeth at St. Paul's Cross. In 1608 he gave a sermon at the University church in Cambridge in defense of the Puritans, after which he was censured by the Vice Chancellor for attacking the policies of Archbishop Bancroft. His preaching at Aldermanbury was said to be "a brazen wall against popery and Arminianism" (Seaver 1976: 184). A letter in 1626 to a priest in Spain complained that "certain zealous persons were stirred up by the sermons of a Calvinistic sot in Aldermanbury to deface our Saviour's picture." (Goss 1944: 153). The "Calvinist sot" was either Taylor or another Puritan lecturer. Collected editions of Taylor's works (with a life and portrait) were published in 1653, with a preface by one of his successors at St. Mary, Aldermanbury—Edmund Calamy. He left the Aldermanbury pulpit in 1630 because of ill health. He died in 1633 and was buried in the Church (Oliver 1969: 22). A prolific writer, he authored over seventeen separate works.

In his highly respected work, The Revolution of the Saints (1966), Michael Walzer heralds Taylor, Harris, and their famous successor at Aldermanbury, Edmund Calamy, as the first "radical politicians," men who called and worked for a complete transformation of the state in light of their vision of a righteous society.

Sometime in the 1620's, during the tenure of Thomas Taylor, Sir Robert Harley (1579-1656) moved into the parish. Harley was a Herefordshire farmer who served in the Long Parliament and gained fame as a patron of Puritan ministers. He was "earnest for presbytery." He worked closely with Taylor and Taylor's successor, John Staughton. He functioned as "a kind of clearinghouse for Puritans seeking livings and patrons seeking preachers" (Seaver 1976: 50). Knighted by James I in 1603, he served as master of the mint from 1626-1635 and 1643-1649. He participated in the drafting of the ban on the wearing of surplices by clergy and supported the demolishing of "idolatrous monuments" in Westminster Abbey and London churches. In 1641 he was instrumental in securing an invitation for Aldermanbury curate Edmund Calamy to speak at the first House of Commons fast days. Although he supported the Parliamentary cause during the Civil War, he opposed more extreme measures and was dismissed from his position at the mint for refusing to cast new, parliamentary coins.

During this period of religious fervor, the church building itself apparently had fallen into disrepair. On 19 June, 1629, £200 was voted for repair of the church and steeple from an assessment. Some parishoners must have objected, for five days later the assessment was voided and another plan adopted to raise the money from leases. That plan was thrown out on 10 July and still another adopted (Ms. 3570aI:46-47).

At a general assembly of the parish on 13 August, 1632, Dr. John Staughton appeared and agreed to become curate and lecturer. His stipend was to be equal to that of his predecessors. On 5 December, 1632, at Dr. Staughton's request, a general meeting of the parishoners was held to confirm his call and stipend. At the meeting he was asked to move into the parish from the country and to surrender his other livings. It was agreed that his stipend would be raised from subscribers and collected quarterly by the churchwardens. (Carter 1913: 45). Staughton was questioned by Bishop Juxon for "breach of the canons of the church." Despite the efforts of John Winthrop to lure him to New England to join the "noble experiment in creating the righteous society," he remained at Aldermanbury until his death in 1639 (Seaver

1976: 257).

By the 1630's parish vestries had control over the advowson in only thirteen London parishes, and one was Aldermanbury. In effect, these parishes provided working models for the creation of presbyterian polity within the established church, implementing the approach of reform "from within." They also provided a haven for some of the most famous nonconformist preachers of the day, like Harris, Taylor, and their successors, Staughton and Calamy (Seaver 1976: 138).

The account book of 1632 shows our first example of a fine being paid by a parishoner for relief from serving in a parish office. A Mr. Witham, merchant, paid £15 to be excused from "all offices in the parish whatsoever." (Carter 1913: 111). This practice of avoiding parish service by paying a fine was to become widespread in later years, especially during tumultuous times.

A bond concerning the apprenticeship of John Aldermanbury, a foundling, to John Payne was entered into record on 30 January, 1633/4 (Ms. 23,737A: 176).

Sir John Davy left £100 "for the poor" in 1637 (Ms. 3570aI:49-50). On 19 May, 1638, the Vestry agreed to place a valuation on houses in the parish of at least £100, in order to "maintain a preaching Minister" in conformity with an order of the Privy Council. The order was dissolved several months later.

A study of parish demography, based on a 1638 catalogue of the inhabitants of London parishes, has shown that roughly 20-30% of those living in Aldermanbury were "substantial householders," making the parish one of modest to high economic means (Jones 1980). The medieval practice of intermingling rich and poor continued well into the 17th century (Pearl 1979). Parishes were microcosms of the whole city rather than social quarters. The social mix prevailed even within the most prosperous houses. On the ground floor was a shop or work room, with the proprietors living on the first floor, journeymen on the second, and servants in the attic (Jones 1980: 126). Nevertheless, the richer houses were concentrated in the center of the walled city, with the poorer residences on the periphery. Movement within the city was still difficult, causing the elite to congregate at the center, the less well-to-do around the edges, and the poorest in the suburbs. However, by 1638 high status residential suburbs, with town houses for the prosperous, had begun to develop to the West.

Conclusion

By 1638 St. Mary, Aldermanbury, had become an important parish, both politically and religiously. It was one of the leading Puritan parishes in the City of London. Its importance in the efforts to reform the Church of England from within was already established. Its role in modeling ecclesiastical self-government had begun, with effects which were to be long lasting both religiously and politically. In both areas the next phase in the history of Aldermanbury would be even more amazing.

Bibliography

Brigden, Susan
    1989   London and the Reformation. Oxford: Clarendon Press.

Bryant, James C.
    1984   Tudor Drama and Religious Controversy. Macon, GA: Mercer University Press.

Carter, Pierson Cathrick
    1913   History of the Church and Parish of St. Mary the Virgin, Aldermanbury. London: W. H. and L. Collinbridge.

Collinson, Patrick
    1967   The Elizabethan Puritan Movement. Berkeley: University of California Press.

Connell, Charles
    1982   They Gave Us Shakespeare: John Heminge and Henry Condell. Stocksfield: Oriel Press.

Darlington, Ida, ed.
    1967   London Consistory Court Wills. London: London Record Society.

Finlay, Roger
    1981   Population and Metropolis: the Demography of London, 1580- 1650. Cambridge: University Press.

Forbes, Thomas Rogers
   1971   Chronicle from Aldgate: Life and Death in Shakespeare's London.
           New Haven: Yale University Press.

Goss, Charles
   1944   "A History of The Parish of St. Mary the Virgin, Aldermanbury."
           Transactions of the London and Middlesex Archaeological Society.
           9 (1944-47), 113-164.

Holmes, Martin
   1969   Elizabethan London. New York: Frederick A. Prager.

Jones, Emry
   1980   "London in the Early 17th Century: An Ecological Approach,"
           London Journal 6, 121-133.

Kitching, C. J., ed.
   1980   London and Middlesex Chantry Certificates, 1648. London Record
           Society Publications XVI. London: The London Record Society.

Malcolm, J. Peller
   1803   Londinium Redivivum: An Ancient History and Modern Description.
           London: John Nichols and Son.

Morgan, Robert
   1986   Godly Learning—Puritan Attitudes towards Reason, Learning, and
           Education, 1560-1640. Cambridge: University Press.

Museum of London
   no date   Map of Elizabethan London, engraved for an Atlas of
           European Cities, by G. Brown and F Hogenberg, 1572. London.

Oliver, Dame Beryl
   1969   The Winston Churchill Memorial and the Church of St. Mary the Virgin,

Aldermanbury: A Brief History. London: The Faith Press.

Pearl, Valerie
    1961   London and the Outbreak of the Puritan Revolution: City Government and Politics, 1625-1643. London: Oxford University Press.

    1979   "Change and Stability in 17th Century London," London Journal 5.

Pendrill, Charles
    1937   Old Parish Life in London. London: Oxford University.

Perle, Charles
    no date   "The Shrine in Shakespeare's London: a history and description of the Heminge and Condell Monument." Guildhall Library Pamphlet 5562.

Prockter, Adrian and Robert Taylor
    1979   The A to Z of Elizabethan London. London: London Topographical Society (publication no. 122).

Rowse, A. L.
    1957   The England of Elizabeth: The Structure of Society. New York: Macmillan.

    1988   Shakespeare the Man. rev. ed. New York: St. Martin's Press.

Rude, George
    1971   History of London: Hanoverian London, 1741-1808. London: Secker and Warburg.

Seaver, Paul, ed.
    1970   The Puritan Lectureships: The Politics of Religious Dissent. Stanford: Stanford University Press.

1976   Seventeenth Century England: Society in an Age of Revolution. New York: New Viewpoints.

Stow, John
1598   A Survay of London by John Stow, Citizen of London. London: John Windet, 1598 (1603).

Walker, Charles
1896   "John Heminge and Henry Condell and what the world owes them," London.Pamphlet distributed at dedication of monument.

Walters, Henry B.
1939   London Churches at the Reformation. London: Church Historical Society.

Walzer, Michael
1966   The Revolution of the Saints. Cambridge: Harvard University Press.

CHAPTER FOUR: A PRESBYTERIAN PARISH DURING TUMULTUOUS TIMES: THE EDMUND CALAMY ERA (1639-1662)

Introduction

The City of London and its Churches were destined to play a salient role in the dramatic half-century between the election of the Long Parliament and the Glorious Revolution. This influence was most marked in parishes like Aldermanbury that held their own advowson, or where the advowson was owned by a Puritan notable. St. Antholin, Budge Row, is often cited as a bellweather. Not only was it a long-time Puritan parish, it also had an endowed lectureship. These Sunday afternoon and weekday lectures were important instruments of Puritan persuasion. They were Calvinist orations, and hence were generously laced with political commentary. Like St. Antholin, St. Mary, Aldermanbury, owned the advowson and possessed a lectureship.

In 1639 the parish chose as perpetual curate a minister who would place Aldermanbury at the fulcrum of great events. At a general assembly of the parishoners of St. Mary's on 27 May, 1639 the election of Edmund Calamy (spelled Callomee in the Minutes) as minister was confirmed. He was to be paid £160 per year, now the going rate for a St. Mary's curate, and "probably the highest annual stipend a London minister received so early in this period." (Liu 1986: 151-152). Calamy agreed to provide (by himself, or some other preacher) three sermons a week—two on Sundays and one on Wednesday afternoon. He was to arrive by Midsummer next.

Without a doubt Edmund Calamy is the most famous clergyman to serve St. Mary, Aldermanbury in the nearly one thousand year history of the church. As a leading historian of the period has stated, "in any study of Puritan London, Edmund Calamy would deserve the foremost attention" (Liu 1986:74). Our treatment of this critical period in the life of the parish will, therefore, focus largely on the career of this distinguished minister. (We are principally indebted to the following scholars in our treatment of Calamy and the turbulent times in which he served St. Mary's: Richard Greaves for his very thorough research on Calamy's life, upon which we have drawn in the following portrait; Tai Liu for his study of Puritan London; and Brian Manning for his research on the relation between religion and politics during the Puritan period.)

Calamy was deeply involved in the political and religious turmoil of Puritan England. "Throughout the 1640s and 1650s Calamy worked tirelessly in the Presbyterian movement, distinguishing himself as one of London's most prominent religious leaders" (Greaves 1985: 9). In a time of extremism he had the misfortune to be a principled moderate who would not compromise with extremists. He paid a price for his obstinancy, but he also earned the respect of both Parliamentarians and Royalists, Independents and Anglicans. Although he offended some of the parishoners of St. Mary's, almost all had genuine affection for the man and great admiration for the preacher and politician.

Edmund Calamy's Background before coming to St. Mary's (1600-1639)

Edmund Calamy (see Figure 4.1) was born in 1600 in London, the only son of tradesman and London citizen George Calamy, an immigrant from Guernsey who was possibly of Huguenot origin. He was baptized at St. Thomas Apostle on 24 February 1600. Calamy must have been precocious. He entered the prestigous Merchant Taylors' School in London at age 13. On 4 July, 1616 he was admitted to Pembroke Hall, Cambridge, where he earned a B.A. in 1620 and an M.A. in 1623. In 1625 he was named a fellow of Pembroke. Calamy married into politics. His first wife, Mary, was the daughter of Robert Snelling, a member of parliament from Ipswich in the last several parliaments of James I (Walzer 1966: 136-137). By his first wife Calamy had a son (Edmund) and a daughter (Susan). His second wife, Anne, was from Lancashire. Their children included three sons (Benjamin, James, and John) and four daughters (Elizabeth, Rebecca, Anne, and Mary).

Calamy was ordained as a minister on 5 March, 1626. Bishop Nicholas Felton of Ely became his patron and appointed him a Chaplain to the Bishop and vicar of St.

Mary's, Swaffham-prior, in Cambridgeshire. According to his grandson, Calamy lived in Felton's home and spent up to sixteen hours a day studying Scripture, Thomas Aquinas, and the works of Augustine (which he read five times). The Bishop instructed his servants not to call Calamy to family prayers or other occasions without a half-hour warning, so that his studies might not be broken off too abruptly (Matthews 1934: xlix). Felton's home became a center of Puritan study during this period.

Calamy left Ely in 1627 to assume a lectureship at Bury St. Edmunds, Suffolk, where he preached three times a week. One of his associates at Bury was Jeremiah Burroughs, who later became one of the leading Independents.

Two years later he received a license to preach in the diocese of Norwich, under the authority of Christopher Wren's uncle, Bishop Matthew Wren. During his tenure at Bury, in 1632, he was awarded the honorary degree of B.D. by Cambridge University. Calamy's Puritan sympathies are evident during this period. He resisted having to read required services from the Book of Common Prayer and refused to bow at the altar. When Bishop Wren, second only to Archbishop Laud (see below) in his defense of High Church practices, required that chancels be raised and the communion table placed at the East end as an altar, with a railing, Calamy apparently refused. He was called before the Bishop's commissioners with two other ministers. He retained the favor of the Bishop and the support of his parishoners, however, for when in 1637 he announced plans to leave Bury St. Edmunds, he was offered a £400 yearly stipend to remain.

In part because of his disenchantment with Bishop Wren, he left Bury in November, 1637 to assume the rectory of Rochford, Kent, under the patronage of one of the most prominent Puritan peers, Robert Rich, Earl of Warwick (see below). While in Rochford he contracted a disease which troubled him the rest of his life. His grandson called it "a tedious Quartan Ague, which brought upon him a Dizziness in his Head" (Matthews 1934: l). As a result, from this point on in his ministry, he refused to preach from an elevated pulpit, speaking instead from a seated position, at his reading desk.

The Stuarts (continued)

From the story of Edmund Calamy we step back to look once again at the broader historical context, continuing the story of national events during the tumultuous

Stuart dynasty, turning to the successor of James I—his son Charles I.

Charles I (1625-1649): Prior to the Civil War (1625-1642)

One of the most tempting historical "what ifs" in Stuart history is, what if Prince Henry (1594-1612) had lived to succeed his father and enjoy a life and reign of normal length, leaving after him an heir sired in his own image? For Henry was all that his father and a great deal that his brother Charles were not. Unlike the dissolute and extravagant royal court, Henry's household would have been decorous and circumspect and the Prince himself a model of morality and Protestant zeal.

Henry had a royal charisma and flair for public relations which contrasted with James' reclusive tendencies. Created Prince of Wales in 1610, with his own court at St. James, Henry became so popular that the King exclaimed, "Will he bury me alive?" He took an early and enthusiastic interest in matters of statecraft, staking out positions which were generally on the popular side. He opposed James' pro-Spanish policies, advocating a stronger navy and army and favoring military adventurism. Perhaps his most enduring legacy lay in instructing his brother, Charles, in the appreciation of art, for Charles not only inherited Henry's collection of paintings, but augmented it, forming the basis for today's Royal Gallery.

Henry died suddenly and unexpectedly, perhaps of typhoid fever. Public expressions of grief were widespread, compounded by rumors of poisoning, some implicating the King. A King Henry IX may not have entertained any less exalted views of royal prerogative than James or Charles I, but he may have guided England in the transition toward modernity without a ruinous civil war.

When James passed quietly from the scene, Buckingham took the initiative. Although his efforts to secure a Spanish Catholic wife for Charles had failed, within ten weeks of Charles' ascent to the throne, Buckingham had arranged a marriage with the French Catholic Henrietta Maria, sister of Louis XIII. The marriage was a happy one, but the Queen's Catholicism increased popular suspicion and hostility, especially in Puritan quarters. Buckingham's string of failed military adventures brought Parliamentary resistance, which ended only when Buckingham died at an assassin's hand in 1628.

Three Parliaments were crowded into Charles' first four regnal years. The first two were tight-fisted and Charles riposted with stepped up illegal impositions, particularly extorted loans. Martial law was imposed and troops quartered upon the populace with predictable looting, rapes, and other acts of violence. The Parliament of 1628 arrived in Westminster determined to rectify matters. It drew up the Petition of Right and made it plain that unless the king gave his assent there would be no revenue. Like the Magna Charta, the Petition addressed specific wrongs and abuses: arbitrary imprisonment and taxation, the quartering of troops and martial law. In giving his assent on 7 June, 1628, Charles in effect confessed to wrongdoing and admitted that the king was under, not above, the law.

It might be said that James, though hostile to Parliament, was resigned to it as an inevitable part of the English political landscape. After the Parliament adjourned itself in 1629, Charles resolved to reign without one. So began eleven years of "personal rule." It was a period of peace because the king could not afford a war. However, he did feel obliged to squeeze illegal revenue sources even harder than in the past, with progressive loss of public affection.

Charles was not well-served by his chief ministers, although they were infinitely more able than Buckingham. They were efficient administrators of detested measures. William Laud (1573-1645), a viruently anti-Calvinist Churchman, had become privy counselor in 1626, and rose rapidly to bishop of London, chancellor of Oxford, and finally archbishop of Canterbury in 1633. "High church" has had a variety of meanings in Anglican history. For Laud it meant an exalted view of royal and episcopal authority and the subordination of the laity to the priesthood. It included rigid conformity to the words and rubrics of the prayer book and to episcopal commands. Laud did not call for a reversion to medieval liturgy and vestments, but he did demand more in the way of chancel adornments, clerical vestments, and ceremonious actions than a majority of his clergy cared for, which is to say a great deal more than a Puritan conscience like Calamy's could tolerate. His decrees were resisted, and Laud responded with stern disciplinary actions.

Laud did not confine himself to sacred matters. He sat on both the Star Chamber and High Commission, and was associated with exquisite torture and cruel and unusual punishments, some against recalcitrant clergy. He joined the King and Earl of Strafford as a sort of governing triumvirate. If Laud was the most hated Churchman in England, second place fell to Bishop Matthew Wren of Ely, uncle of Christopher, of whom, as we have seen, Edmund Calamy ran afoul. Sir Winston Churchill described Laud as Charles' evil genius. It was his insane drive for uniformity that provoked Scotland to armed conflict and set in train the events leading to the Civil

War.

The Earl of Strafford (Sir Thomas Wentworth) was a more ambiguous figure. He had been a strong opponent of the crown in the Parliament of 1628, who was won over by the King by Christmas of that year. His remarkable success as the ruthless lord lieutenant of Ireland led to his appointment as Charles chief minister in 1639. However, his tactics made him an easy target of the Long Parliament, which passed an act of attainder. Intimated by the London street mobs, Charles gave his assent and in 1641 Wentworth became the first of the triumvirate to lose his head. On the block he quoted the words of Scripture: "Put not your trust in princes."

Unlike Puritan Independents, Presbyterians had no inherent antipathy to prayer books and forms of worship. John Calvin had promulgated liturgies in Strausbourg and at Geneva, and John Knox had worked with Thomas Cranmer on the second prayer book of Edward VI. But the staunchly Presbyterian Scots would not countenance the prayer book that Laud tried to impose, with all of its episcopal and priestly overtones, and without the authority of the Scottish Kirk. In 1638 nobles and commoners, ministers and laity gathered in Edinburgh's Greyfriars Churchyard to subscribe to the National Covenant, affirming Presbyterianism and rejecting Laud's innovations. It was an open act of rebellion against the crown. So Laud's gratuitous meddling with the existing ecclesiastical equilibrium provoked the Scots to set in motion the events which brought a Scots king to ruin. The issues were not entirely religious. Scots patriotism and nationalism, resentment of English domination, and the emerging ideology of human rights over royal authority were major factors.

Charles' attempt to riposte the Scots uprising with the resources at hand resulted in the two "Bishop's Wars" (1639, 1640). The English proved no match for the Scots army, led by officers and troops with experience fighting on the Protestant side in the continental war. The first war ended in a patched-up peace. Bent on revenge Charles accepted Strafford's advice and called what was to become known as the "Short Parliament." It was a disaster from the royalist point of view. The Commons would grant the King nothing until the grievances of 11 years of personal prerogative rule were redressed. A frustrated Charles dismissed the Parliament after only three weeks, resulting in riots which Strafford ruthlessly suppressed.

A conscripted English army was raised to attack Scotland, but before they could act the Scots army marched as far south as Durham. They might have gone further, perhaps even to London, but the Scots did not want to antagonize the English people.

They merely wanted to force Charles' hand. The Scots army encamped at Durham and demanded that Charles pay their bills (estimated at £850 a day).

The King, lacking money either to pay the blackmail or raise an adequate army, was forced to call another Parliament. The "Long Parliament" convened in November, 1640. Its sitting would eclipse by nine years Charles eleven years of personal rule. At its head emerged the formidable John Pym (1584-1643), a Puritan squire for whom (in the best Calvinist tradition) sound government was an article of religious faith. So powerful did he become that some wags declared there were two kings in England: King Charles in Whitehall, and King Pym in Westminster.

No one, in all probability, desired the civil war about to come. The adversaries blundered, as it were, into war. But in a sense it was war from the first. Those on the extremes were bent on destruction of their opponents, and the more moderate opinions of the majority in the middle were overridden by circumstances. They would be forced to take sides or, as a few did, take refuge in the colonies or on the continent. The extremes were met. On one side were Charles, with his absolute claims, and his ministers who supported them. On the other were men who would lodge the power of state in Parliament. On the one side was Laudian high churchmanship. On the other were the extremes of Puritanism. Most Englishmen would probably have voted for "none of the above," had they been given the choice. The Parliamentary leaders struck first and felled both Strafford and Laud. The proceedings by which they were brought to justice reflect no more credit on the law than the arbitrary actions of the accused. But once these deeds were done, the Long Parliament made, in the early years of its sitting, a number of contributions to England's evolving polity. The prerogative courts with their lawless license were abolished. Thereafter, justice would be adjudicated in the courts of common law with their developing precedents protecting the defendants and not the prosecution. The various forms of irregular taxation and revenue enhancement were outlawed. Regular sittings of Parliament were ordained whether or not the crown sought them.

Excursus: The City Polity

Even as the Long Parliament joined deadly combat with the architects of prerogative rule and hammered out some aspects of the shape of England's future national polity, equally significant precedents were being established for the government of the City itself. Here, the seminal study by Valerie Pearl (1961) is an invaluable resource.

By the 17th century the ancient Court of Hustings was an atavistic survival from the Middle Ages. The courts of the Lord Mayor, the (two) Sheriffs, Requests, the Coroner and Escheaton were of relatively minor importance and that largely judicial. One must remember that in historic English, "courts" describes entities with governing as well as judicial functions.

The three main London courts by the 17th century were, in ascending order of prominence, Common Hall (largely electoral in capacity), Common Council (legislative), and Lord Mayor and Alderman (putatively administrative, but also involved in the electoral and legislative processes).

Common Hall had roots in the Folkmote, the assembly of City freeholders. But Common Hall (called "Congregation" in its minutes until 1738) was restricted to liverymen of the City, of whom there were about 4,000 in the mid-17th century. But there was no effective way to prevent persons of lower rank from attending and voting, and apparently some did. The notion that Common Hall should be open to all free men of the City was widely heralded in the tumultuous 1640's. The Common Hall met on 29 September (the Feast of St. Michael and All Angels) to nominate two candidates for Lord Mayor, normally the senior alderman and a pro forma second candidate. The names were forwarded to the Court of Alderman which ordinarily elected the senior alderman. A second annual meeting of the Common Hall was held on 24 June for other elections, including (from the 16th century on) the City's four representatives in Parliament.

Common Hall did not hold a monopoly on City electoral procedures. Wardmote commanded the presence of all householders and males over 15 years of age in the ward, though only freemen could vote on the higher offices (i.e., aldermen and Common Councilmen). The Common Councilmen (4, 6, or 8 per Ward, depending on size of the ward) were usually liverymen who once elected served until they were elected to higher office or died. When an aldermanic vacancy occurred, a special wardmote was called and the freemen chose a slate of four names to send up to the self-perpetuating Court of Aldermen. The process of aldermanic election was complicated by the fact that an alderman need not live in the ward he represented. Wardmote also elected ward officers such as the clerk, the beadle, the constables, and the Inquest.

Wardmotes might be divided into precincts, which were supposed to nominate candidates for election by Wardmote. Precincts did not coincide with parishes, but influential parishes might control a precinct up to the point of the vestry, even a "select" vestry, usurping the entire electoral process. In ten parishes where early 17th century minutes are preserved, precinct minutes are recorded in the vestry records and Common Councilmen declared elected before wardmote even met. (St. Mary, Aldermanbury is among these parishes.) In some wards an unofficial committee of the wardmote, composed of the alderman, his deputy, the Common Councilmen and a few of the other wealthier and more influential citizens, might convene as "the Common Council of the Ward" to guard against "excessive" democracy.

The Court of Common Council supposedly represented all the freemen of the city. It evolved out of 14th century efforts to control financial exactions by the Court of Aldermen. Across the centuries it grew from 100 members in the 1400's to 196 in the early 1600's and 237 by the mid-1600's. Common Council claimed jurisdiction over some municipal property.

The Court of Aldermen sat as part of Common Council, but the two courts were polled separately and an aldermanic majority could veto acts of Common Council. Common Council was limited to discussion of issues proposed by the Aldermen. Just as the self-styled worthiest men conspired against too much democracy in the wards, so the Lord Mayor and Aldermen sometimes guarded the city from its elected legislators by convening in place of Common Council a hybrid assembly of themselves and their wealthier associates. The Common Council ordinarily sat two to six times a year.

The Court of Aldermen sat each Tuesday and Thursday except during the holiday seasons. There were 26 members. Except for the years 1354-1494, election was for life. The Court considered itself the sole judge of the fitness of its self-perpetuating membership. Though not required to reside in the City, an alderman had to be an Englishman, the son of an Englishman, a freeman of the City, and, prior to the 17th century, a liveryman of one of the twelve "great" companies. A property requirement of £10,000 screened out all but the wealthy. A fine of £600 to £1,000 might be levied against the nominee who shirked this public duty, just as fines were levied against those who refused election to parish office. So great were the entertainment and other expenses of some offices, that a number of City worthies ducked the honor and paid the fine more than once. Aldermen sat on a number of courts, issued ale-house licenses for the City, approved all ordinances of City guilds and controlled the patronage of over 140 City offices. They could borrow from City funds at favorable rates and secure leases on City property. They could collectively petition the throne, and through the Sheriffs, the House of Commons. Royal favor might come easily to men of such station, but they were as well exposed to royal wrath.

The principal City offices were Lord Mayor, Sheriff (two), City Chamberlain, Recorder, and Remembrancer. The office of Remembrancer was abolished in 1642, but since has been restored.

The Lord Mayor was at the head of the Court of Aldermen and the chief magistrate of the City. The office was powerful and expensive, but also lucrative. Four-fifths of the price of offices in his gift plus over £500 from rent farms and market leases went to offset his expenses.

The City also was a county in terms of national polity and so required the ancient office of shire reeve (sheriff). There were two, and the office was expensive. The cost of entertaining the Court of Aldermen alone could run to £3,000 a term! Sheriffs were sole judges in their own courts and judges under the Lord Mayor in the Court of Hustings. They represented the crown in judicial proceedings and presented the petitions of the Aldermen and Common Council to the Commons.

The City Chamberlain was elected for life. He was paid no fees but had the cash balances in Chamber accounts at his disposal. A major responsibility was to keep City orphan estate accounts.

The Recorder was also elected for life. He was the chief legal advisor to the City and represented the City in negotiations with the crown and Privy Council.

The Remembrancer was the full-time agent of the municipality before Privy Council and the royal court. He was considered an assistant to the Recorder and an attendant of the Lord Mayor. The office was abolished as an unnecessary expense in 1642 when the Parliamentary party gained ascendancy in the City. It was later restored.

Thus far we have dwelt principally on the linear development of City polity. But already there have been hints of extraordinary forces at work in the City during the tumultuous 1640's. We must turn now to those years, once more with special deference to the work of Valerie Pearl (1961).

Thomas Taylor, Perpetual Curate of St. Mary, Aldermanbury from 1626 until 1632, wrote in dismay that the loan which Charles extorted from the City in 1627 would spare the king from ever calling a Parliament. Dr. Taylor little understood royal finance. Charles was broke again and obligated to call a Parliament the next January, with consequences already noted for the country at large. Constant royal milking of the City for loans (which were always defaulted) and other irregular means of revenue enhancement during the years of personal rule led to growing disaffection. The Lord Mayor and Aldermen, visible and vulnerable as they were, generally knuckled under to royal demands. Some were devoted royalists, but the general temper of the higher orders of the City tended to be parliamentary and Puritan, what has been called "political Presbyterianism," a sort of moderate conservatism that was ready to accomodate differences, but not at any price. But there were more radical elements in the City, some among the highest orders, and increasing as one descended through the socioeconomic ranks. The easily manipulated City street mob, frequently called "the unruly apprentices," though many were probably apprentices of no recognized trade or craft, turned out to be a powerful weapon with which the City Puritans could support their Parliamentary allies. "Law and order" waned in the City as the Trained Bands, the City militia, grew increasingly disinclined to arrest dissidents.

Growing social and political tensions produced what Pearl (1961:107-159) described as a City constitutional crisis in the years 1640-1642. Matters came to a head in 1641 when Common Hall refused to nominate the notoriously royalist senior alderman, Sir William Acton, for Lord Mayor. Instead they sent up names of persons who had resisted the crown, some to the point of imprisonment. On a compromise, the second ranking alderman (no favorite of Parliamentary Puritans) was nominated and elected. But the Parliamentary delegation included three Puritans. Common Hall also bypassed the aldermen and adopted a grievance petition.

The Lord Mayor and Aldermen, against strong popular opposition, extended the King a great banquet on 25 November, 1641. This may have been an event of national significance. Coming as it did after the fall of Strafford and Laud it made some sort of national reconciliation possible at a moment when the balance between royalist and antiroyalist forces in Parliament was quite close. The Grand Remonstrance, rehearsing royal evils and Parliamentary reforms, and proposing further reforms, a sort of Puritan party platform, was narrowly adopted. (Oliver Cromwell confided he would have emigrated to Puritan New England had it failed.) Charles seems to have overestimated the importance of signs of popular support, and the City banquet was such an event. But a clearer sign of the political temper of the City was the Common

Council election of 21 December, 1641. Pearl (1961:132) described it as a "weather change." Old leaders were swept out and "parliamentary Puritans" (describing their political more than their religious sympathies) were swept in. And hard on the heels of this development, dramatic events in the City and in Whitehall and Westminster began to converge with dolorious consequences for the nation at large.

Calamy's Early Years at St. Mary, Aldermanbury (1639-1642)

From Rochford Edmund Calamy returned to London to become perpetual curate of St. Mary, Aldermanbury, succeeding Dr. John Stoughton. He assumed the living on 26 October, 1639.

The Aldermanbury parish was one of the most important in Puritan London. It was a prestigious area, both for trade and residence (Liu 1986: 29). It was already a focus of Puritanism in London. Since purchasing the advowson in 1620, as we have noted, the parishoners had selected a series of Puritan clergymen—Robert Harris, Thomas Taylor, and John Stoughton. A number of civic leaders resided in the parish, among them three Aldermen (Symon Edmonds, George Witham, and Walter Boothby); five Common Councilmen (the above three as well as Gabriel Newman and James James); and three parliamentary assessors (Edmonds, Witham, and Boothby). Boothby in particular was heavily involved in raising support for the parliamentary cause in the parish (Liu 1986: 75-76). Boothby was apparently the benefactor of a set of 17th century silver communion plate, which were in the church until they were stolen in the late 19th century (see Ch. 7), for the the name "W. Boothby, Merchant" was engraved on one of the flagons.

It did not take long for Calamy to rise to prominence among the London clergy. On 6 August, 1640, Calamy met with other Puritan leaders to formulate a response to the seventeen canons and "etcetera oath," which had been promulgated by supporters of Archbishop Laud. Among other things, the canons required railed altars at the east end of the church as well as bowing by worshippers toward the altar when entering and leaving the church. The "etcetera oath" required that clergy accept the polity of the church as established. Several months later Calamy was involved in promotion of a moderate plan to reform the church government, with a modified episcopacy.

In early 1641 Calamy hosted in his home a group of Puritan ministers who met to draft a reply to a publication written by Bishop Joseph Hall, titled "An Humble

Remonstrance." Bishop Hall argued in the pamphlet that episcopacy was the form of church government instituted by God. The Calamy group's response was published in March, 1641, under the pen name Smectymnuus (a compilation of the initials of the five authors: Stephen Marshall, Edmund Calamy, Thomas Young, Matthew Newcomen and William Spurstow). Their argument was for parity among the clergy and reform of the episcopacy. In particular, they were critical of the contention that episcopacy and monarchy were linked. They called for a reform of the liturgy, claiming that the current form was too "popish." Calamy considered this tract "the first deadly below to Episcopacy in England" (Greaves 1985: 14). One of the authors, Spurstow, was a tutor of John Milton, who wrote three pamphlets in support of Smectymuuus (Oliver 1969: 31). Milton edited the work.

In March, 1641, Calamy was named to a subcommittee of the House of Lords to study "innovations" in the Church. The paper prepared by the committee called for a modified episcopacy and changes in the Book of Common Prayer and condemned doctrinal innovations.

One of the Calamy's supporters in the House of Lords was Lord Kimbolton, 2nd Earl of Manchester, who was buried in the Aldermanbury church in 1671. In 1641 while John Pym was attacking Charles in the Commons, Baron Kimbolton, later Viscount Mandeville, was leading the charge in the House of Lords (Oliver 1969: 38). Mandeville went on to become one of the military heroes for the Parliamentarians in the Civil War, but later joined with Calamy in arguing against the execution of King Charles I in 1649. Like many others, he thought Cromwell (who had served under him in the Army) was an extremist. Like Calamy he would also call for the Restoration of King Charles II and was in the party which welcomed him back to London. Calamy was also a friend of the prominent Puritan landholder, Sir Simonds D'Ewes, who had heard him preach at Bury St. Edmunds (Cliffe 1984: 226).

Calamy's centrality among London clergy is further shown by a meeting held at his house in November, 1641. "His residence by now had become the [ecclesiastical] counterpart of [John] Pym's home, where leading proponents of political reform met." In fact, Calamy's home became known as "the general Receptacle for all Presbyterian Ministers ...." (Greaves 1985: 15). At these meetings Calamy generally presided (Liu 1986: 74). The November, 1641 gathering brought together a group of Presbyterian and Independent clergy. Its purpose was to devise a common strategy. According to Thomas Edwards, a conservative Puritan present: "The ministers on both sides [were] desirous of reformation in church government and worship, being sensible how much our differences and divisions might distract the Parliament and hinder the taking away of episcopal government and the reformation intended ... " (cited in Tolme 1977: 88). As a result of the meeting an agreement was signed stipulating "that (for the advancing of the publike Cause of a happy Reformation) neither side should Preach, Print, or dispute, or otherwise act against the other's way; ...." (Greaves 1985: 15). They also agreed to placate moderate Anglicans by continuing to use the "least offensive" portions of the Book of Common Prayer.

Excursus: Calamy's Patron—Robert Rich, Earl of Warwick

Shortly after Calamy began preaching at St. Mary's the above mentioned Robert Rich, second Earl of Warwick (1587-1658), applied for a pew in the Church, although there is no record that he took up residence in the parish. Rich was a Puritan and was a passionate supporter of the Parliamentary cause. In 1640 he was arrested after the dissolution of the Short Parliament. In June, 1640, he was one of seven peers to sign a letter to Scottish leaders. In February, 1641, he was named a member of the Privy Council. When Charles I fled Whitehall, Rich joined the parliamentary side. He served for a time as captain-general of a planned second parliamentary army. However, his service as commander of the navy was his greatest military contribution. Under his command, the navy succeeded in blocking Prince Charles' efforts to aid his father's forces. He was named admiral in 1642 over the King's objection and brought the navy under parliamentary control.

In 1647, with other Presbyterian leaders, Rich was active in the effort to work out a settlement with the King. When Cromwell and the Independents gained power in 1649, they removed Rich from command of the navy. At first, Rich steered clear of Cromwell, but in 1657 he was present at the investiture of Cromwell as Lord Protector. Cromwell's daughter married his grandson and heir.

Rich protected and promoted Puritan clergymen; he was undoubtedly Calamy's principal patron. One of Archbishop Laud's supporters called him "the temporal head of the puritans." His home became a rendezvous for silenced ministers. He often went to hear his favorite Puritan divines, including Calamy, preach. He spent a good part of his estate in supporting these clergy. Calamy called Rich "a great patron and Maecenas to the pious and religious ministry" and a man of high personal piety. His opponents called his puritanism mere hypocrisy.

Rich also played an important role in the development of the American colonies, as a member of the Council of Virginia and the Council of the New England Company, to which he was appointed in 1620. He was elected president of the New England Company in 1630. He was a founder of the colonies of Plymouth (Mass.), Connecticut, Virginia and Rhode Island. In 1619 his ship, Treasurer, brought over some of the first Africans to Virginia. In 1643 Warwick was appointed Lord High Admiral and Governor-in-Chief of all the English royal colonies. In 1643 he granted Roger Williams a patent. He was a staunch supporter of religious freedom in the colonies, and a strong advocate of conversion of the Indians to Christianity.

Rich died on 19 April, 1658, and on 1 May, 1658, Calamy preached a sermon entitled "A Patterne for All, especially for Noble and Honourable Persons" at his funeral. In his remarks Calamy showed a rare touch of humor. He quoted someone, who after seeing the Earl's gardens, said, "You had need be very good, it is ill going to hell from such a Paradise" (quoted in Calamy Service, 4). He also used a theme recurrent in his sermons, saying, "Great men are like looking glasses according to which all the country dresse themselves, and if they be good they do a world of good" (34, quoted by Greaves 1985: 38-39). This was a common theme among Puritan preachers, who inveighed most heavily against the sins of the nobility and gentry, arguing that their bad example had corrupted the mass of people (Manning 1973: 104).

Calamy's Early Years (continued)

Calamy's skill as an orator caused people from throughout the city to come to hear his lectures. His grandson reported (Matthews 1934: l):

> No Minister in the City was more follow'd; nor hath there ever been
> a Week-day lecture so frequented as his; which was attended not only
> by his own Parish, but by other Eminent Citizens, and many Persons of
> Greatest Quality, and constantly for 20 years together; for there seldom
> were so few as 60 coaches.

Fortunately, a number of the sermons Calamy preached have survived. Most of those surviving were preached before the House of Commons, the House of Lords, St. Paul's, and the Lord Mayor, but several of his Aldermanbury sermons are extant. So we can learn of St. Mary's most famous curate from his own words.

One visitor, who heard Calamy preach on 17 November, 1640, wrote in his diary,

"I was at Aldermanbury church about 14 hours together, where three ministers prayed and preached one after another—Mr. Calamy and two strangers." This was probably an example of a practice known as "prophesying." A group of Puritan clergy would gather and deliver a series of "exercise" sermons before their clergy colleagues and others. These "colloquies" were based on a practice present in John Calvin's Geneva. They provided a model for the development of the "classis" or "presbytery." (Collinson 1967: 168-169, 177).

At a meeting of the Vestry on 17 December, 1640, the discussion turned to Mr. Calamy's salary. At Calamy's urging (Malcolm 1803: 120) the Vestry decided to petition parliament to provide "sufficient mayntainance" for the Minister. "The parish being parson," it was appropriate for the Vestry to initiate this action. It was apparently unsuccessful.

It is easy to understand why Calamy might have felt Parliament would have approved a stipend for him. He was a frequent speaker before both houses of Parliament. Twice in 1641 he was invited to speak before the House of Commons during the brewing controversy between King Charles I and Parliament. He clearly sided with the Parliament, although he had harsh words for them. His were among the 240 sermons preached before the Long Parliament during the 1640's (Wilson 1969: 7).

The House of Commons first invited Calamy to preach before them at a 6:00 a.m. service in St. Margaret's Church, on Sunday, 8 August, 1641, but due to the press of business there was no time for the sermon. This was an occasional rather than a fast day sermon, so it shows the special esteem in which the members held Calamy. Calamy was dismissed with an apology for holding the session on the Lord's Day. (Wilson 1969: 14).

On 22 December, 1641, in connection with a fast day called because of the Irish crisis, Calamy delivered a sermon entitled "England's Looking-Glasse." This set the stage for the tradition of monthly "fast sermons". 129 such sermons were published (Wilson 1969: 9). Calamy's sermon was so widely read that after being printed in 1642 by order of the House it ran through five editions. It set the tone for the Parliamentary program, until Cromwell seized power, asserting that "the parliament stood for the nation before God" and that it was incumbent upon Parliament to reform itself as well as the nation (Wilson 1969: 55-56). Edward I had decisively rejected the idea of fast sermons. Charles' acceptance of them gave credibility to the view that

Parliament represented the nation. Probably without grasping the full consequences of his action, Charles granted a charter for the monthly fasts on 8 January, 1642. On fast days parliamentary business was usually suspended and members were expected to attend morning and afternoon services at St. Margaret's Church, next to Westminster Abbey.

We will examine Calamy's "Looking-Glassse" sermon rather closely because of its importance in the early stages of the English revolution and in order to experience Calamy's sermonic style. In the preface to the published edition Calamy described his subject as "the ruine and repaire of Kingdoms and Nations; a matter suitable for you that are the representative Body of the Kingdom." (A2). As was his practice, Calamy began his sermon with doctrinal assertions based on a Biblical text. His text was Jeremiah 18:7-10, which he called "a looking glasse for England and Ireland, or for any other Kingdome."

The doctrinal assertions were 1) that God has absolute power over all Kingdoms and nations to pluck them up, pull them down and destroy them; 2) that though God has this power, he seldom uses it without first giving warning; 3) that if a kingdom repents upon being given warning, God will build it up; 4) that when God begins to build up a nation, if that nation does evil, God will repent of the good he intended to do (2-3).

Calamy's rhetorical flourish is evident in his comments on each of his assertions. On the first, "Oh England, heare the God of heaven and earth! O you House of Commons, tremble and sin not: ... we are all in God's hand as a flye in the paw of a roaring Lion, as the clay in the hand of the Potter" (4).

On the second, "As Ambrose observed, God puts his bow in the heavens, not his arrow but his bow to forewarn us of the arrow" (6). Calamy frequently quoted the early Christian fathers and often classical sources as well.

On the third, "God doth sometimes will a change, but he never changeth his will" (11). He called upon the House to show humility so that reformation will follow. To this end he described "seven buckets for the tears of humiliation." He warned against reformation which is only superficial, reflecting his stubborn holding to principal regardless of which way the wind blew. "We live in a time of much turning. Some like the Dog to his vomit—atheists, papists, Socinians, Arminians. Some turn like a Weathercock—any direction the wind blows. Some like Chamelions, any colour except white. Let us turn sincerely to the Lord. Fasting not merely from meat and mirth but from Sin." "Repent of your security, that you may live securely." (20)

Playing on his title, he proclaimed, "Great men are the looking-glasse of the Country where they live, according to which most men dresse themselves ..." (22). It is time, he said, to "reform the reformation." Just as Christ rose and left his linen cloths we must leave behind 'superstitious ceremonies'," Calamy said, and have a "perfect Reformation according to the Word of God. He called for a National Synod of Ministers to instruct Parliament on how to leave the grave clothes behind. (24)

On the fourth assertion, Calamy avoided any predictions of destruction. Instead he toned down his rhetoric and complimented the House, saying, "Wee have been in the Dungeon of despaire, and wee blesse God for the little crevise of light let in by your measures." He asked them to send "a faithful and painefull Ministry thorow out the Kingdome." (27)

In his conclusion Calamy appealed to a spirit of national unity. "We are all of one nation, of one body, one flesh, one Church." (31)

In a postscript in the printed edition Calamy answered the charge that he had failed to talk about predestination. How could anyone repent unless it were predestined to do so? To this objection Calamy replied that we must first go to the Grammar school of Repentance before we can be admitted to the University of Predestination. A century later Puritan preachers in the American colonies were using Calamy's theme of calling the nation to task because of its sins to support the argument for independence from England (Wilson 1969: 63).

For his sermon Calamy received a large almsdish worth £20. It was inscribed with his arms and the words: "This is the Gift of the House of Commons to Edmund Calamy, B.D., 1641."

On the 27-29th of December riots took place in London. Westminster Abbey was entered by a mob intent on destroying the altar and organ. The riots occurred after a petition bearing 30,000 names protesting the presence of bishops and Catholics in the House of Lords was announced. Calamy was one of those named by conservative critics as responsible for the petition (Greaves 1985: 17).

Calamy and Stephen Marshall, who had also preached before Commons in December, were invited to inaugurate the series of monthly fast sermons at St. Margaret's Church on 23 February, 1642. The service lasted from 9:00 a.m. until 4:00 p.m. with Calamy speaking in the morning. The title of his sermon was "God's Free Mercy to England, Presented as a Pretious and Powerfull motive to Humiliation."

Calamy pulled no punches with the Commons. "My purpose," he began, "is to lay the sinnes of England against God in one scale, and the mercies of God to England in the other scale, and to call upon you this day to be humbled, and ashamed, and broken in heart before the Lord." (2)

Calamy again used vivid language. "You can cure a stony heart like a stony bladder, by cutting it out or dissolving it with soft medicine." (2). His intention, he said, was to use the "heart melting mercies of the Gospell" rather than the "heart cutting threatenings of the Law" to convince them. He then rehearsed the history of Christianity in England, claiming that the Faith was brought to England by Joseph of Arimathea. He heralded Henry VIII for throwing off the subjection of the "Antichrist" and James I as the first monarch to call the pope the Antichrist. In the last two years, he said, God's mercies have richly been bestowed on England. He listed the happy pacification between England and Scotland, the turning away from "popery," the hope of reformation of church and state, and "the discovery of the secret underminers who have for these many years laboured to blow up our Religion" and under the name of Puritan scare people from being Protestant. He cited as the circumstances of these mercies that it was all done legally, peaceably, with prayer, and despite the great sins of England, such as calling bishops and tithes the law of God and the Lord's day the law of man and exalting the holiness of places and depressing the holiness of persons. He said that Parliament had been the bearer of these mercies and deserved the praise and thanks of all. (5-7)

But then Calamy uttered a stern warning: "Be it known unto you, O house of England, It is not for your sakes, for you are a stiff necked people, but for my holy Name's sake." (17)

Later he called them to commitment and service, saying, "What a shame it is for a poore Cobbler to do more service for God then it may be some of you doe, that have received so much from God .... O let not your honours and riches, & ye silken halters to strangle your souls" (41).

Finally, he listed the steps England and the Parliament should take. His refrain was that the House should "do something," for the honor of the Lord's day, for purging the land of the blood of the martyrs shed in Mary's day, for the reformation of the house of God according to the Word of God, for the setting up of a preaching ministry throughout the kingdom with "competent maintenance" for this ministry, for purging the defilements in worship, and finally for bleeding Ireland.

In this sermon Calamy was clearly countering the Arminian view, which was gaining strength in the puritan movement, by stressing that "national mercies come from free grace, not from free will; not from man's goodness but God's goodness" (Wilson 1969: 17).

Calamy's sermons typically ran to 50 pages in print and took several hours to read aloud. The "Mercies" sermon was 51 pages and, according to Calamy, took over two hours to deliver (51).

Although Calamy's sermons were not directly political, they had immense political impact. His was a "revolutionary rhetoric" which implicitly called for nothing short of a complete reconstitution of Stuart society (Wilson 1969: 146). His "plain style" was in marked contrast to the "witty style" of the court sermons and assumed the "intellectual priesthood of all believers" (Wilson 1969: 140). In his view, there was no distinction between natural and revealed truth, for the truths of Scripture conform to the experience of rational people. He assumed that any clear thinking hearer would see, as he did, that England was at a crossroads. Either England would respond to God's mercies and through ongoing reformation cooperate in the creation of God's kingdom on earth, or England would reject God's grace and follow a road to destruction. (See Wilson 1969: 137-196). He might have a similar message if he was able to preach in his beloved Aldermanbury church in its new home!

King Charles I and other royalists considered Calamy and other prominent Puritan clergy largely responsible for the conflict which swirled around him. Calamy and several other clergy (including Marshall, Hugh Peter, Henry Burton, and Thomas Case) responded to the charge of treason in a pamphlet entitled "An Answer to the Articles." They blamed the bishops for the turmoil, for they had replaced the gospel with popery, ceremonial superstition, and canonical innovations. Moreover, they were guilty of deluding the king.

Despite Calamy's growing fame the parishoners at St. Mary's were not impressed enough to raise his salary. At a meeting on 19 April, 1642, the Vestry discussed Calamy's stipend and decided "that it shall continue as it hath done without alteration for the present ..." There is also a hint of unrest within the Church over Calamy's leadership, as the minutes record that "the generallity hath promised to secure and save harmless those ten men that stand bound unto Mr. Calamy for the payment of his £160 per annum." The background for a dispute over Calamy's salary may have been Parliament's decision to provide direct support for the Sunday lecturer at St.

Paul's, Cornelius Burgess, in the amount of an annual stipend of £400. This may have ruffled Calamy's feathers. However, while Calamy was receiving £160, some other prominent Presbyterian clerics were receiving as little as £60 a year (Liu 1986: 152).

At this same Vestry meeting the parish became the first to reorganize parish government, "the most thorough reorganization among all the London parishes during the revolutionary period" (Liu 1986: 173). The select Vestry was abolished in a movement to democratize decision making. The requirement that no one could be elected to an office unless he could both read and write was also annulled. The lay leaders of the parish were not members of the nobility, but were merchants. According to Manning, such members of the "middle ranks" of society were the supporters of democracy in parish government, as a way of taking control from the bishop and gentry. Indeed, the democratic tradition which eventually found its way across the Atlantic was nurtured in the campaign to change church government during this period (Manning 1973: 110-111). Therefore, St. Mary, Aldermanbury, contributed in an important way to the democratic heritage cherished in the land where the church now resides! Although Presbyterian leaders like Calamy denied that democratic reorganization in the church lent support to political democracy, others (like the Levellers) drew the parallels.

During Calamy's tenure, St. Mary, Aldermanbury was the site of many spiritual awakenings, inspired by the preaching of Calamy and other invited preachers. For example, in 1642, John Owen came to St. Mary's to hear Calamy, only to find that a "country preacher" had taken Calamay's place. As a result of the preacher's sermon on Matthew 8:26 ("Why are ye fearful, O ye of little faith?"), Owen experienced a transformation which redirected his life. "Owen's doubts, fears and worries as to whether he was truly regenerate and born anew of the Holy Spirit were removed as he felt himself liberated and knew he was an adopted son of God. This spiritual experience ... gave Owen the inward conviction that he was a true child of God, chosen in Christ before the foundation of the world, that God loved him and had a loving purpose for him, and that his God was the living God." (Exeter 1971: 13). Owen later became a prominent minister and inspirational preacher.

Charles I: The Civil War and the Westminster Assembly (1642-1649)

On 3 January, 1642, Charles botched an illegal impeachment of Pym and other important Parliamentary leaders. The next day Charles invaded the Commons with a gang of Cavalier bullies in an effort to arrest the offending Parliamentarians illegally. Word had leaked out, and Pym and company had taken to the Thames and boated downstream to take refuge in the City. Charles was left to mutter lamely, "the birds have flown." Meanwhile, the City welcomed the fugitives as heroes. London offered Parliament its protection, a significant offer since the Trained Bands constituted the best fighting force in the country. Meanwhile, volunteers from adjoining counties numbering in the hundreds came to join in the protection of Parliament.

On 4 January Common Council met ahead of the customary Plough Monday to form a Committee on Safety with a pro-parliamentary majority. The King was in the City and present at a Common Council meeting on 5 January. But on 10 January Charles fled his Whitehall palace and the stage was set for civil war. The next day the fugitive parliamentary leaders returned to Westminster in triumph, and Edmund Calamy was invited to preach the service of thanksgiving for their safe deliverance.

The House of Commons ordered that the Lord Mayor should call Common Council whenever the Committee on Safety ordained. The Committee was also given the power to rule on disputed seats in the 21 December election and authority as Commissioners on Militia. So as the nation lurched toward civil war, the very foundations of City polity were shaken as well. The parliamentary puritans succeeded in having impeached Lord Mayor Gurney for "obstructing the will of Parliament." However, within a year the more moderate forces were reasserting themselves. Indeed the "political Presbyterianism" of the City brought the Army of Parliament against the City in 1648, as we shall see.

The King's flight from Whitehall set the terrible Civil War in process. In a general way, the great nobles tended to side with the King, the gentry and the urban middle class with Parliament. But this was not true in an exclusive sense. Some great burghers of the City, for instance, were devoted royalists, while lords of high rank embraced the parliamentary cause. Again in a general way, the more conservative north and west stood with the King, while London and the south stood with Parliament. In the language of the time, one army stood for the King, the other for King and Parliament.

The Trained Bands were, as noted, the ablest military force in England. But the military balance nonetheless favored the royalist side at first, in part because of its skilled leadership, including Charles' German kinsman, Prince Rupert. The Cavalier army made a southward dash toward an undefended London, taking Oxford as

Charles headquarters. However, the royalists were blocked at the Battle of Newberry in which a company of London apprentices played a gallant role.

With the War going against them, the Parliamentary leadership made an expedient decision for the short term, which had ill-fated long term consequences. The decision was to enter into alliance with Scotland, sealing the agreement with the Solemn League and Covenant (1643). The Scottish price was that the Church of England become Presbyterian. The Westminster Assembly (to be discussed below) was called to carry out the transformation. Despite their affluence and influence in the Parliamentary cause, Presbyterians were a minority in the Puritan camp and in the country at large. In the heady days of Puritan ascendancy the substitution of presbyter for priest did not strike the majority as a sufficient response to the Laudian excesses.

The name of Oliver Cromwell is synonymous with the Puritan cause for many persons, especially Americans, who find it difficult to realize that he was never commander in chief of the Parliamentary army. In fact, he was a relatively obscure figure at the outset, sitting in Parliament for his home county of Huntingdonshire. But Cromwell had two traits which brought him to the fore. He had an intuitive grasp of the art of warfare, and he was convinced that the solutions he discerned to problems were coterminous with the will of God.

Oliver commanded a small cavalry squadron in the indecisive battle of Edgehill. But he saw enough to convince him that the Parliamentary army would have to develop a cavalry force such as Prince Rupert led in the King's army in order to prevail. Oliver envisioned a Parliamentary calvary, not only with the mobility to break the flanks of an opposing force, but the discipline and determination to wreak destruction anywhere on a battlefield. Fortified with the religious teaching of Puritanism and the tactical doctrines of the Swedish King Gustavus Adolphus, Cromwell retired to his home country to raise and train such a heavy calvary. The result was the legendary "Ironsides," which proved their worth at Marston Moor, west of York (1644). With Scottish help, the Ironsides broke the Royalist infantry when the battle was going against the Parliamentary side.

Cromwell's spectacular success led to his appointment as deputy commander of a reorganized parliamentary army, the New Model Army (the first "redcoats"). The New Model Army essentially ended the war at Naseby in June, 1645. Cromwell's cavalry tactics were again decisive. Charles fled north and took refuge with the Scots. Parliament had won the war, but it soon lost the peace and all England suffered.

In the negotiations to end the war, four parties emerged—the King, Parliament, the Scots, and the army. Charles took a devious course, making it impossible to deal with him. The latter three were united only by their opposition to the absolutist policies of Charles. The Parliament was controlled by Presbyterians, not even a plurality in the Puritan movement. The Independents and other more radical Puritans were dominant in the army. The Scots, fed up with the antipresbyterianism of Charles, in effect, sold the king to Parliament. Thus armed, Parliament set upon a course of heavy taxation and religious persecution, and above all upon a surly policy toward the victorious army.

The army's patience broke during the Summer of 1647. They took charge of negotiations by seizing the king. By this time Cromwell was in charge of the army, so the army's action placed him effectively at the helm of the opposition. He had as little patience with extreme radicals (such as the Levellers and "Fifth Monarchy Men") as he did with a staunch Cavalier. His blunt and inarticulate manner left the image of an authoritarian radical. In fact, he was a moderate man. His proposal to Charles was amazingly generous and tolerant, but the obstinant monarch refused it, holding out hope for a Scottish invasion.

As a result a "Second Civil War" broke out in 1648. It was shortlived. Cromwell's army decisively defeated a Scots-Royalist alliance at Preston. When Parliament and the King seemed on the verge on striking a deal, creating a sort of Presbyterian monarchy, the army moved. London, the Presbyterian power base, was occupied and the king secured. On 6 December, 1648, Colonel Pride forced out of Parliament those with royalist or Presbyterian sympathies. "Pride's Purge" (with Cromwell behind it) left just under 20% of the original Long Parliament, hence the nickname "The Rump." Cromwell gave Charles one last chance to accept terms. The king's refusal seemed to Oliver a sign from heaven that the more radical elements were correct—the monarch must be brought before a court of law.

The king's trial on charges of treason has been denounced as a legal travesty, though its proceedings were no more irregular from the standpoint of common law than those of the King's prerogative courts. The trial was held in open court. Cromwell and the Rump leaders were convinced of the justice of their action, just as Charles was certain that in his stubborness he was defending royal rights and the nation founded on them. The outcome of the trial was, of course, predetermined, and on 30 January, 1649, on a scaffold outside Inigo Jones' Whitehall Banqueting House,

King Charles I was beheaded. As we shall see, this act of regicide alienated the Puritan moderates (including Calamy), planting the seeds which would lead eventually to the restoration of the monarchy.

Calamy and Aldermanbury during the Civil War

Throughout the war Edmund Calamy made no secret of his support for the parliamentary cause. In his sermons he described it as "the Lord's battle in which those who died were martyrs" (Greaves 1985: 19).

His support caused him in one instance to be deceived. A man named Melmore came to Calamy demanding a collection of £9.9s for "distressed captains." Before Calamy learned the man was an impostor he had collected the money. The Vestry decided to dispose of the sum for the poor rather than return it to the donors (Malcolm 1803: 120).

The parish's enthusiasm for the parliamentary cause was evidenced in November, 1642, when 64 of the inhabitants gave £924 to Parliament, one of the largest contributions among the parishes of London (Liu 1986: 29).

That same month, Matthew Newcomen, Calamy's brother-in-law and soon-to-be lecturer at St. Mary, Aldermanbury, was invited to speak at a special parliamentary service. In his sermon, entitled "The Craft and Cruelty of the Churches Adversaries," Newcomen argued that the King was being deceived by evil adversaries. He called Charles to return to London where his true Protestant subjects resided (Wilson 1969: 66-67). Newcomen (1610?- 1669) had married the sister of Calamy's wife in 1640 and a year later was one of the "Smectymnuus" authors. He had been educated at St. John's, Cambridge, and was one of the leaders in the church reform party in Essex. Seven of his sermons were published. He held the Aldermanbury lectureship from 1643 until he returned to his lectureship in Dedham in 1648.

Calamy had strong supporters within the Church. In 1642 a Mr. Colborne was voted a "piece of plate" for "his love" in granting an eight year lease to Mr. Calamy for a house (Malcolm 1803: 120). Apparently parishoners were given a choice whether to support Calamy's ministry or not. In what sounds like a compromise, three boxes were placed at the church doors in 1642, a poor box, a box for the churchwardens, and a box for Mr. Calamy, for distribution.

Early in 1643 Calamy was named as a receiver of donations to support the transportation of urchins from Ireland and England to New England. The same year he was made a member of the Board of Governors at Sion College. He asked the Board to allow him to have a door opened between his parsonage and the College grounds, so that he could come and go as he pleased. The request was granted, but withdrawn in 1661 (Pearce 1913: 92).

On 12 June, 1643, when the Westminster Assembly of Divines was called to meet in the Abbey by the Long Parliament, Calamy was appointed one of four London members. He and Marshall were the two members through whom Parliament channeled funds for the Assembly's work. Two days later Calamy was also named one of twelve clergy responsible for licensing books. This group was instrumental in restricting the publication of works by religious extremists. Calamy was known not only as an opponent of the bishops, but as "a great Enemy to the Sectaries...." (Greaves 1985: 20).

Calamy was invited to preach on 15 June before the House of Lords at a "Solemn Day of Thanksgiving, for the discovery of a dangerous, desperate and bloody plot designed to the utter subversion of the Parliament and of the famous City of London, of the Army, of the whole Kingdome, and which as above all to the utter ruine of the true reformed Protestant religion." (1). The conspiracy, known as Waller's Plot, involved members of the House of Lords.

The theme ("The Noble-Man's Patterne of True and Reall Thankfulnesse") echoed his "Looking-glasse" sermon. In developing the theme he quoted Sir Thomas More, saying "I will not pin my salvation upon any man's sleeve because I know not whither he will carry it."

The political purpose of the sermon was obviously to recruit for the Parliamentary cause. If the great and rich men would support the war undertaken by Parliament "how quickly would the whole Land arise as one man to take part with them" (17).

Calamy could be blunt. He reminded the Lords that Alexander the Great had two friends, one who labored to satisfy his lusts and another who tended to his honor and the peoples' safety. "Our Soveraigne King hath two such kind of friends," Calamy said pointedly. (19) He then directly attacked the army of Charles I, based at Oxford, calling them an "Army of Papists." (24)

Calamy's conclusion was, "This is is the greatest Nobility to be a true servant of the great God. A King may give Titles to a great man, but he cannot make a great man." (42). This was a key sermon, because it was a calculated effort to support Pym's plan to bring the Lords under the Puritan discipline (Wilson 1969: 70).

The work of the Westminster Assembly took on added importance in September, 1643, when the Parliament entered into the Solemn League and Covenant with Scotland. As we have seen, according to the terms of that agreement, the English Church was to be reformed on the Presbyterian model of the Scottish Kirk in exchange for Scottish support of the Parliamentary cause in the war against the Royalists. Those members of Commons who refused to swear allegiance to the Covenant were expelled. Some considered it an indication that God's kingdom had come to earth.

On 14 September, 1643, Calamy had been appointed to chair the Assembly's committee on Antinominianism, because of his strong opposition to the libertarian wing of the puritan movement.

On 6 October Calamy was asked to speak at the Guildhall in support of raising a loan in the City to subsidize the Scottish army. Although he called the funds "happy money that will purchase my Gospel, ... and Purchase a Reformation to my Posterity," he considered it a shame that England had to rely on another country to safeguard the Protestant faith (Greaves 1985: 20). He lashed out at those who remained neutral in the conflict.

Calamy apparently took very seriously the charge to ministers to examine parishoners as to their suitability to receive the Sacrament of the Lord's Supper. On 23 January, 1644, the Vestry responded to his request for "three pious persons" to assist him in examining and preparing parishoners for Communion. This was a prelude to the action taken a year later to elect lay elders to administer the discipline of the church with the minister. Those refused admission to the Sacrament by Calamy and the examiners objected to the Vestry, but the Vestry confirmed the decisions and noted that 200 persons had been admitted from December through February. Some parishoners apparently refused to pay in support of Calamy for a deputation of several aldermen and others was appointed to enforce payments (Malcolm 1803: 120). The dispute suggests the presence of Independents in the parish. In other parishes Independent civic leaders opposed the practice (Liu 1973: 163). The fact that the Vestry supported Calamy shows the Presbyterian domination of the parish.

Matthew Newcomen again preached before Parliament on 12 September, 1644, at a special joint session. His sermon was called "The Root of Apostasy." His theme was that twelve months after the members had sworn allegiance to the Solemn League, violation of it was rampant. He warned his audience that they might provoke the Lord to strike parliament because of their sins. (Wilson 1969: 185).

On 5 October, 1644, Calamy was named along with other clergy to examine and ordain ministers. On 22 October, 1644, Calamy preached once more before the House of Commons at St. Margaret's, again at a fast day, delivering a sermon entitled "England's Antidote Against the Plague of Civil Warre" on the text, "but now commandeth all men everywhere to repent ..." (Acts 17:30b). He echoed the basic theme of his earlier sermons before Parliament calling on the members to repent, warning that God expects great men to repent. "God's Argument is this," Calamy said, "Repent, o ye Lords and Commons, or else I'le give you over to Begging: Repent or else I'le give you over to Popery; I'le give you over to slaverie; Repent, or else I'le plunder your houses; I'le give up your wives and daughters to be deflowered; Repent, or else I'le burn your Cities; Repent, or else I'le remove the Gospel from you" (9). "Great men doe more hurt by their sins than others, and therefore God will punish them more than others; and therefore they are to repent more than others," Calamy said (21). He called for repentance not only from the Commons, but also from the army and among the people. He called for it from the Assembly of Ministers at Westminster and from the "pretended Parliament" at Oxford (31). In the sermon he also called on Parliament to suppress the Anabaptists and Antinomians. The sermon was preached on the eve of the Battle of Newbury, at a time when the anti-royalist forces were embroiled in controversy and "may have helped to avert even more serious rifts" (Greaves 1985: 21). This sermon may have been the beginning of the final episode in the prosecution of Bishop Laud). Three days later the Lords adopted the practice of a formal fast day (Wilson 1969: 80). The plan to bring the Lords into the parliamentary camp was complete.

On Christmas Day, 1644, Calamy preached before the House of Lords at Westminster Abbey. The sermon was entitled "An Indictment Against England Because of Her Selfe-Murdering Divisions, together with an Exhortation to an England preferring Unity and Concord" and published in 1645 at the behest of the House. In his introduction Calamy said he was glad Parliament was not celebrating December 25 as "Christmas" but as a monthly fast day. Like other Puritans Calamy found no Biblical basis for the holiday of Christmas. He claimed that his intention was to be a peacemaker, although he realized (prophetically in his case) that "he that will step in to reconcile two parties that are a fighting, doth prove the party against which both of them will fight." In the sermon itself he supported the negotiations underway with King Charles I at Uxbridge. He reproved those who were telling the King that Parliament was seeking his life (18) and called on Parliament to "be at Peace with the King's Majesty as much as is possible" (21). Civil War is a plague, Calamy told his audience, which must be brought to an end as soon as possible (8-9). He also contended that the ultimate destruction of England could be avoided only if there were loyalty to the Solemn League and Covenant. He said that although the Church had been reformed "our hearts are no whit Reformed . ... Our high altars are taken down, but our high minds are not taken down" (11). He chided Parliament for being as repressive as the High Commission and Star Chamber of the Royalist Parliament had been (12). He deplored the divisions in the Puritan movement, with particularly harsh words for anabaptists, Brownists, and those who wanted toleration for all religions (13). Calamy was undoubtedly frustrated at the lack of progress in the Westminster Assembly because of these divisions. His goal of a truly reformed Church of England was slipping away.

The sermon was delivered amidst deliberations over the fate of Bishop Laud. A bill of attainder was pending against Laud. On 4 January the Lords approved the bill, and on 10 January he was executed.

In January, 1645, the Aldermanbury parish adopted a Presbyterian form of government by electing lay ruling elders. It was one of the first of the 64 city parishes to do so and occurred nearly a year and a half before Presbyterian government was established in the City (Liu 1986: 54 and 76). Since Calamy was a strong advocate of a system of church government with lay elders in the Westminster Assembly, it is not surprising that his own parish adopted the practice as an example to other parishes. Of course, as we have noted, Calamy had in his parish a group of Presbyterian-minded lay leaders from whom elders could be drawn.

A well-documented incident in 1645 shows that Independents among the Puritans were speaking out against Calamy (as he was against them), even in his own church. On/Tuesday, 23 September, 1645 an Independent clergyman, Henry Burton, was giving a lecture in the Church, as he did every other week, supported by a trust. He was speaking about the Second Commandment's rejection of idolatry, applying the prohibition to various situations in the history of England. Mr. Calamy was not present, but the Parish Clerk reported to him that Burton had attacked Parliament and the Assembly of Ministers in his lecture. In fact, Burton had urged his hearers to base their faith on their own introspection rather than simply relying on any body,

Parliament or the Assembly included, to tell them what to believe.

As a result, in his own lecture the next day, Calamy added to a list of seven particular sins another concerning those who would disparage Parliament. On October 6th, the Monday before Burton was to speak again, the Sexton of St. Mary's informed Burton that the Churchwardens had locked the doors of the Church and barred him from preaching. Calamy apparently did not know about this and sent word to Burton that he did not object to Burton's speaking so long as he refrained from attacking Parliament.

This apparently infuriated Burton, who responded to Calamy by saying that he would not be restrained from preaching the truth of God as it came to him. On October 13th Burton and two members of the Committee which underwrote his lecture went to see Calamy. Calamy claimed that he had no power over the keys for he was "but the curate of the parish." Burton demanded to know why Calamy had not come to him before reprimanding him from the pulpit, to which Calamy replied that there was not time and he had seen notes of those in attendance. Burton objected that his words had been distorted and he had not derogated Parliament or the Assembly. Calamy responded saying that Burton had been barred for other reasons and Burton charged him of being just like Bishop Laud who had apparently suspended Burton for attacking the practice of bowing when the name of Jesus was spoken. Burton said that at least Calamy could have called the remark an indiscretion rather than a sin, and at that the meeting ended. Later Burton asked Calamy to allow him to resume the lecture, but Calamy said his conscience could not allow him to do this.

The custom during this turbulent time was to take such disputes into public through pamphlets. The above reconstruction is based on a pamphlet by Burton entitled "Truth Still Truth, Though Shut Out of Doores" (1645). After giving his version of events, Burton concluded, "Let us be ashamed and confounded that we have been ashamed of the truth, more precious than our lives, and have shut it out of our doores."

Calamy was not about to let Burton get the better of him. Shortly after Burton's pamphlet was published, another appeared, with the title, "The Door of Truth Opened, or ... how Mr. Henry Burton came to shut himself out of the Church-doors of Aldermanbury" (1645). The pamphlet was "in the name, and with the consent of the whole Church of Aldermanburie." Calamy is not named as author, but the words are almost certainly his.

In his typical methodical style, Calamy listed seven points in response to Burton's charge that in denying him the opportunity to speak at Aldermanbury truth itself had been barred.

1) "An opinion is not ... a truth, because Mr. Burton saith it." It is the practice in Reformed churches not just to be swayed by "bold and confident" assertions but to consider "the weight and strength of the arguments." Burton has simply assumed that "the shutting of Independency out of doors is the shutting of truth out of doors."

2) Burton had promised not to preach his Independent ideas, and as a Presbyterian Calamy had to insist on this in order to preserve the peace and piety of the church.

3) Various witnesses had heard Burton say that to wait on Parliament or the Assembly to establish a form of worship was idolatry.

4) Other Independents had called Aldermanbury a "pure church." Burton had distorted Calamy's words.

5) Burton had slandered the Churchwardens.

6) When Burton spoke it was "the Spirit of Error that haunted Aldermanbury," and thus Calamy had no choice but to counter this untruth.

7) Burton "stole" one of the Aldermanbury parishoners, a most unseemly act for a guest!

Calamy also responded to Burton's charge concerning his support of Bishop Laud during the 1630s in a a pamphlet entitled "A Just and Necessary Apology Against an Unjust Invective" (1646).

On 3 December, 1645 Calamy was prepared to debate at Aldermanbury with three Baptists on the subject of infant baptism. However, the Lord Mayor withdrew his sanction for the debate on the evening before in order to preserve peace (Greaves 1985: 22). As we have already seen, Calamy was also a leader in the fight against Antinomians, clerics who argued that Christ freed believers from allegiance to the commandments of the Biblical law (Greaves 1985: 23).

For his attacks on sectaries Calamy was satirized in October, 1645, as "a man but newly Metamorphosed ... from Episcopality to Presbytery ... ."

Also in 1645 Calamy was appointed to a Suffolk commission for the trial of some women accused of being witches.

On 14 January, 1646, Calamy preached a sermon entitled "The Great Danger of Covenant Refusing and Covenant Breaking" before the Lord Mayor, Sheriffs,

Aldermen and the rest of the Common Council. The sermon was on the occasion of the renewal of the Solemn League and Covenant. In the sermon he attacked the Independents' contention that a group of people could use the concept of covenant to create their own separate church. This was, he contended in his Introduction, a distortion of the Biblical understanding of covenant. He also claimed in his Introduction that since the sermon was delivered he had "undergone many harsh and bitter censures."

England's troubles, he wrote, are as a result of her breaking the covenant. "England hath broken Covenant with God, and now God is breaking England in pieces" (22). He likened the chaos in the country to what happened when Jesus whipped the money changers in the Temple. "As Christ whipt the buyers and sellers out of the Temple, with whips made of the cords which they brought to tye their oxen and sheep with all, a Covenant is a cord to ty us to God, and now God hath made an iron whip of these cords which we have broken asunder to whip us with all" (22-23). He chided the neutrality of politicians who fear "to come too near the heels of Religion, lest it should dash out their braines" (31). He concluded by roundly condemning the self-love which causes people to "pretend God and his glory, and the common good: but intend ourselves, and our own private good and interest; ... ." (40).

During this period Calamy was deeply involved with the work of the Westminster Assembly. He joined with the Scottish commissioner Robert Baillie in advocating a presbyterian polity with a strong lay eldership (which, as we have noted, had already been implemented in his parish in January, 1645). In this capacity he represented the Assembly's position before the House of Commons in June, 1645. In May, 1646, he was delegated by the Assembly to pray with the Lords, Commons, and Committee of Both Kingdoms as the first Civil War was coming to an end. (Greaves 1985: 25). The same month he was named a member of the committee which was to determine scandalous sins.

According to the minutes of the Proceedings of the Assembly, Calamy contributed to debates on marriage, excommunication, censure, predestination, and the fall of Adam (Greaves 1985: 26). In the debate on redemption (October, 1645) Calamy argued that Christ died for all persons, not only for the elect. The difference is that God's grace is made effectual only for the elect. Thus he distinguished between a general election of all and a special election for the chosen. Although redemption is offered to all, it is not accepted by all.

Calamy served on a number of the Assembly Committees: on printing the Bible and the Confession of Faith, fasting, determining which children qualified for baptism, antinomianism, examination of ministers and Christian liberty. In March 1647 he was named to the committee which disciplined ministers who had come over from the Royalist side.

He was assigned the task of drafting the chapter on the Lord's Supper in the Westminster Confession of Faith and the commentary on the second commandment in the Larger Catechism. He also assisted with the commentary on the sixth commandment and was on the committee which drafted the preface to the Shorter Catechism (Greaves 1985: 27).

In 1646 the Parliament authorized the establishment of Presbyterian government in London. Among the 136 churches, twelve Classes (Presbyteries) were established, with the classes represented in a London Provincial Assembly. Each church was to elect between six and twelve lay elders. A Classis was to be composed of 10-20 churches. Ideally, each Provincial Synod (or Assembly) was to have about 24 Classes. There was to be a National Synod with three ministers and three lay elders elected from each provincial synod. (Liu 1986: 51-89). St. Mary, Aldermanbury, was in the Sixth London Classis, which was probably the strongest because of its "favorable coalescence of clerical and civic leadership" (Liu 1986: 73). The clerical leadership of the Sixth Classis included Calamy and Matthew Newcomen. Despite Calamy's involvement with the Sixth Classis and the London Provincial Assembly, there is little evidence in the Vestry minutes of these institutions. Apparently, parish affairs and those of the higher judicatories did not intersect very often (see Liu 1986: 54).

Also in 1646 the parish decided to have Daniel Votier, an orthodox Anglican, serve as lecturer (although it is doubtful he ever actually assumed the post) (Liu 1973: 135). Apparently, Calamy and the lay Presbyterian leadership were trying to be inclusive, allowing both an Independent (Burton) and a supporter of episcopacy as lecturers. This is also another indication of the presence of non-Presbyterians in the parish.

Stress was taking its toll on Calamy. On 29 May, 1646, he was excused from preaching at the next scheduled fast day due to ill health. He may have been seriously ill, because he also declined to preach before the Lords on 29 July and again before Commons on 26 August (Wilson 1969: 89). However, his reluctance may have also been because of the ascendancy of radicals calling for the death of the King and congregational church government.

When the army seized the King in June, 1647, Calamy was again sent by the Westminster Assembly to pray with Parliament. As the Assembly drew to a close in 1648 he was delegated to thank the Church of Scotland for its support. It is certainly accurate to say that "Calamy was a major force in the deliberations and accomplishments of the Assembly" (Greaves 1985: 28). The High Church tract Persecutio Unadecima named him as the evil genius behind the whole operation.

As noted above, in July, 1647, London was in an uproar. On the 21st a group of working class Londoners in alliance with lay Presbyterian leaders of the City government, stormed the House of Commons and held the Speaker in the chair until a resolution calling for the restoration of the King to the throne was passed. Many members of the Commons then fled London and joined the army which was marching on the city. On the 28th Calamy preached at the Guildhall and called for recruits for a London militia to stand against the army. When the New Model Army marched into London on 6 August, bloodshed was avoided, but Calamy denounced the occupation in a sermon at St. Michael Cornhill. In response a pamphleteer sympathetic to the army chided Calamy, writing: "When we come to hear you, we expected to be instructed in Divinity, and not to be corrupted in Civility; if we had a desire to learn the language of Billingsgate, we should not have gone to Michael Cornhill in London, especially when Mr. Calamy was the Teacher" (cited in Liu 1986: 74).

The divisions of the Civil War between supporters of the Crown and of the Parliament were not foreign to Aldermanbury parish. A few doors from the church lived Alderman Christopher Pack, who submitted the proposal that Oliver Cromwell become King. In a house close by, with parlor windows opening into the Church yard, had lived Sir Hugh Windham, a Royalist who was imprisoned by the Parliamentarians. Windham had asked the Vestry not to use the Churchyard for interments, but the Vestry refused saying that he had no right to use the churchyard for his own convenience. The Vestry bricked up the doorway in 1648 (Goss 1944: 143; Malcolm 1803: 127).

Calamy's opposition to radical Protestantism remained strong during the late 1640s and placed him in the eye of various controversies. In 1648 Calamy was preaching in St. Benet Fink when a General Baptist named Edward Barber interrupted his sermon. Calamy accused Barber of coming to make a disturbance and insisted that he be allowed to finish his sermon. The congregation responded by calling for Barber to be pulled limb from limb. A constable rescued him but not before a woman scratched his face. (Tolme 1979: 78 and Greaves 1985: 29). Barber's version of the event is found in "A Declaration and Vindication of the Carriage of Edward Barber" (1648).

During 1648 and 1649 Calamy was increasingly made the target of a campaign by Independents and Sectaries. Once again, Calamy's desire for moderation was the source of dispute. Along with other Presbyterians he was critical of the army leadership in the aftermath of Pride's Purge (6 December). A meeting of Presbyterian clergy, held at Calamy's house, was broken up by a troop of soldiers under Hugh Peter. Calamy was not cowed, for in a protest to General Fairfax, commander of the Army, he called Peter a "knave" (Greaves 1985: 30). Also in December, 1648, Calamy was appointed by the Army Council to a group which was to determine how much religious freedom should be granted to individuals. Calamy must have been instrumental in drafting the group's recommendation, for it was a moderate endorsement of religious liberty, not the full blown defense of religious freedom called for by some Sectaries and Independents.

On 11 January, 1649, Calamy and Marshall were delegated by their fellow Presbyterian ministers to meet with General Fairfax concerning the fate of the King. On the 20th Calamy signed a document which called the trial of the king a violation of Scripture and the law of the realm. Calamy considered the execution of the king a denial of "the principles of the Protestant religion, never yet stained with the least drop of the blood of a king" (Greaves 1985: 32). On the day of the execution of King Charles I Calamy went to St. James palace where the king was being held to offer his pastoral services. However, the king refused, preferring instead the company of the Bishop of London.

The Commonwealth and the Protectorate (1649-1659)

The Cromwells (1649-1659)

If Oliver Cromwell suffered temporal punishment for his part in the regicide, surely it was that he, like Charles, had to deal with parliaments that would not be dealt with. The period of the Interregnum is conventionally divided into the Commonwealth (1649-1653) and the Protectorate (1653-1660). The Commonwealth was a sort of republic with a de jure executive, the Council of State, and Cromwell as de facto leader. The executive ruled, or tried to, first with the Rump, and then with a Commonwealth Parliament. Cromwell expelled both from Westminster by force. So ended all pretext and so ended the Commonwealth. The army was in charge. But the army was not eager to install a dictatorship. Leading officers drafted a constitution, "The Instrument of Government." It provided for the lifetime office of Lord Protector (Cromwell) and a Parliament, with power divided between them. There were two Protectorate Parliaments. The first tried to undercut the executive. The second offered Oliver the crown. He declined any higher title than Lord Protector. It simply did not work out. In the end Cromwell resorted to a military dictatorship, souring Englishmen with the notion of a large standing army ever thereafter. The country was divided into administrative districts, each under a major general. The army was the stronghold of the more radical Puritan elements. Military rule took on aspects of a coerced moral crusade. Frivolous and sinful entertainments (the theater, cockfights, even Church festivals) were outlawed.

A copy of one of the rules passed, "An Act for the Better Preventing and Suppressing of Prophane Swearing and Cursing" is in the archives of the Churchill Memorial. Announced on 28 June, 1650, it imposed fines on those found guilty of public profanity, ranging (for a first offense) from 3s4p for a commoner and 6s8p for a Gentleman up to 20s for a Baronet or Knight and 30s for a Duke, Marquis, Earl, or Viscount. Higher fines were to be imposed for each successive offense up to nine times. On the tenth offense the guilty party could be publically proclaimed "a Common Swearer or Curser."   Repressive ordinances limiting activity on the Lord's Day were passed, the root of the Sunday blue laws adopted in many American states. They were unpopular and helped destroy any chance of acceptance of a Puritan republic. But under the major generals, there was plenty of law and order.

Things went much better for the new government outside England. Oliver and the army first settled accounts with Ireland. In the upshot, much of the land in Ireland came under the control of English Protestant landlords, further alienating native Irish. Then it was Scotland's turn. Cromwell and the army thrashed the Scots at Dunbar in 1650. Then, in 1651, a combined army of Scots and Royalists invaded England with the Prince of Wales, the future Charles II, at their head. Charles was one of the few survivors of the carnage and both Scots uprisings and armed attempts to restore the monarchy became decidedly unfashionable under the Protectorate.

John Milton, better remembered as a poet, served ably as Cromwell's foreign secretary. With Oliver leading the army and a rehabilitated navy, England was once more a power to be reckoned with. However, Oliver was not able to assemble the great Protestant coalition of which he dreamed.

Cromwell's health went into rapid decline and he died in 1658. He had for a decade held the Puritan political experiment together almost by force of personal will. The divided opposition to the house of Stuart was never able to compose its fragmented condition and devise a polity or policies that could gain widespread popular assent. Even with creative minds like Milton, the Puritan camp lacked creative constitutional imagination.

The best solution that could be devised for filling the vacancy in the office of Lord Protector was the royalist principle of inheritance. Oliver's son Richard (1626-1712), mockingly known as "Tumbledown Dick," was unable to fill his father's boots. The Rump was recalled to Westminster, and the stage was set for the restoration of the Stuart monarchy. Richard's attempt at rule lasted from September, 1658, to May, 1659.

Calamy and Aldermanbury during the Commonwealth and Protectorate

The Civil War had left London and the parish of St. Mary relatively unscathed. Indeed, London profitted from the war trade, and its civilian commerce was largely uninterrupted. The Commonwealth and Protectorate can also be put down as a net plus. London merchants benefitted from British victories over the Dutch. England's increased stature in Europe was good for business.

Amidst the political turmoil of the Commonwealth and Protectorate, the Vestry continued to concentrate on internal matters. On 23 January 1649, the position of Churchwarden was formally split into "upper" and "under" churchwarden (Carter 1913: 61). On 11 March 1649 the Vestry established a Committee to determine what was owed Mr. Robert Mercer, Calamy's assistant. An agreement was made for the Vestry to pay him 5.10.00 and Calamy 7.10.00. The Vestry agreed that a way needed to be found to pay the assistant on a regular basis. The money borrowed from the poor fund was ordered repaid.

Also during 1649 Calamy served as moderator of the provincial Synod of London and signed a Vindication of the Presbyteriall-Government on 2 November.

At a meeting held on 3 September, 1650 the Vestry put the wife of the late Churchwarden under bond for money collected by her husband for Mr. Calamy (Carter 1913: 61). Also on 3 September a 40s charge was established when a man, woman, or child was buried in the Vaults (Carter 1913: 74).

Also in 1650 Calamy was named President of Sion College (see ch. 2) for a one-year term. He had been on the Court of Governors of the College since 1643, when the Royalist members of the college had fled London. He also had served as junior dean of the college in 1644 and senior dean in 1649. At the end of his term he received 1.0.3 for the customary Latin sermon preached by the outgoing President. The college, which not only aided the indigent and provided books for students but was also a sort of gathering place for London clergy, had been a center of Presbyterian activity (Greaves 1985: 33). At the end of Calamy's presidency soldiers were quartered in the College (Pearce 1913: 112).

Calamy was caught up in a controversy involving prominent Presbyterian clergy in the Spring of 1651. On 2 May three Presbyterian leaders, co-signatories with Calamy of the Vindication were arrested on the charge that they were engaged in a royalist conspiracy. The assumption that Calamy and his friend Stephen Marshall were also involved was widespread, but Calamy was never arrested. One of the Presbyterian clergy (Christopher Love) was executed on 22 August. Calamy was with him on the scaffold and in following years helped to see that Love's writings were published posthumously (Greaves 1985: 33-34). (On Love, see Liu 1986: 66-67.)

Two of Calamy's own sermons were published in 1651: "The Saint's Rest" and "A Sermon Preached ... August 24, 1651." The latter was probably motivated by the execution of Christopher Love (Richardson 1928: 103).

Also in 1651 Simeon Ashe became a lecturer and assistant to Calamy at St. Mary's (Seaver 1970: 271). Like Calamy he was a Cambridge graduate (Emmanuel), who was an early supporter of the Presbyterian cause. He also spoke frequently before parliament (Wilson 1969).

On Gunpowder Treason Day in 1651 (5 November) Walter Jenkins, minister of Christ Church, London, preached a sermon at St. Mary, Aldermanbury. He warned that just as Papists had once sought to destroy the Church of England, now heresies and "filthy blasphemies against the name of God" threatened to undermine the Church (17). In a note attached to the published sermon Calamy explained that it had been printed to build people up "in these backsliding times."

In 1652 the Account Book shows 5p paid to bellringers on November 5th, Gunpowder Treason Day and 1.13.00 paid to a carpenter for work done on the Curate's house (Carter 1913: 112).

Excursus: Allen and Margaret Robinett

The Aldermanbury Parish Register recorded the wedding on 29 September 1653 of Allen Robinett (spelled Robanett in the Register and Robanet by him) and Margaret Symm, both of the parish of St. Michael Queenhithe (amalgamated with St. Michael Paternoster after the destruction of the church building in 1876) (Robinett I 1982: 5). Allen Robinett (identified as a Grocer) was, according to family tradition, of Huguenot ancestry (Robinett I 1982: 5, 7). In addition, Allen's handwritten comments in his Bible, dated 1653, seem to reflect Puritan sympathies (Robinett I 1982: 7, 26-28). This can be considered circumstantial evidence that Allen and Margaret were in sympathy with the Puritan Presbyterian leanings of the Aldermanbury parish, and chose to be married by another descendant of the Huguenots— Edmund Calamy.

The Robinetts eventually settled in Bunbury in Cheshire. In 1682 they were among those who migrated to Pennsylvania, acquiring property from William Penn. Allen was a "first purchaser" of 250 acres of land near the present town of Media, where he and Margaret settled with two of their children, Samuel and Sarah.

Whether the couple had become members of the Society of Friends and joined the migration out of religious conviction, or simply associated themselves with the Penn company for other reasons, cannot be ascertained for certain. It is the conviction of the Robinett family history that they were not members of the Society because their names are not included in the rather extensive Quaker records in Chester County where they settled (Robinett II 1982: 26). They must have at least been sympathetic to the Society of Friends cause, for they settled among Quakers. Allen and Margaret's daughter Susanna, who immigrated to Pennsylvania separately from her parents, married a Quaker named Robert Ward, perhaps before departing from England (Robinett II 1982: 1.2).

When the American descendants of Allen and Margaret Robinett discovered that the church in which their ancestors' marriage was registered had been moved to the United States they began holding biennial meetings of the Robinett Family Association on the Westminster College campus. The first gathering in 1982, celebrating the 300th anniversary of Allen and Margaret's arrival in America, attracted over 300 Robinett descendants. Gatherings have been held every other year since, each with genealogical updates, presentations on the history of the Church of St. Mary, Aldermanbury, and a special service of worship in the restored Church. In one service the marriage of Allen and Margaret was re-enacted, with the present perpetual curate, Dr. William Young, taking the role of Edmund Calamy and two teenage Robinett descendants assuming the parts of their ancestors (See Figure 4.2).

Calamy and Aldermanbury during the Commonwealth and Protectorate (continued)

During 1654 Calamy was apparently absent from the pulpit for a time. The Accounts show 17s4p spent "for wine and bread fetched at several times to entertayne Ministers that have preached in Mr. Calamies absence." (Carter 1913: 112). Also in 1654 5s was spent to rent Brewer's Hall on St. Thomas Day and 2s for a lock for the door when a woman lay there. The Accounts also speak of 1.07.08 spent for "bread and beere" on perambulation day. This is an early indication of the parish tradition of walking around the parish boundaries on Ascension Day to check to see if parish markers were in place. It was a festive occasion with children bedecked with ribbons and sticks used to "beat the bounds," that is, actually touch all the boundary markers. The tradition continued into the twentieth century.

On 19 October, 1654, Calamy preached the funeral sermon for Dr. Samuel Bolton, late Master of Christ's College, Cambridge. It was published the following year under the title "The Saint's Transfiguration." The sermon was dedicated to Calamy's patron, the Earl of Warwick.

On the 10th of December of the same year he preached before the Lord Mayor a pessimistic sermon published under the title "The Monster of Sinful Self-Seeking, Anatomized" (1655). In the sermon Calamy claimed that the reformation had been obstructed and Parliament, the ministry, and the gentry destroyed by self-seeking. (Greaves 1985: 34-35).

Calamy was aware of and supported the conversion of Indians by English settlers in America. He signed an epistle to a 1648 work by Thomas Shepherd, a Cambridge, Massachusetts minister. The work was entitled "The Sun-shine of the Gospel Breaking Forth upon the Indians in New England." The epistle, dedicating the work to Parliament described the Indians as "the saddest spectacles of degeneracy upon earth ...." Calamy also signed the epistle to the readers which included a word for the merchants involved in trade with the New World, calling for their support of the missionary activity: "Whither you traffick you take much from them [the Indians, but] if you carry this [the gospel] to them, you will make them an abundant a recompense" (Greaves 1985: 35). Works through 1655 on the activity of missionaries among the New England Indians carried Calamy's endorsement.

Entries in the Vestry records from 1655 give an indication of the use of the poor fund in the parish. There are numerous entries relating to nursing, clothing and feeding parish foundlings. (Carter 1913: 112). To help finance care of the poor £20 was given by Mr. Dyer from a legacy given by Lady Swynerton.

Several entries for 1655 show children named John Aldermanbury or Rebecca Aldermanbury or Mary Aldermanbury. It was the custom to give parish foundlings as a surname the name of the parish in which they were found. At first "Aldermanbury" was the surname given by the St. Mary's Vestry. But later it was shortened to "Berry." The foundling was put out to nurse and then, if a boy, apprenticed when old enough, or, if a girl, given a dowry. The earliest evidence for a parish foundling (an abandoned infant) in Aldermanbury is 1586. The practice reached epidemic proportions during the Civil War and Commonwealth periods.

The practice of hiring someone to walk through the parish and put out pregnant women is documented in the records. For example, an entry for 1658 reads (Carter 1913: 113): "Paid ye Bellman to get a woman out of ye parish that was ready to be delivered .... 2s6d." Apparently the effort failed, for the note continues "and a woman to carry her child."

The prevailing view among scholars is that the Puritan revolution was a time of repression of the poor and a triumph of a laissez-faire attitude. As R. H. Tawney wrote in <u>Religion and the Rise of Capitalism</u>, "charity and relief fell on evil days" (cited by Pearl 1961: 206-207). Certainly, the practice of putting pregnant women out of the parish does not speak well for the parish's concern for the poor. However, we must be aware that the practice of forcing out women about to deliver was already well-established, the result of limited resources and the law which made the parish of birth responsible for the welfare of the infant until he was apprenticed (if a boy) or married (if a girl). Parishes became quite astute in finding ways to assure that indigent babies were not born within their bounds.

On the other hand, St. Mary, Aldermanbury, and other Puritan parishes considered the care of the poor the highest of parish responsibilities. At one point, when £15 was drawn from the poor stock to pay Calamy's stipend, it was ordered repaid immediately so as not to diminish the funds available (Liu 1986: 187). What the Puritans did try to do was to organize care of the poor more effectively and combine almsgiving with imposition of work discipline and education (Pearl 1961: 208-209). In 1647 Parliament had created the Corporation for the Poor in an effort "to educate and train the children of the poor" (Pearl 1961: 219).

Also in 1655 we find an unusually long list of parishoners paying the fine to be excused from parish offices. Six men paid fines ranging from two to eight pounds to be excused from the office of Constable, and two to be released from serving as Scavenger. An Alexander Bramme paid £5 to be excused from all offices (Carter 1913: 113).

Mr. Calamy was again absent from the parish in 1655 as the records show 1.03.04 for "several pints of wine for the Ministers who have preached in Mr. Calamies absence."

During 1654-1655 there is evidence that Calamy's attitude toward Independents and others to his religious left was moderating. Along with a number of other Presbyterian but also Independent leaders, he endorsed the formation of an English-European Protestant league "against the Antichrist" in April, 1654. He also joined with Independents and Baptists to help raise funds to support persecuted Protestants on the continent in 1655. Most surprisingly, he intervened in support of an exiled Socinian scholar, Joseph Biddle (Greaves 1985: 36).

Calamy's concern for education is documented by two events in 1656. In January he joined with other London clergy in urging an inquiry into a schoolmaster he considered unqualified. In March he was named to a committee charged with developing statutes for a new college in Durham.

On 30 January 1656 a new assistant was chosen for Calamy at a stipend of £40 annually, to be paid by the parish (Carter 1913: 47).

On 8 October 1656 the following entry in the Vestry minutes shows the affection in the parish for Calamy:

> It was considered of that Mr. Calamy having now continued our
> pastour this 17 years and yet the parish had never testyfied
> their Love unto him or to present him with any gift in name
> of the whole parish it was then and there freely consented

unto that the Churchwardens shall in the name of the parishoners deliver unto Mr. Edmund Calamy now Pastour the sum of twenty pounds of Good and Lawfull money of England out of the parish stock.

Excursus: John Milton's Assocation with Aldermanbury

The Aldermanbury register records that the banns for the marriage of John Milton (1608-1674) and his second wife, Katherine (also spelled Catharine) Woodcock, "of the Parish of Marys in Aldermanbury" were published in the church three times in October and November, 1656 (see Figure 4.4). The register further states that the couple was married on 12 November, by Sir John Dethicke, an Alderman and Justice of the Peace. This bit of evidence connects one of the most influential English writers of any age to St. Mary, Aldermanbury. Let us examine Milton's association with the parish in the context of a brief recounting of his life and work.

A Londoner by birth, and Cambridge educated, John Milton attained fame as a poet and political writer. While a student at Christ's College, Cambridge, he already displayed literary ability. He trained to be a minister, but decided that he could not serve under the restraints imposed by the Church of England. Since Edmund Calamy was still in the Cambridge area during Milton's tenure at Cambridge, it is possible (though not documented) that the two Puritan-sympathizers met there. While at Cambridge Milton composed "L'Allegro" and "Il Peneroso," companion poems contrasting the pleasures of a man of mirth and the joys of a thoughtful person.

He left Cambridge in 1632 and went to his father's country home, Horton. There he wrote Comus, a masque on the nature of virtue, and "Lycidas," a pastoral elegy. In 1638 and 1639 he spent 15 months touring Europe. He returned to London in time to join the Puritan cause at the onset of the Civil War. When Calamy and his friends wrote against episcopacy under the acronym Smectymnuus (see above), Milton edited their work and, according to one report, expanded it by twenty pages (Saillens 1964: 89). Milton also defended Smectymnuus and their cause in a series of political pamphlets, culminating in Apology for Smectymnuus (1642). In 1644 he wrote his most famous prose work, Areopagitica, a spirited defense of freedom of the press.

When Milton wrote The Tenure of Kings and Magistrates (1649), arguing that the people have the right to select and depose their rulers, Commonwealth leaders rewarded him with appointment as official translator of official dispatches into Latin.

He also wrote a number of tracts defending the Commonwealth.

Milton had married a a sixteen-year-old girl, Mary Powell, in 1643, but the marriage was not a happy one. Mary died in 1652, leaving Milton with two young daughters. The same year Milton's eyesight failed, and he went blind.

There is no record of how Milton met Katherine Woodcock. Apparently he was already blind when they became acquainted. She was a Londoner, born in 1628 and baptized at St. Dunstan's in the East. Her father, a Captain Woodcock, had died and left her mother, Elizabeth, destitute, forced to raise Katherine and her sisters by herself. A Cromwellian Marriage Act, effective on September 29, 1653, required that marriages be solemnized by Justices of the Peace rather than ministers. Hence, when Milton and Woodcock married, Sir John Dethicke, a Justice of the Peace, conducted the ceremony. Although the marriage may have been conducted in St. Margaret's, the Parliamentary church, it was more likely held in the Guildhall, since Dethicke was an Alderman.

After the marriage Katherine moved into Milton's lodgings in Petty France, near Westminster Abbey (and St. Margaret's). Although she was twenty years Milton's junior (her mother was approximately the same age as the poet), Katherine proved a good wife and mother to his children. By this time Milton had become convinced that polygamy was God's plan (Wilson 1983: 188), but in Katherine he found the domestic helpmate he had not in Mary Powell. His marriage with Katherine may have inspired him to write in Book IV of Paradise Lost:

>Hail wedded love, mysterious law, true source
>of human offspring, sole propriety
>In Paradise of all things common else.

On 19 October, 1657, Katherine gave birth to a daughter, also named Katherine. Soon after, the elder Katherine fell ill with consumption, and died on 17 March, 1658. Ten days later the infant Katherine also died. Milton's last sonnet, "Methoughts I Saw My Late Espoused Saint" (1658) was inspired by his wife Katherine's death:

>Methought I saw my late espoused saint
>>Brought to me like Alcestis from the grave,
>>When Jove's great son to her glad husband gave,
>>Rescued from death by force through pale and faint
>>Mine as whom washed from spot of childbed taint
>>Purification in the Old Law did save,

> And such, as yet once more I trust to have
> Full sight of her in heaven without restraint
> Came vested all in white, pure as her mind:
> > Her face was veiled, yet to my fancied sight
> > Love, sweetness, goodness in her person shined
> So clear, as in no face with more delight.
> > But O as to embrace me she inclined
> > I waked, she fled, and day brought back my night.

Katherine was buried in St. Margaret's on 10 February in a coffin with twelve locks. Milton gave the keys to twelve different young men.

After the restoration of Charles II in 1660 (see below), Milton was arrested but not imprisoned. According to one source he married his third wife, Elizabeth Minshull on 24 February, 1663, in St. Mary, Aldermanbury (Saillens 1964: 250). However, the wedding actually took place in St. Mary, Aldermary (Axelrad 1980: 146), a church frequently confused by careless historians with St. Mary, Aldermanbury. About this time, after his expulsion from the Aldermanbury pulpit, Edmund Calamy may have visited Milton in his home on Jewin Street (Saillens 1964: 252).

In his declining years Milton dictated the great epic poems <u>Paradise Lost</u> (1667), <u>Paradise Regained</u> (1671), and <u>Samson Agonistes</u> (1671) to his daughters. The first is a twelve-book poetic retelling of the story of the creation and "fall" of Adam and Eve in the Book of Genesis. The second focuses on Christ's overcoming the power of Satan. The last is based on the Biblical story of the blind Samson who overcomes the deceit of his wife Delilah (Daila in the poem) and the might of the Philistines. They establish his reputation a one of the greatest of all English poets.

Although Milton was more radical in his rejection of the structure of the Church of England than his friend and fellow Puritan, Edmund Calamy, the two shared the same views of the necessity of ongoing reformation of the Church and the importance of the individual believer's commitment to the highest moral standards. Whether by accident or design, Milton's marriage to Katherine Woodcock linked him permanently to Calamy's beloved Aldermanbury.

Calamy and Aldermanbury during the Commonwealth and Protectorate (continued)

In the Spring of 1657 Calamy was involved in consultations with Oliver Cromwell concerning whether Cromwell should assume the throne. According to a member of the Council of State present at the meeting Cromwell held with prominent London clergy, Calamy told the Lord Protector that the plan was both illegal and impractical. When Cromwell said that the safety of the nation made the proposal legal, Calamy is reported to have said, "Oh it is against the Voice of the Nation; there will be Nine in Ten against you." Calamy was willing to stand up to anyone, no matter how powerful! (Greaves 1985: 37-38 and Richardson 1928: 40 n.76).

During this same period Calamy was instrumental in convincing Cromwell's government to side with the moderate Resolutioners of the Church of Scotland against a more radical party (the Protesters). (Greaves 1985: 39-40).

Also in 1657 the first edition of a collection of five sermons of Calamy appeared under the title, <u>The Godly Man's Ark</u>. It went through five editions during the next twenty-five years.

He also wrote the preface for a work entitled Evidence for Heaven, written by a "Gentlewoman" in the congregation who desired to remain anonymous.

Calamy again spoke before the House of Commons on 27 January, 1658, on another fast day. Some Cromwellians thought the sermon "smelled Presbyterian," to which Calamy apparently responded by reminding them that he was no "Court flatterer." Although requested to do so, Calamy apparently did not publish the sermon (Greaves 1985: 40).

Also in 1658 Calamy wrote the preface to Samuel Hudson's <u>A Vindication of the Essence and Unity of the Church Catholick Visible</u>, warning Independents of the dangers of separation.

On 11 October 1658 Calamy joined with other Presbyterian leaders in expressing support to Richard Cromwell, when he succeeded his father as Lord Protector. However, against the advice of General George Monck and others, the new Protector refused to summon a new assembly of divines to work out a plan of accomodation among the various religious factions. On 24 November, 1658, Calamy's stipend was raised to £200 from 182 (Carter 1913: 47).

The next January a dispute arose in Commons over whether to invite Calamy or an Independent cleric to fill out a group of three to speak on 4 February, a fast day. After an acrimonious debate both were invited. Three were Presbyterians. One of the Presbyterians (Edward Reyondos) urged that the Commons crack down on religious radicals. Calamy's sermon has not survived (Greaves 1985: 41).

On 1 January, 1660 the first example of "streaking" may have occurred at St.

Mary's. A Quaker named Solomon Eeles came into the church "naked in ye time of Mr. Calamy's preaching." The account books show an expenditure of 1.5.10 spent by the parish prosecuting Mr. Eeles (Carter 1913: 114). The event was likely a graphic response to Calamy's participation, along with Baptist and Independent leaders, in opposition to the young Quaker movement (Greaves 1985: 41). Whether Eeles was also associated with the Adamites, a group which worshipped in the nude to symbolize a desire to return to the days of pre-Fall innocence, is not known.

This same year controversy apparently grew in the congregation over Calamy's leadership. A Vestry minute for 19 July records that nine men were appointed to speak to those who refused to pay for Calamy's services, and a widow, Mrs. Gilburd, was ordered locked out of her pew because she "will not give noe thing to Mr. Calamy" (Carter 1913: 47). The controversy may have stemmed from the fact that Calamy was joining actively in the call to bring Charles II back to England.

The Restoration and early Reign of Charles II (1660-1666)

General George Monck and the Restoration (1659-1660)

Inability to cope with the political vacuum created by Oliver Cromwell's death produced a dangerously unstable situation in England. The army was arrayed against discontented civilians. The Rump took the civilian side. Disparate elements of the army jockeyed for position and power. Either a military coup or renewed civil war were genuine threats. As noted, Anglican and Presbyterian leaders in the City (Calamy prominent among them) conspired against the Quakers and for Stuart restoration. Support grew for Restoration, but no one seemed to have the means to achieve it peacefully. A group of officers led by the ambitious General Lambert entertained a variety of self-serving schemes to gain power.

It was at this point that Major General George Monck stepped forward to guide England's destiny. Monck was a soldier's soldier. He helped put upon the military profession the particular stamp it still bears in the English speaking world: deference to civilian authority, the placing of principle above personal ambition, and putting the long range national good above political dogma. He had attracted Cromwell's attention during the Irish campaign, and proved himself at the Battle of Dunbar. In 1652 Cromwell had entrusted to Monck the task of pacifying Scotland, which he did less by force than by winning the trust of the people.

Monck began to concentrate the Army of Scotland at the village of Coldstream on the Tweed in December, 1659. Though most English forces were withdrawn from Scotland, the country remained tranquil, a tribute to Monck. Monck consulted with his trusted officers at Coldstream, and later with other old comrades at arms like Fairfax. But publicly he kept his actual intentions secret. On 1 January 1660, the "Coldstreamers" crossed the Tweed and began a fateful march south. (As a result of their work under Monck they became The Coldstream Guards, the only Parliamentary regiment retained in the Royal Army, and still an active regiment today. Monck would be created Duke of Albermarle and Captain General.) Monck proclaimed that he was marching to London to support Parliament and the law, that is to oppose a military coup or some sort of dictatorship.

London stood firm for civilian rule, withstanding the threats of the army. In the meantime, Monck brushed aside Lambert's forces and continued his march on London. He arrived on 6 February, and deployed his troops to keep peace. Immediately he went into consultation with restorationist leaders (including Calamy). When he disclosed to the Rump his intention to recall the entire Long Parliament, his command and very life were put in danger. To assure the Council of State of his loyalty he arrested members of the Common Council and took down the gates and street chains that symbolized London's autonomy. Then, on 11 February he called a fateful meeting in the Guildhall with the Lord Mayor, Aldermen, and Common Council He announced that he would order the Rump to recall the full Parliament so that a free and fair election could be held. London went wild with celebrations.

All surviving members of the Long Parliament were called yet once more to Westminster. The Presbyterian members insured a majority of moderately royalist temperament. In its last act the Long Parliament called for a "convention Parliament," which in turn invited Charles II to return to England from exile in Holland. Charles returned to popular acclamation and was duly installed with proper pomp and ceremony. (See Figure 4.3)

Calamy's Role in the Restoration

By the Summer of 1659 Royalist leaders had determined that without the support of Presbyterian leaders like Calamy they would not succeed in restoring the monarchy. Outside London some Presbyterian leaders had joined forces with Royalists in rebellion during the summer. On 26 August, Alderman James Bunce wrote to Calamy and other Presbyterian leaders soliciting their support for the insurrection, but by that time it had been crushed. In January, 1660, Calamy had been one of the first consulted when the future Charles II had sent one of his key advisors to London to meet with Presbyterian leaders (Greaves 1985: 41-42).

Calamy apparently believed that the new king would support an ecclesiastical settlement similar to that in Scotland. This had been the promise of one of the messengers sent from Holland and the stated preference of General Monck when he arrived in London. Monck named Calamy one of his chaplains, received the Lord's Supper from him, and consulted with him on ministerial appointments (Greaves 1985: 42).

On 21 February, after the return of members to Parliament who had been excluded in Pride's Purge and the creation of a Presbyterian majority in Parliament, Calamy preached a sermon of thanksgiving. He was undoubtedly ecstatic when the new Long Parliament, convened by General Monck, adopted the Westminster Confession he had helped to write, ordered the annual reading of the Solemn League and Covenant, and created a new commission to approve ministers to replace the Cromwellian apparatus. Calamy was on the thirty-one member commission. He was also asked to serve with three other clergy to advise Parliament's Committee on Religion (Greaves 1985: 43).

By April 1660 General Monck was pressuring Charles to write a letter in care of Calamy for all the Presbyterian clergy, in which he would pledge to uphold the Protestant faith in England. On 30 April Calamy again preached to the Commons on a fast day (Greaves 1985: 45).

On 7 May, at a meeting held at Sion College, Presbyterians meeting in "General Assembly" approved the Declaration of Breda and delegated Calamy and three other ministers to go to Holland and consult with Charles. The delegation met with Charles in his bedchamber and gave him a letter of support signed by more than eighty ministers (from the Sion College meeting). In return for their pledge of support for a restored monarchy and a moderate episcopacy, Charles agreed that Parliament would settle the question of church government in a manner favorable to Presbyterians. However, he resisted their efforts to stop using the Book of Common Prayer, insisting that he wanted the same measure of liberty they were asking for themselves. Nevertheless, Calamy and the others returned home feeling that the Presbyterian position was secure (Greaves 1985: 45-46).

During May Calamy again preached a fast day sermon to Parliament, meeting in St. Margaret's. His grandson claims that Calamy was one of the clergy sent to escort Charles from Holland (Matthews 1934:1). On 29 May he was probably present along with other Presbyterian clergy to greet the King when he arrived in St. Paul's churchyard (Greaves 1985: 47).

The Early Reign of Charles II (1660-1666)

A brilliant, talented and pleasure-loving court assembled around the new Stuart king at Whitehall. The Puritans had outlawed games, sports, and the theater and put sensuality under the pall of suspicion. The Restoration reversed the trend! It was as if, after the Puritan repression, England launched upon a grand and glorious party with the king as the master of revels.

Two anecdotes concerning royal mistresses perhaps catch the spirit of the age better than discursive prose, even if the tales are apocryphal.

The royal mistress, Barabara, Lady Castlemaine, had a more than cousinly affection for her cousin, handsome and dashing young Captain Jack Churchill, the future Duke of Marlborough, and an ancestor of Winston Churchill. One evening Barbara and Jack were between the sheets when they heard the unmistakable tread of the king on the stairway. Barbara urged Jack to hide, but fearing discovery he climbed out the window and jumped to the ground. The next day at court the king congratulated Captain Churchill on his "heroic leap."

On another occasion a street mob assaulted a curtained sedan chair, suspecting it bore a detested Catholic mistress to the king's bosom. Out of the curtains popped the red headed comedienne, Nell Gwenn. "Stop!" she cried, "I'm the Protestant whore!" The mob took the chair from the bearers and, cheering, escorted saucy Nell to the royal apartments.

The central policy of Charles' reign was, as he once remarked, to avoid resuming his "travels." Thus, however dear to his heart the policy, however deep the moral obligation, Charles always backed away from any public action that would push the nation beyond its point of toleration. Secret acts of state were another matter. For example, the Treaty of Dover, negotiated with France in 1670, included a secret promise by Charles to convert to Catholicism and to force England to convert with him. Whether Charles had authentic Catholic convictions is a matter historians debate. A fundamental commitment to any faith may have been impossible for an opportunistic cynic like Charles.

Whatever his failings, Charles had the saving grace of a sense of humor and apparently a genuine spirit of tolerance. He certainly had the best political judgment of any of the Stuarts. Part of his political success, it must be noted, came from shunting responsibility for failed or unpopular policies onto his advisors.

Though not as erudite as his grandfather, Charles had a good mind and was genuinely interested in the burgeoning discoveries of the new science that was coming to be in his time. He issued the charter of the Royal Society (1661), England's oldest learned society.

The Convention Parliament had, at best, an irregular pedigree, so a new election was duly called by the King. In the flush of royalist enthusiasm the nation's electors returned the royalist and Presbyterian "Cavalier Parliament," so sympathetic to the king's cause that he let it sit for 18 years. On the whole, they let the king have what he wanted so long as it was not a lot of money.

Charles issued a general amnesty (except for those involved in the execution of his father), but the Cavalier Parliament and the bishops meeting at the Savoy Conference were less humane. Charles owed a genuine debt of honor to the Presbyterians like Edmund Calamy who had been so instrumental in his return, and he tried to honor that debt. But the Cavaliers and Bishops had the bit in their teeth and simply overrode the king, who placed not resuming his travels above unyielding support for Presbyterians. Ironically for its Presbyterian members, Parliament passed disabling legislation against all "Dissenters" (later labelled "Nonconformists"), and not just the Independents, Anabaptists and other true "Roundheads". We will return to the work of the bishops in the next chapter.

The remains of Cromwell and two of his chief lieutenants were disinterred, gibbeted, and desecrated. About twenty of the sixty men directly involved in the regicide were apprehended, the others having died or fled. Nine were executed. "I am weary of hanging," declared Charles, and the executions ceased. The hangmen were mostly former colleagues of the victims with their coats now turned, an irony not lost on many contemporaries and most historians.

Some consequences of the Interregnum were undone. All parliamentary acts since 1642 were deemed null, since they had not gone through the normal process of approval by both houses and royal assent. Expropriated crown property and private estates were restored. However, many royalists had been obliged to sell property to pay high taxes and fines. These properties were left in the hands of their new owners, largely Presbyterian gentry.

Because of parliamentary parsimony, Charles turned to his patrons in France to support his government. The British military hired out as mercenaries in French service. The result was good training for a number of young British officers, including John Churchill (later to be a nemesis to the French!).

Charles first "ministry" was led by his faithful friend, the Earl of Clarendon. He was blamed for the sorry state of much of the British navy, which led to defeat in the second Dutch war, and for Charles' unpopular marriage to the Catholic Catherine of Braganza. Some even seemed to feel he was somehow responsible for the terrible plague in 1665 and Great Fire of London the next year. However, as we will see in the next chapter, it was more fashionable to blame "Papists" or the French for these calamities.

Calamy's Final Years

We will continue the story of the reign of Charles II in the next chapter. Let us now return to events in Aldermanbury and to the remarkable career of Edmund Calamy. We are again especially indebted here to the reconstruction of these years of Calamy's life by Richard Greaves.

Out of gratitude for their support Charles II made Calamy and nine other Presbyterians his royal chaplains. Calamy accepted, possibly with some reluctance, for we know that his brother-in-law Matthew Newcomen refused the offer. Calamy preached before the King at Whitehall only once in this capacity (on 12 August, 1660). Although the King allowed him to preach without a surplice, informants reported that while Calamy and the other Presbyterians preached the king looked at pictures in his Bible. According to Samuel Pepys, Calamy was very officious and lectured the King too much (Greaves 1985: 49).

Calamy was no less polite to General Monck, when the general came to hear one of Calamy's Aldermanbury sermons after the Restoration. Calamy's grandson records that his grandfather was preaching on "filthy Lucre." "And why," said he, "is it call'd filthy, but because it makes Men do base and filthy things? Some Men," said he, "will betray Three Kingdoms for filthy Lucre's sake." With this he threw his handkerchief, which he waved up and down when he preached, towards the General's pew (Matthews 1934: l).

During the negotiations between Anglican and Presbyterian leaders, which began in June, over the form of church government to be adopted, Calamy again was a voice of moderation. He did not endorse the more radical Presbyterian position that the settlement follow the Scottish model. However, in meetings moderated by the King, Calamy firmly insisted that nonessentials not be required in the church, that biblical discipline be followed, and that only godly clergy should have appointments.

In meetings with Presbyterian leaders from throughout England, held at Sion College during June, 1660, Calamy helped shape proposals to be taken to the king. They agreed to episcopacy balanced with "a due commixtion of Presbyters." They insisted that there be not oaths of obedience to bishops required for the ordination of clergy. They also called for a revision of the Book of Common Prayer as well as abolition of the surplice, the sign of the cross in baptism, and bowing toward the altar and at the name of Jesus. The king received them politely and promised to bring the Anglicans and Presbyterians together to work out a compromise (Greaves 1985: 48).

Calamy's realistic and pragmatic approach is evident in a letter dated 10 August, 1660, sent in reply to some Scottish divines who asked about the prospects for a Presbyterian settlement in England (Matthews 1934: x).

> The general stream and current is for the old prelacy in all
> its pomp and height, and therefore it cannot be hoped for,
> that the presbyterial government should be owned as the public
> establishment of this nation, while the tide runneth so
> strongly that way; and the bare toleration of it will certainly
> produce a mischief, whilst papists, and sectaries of all
> sorts, will wind in themselves under the cover of such a favour:
> therefore no course seemeth likely to us to secure religion and
> the interests of Christ ... but by making presbytery a part of
> the public establishment; which will not be effect but by
> moderating and reducing episcopacy to the form of synodical
> government. ... This is all we can for the present hope for.

Apparently not all in the parish supported their curate's stand. On 19 July, 1660, the Vestry directed nine gentlemen to speak to those who were refusing to pay their portion of Calamy's stipend. The Vestry also ordered the Churchwardens to lock the pew door of Mrs. Gilburd, because of her refusal to pay (Chancery Petition 1887: 71).

After receiving the King's initial proposals for accomodation, and finding them unacceptable, Calamy and other moderate Presbyterians proposed in September that five concessions be made to the Presbyterian side: bishops and presbyters together ordaining and imposing discipline; suffragan bishops in larger dioceses; confirmation only with the local minister's approval; revision of the Book of Common Prayer with provision for alternative forms of worship; making kneeling at communion optional.

On 22 October Charles met with Calamy and six other Presbyterians. Eight Anglicans were also invited. The atmosphere was tense, as the Anglicans defended their view of episcopacy and Calamy defended from Scripture the Presbyterian case for the equality of presbyters and bishops (Greaves 1985: 50-51). The result of this meeting was the appointment of Calamy and another moderate Presbyterian to meet with two Anglicans. On 25 October their draft was published, with major concessions to the Presbyterians, including a commitment to revision of the Prayer Book. Calamy then became active in the effort to win Parliamentary approval of the King's Declaration.

In gratitude for their support the King offered to make Calamy Bishop of Lichfield. Although another moderate accepted the see of Hereford, Calamy ultimately declined appointment after much agonizing. He apparently concluded that although he could in conscience accept the appointment under the terms of the Declaration, his opposition to episcopacy had been so strong, his acceptance would be misunderstood and hurt the Presbyterian cause. Moreover, his wife and brother-in-law were against his acceptance (Greaves 1985: 52-53).

Perhaps influenced by Calamy's refusal to accept the see, the House of Commons rejected the royal declaration. Calamy himself, however, continued to participate in efforts at accomodation. When the Savoy Conference convened in April, 1661, to undertake the revision of the liturgy, he was instrumental in drafting the eighteen "Exceptions" to the existing liturgy. His position was that there should be nothing in the liturgy that was "doubtful or questioned among pious, learned and orthodox persons." The Anglicans rejected the proposals, the Reconcilers became divided, and the Conference ended in July without success (Greaves 1985: 54-55).

On 17 April Calamy asked the Vestry to be relieved of his lecture until October, presumably to participate in the Conference, although his health was also poor. He

153

had fallen earlier in the year, probably because of his dizziness, and feared his leg was out of joint. The Vestry granted his request (Malcolm 1803: 120).

Hopes of compromise dimmed as Bishop Sheldon excluded Calamy from a Convocation called while the Savoy Conference was in session. Although Calamy had been nominated by London ministers, the Bishop exercised his right to select the delegates attending from his diocese. As we have seen, the recently elected Cavalier Parliament was also antagonistic to accommodation with Presbyterians (Greaves 1985: 54).

During the Fall of 1661 London playgoers were treated to a revised version of Ben Jonson's "Bartholomew Fair" which satirized Calamy and other Presbyterians. The King himself was in attendance in October with Sheldon and other prelates to see imitations of Calamy and others praying and quoting Scripture (Greaves 1985: 55).

Another cruel blow was struck by the Governors of Sion College, who on 2 April, 1661, ordered Calamy to close the passage way which had connected his residence to the College since 1643. Because of his lameness, the Board at first relented, but then a year later issued an order closing the opening (Pearce 1913: 92).

On 31 October 1661, Calamy preached another sermon which was published, "The Happinesse of Those Who Sleep in Jesus" (published in 1662). He delivered it at the funeral of Lady Anne Waller, wife of his friend Sir William Waller. Amidst the political turmoil, Calamy may have himself taken some comfort in his portrayal of the "blessed, comfortable sleep" which he said awaits the saints after death while they await resurrection to heaven. (Greaves 1985: 55).

In January, 1662, the House of Commons passed a bill ordering the ouster from churches of any ministers not in episcopal orders. The Lords amended the bill to exempt Presbyterian clergy, and Calamy and others expressed their gratitude. However, Commons refused to accept the revision, and on 19 May Charles agreed to accept the Act of Uniformity, as the bill was called, giving it royal assent on 29 July, 1662. (Greaves 1985: 56).

The Act sought to perpetuate the Elizabethan Settlement of 1559. Only Episcopal ordination was recognized as valid. Clergy had to make a public declaration of assent to the contents of the revised prayerbook, with its anti-Puritan slant. They also had to renounce violence against the King, reject the Solemn League and Covenant, and promise to conform to the Church of England's liturgy. Ministers who did not comply by 24 August, 1662, were to be deprived on their living and subject to three months in prison if they preached again. (Matthews 1934: xii). A total of 936 ministers were ejected, 50 in London. In addition to Calamy, an Aldermanbury lecturer, a Mr. Lee (or Loe) was ejected (Matthews 1934: 329; Hatton 1708(I): 363).

Standing once more on principle, Calamy refused to endorse the Act of Uniformity. However, a plan was developed, with the support of King Charles, through which Calamy and other selected ministers would be exempted, if they agreed to read Common Prayer in their churches. On 27 August, 1662, Calamy and the others sent a petition to the King requesting exemption. The petition read as follows:

> May it please Your most Excellent Majesty,
>
> Upon former Experience of Your Majesty's Tenderness and Indulgence to Your Obedient and Loyal Subjects, (in which Number we can with all Clearness reckon ourselves) we some of the Ministers within Your City of London, who are likely by the Act of Uniformity to be cast out of all publick Service in the Ministry, because we cannot in Conscience conform to all Things requir'd in the said Act, have taken the Boldness humbly to cast ourselves and Concernments at Your Majesty's Feet, desiring that of Your Princely Wisdom and Compassion, you would take some effectual Course whereby we may be continu'd in the Exercise of our Ministry, to teach your People Obedience to GOD and Your Majesty. And we doubt not but by our Dutiful and Peaceable Carriage therein, we shall render ourselves not altogether unworthy of so great a
>
> Favour. (as cited by Greaves 1985: 57).

Charles presented the petition to the Privy Council the next day, but Calamy's old nemesis, Bishop Sheldon, who had already dismissed Calamy and the others, opposed it. The King relented and the petition was denied. Thus ended Calamy's 23 years as perpetual curate of St. Mary's.

The Aldermanbury parishoners stood behind Calamy as best they could. At a "full and ample Vestry" on 4 June, 1662, with 110 names given and 30-40 other "substantial householders in attendance" it had been decided to give "Edmund Calamy our Pastor" use of the house on Addle Street (3560aI, 64). This explains why Calamy continued to live in the parish after his dismissal.

Even before submitting the petition to the King, on 17 August, Calamy preached his farewell sermon on the text 2 Samuel 24:14. He apparently sensed that the petition would be denied. In his message Calamy asserted that "straits and sufferings for God are not worth the name of straits, "for when we suffer for God's sake, or a good conscience, these troubles are so sweetened by the consolations of Heaven, that they are no troubles at all." The preacher who stood before Parliament and called for the members to repent could not resist one last prophetic opportunity. We might expect Calamy to show gratitude for the parish's support. Instead, to the parishoners of St. Mary's he said:

> You have had the Spirit of God seven and thirty years in faithful
> Ministry of the Word, knocking at the door of your hearts, but many of you
> have hardened your hearts. Are there not some of you ... I only put the
> question, that begin to loath the Manna of your souls and look back
> towards Egypt again? Are there not some of you have itching ears, and
> would fain have Preachers that would feed you with dainty phrases, and
> begin not to care for a Minister that upsets (?) your Consciences, speaks
> to your hearts and souls, and would force you into heaven by frighting you
> out of your sins.

Some of the parish were "sermon proof," he claimed, for they sleep and scoff away sermons. Like the Church of Laodicea, mentioned in the Book of Revelation, they were, he said, neither hot nor cold, but lukewarm. "Therefore," he said, "God may justly spew you out of his mouth."

However, this was not to be Calamy's last sermon at St. Mary's. After his ejection from the pulpit he continued to attend church and to speak in his home and in the open. Meanwhile, the church could not find a replacement. Calamy's friend John Tillotson was elected but refused to serve (Greaves 1985: 57). Tillotson was Vicar of St. Lawrence Jewry, just around the corner from Aldermanbury on Gresham Street, and a monument to him is still in that church. He went on to become Archbishop of Canterbury and author of the Great Thanksgiving in the Book of Common Prayer.

The account books for 1662 show no less than 17 preachers during 1662 (Carter 1913: 114). On 1 December, the Vestry sent five members of the committee of sixteen chosen to select a new minister to meet with Calamy and seek his advice on how to proceed (Chancery Petitions 1887: 71). Calamy could hardly have been surprised when on 28 December, 1662, the preacher invited to preach at St. Mary's failed to appear. The congregation pleaded with Calamy to preach, and he gave a sermon he had obviously been waiting to deliver. It was entitled "Eli Trembling Before the Ark." Calamy apparently had already consulted with lawyers who advised him that an occasional sermon would not violate the Act of Uniformity (Greaves 1985: 58).

Church authorities saw the situation differently. Bishop Gilbert of London charged Calamy with preaching without a license. The mittimus charged that Calamy did twice (26 August and 28 December, 1662) in the Church of St. Mary Aldermanbury "presume and take upon himself (without any lawfull approbation and license thereunto) to preach or read two Several Sermons or Lectures before the Congregation." Presumably the August date was as a result of Charles urging him to continue to preach after dismissal until the Petition could be acted upon.

Calamy was found guilty and was sentenced on 5 January 1663 to three months at Newgate prison. Calamy asked the court if he could voluntarily surrender on 6 January, which he did.

What did Calamy say in his celebrated sermon? According to the published version Calamy interpreted the ark of God as a type for the Church of Christ. Calamy warned against loss of the ark of God from the nation. He left no doubt as to his view of his dismissal, saying that when the Ark is gone "ministers are driven into corners." He also warned against the presence of Jesuits and priests in England. He claimed that his words were not premeditated to them. In the several months since his dismissal, his attitude toward the parish had softened, for he said, "it was the great respect I had to you of this parish, whom I shall ever own, and praise God for, as long as I have breath in me ... [that] would not let me send you home this morning without a sermon."

Soon after Calamy's entrance into Newgate prison, Newgate Street was blocked with the coaches of people visiting him. As a result of the popular support for Calamy and perhaps to garner Presbyterian support for his Declaration of Indulgence issued on 26 December, two days before Calamy's "illegal sermon," the King ordered his release on 13 January (Goss 1944: 154 and Greaves 1985: 58-59).

Calamy's sermon and imprisonment inspired a public controversy. A pamphlet entitled "Perez Uzza. Or, A Serious Letter Sent to Master Edm. Calamy Touching his Sermon at Aldermanbury December the 28th" appeared. The pamphlet attacked Calamy for showing contempt of Parliament, offending a gracious sovereign, disturbing a quiet government, violating the trust and affection of his many admirers, and troubling the Bishop. In his sermon Calamy had sarcastically pointed out the decline in church attendance since the Act of Uniformity. The author of the above pamphlet claimed that congregations were thin "not because their ministers are removed into corners, as you say, but because they came to hear men not the Word of God." Calamy, the author claimed, was guilty of meddling in political matters. "Our business," he wrote, "is to discover to the people the state of their souls; let those in Authority shew them the state of the Government; ..." Ironically, the letter is signed "Your affectionate friend in our Common Savior."

Calamy's imprisonment also sparked support. An undated Broadside called "A poem upon the imprisonment of Mr. Calamy in Newgate," written by Robert Wild, who himself had been dismissed under the terms of the Act of Uniformity, offered the following doggerel in Calamy's defense.

> Thanks be to the Bishop and his good Lord Mayor
> Who turn'd the Den of Thieves into a House of Prayer:
> And may some Thief by you converted be,
> Like him who suffer'd in Christ's company.
> First, it is prov'd that you being dead in law
> (As if you car'd not for that death a straw!)
> Did walk and haunt your church, as if you'd scare
> Away the Reader and his Common Prayer.
> Nay 'twill be proved you did not only walk,
> But like a Puritan your Ghost did talk.
> Dead, and yet preach! there Presbyterian slaves
> Will not give over preaching in their graves.

With reference to the multitude of visitors, the author says:

> Good men, good women, and good Angels come,
> And make your Prison better than your home.
> Now may it be so till your foes repent
> They gave you such a rich imprisonment.

On 2 March, 1663, Calamy and several other nonconformists were called before the King. Charles told them that if they would support his policy of indulgence, he would allow them to return to their livings (Greaves 1985: 59). However, no agreement was reached, perhaps because Calamy and his colleagues feared the toleration for Catholics which would result from the Indulgence.

The same year an Anglican attack on Calamy and other Presbyterians was published under the title "Evangelium Armatum. A Specimen or Short Collection."

It was a collection of excerpts from their writings on reformation in the church with rebuttals.

There is no evidence to suggest Calamy again preached at Aldermanbury, but he did continue to live in the parish and speak in his home after Sunday evening services as long as he was able. He also channeled funds for the support of needy nonconformist ministers. Little else is known about his final years.

Edmund Calamy died on 29 October 1666. After the Great Fire of 3 September he had been driven through the devastation of his beloved parish and fell into despair. His grandson wrote, "He went home and never came out of his Chamber more; but dy'd within a Month" (Matthews 1934: li). He had asked to be buried beneath the reading desk where he had delivered so many erudite and pointed lectures and sermons. The debris was so deep after the Fire that the exact location of the desk was unknown. He was buried as close as could be guessed on 6 November (Goss 1944: 154).

An admirer of Calamy wrote the following epitaph for St. Mary's most illustrious curate: (Anonymous n.d.: Elegie)

> Here a poor Minister of Christ doth lie,
> Who did indeed a Bishoprick deny.
> When his Lord come, then, the World shall see,
> Such humble ones the Rising Men shall be.
> How may Saints whom he had sent before,
> Shouted to see him enter Heaven's door?
> There his blest Soul beholds the face of God,
> While we below groan at our Ichabod.
> Under his burned Church his body lies,
> But shall itself a Glorious Temple rise.
> May his kinde Flock, when a new Church they make,
> Call it St. Edmundsbury for his sake.

Some of Calamy's writings were posthumously published. The Art of Meditation or A Discourse of the Nature, Necessity, and Excellency thereof, With Motives to, and Rules for the better performance of that most important Christian Duty (1680) is a collection of sermons on Genesis 24:63 based on notes of a listener. Calamy explained that God requires all people: men and women, nobility and commoners to meditate. He distinguished between sudden, short, and occasional meditation and solemn, set and deliberate meditation. In his typically pragmatic manner, Calamy clearly explained how to meditate seriously, emphasizing that it must not only be emotional and speculative but practical and reflective. Among the topics upon which he thought people should meditate are death, judgment, heaven, hell, God, Christ, the Holy Ghost, and one's self. The work includes a frontispiece engraving of Calamy, shown in his Puritan clerical robe, looking rather tired and forlorn (see Figure 4.1).

Conclusion

Some of Calamy's more memorable sayings were included in a collection of aphorisms published as Saints Memorials: or, Words Fitly Spoken, Like Apples of God in Pictures of Silver (1674). Among the collected sayings of Edmund Calamy is one which reflects the character of the prophetic Presbyterian prelate of Aldermanbury:

Though Truth in these Erronious days be unsettled,

yet labour to get your Consciences settled.

Edmund Calamy certainly lived by that precept. He stood on principle, regardless of the consequences, and he stood for moderation, at a time when extremism was the fancy. He helped modify strict Calvinism during the Westminster Assembly, in which he played so crucial a role. He supported Parliament and the First Civil War, but refused to endorse the radical positions of many leaders. He stood in opposition to his King, when his principles dictated, but supported the Sovereign when he felt it was right. He opposed rigid supporters of episcopacy on his right and sectaries on his left. His strong leadership helped prevent Presbyterian collapse in the 1650's and preserve Presbyterian independence and integrity in the 1660's. "Moved by conscience, his commitment to the Presbyterian cause remained unshaken ...." (Greaves 1985: 62).

In the Aldermanbury parish Calamy established a high standard for preaching and leadership. He would not be easy to replace, as we shall see in the next chapter.

Bibliography

Anonymous

    1650   "An Act for the Better Preventing and Supressing of Cursing," London: Edward Husband and John Field. 28 June.

no date "An Elegie on the Death of Edmund Calamy," London.

Axelrad, Arthur
 1980 "Elizabeth Minshull," <u>A Milton Encyclopedia</u>, vol. 6. ed. William Hunter, Jr. Lewisburg: Bucknell University, 146.

 1980 "Katherine Woodcock," <u>A Milton Encyclopedia</u>, vol. 8. ed. William Hunter, Jr. Lewisburg: Bucknell University, 176-177.

Beveridge, W.
 1904 <u>A Short History of the Westminster Assembly.</u> Edinburgh: T and T Clark.

Burton, Henry
 1645 "Truth Still Truth, Though Shut out of Doors." London.

Calamy, Edmund (1639-1662)
 1641 "God's Free-Mercy to England," preached before the House of Commons on 23 February, 1641.

   "Groanes for Liberty, presented to Parliament, by reasons of the prelates tyranny," (1641). Published under the acronym *Smectymnuus*, standing for Stephen Marshall, Edmund Calamy, Thomas Young, Matthew Newcomen, William Spurstowe.

   "England's looking-glasse," preached before the House on Commons on 12 December, 1641.

 1643 "The Noble Man's Pattern of True and Real Thankfulnesse," preached beforethe House of Lords on 15 June, 1643.

   "A Speech delivered at Guildhall on the occasion of desirig assistance from our brethren in Scotland in this warre," 16 October, 1643.

1644 "England's Antidote; Against the Plague of Civil Warre," preached before the House of Commons on 22 October, 1644.

"An Indictment Against England because of her Self-Murdering Divisions,"preached before the House of Lords on 25 December, 1644.

1645 "The Door of Truth Opened," in response to Henry Burton's "Truth Shut out of Doors," London, 1645.

1654 "The Monster of Self-Seeking, Anatomized," preached at St. Paul's on 10 December, 1654.

"Jus divinum ministerii evangelici, or the divine right of the Gospel-ministry,"London, 1654.

"The Saint's Transfiguration," preached at the funeral of Dr. Samuel Bolton, Master of Christ's College Cambridge at St. Martin's, Ludgate on 19 October, 1654.

1655 "Precepts for Christian Practice," London, 1655.

1658 "A Patterne for all, especially for Noble and Honourable Persons, To teach them how to die Nobly and Honourable," preached at the interment of the RighHonourable Robert Rich, Earl of Warwick. 1 May, 1658.

1662 "Farewell Sermon," preached at St. Mary, Aldermanbury on 17 August, 1662.

1662 "Eli Trembling before the Ark," preached at St. Mary, Aldermanbury on 28 December, 1662.
1680 The Art of Divine Meditation. London: Tho. Parkehurst,1680.

Calamy, Edmund (the younger)

1713 <u>Account of the Ministers, Lecturers, Masters and Fellows of Colleges, and Schoolmasters who were Ejected or Silenced</u>. 2 vols., with a 2 vol. continuation. London.

1718 "A Letter to Archdeacon Echard, upon the Occasion of his <u>History of England</u>: Wherein the true Principles of the Revolution are Defended; the Whigs and Dissenters Vindicated; Several Persons of Distinction Cleared from Aspersions; and A Number of Historical Mistakes Recify'd," 2nd ed. London: John Clark.

Carter, Pierson Cathrick
1913 <u>History of the Church and Parish of St. Mary the Virgin, Aldermanbury</u>. London: W. H. and L. Collinbridge.

Chancery Petition
1887 "Petition of the Parishoners to the Chancery Court in the matter of the Rectory Church and the City of London Parochial Charities Act of 1883," 26 November, 1887 (GL Pamphlet 113360)

Cliffe, J. T.
1984 <u>The Puritan Gentry: The Great Puritan Families of Early Stuart England</u>. London: Routledge and Kegan Paul.

Collinson, Patrick
1967 <u>The Elizabethan Puritan Movement</u>. Berkeley: University of California Press.

Drysdale, A. H.
1889 <u>History of the Presbyterians in England</u>. London.

Exeter, Peter Toon
1971 <u>God's Statesman: The Life and Work of John Owen</u>. Paternoster Press.

Greaves, Richard
    1985   Saints and Rebels: Seven Nonconformists in Stuart England. Atlanta: Mercer University Press.

Hatton, Edward
    1708   A New View of London. 2 vols. London: R. Chiswell, 1708.

Hill, Christopher
    1964   Society and Puritanism in Pre-Revolutionary England. 2nd ed. New York: Schocken.

    1965   Intellectual Origins of the English Revolution. Oxford: Clarendon.

    1980   The Century of Revolution, 1603-1714. New York: Norton.

Hole, Robert
    1989   Pulpits, Politics and the Public Order in England. Cambridge: Cambridge University Press.

Jenkins, William
    1652   "A Sermon Preached at St. Mary, Aldermanbury on the 5th Day of November, 1651, Being a Day Set Apart in Remembrance of that Great Deliverance from the Gunpowder Treason," London.

Kendall, R. T.
    1979   Calvin and English Calvinism to 1649. Oxford: University Press.

Kitching, C. J., ed.
    1980   London and Middlesex Chantry Certificates, 1648. London Record Society Publications XVI. London: The London Record Society.

Liu, Tai
    1973   Discord in Zion: The Puritan Divines and the Puritan Revolution, 1640-

       1660. International Archives of the History of Ideas, 61. The Hague: Nijhoff.

  1986   Puritan London: A Study of Religion and Society in the City Parishes. Newark: University of Deleware Press.

Malcolm, J. Peller
  1803   Londinium Redivivum: An Ancient History and Modern Description. London: John Nichols and Son.

Manning, Brian
  1973   Politics, Religion and the English Civil War. New York: St. Martin's Press.

Matthews, A.G.
  1934   Calamy Revised, Being a Revision of Edmund Calamy's "Account of the Ministers and others Ejected and Silenced, 1660-1662. Oxford: Clarendon.

Oliver, Dame Beryl
  1969   The Winston Churchill Memorial and the Church of St. Mary the Virgin, Aldermanbury: A Brief History. London: The Faith Press.

Pearce, E. H.
  1913   Sion College and Library. Cambridge: University Press.

Pearl, Valerie
  1961   London and the Outbreak of the Puritan Revolution: City Government and Politics, 1625-1643. London: Oxford University Press.

Pennington, Donald and Keith Thomas, ed.
  1978   Puritans and Revolutionaries: Essays in 17th Century History Presented to Christopher Hill. Oxford: Clarendon.

Richardson, Caroline
    1928   English Preachers and Preaching 1640-1670. New York: Macmillan.

Robinett, Allin P.
    1982   Allen Robinett and His Descendants in America. Unpublished manuscript Two Parts. Reproduced and revised in 1968 and 1982 by James M. Robinett.

Saillens, Emile
    1964   John Milton: Man, Poet, and Polemist. New York: Barnes and Noble.

Seaver, Paul
    1970   The Puritan Lectureships: The Politics of Religious Dissent. Stanford: Stanford University Press.

    1976 (ed.) Seventeenth Century England: Society in an Age of Revolution. New York: New Viewpoints.

Todd, Margo
    1988   Christian Humanism and the Puritan Social Order. Cambridge: University Press, 1988.

Tolme, Murray
    1977   The Triumph of the Saints. The Separate Churches in London: 1616-1649 Cambridge: University Press.

Udall, D.
    1663   "Perez uzza, or, A Serious letter sent to E. Calamy, 17 January 1663 touching his sermon at Aldermanbury." London.

Wild, R.
    1663   "A poem upon the imprisonment of Mr. Calamy in Newgate." London.

Wilson, A. N.

1983   The Life of John Milton. Oxford: Oxford University Press.

Wilson, John
1969   Pulpit in Parliament: Puritanism during the English Civil Wars, 1640-48. Princeton, N. J.: University Press.

Young, Percy
1980   Unpublished lecture on Edmund Calamy presented at the Church of St. Mary, Aldermanbury on November 14, as part of the University of Missouri, Columbia Chancellor's series on British Church Music.

Yule, George
1981   Puritans in Politics: The Religious Legislation of the Long Parliament. The Courtenay Library of Reformation Classics. Appleford, England: Sutton Courtenay Press.

CHAPTER FIVE: THE PHOENIX OF ALDER-MANBURY (1662-1677): THE PLAGUE, GREAT FIRE, AND REBUILD-ING BY SIR CHRISTOPHER WREN

Introduction

Finding a replacement for Edmund Calamy proved no easy task for the Vestry. Since about two thousand ministers had, like Calamy, refused to endorse the Act of Uniformity, the supply was low. In addition, Calamy's long tenure and reputation would have caused any potential successor to think carefully before accepting the curacy of Aldermanbury.

The events which transpired in the decade after Calamy's death were, in many ways, the most tumultuous and most glorious in the parish's long history. The parish survived the Plague of the Summer of 1665 only to be devastated by the Great Fire of September, 1666. The total destruction of the Church of St. Mary, Aldermanbury, became the occasion for the creation of the building which still stands, designed by the greatest English architect of any age—Sir Christopher Wren (See Figures 5.1 and 5.4). From the records of the church and the extensive documentation of the plague, fire, and Wren rebuilding of London, we can paint a fairly complete picture of this remarkable epoch, perhaps the centerpiece in the story of the Phoenix of Aldermanbury.

Before we turn to the story of the devastation of the parish and the rebuilding of the church, we will set the context by returning to the story of England and London during the reign of Charles II.

The Stuarts (continued)

<u>The Later Years of Charles II (1666-1685)</u>

Party politics as it would develop over the following years began to emerge during Charles' Cavalier Parliament. Charles' second "ministry," called the Cabal (the letters happened by chance to be the initials of its five members), was felled by the king's religious policy. Whether prompted by the Treaty of Dover (see. ch. 4), or by his own tolerant temper, the king issued in 1672 "A Declaration of Indulgence for Tender Consciences," a decree of toleration for Catholics and Dissenters. Charles' brother James, Duke of York, converted to Catholicism (or publicly acknowledged his faith). Dissenters and Anglicans alike assumed the decree was mostly for Catholic benefit. Parliament riposted with the Test Act (1673), excluding from public office all who refused Anglican communion. The Catholic disabilities were removed only by the early 19th century reform laws. The Cabal collapsed in the initial controversy.

The seeds of the Tory party, party of the King and High Church, were sown when Thomas Osborne, soon to be the Earl of Danby, became the king's new parliamentary leader, precisely because he was a prominent supporter of the king. Osborne also pioneered another important aspect of party politics, the lubrication of the legislative process with bribes and patronage. Opposition was organized by the Earl of Shaftesbury.

The Green Ribbon Club (1675) is said to mark the birth of the Whig Party with its platform of "No Popery," parliamentary supremacy, and personal liberty. Both party names were slurs, coined by the opposition. "Tory" came from a Gaelic word meaning "a pursued person" and was used to describe an Irish outlaw. It is no surprise that "Tories" have preferred to be called "Conservatives." "Whig" comes from a Scottish word used to describe persons who opposed Charles I in 1648. The term eventually gave way to "Liberal" in the 1850's.

The long honeymoon between Charles and the Cavalier Parliament was obviously coming to an end. He dissolved it in 1679. Charles was thereafter plagued by the sort of Parliaments that Stuart kings seemed to attract (and possibly deserve). The first "Whig" Parliament was returned in 1679. Before Charles could stop it, it had passed the Habeas Corpus Act, establishing in legislation the old common law right requiring that persons arrested be shown both the reasons and the authority for the arrest. It also seemed clear that they would pass an act excluding the Catholic Duke of York from succession to the throne and naming Charles' illegitimate son, the Protestant James, Duke of Monmouth, as the heir, so Charles dissolved his second Parliament in one year.

Another Whig Parliament in 1680, bent on exclusion, was dissolved before it could be seated. Charles called yet another in 1681 and the country once again returned a Whig majority. This Parliament was called to meet in Tory Oxford, a safe distance from the London mob. But Charles suddenly dismissed it before any work was done. The king struck at Whig power by revoking town charters and issuing new ones that insured Tory magistrates who would mete out the Stuart version of justice. Whigs and Dissenters were harshly treated, while Tory clergy and squires praised a doctrine of subservience to royal authority.

Protestant extremism did have its own last hurrah in 1678, with the publicizing of the "Popish Plot," a supposed Jesuit plot to murder the King, burn London, invade England with French and Irish troops and give Protestants a choice between conversion and death. The plot appears to have been the invention of a professional informer, Titus Oates, who will figure later in our narrative, when we return to this period in the next chapter. An anti-Catholic campaign followed, with wide popular support.

The last years of Charles' reign were peaceful and apparently enjoyed by those not targeted by the likes of Oates, or Stuart "justice." Thanks to Charles' French patron Louis XIV, French taxpayers supported the English government. Sycophants in the English court spoke of a "second Augustan age," an assertion for which the architecture of Sir Christopher Wren and his associates may have been the only visible evidence. Stuart absolutism had crept back into English life, unheralded except by Whig leaders in continental exile.

Charles was felled by a stroke at the age of 56, in February 1685. His good humor seems to have stayed with him to the end, for he apologized for taking so long to die. However, his failure to deal adequately with the problem of succession would bring England once more to the verge of Civil War.

What saved England and enabled the nation to enter the modern political age will occupy us in the next chapter. In the remainder of the present chapter we will focus our attention on the "death and rebirth" of the City of London and the Aldermanbury parish and church during the decade following the death of Edmund Calamy.

Finding a Successor for Calamy

The Accounts for 1662 show that John Tillotson, Vicar of St. Lawrence, Jewry, had preached twice after Calamy's expulsion (Carter 1913: 114). However, when a "full Vestry" voted on 6 December 1662 to make Tillotson Calamy's successor at a stipend of £100 annually and perquisites, with the promise to pay a reader, Tillotson refused. He probably knew how much Calamy was being paid and was offended by the offer. Perhaps it was not a serious one. In any event, as we have already noted, Tillotson later became the Archbishop of Canterbury.

On 28 January, 1663, another full vestry met and agreed to offer the position to Richard Martyn "for soe long tyme as the pishe and he can agree." In other words, Martyn was to be a temporary curate. Like Calamy Martin had been ejected. He was later to serve at St. Michael's Wood Street (Matthews 1934: 342). On 22 April the Vestry decided to hold off on the choice of a "settled minister" (Carter 1913: 47-48). Whether this was a protest against the dismissal of Calamy or a matter of necessity we cannot judge, but by early 1664 the Bishop had communicated with the parishoners demanding to know "why the parish did not chuse a Minister and also to let them know hee had power to put one in but he did rather desire the parish would chuse one themselves and he would confirme him." (Carter 1913: 48). The Vestry responded that a minister would be chosen by Easter.

On 11 February 1664 four names were placed in nomination for the curacy—Dr. Walker, Mr. Potter, Mr. Richard Martyn, and Mr. Pearholl. Dr. Anthony Walker was chosen at a salary of £100 plus payment of a reader. Walker apparently did not think this was enough, for on 22 February the Vestry agreed to raise the offer to £150 if Dr. Walker would preach three sermons a week (the earlier offer mentioned two) (Carter 1913:48). The pulpit was filled by various ejected ministers, including Richard York on 3 July 1664 (Matthews 1934: 552).

By Fall the call of Dr. Walker was still not resolved. At a Vestry on 21 October it was reported that Dr. Walker wanted £200 (the same as Calamy had made) with the provision that he pay the reader and find a house, and that he would preach three sermons a week for three quarters of the year. After "serious debate" a vote was taken and the Vestry agreed to Walker's terms. Dr. Walker then joined the meeting and offered to preach the three sermons "if it please the Lord to continue his strength." He asked for security for the £200.

The Vestry apparently resisted this demand until Walker went to the Bishop. On 3 November a "general Vestry" agreed to give the security and ordered the Churchwarden to tell Walker to come at once to begin his duties. Still Walker was not satisfied and the dispute dragged into 1665, with the parish finally agreeing to put the parish lands up as security. Walker apparently assumed the duties of curate, but not fully. On 14 March 1666 the parishoners were informed that the Bishop would not allow Walker "to stay till Michaelmas before he comes thoroughly to this parish." On 1 April 1666 Walker informed the parishoners that he could not comply with the Bishop's order and asked them to "chuse whom they please." It was then decided "that any parishoner may bring his friends to preach for approbation he giving timely notice to the Churchwardens" (Carter 1913: 50).

The uncertainty over Walker did not keep the Vestry from attending to other business of the Church. At a meeting on 9 June 1665 it was decided to repair the Vestry and Church, with heated debate over how to pay for the repairs (Ms. 3570aI:67). Malcolm writes that a vestry room was added to the church over part of the former cloisters at this time (Malcolm 1803: 127).

The Plague and Great Fire of London (1665-1666)

The plague which swept through London in 1665 took its toll in Aldermanbury. The General Bill of Mortality for the year ending 19 December, 1665, showed that of the 181 persons buried in the parish, 109 had died of the plague. Several surrounding parishes were harder hit. In St. Michael, Bassishaw 164 were listed as plague victims; in St. Alban's, Wood Street, 121; and in St. Alphage, London Wall, 115. In St. Lawrence Jewry, however, the Bill listed only 48 plague deaths. (Bell 1951: after 320). The official total for all of London was 68,596 dead from the plague. So in comparison to other City churches, the official toll in Aldermanbury was about average.

The first signs of the plague appeared in London in March, 1665. However, the first recorded plague death occurred in early May. The first recorded burial due to the plague in Aldermanbury was during the week of 27 June. The first to die may have been a temporary curate. One source claims that on 21 June 1665 "John Pechell, curate of St. Mary, Aldermanbury (it had neither rector nor vicar), died at his post" (Hennessy 1898: 299). While many clergy fled with their well-to-do parishoners to the country to avoid the plague, some, like Mr. Pechell, stayed. Former Aldermanbury curate Dr. Anthony Walker, now serving at St. Katherine, Coleman Street, was another who remained to minister in spite of the plague (Bell 1951: 227n).

Almost all of the plague deaths in the parish were between 1 August and 3 October. During that period, the Bills of Mortality listed 106 plague deaths in Aldermanbury. During the same weeks nearly 9,000 people died in the 97 parishes within the wall. The worst single week in Aldermanbury was 12-19 September, 1665, when 16 of the 20 deaths officially recorded in the parish were attributed to the plague.

The plague came on its victims insidiously. First there were chills, then shaking, followed by nausea and vomiting. Some people became drowsy. Headaches were common, as was a high fever. Two to four days after the onset of symptoms a rash, called "botches" or "tokens," appeared. This gave rise to the phrase "spotted death" to refer to the plague. In the final stages victims became delirious and their hearts palpitated rapidly. Death came as a relief from the intense suffering.

The houses in which plague victims were found were closed and padlocked for forty days, a red cross marking them. Those inside who had not yet come down with the plague were almost certainly condemned by their entrapment. The practice of sealing houses caused many to hide plague victims, resulting in the likelihood of a lower official count than actually died. The most thorough historian of the plague, Walter Bell, estimates that the death toll in greater London was closer to 100,000 (Bell 1951: 20). Each morning cries of "bring out your dead" would be heard as death carts made their way through the streets.

Care for the plague victims was worse than the disease. "Nurses" were poor persons paid by parishes to go into plague houses. Often their ventures into homes was only to strangle the sick and steal their goods, then shut up the houses once again. (Bell 1951: 108-110). As in most other times of disaster, the weak and the powerless suffered the most. Almost all persons of means fled the city, some taking the plague with them.

Many London clergy interpreted the plague as the judgment of God on a sinful city. Calamy would certainly have done so had he still been preaching. The records show that on 16 September 1665 the Rev. Thomas Vincent, preaching at the funeral of another minister, Abraham Janeway, "frightened his listeners, ... by a Vision of Hell from beneath moved by the numbers of guests received into its chambers" (Bell 1951: 222). A letter from the printer in the collected bills of mortality advises readers,

"O let us not imagine that they [who died of the plague] were greater Sinners than we the Survivors! ... Except we speedily and seriously Repent; we shall all likewise perish ..." (Bills of Mortality 1665: 17).

The Churchwarden's Accounts for 1665 show 14.19.00 spent for "sea coals to burn in the streets for four days and four nights by order from ye Lord Mayor" and 127.10.03 for "relief of poor, visits by Drs. and nurses, and charges for burial." After the repair of the Church 5s was paid for perfume for the church (Carter 1913: 114).

From 12 January until 9 May 1666 25.10.00 was spent for ministers to preach (Carter 1913: 114). On 3 June Mr. John Harper was selected as minister at a stipend of £140 yearly.

The fire which became known as the Great Fire of London broke out in a baker's shop on Pudding Lane on 2 September, 1666. It devastated the City north of the Thames for five days, destroying virtually the entire parish of Aldermanbury. The Church of St. Mary was totally consumed, leaving only a mound of debris.

Even before the Plague the City was in poor condition. In 1661 John Evelyn wrote to Parliament expressing dismay. "That this glorious and ancient City ... should wrap her stately head in clouds of smoke and sulphur, so full of stink and darkness, I deplore with just indignation," he said. He complained of the congestion of the buildings and the narrowness of the streets. (cited in Milne 1986: 14). The city was indeed a fire trap.

Whether the fire began by accident or negligence in Thomas Faryner's bakery we do not know. Nevertheless, when it started it spread rapidly. The riverfront was packed with combustibles—timber, oil, and pitch. The houses were tinder dry after a hot summer. Fire equipment was pathetic—leather buckets, axes, and fire hooks. Each parish had its own equipment, and coordination was difficult. An unusally strong east wind fanned the flames, spreading them over the greater part of the City. By the afternoon of 2 September, the fire had destroyed the water front buildings and was on its way toward Cheapside.

The fire started on a Sunday. By Tuesday it was the sweeping up Ludgate Hill, destroying the medieval, already damaged St. Paul's Cathedral. The Guildhall was consumed the same day. Almost certainly, St. Mary, Aldermanbury, burned down at about the same time. The efforts of the Lord Mayor to fight the fire proved futile, so the King put the Duke of York (the future James II) in charge. He ordered gunpowder used to blow up houses and create a fire break. The fire burst through the city gates to the west and north. The northern edge of the City and areas to the east, including the the Tower, were saved by the direction of the wind. The wind died down Tuesday night, and the fire was out by Friday.

Rev. Vincent also saw the judgment of God in the Fire. On the first day he wrote that "the time of London's fall is come: the fire hath received its commission from God to burn down the City; therefore all attempts to hinder it are in vain" (cited in Milne 1986: 34). On Monday he vividly described the fire in these words: "Rattle, Rattle, Rattle was the noise which the fire struck upon the ear round about, as if there had been a thousand iron chariots beating upon the stones" (Milne 1986: 38). On Tuesday, when half the City (including Aldermanbury) was consumed, he wrote, "... the yellow smoke of London ascendeth upon the heaven like the smoke of a great furnace; a smoke so great, as darkened the sun at noon-day ..." (Milne 1986: 57). When the wind turned on Wednesday and the fire began to ebb, he claimed that the Lord was taking pity on London, leaving a pious "remnant" (Milne 1986: 57).

The cost of the fire was staggering. Over 13,000 homes had been destroyed. 87 parish churches and St. Paul's Cathedral were consumed, as were 52 company halls. The Guildhall, Royal Exchange, Custom House, Sessions House, Newgate Jail, three city gates, and four bridges were in rubble. Over £2,000,000 of printed books were burned. The total cost was estimated at £10,000,000. Miraculously, despite the property damage, few lives were lost, as people had time to flee the raging conflagration. (Milne 1986: 77).

Although a Frenchman, Robert Hubert, confessed to having started the fire as part of a "popish plot" and was executed in October, the official Parliamentary report declared it an accident, caused "by the hand of God upon us, a great wind and the season being so very dry" (Milne 1986: 78).

The Effects of the Fire on Aldermanbury

After the fire the parishoners of St. Mary's were instructed to go a half mile east for services at St. Peter le Poor on what is now Broad Street (Malcolm 1803: 116). There is no evidence the parishoners followed this directive. Instead, they soon began the monumental task of building a new church on the site of the old. Some congregations set up temporary "tabernacles" in the ruins of their churches for services, but the vestry minutes do not mention such a practice in Aldermanbury.

In 1671 arrangements were made to hold services in Brewer's Hall, in the parish until the church was rebuilt. The minutes of the Court of the Brewer's Company record that on 4 July, 1671, an application was received from "Dr. Ford, minister; Mr. Page and Mr. Holgate, common consollmen [sic] and Mr. Atkinson Churchwarden of Aldermanbury parish for leave from the Company for the Parishoners of the said parish to be meeting (?) in the Rooms now used by the Company for their Court Room on Sabbath dais [sic] for that their parish church is not yet rebuilt" (Ms. 5445/20: 424). The leave is "until further order." The parishoners agree to be be careful not to damage company goods and pay for them if they do.

The parish apparently had an association with Brewer's Hall which pre-dated the Great Fire. Ward meetings and important parish meetings often met in the hall, and Ascension Day feasts for parishoners were also sometimes held in Brewer's Hall. (Carter 1913: 95).

It was not uncommon for city livery companies to allow dissenting congregations to hold services in their halls. By 1689 a dozen companies had let their halls to Presbyterian, Independent, and Baptist groups. In part this reflects the close association of the mercantile community with such groups (Rude 1971: 112-113).

On 14 November 1666 Churchwardens Edward Jackson and Dan Davis were ordered to "take present care for the taking up of the lead in and about the Church and for the casting of it into Pigs" (Ms. 3570aI, 68). This was completed by December. The accounts show that £8.2.6 was paid to laborers for removing stones and rubbish and gathering up the lead and bell metal. 6.18.00 was paid "to the plummer for casting the ould lead into piggs." It was a good investment, for £105 was received for the lead and 41.10.00 for the bell metal (Carter 1913: 115). The Vestry ordered that the money realized "be disposed of towards the payment of monies due and owing for the building of a new Vestry and repairing the Church and also for clearing the Parish from the charge of those children that appertain to them" (Ms. 3570aI, 68-69). So before a new building project could begin, the old one had to be paid for (in spite of the fire) and the parish accounts cleared.

The Vestry also had to deal with questions surrounding the rebuilding of houses in the parish owned by the Church. At a meeting on 4 June 1667 of seven householders and the two churchwardens it was ordered that Mrs. Elizabeth Herring be awarded a lease of 61 years for "her late dwelling house which was demolished by the late dreadfull fire." The house was located on Love Lane, next to the Church. It was agreed to add a part of the Churchyard to her lease. She agreed to pay a rent of

£6 yearly and £30 as a fine. Minutes of the Court set up by the Fire Act (Jones 1966: Fire Act A-357 BM 5065-47) show that this arrangement was validated on 12 November 1667.

On 15 March 1669 Churchwardens Dan Davis and William Thacker were charged with removal of stones from the Church of St. Mary Magdalen, Milk Street, which were being cleared for a market (Ms. 3570aI:70-71). These stones were later used in the rebuilding of St. Mary, Aldermanbury. The stones were purchased at a cost of £28.13.04. This amount was later recovered from the city funds set aside for the churches by then Churchwarden John DuBois (Ms. 25,539:56.2). According to the city accounts, 12.03.06 was paid to workmen and laborers and 12.17.00 for carriage of the stones.

On 6 October 1669 a general Vestry chose Walter Pell, a Merchant Taylor, as Treasurer and Thomas Page as Deputy Treasurer for the purpose of receiving all money "voluntarily given collected or raised for and towards repairing or new building of the Parish Church of St. Mary the Virgin Aldermanbury" (Carter 1913: 25).

Also in 1669 Edmund Calamy's son Edmund (himself a nonconformist minister) was holding services next door to an inn called the Seven Starres in Aldermanbury (Matthews 1934: 98). He had received a lease of a house in Bury Court from his father, and apparently remained in the parish after the fire. These may have been the services attended by the majority of Aldermanbury parishoners, but again the Vestry Minutes make no reference to them.

A note appended to the Churchwarden's Account Books claims that on 7 December, 1669, the Lord Mayor and Aldermen met and voted that St. Mary Aldermanbury "be one of the Parish Churches to be continued within the City of London."

The Parish after the Great Fire

From a roll found in the church safe, dated 1671, and the Ogilby and Morgan map of 1677, we can develop a fairly complete picture of the rebuilt parish (cf. Carter 1913:1-3 and Goss 1944:127-146).

At the southern end, on the East side of Aldermanbury was a coffeehouse and hotel, called the Baptist's Head, a name given during the Commonwealth. It was later called Aldermanbury Coffeehouse. It was situated next to Fountain's Court, built on the site of a mansion house. Next to the North were eleven houses, six owned by William Dyer, called Dyer's Court. To the North of Dyer's Court were two houses owned by the parish, several small tenements, then three more houses of the parish. Two faced Aldermanbury and the other, with a large garden, was inhabited by Judge George Jeffreys (see below). The side court of the Jeffrey's mansion led to Bassishaw Alley, which connected Aldermanbury with the Church of St. Michael Bassishaw.

To the North of Bassishaw Alley, at no. 20 Aldermanbury, was the rebuilt Axe Inn. A Vestry minute says that in 1670 Edward Jackson, who had acquired a 21 year's lease on the Inn in 1656, "atte ye Axe lent £10 towards the rebuilding of the church." The reconstructed Inn was surrounded by other buildings with sleeping quarters for nearly 100. It was a coaching inn, used by travelers between London and Liverpool (Lillywhite 1963: 94).

North of the Axe Inn lay the site of another Inn, George Inn, with an accompanying yard, called George yard. Records show that by July 1677 the Inn had not yet been rebuilt, but the Ogilvy and Morgan map of 1677 shows the location of the yard and Inn.

Again to the North on Aldermanbury were a series of small residences and Miller's Court, consisting of four houses. At the far northeast corner of the parish was Green School Court, with an entrance from London Wall.

On the West side of Aldermanbury, at the northern parish line, were four houses owned by Brewers Hall, just north of the intersection of Aldermanbury and Addle Street. In this northwest corner of the parish, north of Addle Street, was also some property owned by Sion College (formerly Elsing Spittal) and the Brewers Hall, which, as we have seen, served as the location or parish worship services from 1671 until the church was rebuilt. Adjacent to Brewers Hall may have been "Ye Old Cheshire Cheese Hotel," which was claimed to have been rebuilt by Wren by 1673. The Hotel is not shown on the Ogilby and Morgan map, however.

To the West of Brewers Hall, across Philip Lane, stood the Plaisters Hall, which was also rebuilt by Wren. It was partly in St. Alban's parish. At one time some children born in the hall became the source of dispute between the two parishes as to who was responsible for them. To the north of the Church on the West side of Aldermanbury were five houses (nos. 58-62).

To the West of the Church on Love Lane were two houses belonging to the Church (nos. 10-11 or 11-12). These are the houses rebuilt by Mrs. Elizabeth Herring and leased along with a portion of the churchyard. Running south from the south side of the street was Berry Court.

South of the Church on the west side of Aldermanbury was a house owned by Nicholas Stanton, standing at the corner of Aldermanbury and Love Lanes. He owned other parish houses. Two doors down was the house of Dr. Timothy Timms. Two brothers, John and Richard Chandler, lived in the next houses.

At the Southwest corner of the parish was the "Flying Horse," another inn. Behind it on the parish boundary was still another inn, the "Swan with Two Necks," located on Lad Lane (which in 1845 was absorbed into Gresham St.) (On the "Swan with Two Necks" see Lillywhite 1963: 562-564.)

The Rebuilding of the London Churches

The first act of Parliament for the rebuilding of London, passed in 1667, put a tax on coal coming into the City, but made no provision for the rebuilding of St. Paul's Cathedral and the city churches. A further act in 1670 increased the coal tax from one shilling per chaldron of coal to two shillings, and ordered that a portion be made available for reconstruction of the Cathedral and churches. The tax was increased again in 1677 to three shillings.

The warrant for the rebuilding of the city churches came on 17 May 1670. The warrant authorized the Archbishop of Canterbury, the Bishop of London, and the Lord Mayor of London to spend funds generated by the coal tax between 1 May 1670 and 24 June 1687. These three named Dr. Christopher Wren, Surveyor General of all his Majesty's works, "to direct and order the dimensions, formes, and modells" of the city churches "upon strict and diligent view and Surveigh of the present foundations and part standing of the said churches, with due care had to the Extent of the respective parishes, as now they are united" (Ms. 25,540/1:1-2). Wren must "contract with such Artisans, builders, and workmen as shall be employed therein" and "likewise to surveigh and take care for the orderly execution of the works and accompts ..." Appointed as Wren's assistants were Robert Hooke, one of the surveyors of the City of London, and Edward Woodroffe. Because of their significance, we will pause in our narrative to give attention to Wren and Hooke.

Excursus: Sir Christopher Wren and Robert Hooke

Sir Christopher Wren (1632-1723) is remembered today for his achievements in architecture. There lies the connection with St. Mary, Aldermanbury. However, that reputation came to him only in his middle years. In his earlier life he was noted for two things. He was a mathematical and scientific prodigy, accepted as an equal by the most distinguished researchers (John Evelyn described him as "that miracle of a youth"), whose scientific stature continued to grow. He was a charter member of the Royal Society, which did more to foster the development of the experimental method during this period than any other single group, and its president, 1681-1683. He was also a person of the most rational, irenic, and tolerant temperament. He literally embodied the ideal spirit of his time, the Enlightenment, the Age of Reason. His scientific bent and benevolent personality may explain why he so successfully transcended the rancor of the times.

Wren was the son of a Wiltshire priest, turned out of his living for royalist sympathies by the Puritan administration, and the nephew of Bishop Matthew Wren, devoted disciple of Laud. As a boy, while his father was a royal chaplain at Windsor, Wren played at the Castle with the future Charles II.

Despite his royalist associations during a time of Puritan ascendancy, young Christopher achieved a series of fellowships, his Oxford degrees, and his first professorship under the Cromwellian government. With the Restoration he achieved a place under Charles II and survived the convolutions of policy and personnel under the Anglican Charles, Catholic James II, and Protestants, William and Mary, Anne, and the Hanovers. He was finally deposed by his Whig detractors as a feeble old man who probably should have retired voluntarily.

During his student days at Oxford Wren had been an associate of the great scientific circle known as "the Invisible College." His flair for drawing and his knack with machinery made him valued as a scientific illustrator and an inventor and assembler of apparatus. In addition, he was a mathematical genius and skilled astronomer. Wren was reluctant to leave the Oxford setting, but in 1657 he assumed the professorship of astronomy at Gresham College, London. In 1661 he was given the prestigious Savilian Professorship of Astronomy at Oxford. The same year, before he had attained fame as an architect, he was given honorary doctorates for his work in science by both Cambridge and Oxford. Before he had designed a single structure, Wren had distinguished himself with innovations in physics, meteorology, geometry, and physiology.

Historians debate why Wren turned from his successful career in science to the more practical field of architecture. One reason may have been the absence of serious architectural theory in England. With the death of Inigo Jones in 1652, no one had stepped forward. Many were engaged in scientific inquiry. Architecture was a field Wren could dominate. Moreover, his interest in mathematics and physics together with his skill as a draughtsman and model builder were the perfect combination for success in building.

In 1661 Wren was invited to survey the harbor and fortification of Tangier, in North Africa, but he declined due to ill health. A year later he was given the assignment of designing the Sheldonian Theatre at Oxford. The structure, still in use over three hundred years later, was for university ceremonies. Reflecting Renaissance influence, Wren adopted a classical form, patterning the theatre after the Theatre of Marcellus in Rome. However, his innovation was an imaginatively designed set of timber trusses, which allowed for a large, unsupported and thus unobstructed ceiling space (on which a painting of the sky was done, to give the theatre a sense of natural openness).

About the same time Sheldon, now Bishop of London, was consulting Wren on the repair of the dilapidated Gothic St. Paul's Cathedral. Wren suggested remodelling the building as a quasi-Renaissance structure with round head windows and a dome, to harmonize with Inigo Jones' classical west porch.

In 1663 Wren accepted a commission from his uncle Matthew to design a chapel for Pembroke College, Cambridge, his first of several college buildings in Cambridge.

Wren's only trip abroad came in 1665 when he visited Paris for six months. In Paris he had a brief audience with the great Italian classicist architect and sculptor Bernini and studied French Renaissance designs.

Back in London, Wren's proposal for a remodeled St. Paul's was accepted in principle on 27 August, 1666, a week before the Great Fire. Between 5 and 11 September Wren determined the area of destruction in London and worked out a plan for rebuilding the City in a regular shape, with piazzas and long, wide avenues. However, like the plans submitted by Robert Hooke and others, Wren's was doomed because of the need for rapid reconstruction of the City along existing property lines.

After the fire Wren's life was busy. In addition to supervising the rebuilding of London churches, he somehow found time to design a new chapel for Emmanuel

College, Cambridge (1668) and a new library for Trinity College, Cambridge (1676), as well as surpervising various royal projects.

Of the 87 churches destroyed in the Great Fire, 51 were rebuilt under Wren's supervision. Those not rebuilt included some in the neighborhood of St. Mary, Aldermanbury (e.g., St. Mary Staining and St. John Zachary). Wren undoubtedly initiated the design of each church, although others, including Hooke, executed the basic plan. Although Wren was confined by the sites of the existing churches, often irregular and butted against other buildings, he had great freedom of design because no architectural precedents existed for Protestant churches in a classical style. Wren put his own stamp on each church, with remarkable results, as in St. Stephen, Walbrook (1672-1679), where he experimented with a dome. Wren's particular genius was to give each city church a unique tower, some Gothic and others enriched with classical expressions, creating a distinctive London skyline.

Wren began in the classic Paladian style favored by Inigo Jones. But in the course of his work he moved into the Baroque style. Indeed, he invented English Baroque architecture. St. Mary, Aldermanbury, is one of his transitional designs, with both Palladian and Baroque features.

While the city churches were under construction, Wren painstakingly and stubbornly worked to create his masterpiece, a new St. Paul's Cathedral. It took him over forty years to complete (1670-1711), but it remains one of the most remarkable buildings ever constructed, both from aesthetic and engineering perspectives. His initial St. Paul's design, the "First Model" of 1670, was first accepted, then rejected as too modest. His "Great Model (1673)," with a mammoth central dome, surrounded by eight domed sections supported on eight arches and a domed vestibule, was rejected by the Dean and Chapter of the Cathedral as "not enough of a Cathedral fashion." The "Warrant Design" (1674), a restrained Classical-Gothic amalgamation in the traditional cathedral style, was accepted, and actual work began in 1675. However, the cathedral Wren fashioned bears only a limited resemblance to the Warrant Design. The upper sections of the mammoth walls were mere screens, hiding the flying buttresses. The huge walls were necessary to support the drum and magnificent dome, which Wren did not begin until 1698 and which were not completed until 1711, when Wren was 79. The dome, with its hidden brick cone, surrounded by a timbered, outer shell, is considered one of the greatest architectural and engineering achievements of all time.

As Surveyor of the King's Works Wren completed a number of royal projects, among them: Chelsea Hospital for army veterans, new construction at Hampton Court Palace, and a hospital for seamen at Greenwich. All still stand as monuments to Wren's genius.

When Wren was finally dismissed as Surveyor General in 1718, he wrote, "as I am Dismiss'd, having worn out (by God's mercy) a long Life in the Royal service, and having made some Figure in the World, I hope it will be allow'd me to Die in Peace." That he did five years later. He was buried in the crypt of St. Paul's, in a simple tomb. A nearby Latin inscription, penned by his son, says it well: *Lector, si monumentum requiris, circumspice* ("Reader, if you seek a monument, look around").

Robert Hooke (1635-1703), in contrast to Wren, is remembered primarily as a scientist, mechanic, and inventor. The Royal Society made him its curator of experiments in 1662 and in 1665 he was appointed professor of geometry at Gresham College, London. His Micrographia is a classic work on the use of the microscope in which he also gave an accurate account of combustion (and praised Wren's achievements as a scientific illustrator). He stated the theory of elasticity, now known as "Hooke's Law." Hooke anticipated Isaac Newton in stating the Law of Inverse Squares, and claimed to have beat him to the draw on the entire theory of motion. Newton and Hooke, both known for their prickly personalities, nourished mutual detestation. That Wren maintained friendships with both is a testament to Wren's liberal and tolerant temper.

Like Wren Hooke was also an architect (or "surveyor" as it was then called). In 1667 he became Surveyor of the City, two years before Wren was named Surveyor General of the King's Works. Among Hooke's major designs were the College of Physicians, the new Bethlehem Hospital ("Bedlam") and Montague House. He also launched the rebuilding of a few affluent City Churches that could pay the cost before Parliament levied the Coal Tax.

Wren and Hooke carried on a productive scientific collaboration from the time they were both in London. They assembled astronomical telescopes of prodigious focal length in the yard at Gresham College and conducted joint experiments in other branches of science. Historians of science suspect that Wren assisted with the apparatus for many of Hooke's independent experiments.

As City Surveyor Hooke had an interest in all 51 of the churches slated for reconstruction. In fact, Hooke probably played a larger role than did Wren in the actual reconstruction. He kept a diary and records numerous joint tours with Wren of the works, interspersed with stops at coffee houses and inns where they discussed both construction projects and scientific matters.

Wren and Hooke's Rebuilding of St. Mary, Aldermanbury (1670-1677)

It would take twenty-five years and £265,000 to rebuild the 51 London parish churches. The main surge of church rebuilding came after 1677, when civic reconstruction had been completed. Only a relatively few churches were rebuilt by 1677. One was St. Mary, Aldermanbury.

The first stage in the rebuilding was the tearing down of ruins left standing after the fire. On 2 March 1670 the Commission overseeing the rebuilding of City Churches ordered Joshuah Marshall (see Figure 5.2) and Thomas Knight, Masons, to take down the walls and tower of St. Mary, Aldermanbury. The estimate of rubble was about 1068 cubic yards. They were to sort the rubble, separate the stone suitable for use in rebuilding and carry off the rest. Dr. Wren would then survey the stones they had set aside and instruct them to carry off any more material he deemed unsuitable for use in the reconstruction. The masons had to agree not to carry off any rag stone, iron, lead bell metal, or other materials belonging to the Church found in the ruins. They were to be paid £80, £30 up front, £20 when the stones were sorted, and £30 when the masons work was completed. (St. Paul's WE 16 f. 156).

On 13 June, 1670, the Archbishop, Bishop and Mayor approved a list of the first 15 churches to be rebuilt. They included several churches near St. Mary's (St. Lawrence, Jewry; St. Anne and Agnes; and St. Vedast alias Foster) but not Aldermanbury (Ms. 25,540/1:3). On the 17 June they decided to commit coal tax revenue to other churches which could advance money. However, parishes objected that it was difficult to raise money when the 15 had a lock on the coal tax income for the foreseeable future. So on 13 July it was decided to pay churches in £500 lots, in the same order as these parishes raised the money. (7).

This explains the entry of 30 November 1670 in the Vestry minutes: (Carter 1913: 25).

> At a meeting then holden the raising of monie for the rebuilding of the church the £500 being not yett raised and after the order read that no parish wch expectes the benefitt by yt imposition upon Coles shall pres (?) to meddell to rebuild their church and

alsoe the forme of subscription apoynted by the Ld Bishopp of Canterbury Ld Bishopp of London Lord maior of London was alsoe read. It was then desired that those persons whose names are registered will be pleased to take the pains or any three of them to receive the monies or subscriptions of and from all such persons who will give or lend any sum of monie for and towards the rebuilding the Church as aforesaid

Wm. Page	Mr. John Davies
Alderman Chandler	Mr. Tanckard
Esqr. Aske	Mr. Holgate
Mr. Duboyse	Mr. Winter
Mr. Jackson	Mr. Dan Davies

and the Churchwardens

Of this group Mr. Aske was an especially distinguished member of the Haberdashers. He initiated the famous Haberdashers School in 1690.

Also on 30 November 1670 "the choice of a minister was taken into consideration it being now some considerable time since Mr. Harper died." Dr. Conant was chosen, but since "he was a stranger to most of the Vestry" it was decided to hold action until the next meeting. (Carter 1913: 51) The delay proved costly. On 19 December Dr. Conant was chosen, but he had already been selected at Northampton. So on 29 December Dr. Simon Ford was elected at a yearly stipend of £150. It was also stipulated that if Dr. Ford accepted any other responsibility which would keep him from his duties, he must resign the living (Carter 1913: 52). Before calling Dr. Ford the Vestry had to satisfy a Committee appointed by the Common Council on City Ministers' maintenance that the parish would support a minister. The Vestry was ordered to appear at a meeting at the Guildhall "with an Account in writing under your hands of the name of the present Incumbent the value of the said tithes and Glebe per annum and your estimate of the Ministers perquisites in your parish per annum." The Vestry met on 26 December 1670 and drafted a response: (Carter 1913: 14)

The Parishoners of Aldermanbury are patrons to the living.
That the tithes of the Parish are £21 per annum, £11 is
appointed by the Will of the donor to 10 poor people and
a Sermon, £10 per annum is at the discretion of the Parish.
The Parish hath no glebe belonging to it. We are without

a Minister at present, but the Parish have unanimously chosen

Dr. John Conant for their Minister but have not yet his answer ...

This shows that Ford's name must have come to the Vestry unexpectedly. It also shows the parish's willingness to bend the truth. The parish still possessed the land upon which parish houses owned had stood before the fire, so there was indeed a glebe.

Dr. Ford was an accomplished preacher before he accepted the curacy at St. Mary's. Born about 1619 in Devonshire he had been educated at Magdalen Hall, Oxford (B.A., 1641). Because of his strong Puritan leanings he was expelled, but later returned to receive an M.A. (1648), B. D. (1650), and D.D. (1665). He had published major works on infant baptism, prayer, and the Psalms of David and a number of sermons. However, his most famous works were a series of four poems on the Great Fire. They earned him the title "laureate of the fire" (Aubin 1943: 4). They vividly describe the "sickening hurry, bewilderment, and terror of those frightful September days" (Aubin 1943: 6). He has been described as "a very able scholar, a noted preacher, and a most eloquent Latin poet" (Malcolm 1803:125).

This was a very busy and productive period in the life of the parish. On 1 January, 1671, the Vestry met and a list was presented of persons willing to loan money so that £500 could be guaranteed. The following were listed among the initial donors: Sir John Langham Kt. (£150), Walter Pell Esq. (£100, Robert Aske Esq. (£40). (Carter 1913: 26). On 1 July 1671 the Archbishop, Bishop and Lord Mayor authorized £500 to be repaid to St. Mary's after £28,150 had been received from the coal tax (Ms. 25,540/1:18). Subsequent £500 reimbursements were approved on 4 November, 1671 and 18 August 1673. The Vestry minutes (Carter 1913: 26) show another list of subscribers for £50. The entire amount was repaid to the parish in December, 1674.

The actual rebuilding of the church apparently began in 1672. Several pieces of evidence converge to support this assertion. The accounts for 1672 (Carter 1913: 115) show expenditures for "digging a pitt to burie ye bones." This suggests excavation of the church site in preparation for the rebuilding. The accounts also show 4.12.00 spent for a dinner of some of the parishoners with Dr. Renn (sic) and Robert Hooke, probably to discuss the design of the Church and to encourage them to get on with the project. Dinners for Wren and his assistants and craftsmen with vestries were not uncommon to speed up the rebuilding process (Cobb 1977: 34). The Churchwarden Account Book notes that £2.8.0 was spent in 1672 for what was apparently another dinner with the "Surveyor and Workmen."

The account of the charges for the rebuilding of the city churches (Ms. 25,539) confirms that the actual restoration began by 1672, and possibly even in 1671. One entry for smith work lists work done from 31 July 1671 onward.

The work went quickly. The basic stone work must have been completed by late Spring, 1672, for on 20 June, 1672, the City Churches Commission contracted with Matthew Bankes, Carpenter, for the roof. It was to include two compass windows on the bay of the roof on each side. All work was to be done "according to the direction of Dr. Christopher Wren." On 12 August, 1672 the Commission contracted with Mr. Nathaniell Cham, "Plomber," to lead the roof and provide the gutters "following the direction of Dr. Christopher Wren and such as he shall appoint." On 16 November the Commission appointed Danniell Davis to supply glass for the windows and John Turner as"joyner." Mr. Cham apparently failed to complete the "plombing" work, for on 21 November of the same year the Commission hired John Talbott to provide the "best Darbyshire lead" for the church, with all work "to be seen by persons as shall be appointed by Dr. Christopher Wren." (St. Paul's WE 16, f. 156).

The accounts for 1672 also list rent of Brewers Hall for at least 21 morning services. A Robert Thompson was paid 6.17.9 for a pulpit and 14 benches.

On 14 March 1672 at a Vestry meeting "it was decided that as the church was being rebuilt but not ready for use, and as Dr. Ford was still doing duty elsewhere, that part of his stipend should be kept back and allowed to accumulate so as to form a fund towards building a Vicarage" (Carter 1913: 52).

This scheme fell through and the next year (2 March 1673) the Vestry faced the fact that it did not have money enough to build a house for the curate. The Vestry decided to ask Dr. Ford to come "by the time as the Church shall be fitting to be preached inn."

The role of famous carver and sculptor, Grinling Gibbons (1648-1721), in the furnishing of the Church of St. Mary, Aldermanbury, is not clear. Gibbons' carvings in St. Paul's Cathedral, Windsor Palace, Hampton Court, Trinity College and elsewhere have rightly earned him the acclaim of history. He was indeed a master of his craft, whose artistry was and is unsurpassed. It is certain that Gibbons and his associates worked with Wren in providing carvings in some of the City churches. However, "the only ones that are documented and can be attributed to him with certainty are the altarpieces of St Mary Abchurch and St James's, Piccadilly, and the organ-case and font at the latter church" (Beard 1989: 33). It is common to attribute the carvings in St. Mary, Aldermanbury, and other of Wren's City churches, to the "shop of Gibbons." Whether, in fact, any of the carvings in St. Mary, Aldermanbury, came from the hand or shop of Gibbons is a matter of mere speculation. No direct evidence exists, such as a signed receipt or attestation in a contemporary source, to link Gibbons to the Church's furnishings. In fact, the available evidence (see below) suggests that the carvings came from the hands of independent craftsmen not said, in the available sources, to have been associated with Gibbons. However, the decorations on the reredos and other carvings in St. Mary's certainly were in the "Gibbons style," if they did not come from Gibbons himself or his shop.

John Dubois, Churchwarden between 1672 and 1674, was the principal contact between the parish and the architects. Robert Hooke's diary shows that Hooke met with DuBois at a coffeehouse in Aldermanbury on 13 March 1673. Three days later the Vestry met and received a report of a number of contributions of £20 each (including £20 from George Jeffreys) to pay Mr. Cleare the joyner (Carter 1913: 26).

On 30 April 1673 the Minutes record "Att a Committee in Pursuance to consider about facilitating the finishing of the Church having considered the kindness of Dr. Xtopher (sic) Wren and Mr. Robert Hooke expediting the building of the church ... it is now ordered that the Parish by the Churchwardens doe present Dr. Xtoper Wren with twenty guineas and Mr. Robert Hooke with ten guineas" (Carter 1913: 26-27). The Accounts show that Wren was actually paid £21 and Hooke £10.10. £1.7 was spent for wine (12 claret, 4 canary, 2 Renish) perhaps as gifts for the architects or craftsmen.

Goss states that "Wren not only returned the whole of the sum presented to him, but he also gave £25 towards the purchase of the clock" (1944: 154). This assertion needs to be corrected. There is no confirmation yet found in the parish records that Wren returned the £21. As we shall see below, the supposed £25 "gift" was actually Wren's reimbursement from coal tax funds to John Dubois for charges the parish incurred in removing the materials from the Milk Street Church (Ms. 25,539:56.2).

Although not among the first ten churches authorized, St. Mary's was the ninth church actually rebuilt (Ms. 25,540/1:51; Goss 1944: 154). This speaks well of the Vestry's efforts to raise money. The speed with which a church was rebuilt was in direct relation to the parish's ability to raise money against the guarantee of the coal tax (and the influence exerted on the architects and craftsmen).

The Vestry could be ingenious in paying for work. On 22 April the Vestry agreed to acquit charges to a Mr. John Emery, Bricklayer and parishoner, and allow him to be buried in the church, for £5 worth of work he had done.

On 4 April 1673 a William Walker was hired as Warden "to keep beggars from ye Parishoners doors ... and to prevent children to be laid in the parish" (Carter 1913: 69). The same year the accounts show 10d spent "getting a woman in labour out of the parish" and 2s for removing a "great bellied woman" (Carter 1913: 115).

On 13 May 1673 a committee reported on having received estimates for the Joiner's work in the church from Mr. Cleare, Mr. Harris, and Mr. Sanderson. Mr. Cleare was chosen to make the Pews for the church in an election in which he received five votes and the others three. According to the minutes, "the Articles [were] to be drawn for the performance according to St. Michael's Church in Cornhill." (Bolton and Hendry (vol. XIX) 1942: 36).

On 15 May, 1673, decisions were made on the "dimensions for the ground platges and joyses and flooring for the Pews." The Flooring was to be made of "good yellow whole deale" by Mr. Miller, a Carpenter who resided in the parish. The Vestry also specified that locks, hinges, and the ironwork for the pews "be not medled with till Mr. John Harris be first consulted." (Bolton and Hendry 1942: 37).

On 22 August 1673, the Vestry gave the committee dealing directly with the craftsmen authority to pay a gratuity to Mr. Marshall, the Mason, and other workmen who were refusing to finish the church. The amount was limited to £400 and was to be paid out within a two year period.

On 2 March 1674, it was reported that the Joyner, William Cleare, was in great need of £100 in payment of his work, because the money which was collected as an advance against the coal tax revenues had not arrived. The committee reported that persons who had newly moved into the parish had been approached and had been prevailed upon to give the £100 needed. Two weeks later a Mr. Sam Wyng, an Ironmonger, appeared before the Vestry to receive authorization for the locks, hinges catches and other things necessary for the pews at 6s. 6d. per set. On 23 March Mr. Cleare produced a model of the Altarpiece, and it was accepted. A Mr. Turnly was hired to produce a "good clean wainscott for the King's Arms" for £34, and £6 for carving it. A fence wall between the Fore Door and the Church to be made of brick was ordered, with a Door in the middle made of two ashen Posts with Balls on top and folding doors.

While the poor and pregnant were being put out the parish was investing parish funds in the "Assention Day" (sic) dinner (7.3.2) and a dinner "with ye Surveyhors and workmen for ye building ye church" (Carter 1913: 115). Also in 1673 £37 was spent for "ye Tribble Bell" and 3.18 for "bellhangers."

By late 1674 or early 1675 the Church must have been fairly well completed. John Dubois noted in the Churchwarden's Account Book that during the period between Easter 1672 and 1675 "the Parish Church was restored from the total ruine it received by ye general and dreadfull Conflagration in anno 1666 and was rebuilt and adorned by the Mercy of God to this Parish as it is this day" (Bolton and Hendry 1942: 38).

The accounts for 1674 show expenditures for trees—8 lime trees and others—for the Churchyard. (Carter 1913: 115). In June the Committee in charge of completing the steeple agreed to pay Mr. Marshall an additional £35 to complete the work. On 22 June the Vestry appointed two members to measure the Joyner's work, and on 13 August Mr. Cleare appeared before the Vestry to settle the bill. Additional vestrymen were appointed at this meeting to examine the Pulpit and determine what adornments should be added. During this period a number of other bills submitted by craftsmen were ordered paid, but money was tight. On 14 September Mr. Cleare again appeared asking for payment of what was owed him, and £150 was ordered to be given to him from the next £500 of coal money received. At this meeting John Harris was assigned the task of making the two screens for the two doors at the east end of the Church in wainscott. By 18 November 1674 the Vestry was trying to raise £250 for "pews and other ornaments" (Ms. 3570aI: 77), which had already been installed. A Vestry meeting on 26 August 1674 had heard the report of a debt of £240 on the church (Ms. 3570aI: 76-77).

Also in 1674 the Vestry petitioned the Lord Mayor and aldermen to force Plaisters Hall to pay duties to the parish (Ms. 3570aI: 75-76). At a meeting after the Ascension Day dinner (28 May) at the Axe Inn the parishoners voted to hire a Sexton. Taking advantage of the good spirits Dr. Ford appealed for subscriptions for a house in the parish for his family (Ms. 3570aI: 76).

On 12 December 1674, Hooke wrote in his diary that he had approved the Grove account for Aldermanbury (Robinson and Adams 1935: 135). Grove was a plaisterer who was responsible for the moulding, flowers, cornich and whiting of the stonework (Ms. 25,539/55: 1). Three days later Hooke again met John Dubois and other parishoners at the Lord Mayor's (Robinson and Adams 1935: 135). Hooke says he again went to Dubois' home on 2 March 1675 (Robinson and Adams 1935: 150) and that on 13 December 1675 Dubois came to him to complain about the Church gutter leaking. (Robinson and Adams 1935: 200). On the 23 December Hooke went to see Wren "about Mr. Dubois," presumably to discuss this complaint (Robinson and Adams 1935: 203). Hooke reports several other visits with Dubois through 1679.

The accounts for 1674 listed the following parish houses or ground rents: (Carter 1913: 116).

3 houses ground rent leased to the city

3 ground rents leased to Squire Pask, let to Esqr. Aske

3 ground rents leased to Mr. Own Hanning

2 ground rents leased to Wm. Brett as Exor to Abraham Nunn

On 22 February, 1675, the Vestry ordered the Clerk to go with the Churchwardens to the Lord Mayor's with the names of those in arrears of tithes "in order to take out a warrant to compel them according to law" (Carter 1913: 14). On 24 March the Vestry ordered them to be prosecuted.

Perhaps in celebration of the near completion of the Church the parish treated itself to an elaborate Ascension Day dinner, with parish funds expended for "meate, Sparagrass, Tobacco, pigeon pies, wine, bread, beare and dressing" at an expense of over £11. Two years later an even more elaborate feast cost 18.10.10. (Carter 1913: 116). Also in 1677 5s6d was spent for a "Chamber pott for ye vestry."

The Vestry did not resolve its dispute with Mr. Cleare about payment of his bill until April 1675. Cleare apparently disputed the Vestry's measurements of his work, for in March 1675, the vestry hired a Mr. Beale (with the knowledge of Mr. Cleare) to measure the joiner's work in the church. On 19 April an additional £16 was paid Mr. Cleare as full and final payment of all his work.

On 29 April the bills of Mr. Talbot, the Plumber were audited and allowed, as were bills of Mr. Miller and Mr. Emery. The Commandments, Lord's Prayer, and Creed were ordered to be added to the reredoes after the design at St. Dionis Backchurch. A Mr. Huntley was employed for the work at £10.

On 12 October 1676 the Vestry debated whether to ask Dr. Ford to resign since he had accepted another living. A week later Esquire Jeffreys reported that Ford would resign the next Lady Day. The minutes for 30 March 1677 say that Ford submitted his voluntary resignation.

The Vestry minutes for 15 December 1676 read, "Mr. John Dubois made a proposition concerning a clock, having a prospect of £25 from Sir Christopher Wren for charges in pulling down and removing ye materialls of Milk St. Church and of his own freed good will doth promise to give five pounds more to make it £30" (Carter 1913: 27). Wren's account shows that on 6 December, 1676, £28.13.04 was authorized "to Mr. John Dubois Churchwarden of Aldermanbury for money by him disbursed about removing ye rubble stone from Milkstreet Church, carrying the same to Aldermanbury where it was used..." (Ms. 25,539/56:2). Mr. Dubois himself added £5, creating a "clock fund" of £30.

We can conclude then that the church was essentially completed by early 1677. The 1677 date for the completion of the rebuilding is confirmed by the reference below from <u>Parentalia</u>.

However, the cupola was apparently not added to the tower until 1679. On 26 February, 1679, John Slater, "Plomber" was hired by the Commission to do work on the "Tower Lanthorne (sic)." (St. Paul's WE 16 f. 156). A note in the 23 September 1679 minutes reveals that the cupola had been framed by Mr. Matthew Banks for twelve months, but he was refusing to put it up until he was paid. Mr. Dan Davies was instructed to consult with Mr. Banks and tell he he would be paid £5 as soon as the work was done.

On 19 May 1680 the Vestry debated whether to paint the dials on the clock, and a committee was chosen to pursue the matter. On 10 August the bills of the bellfounders and bellhangers were referred to committee.

The final bills for craftsmen are dated 1680 (Ms. 25,550), so work must have gone on, perhaps in the churchyard for several years. The final dated bill was to Samuel Tulkey, a mason; it was dated 14 January, 1681.

The craftsmen involved in the rebuilding and the amount paid to them, as recorded in the abstract of bills (Ms. 25,550) were:

John Talbot, Plumber	695.7.0
Joshuah Marshall, Mason	3190.3.7
Matthew Banker, Carpenter	614.18.3
Grace Smith, Smith	101.4.0 (see Figure 5.3)
Daniel Davy, Glaizer	55.1.6ii
Thomas Hodgkins, Smith	146.4.5
William Cleere, Joyner	31.0.0ii
John Grove, Plaisterer	174.15.5ii

Robert Streeter, Painter	22.4.4
Robert Day, Carpenter	8.17.0
Robert Bird, Coppersmith	11.2.0iiii
William Cocker, Plumber	120.9.8iii
John Slaughter, Painter	8.8.11iii
Samuel Tulkey, Mason	14.15.1iiii

No plans or drawings for St. Mary, Aldermanbury, survive in the archives of Wren drawings at All Souls College, Oxford; the Royal Institute of British Architects; Guildhall Library; or any other repository. Christopher Wren, Jr. included a poor drawing, not one of his father's, in the Wren family volume Parentalia. St. Mary's is not the only structure so lacking. Very few final plans or drawings of the City churches have survived. They were used as blueprints in the construction process and were probably not in very good condition at the end of the work. The majority of "Wren's drawings" were in fact executed by clerks and assistants employed in the Office of Works. They represented the the decision if not the original conception of the Surveyor General "Dr. Wren" (as his associates and assistants called him), but not his actual work. Although he may not have executed the drawings there is no question that he was the guiding genius behind the work.

The description of the Wren design of St. Mary, Aldermanbury, found in Parentalia (Wren 1965: 315), reads:

... rebuilt in 1677, of stone, with the Steeple, consisting of a
Tower and Turret. The Roof within is camerated, and supported
with twelve columns of the composite order, at the East end is a
large Cornice and Pediment; also two large cartouches, and Pineapples
of Stone carved, the inside of the Roof is adorned with Arches of
Fret-work, and the said Columns with an Entablature; the Cornice
Cantalever. The Length 72, Breadth 45, Height 38 Feet; and of the
Steeple, about 90 Feet.

In 1711, when it was proposed that more parish churches be built, Wren wrote a memorandum in which he expressed his view of church architecture. "... in our reformed Religion, it should seem vain to make a Parish Church larger, than that all who are present can both hear and see" (Whinney 1971: 48). Surely St. Mary, Aldermanbury, as redesigned by Sir Christopher fulfills this principle.

St. Mary's long nave with aisles represents Wren's favorite solution to the construction of a small parish Church where the lot would permit (Bennett 1982). Indeed, he adopted the same solution with the addition of galleries to the large parish churches as well, including St. James Piccadilly, his personal favorite among the parish churches. However, at St. Mary's the solution was dictated by the survival of sound foundations from the 15th Century perpendicular church, and a third of the tower. Wren frequently reused sound walls and foundations where possible, effecting a substantial saving in time and money. So Wren in effect accepted the challenge of constructing a Renaissance Church on Perpendicular Gothic foundations, resheathing the lower part of the tower and rebuilding anew upon it. The west (or "invisible") face of the Church (it was hard up against a house or other buildings) was designed in simple Renaissance classical style, emphasizing geometric elegance, as is also the case with the tower and its lead clock cupola. The east face of the Church, overlooking Aldermanbury, was unashamedly Baroque, with its "jolly" voluted scrolls (as some architectural critics have called them) serving no structural purpose. The north and south walls, with their roundhead windows, are conventionally Renaissance classical. But the interior adornments, including the plastering and carved wood work so far as they can be recovered from surviving sketches, once more bespeaks Baroque flamboyance.

Professor Grimes' archaeological investigations have revealed that Wren used the south wall of the earliest stone Church of St. Mary on the site as the stybolate to support the columns of his south aisle, thus saving further time and expense on the project. He could not so use the north foundation of the old Church for reasons of symmetry. St. Mary's was built at the time Wren was making his personal transition from the Classical to the English Baroque style he invented. St. Mary's is to some degree a record of his pilgrimage.

Conclusion

Like the mythological phoenix, St. Mary, the Virgin, Aldermanbury, emerged from the ashes of the Great Fire of 1666 because of the genius of one of the greatest architects in history, the skill of dedicated craftsmen, and the perseverance of the parishoners. This would not be the last time the church suffered near total devastation, nor the last time architectural genius combined with craftsmanship and determination would cause St. Mary's to rise again.

The church rebuilt by Sir Christopher Wren was to stand for nearly 300 years in

London, then, after its destruction, have a rebirth in the United States. In the next two chapters our story will reveal how the Wren church fared during the transition of the Aldermanbury parish into a commercial and industrial center with a declining residential population.

Bibliography

The Plague and Great Fire (1665-66)
Aubin, Robert, ed.
    1943   London in Flames, London in Glory: Poems on the Fire and Rebuilding of London, 1666-1709. New Brunswick: Rutgers University Press.

Bedford, John
    1966   London's Burning. London: Abelard-Schumann.

Bell, Walter
    1951   The Great Plague in London. 2nd ed. London: Lane.

    1971   The Great Fire of London in 1666. Westport, Conn.: Greenwood Press.

Bills of Mortality
    1665   London's Dreadful Visitation: or a collection of all the bills of mortality beginning 27 Dec., 1664. London: Cotes.

Cowie, Leonard
    1970   Plague and Fire: 1665-6. London: Waylund.

Jones, Philip, ed.
    1966   The Fire Court. Calendar to the Judgments and Decrees of the

the Court of Judicature appointed to determine differences between landlords and tenants as to rebuilding after the Great Fire. vol. I. London: William Clowes and Sons.

Milne, Gustav
    1986   The Great Fire of London. New Barnet: Historical Publications.

Ross, Sutherland
    1965   The Plague and Great Fire. London: Faber.

Leasor, Thomas
    1962   The Plague and the Fire. London: Allen and Unwin.

Christopher Wren and Robert Hook

Allsopp, Bruce and Ursula Clark
    1979   English Architecture: An Introduction to Architectural History of England from the Bronze Age to the Present Day. Boston: Oriel Press.

Beard, Geoffrey
    1982   The Work of Christopher Wren. Edinburgh: John Bartholomew and Son, Ltd.

Bennett, J. A.
    1982   The Mathematical Science of Sir Christopher Wren. Cambridge: University Press.

Bolton, Arthur T. and H. Duncan Hendry, ed.
  1924-43   The Wren Society Publications. 20 vols.

Booth, Arthur H.
    1967   Sir Christopher Wren. London: Frederick Muller.

Crowthers, J. G.
 1982 Founders of British Science. Westport, CN: Greenwood Press.

De Mare', Eric
 1975 Wren's London. London: Folio Society.

Dircks, Rudolf, ed.
 1923 Sir Christopher Wren, AD 1632-1723. Bicentenary Memorial Volume published under the auspices of the Royal Institute of British Architects. London: Hodder and Stoughton.

Dorn, Harold and Robert Mark
 1981 "The Architecture of Christopher Wren," Scientific American 245(1981), 160-173.

Downes, Kerry
 1966 English Baroque Architecture. London: Zwemmer.

 1971 Christopher Wren. London: Allen Lane.

 1982 The Architecture of Wren. New York: Universe Books.

 1982 Sir Christopher Wren, an exhibition. London: Whitechapel Art Gallery.

Furst, Viktor
 1956 The Architecture of Sir Christopher Wren. London: Lund Humphries.

Gould, Heywood
 1970 Sir Christopher Wren: Renaissance Architect, Philosopher and Scientist. London: Watts.

Gray, Ronald D.
 1982 Christopher Wren and St. Paul's Cathedral. Minneapolis: Lerner Publications. In cooperation with Cambridge University Press.

Hutchison, Harold
    1976   Sir Christopher Wren: A Biography. New York: Stein and Day. .

Little, Bryan
    1975   Sir Christopher Wren, A Historical Biography. London: Robert Hale.

Richards, J. M.
    1981   The National Trust Book of English Architecture. New York: W. W. Norton.

Robinson, Henry W. and Walter Adams, ed.
    1935   The Diary of Robert Hooke. London: Taylor and Francis.

Sikler, John
    1956   Wren and His Place in European Architecture. London: Faber.

Summerson, John
    1951   Sir Christopher Wren. London: Collins Press.

Whinney, Margaret
    1971   Christopher Wren. New York: Praeger.

Wren, Christopher and Stephen Wren, ed.
    1965   Parentalia: or, Memoirs of the Family of the Wrens. Farnborough, Hants: Gregg Press, 1965. First published in 1750.

Other

Beard, Geoffrey
    1989   The Work of Grinling Gibbons. Chicago: The University of Chicago Press.

Carter, Pierson Cathrick
    1913   History of the Church and Parish of St. Mary the Virgin, Aldermanbury.

London: W. H. and L. Collinbridge.

Cobb, Gerald
1977   London City Churches. rev. ed. London: B. J. Batsford.

Hennessy, George
1898   Novum Repertorium .... London: Swan Sonneschein.

Lillywhite, Bryant
1963   London Coffeehouses. London: George Allen and Unwin, Ltd.

Malcolm, J. Peller
1803   Londinium Redivivum: An Ancient History and Modern Description. London: John Nichols and Son.

Matthews, A.G.
1934   Calamy Revised, Being a Revision of Edmund Calamy's "Account of the Ministers and others Ejected and Silenced, 1660-1662. Oxford: Clarendon.

Rude, George
1971   Hanoverian London, 1714-1808. Berkeley: University of California Press.

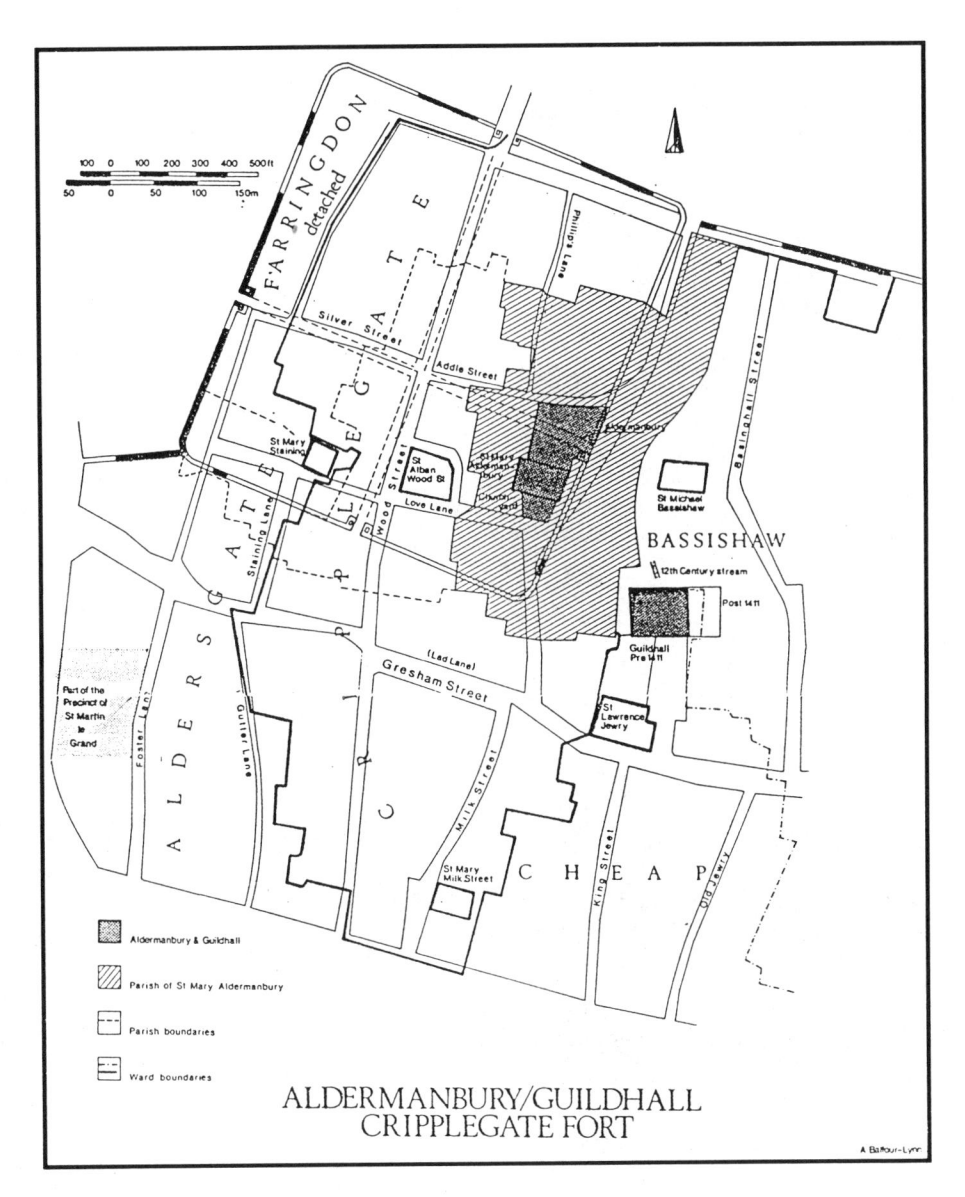

Figure 1.1
Cripplegate Fort in relation to the Aldermanbury parish. This map portrays the northwest corner of the City of London within the walls, including the locations of the Church of St. Mary, Aldermanbury and its parish (hatched), the Aldermanbury tenement, and Guildhall, as well as the layout of the earlier Roman fort ("Cripplegate fort"). The deviation of Aldermanbury to the west and Basinghall Street to the east would be explained by the location of the Roman amphitheater in the Guildhall area. (Courtesy of Mr. Tony Dyson, FSA)

Figure 1.2
Overview of the site of St. Mary, Aldermanbury, during the excavation directed by Prof. W.F. Grimes. After the removal of the Wren fabric of the Church, Prof. Grimes conducted an archaeological excavation of the site. Note the Shakespeare monument in the south Churchyard. (Courtesy of Guildhall Library, Corporation of London)

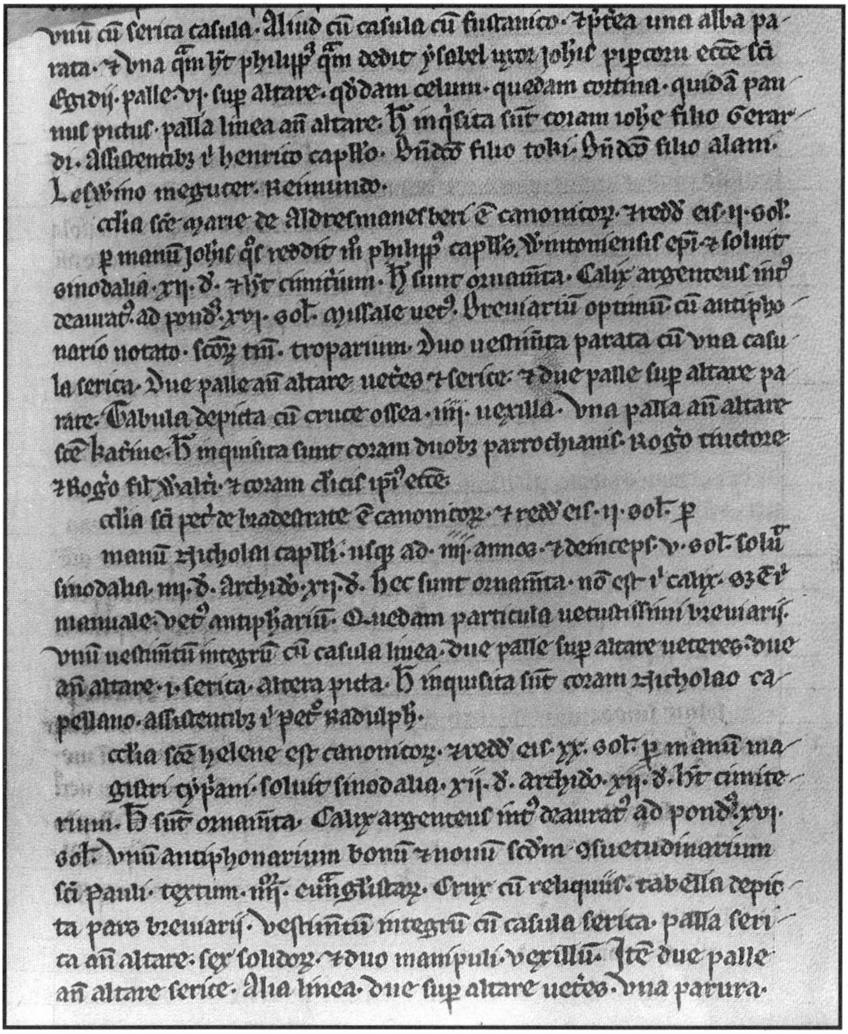

Figure 1.3
The 1181 Inquisition of London Churches. Dean Ralph DeDiceto (the "good dean" of St. Paul's Cathedral) ordered an inquisition (inventory) of churches in the diocese in 1181. This document includes the earliest known written reference to the Church of St. Mary, Aldermanbury. St. Mary's was by this time a flourishing parish Church and so must have had some history already behind it. (Courtesy of Guildhall Library, Corporation of London Guildhall Library MS 25.504, FO84R [Modern 87R])

Figure 2.1
A reconstruction of the 1437 Church of St. Mary. Mr. Bryce Gordon executed this conjectural drawing of the 1437 Perpendicular Gothic Church of St. Mary, Aldermanbury, utilizing information collected by Prof. Hauer (the Copper Plate Map, the description in the Wren family work (Parentalia), the 1929 report of the Royal Commission on Historical Monuments, and Prof. Grimes' archaeological excavation). The precise sort of stone and the size of the blocks used in the structure is not known. (Courtesy of The Churchill Memorial Archive)

Figure 2.2
The tower stairs from the medieval Church of St. Mary, Aldermanbury, as incorporated into the present reconstruction. Information from Christopher Wren, Jr., in the Wren family volume Parentalia, the 1929 report of the Royal Commission on Historical Monuments, and Prof. Grimes' investigations combine to suggest that this spiral staircase, originally in the lower course of the tower, was part of the 1437 Gothic St. Mary's. It now rises from the gallery level in the tower of the reconstructed Wren Church. (Courtesy of The Churchill Memorial Archive)

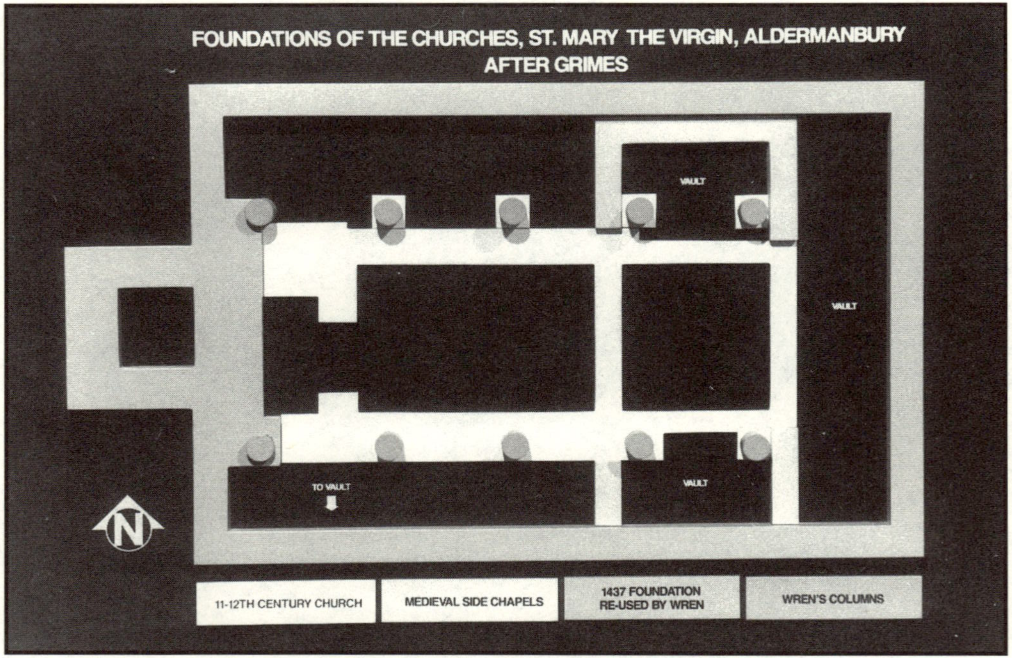

Figure 2.3
The foundations of the Church of St. Mary, Aldermanbury. This small relief in the permanent exhibit of the Churchill Memorial Museum shows the foundations of the successive St. Mary Aldermanbury buildings, from the early rectangular Church (later enhanced with side chapels) through the 1437 Gothic foundation reused by Wren. Note that Wren also used a wall of the earliest building to support one row of his columns. The relief is based on Prof. Grimes' site plan. (Courtesy of Mr. Bruce Hackmann)

Figure 3.1
The Copper Plate Map (1553). The "Moorgate Plate" of the Copper Plate Map (1553) supplies the earliest known view of the Church of St. Mary, Aldermanbury. It exaggerates the size of the tower in relationship to the nave of the Church, a convention typical of 16th/17th century view maps. (Courtesy of the Museum of London)

Figure 3.2
A Portrait of William Shakespeare from the First Folio of Shakespeare's Plays (1623). John Heminges and Henry Condell were Aldermanbury residents and officers in the Church of St. Mary, Aldermanbury, who were close friends of William Shakespeare and actors in many of his plays. In order to preserve and protect the authenticity of their friend's plays, they edited the plays and published this First Folio edition after his death. Theirs was the first publication of such plays as "Macbeth," "Julius Caesar," and "As You Like It." This portrait of Shakespeare, by Martin Droeshout, is one of two images of the dramatist considered authentic. (Courtesy of Folger Shakespeare Library, Washington, D.C.)

Figure 3.3
The Shakespeare monument in the Aldermanbury Churchyard. This monument, erected by Mr. C. C. Walker in 1895, stands in tribute to the work of John Heminges and Henry Condell in preserving the plays of William Shakespeare. It was left in place after the removal of the Wren fabric and can be seen today in the park created on the site of the Church in London. (Courtesy of The Churchill Memorial Archive)

Figure 4.1
Edmund Calamy. Dr. Edmund Calamy was perpetual curate of St. Mary, Aldermanbury, from 1639 until 1662, and a leader of the Presbyterian wing of the Puritan movement in the Church of England. (Courtesy of The Churchill Memorial Archive)

Figure 4.2
The Robinett Wedding. The 29 September, 1653 wedding of Allen and Margaret Robinett is recorded in the Parish Register in the Church of St. Mary, Aldermanbury. During a service of worship at a biennial meeting of the Robinett Family Association at the Churchill Memorial, the wedding was re-enacted in the Church of St. Mary, Aldermanbury, with Dr. William Young playing the role of minister Edmund Calamy, and two teenage descendants of Allen and Margaret Robinett representing their ancestors. (Courtesy of The Churchill Memorial Archive)

Figure 4.3
King Charles II. The dedication plate of William Morgan's map and panorama, "London &c Actually Survey'd" (1682), shows Morgan's step-grandfather and professional mentor, John Ogilby, presenting the subscription book for his own survey to King Charles II and Queen Catherine of Braganza. Dr. Edmund Calamy (see Figure 4.1) was active in the Restoration of the monarchy, which brought Charles II to the throne. (Courtesy of The Museum of London)

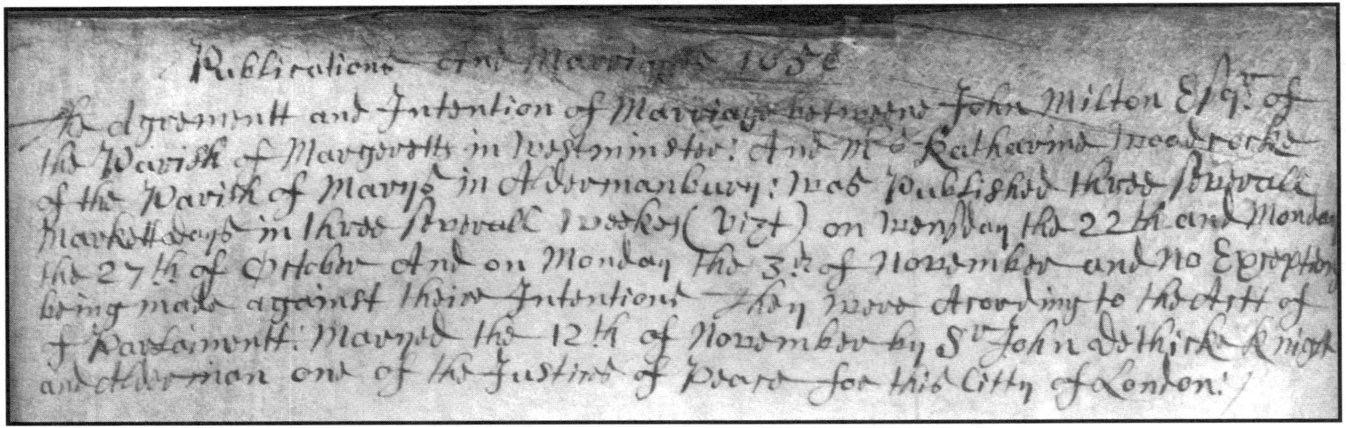

Publications and Marriages 1656
The Agreement and Intention of Marriage betweene John Milton Esqr of the Parish of Margaretts in Westminster: And Mrs Katharine Woodcocke of the Parish of Maryes in Aldermanbury: was published three severall Markett dayes in three severall weekes (Vizt) on Wensday the 22th and Monday the 27th of October And on Monday the 3d of November and no Exception being made against their Intention They were according to the Act of Parliament: Married the 12th of November by Sr John Dethicke Knight and Alderman one of the Justices of Peace for this City of London.

Figure 4.4
The Second Wedding of John Milton. This page from the Aldermanbury parish register records the wedding of famous author John Milton and Katherine Woodcock, a resident of the Aldermanbury parish, which took place on 12, November 1656. (Courtesy of Guildhall Library, Corporation of London, Guildhall Library MS 53, 572, Voc 1)

Figure 5.1
Sir Christopher Wren (the Pierce Bust). The original of this bust of Sir Christopher Wren (1673), by sculptor Edward Pierce, stands in the Ashmolean Museum, Oxford. This reproduction is in the Wren section of the Churchill Memorial Museum. (Courtesy of The Churchill Memorial Archive)

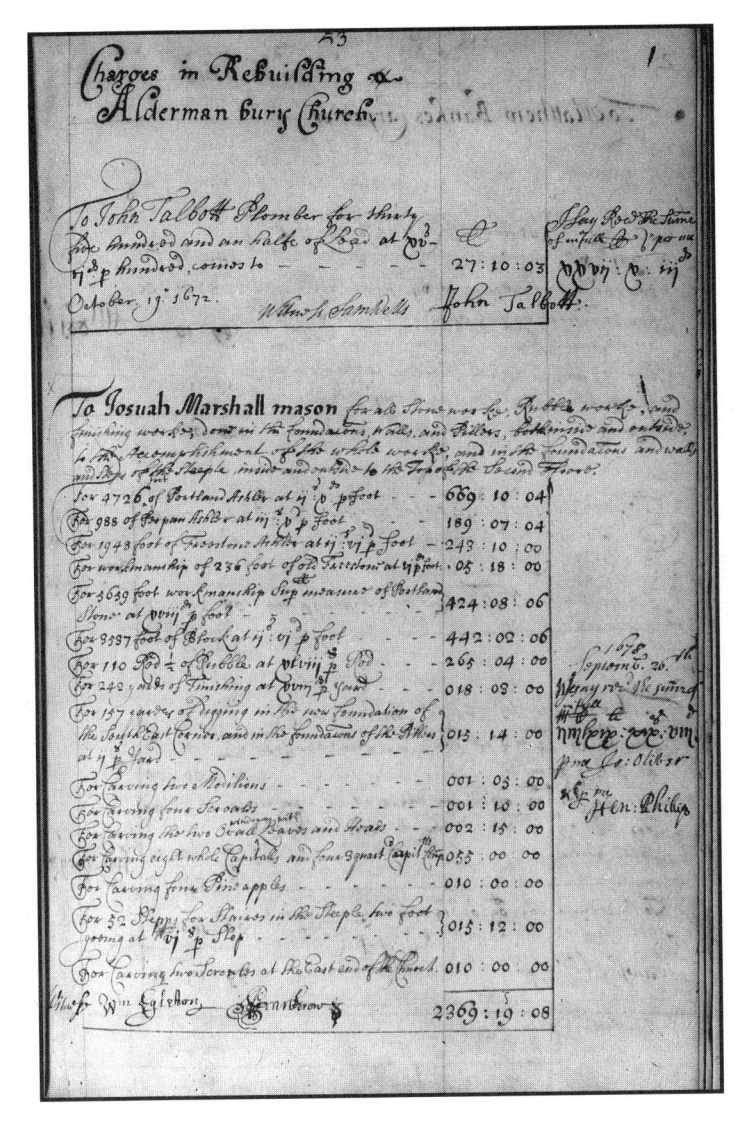

Figures 5.2 and 5.3

The Wren City Church Account Books. Two pages from the Account Books for the Reconstruction of the London City Churches, show charges for the rebuilding of the Church of St. Mary, Aldermanbury, according to the plan of Sir Christopher Wren. Figure 5.2 shows charges paid to the famous mason Joshua Marshall, and 5.3 shows the mark of Grace Smith, one of the craftswomen who participated in the reconstruction of the City churches. It is the only signed receipt in the St. Mary, Aldermanbury, account books. (Courtesy of Guildhall Library, Corporation of London, Guildhall Library MS 25.539, Vol 1)

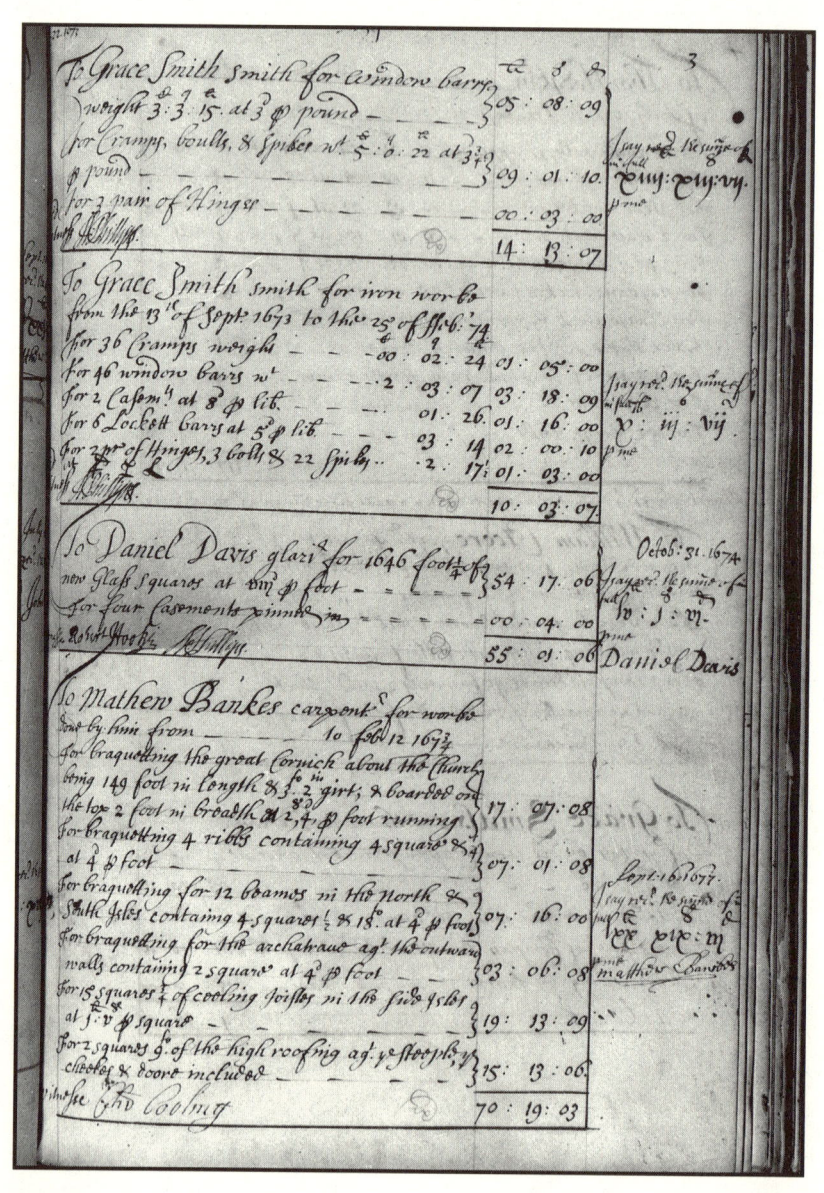

To Grace Smith smith for Window barrs
weight 3: 3: 15 at 3ᵈ ꝑ pound .... 05 : 08 : 09
for Cramps, boults, & Spikes w⟨t⟩ 0: 0: 22 at 3½ᵈ
ꝑ pound .... 00 : 01 : 10
for 3 pair of Hinges .... 00 : 03 : 00
                                                14 : 13 : 07

To Grace Smith smith for iron works
from the 13ᵗʰ of Sept: 1673 to the 25 of Feb: 74
for 36 Cramps weight .... 00 : 02 : 24 01 : 05 : 00
for 46 window barrs w⟨t⟩ ..... 2 : 03 : 07 03 : 18 : 09
for 2 Casem⟨t⟩ at 8ᵈ ꝑ lib ..... 01 : 26 : 01 16 : 00
for 6 Lockett barrs at 5ᵈ ꝑ lib 03 : 14 02 : 00 : 10
for 2ꝑ⟨r⟩ of Hinges, 3 boltꝪ & 22 Spikꝫ 2 : 17 : 01 03 : 00
                                                10 : 03 : 07

To Daniel Davis glazi⟨er⟩ for 1646 foot ¼
new Glass squares at viij ꝑ foot .... 54 : 17 : 06
for four Casements ⟨mended⟩ .... 00 : 04 : 00
                                                55 : 01 : 06

To Mathew Bankes carpent⟨er⟩ for works
done by him from .... to Feb 12 1674
for braquetting the great Cornich about the church
being 149 foot in length & 3½ girt; & boarded on
the top 2 foot in breadth at 2ᵈ ꝑ foot running ... 17 : 07 : 08
for braquetting 4 ribbs containing 4 squares ¾
at 4ᵈ ꝑ foot .... 07 : 01 : 08
for braquetting for 12 beames in the North &
South Isles containg 4 squares ½ & 18 at 4ᵈ ꝑ foot 07 : 16 : 00
for braquetting for the archatraue ag⟨t⟩ the outward
walls containing 2 square at 4ᵈ ꝑ foot .... 03 : 06 : 08
for 15 squares ½ of cooling Joistes in the sides Isles
at 5 : v ꝑ square .... 19 : 13 : 09
for 2 squares ¾ of the high roofing ag⟨t⟩ y⟨e⟩ steeple
cheekes & doore included .... 15 : 13 : 06
                                                70 : 19 : 03

Figures 5.3

Figure 5.4
Sir Christopher Wren (Royal Society Portrait). Wren was a founder of the Royal Society and served as president, 1681-1683. His " presidential portrait" is attributed to Closterman. (Courtesy of the Royal Society)

Figure 5.5
Morgan Panorama. The Morgan map and panorama (1682) furnish the earliest views of the Wren fabric of St. Mary, Aldermanbury. They show the building before the lead lantern was installed atop the stone tower. This detail from the panorama shows the tower (shaded). (Courtesy of The Museum of London)

Figure 6.1
Judge George Jeffreys. Baron George Jeffreys became known as the "Hanging Judge" because of his role in the "Bloody Assizes" after Monmouth's Rebellion in 1685. Jeffreys took up residence in the Aldermanbury parish in 1671 and was an active member of the Church of St. Mary. Although he moved from the parish in 1685, he was buried in a vault beneath the chancel in 1698, a decade after his death in the Tower of London. This portrait, by an unknown artist, is in the National Portrait Gallery. (Courtesy of the National Portrait Gallery)

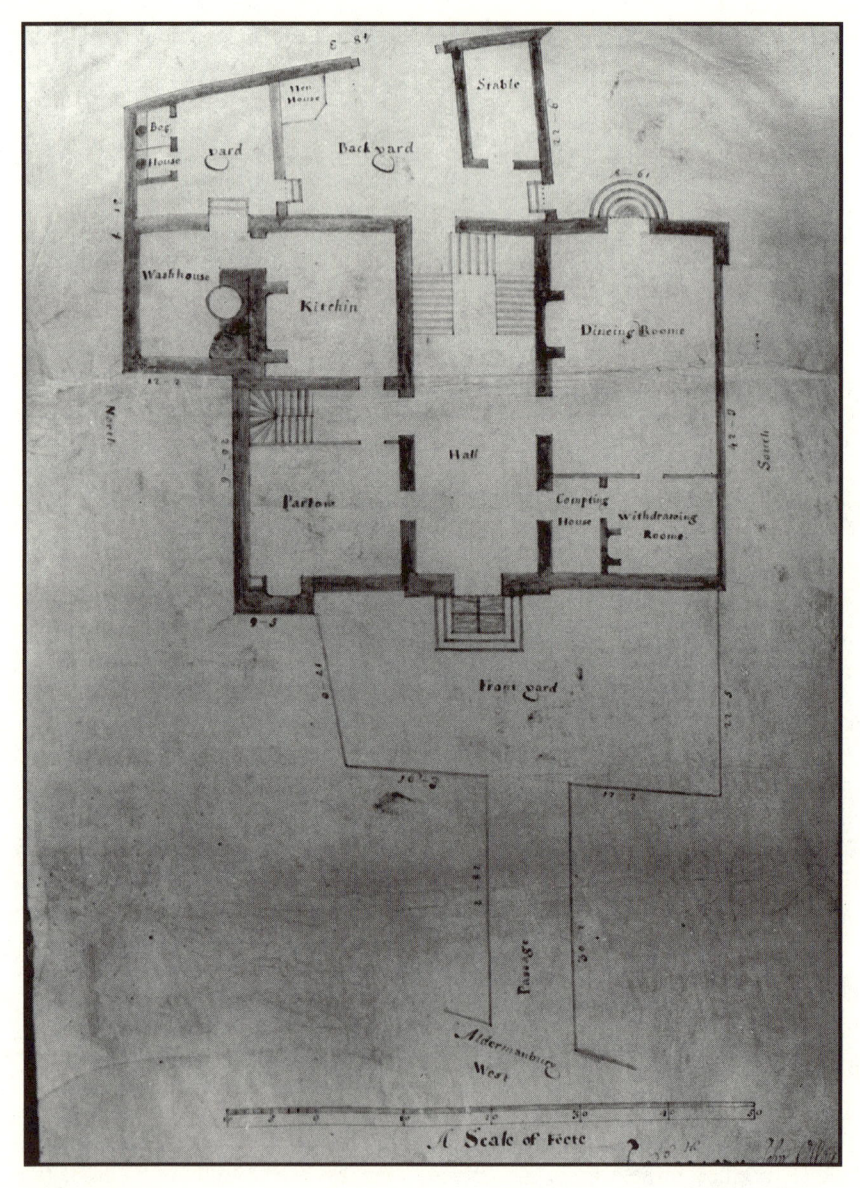

Figure 6.2
Judge George Jeffreys' house in Aldermanbury. In 1671, when he became Common Sergeant of the City of London, Judge Jeffreys received title to a tenement located behind Nos. 18 and 19 Aldermanbury. He remained in the house until he moved to Westminster in 1685. (Courtesy of the Corporation of London Records Office)

Figure 6.3
Swan with Two Necks Inn. This prominent coaching inn was located on the southern boundary of the Aldermanbury parish. (Courtesy of Guildhall Library, Corporation of London)

Figure 6.4
A Table of Fare for coaches leaving from the Swan with Two Necks Inn. (Courtesy of Guildhall Library, Corporation of London)

Figure 7.1
An 1886 map of the Aldermanbury parish. (Courtesy of Guildhall Library, Corporation of London)

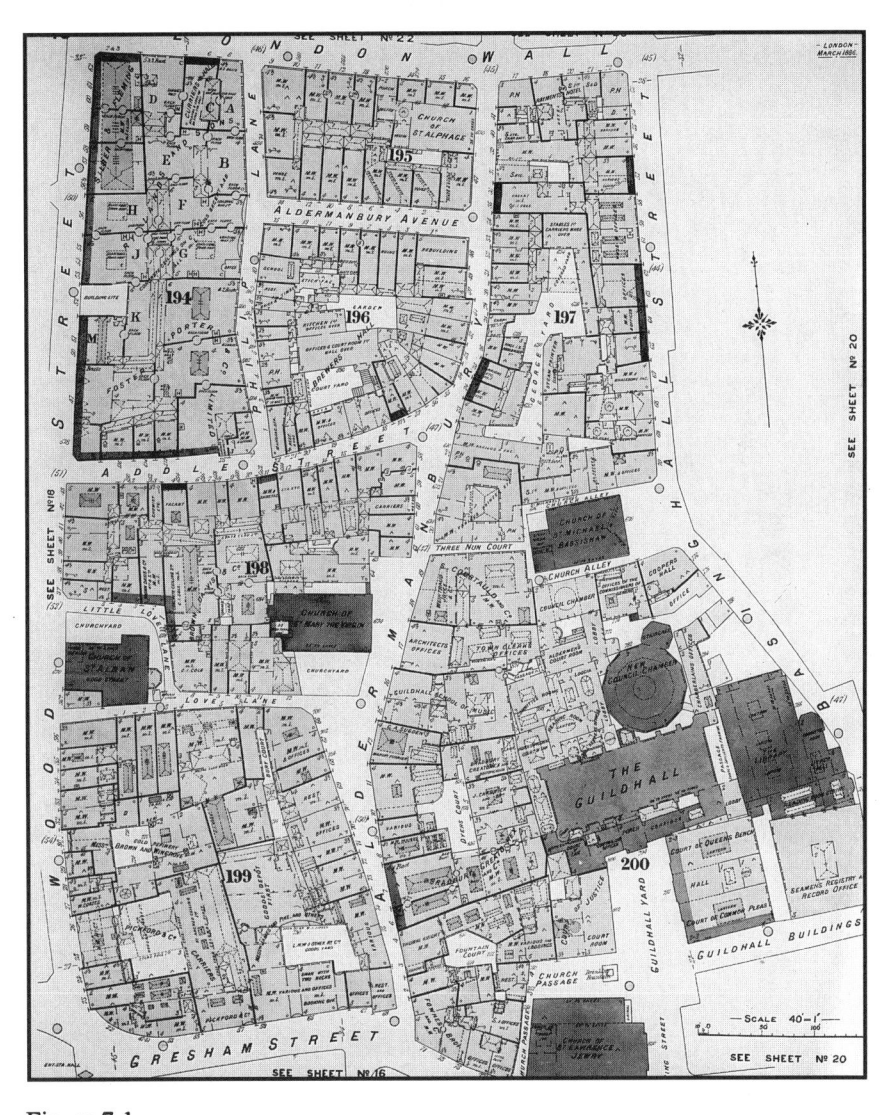

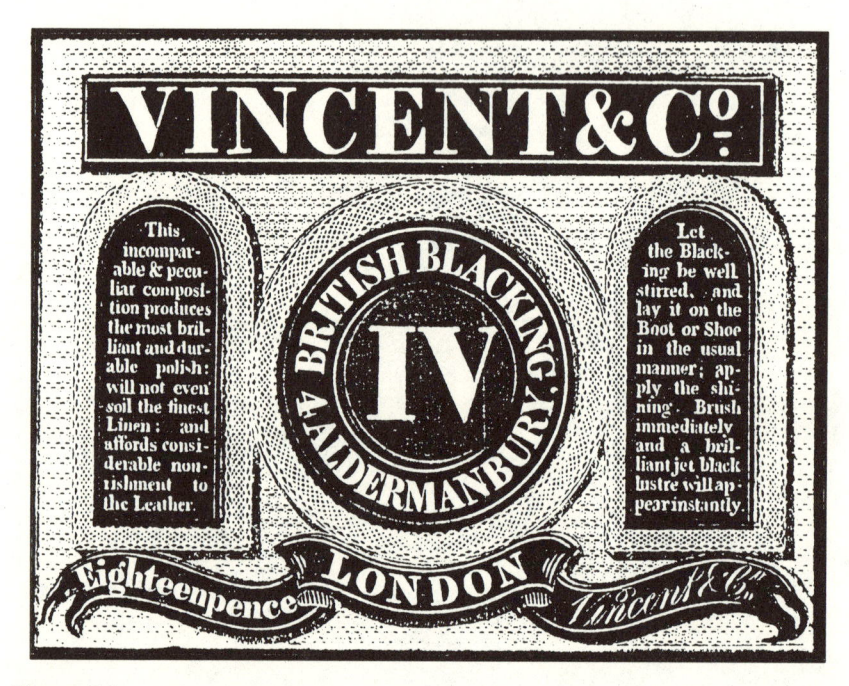

Figure 7.2
Aldermanbury Business Card. A card from one of the many businesses in Aldermanbury illustrates the 19th century commercialization of the parish. (Courtesy of Guildhall Library, Corporation of London)

Figure 7.3
The Church of St. Mary, Aldermanbury (1814). This is the best rendering of the Wren fabric of the Church, prior to the Victorian "improvements." The impression was prepared for a publication on London Churches which appeared in 1830, but the originals were engraved in 1814. (Courtesy of The Churchill Memorial Archive)

Figure 7.4
Grave Robbers. An early nineteenth century engraving shows grave robbers stealing a lead coffin from St. Mary, Aldermanbury. (Courtesy of Guildhall Library, Corporation of London)

Figure 7.5
A 19th century warehouse in Aldermanbury. (Courtesy of Guildhall Library, Corporation of London)

Figure 8.1
The east end of the nave of St. Mary, Aldermanbury. This sketch was drawn following the Victorian refurbishment of the church, described by the Wren Society as "a most unfortunate restoration." The pulpit, altar and reredoes were of stone. They were removed to make way for oak furnishings from St. Alphage, London Wall, after the amalgamation of the two parishes early in the 20th century. (Courtesy of The Churchill Memorial Archive)

Figure 8.2
The interior of St. Mary Aldermanbury (early 20th Century). This widely published photograph was taken following the installation of the oak pulpit, reredoes, altar and pews from St. Alphage, London Wall. The organ occupied the easternmost bay of the north aisle, the Lady Chapel two bays at the east end of the south aisle. The wooden chancel furnishings were less alien to the Wren ambience than their stone predecessors, but the two latter innovations represent departures from the Wren style. (Churchill Memorial Archive)

Figure 8.3
St. Mary, Aldermanbury (1930). This photograph was taken from a point near Gresham Street, looking north on Aldermanbury. (Courtesy of The Churchill Memorial Archive)

PERSONAL.

"O Israel, return unto the Lord thy God." "I will heal their backsliding, I will love them freely; for Mine anger is turned away from him."
Hosea xiv. 1, 4.

†

St. Mary-the-Virgin, Aldermanbury, E.C.

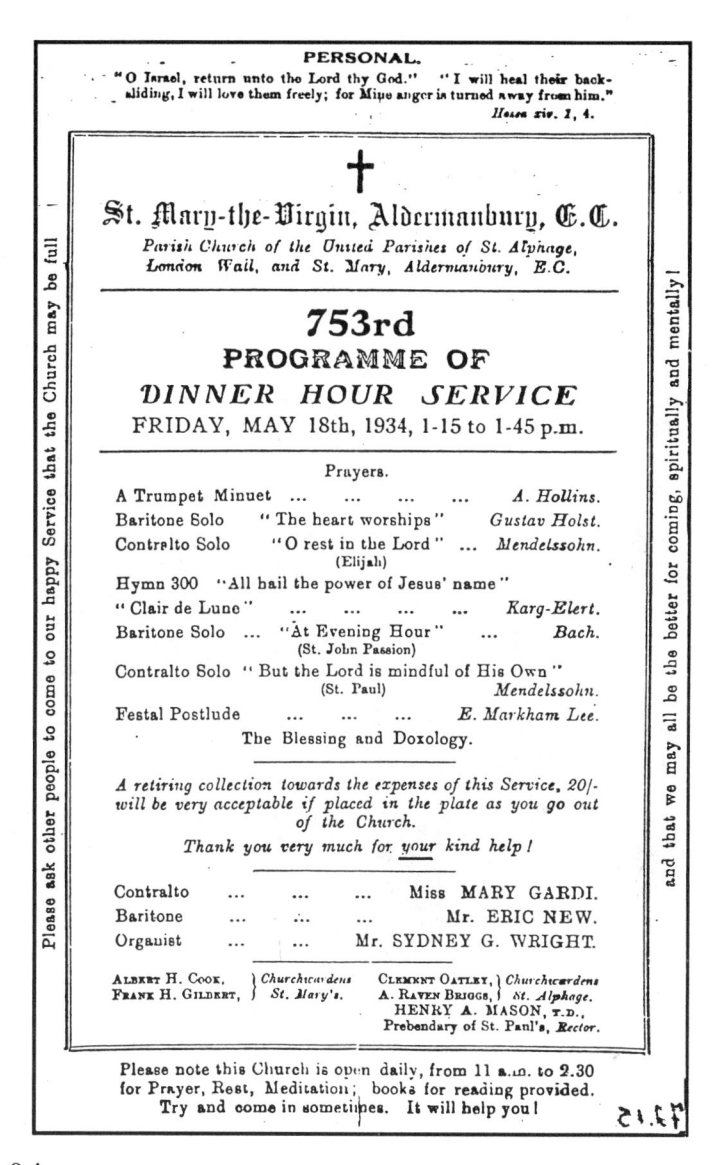

Parish Church of the United Parishes of St. Alphage, London Wall, and St. Mary, Aldermanbury, E.C.

753rd
PROGRAMME OF
DINNER HOUR SERVICE
FRIDAY, MAY 18th, 1934, 1-15 to 1-45 p.m.

Prayers.

A Trumpet Minuet	... ...	*A. Hollins.*
Baritone Solo	"The heart worships"	*Gustav Holst.*
Contralto Solo	"O rest in the Lord" (Elijah)	*Mendelssohn.*
Hymn 300	"All hail the power of Jesus' name"	
"Clair de Lune"	... ...	*Karg-Elert.*
Baritone Solo	"At Evening Hour" (St. John Passion)	*Bach.*
Contralto Solo	"But the Lord is mindful of His Own" (St. Paul)	*Mendelssohn.*
Festal Postlude	... ...	*E. Markham Lee.*

The Blessing and Doxology.

A retiring collection towards the expenses of this Service, 20/- will be very acceptable if placed in the plate as you go out of the Church.

Thank you very much for your kind help!

Contralto	Miss MARY GARDI.
Baritone	Mr. ERIC NEW.
Organist	Mr. SYDNEY G. WRIGHT.

ALBERT H. COOK, } *Churchwardens* CLEMENT OATLEY, } *Churchwardens*
FRANK H. GILBERT, } *St. Mary's.* A. RAVEN BRIGGS, } *St. Alphage.*
HENRY A. MASON, T.D.,
Prebendary of St. Paul's, *Rector.*

Please note this Church is open daily, from 11 a.m. to 2.30 for Prayer, Rest, Meditation; books for reading provided. Try and come in sometimes. It will help you!

Please ask other people to come to our happy Service that the Church may be full

and that we may all be the better for coming, spiritually and mentally!

Figure 8.4

1934 Programme. Before it was bombed in 1940, the Church of St. Mary, Aldermanbury was open on workdays to provide shelter for workers who came into the City on the cheaper early hour fares and needed a place to stay until their places of employment opened. There was also a program of weekly concerts and services on weekdays rather than Sundays. These efforts to offer a relevant ministry to a changing parish were quite successful. (Courtesy of The Churchill Memorial Archive)

Figure 9.1
Sir Winston Churchill on the Westminster Campus. Sir Winston Churchill approaches Washington West House, then the home of the President of Westminster College, on March 5, 1946, for a luncheon, with President Harry S. Truman on the left and Westminster President Franc L. McCluer on the right. The menu included Callaway County country ham, about which Sir Winston remarked: "The pig has reached the highest state of evolution." (Courtesy of The Churchill Memorial Archive)

Figure 9.2
The "Iron Curtain" Speech. Sir Winston S. Churchill stands at the podium in the gymnasium of Westminster College on March 5, 1946, delivering his Green Foundation lecture, "The Sinews of Peace," better known as the "Iron Curtain" speech. The podium, once a pulpit in the College's Swope Chapel, is on permanent display in the Churchill Memorial Museum and was used by other prominent speakers, including former Soviet president Mikhail Gorbachev on May 6, 1992. (Courtesy of The Churchill Memorial Archive)

Figure 9.3
Westminster College President R. L. D. Davidson and reconstruction architect Marshall Sisson, conferring in the ruins of the Church in London. (Courtesy of The Churchill Memorial Archive)

Figure 9.4
The fabric of the Church showing the devastation caused by the bombing raid of 29 December, 1940. (Courtesy of The Churchill Memorial Archive)

Figure 9.5
The park created on the site of the Church, after removal of the Wren fabric to Westminster College. (Courtesy of The Churchill Memorial Archive)

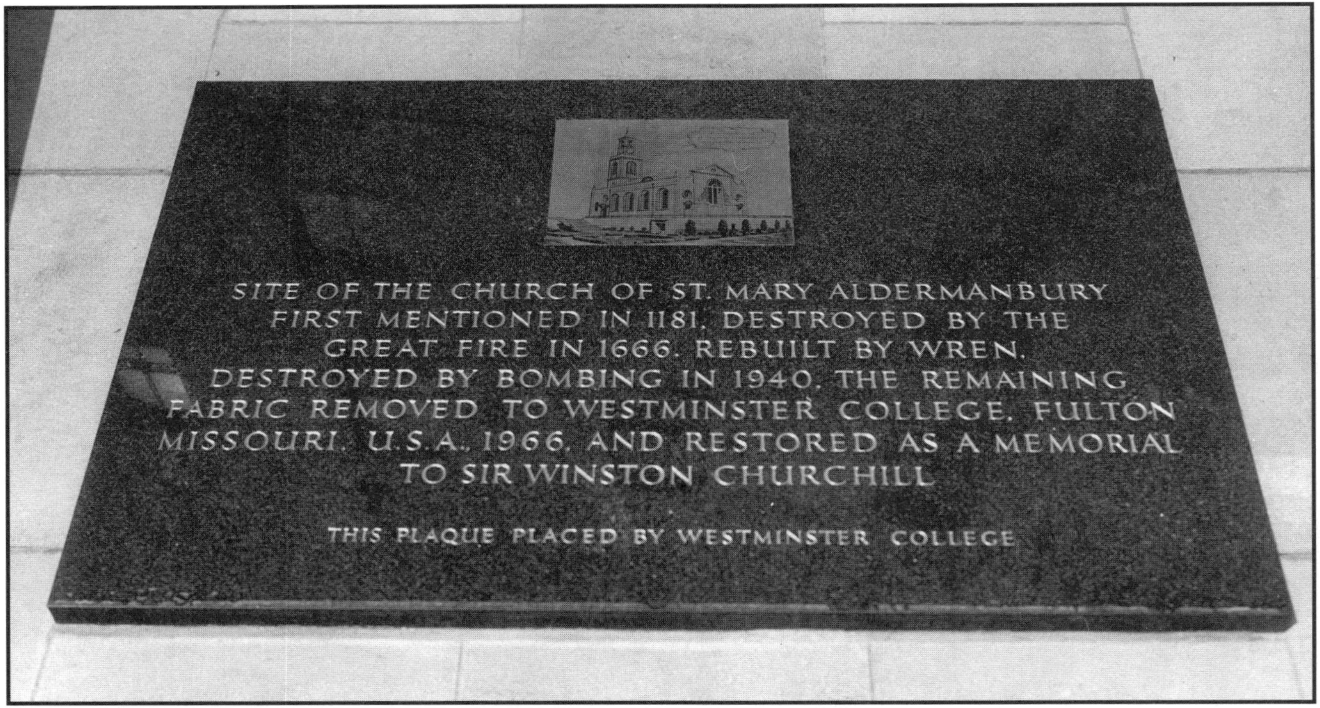

Figure 9.6
The plaque placed by Westminster College in the park created at the site of St. Mary, Aldermanbury in London, after the removal of the fabric of the Church. (Courtesy of The Churchill Memorial Archive)

Figure 9.7
President Harry S. Truman turning the symbolic first shovel for the Churchill Memorial on 19 April, 1964. The ceremony was held at the historic Westminster Columns, since the site on campus for the Memorial had not been finally settled. Mr. Truman cheerfully turned spadeful after spadeful as photographers called out, "One more, Mr. President!" (Courtesy of The Churchill Memorial Archive)

Figure 9.8
Master stonemason Eris Lytle. Mr. Lytle of the John Epple Construction Company, was responsible for laying the stones of the reconstructed Church of St. Mary, Aldermanbury, which had been transported from London. He proved himself a worthy successor to the great master masons who worked with Sir Christopher Wren. Lytle's recorded memories of the project are held in the Churchill Memorial. (Courtesy of The Churchill Memorial Archive)

Figure 9.9
The "greatest jigsaw puzzle in the history of architecture." The stones of the Church of St. Mary, Aldermanbury, are laid out on the campus of Westminster College in preparation for the reconstruction. (Courtesy of The Churchill Memorial Archive)

Figure 9.10
Westminster College President R. L. D. Davidson; College Board of Trustees Member and Project Chairman, Neal Wood; British Reconstruction architect Marshall Sisson; and American architect Frederick Sternberg announcing the Churchill Memorial project. (Courtesy of The Churchill Memorial Archive)

Figure 9.11
The Church of St. Mary, Aldermanbury, reconstructed according to the design of Sir Christopher Wren. This view of the Church from the southwest, shows the statue of Sir Winston Churchill by sculptor Franta Belsky. (Courtesy of The Churchill Memorial Archive)

Figure 9.12
Lord Mountbatten of Burma, Churchill's daughter Lady Mary Soames, Gen. Mark Clark, official representative for President Richard Nixon, and R.L.D. Davidson, Westminster College president at the rehallowing of the church and the dedication of the Churchill Memorial on 7 May, 1969. (Courtesy of The Churchill Memorial Archive)

Figure 9.13a & b
The Breakthrough Sculpture. This sculpture, made from panels of the Berlin Wall, was designed and executed by Churchill's granddaughter, Edwina Sandys. It symbolizes the end of the era of the Iron Curtain. It was dedicated on 9 November, 1990, by former U.S. President Ronald Reagan, one year after the Berlin Wall "came down". (Courtesy of The Churchill Memorial Archive)

Figure 9.14a & b
Former President of the U.S.S.R. Mikhail Gorbachev speaking before the Breakthrough Sculpture. On May 6, 1992, President Gorbachev came to Westminster College and spoke before a crowd of 20,000. As Sir Winston Churchill had done in 1946, Mr. Gorbachev delivered a Green Foundation lecture in which he called for international cooperation in facing the common enemies of humanity. History had come full circle! (Courtesy of The Churchill Memorial Archive)

Figure 10.1
The altar of the reconstructed Church of St. Mary, Aldermanbury. The reredoes above the altar was designed by reconstruction architect Marshall Sisson, with carvings by Arthur Ayres, in the style of Grinling Gibbons, the master woodcarver who worked with Sir Christopher Wren in the rebuilding of St. Paul's Cathedral and at least a few of the City churches. The communion silver on the altar is the 17th century set from the Church of St. Anne and St. Agnes. The Ten Commandments above the altar were a typical feature of 17th century churches in England. (Courtesy of The Churchill Memorial Archive)

Figure 10.2
The Mander tracker organ. This organ, built under the direction of Noel P. Mander at St. Peter's Organworks, London, is one of the finest Baroque organs in North America. The central part of the case dates to the 18th century and is from the parish church in Woolwich, Kent. Two flute pipes by George England, who built St. Mary's first organ, are incorporated into the instrument. The crown and bishops' mitres atop the organ, symbolizing the Restoration of 1660, are from the London City Church of St. Michael Paternoster Royal. (Courtesy of Mr. Bruce Hackmann)

Figure 10.3
A 17th century cherub from one of the vestry screens. This carving, from Wren's St. Dionis Backchurch, was incorporated into the reconstructed Church of St. Mary, Aldermanbury. Perhaps from the shop of Grinling Gibbons, this cherub and the surrounding adornments served as the basic motifs for Arthur Ayres' 20th century reproduction carvings on the reredoes gallery and pulpit. (Courtesy of The Churchill Memorial Archive)

Figure 10.4
Pulpit carving in the reconstructed Church. A 20th century cherub, by artist Arthur Ayres, adorns the pulpit of St. Mary, Aldermanbury. (Courtesy of The Churchill Memorial Archive)

Figure 10.5
Victorian Communion Silver. This communion silver was in the St. Mary, Aldermanbury safe on the night of 29 December, 1940. It still bears the scars of the Blitz. The 18th century bust of the Virgin Mary, which once again caps the Churchwarden's staff, can be seen in the right rear. (Courtesy of The Churchill Memorial Archive)

Figure 10.6
Candlesticks from Westminster Cathedral. The Roman Catholic Westminster Cathedral was the source of St. Mary's handsome candlesticks. They were a gift to the Church of St. Mary, Aldermanbury, from the Cathedral. The communion silver is the St. Anne and St. Agnes plate, a memorial to Canon C. B. Mortlock. Some of the pieces were originally from St. John Zachary, a Church not rebuilt after the Great Fire of 1666. (Courtesy of Dr. Christian Hauer, FSA, FRSA)

Figure 10.7
Lord Mayor's Sword and Stand. As a London city church, St. Mary, Aldermanbury, required a sword stand for the Lord Mayor's ceremonial sword during official visits. The St. Mary's stand bears the arms of the Worshipful Company of Haberdashers and is a replica of a 17th century stand in Haberdashers Hall. St. Mary's was the guild Church of the Haberdashers; they and a company of other British donors catalogued in chapter 10 made the gift of the stand. The restored 18th century sword was presented by the Corporation of the City of London. (Courtesy of Dr. Christian Hauer, FSA, FRSA)

Figure 10.8
Dr. Noel P. Mander, MBE, FSA. Dr. Mander, organbuilder for St. Mary Aldermanbury, Christ Church, Canterbury, and St. Paul's Cathedral, is official representative of the Churchill Memorial in the United Kingdom. He was an early advocate of the project to bring the Church to Westminster College and is responsible for many of the furnishings and adornments which enhance the beauty of the Church. (Courtesy of N. P. Mander, Ltd.)

CHAPTER SIX: A PROSPEROUS PARISH
(1677-1790)

Introduction

During the late seventeenth and eighteenth centuries the Church of St. Mary, the Virgin, Aldermanbury was an influential church in a growing city. The first post-fire curate was Edmund Calamy's son, Benjamin. Unlike his father Benjamin opposed nonconformity and advocated this position during his curacy at Aldermanbury. During Benjamin Calamy's tenure the most infamous parishoner in the history of Aldermanbury, Sir George Jeffreys (known as "The Hanging Judge") was active in the church (see Figure 6.1). Was Jeffreys as terrible as tradition has made him out to be? In this chapter we will take up that question. Apart from Judge Jeffrey's notoriety, during this period life in the parish was stable in comparison to the turmoil of the previous century. A great deal of parish energy during the eighteenth century was invested in the care of the poor within the parish bounds and relatively mundane issues of parish life. Therefore, the Aldermanbury story in this chapter is concerned primarily with the relatively ordinary life of a growing parish. The century ended on the dawn of the industrial age, when life would change dramatically in the parish.

Before we turn to the story of parish life during this period, we will set the stage with an examination of political, economic, social and religious developments on the national stage. The reign of the Stuarts continued with the ineffective James II replacing his brother, Charles II. Aldermanbury's Judge Jeffreys was a participant in the events which ultimately drove James into exile and the Judge into the Tower of London. The Glorious Revolution deposed James and installed the Dutch William of Orange and his wife, James' daughter, Mary, as co-sovereigns of a nation which had entered the modern age.

Under Anne, the last Stuart monarch, and the early Hanoverians, England and Scotland were constitutionally joined as the United Kingdom and the threat of a (Catholic) Stuart restoration ended. Parliamentary supremacy took firmer root and "responsible" government under the two party system evolved. Britain took its place as one of (if not the) premier powers of Europe and set the stage to become the most successful imperial power.

The Stuarts (continued)

James II (1685-1688)

England, with the exception of a few radical Whigs, some of them exiles on the Continent, appeared ready to accept a middle-aged Catholic monarch whose heirs were his Protestant daughters, Mary and Anne. Both were safely married by James' accession, Mary to the Protestant champion, William III of Orange, Staatholder of the Netherlands, and Anne to the amiable Protestant prince, George of Denmark. The accomodating Dr. Wren, staunch in his own Protestant convictions, designed a Catholic chapel for the king at St. James Palace. James' first Parliament was most friendly, voting him a generous subsidy. This demonstration of loyalty to the principle of legalistic royal succession triumphed readily over its first challenge, Monmouth's Rebellion.

Monmouth's Rebellion

James, Duke of Monmouth, was the popularly acknowledged (if illegitimate) son of Charles II. Had Whigs been able to pass the act of Exclusion, it was this Protestant prince who would have displaced James, Duke of York, as heir to the throne. He had earned his spurs as a soldier in his father's service. But because of his implication in the abortive Rye House plot of 1683 to assassinate both Charles and James, he was in Dutch exile at his father's death. Whig expatriates quickly persuaded Monmouth that England was ready to rise in his favor should he return. He embarked with a small force, but failed to rendezvous with Whig compatriots in the north due to the royal fleet. By the time he avoided the navy and made his landing in the south, his allies had been suppressed. The Prince of Orange played a skillful diplomatic game in this episode. He made no effort to impede Monmouth's sailing, but he freely honored a treaty obligation to support James with Dutch troops, and even offered to lead them himself. If Monmouth succeeded, William would have a Protestant ally against Louis XIV. If Monmouth failed, William's wife was first in line to succeed her aging father. Monmouth landed 11 June, 1685. His days were sorely numbered.

Monmouth was able to raise a troop of volunteers to augment his small invading force, but his run of bad luck continued. The country did not rise. Cities locked their gates in his face. He probably realized early on that he was doomed. Soon the king's regulars, strong in cavalry and led by Lord Churchill and Colonel Kirke, skilled professional soldiers, dogged his heels, awaiting the arrival of the main force.

At this juncture, Monmouth gained whatever chance he may have had. The custom of trusting supreme command to a senior nobleman, which had afflicted the Parliamentary army early in the Civil War, was alive and well. The Earl of Feversham, a French emigre', commanded the king's army, and he was demonstrating singular skills at doing nothing against the enemy on his front. Monmouth gambled all on a single throw at Sedgmoor, launching a courageous night attack. A deep ditch provided chance protection for Feversham's unprepared force. But Churchill was prepared. He broke the rebel flank and carried all before him. Monmouth's army was scattered with heavy losses and the Duke himself was captured and committed to his uncle's tender mercy. It was the custom for the victim at a beheading to tip the headsman in hope of a quick and painless dispatch. The executioner was usually promised an additional gratuity from a trusted retainer if his work was in fact well done. Monmouth's killer did such a clumsy job that the Duke rose from the block to glare at him before resuming the appropriate posture. One hopes the trusted servant kept the additional money in this case.

At this point, Aldermanbury parish, or at any rate one of its more substantial citizens, the infamous "hanging judge" George Jeffreys, moved to prominence on the national stage. Because of his importance in the story of the Aldermanbury parish we will devote separate attention to the good judge when we return to the history of the parish.

The Policies of James

Seldom has a figure in political life thrown away advantage, embraced catastrophe and snatched defeat from the jaws of victory with the skill and enthusiasm of James II. It might be a going a bit far to say that James at any time enjoyed the affection of a substantial body of Englishmen (even among the poltroon clergy who admonished poor Monmouth on the scaffold concerning the Anglican doctrine of non-resistance). But the mass of Englishmen did accept him (as they had accepted Mary Tudor) as the legitimate heir. To the grief of diehard Whigs, England was willing to endure an aging Catholic monarch when his only two legitimate heirs were Protestant! He had the support of Parliament, which voted him generous revenues, and the loyalty of the army and navy as well as the various orders of civil society. But James seemed to combine within himself the political vices of the Stuart line with none of their redeeming virtues. He was stubborn, arrogant, imperious, dogmatic in his personal convictions and in his will to bend others to them, and devout in his royal absolutism, while lacking the intelligence of his predecessors or the saving wit and tolerance of his brother.

James embarked upon policies that seemed intended to subjugate English freedoms to the royal will and to dragoon England into the Catholic fold. Louis XIV revoked the Edict of Nantes, which had afforded limited protection to France's persecuted Protestant minority shortly after James accession and many fled to England to escape renewed brutality. This example of the fruits of Catholic hegemony was not lost on Englishmen. Neither was the potential for mischief in James' policies, which included the wholesale appointment of Catholic officials under an alleged "dispensing" power, in defiance of the Test Act. James had sought its repeal, but Parliament refused. He also sought repeal of the Habeas Corpus act without result. Perhaps most menacing was the expansion of the army, which stood at 20,000 men and still growing by 1686, many of the troopers Irish Catholic recruits, and a substantial Catholic officer cadre. Summer encampments were held near London in a transparent attempt at intimidation.

An effort to subvert the Protestant succession backfired. James offered to pass over Mary in Anne's favor if she would convert to Catholicism. But Anne was devout in both her high Anglicanism and high Toryism. So Anne and her husband, George, Prince of Denmark, were further estranged from the king. Anne and her confidantes, chief among them John and Sarah Churchill, Sidney, Earl Godolphin, and Bishop Compton of London, became at great risk a sort of resistance cell in the heart of

Whitehall. (Anne's apartment was called "the Cockpit," because it stood where chicken fights were once held—hence "the Cockpit set.") But Churchill, with his courtier's bland and inscrutable demeanor, and his reputation as the hero of Sedgmoor, retained senior command.

James attempted to co-opt the high Anglican episcopate in his policy of Catholic tolerance, or perhaps more accurately, reestablishment. When rebuffed, he sought to bend the Church to his will. Bishop Compton was deposed from the see of London in 1686. James installed a Catholic principal at staunchly Anglican Magdalen College, Oxford. An attempt was made to establish an ecclesiastical court like the old High Commission. And in one fell swoop, James accomplished the improbable feat of making heroes of the bishops. (The clergy of the established Church stood low in public esteem, the bishops even lower.) On 18 May, 1688, James caused the arrest of seven bishops (Archbishop Sancroft of Canterbury among them) who had opposed his policies, charging them with seditious libel. Bells rang and crowds cheered in London on 30 June when, despite the king's power over the courts, they were acquitted. James noted with dismay that there was cheering in the army, too. For the record, even the Pope counseled against James' headlong zeal, and was ultimately part of the coalition that favored his fall.

The event that sealed James' doom transpired even before the Bishops' victory. Queen Mary of Modena, James' long-barren Catholic second wife, allegedly bore a son on 10 June. Official witnesses at the birth, essential in a matter of royal succession, were unwisely restricted to the king's Catholic cronies. A popular rumor circulated that the baby was in fact a foundling, smuggled into the royal bedroom in a bedwarming pan.

The advent of the warming pan prince created, as Americans say, "a new ball game." The Whig opposition had been whipped into a state of rabid enmity. The Tories had been alienated by favoritism to Catholics and attacks on the established Church. But all except a few hotheads seemed content to let nature take its course with the aging Catholic king and his tyrannical ways, and bring a reigning Protestant queen to the throne in due course. But now England faced the prospect of a Catholic dynasty with no end in sight. Not only England. Also the Prince of Orange. His wife, Mary, formerly the heir, was now second in line and unlikely to inherit. (William himself, as a grandson of Charles I, could stake a personal claim on the British throne, though he never pressed it.) For Englishmen committed to some combination of Protestantism and/or liberty, and for William's strategic designs, the waiting game ended abruptly. It was now or never.

The Glorious Revolution

No headstrong dashing hero was William of Orange, but a man of patience and sagacity. History does not rank him among the great battle leaders. But under his leadership, the tiny Dutch Republic had survived the onslaughts of Louis' hordes, and still he schemed to sustain a coalition that could check Louis' ambition if not bring him to heel. Correspondence had flowed between William and those in England opposed to or made uneasy by James' policies, Lord Churchill among them. But William required more than friendly noises to bestir him against James. He required an explicit invitation and assurance from an adequate company of prominent British leaders. On the night that London celebrated the bishops' acquittal, seven magnates, Danby and Bishop Compton among them, met at Lord Shrewbury's house and subscribed a letter to William, assuring him of their support should he come to England. William was willing, but all must be right. Careful negotiations gained the support of the Pope, the Holy Roman emperor, the Spanish government and assorted German princes. Louis XIV of France, who could be as harsh on Catholic prelates who opposed his policies as Protestant leaders, was the key player, for if he made his annual war in the Low Countries, William would be tied down, seeing to the defense of Holland. But in September, the French armies marched off to have their annual war on the middle Rhine. William was free to move.

Alarmed at the temper of the country, Jeffreys and Sunderland persuaded James to reverse some of his most detested policies. But it was too late to turn back the clock. William sailed for England on 19 October, his ships bearing six Scottish and English regiments along with Dutch, Swedish, Danish and Prussian troops from the Protestant side of William's coalition. Unfavorable winds prevented an invasion to the north, but then a "Protestant wind" carried his fleet southward through the Channel while the British fleet failed to intercept. The invading/liberating army landed in Devon on 5 November. When reminded it was the anniversary of the gunpowder plot, Calvinist William remarked to a deputy, "What do you think of predestination now?"

The royal army numbered 40,000 in November, 1688. Of these, 25,000 foot and horse soldiers were sent westward to confront William's force of some 12,000 near Salisbury while 7,000 royal troops were deployed against London, a tribute to the

City's love of liberty. But the sizes of the two armies were not constant. William's grew while James' shrank. The 23rd of November was particularly costly to James, psychologically even more than numerically. Lord Churchill rode over to Prince William's camp with a part of his command while in London Princess Anne decamped from Whitehall in the company of Sarah Churchill and Bishop Compton. The fleet and with it key ports declared for William. Rebellion flared across the country. James retreated to London and then fled south, sending orders to dissolve the army and throwing the Great Seal in the Thames himself. Rumors of Irish atrocities led to a rising of the London mob and a night of turmoil and terror swept the City and Westminster. The royal council, left in session by James, did what it could to restore order and, acknowledging William, asked him to speed his leisurely march toward London. Meanwhile, a citizen posse apprehended James when his escape ship missed the tide. They turned him over to authorities. But the prominent leaders of England were not prepared to conduct a second royal execution in a century. It was arranged for him to "escape" again, this time successfully.

As we shall see below, Aldermanbury's Lord Chancellor Jeffreys did not fare so well as his master. England and Scotland would be plagued for decades by abortive attempts to restore James' male line to the English throne. But a French nobleman who heard out James' arguments for why he should be restored as king observed that he afterward understood why he could never be.

James flight and William's acclamation created an irregular constitutional situation that in England at an earlier and ruder time, and in many lands at any time, would have been settled with a few murders, some perhaps ritually staged as executions. The total and rapid disintegration of James' authority and wholesale defections by both high and low from his cause had spared England civil war even as they spared William the image of a foreign conqueror. To that point the Glorious Revolution had been a bloodless revolution (discounting mob mayhem against Catholics and the embassies of Catholic governments). But social chaos, potentially exacerbated by James' dissolution of the army, turning hordes of unemployed troopers upon the country, threatened. William was invited to take interim charge by an ad hoc company of Whig and Tory peers and MP's, and City notables. A call went out in William's name for a "convention Parliament" such as the one called by General Monck and the Long Parliament. Such a Parliament met to resolve the constitutional crisis and provide England with a proper government. William, ever the shrewd hard bargainer, refused to settle for a regency in the stead of his absent father-in-law or a sort of princely premiership during the lifetime of his wife, the recognized heir. Letting it be known that he was prepared to go home and leave England to stew in its own juices, William gained the offer of joint sovereignty with his wife. Under the agreement, in the event of the death of either, the other would continue to reign for life. But it was not an offer with no strings attached. The sovereigns for their part had to accept the Declaration of Rights, which clearly made the divine right of kings the dead letter it really always had been. James' constitutional transgressions were denounced, and fundamental civil rights guaranteed to all subjects of the British crown.

Parliament declared that James had forfeited all claim to the British crown by subverting the constitution and fleeing the country. William and Mary were now the legal, if limited, sovereigns. The subtleties and niceties of limited monarchy and responsible parliamentary government would have to evolve over the decades which lay ahead. But the die had been cast. The people and their Parliament had triumphed in the long struggle with the crown. Modernity had triumphed over the Middle Ages. In a real sense, the political convictions of the moderate Puritans like the Presbyterians of Aldermanbury had been exonerated and England was prepared like no other country to move into the bourgeois world of commerce and industry that (despite Marx and Lenin) still defines the parameters of advanced societies. This model of a constitutional head of state (whether hereditary, appointed, or elected) and a democratic parliament has become the pattern followed by the majority of the world's democracies, while the American form, forged in the sparks of the Enlightenment and moderate Calvinist political ideas struck from the English experience, informs the rest.

The bargain was good enough from William's point of view. In Holland he was merely Staatholder, circumcribed by a web of control in the Estates General. In England he was a real king even if a limited one with a joint sovereign (who never second-guessed her husband's political judgements and who was endlessly helpful to him in political matters). William could now marshall the wealth and power of Britain into his struggle to put a halter on Louis XIV and insure the future of Dutch independence and of continental Protestantism. Thus England was launched on a policy of continental warfare during the reigns of William and Mary, and on into the reign of Anne. And this was a policy fraught with great significance for the City.

Wars cost money, and the brokering of money was the specialty of the City. Wars consume material, and the merchants of the City were prepared to deliver merchandise for a price. Further, the wars and alliances of the last two Stuart reigns advanced England's colonial fortunes at the expense of France and Spain, and even of Holland, again to the profit of the City. Aldermanbury could not but share in the benefits.

Aldermanbury During the Last Years of Charles II (1677-1685) and the Reign Of James II

The Benjamin Calamy Era (1677-1683)

After the post-Fire rebuilding of the Church of St. Mary, the parish was determined to return to its former stability and importance. At a Vestry meeting on 18 April, 1677 a committee was appointed to "prepare and make ready for the choice of a Minister ... ." The committee recommended that a set of criteria be developed before the next curate was appointed. These included recommendations that the "chosen Minister be obliged to preach the weekday lecture ...," that the minister chosen preach every Lord's Day forenoon and afternoon "by himself or such a fit person as the Parish shall approve," that if the person chosen accept any other living which inhibits his ability to perform these duties he resign within three months, and that any person chosen must relinquish any other cure or promotion. The committee also recommended that the new minister post a bond of £300 to guarantee fulfillment of these conditions.

The appointment of a committee of the General Vestry was related to the concentration of power within parishes which began in the late 17th and continued throughout the 18th centuries. In some parishes the open or general vestry was abolished and replaced by a small or "select" vestry made up of the "principal inhabitants" of the parish. In other parishes a mixed form of government developed, with some business (especially the selection of a minister) conducted by a general vestry and the rest by a smaller, select vestry (Rude 1971: 130-131).

On 25 April the Vestry accepted these recommendations and ordered that they be entered into the Vestry Book as a precedent. The first name on the list of committee members was George Jeffreys, Esq. At this same meeting three names were placed in nomination for the curacy—Mr. Benjamin Calamy, Mr. Heaver, and Mr. Hall.

Calamy was selected, probably at the urging of Jeffreys. At this Vestry it was also ordered that no books be taken from the chest in the Vestry Room without the approval of the Vestry.

Benjamin Calamy (1642-1686) was the second son of Edmund Calamy by his second wife, Anne Leaver. He received his education at St. Paul's School and Catherine Hall, Cambridge. He was still at Cambridge when his father and elder brother, also named Edmund, were ejected after the implementation of the Act of Uniformity. Soon after his appointment at St. Mary's, Benjamin was named one of the king's chaplains. Although he chose conformity to the established church, he remained on good terms with his nonconformist brother and nephew, both named Edmund. In one of his sermons he claimed that if he could find a church "that did lay greater stress upon a pure mind and blameless life, and less upon voluntary strictness and indifferent rites than we do, I would very soon be of that church, ..." (Dictionary of Biography III: 679).

Accounts for 1677 show that George Jeffreys' first wife, Lady Sarah Jeffreys, was buried in the Vault. They also show 5s spent for "hungry Ministers," presumably those who, like Edmund Calamy, had 15 years ago lost their parishes because of refusal to assent to the Act of Uniformity. Funds were also spent for "severall poore Ministers Widdows." A total of 18.10.10 was spent on the annual Ascension Day feasts, including 2s for tobacco, 4.13.0 for wine, and 1.14.0 for "beare Ale and bread." 7.1.6 was received from Parishoners toward the Ascension Day dinner. In addition, 4s was paid "the same day a notice was given concerning the Marage [sic] between the Prince of Orange and Her Highness ye Duke of York's Daughter." A chamber pot was also purchased for the Vestry.

On 20 March, 1678, a Mr. Steven was named lecturer for the Sunday afternoon service.

Excursus: Sir George Jeffreys (1648-1689)

George Jeffreys was perhaps the most infamous resident of Aldermanbury in the history of the parish (see Figure 6.1). A native of Denbighshire, he was educated at Westminster School, Cambridge University (1662-63), and the Inner Temple (1663-68). According to tradition, Jeffreys spent more time in the taverns than studying, and had a knack for cultivating the favor of influential people.

Jeffreys married his first wife, Sarah Neesham, in 1667. She had been a companion to a rich heiress Jeffreys had been courting, and Jeffreys was using Sarah to communicate with the heiress, whose father disapproved of him. When the father of the heiress discovered Sarah's role, he threw her out. The fact that Jeffreys married her has been cited as evidence that he was capable of showing compassion (Balfour 1925: 72). However, Sarah did bring with her a dowry of £300 (Helm 1966: 21). After their marriage the couple lived at 79 Coleman Street, near the Guildhall.

Jeffreys became a barrister in 1668. On 13 December, 1671, Jeffreys, now Common Sergeant of the City, was given "the back tenement in Aldermanbury contiguous to the wall enclosing Mr. Town Clerk's Courtyard which (with two other tenements before the same next the Street) are now built by the City upon the ground lately purchased of Sergeant Goddard for and during so long tyme as he shall continue Common Sergeant and Officer of the City paying the yearly rent of £20 ..." (Balfour 1927-31: 179, quoting the City records). The Common Sergeant had a judicial role in the city courts and also at the courts of Old Bailey.

In 1677 he was named solicitor-general for the Duke of York. On 14 September, 1677, Charles II knighted him. He became involved in the prosecution of the "popish plot" and developed a reputation as a skilled orator and vigorous prosecutor.

In 1678 he was elevated from the post of Common Sergeant to the office of Recorder of London. As Recorder he passed sentences on prisoners at Old Bailey and acted as spokesman for the Common Council on official occasions. He called himself the "Mouth of the City." His opponents called him simply "the mouth" (Helm 1966: 30). When he left the post two years later due to political differences, a committee was appointed to consider what sum to pay Jeffreys because of improvements made to his house. He apparently persuaded the Aldermen to allow him to stay in the house, for records show his name on the lease through the rest of his life. However, he leased the house to a John Normansell in 1685 for £82 a year.

The house stood behind no. 18 and 19 Aldermanbury (see Figure 6.2). To the north was Three Nun Court, where the Axe Inn was located. To the South, abutting Jeffrey's house were two small tenements recently built by William Avery, the town clerk. It was apparently the Town Clerk's official residence.

Jeffrey's house would have had three storeys. A great parlor and small parlor were on the ground level. A large room, probably used for dining, was on the first floor, as were bedrooms. A full schedule of fixtures for the house has been preserved, including "a pissing Cisterne in ye fore Yard" (Balfour 1927-31: 190). The house was extensively remodelled in 1679.

Jeffreys also acquired a country home in Buckinghamshire, and entertained the King there in August,1678 (Helm 1966: 29).

In 1680 Jeffreys became Chief Justice at Chester and counsel for the crown at Ludlow. He was chastized for his overbearing conduct. He had a role in the judicial murder of Algernon Sidney and earned royal attention through his brutality toward Richard Baxter. Although King Charles II once said Jeffreys had "no learning, no sense, no manners and more impudence than ten carted street-walkers," (Oliver, 1969: 37) he appointed Jeffreys Lord Chief Justice of England in September, 1683. The same year Jeffreys became a member of the Privy Council. An incident in 1684 is often cited to show how ruthless Jeffreys was. In condemning Sir Thomas Armstrong to death, he responded to Armstrong's appeal that "he have the benefit of the law and nothing more," Jeffrey's is reputed to have said, "That you shall have by the grace of God. See that execution be done on Friday next, according to the Law."

In 1685 he became Baron Jeffreys of Wem and took a seat in the House of Lords. He moved that year from Aldermanbury to a more fashionable dwelling on Great Queen St. in Lincoln Inn's Fields, then in 1687 to Duke Street in Westminster, near St. James Park. Jeffreys was now at the pinnacle of his power, virtually "ruler of the City" in some historians' estimation.

After Monmouth's Rebellion (1685) failed, Jeffreys earned the nickname "The Hanging Judge." King James II dispatched him to execute a judicial mopping up operation in the wake of the military suppression. The series of trials which followed, with Jeffreys at the bench, became known as the "Bloody Assizes." He apparently amassed considerable personal wealth through extortion of the rebels' families and friends, although his gestures of "clemency" were limited. For example, he agreed to allow one of his female prisoners, an Alice Lisle, to be beheaded rather than burned. The records of the trials suggest that for Jeffreys accusation was tantamount to conviction. Jeffrey's ruthlessness was fully supported by the King. On one occasion, Lord Churchill remarked to a woman (whose appeals to the king for her family he was supporting) that the royal heart was as warm and soft as the marble mantle on which he rested his elbow. As a result of the "Bloody Assizes" over 200 people were hanged and nearly 800 "transported" to Barbados as virtual slaves. In recognition of his loyalty, on 28 September, 1685, King James II made Jeffreys Lord Chancellor of England.

Jeffreys' loyalty, however, was fickle. When James was under fire in 1688, Jeffreys first tried to dissociate himself from the King. He returned the Great Seal to the King on 8 December, and, as noted above, James threw it into the Thames when he fled London. Jeffreys then tried to flee in the disguise of a sailor. He intended to escape abroad, but on 12 December, 1688, he was captured while drinking at a tavern.

Jeffreys was committed to the same Tower of London where many of those whom he had sentenced to death met their fate. Before he could be executed, he died in the Tower on 18 April, 1689, and was buried there. However, he was later reinterred in a splendid lead coffin next to his first wife on 2 November, 1698, near the communion table of the Church of St. Mary. This was undoubtedly done out of deference to the second Mrs. Jeffreys, who remained a respected member of the Aldermanbury parish after her husband's disgrace. The parishoners probably had little love for their former trustee and his vicious loyalty to the Catholic monarch. The coffin was seen as late as 1810 (see Ch. 7), but when Grimes excavated the church after the removal of its fabric to America, he could not find it. Apparently it had been robbed for its lead, but it is also possible that it was actually under the north side of the communion table, rather than directly underneath it as Grimes had assumed.

As we have already seen, Jeffreys was very active in the life of the Aldermanbury parish. For example, at a meeting on 3 April, 1678, "Sir George Jeffreys, Knight" is listed among those named assessors for the poor.

The consensus of historians is that Jeffreys "was a man of considerable talents and some social gifts" but that he was also "devoid of principle, of drunken and extravagant habits, ... reckless of everything save his own advancements" (Dictionary of Biography 1973: 718).

However, is such an appraisal fair? A few modern historians have begun to challenge the accepted assessment of Judge Jeffreys. They point out that the villification of Jeffreys began shortly after his death. He became a convenient scapegoat upon whom all the ills of the past decade could be blamed. Early historians simply echoed the stereotype of the pamphleteers. In 1705 one wrote that Jeffreys was "perpetually either drunk or in a rage, liker a fury than ... a judge. ... He hanged, in several places about six hundred persons. He ordered a great many to be hanged up immediately, without allowing them a minute to say their prayers" (cited in Helm 1966: 193-194).

The most widely read English historian of the 1800's, Thomas Macaulay, secured the image of "the hanging judge" in <u>The History of England from the Accession of James II</u> (1848-1855). Among his statements about Jeffreys were the following (cited in Helm 1966: 194):

> most consummate bully ever known in his profession. All tenderness for the feelings of others, all self respect, all sense of the becoming were obliterated from his mind.

> to enter his court was to enter the den of a wild beast.

There is little wonder that virtually every school child in England and elsewhere learned of the infamous "Hanging Judge" George Jeffreys.

Although Jeffreys was no saint, he may not have been the terrible monster into which legend has made him. His judicial decisions, though harsh, were typical of the time in which he lived. About 200 were executed and 800 sentenced to "transportation" (exile to Barbados) in the "bloody assizes" of 1685, but the punishment was similar to that of governments in similar circumstances throughout the centuries. His oratorical style would today be considered bullying; it was quite in keeping with the courtroom demeanor of the 17th century.

The case can be made that Judge Jeffreys' greatest error was in supporting the wrong side. If he had joined the "Glorious Revolution," contemporary historians would probably have been much kinder to him. As has been said, treason is a matter of timing (Talleyrand, quoted by Helm 1966: 201). Jeffreys himself had prophetically said, "We live in an age wherein men are apt to believe only on one side. They can believe the greatest lie if it makes for the advantage of their party, but not the greatest truth if it thwarts their interests ... ." (Helms 1966: 10).

In 1907 a marker memorializing Judge Jeffreys was set in the church. By this time some historians had begun to challenge the commonly held stereotype. Although the Vestry formally opposed the marker (see Ch. 7), the curate, Rev. C. C. Collins, ignored their protests. The plaque read:

> In memory of George, Baron Jeffreys (of Wem) Recorder of London, Chief Justice of the King's Bench, and Lord Chancellor of England 1685. Formerly a resident of this parish and whose remains are buried in this Church.
>
> "The Lord seeth not as man seeth." 1st Samuel 16:7

The Benjamin Calamy Era (continued)

On 26 September, 1678, the minutes reflect discussion on the steeple and cupola (see Ch. 5), presumably with concern that some finishing work was necessary.

On 18 December, 1678, the Vestry dealt with several matters which had upset members of the parish. The actions probably had the effect of re-establishing the principle of democratic decision making in parish government. The Vestry wanted to make clear that they and not any individual parish officials or members were the governing body. For example, the Vestry ordered that no part of the "Sacrament money" be disposed of by the Churchwarden without authorization of the overseers of the poor. The Vestry also ordered the Clerk and Sexton to inquire within a week which inmates were in the parish and their children. If they neglect their duty the Vestry ordered that half their salaries be withheld. Great concern was also expressed at the discovery that leaves had been removed from the Vestry Book. The Vestry ordered that the missing leaves be appended to the book when they were found (they never were) and instructed the Vestry Clerk to see that such abuses not happen again. The Vestry also voided an earlier seating arrangement and ordered that no person be seated in any pew without the consent of the churchwarden.

On 14 April, 1680, the Vestry ordered that anyone chosen Churchwarden must put in security £200. The Churchwarden handled all the accounts of the parish, and the £200 was an assurance that the funds would not be appropriated for personal use. At the same meeting the Vestry established a rule that no grave stone could be laid in the chancel or churchyard without the consent of the Vestry. A month later, on 19 May, the Vestry established a committee, chaired by John Dubois, to arrange for the painting of the "dyalls [sic]" on the clock. On 25 October the Vestry authorized the principal Churchwarden, Mr. Needler, to rent the back of the churchyard.

During 1681 there were extended discussions on selection of a Sunday afternoon lecturer. After several meetings and creation of a committee, the Vestry drew Dr. Calamy into the discussions. On 8 May, Francis Bridge was chosen to give the lectures for a year. On 13 December, apparently in reaction to the excessive expenditures of recent years, the Vestry ordered that there would be no parish dinner on "Holy Thursday" (Ascension Day) until further notice.

On 29 May, 1682, Calamy preached a sermon before the Lord Mayor and Aldermen on the anniversary of the Restoration of the monarchy. In the sermon

Calamy called the Commonwealth a time of "inslaving this land to the wills and lusts of the basest and meanest of the People" (B. Calamy 1682: 2). He was particularly effusive in his praise of Charles II, calling him "light of our Eyes, the breath of our Nostrils" (3).

On 15 December, 1682, we find the first record in the Vestry records of the election of parish officers. For the rest of the life of the parish in London, these elections were usually held during December in the church. Typically parish officials were elected at meetings held for that purpose. The churchwardens and other church officers were elected at the Easter Vestry. At a General Vestry with 37 members of the parish present (and with the name of George Jeffreys at the head of the list), the parish elected members to represent the parish on the Common Council, Wardmot Inquest, and to serve as Constable and Scavengers for the parish.

In 1683 a dispute over piety arose in the parish, reflecting the continuing tension between nonconformists and conformists over the regulations of the Church of England governing worship. Ironically, Edmund Calamy's refusal to conform cost him the curacy of St. Mary's. Now his son, serving the same parish, found himself a defender of the position his father opposed.

In response to this conflict Benjamin Calamy preached one of his more famous sermons, entitled "A Discourse About a Scrupulous Conscience Containing Some Plain Directions for the Cure of It." The sermon was dedicated to Mr. Jeffreys. He later preached it at St. Mary le Bow, then published it.

In the sermon Calamy stated that his purpose was not "to expose or upbraid the Weakness of any of our Differing Brethren, but rather charitably to contribute what I can towards the healing and curing of it." According to Calamy, a scrupulous conscience was one which focuses on things which God has not commanded us to do or abstain from. It rendered religion "a most troublesome Burden." It "robs men in great measure, of that Peace and Satisfaction which they might otherwise find in Religion, whilst they are daily perplexing themselves with untying Knots which themselves have fastened." Apparently some members of St. Mary's had left the church on this issue, for Calamy spoke of "those who have taken offence at some things in our Church, and have thereupon separated themselves from us, and associated themselves with a purer congregation ... ." He wondered if in their search for purity they will keep refining themselves until "they have sunk down either into Quakerism, Popery, or Atheism." All the quarreling about the incidentals of religion had done mischief to the Reformed Church of England, Calamy asserted.

How does one cure a scrupulous conscience? According to Calamy, the solution was to realize that you too may just be mistaken and need to seek advice from others. You must also distinguish the incidentals of religion, such as whether or not to kneel for the Sacrament, from the essentials, which are based on "thoughts of God Almighty." He asked those who were concerned about Conformity to "think that the Ministers of the Church of England have some Sense and Conscience too as well as other Men." He asserted that in areas where God has not expressly commanded or forbidden an action in worship, that worshippers be guided by "the general Rules of Scripture, the commands of our Superiors, and by the measures of Prudence, Peace, and Charity."

In a response to Calamy's sermon entitled "A Plea for the Non-Conformists" the non-conformist cleric Thomas DeLaune argued that just as the Conformists felt it necessary to separate themselves from the authority of the Pope, Non-conformists considered it essential to distance themselves from the vagaries of the Conformists. He also accused Calamy of hypocrisy for supporting the French Presbyterian dissenters while persecuting English Presbyterian dissenters. He accused Calamy of helping to forward his brethren's afflictions "by your Presses, Pulpit, and Addresses." A note on the response, published in 1704, indicates that DeLaune, his wife, and children, died in Newgate Prison, where DeLaune had been confined because of this publication.

DeLaune was the original author of <u>Angliae Metropolis: or, the Present State of London with Memorials</u>, begun in 1681, which surveyed the ecclesiastical situation in London after the fire. In that work (one of the continuations of Stow's 1598 work) DeLaune reported on the state of the clergy, claiming that the parish rectors and vicars of London "are reputed the most excellent Preachers in Christendom" (DeLaune 1680: 200). He claimed that " ... for the sincere and pure Worship of God, and Profession of the Reformed Religion, there is no City or place in the World can compare with <u>London</u>" (204). He reported that the maintenance of the clergy had been guaranteed. In lieu of tithes, which had been upset by the destruction of property in the fire, an act of Parliament established a schedule of payment for parsons, ranging from £100-200. DeLaune's list had £150 designated as the stipend for St. Mary Aldermanbury's curate. DeLaune also appealed in this work for understanding between Conformists and Dissenters, saying that "it is my hearty wish, that since they all agree in the Fundamentals of Religion, that there may be no clashing or disunion ... . Where we agree in Fundamentals we should have mutual Christian Fellowship, without wrangling about Circumstantials" (204, 206).

Despite the popularity of Calamy's "Scrupulous Conscience" sermon and another publication on the issue entitled Some Considerations About the Case of Scandal or Giving Offence to Weak Brethren (1683), Calamy's days were numbered in the parish. On 20 June, 1683, at a General Vestry, with 79 present, Calamy expressed his intention to surrender the living "into the hands of the parish who are the patrons thereof" to be effective Midsummer "or thereabouts." Ten days later, on the same day Calamy signed his resignation, the parish selected Dr. Nicholas Stratford as Calamy's successor. These circumstances suggest that the sympathies of the parish were still more with the nonconformist position of the late Edmund Calamy than with his son's conformity. The same Vestry ordered that Calamy be paid for his services through 24 June, 1683. After leaving Aldermanbury Calamy assumed the living of St. Lawrence, Jewry (Oliver 1969: 25).

At this same meeting a committee of 11 was appointed to wait upon Sir Christopher Wren concerning a gallery in the church, and an inquiry into the state of parish land was ordered. There was also much discussion as to whether to continue the weekday lecture or to defer it. The Vestry decided to continue the subscriptions for it.

The Nicolas Stratford Era (1683-1689)

Nicolas Stratford was a graduate of Trinity College, Oxford. After taking Holy Orders in 1667 he was appointed by Charles II to a parish church in Manchester, succeeding a Puritan cleric. Charles made him a Chaplain in 1673. He was forced to leave Manchester because of religious controversy and went directly to Aldermanbury (Oliver 1969: 25).

On 14 December, 1683, the records reflect the first instance of what was to become a very common practice. Two men were excused from serving in precinct offices after having been elected to them, through the payment of fines. The offices in question were Constable and Questman and the fine £10. At a meeting four days later one of the fines was waived because of the illness of Henry Smith, and he was given a pension of 4s and some clothes. At this meeting the Vestry tried to draw Dr. Stratford into a controversy over the Sunday afternoon lectureship, but Stratford sidestepped the issue. Nevertheless, the Vestry ordered that the current lecturer, Dr. Bridge, be relieved, and a new lecturer chosen.

On 13 March, 1684, Richard Bird was chosen as lecturer over three other nominees, and several weeks later was confirmed by the entire Vestry. He continued as lecturer until 1702 (Hatton II 1708: 363). On 2 April, 1684, the Vestry appointed a committee to check on a legacy from Mr. Francis Ash, still due from Emmanuel College, Cambridge. Another was assigned the task of finding out why the conduit had not yet been finished and how much it would cost to complete it. By October the Ash bequest was being received and used to pay Dr. Calamy for his services between 29 September 1682 and 24 June 1683. On 4 November, 1684, Calamy signed the Vestry Book to show that he had received from the parish money owed him.

A note in the 25 July, 1684, minutes, indicated that William Berry, a parish boy, was to be apprenticed to Mary Ozell, a widow. She was to be paid £6.4 and discharge the parish from any further charge until the boy was 21. During this period the parish foundlings who had been christened as Aldermanbury were now called William or Charity Berry, and new christenings reflected this shortened surname.

The minutes of the 21 April, 1685, meeting indicate the division of the office of Churchwarden into what was called "open" (later "upper" or "senior") churchwarden and under ("lower" or "junior") churchwarden. The under churchwarden also served as collector for the poor. A committee was established at this meeting to investigate completion of the conduit.

On 17 June, 1685, the Vestry ordered that money designated by gifts for the poor be distributed according to the directions of the overseers of the poor. At this meeting the Vestry also mandated that "ye great pew be taken lower according to St. Lawrence and be not high above the other pews than be at St. Lawrence." Apparently there was concern that the parishoners at St. Mary's not appear to be more ostentatious than the congregation at St. Lawrence Jewry, the church adjacent to the Guildhall. At this same meeting Constable and Questman, Scavenger, and Beadle were elected.

The Vestry created a committee (one of its favorite activities) on 1 April, 1686, to "demand of Mr. Taylor living behind St. Lawrence Church the Ministers tyths in arrears of tyths out of ye minister of St. Mary Aldermanbury for a parcel (?) of ground ... ." A family dispute was referred for hearing to a special panel. A "bastard child" of a parishoner was also discussed.

On 22 November, 1687, the churchwardens were directed to see to the "whitening" and "beautifying" of the church. At the election of parish officials on 14 December, the Vestry received a petition from a widow for a pension, and 2s per week was designated.

Also in 1687 Stratford published a 38 page tract entitled The Lay-Christian's Obligation to read the Holy Scriptures. In the pamphlet he called for the education of women, saying that in the time of Jesus "women were then so learned in the Scriptures, as to be able to instruct their Children" (Stratford 1687: 8). He also said, "... what reason can a Man who knows not the Scriptures give, why he is a Christian, rather than a Mahometan[sic]?" (12). Like others who occupied the Aldermanbury pulpit, Stratford could be rather pointed, as in this timeless series of rhetorical questions (36-37):

> You who pretend you have no leisure for reading the Scriptures
> do not many of you find time enough for worthless impertinent
> matters? if not also for such trivling discourse? Have you
> not time for Feasts, and Merry Meetings, for Cards and Dice; for
> Taverns and Play-houses? How many morning hours (more
> than need) do many persons spend in their Beds, or in attiring
> themselves when they get up?

Apparently by 1688 the practice of an Ascension Day dinner had resumed, for the accounts show that a Mr. Wingrave left his share of the dinner unpaid.

On 27 January, 1688, Robert Aske, Haberdasher, one of the more renowned residents of the parish, died. He rented the glebe house at No. 11-12 Aldermanbury. Aske was a philanthropist and influential citizen. He had been apprenticed in 1634 to John Trott of the Haberdasher's Company and was admitted to the Freedom of the Company in 1643, elected to the Court in 1666, and served as Master in 1684. He was elected Alderman in 1666, but declined to serve and paid a fine. Upon his death he left a large sum of money to care for the poor and educate children of members of the Haberdashers Guild. He was buried in the chancel of the Church. A monument to Mr. Aske was erected in the Church by the Haberdasher's Company early in the twentieth century. (Carter 1913: 3, 94). Its fate, like that of the other monuments left at the site of the Church of St. Mary after the removal of the fabric to Westminster College, is unfortunately unknown. (In 1988, on the 300th anniversary of his death a beautiful stand for the Lord Mayor's sword was erected in the Church in his memory under the sponsorship of the Haberdasher's Company. See Ch. 10.)

William III (1689-1702) and Mary II (1689-1694)

It cannot be said that the joint reign of William and Mary was either a long or a happy one. There was apparently little affection in their royal marriage. William was said to regard Mary more as a political assistant than as a wife. More rigorous historians reject the claim that William was homosexual, suggesting that he devoted most of the limited energy in his sickly body to duty rather than pleasure. After Mary's early death he is said to have missed her greatly.

In the course of the reign, Mary became estranged from her sister, Anne, and ordered her to give up her closest friend and confidante, Sarah Churchill. John Churchill, Lord Marlborough, was dismissed from all his offices. Anne withdrew from the court. William had treated Anne's husband shabbily, and continued to do so. Then, on 28 December, 1694, Mary died of smallpox, confounding expectations that she would outlive her sickly consort, leaving a proper English queen to occupy the throne alone. The tragedy at least resolved a damaging conflict. William and Anne made peace and the Marlboroughs returned in due course to their respective posts. But William seemed on the whole to have an inadequate appreciation of Englishmen, and awarded many high offices to foreigners, chiefly Dutchmen. To be sure, many prominent Englishmen were in correspondence with the exiled court of James, hedging their bets against his ultimate restoration. However, when the chips were down, the chief among them (including Marlborough and Admiral Russell) remained staunchly loyal to William and the revolutionary settlement. William was apparently fully aware of this double game and accepted it as one of the conditions for doing business in a country that had enjoyed two revolutions in less than a century.

The War of the League of Augsburg, the clash between William's grand alliance and Louis XIV's France, began in 1689 and ran through 1697, ending with the Peace of Rywsick (in which Louis recognized William as the legitimate king of England). An Irish rising in 1689, prompted by the turmoil in England and soon led by James himself with French reinforcements, drew William from his continental concerns. William won few battles, but in the Battle of the Boyne (1690) he scored a decisive victory, ending James' Irish adventure. William was no vicious conqueror, but the long term consequences of English administration produced grave misfortunes not only on the Catholic Irish, but also the Protestants. (English trade policies prompted the movement of Ulster Scots Presbyterians to the North American colonies.)

The land war in the Low Countries provided no corresponding triumphs for English or allied arms. At sea, a rejuvenanted French navy defeated an Anglo-Dutch fleet off Beachy Head in 1690, potentially isolating William in Ireland and exposing England to an invasion that did not materialize. Two years later, with a Jacobite invasion prepared to launch, the British under Admiral Russell crushed the French fleet off Cape La Hogue, ending any serious French threats at sea. But the Peace of Ryswick might more properly have been called "The Truce of Ryswick." England and France were at war more than half the time from the outbreak of hostilities in 1689 through the conclusion of the Napoleonic wars in 1815, prompting historians to speak of "the second hundred years war."

A cascade of constitutional developments flowed from the settlement of 1688, chief among them the Act of Settlement of 1701. It insured the Protestant succession by providing that, in default of an heir from William and/or Mary, or Anne, the crown would pass to Sophia of Bavaria (a granddaughter of James I) and her line. It also changed the basis of judicial tenure from royal pleasure to good behavior, neutralizing the weapon by which the Stuarts had extorted favorable legal rulings. Parliament also legislated regular elections. This, with the practice of annual appropriations, increased parliamentary leverage vis-a-vis the crown. The Toleration Act of 1689 extended greated religious freedom to Nonconformists (but not full political rights) through the device of "occasional conformity" (e.g., receiving communion once a year in the Established Church, leaving them to worship as they pleased the rest of the year). The Scots, still a separate kingdom though under a common monarchy, established the Presbyterian Church in 1688-89, thus ratifying a long time fact of life.

There were also important developments in the realm of political economy. From 1693 onward, England financed part of the costs of the war (and of future wars) by means of a "national debt," borrowing against the future rather than attempting to raise revenues on a pay-as-you-go system. The government debt was about one million pounds in 1688. It had reached 18 million pounds by 1702. England began to assume the role of "paymaster of the allies" under William, a continuing part in a long-running drama. Taxes on land rents remained the chief source of war revenue. An income tax, which would have spread the burden more equitably, was proposed but the treasury was unable to figure out an adequate collection scheme. So the Tory squires continued to bear the costs of Whig adventures.

The Bank of England was established in 1694, a private enterprise with many public functions. It managed both government and private credit, issued banknotes, and enabled England to develop a modern financial system. The Bank was the creation of Whig politician and financier, Charles Montagu and the Scots banker, William Patterson. Montagu, in his capacity as Chancellor of the Exchequer, also elicited the aid of John Locke, a philosopher with a talent for practical action, to reform the coinage. Aldermanbury and the rest of the City, and the country as a whole, benefitted from these economic developments. But the Bank, as a Whig institution, was the object of Tory hostility. Their efforts to establish a rival institution proved futile.

The Whigs fell in 1697 and the Tories began to take revenge on an unpopular king by savaging his defense requests. The armed forces were slashed and many officers and soldiers, Huguenot refugees among them, were driven into poverty. Churchill (1957: 24) wrathfully compared this behavior to the action of the Tory party from 1932-37. And well he might, for English strength was required for European peace. Without it, Louis XIV's taste for aggression would be, and was, whetted once more. Indeed, the century had hardly turned before the threat to England's security became so obvious that even the Tories were ready for another war.

William's diplomatic skills were exercised to raise yet another grand alliance. But William was not destined to lead it. A riding accident inflicted injuries which a more vigorous person might have survived. For the king's racked and wasted body they were terminal. Sordid Jacobites raised glasses in toasts to "the little gentleman in black velvet," the mole whose burrow tripped William's horse. Their triumph would be limited to rejoicing over a royal death. Events of the next reign nullified the value of French support and put an end to the realistic hopes of the Stuart pretenders and their partisans. Not, unfortunately to their unrealistic hopes.

Anne (1702-1714)

The death of William brought Mary's sister Anne to the throne. The London which was the center of her kingdom and empire was a vigorous and burgeoning capital. Rude (1971:4) accepted Wrigley's estimates that London's population had grown from 400,000 in 1650 to 575,000 in 1700. A substantial part of the population increase took place within the already built up areas (Rude 1971: fig. 1, after 8).

Anne has been unjustly maligned for her allegedly frumpy appearance and for her lack of intelligence. The first of these is irrelevant for her state responsibilities, and seems to some extent belied by contemporary art, even allowing for artistic charity to a sovereign. The second is discounted by historians who note that she worked devotedly at the tasks of government, a sort of political overachiever. She did so in spite of personal tragedy. She bore at least 15 children, only one of whom—the Duke of Gloucester—survived infancy. He did not survive adolescence. Her successive pregnancies took a toll on her health, leaving her with frequent illness and almost constant pain. Her consort, the amiable Prince George of Denmark, was probably a personal support to her, but not much help in politics. Her own polestar seems to have been her religious faith. She was a devoted high church Anglican, which in those days meant Protestantism, the Crown, Bishops, and the Prayer Book against all comers, papist or nonconformist.

Anne's trophies as sovereign rank first among the house of Stuart, as we shall presently note. Unlike her more flamboyant and allegedly more talented kin whose reigns brought England misfortune, disgrace, dishonor and revolution, Anne came to office with a small but singularly talented set of advisors and she had the wit to follow their advice through roughly two-thirds of her reign. Her laurels faded toward the end when understandable personal weakness and the shifting fortunes of politics placed her in the hands of less worthy companions.

First among the inner triumvirate was John Churchill, Lord Marlborough. Of all the sovereigns he served it was apparently Anne alone to whom this brilliant warrior and statesman gave his total and unswerving devotion. Closest to the Queen was Sarah, Lady Marlborough, her husband's equal in intellect but not in diplomatic sagacity. Sarah was without peer for her sharp tongue and imperious will. The happiness of the Marlboroughs' passionate marriage (on his return from war John was said to bed Sarah, then remove his boots) may have owed much to the fact that he gave way to her in most matters. The third member of the inner circle was Sidney, Earl Godolphin, master of finance and tireless in his parliamentary activities on behalf of the Queen.

The Holy Roman Empire and the Spanish empire had been ruled by separate branches of the house of Hapsburg since the retirement of the Emperor Charles V in the 16th century. The Spanish Hapsburg line, enfeebled in mind and body, was expiring in the person of Charles II of Spain as the 17th century wound to a close. Both the Austrian Hapsburgs and the French Bourbons had a claim on the soon to be vacated throne through assorted royal marriages. But if Louis XIV thought it was a good idea for a prince of his line to ascend the throne of Spain, much of the rest of Europe considered it a simply terrible idea for the power of France to be joined with what was left of Spanish power, and with the wealth of Spain's New World empire. Thus, the war which racked Europe from 1701-1713 is known as "The War of theSpanish Succession." When it was all over, Spain ended up with a Bourbon king. But the successes of British and allied armies under the inspired and inspiring leadership of Marlborough and of his close colleague, Prinz Eugen of Savoy, were such that the combination of France and Spain made little difference.

Continental warfare of the period was largely a matter of maneuver, countermarch and sieges against carefully fortified strongpoints. It was widely assumed in the summer of 1704 that the substantial force being assembled under Marlborough in the Low Countries would be so used in that general neighborhood, certainly no further away than the valley of the Moselle. But the allied cause was deeply imperilled by events in central Europe. The King of Bavaria, an elector of the Holy Roman Empire, had renounced his ancestral allegiance and declared for France. The upper Danube was open to the armies of France, and Vienna itself was exposed to attack. Marlborogh took care to disentangle his army from the rather short apron strings of the Dutch Estates General which could make effective military operations impossible and embarked on a march up the Rhine. But he did not make the expected right turn at Coblenz to campaign along the Moselle. Instead, he crossed to the east bank and continued his upstream march, linking up with allies among the German states on the way. New boots for the infantry and new tack for the cavalry awaited along the route, the high quality amazing persons accustomed to grafting generals less concerned for their troops. The allied force passed through the Swabian mountains and to the upper Danube. There Marlborough linked up with the Imperial army under the Margrave of Baden and Prince Eugene.

Having sent the burdensome Margrave on a siege, Marlborough and Eugene engaged the Franco-Bavarian armies near Hochstadt on the Danube in a day-long battle on 13 August, 1704. The little village of Blindheim, or Blenheim, was a main target of the British attack, and the botched French defense a major factor in their undoing. In the end, Marlborough used his trademark ploy of enticing the enemy to thin part of the line to meet assaults elsewhere, then aiming his main blow at the depleted sector, in this case the French center. The French army under Marshal Tallard was utterly broken and the Franco-Bavarian force under Marshal Marsin and the king of Bavaria compelled to retreat toward the Rhine, with no opportunity to make a stand. Over 40,000 French soldiers had become casualties or stragglers. Marlborough marched after the retreating enemy, sweeping up the prizes of fortress after fortress on the way back to Holland via the Moselle. The tide of the war was turned and French morale severely tested. Marlborough was elevated to the rank of Duke and bestowed a lifetime income by a grateful Queen and Parliament. In the same month as the great land victory of Blenheim, the fortress rock of Gibralter fell to an allied combined operation, the climax of an Anglo-Dutch naval operation in the Mediterranean.

Marlborough's military genius reasserted itself at Ramilles in 1706, where he crushed another French army and gained Belgium for the allies. 1708 saw his resounding victory of Oudenarde and the capture of Lille, in France. Finally, in 1709, Marlborough achieved the costly victory of Malplaquet, Europe's bloodiest battle of the 18th century. After "the Great Frost" of 1709 France was ready to concede much for peace, a circumstance which encouraged the allies to make unreasonable demands, steeling France for more stubborn fighting. As late as 1711, despite political reverses at home, Marlborough outmaneuvered the French, conducted a masterful siege, and might even have marched unopposed on Paris. But the summer and autumn of 1711 was to be the last campaign of England's most successful general, who as his distinguished descendant, Sir Winston Churchill, wrote (1937:90-91), "... never fought a battle he did not win or besieged a town he did not take." On 30 November, 1874, Winston was born in Blenheim Palace, the Oxfordshire mansion built for the Duke of Marlborough in honor of his great victory.

The triumphant triumvirate fell piecemeal. Sarah was brought down in 1707 by Abigail Masham, a poor relative whom she introduced into the queen's entourage. Abigail catered to the queen and flattered her where Sarah had dominated. Mrs. Masham was also the sometimes agent of Robert Harley, "Robin the Trickster." Originally a Whig and Dissenter he gained his political fortune as a Tory and High Churchman. Marlborough and Godolphin found themselves obliged to work with Harley because of his power in Parliament.

There had been a basic ambivalence in Anne's triumvirate, for like the Queen they were all Tories and Anglicans in their basic sentiments. But Godolphin and Marlborough were increasingly obliged to depend on the Whigs for support of their war policy, and in the end Marlborough declared for the Whig party. The Whig-Tory division had been close through much of the reign. A sea change in the political landscape was signalled by the popular reaction to a sermon at St. Paul's on Guy Fawkes Day, 1709, by one Dr. Sacherverell. It was a virulent assault on Godolphin personally, and on the Revolutionary Settlement. Sacherverell was a popular hero and got off with a slap on the wrist for his offense against the government; so lightly were many, both low and high, prepared to cast off their hard won liberties!

The 1710 election brought a strong Tory majority into parliament. But Godolphin had already been summarily dismissed by the queen. Swift and other writers sold their pens for political pottage, aiming particular venom at Marlborough. Harley stood first in Anne's favor, and close beside him the brilliant but even more devious Henry St. John, Viscount Bolingbroke. The Queen found their Toryism and high Churchmanship congenial and accepted their policy of peace at any price. Together with Mrs. Masham, they gave Anne her second triumvirate. Under Bolingbroke's influence, Parliament enacted several laws aimed at Nonconformist liberties, perhaps hoping to provoke rebellious activity that would justify calling the Pretender to the throne. (Louis had promised the support of French troops.) But the laws were not assiduously enforced and the scheme came to nothing.

Marlborough was accused of graft and of accepting bribes and was dismissed by a deluded queen without investigation in 1711. The Duke sought refuge in exile on the continent, where he was received royally in the capitals of the alliance he had served so well. Meanwhile, England earned the nickname "Perfidious Albion" by pulling unceremoniously out of the war and leaving her allies to sink or swim as they might.

The treaties negotiated at Utrecht were concluded in 1713. England reaped substantial benefits in the colonial realm. France conceded English claims in Hudson's Bay, Newfoundland, and Nova Scotia. Gibralter and Minorca, prizes of war in the Mediterranean, were retained. And England was granted trading concessions in Spanish America. The City would benefit in all these matters.

A significant constitutional development accompanied the run-up to the final peace settlement. Anne, on the advice of Harley, created 12 new peers (Mr. Masham among them) on New Years, 1712, insuring a majority in the Lords to support the peace moves in the Commons. Though the ploy was never repeated, it remained the sovereign's only means of affecting legislation directly.

Much more significantly, the Kingdom of Great Britain came into being on 1

May, 1707. England and Scotland were united as a single kingdom under a single parliament (though the Scots steadfastly retained the Presbyterian Kirk as their established Church). Scotland would reap substantial economic gains from the union, and Scots energy and ingenuity would contribute to overall national benefit, while Scots regiments would render the British army even more formidable.

It is said that Queen Anne's death was precipitated by a violent confrontation in council on 27 August, 1714, between Harley, now the Earl of Oxford, and Bolingbroke, when the Queen demanded Oxford's resignation as Lord Treasurer, the culmination of a conspiracy by Bolingbroke and Mrs. Masham. The Queen had to be assisted from the council chamber to her bed, and her condition deteriorated steadily. On the continent, Marlborough, the Elector of Hanover, the British officers still on duty in the Low Countries, and the Dutch were posed to intervene on behalf of the Protestant succession should an attempt be made to install "James III." Some historians believe that England trod the brink of civil war during Anne's last years. And it appeared that Bolingbroke had some sort of great scheme afoot in the hours that the Queen's life ebbed away, though whether it was a coup in favor of "James III," or simply a plot to control all the options under the new Hanoverian dynasty remains unclear to the present. Whatever the case, he was overtaken by events. The Dukes of Somserset and Argyll, uninvited privy councillors, intruded upon a council session on 30 July and joined forces with the Lord Chamberlain, the Duke of Shrewsbury. The council came to the Queen's bedside, urging her to appoint Shrewsbury Lord Treasurer in Oxford's place. This she did, her last act of state.

With the moderate Shrewsbury in control, the privy council took measures that made it unnecessary for the Elector of Hanover and Marlborough to reenact William's friendly invasion of England. The Queen had sunk into a coma, but the fleet was on patrol against French adventurers, army units and the London trained bands were on alert and diplomatic messages were sent to friendly powers. Anne died on 1 August and George I was proclaimed king. The Protestant succession was secure. Bolingbroke, his scheme and career in ruins, joined meekly in the actions ordained by council and like the other great magnates ordered a bonfire lit before his London house in celebration.

Anne's first triumvirate had brought her trophies exceeding those of any previous English sovereign. Her second triumvirate brought shame and degradation. But French dominance had been broken and England's place among the first powers of

Europe, if not as the first power, was secured. Indeed, it was no longer simply England, but Great Britain, the union of England and Scotland. And this legacy she bequeathed to the new dynasty that assumed the British crown.

Aldermanbury During the Reign of William and Mary and Anne

<u>*The Short Incumbency of Ezekiel Hopkins (1689-1690)*</u>

At a General Vestry on 8 September 1689, with 61 present, eight ministers were nominated to replace Reverend Stratford who had been named Bishop of Chester. Ezekiel Hopkins, the Bishop of Derry since 1681, was elected, but died several months after being selected. At this same meeting the following guidelines for ministers were adopted:

> That the minister chosen, upon his acceptance of any
> living or promotion, whereby his personal attendance
> to officiate as a minister of the said parish, cannot
> be so effectually performed, that, within three
> months after such acceptance, he shall resign to the
> parishoners of the said parish his right, title, and
> pretence to the incumbency, to the said parish.

Hopkins was a student Merchant Taylors' School, London, and graduated from Magdalen College, Oxford. He accepted the Act of Uniformity in 1662. By 1669 he had become chaplain to Lord Robartes, Lord Lieutenant of Ireland. Within two years he had been named Bishop of Raphor, then ten years later Bishop of Derry. When the rebellion against James II broke out, he sided with the King and counseled non-resistance. At this point he returned to England and assumed the curacy at Aldermanbury. He died on 19 June, 1690 and was buried in the church. He authored a number of books. (Oliver 1969: 25-26).

<u>*The Lilley Butler Era (1690-1717)*</u>

On 2 July, 1690, the Vestry decided to allow any gentleman of the parish to reserve the pulpit on a given Sunday afternoon for his nominee for the curacy to preach an "approbaytionall" sermon. Eleven candidates were nominated. On 6 August 83 parishoners were present to elect Dr. Lilley Butler the new perpetual

curate. The Vestry stipulated that Butler either preach the two Sunday sermons or appoint a "fit person," resign within 3 months if he take another living, and take up residence in or near the parish. The account book showed that 18s was paid at Three Nun Tavern when Dr. Butler was selected.

On 15 April, 1691, the Vestry directed that 4s be paid each quarter to a custodian who would open and shut the conduit into the parish.

A note dated 2 April, 1693, suggests a conflict between the Churchwardens of Aldermanbury and St. Michael, Bassishaw, over a child who was laid at a certain place. Each churchwarden argued that the location was in the other's parish, in order to avoid liability. The note was a ruling from someone appointed to resolve the dispute, who ruled that the place was "wholly in the Parish of St. Michael, Bassishaw."

At the 19 April 1693 meeting, the Vestry acted to restrict the Clerk or Sexton from giving the key to a pew to any parishoner or others without an order of the Churchwarden, and that they be fined £2s if they do. A marginal note on the minutes indicated an expenditure of £15 for building the conduit. On 24 December, after electing Ward officers (the heading now used), it was ordered that every grave in the churchyard would have to be six feet deep where the ground allowed. The Sexton was to be paid 1s for every grave he dug.

Between May and July, 1695, parish assessments were made, and an alphabetical list of all parishoners and the amount assessed, is extant. Analysis of this list shows that the Aldermanbury parish was composed of 20-30% "substantial households" (Glass 1966).

At a Vestry held on 17 December, 1695, a Mr. Jacobs was awarded a "pugh" [sic] for his family at a cost of £10. The practice of renting pews to wealthy parishoners was widespread during this period, and was a deterrent to attendance at the services by the poor (Rude 1971: 106).

On 18 December, 1696, the Vestry directed the churchwardens to go around the parish once a month or so in order that "no charge be brought upon the parish that may be prevented." The reference, of course, was to the parish's responsibility for the poor within its bounds.

During 1697 and 1698 the accounts show funds spent to burn fires for "ye News of peace" in the war with France.

On 14 December, 1698, Abraham Gubinant was chosen as a Warder for the parish. According to the minutes, "he is every night to see that no children be left in ye street till ye watch be sett and likewise be up in ye morning att five o'clock about ye same business for which he is to receive five pounds for his years service." At this meeting Sir James Bateman and Alex Jacobs were released from serving offices having "lent" to the parish £15.

In the Vestry Minutes for this period, there is an entry for a July, 1701, meeting of the overseers of the poor, giving a sense of the type of business conducted by this group. At this meeting a young man named Moses Bury (or Berry) was ordered apprenticed and his rent paid, at the discretion of the churchwardens.

The Charity Schools movement began in London in the 1690s, under the sponsorship of the Society for Promoting Christian Knowledge. The schools were for children ages 7-12 and were set up to teach them basic Christian values and prepare them for "services of the lowest kind." No attempt was made to teach crafts or reading. By 1704 there were 54 Charity Schools in London, with 2000 children attending. (Rude' 1971: 115-116).

On 28 September, 1702, John Dubois, who had played such a crucial role in the rebuilding after the Great Fire, was buried in the Churchyard. The list of expenditures shows the fees involved in a burial:

Ground and bell	2.3.4
Minister	6.8
Clerke	6.8
Sexton	8.0
Registering	2.0
Each barer (sic)	4.0

In 1702 Edmund Calamy, grandson and namesake of the famed Presbyterian prelate of Aldermanbury, published a work entitled <u>Abridgement of Mr. Baxter's History of his Life and Times</u>. It was based on the notes of the non-conformist Richard Baxter (who had been one of the victims of Judge Jeffreys) and focused on the ministers silenced before or ejected after the Act of Uniformity, including his grandfather. A second edition was published in 1713. As a boy Edmund had often gone to visit and taken gifts to the ejected ministers confined in Newgate prison. He was deeply moved by their witness.

At the meeting on 1 February, 1703, because of a dispute over adding a door from the house joining the church to the West, the parishoners were made aware that most of the trustees of the parish estates had died. There was no term of service for this office, and it was not untypical for trustees to die and not be replaced until a need arose. At this meeting 12 new trustees were added to the 3 living trustees. On 27 August, permission was granted for the door, provided the tenant "give a bottle of wine yearly of the Churchwardens' choice."

During this period the parish accounts show frequent expenditures at various inns and taverns for meals and drinks at the time of parish meetings. The vestry considered it a perquisite of parish office to be entertained at a parish establishment after the meeting. Here are two entries from 1703:

    Paid at ye Baptist head   2.12.6

    Paid at ye tavern at ye choice of Ward Officers   0.1.6

During 1703-04 104 members of the parish gave a total of 46.16.9 for the relief of the Protestants of the Principality of Orange.

On 11 April, 1705, the Vestry ordered the Church "be Trimmed up forthwith." The accounts show 7s8p spent for "ye funerall of a parish child" and 4s8p for a "Shroud and coffin and bread and beer." On 18 December, 1705, the Vestry received a complaint that the Sexton was not ringing the church bells at 7:00 a.m. each Sunday.

At the 27 March, 1706, meeting an Isaack Eeles was elected Under Churchwarden. Whether he was related to the Solomon Eeles who ran through the church naked on New Year's Day, 1660, was not stated.

On 22 February, 1707, the vestry released Dr. Butler from paying for the Sunday afternoon lecturer because of his large family. The lectureship was to be funded by subscriptions instead.

Hatton's New View of London, published in 1708, included a detailed description of the church (Hatton I 1708: 362):

> It is a structure well built of stone, as the Steeple is;
> Consisting of Tower and Turret. The Roof within is camerated
> and covered with lead which is supported with twelve pillars
> of the composite order. It is paved with stone—The Floor of
> the Chancel is one step higher than that of the body of the
> Church and the apperturances are numerous and well placed
> rendering it very pleasant. The ornamental part is handsome.
> At the East end fronting Aldermanbury is a large Cornish and
> Triangular Pediment, also 2 large Cartouches and as many Pine
> Apples of stone carved. The inside of the Roof is adorned

with Arches of Fretwork and the said Columns with an Entablament the Cornish being Cantalievere. It is wainscotted near 9 foot high and pewed with oak. The pulpit is also of that timber with Enrichments of Cherubims. Here are also 3 plain wainscot inner door-cases.

The Altar-piece is adorned with 2 fluted Pilasters Entableture and open circular Pediment of the Corinthian Order. The Inter-Columns are the Commandments between the Lord's Prayer and Creed done in gold letters on Black. Above the Commandments is a Seraphim between 2 carved and embellished with enrichments of Fruit, Leaves, etc. The Communion Table is finnier'd and its Foot-pace paved with Marble, enclosed with rail and bannister.

The dimensions of the church were given as 72 feet long, 42 feet broad, and 38 feet high, with a 90 foot steeple, consisting of tower, turret, and two bells. In the same work, Hatton claimed that there were 132 houses in the parish (364).

The 1709 accounts show a long list of payments by the churchwardens for the poor, including £6.8 to a woman for nursing a sick child for 38 weeks and 3s to get a woman in labour out of the parish. 8p was spent for a slate for a parish foundling, Joseph Berry. The same accounts show parish expenditures for the Ascension Day meal, including £5 to the cook.

The encroachment of neighboring properties on the church is evidenced in a 15 December, 1712, agreement in which John Dent agreed to pay the parish £20 to the Parish for "four Little ____ Lights" in his houses. The Parish, in turn, agreed to pay Dent or his estate £15 if the lights were ever stopped up or darkened. The lights apparently were over against the steeple.

During 1712 the parish spent £17 to keep Richard Parnell in a mad house and £1 to a surgeon for "cure of his toes and a ulcer in his legg." In 1709 6s6p had been paid to get a coat that Parnell had pawned, and over £6 spent for other provisions for Parnell.

By 1714 the Vestry was becoming concerned by the number of persons electing to pay fines rather than serve in offices. The going rate to be excused from all offices was now £15. On 17 December, 1714, 56 parishoners ordered the Churchwardens not to take any fines for Ward offices or the office of churchwarden without the consent of the Vestry.

18th century medical practice was reflected in the reference in the 1717 accounts to 7s6p paid to shave and bleed the head of one of Elizabeth Perry.

The Early Hanoverians (1714-1760)

The Electress Sophia dearly longed to be queen of England. But she was thwarted by Anne, who outlived her by four months. So the crown of England came to an unenthusiastic heir, her son George. The throne of England was a prize too great to be spurned, but **George I (1714-1727)** was not fond of the job or of England. He never learned English, complicating the task of communication for his ministers. Distant, peevish and disinterested, inclined to use British power to advance purely German interests (hardly a popular policy), the king was not a beloved figure. His aging German mistresses (soon created duchesses) were dubbed by wags "the elephant" and "the maypole." They were alternately butts of humor and objects of hostility because of their alleged cupidity.

There was, however, a positive side to the situation, so far as the development of British polity was concerned. George's disinterest and basic dullness advanced the cause of the Revolutionary Settlement and parliamentary supremacy. A king who was not interested in governing left the job to his chief ministers. Since they sat in Parliament, either in the Lords or Commons, the power of government came into the hands of prominent parliamentarians. Thus under George I there evolved in Britain the form of cabinet government characteristic of parliamentary democracy in many lands down to the present day. The government ministry was constituted of the leaders of the majority party in the Commons, with the leader of the party at the head. (The title "prime minister" would be a while in coming.) The government fell if it lost majority support on a key issue, or if a majority voted "no confidence." A new government might be formed in the existing Parliament, or new elections might be held. Government was responsible to Parliament, but under the corrupt electoral practices of the time, Parliament was not yet fully responsible to the people.

Bolingbroke and many other Tory leaders had so discredited themselves that unchallenged governing power fell to the Whigs for decades. This led to an unlikely, but still unlovely, Kulturkampf in the realm of architecture. Lord Burlington, in his writings on the subject, practically equated Baroque architecture with Stuart absolutism and a taste for Palladianism with proper British patriotism. The aged Sir

Christopher Wren, who had almost singlehandedly developed the English Baroque style, was turned out of office as Surveyor General of the King's Works in 1718. (His masterpiece, St. Paul's Cathedral, had been "topped out" in 1710.) Fortunately, the Whig architectural critics did not set about to "correct" Wren's architecture as the Victorian vandals would do a century and a half later. And Wren's most brilliant protege, the flamboyantly creative Hawksmoor, continued to flaunt his style, only gradually curbing his work to Palladian taste.

Yet another attempt to reimpose the male Stuart line was mounted in 1715. There was almost a comic opera aspect about it. Most of the chief figures on both sides, with the exception of George I and the Pretender, seem to have been double agents. Even some of the Jacobite leaders seemed uncertain about whether they really wanted "James III" on the throne. Historians do not universally agree on the strength of the Jacobite movement. It is difficult to suppose that many of the leaders of the Jacobite cause (or the great men like Marlborough, who played a double game) really favored Stuart policies, royal absolutism and, from James II onward, the imposition of Catholicism as the state religion. Perhaps it was driven by Tory thirst for revenge on the triumphant Whigs. Perhaps it was something like the Reagan phenomenon in modern American politics, people enamored of a popular leader while rejecting some of his most treasured policies. Perhaps the habits of revolution had become so deeply ingrained in the previous century that sedition had become second nature.

Both the planning and execution of the rising were bungled, and the London government was apparently in possession of the rebel plans such as they were. The rising broke out piecemeal. Louis XIV died, depriving the Jacobites of their strong ally; the regency for Louis XV did not act. There had been tumults in London, Oxford and the English west country in the run up to the rising, with the Dissenters and the memory of King William the main targets. But despite their communications with, and even financing of, the Pretender, the great leaders in England stood in the moment of crisis for the Revolutionary Settlement and the Protestant succession. Action centered in the north and in Scotland. Only a skeleton force of royal regulars was available in England, and it proved adequate. The Pretender had barely landed when he was obliged to reembark for France, where he lived out his days. There were some trials and executions, but the tidying up was much less violent than might be expected, a circumstance which some think encouraged Bonnie Prince Charlie's adventure thirty years later.

Perhaps more threatening to the civil order generally and the throne of the Hanoverians in particular was the financial catastrophe and subsequent scandals known as the "South Sea Bubble." The South Sea Company had been started by Harley in 1711, looking toward the opening of trade with the Spanish colonies in the New World. In 1720, the company joined the Bank of England and the East India Company in taking over portions of the national debt, receiving in return government securities and special privileges. The Bank and the East India Company played their part with discretion. Not so the South Sea Company. Its stock was driven upward in price by a combination of manipulation and wild speculation. Shares with a par value of £100 rocketed to over £1,000. Other companies were dragged in the train and new ones (some of apparently fraudulent purpose from the outset) were established in the speculative fever. Instant riches beckoned to ruin. Insiders profitted mightily. Then the "Bubble" burst and England took a financial bubble bath. Panic, failure and bankruptcy spread among investors and among other companies. One would hope that sufficient Calvinist prudence lingered in Aldermanbury to spare its parishoners the catastrophe which swept the City and the country as a whole.

High government officials and the none-too-popular royal mistresses were implicated in the scandal which followed. The nation required an able leader unbesmirched by the scandal to restore public confidence and to restore the houses of government and finance to order. Fortunately for Britain and for the House of Hanover, such was forthcoming in the person of Sir Robert Walpole. He never bore the title of "prime minister." Indeed, he would have eschewed it, for the title in those days had connotations of "royal favorite." But historians of England almost universally regard him as Britain's first prime minister and place him at the head of their list of governments. Sir Robert retained the confidence of his sovereign (with whom he could communicate only in imperfect Latin since his knowledge of German equalled the king's of English) and his mastery of Parliament for 21 years (1721-1742). His policies might be summarized as "peace and prosperity," or "prosperity through peace." He emphasized commercial policies and manipulated the tax system as far as he was able to maximize trade and profit. Above all, he strove to avoid a major war. But in 1739, the pressure for war grew irresistible and Walpole, the man of peace, was obliged to manage a war he neither wanted nor approved. Then, in 1742, he took refuge in the House of Lords, leaving the management of government to others. Meanwhile, George I had died and **George II (1727-1760)** reigned.

The early Hanoverians may have been dull monarchs, but many aspects of the artistic life of London were anything but dull during this period. The Tory parliament in 1711 had passed the "50 Churches" act to build 50 new churches in the London suburbs and pay for them with a tax on coal, like the coal tax which funded Wren's rebuilding of the City churches after the Great Fire of 1666. It is not clear whether the motivation was the cure of souls, or the fear that the curing would be done by the Dissenters, whose meeting houses peppered London's expanding residential suburbs. Had the scheme been carried through, the imaginative Hawksmoor might have created an architectural record to match Wren's. But it was not to be. Hawksmoor's six churches (most notably St. Mary Woolnoth in the City and St. George, Bloomsbury), Gibb's St. Martin-in-the-Fields and Archer's St. John, Smith Square, constitue a magnificent early Hanoverian addition to the face of London.

Meanwhile, William Hogarth, arguably England's greatest native-born painter, combined art with withering social commentary. Swift, Pope, Fielding, Goldsmith and Jane Austen were among the adornments of Hanoverian letters. John Blow and Henry Purcell had brought baroque distinction to British music in the previous century. However, England's greatest composer arrived, albeit indirectly, from Germany at just about the same time as George I. This musical George, George Frederick Handel, was in fact from Hanover and had formerly served in the electoral court. Indeed, the two supreme Baroque masters, Handel and Bach, had been born only a few miles apart in the same year, 1685, and would both die in 1759! Handel came to England as a musical entrepreneur, to write and stage grand operas in the Italian style. But he won the hearts of British music lovers as the great exponent of "sacred oratorio," a form especially congenial to their sensibilities. Messiah (1741-42) was his masterpiece, perhaps the greatest setting of an English text in all musical history. Royal fiascos became something of a Handel sideline beginning with the coronation of George II and Queen Caroline when, after a flawless rehearsal, the performers accomplished a Hogarthian botch of Handel's splendid anthems on the occasion itself. But this was surpassed at the Royal Fireworks concert in St. James Park on 27 April, 1749, celebrating the end of the War of the Austrian Succession. The pyrotechnicians overdid things a bit and the elaborate pavilion put up for the occasion went up in smoke. At least the barges used for George I's Water Music party (1717) did not sink!

We noted mob actions during the rising of 1715. The London street mob would be a factor in the political and social life of the metropolis through the 18th century, even as in the 17th. Such tumults might be occasioned by popular prejudice against Catholics and foreigners, labor discontent, or economic conditions. A mob might undertake social reform by pulling down a notorious bawdy house. But the focus was most often political. A favorable disposition was sometimes dramatized by unhitching the team from a popular leader's coach and drawing it by hand to its destination. Disfavor was shown by pelting unpopular politicians with stones and filth, ripping their clothes, smashing house windows and even setting fire to or pulling down houses. But Rude (1971:224-227) noted that mob actions were ordinarily aimed at particular targets and stopped short of fatal violence. When there were deaths, it was usually rioters who died in confrontations with militia or with regular soldiers. And the credentials of persons brought to trial fail to comport with the stereotype of a rabble promulgated by the authorities; most were wage earners, petty employers, apprentices and minor craftsmen, the lower end of the "middling" classes. But there were frequently class overtones to the disorders, the humble venting their rage on the affluent. It may be argued that "the good old cause" of the Roundheads had been passed through the generations and was expressing itself in some cases. And there were a few of what may be regarded as gangs, or "rioting clubs," bands of rowdies with their hangout pubs, at the disposal of one or another faction. Most notorious were the "Jacks," Jacobite partisans. But the conviction and hanging of five Jacks after a particularly violent outburst in 1716 put an end to Jacobite disorders in the City and to the "ale house riots" between factional gangs.

The end of Walpole's long peace marked the resumption of the "second Hundred Years War." Throughout the ensuing hostilities, terminating only with the final defeat of Napoleon, Britain exploited her naval power to gain most of France's colonial empire. But British achievements were much less spectacular on land. There was no longer a Marlborough and not yet a Wellington. To be sure, George II made his mark as the last British sovereign to lead personally forces in the field before yielding to his younger brother, the Duke of Cumberland. Serious continental hostilities lasted from 1740-1748, with official Anglo-French involvement in what was known as the War of Austrian Succession, 1744-1748. But Britain had learned during Queen Anne's wars that it was cheaper to finance allied regiments than to raise, equip and supply your own. Her commerical success permitted her to continue in the role of "paymaster of the allies." But events half a world away would turn out to have much greater significance over the long haul than any European developments of the period. The War of Austrian Succession spread to India where both France and England had colonial outposts. The struggle did not end when temporary peace came to Europe. It really did not end until the French were expelled and the Subcontinent was a British fiefdom.

War came home to England in 1745 with what turned out to be the last Stuart rising. "Bonnie Prince Charlie," the son of "James III" came to Scotland, assembled a rebel army (mostly of Highlanders), and defeated the skimpy Redcoat contingents in the north. There was no popular rising in England to support him, but neither did the people spring to arms in defense of the government. Most of the regular army was on the continent and the Prince was able to march within less than a hundred miles of a very uneasy London before prudently retiring to Scotland in the face of a hastily assembled force from scattered outposts around England. Cumberland was recalled from the continent with a force of regulars and the uprising was doomed. The bloody final act was played out at Culloden in the Highlands on 15 April, 1745. The Prince was spirited to safety in France by loyal followers, but the rebel army was utterly crushed and along with it the hopes of the Stuart line which expired early in the next century. Some dubbed Cumberland "the butcher" for the ferocity of his campagin. But George, Prince of Wales, commissioned Handel to write his great oratorio, "Judas Maccabeus," in celebration of the victory, and Handel recycled the triumphal march, "See the Conquering Hero" from his earlier work, "Joshua," for the occasion.

We have noted that the end of the War of Austrian Succession did not mean the end of the Franco-British struggle in India. Nor did it mean peace in North America. French colonial interests threatened to isolate the English colonies in their narrow strip along the Atlantic coast even as they pressured them from the north. The upper Ohio Valley became the main center of conflict between the rival interests. Students of U.S. history will recognize that young George Washington's heroics in delivering a warning message from the governor of Virginia to the French "trespassers" in 1753, his mixed military success against them a year later, and his role in extricating the shattered remnants of Braddock's regulars after their catastrophic introduction to frontier tactics, were all events of the interwar years. And when the Seven Years War (1756-1763—known as the French and Indian War in U.S. history) had its official beginning, the European side of it went little better despite the fact that England had the best navy in Europe, and had in effect employed as her ally Frederick the Great of Prussia, who had Europe's finest army. Corruption and maladministration among the long entrenched Whigs was a factor in the inept prosecution of the war. But England's fortunes began to turn with the rise of the first William Pitt, notable for his honesty and his statesmanship as well as his oratory. It would be more than a decade before Pitt, by then the Earl of Chatham despite his monicker, "the Great Commoner," would head a ministry in his own name. However, he was the driving force behind the two Whig ministries that governed from 1756-1761. Another government would negotiate the peace, but Pitt's genius had set the course to victory. Britain emerged from the war in possession of the former French colonial empire in India and North America. England also emerged from the war with a new king, **George III (1760-1820)**, grandson of George II, and unlike the two previous Georges, an Englishman. This Hanoverian would outlive the last Stuart pretender, and oversee some of the most significant events of British, European and world history.

Aldermanbury during the Early Hanoverians

<u>*The Joshua Smith Era (1717-1731)*</u>

On 20 May, 1717, a Vestry was called to consider a successor to Dr. Butler, who had died. A few days later Mr. Joshua Smith, then lecturer at St. Mary le Bow, was elected. There was only one other nominee. Smith signed the same agreement as Dr. Butler had, outlining the parish's requirements of its curate.

By 1718 the practice of entertainment in association with parish business had gotten out of hand. At the 18 September meeting, the Vestry ordered that no tavern expenses be allowed the Churchwardens whatsoever. The Churchwardens were not to allow any poor upon the pension roll without the order of the Vestry and unless they come "with the Parish badge upon there [sic] arms." Following this ruling was a list of persons whose rents were no longer to be paid by the parish or whose allowances were to be reduced. (Carter 1913: 64). 40s was also deducted from the salary of the Warder, Mr. Guillford.

The following statement from this same meeting reflects the growing commercialization of the parish and the associated problems:

> Whereas there was a complaint made at the Vestry this day
> of several of the Inhabitants of this Parish that Mr. Pickerin
> or his servants Loading and Unloading and packing up of Goods

in the Street and Church Way was a great anoyance to their goods as well as stopping of Coaches and foot customers coming to their several Shopps it was therefore by the said Vestry Ordered that Churchwardens for the time being should give him notice in writing by the Warden Abraham Gulleford to take care and give order that no such Pracktises be used for the time to come and if he or his servants doe that upon the first offence, the Churchwardens as above Mentchond doe forthwith Prosecute the said Pickering according to law.

At this same meeting alterations to the Gallery, which had apparently been added after consultation with Wren, were authorized although not specified. However, the parish also decided that no expenditure of parish funds exceeding £10 would be allowed unless it had been approved by a second Vestry not sooner than three or more than twenty days after the initial decision.

In 1718 Edmund Calamy's grandson Edmund published another work in response to a history of England written by an Archdeacon Echard, in which he set out to vindicate the dissenters and Whigs and clear "several persons of distinction from Aspersions; ..." As he did in his own history of non-conformist clergy, Calamy vigorously defended his grandfather in this publication. Echard had called the elder Calamy a man of no small learning, but then styled him "an incendiary and promoter of the great rebellion." The younger Calamy responded, "I should have tho't a softer word might have been to the full proper in his case, who was more remarkable for nothing, than for his great love of peace and moderation" (Calamy 1718: 88). Earlier, in defending the Westminster Assembly against Echard's assault, Calamy had written that he was honored to have been descended from one of the leaders of that assembly (19), which he considered the most intelligent and morally qualified convocation before the Restoration or since (82).

The 1719 accounts suggest that the Vestry was concerned about their charges' spiritual as well as physical needs. The records show that a hat and Bible were purchased for William Rock. The same year 8s6p was paid to "old Ling for Intelligence of Mary Slade being married." She was taken off her allowance of 12p a week. On 2 June 1719 the Vestry ordered that anyone not paying the poor rate be prosecuted at parish expense. The Churchwarden was directed to make up his accounts within 40 days after leaving office and deliver the parish books to his successor.

The same year a probably all too typical tragedy is reflected in the accounts. A foundling named Charles Berry, left in Millers Court, was baptized and nursed for several weeks, but then died, with payment authorized for a coffin, searchers (those hired to view the body and report cause of death), a grave, and drink. Mr. Hesketh was paid 10s for "shaving Mad Betty for two years."

At the 5 May, 1720, meeting of the parish we find an indication of tension between the parish and civic officials over parish property. The Upper Churchwarden reported that the Chamber of London was refusing to pay ground rent of £6.13.4 for a year for parish houses.

On 13 April, 1721, the Vestry authorized beautifying and repairing the church with funds to be raised by a "half year's overrate," apparently a surcharge on the poor rate. Total cost of the repairs was about £120. The Vestry also entered into an agreement with an apothecary to provide medicine for the parish poor at £12 per year. The Warden was entrusted with the care of the parish fire engine.

A 15 December 1721 Vestry ordered that no Lodgers should have a pew to themselves in the future.

When a charge of the parish died owning property, the Vestry was not above taking action to claim ownership. When Tabitha Thompson died in 1722 1s was spent to "lay her out," but the records also show a suit was filed against her executors by the parish. In the end the parish realized £7.17.6 from the sale of her property.

On 24 June, 1722, Nathaniel Marshall, Canon of Windsor and Chaplain Orindary to His Majesty, and for seventeen years a lecturer at St. Mary, Aldermanbury, preached a farewell sermon. He urged his audience to "remember ... that every Passion, exceeding its Rule and Boundary, is *noted* in a *Book*, and recorded for a Reckoning; that the *Lust of the Flesh, the Lust of the Eyes, and the Pride of Life* (one as well as the other) are Articles, which if here left uncancell'd, will *there* be found sanding out against you; never to be struck off, never to be forgiven you. For there *the Worm dieth not, and the Fire never shall be quenched* [italics in the original]." (Marshall 1722: 20)

On 9 April, 1724 the dispute with the City over payment of rent led the Vestry to reinstate the practice of passing control of parish land by deed from old to new trustees. On 6 November, 1724, having discovered that the Trustees had died, new Trustees of the Rectory, parish estates, and Sir John Davy Charity were elected. The next January the Churchwardens were ordered to look into the ground rents due from the City. Again in 1726 the Churchwardens were ordered to look into the situation of the rent due from the City.

On 14 January 1726 the Vestry ordered the "viewing" of the parish by "such proper persons as the Churchwardens should think of."

On 5 October 1727 the attention of the Vestry was drawn to the situation of two children of Mr. Harlows who were living in the Plaisterer's Hall. It was put to a vote whether the parish should keep the children or "pass them away." It was agreed to pass them to the parish of St. Alban's, Wood Street, the neighboring parish to the West. However, St. Alban's appealed and on 11 March 1728 the case was resolved by a Deputy Recorder who wisely ruled that "ye settlement must be in that part of the Dwelling that the persons Lyeth." The Vestry agreed to abide by the opinion. The trial cost the parish 23.7.4.

On 16 May 1728 a meeting of the Parish Trustees at the Baptist Head Tavern was reported to the Vestry to be confirmed. Leases for three houses for 21 years at £32 and 24 were granted.

On 4 September of the same year the bill of the Bell Hangers was considered. The Vestry agreed to pay a debt with interest to a Francis Dillings as husband of Ann Beeton, widow of Major Cor. Beeton. On 27 September £500 left by Sam Lambert was ordered to be spent for supporting and repairing the Church. The sum was put out for South Seas Annuities. (The parish was apparently not immune from the allure of investment in the speculative South Sea ventures!)

On 7 September, 1728, John Smith, a twenty-four-year old lieutenant in the British navy and member of the parish drowned off Staten Island, New York. A monument erected in 1789 memorialized him as one "who discharged the active duties of an officer with zeal and fidelity, gave vigour to the military discipline by the force of his won example and taught mankind that valour tempered with humanity is the true characteristic of a British seaman" (Henry 1828: 114-115). The 1728 accounts show that while about £131 was spent on the church that year, over £268 was expended on the care of the poor of the parish (Maitland 1775: 1134).

In 1729 the parish authorized payment to the Churchwardens out of parish funds if their accounts be in arrears. On 30 May the Vestry was informed that there was no room left in the Churchyard for burials, so the parishoners ordered the erection of a vault under the part of the Churchyard next to the Rashleigh house, the opening of which was to be under the South window of the present Vestry. At the same meeting the Vestry decided to move the Vestry Room to the Northwest Corner of the church. The Churchwarden also reported that seven of the parish boundary markers had been removed; the Vestry authorized replacements. The Vestry also agreed to insure "the Saverall houses belonging to the parish" at the "Hand in Hand fire office" for 3.8.10.

On 15 June, 1729, the Churchwardens reported that several inhabitants wanted to repair the pews and erect a gallery. The majority voted not to repair the pews at this time. There was no mention of a gallery. At this same meeting a discussion was initiated but not resolved on whether the parish should erect a workhouse for the poor.

On 16 December, 1729, the Vestry agreed to use £200 of South Sea Stock to pay workmen, whose bill was 377.2.4. This expense apparently related to a fire in the church, for the accounts reflect payment of 10s "paid the Turncock for taking up ye plug when the Church was a fire."

At the same meeting the Churchwarden reported on the state of the poor in the parish. Dues were also set for burials in the new vaults, with "strangers and lodgers" to be assessed double. The order that no expenses of more than £10 be paid unless they are authorized by two subsequent Vestries was reaffirmed.

In 1730 16s3p was paid for half a ton of Scottish coal, the first indication of the heating of the church with coal. Also in 1730 the Vestry received a letter "out of the country saying that Shanks wife and children would be passed to London unless something was paid for their keep." This is the first mention of a family who benefitted from the parish's charity for 80 years. Old Shanks died and was buried at parish expense; at least two more generations of Shanks lived off the generosity of the parish. Later in 1730 the Churchwardens reported that the Workhouse of St. Sepulcher's could accomodate some of the parish's poor. The Vestry accordingly decided to house the poor there for one year at 4s each and not to have a workhouse of their own. The Churchwardens and overseers were given permission to excuse those whom they thought proper.

On 30 April, 1730, the Vestry ordered that lamps be paid for out of parish stocks. This was apparently the first reference to street lights in the parish. Five years later the parish had to pay the Chamber of London over £53 for the lamps.

The William Sandford Era (1731-1754)

In 1731 Joshua Smith was replaced by William Sandford as perpetual curate, with ten nominated to the office. He defeated Dr. Middleton in the final vote, 48-43. On 3 June he signed a detailed statement of agreement. Henry Bund was chosen as lecturer. Sandford was, during his tenure at St. Mary's, chosen to serve as chaplain to the Lord Mayor. Several of his sermons were published. At this meeting the Vestry also agreed that more windows were needed. Later in the year a new chimney was authorized.

In 1733 the Vestry agreed "that notice of the holding of Each Succeeding Vestry and the Occasion of Such Vestry shall be Either published by the Clerk in the Desk immediately after Divine Service is ended on the foregoing Sunday or Else, Such Notice shall be left in Writing at the house of Every Parishoner at least the day before the holding of Such Vestry." The Vestry also decided to establish its own workhouse in the town of Hoxton in the parish of St. Leonard Shorditch. Apparently, it was the house of John Benn, Churchwarden, who was allowed to retain an apartment in the dwelling.

On 24 January, 1734, the Vestry agreed that if the poor were willing to accept 30s a year they would not have to go to the workhouse. On 18 April a matron was appointed for the workhouse at a salary of £8. It was ordered that both Churchwardens agree before anyone was released from the workhouse. The books of the workhouse would have to be brought to the church at least once a month so that any parishoner could examine them. At the same meeting a limit of £4 was set for the Ascension Day feast. At the 3 October meeting the Vestry authorized repair of a decayed portion of the stonework in the Church's northwest corner. On 12 December the Vestry agreed to pay the under churchwarden £50 to reimburse him for his considerable expenses out of pocket for the poor.

In 1736 the Steeple of the Church was repaired and a new clock added at a cost of nearly £200, with some of that spent for drink for the workmen and dinners for the planning committee at a Coffeehouse.

In 1737 the Vestry agreed to remove the churchyard wall and "rail it round with iron palisades." At the same time a pair of Pine Apples to ornament the entrance to the church was purchased for 3.13.8.

A new office was added during 1737 to the Ward offices, Collector for the Lamp Lights. The same year over £6 was spent for both the Easter Vestry and the Christmas Vestry, and 16s was spent for a ham for the latter. It was also decided to pay for half of the year's lamp lights out of the rents from the parish estates.

At the 12 December, 1738, meeting to elect Ward officers, by a majority of hands it was agreed that "no Fines should be taken for any offices for the Future."

On 20 March 1739 the Vestry ordered the Churchwardens to proceed with the "Cupollow" [sic] which was leaking. On 25 September the Under Churchwarden's request to be relieved from the office, because he could not afford the expense, was granted, but later in the meeting the action was revoked on the principle that each must take it in turn even when incovenient. At the next meeting the Vestry authorized the reimbursement of the under churchwarden out of parish rents.

On 13 December the parish discussed problems with the workhouse. It was too far away for proper supervision. It was decided to see if another house closer to London could be found. On 15 June, 1740, the Churchwardens reported that the workhouse was "a Detriment to the parish and not of Any Service." At that meeting the Vestry decided to "quit the workhouse and provide for the poor as was done before the workhouse."

Apparently the Winter before had been particularly harsh. On the 10th of April, 1740, the Churchwardens "layd before the Vestry an Account of about Nine pounds which was layd out in the hard season of the Winter about the Shores."

The parish's responsibility for fighting fires is evidenced in the meetings of the Vestry on 17 June and 1 July, 1740. On 17 June the Vestry decided to purchase a new (fire) Engine. On 1 July the Vestry agreed on the "largest Size Engine and 80 feet of pipe," and authorized 20s a year to keep it in order. Jonathan Brown was hired for half a guinea every time the Engine went out to a fire.

The 1740 accounts show that the Church was now being lighted with lamps rather than candles, as £4 was spent for lamps.

A 1741 survey of London showed that of the 21,649 houses in the City and 748 in Cripplegate Within, 136 were in Aldermanbury (the same number as in 1787) (Smart 1741).

On 2 June, 1742, the Vestry voted that "the parish should be at no expense at the Christmas and Easter Vestries nor on Ascension Day for the future. No more than two pounds two shillings were to be allowed for a dinner for the Minister, Churchwardens, Overseers, and Clerk. And only wand for the children and Rols and ale as usual." The wands were the sticks carried by the children on Ascension Day to "beat the bounds" of the parish.

By 1744 the Vestry was becoming concerned about the amount of parish money spent to carry out its responsibility to care for the poor. On 29 March, 1744, a Committee composed of the Churchwardens, the Overseers, and four others was appointed to see how "to lessen the Expense of the parish poor." The accounts for 1744 show payments for numerous occurrences such as 2.17.0 for "expenses on the woman that cried out at Mrs. Granger." The situation had not improved by December, for on the 17th Churchwarden Dimock reports that he was £130 out of pocket in addition to being £70 short in receipts on the poor rate. By 5 November, 1745, he had had to move out of his house, and the Vestry agreed to pay him £50. The next year the minutes reflected for the first time an assessment for the London Workhouse. The amount was 17.8.6.

On the 30th of April, 1745, the parish was £500 in debt, and a special committee was appointed to "retrieve the parish affairs." The committee reported on 28 May that the debt was actually £640, owed mostly to past Churchwardens who had dipped into their own funds to meet the parish's responsibilities. The Committee blamed the debt on "the increase of the poor, to several Exceedings of Expenses in Parish Meetings and other Extraordinary Charges in some of the late Churchwarden accounts." One unusual expense was noted on 6 August, 1744, an unusually high bill for repair of the top of the church. The recommended long term remedy for "this evil" was for the Vestry to order the Churchwardens be limited to certain sums established at parish meetings.

The short term solution was to raise £500 from a Life Annuity and to "farm" the parish poor for a set fee. The Vestry approved the annuity and received two bids for care of the poor, one for £210 annually from a Mr. Tull of Tottingham and another for £300 from Mr. Benn of the parish. The vestry voted to take the low bid "to farm the parish poor to Mr. Tull for £210" and to settle all parish expenses. The minutes include a copy of the deed with Tull, which he signed on 18 June, agreeing to "provide the poor with meat, drink, washing, lodging and apparell at his house in Ivy Lane in the parish of St. Faiths under St. Paul's." The parish agreed to pay Tull quarterly and reserved the right to visit and inspect his house. Tull continued to be the parish's representative in the care of the poor until 1754. This seems to have resolved the crisis.

Also in 1745, on 22 January, the Vestry was informed of a petition before the Court of Aldermen from the Ward of Bread Street "for the Carts to stand in the uper [sic] part of Aldermanbury." The Churchwardens were instructed to consult with the residents to determine their views. The results of their inquiries were not reported.

During the next several years the Vestry met for the Easter and Christmas Vestries, to elect church and parish officers, and only on a few other occasions to take care of mundane business such as authorizing £7 to fix a leak from the "Cupillow" into the Clock loft on 15 July, 1747.

In 1750 the pace of business again picked up. On 13 February, the Vestry acted on fixing the "Great Engine" and heard the need for a new "Lessor Engine." At the same meeting the Vestry scheduled times to hear candidates to replace Dr. Nichols who had resigned as lecturer. On 29 March the Vestry asked Dr. Nichols to print the sermon he preached on his last Sunday. Mr. Ellison was chosen over Mr. Holme to replace Dr. Nichols by a vote of 50-30, with all voting signing their names beside their choice.

On 19 April, 1750, a committee was appointed to "inspect into the state of the parish" and reported on 27 May that over £355 was owed to the present and former churchwardens and that £100 in rents (a half year's) had not been collected.

On 11 December, 1750, the Vestry heard that concerns had been raised about Mr. Tull's care of the poor. The Vestry then agreed to revise the earlier agreement with Tull, and he agreed to provide "for the Maintenance of the said Poor in a Decent Orderly Manner and when Dead to Bury Them." Any poor who were bedridden were to be cared for at parish expense and not Tull's. Tull had to pay for appeals for the poor under his care, but not for the appeals of poor whom the parish had not responsibility to maintain. This policy was tested when on 14 February, 1751, an attorney appeared before the Vestry, asking for payment for an appeal. At the same Vestry the purchase of tree trunks for water pipe for the Church at an expense not to exceed £5 was authorized.

On 15 April, 1751, the church was found to be "very fowl" and the Vestry ordered that it be whitewashed.

On 31 March, 1752, the Vestry received a report that the Churchwardens had been summoned before the Lord Mayor because of complaints against Mr. Tull about his care of the poor. His Lordship told the Churchwardens that he felt it was improper to farm out the poor in mass, but rather that they should be provided for "by the head." As a result a new agreement with Mr. Tull was recorded in which he was to receive "three shillings and sixpence a Head by the Week and for this pay He is to receive them [the poor of the parish] as they come to the Churchwardens at some convenient place in the parish of Shoreditch ... and to find them with Victuals, Drink, Washing, Lodging and Cloaths, and a Surgeon, and an Apothecary, and Physick, during their stay with him." It further stated that if they were in Hospital he was to receive the same. If any died in his house, he was to be paid twenty shillings for their burial. For "a Lying in Woman in his House, He was to be paid six shillings and sixpence a week more for the month.." Furthermore, "Pains are to be taken for the children to read ... And when any leave the said Mr. Tull's House he is to provide for each One pair of shoes, One pair of stockings, and one of each sort of cloathing proper for the sex ... ."

On 28 May, 1754, Thomas Benn replaced Tull as caretaker for the poor, at the same rate as Tull. At the same meeting a new warder was chosen, with John Newton elected by a vote of 42-36. As was to be the parish practice for all contested elections, a poll was taken among parish householders. In the list of those voting, twelve were women.

Conclusion

Except for the escapades of Judge George Jeffreys and the dispute over the leadership of Benjamin Calamy, the late seventeenth and early eighteenth centuries were an era of relative stability in the life of the Aldermanbury parish. We have told the parish's story at this prosperous time in the context of the history of England during the last Stuart monarchs and the rise of the Hanoverian dynasty. As we reach the end of the eighteenth century the Industrial Revolution is about to transform the City and the parish. That transformation will be our concern in the next chapter.

Bibliography
Butler, Lilley

    1696   "Sermon Preached at le Bow before the Lord Mayor," 26 June, 1696. GP 699.

    1694   "Funeral Sermon," 27 March, 1694. GP 10214.

    1709   "A Discourse, Proving that the Faith and Practice of some Christians are not just a matter of Shame and Reproach," eight sermons preached at

St. Paul's in 1709 (Boyle Lectures).

1710 "Sermon Preached at St. Paul's before the Lord Mayor," 5 November, 1710.

Calamy, Benjamin
1682 "Sermon before the Lord Mayor at Bow Church," 29 May, 1682. GP 4566.

1683 "A Discourse about a Scrupulous Conscience"

"Some Considerations about the Case of Scandal or Giving Offence to Weak Brethren," London.

1683 "A Sermon preached before the Lord Mayor at Guildhall Chappell," 30 September, 1683. GP 2371.

1684 "Sermon before the Lord Mayor at le Bow ," 2 September, 1684 (the anniversary of the Great Fire)," GP 5091.

"A Narrative of the Sufferings of Thomas Delaune, for writing, printing, and publishing A Plea for Nonconformists, 1684. GP A.4.4.no.60.

Calamy, Edmund (the younger)
1713 Abridgement of Mr. Baxter's History of his Life and Times. 2nd ed. London.

1718 A Letter to Archdeacon Echard, upon the Occasion of his History of England; wherein the true Principles of the Revolution are Defended; The Whigs and the Dissenters Vindicated; Several Persons of Distinction clear'd from Aspersions and A Number of Historical Mistakes Rectifyd. 2nd ed. London: John Clark.

Chancellor, William

1787 Accounts of the Several Wards and Precincts and Parishes in the City of London from 1660 to the Present. London: Kearsley.

Churchill, Winston
1956-58 A History of the English Speaking Peoples. 4 vols. London.

Delaune, Thomas
1690 Angliae metropolis: or the present stere of London. London: Harris.

Dictionary of National Biography
1923 "Benjamin Calamy," The Dictionary of National Biography, vol III. Oxford: University Press, 678-683.

1923 "Edmund Calamy (1671-1732)," The Dictionary of National Biography, vol. III. Oxford: University Press, 683-687.

Glass, D. V.
1966 London Inhabitants Within the Walls, 1695. London Record Society.

Goss, Charles
1944 "A History of The Parish of St. Mary the Virgin, Aldermanbury," Transactions of the London and Middlesex Archaeological Society. 9 (1944-47), 113-164.

Hatton, Edward
1708 A New View of London. 2 vols. London: R. Chiswell.

Henry, Thomas
1828 The Wards of London. London: Gifford.

Hyde, Ralph, ed.
1982 The A to Z of Georgian London. London: London Topographical Society (publication no. 126).

Maitland, William
    1775   The History of London. London: Wilkie.

Marshall, Nathaniel, lecturer
    1722   "A Farewell Sermon," delivered on 24 June, 1722. GP 3764.

Oliver, Dame Beryl
    1969   The Winston Churchill Memorial and the Church of St. Mary the Virgin, Aldermanbury: A Brief History. London: The Faith Press.

Rude, George
    1971   History of London: Hanoverian London, 1741-1808. London: Secker and Warburg.

Smart, John
    1741   A Short Account of the Several Wards, Precinct, and Parishes in London. London.

Stratford, Nicolaus
    1687   The Lay-Christian's Obligation to read the Holy Scriptures. London: Richard Chitwell.

Works on Judge George Jeffreys
Balfour, M. Melville
    1925   "An Incident in the Life of a Great Lawyer," Law Quarterly Review 41, 71-78 (GL Pamphlet 3709).

    1927-31   "Jeffrey's House in Aldermanbury, An Historical City Mansion," London and Middlesex Archaeological Society Transactions. (New Series). 6, 177-198.

Dictionary of National Biography
    1923   "George Jeffreys," The Dictionary of National Biography, vol. X. Oxford: Oxford University Press, 714-721.

Helm, Peter
    1966   Jeffreys. London: Robert Hale.

Macauley, Thomas
    1968   The History of England from the Accession of James II. New York: Washington Square Press. ed. Hugh R. Trevor-Roper.

Irving, Henry
    1898   The Life of Judge Jeffreys. London: Heinemann.

Schofield, Seymour
    1937   Jeffreys of the Bloody Assizes. London: Butterworth.

Tuchin, John
    1693   A New Martyrology, with added the life and death of George Geffreyes [sic]. London: Denton.

Woolrych, Humphrey
    1827   Memoirs of the Life of Judge Jeffreys. London: Colburn.

CHAPTER SEVEN: EXPANSION AND DECLINE DURING THE INDUSTRIAL REVOLUTION (1791-1887)

Introduction

The late eighteenth and nineteenth centuries brought sweeping changes to England, to London, and to the parish of Aldermanbury and the Church of St. Mary. This era saw Britain become Europe's principal power and London Europe's (perhaps the world's) greatest city. The British Empire far outstripped all competition in the realm of imperial achievement. Britain led the world into the industrial revolution and experienced an agricultural revolution as well. Then came the railroads and yet another revolution in transportation and communication. Gradually, a long delayed agenda of social and political reform was addressed, and London took up a variety of civic improvements. But the City remained zealous for its historic autonomy.

All of these developments bore upon life in the parish of Aldermanbury, not always in a positive manner. With the dawn of the Industrial Age the parish began a change from a residential area with some warehouses and other commercial establishments to a heavily commercialized section with few permanent residents (see Figures 7.1, 7.2, 7.5). The transition did not come overnight. Until the mid-19th century the Aldermanbury parish continued to grow and flourish. During the rest of the of the 19th century, however, the population of the parish steadily declined as the neighborhood became increasingly commercialized, and warehouses and businesses replaced residences. Throughout the period the machinery of city government became ever more elaborate, increasingly restricting the power of the vestry to management and repair of the church and distribution of charities to the poor.

By the middle of the 19th century it was apparent that there were too many churches in the city of London. Ecclesiastical authorities began to plan for the consolidation of parishes and the destruction of churches, so that the very valuable land upon which they stood could be sold. In 1862 the Vestry of the Church of St. Mary was informed of a plan to merge the parish with the neighboring St. Michael, Bassishaw, and destroy the Church of St. Mary. This marked the first of several efforts to consolidate St. Mary's with other parishes. However, the Vestry's efforts to resist merging with St. Michael's and destruction of the church were successful.

Also during the 19th century responsibility for the care of the poor of London shifted from the individual parishes to a Charities Commission. By the middle of the 19th century, to assist in financing this care, the Charities Commission moved to take control of the property of the parishes. The Aldermanbury parish resisted these efforts, and in 1885 a lawsuit resulted. On the basis of its historic control of the advowson of the parish, and deeds showing ownership of parish properties, the Vestry refused to cooperate with the Charities Commission and took the case to the Chancery Court. The Chancery Court's ruling against the parish marked the end of an era.

The Later Hanoverians (1760-1837)

George III (r. 1760-1820) prided himself on his Britishness. No longer would the Hanoverians be alien princelings. Legend has it that he was admonished by his mother, "George, be a king!" Supposedly, he was also deeply affected by Bolingbroke's book, <u>The Patriot King</u>. (The extent of Bolingbroke's grasp of patriotism offers an interesting subject for speculation.) Bolingbroke had posited a king who would be above party and govern in the larger national interest through ministers of his own choosing. But too much partisan water had gone under the bridge to return to such a Stuart Utopia, and George knew it. To get his way, he had to bring down the Whig magnates and replace them with a more tractable Tory ministry. This he achieved in the first decade of his reign by turning the Whig's great weapon against them: patronage, but royal patronage in place of party patronage.

And so it was that in 1760 there came to power, and stayed in power for a dozen years, a Tory ministry of "King's Friends." With such friends, the King did not need enemies! The Prime Minister, Lord North, was a person of ability, but flawed by excessive devotion to his sovereign. History's judgment on other members of the ministry must be more severe. Under their stewardship, England found herself at war with half of Europe and on the outs with the rest. British arms, even the navy, suffered an unaccustomed series of misfortunes. The American Revolution broke out just over a decade after the conclusion of the Seven Years War had brought Britain's North American Empire to its zenith.

Recent historians have tended to be more generous than their predecessors in judging George III. He is now seen as a devoted and hard-working monarch who was sometimes overwhelmed by events beyond his comprehension, and ill-served by some of his ministers. Still, the policies that produced the American catastrophe were either the king's own, or approved by him. He was the monarch most active in the actual governing of the realm since William III, and he is credited with knowing the British constitution well and seeking his purposes within its limits.

Any consideration of the later Hanoverians must take account of George III's "madness." A majority of modern medical historians now seem to agree that the king's problem was in fact caused by aporphuria, a rare metabolic condition. Physicians in the late 18th century could not diagnose, let alone properly treat, such a condition. Indeed, the 18th century therapeutic regimen of poltaces, leaches and bleedings probably served only to make the patient more miserable. The affliction was intermittent, with long remissions between short periods of acute disorientation. Some general histories sow confusion concerning how many episodes of mental disability the king actually experienced. A brief episode in 1765 is disputed. Four major periods of affliction are well-documented in 1788-89, 1801, 1804, and a final almost unbroken spell from October 1810 until his death on 29 January 1820, by which time he was both blind and deaf, and the object of well-deserved public sympathy and even affection.

Hostility between the monarch and the Prince of Wales was traditional among the Hanoverians to the point of the Prince cultivating the parliamentary opposition. George III was offended by the Prince's Whig liaisons on two grounds. He abhorred Whig political principles. And he had strong moral objections to the flamboyant and sensuous social life of the high living Whig leaders in which the Prince participated. (The future George IV admitted that early in life he acquired an excessive love of women and wine.) The Whigs thus attempted to install the Prince as regent in 1788, but the ploy failed, and it was not until 1811 that he became Prince Regent.

By the time the Prince became George IV, he was a bloated and burned out rake. His exquisite taste had helped advance art and architecture in Britain and is credited with the birth of the National Gallery (even as George III's enhancements of the Royal Library led to the fulfillment of Sir Robert Cotton's late Elizabethan dream of a national library). But his personal extravagance and his tumultuous love life sapped his popular appeal. The Duke of Wellington, whose military achievements led him to the premiership, remarked that George IV and his brothers were "the damnedest millstones about the neck of any government that can be imagined."

Presumably the future William IV, the beloved old sailor, was an exception to these remarks. **George IV** reigned from **1820-1830** and his brother, **William IV**, from **1830-37**. When young Princess Victoria received the news (tradition has it, in her night dress) that her uncle William was dead and that she was Queen, few probably imagined that Britain stood on the threshhold of unparalleled achievement. But there was a good omen. A woman could not reign in Hanover, and so England was liberated from the built-in German complications to her foreign policy.

The promise of Victorian greatness hardly denigrates the signficance of developments between 1750 and the late 1830's. It was in many respects an age of revolution: an agricultural revolution, an industrial revolution, and a religious revolution. Some also speak of a revolution in transportation and communications. To be sure, there was a great spate of canal building which facilitated transport of coal and agricultural and industrial cargoes. Toward the end of the period, Mr. McAdam gave his name to a process for constructing harder roads that stood up better to weather. And the "clipper" design and rigging produced a new generation of faster sailing vessels. But the real revolution consisted of a series of improvements in farming methods which greatly increased yields, encouraged the farming of larger plots by more efficient means, and, in the process, played hob with the medieval village farming system. Crop rotation (including fodder crops for feed) eliminated the need for fallowing fields. The use of manure, lime and marl enriched the soil. Selective breeding produced larger, more vigorous livestock. The average sheep offered at Smithfield market (just to the northwest of Aldermanbury) weighed 28 pounds at the beginning of the 18th century, 80 pounds at the end. The cattle average went from 370 pounds to 800 pounds. The enlargement of plots was achieved by a new series of enclosures of former open and common land. Parliament passed some 2,000 enclosures acts in the 18th century, and more would come early in the next century. Only the landlords and larger tenants could afford to assume the larger land holdings and to practice the more expensive and more productive new techniques. The former holds of smaller farmers were absorbed into larger units and small tenants and cottagers were simply squeezed off the land. Some of these displaced persons remained as hired laborers. Many more migrated into the towns and cities or immigrated to North America. There was thus a symbiotic relationship between the agricultural revolution, underway from mid-century, and the industrial revolution, which began roughly two decades later. The dislocated former agrarian population provided a substantial part of the work force in the growing industrial towns. And the more productive farming methods permitted a smaller agrarian work force to supply food for a growing urban population. Indeed, it was a growing national population. There were 8,890,000 Englishmen when the first census was taken in 1801, 13,800,000 by 1831, despite rampant disease, unsanitary living conditions, and wretched working conditions.

The industrial revolution was the product of a series of technological innovations, initially in the textile industry. England had long been a major exporter of woolens, produced under the "domestic system" (see ch. 3). Her adventures in India had created an interest in cotton fabrics, and cotton grew well in the former Southern colonies, now American states. A mechanical innovation, the cotton gin, brought American production to its full potential and gave the institution of slavery a new lease on life.

Larger and more efficient machinery for spinning and weaving increased production. But it also grew beyond the capacity of human muscle power, and began to be linked to water wheels. The water wheel gave way in due course to the steam engine. The steam engine increased the demand for coal, but more powerful steam operated lifts and pumps made deeper and more productive mines possible. A shortage of oak for charcoal threatened the British iron industry until coke, made from coal, proved a superior substitute. The bulk of coal made it desirable to locate coal burning industries near the mines and so the burgeoning industrial centers sprang up in the Midlands and the north, occasioning a substantial migration of former agricultural workers from the south. London was thus spared the heavy industrial activities that would have caused even more dreadful environmental degradation than it experienced. London also ceased to be Britain's sole major city, as Birmingham and other centers mushroomed. But London remained the premier metropolis of the realm.

The bungling that led to the loss of the American colonies and the social dislocation produced by the early stages of the agricultural and industrial revolutions made England a country ripe for reform if not for revolution in the latter decades of the 18th century. Early ripples of reform were in fact evident, especially in Whig circles. But the excesses of another revolution in France, and England's long involvement in warfare against the revolutionary regime and then Napoleon postponed any serious change well into the next century. In a manner not unlike the American "Red scares" of more recent times, any sort of reformist tendencies, let alone radicalism, were tarred with the brush of French radicalism and the Reign of Terror. Hating Tom Paine became a favorite indoor and outdoor sport. Only the great Whig leader, Fox, whose patriotism was above reproach, seemed to enjoy a public dispensation to think reformist thoughts, even out loud if he wished. Laws against "combinations" strangled embryonic trade unionism. Advocates of the Great Man/Woman theory of history give Edmund Burke, the only Whig whom Dr. Johnson could abide, much of the credit for the negative British attitude toward the French revolution. But it may be that his <u>Reflections</u>, which marked his emergence as a Johnsonesque traditionalist, simply gave eloquent voice to ideas already held by many prominent Britons.

And so the problems of urban poverty, the exploitation of labor (above all women and children), political corruption abetted by an unrepresentative Parliament, went unchecked. So did ethically more neutral, but in the long run crucial, social changes such as the rising wealth, power and influence of the entrepeneural class, the "bourgeoisie," and the concomittant dimunition of the landed aristocracy.

England's religious revolution, in which John Wesley (1703-1791) was a key figure, flourished in the second half of the eighteenth century and beyond. It was largely the British expression of a movement in European religion known as "pietism." Pietism emphasized the personal, the individual, the emotional, the experiential side of religion. It placed a premium on an individual sense of salvation. It emphasized the living of a holy life in the workaday world. (American revivalism and the "born again" movement are among its legacies.) Romanticism, which also appeals to the individual, the emotional, even the irrational, was making its influence felt in literature, art, music, and philosophy. The two trends complemented and reinforced one another. The Anglican Church of the period is condemned for its coldness and aloofness in conventional ecclesiastical histories. But in a sense it was the product of an earlier age and simply failed to respond adequately to changing times (much as "mainline" American denominations appear to be failing to respond to the pietistic movements of the current era). It bears noting that there was a strong evangelical party in the Church of England, with leaders like the eloquent George Whitefield, a sometimes colleague of Wesley. Wesley himself died as he had lived, a loyal priest of the Church of England. Perhaps it was bureaucratic rigidity more than theological and liturgical aridity that underlay the shabby treatment accorded Wesley and his Methodist societies by the Established Church, insuring that the Methodists would become a separate denomination despite Wesley's own best efforts to the contrary. That Anglicanism has thought better of things in modern times is witnessed by the Calendar, which commemorates "John and Charles Wesley, priests," on 3 March.

Much of Wesley's career revolved about locations in and near the City, often in hailing distance of Aldermanbury parish. This is the case with his storied conversion experience in Aldersgate (1738), within several blocks of Aldermanbury. At the time, John and his brother, Charles, had rooms on Little Britain street nearby, and were affiliated with the parish of St. Bartholomew the Less. His original London mission was in the Old Foundry, just north of Moorgate. Later, he moved further north on City Road, building a chapel directly across from Bunhills Cemetery and taking a substantial house next door. (Both are still standing and may be visited.) Wesley's secure place in ecclesiastical history is well-known. The place assigned him in social history may be growing. Some social historians have long since been willing to speculate that Wesley helped spare England the sort of convulsion that struck France both by turning attention from social ills to personal improvement, a process which in the long run helped ameliorate those ills. And historical sociologists are prepared to argue that Wesley supplied the British working class with the same sort of ideological underpinning and personal displine that Weber said earlier Protestantism gave the middle class. Certainly Wesly and Wesleyanism strengthened the hand of the evangelical persuasion throughout England, and the evangelicals were a significant part of the coalition that in later decades brought political and social reform to England.

A succession of ministries directed Britain's destinies during the war years, two of them, including the longest (1783-1801) under the younger Pitt. Initially, the war went badly. The Powers, who hoped to overturn the revolution, underestimated the elan of the French "people's army" and its zealous columnar charges. And once Napoleon assumed control, England and her allies found themselves confounded on land by a military genius who carried all before him. The British navy once more demonstrated its superiority. Nelson drove Napoleon from the Near East in the battle of the Nile and lost his life in the definitive engagement at Trafalgar. Arthur Wellesly, Duke of Wellington, proved to be England's most resourceful soldier in the war, defeating the French in Portugal and Spain in his ingenious "peninsular campaign." But it was General Winter who finally did Napoleon in on his ill-fated Russian adventure. Following his initial defeat and exile, the resiliant Corsican returned for the Hundred Days, only to be finally thwarted by Wellington and the "thin red line" at Waterloo. The American War of 1812 was from the European standpoint a sideshow on the Napoleonic wars, though a significant event in the history of the new Republic.

Once Napoleon was disposed of and the attempt to reassemble Humpty Dumpty at the Congress of Vienna done, England turned to the long postponed agenda for reform, and before long the Hanoverian era was properly over. Reform did not come easily. The opposition, largely Tory, rallied around the Duke of Wellington, who returned from a career as a remarkably successful general to become a remarkably reactionary politician as Prime Minister (1828-1830). The first reform bill was aimed at making the Commons more representative and at extending the franchise. It was successfully derailed in 1831, and the King was persuaded to dissolve Parliament. Earl Charles Grey, the fallen Whig prime minister, fought the election on the issue of the reform bill and swept back into power with a strong majority. The bill passed Commons easily. Rallied by Wellington, the Lords rejected it. England teetered on the brink of revolution. Civil disorder was widespread. Reintroduced in 1832 with minor modifications to appease moderate Tories, it passed Commons by a 2-1 margin. The Lords set about to gut it with amendments. Stymied, Lord Grey resigned and King William invited Wellington to form a new government. He never had the chance. Churchbells pealed throughout England. Workers went on strike. Crowds shouted insults at the royal coach. But it was a run on the Bank of England, symbolized by the slogan of artisan and reformer, Francis Place, "To stop the Duke, go for the gold," that was probably the key element. Wellington withdrew. The King once more sent for Grey, who demanded one concession. There must be a credible threat that, like Queen Anne in 1712, William IV would create enough new peers to pass the bill over the current majority. The king assented. Wellington and his associates stayed home and let the bill pass in their absence rather than sit in a parvenu house of Lords filled with men of no war record and no grandfathers worth mentioning, who were Whigs or liberal Tories to boot.

Additional reform laws followed in the train of the Reform Bill: a rather limited industrial reform act in 1833 and the Poor Law of 1834. Parish charity had been overtaxed by the growing problem of poverty, and the new act doubtlessly saved many lives, though at substantial expense to human freedom and dignity. It has been said, "Poverty was treated as crime." We shall treat below the problem of poverty during this period in microcosm, as it affected the life of St. Mary, Aldermanbury.

Although a few years beyond the present span, this is the appropriate place to mention the repeal of the Corn Laws in 1841. This body of law kept cereal grain prices artificially high through a scheme of quotas and import duties. The repeal was a boon for trade as well as a benefit for the less affluent.

So England embarked on a century (or "baker's century") of reform. Religious disabilities had been removed. England had set herself against human slavery. Laws against trade unionism had been repealed. But more remained to be done, culminating with universal suffrage, enacted in 1928, and the National Health Scheme adopted in the aftermath of World War II.

London continued to grow and to prosper through the later 18th century and on into the 19th. By the 18th century most householders had become freemen either through apprenticeship or through purchasing the freedom of a livery company at a figure of from £5 to £50. This gave one the right to trade in the City, to vote for aldermen and common councilmen, and to be protected from the naval press gangs in wartime. One also became subject to certain taxes and civic duties (hanging a lantern on dark nights, maintaining the street before one's property, serving on night watch). But the duties diminished from 1836 onward, with the passage of the Lighting, Paving, and Watch Acts (Rude 1971:126-127).

London had ever been the objective of immigrants, and much of its growth was from that source. By 1790, births in London exceeded burials, but this had not always been the case. The end of the 18th century found it Europe's largest city, possibly the largest in the world. The census of 1801 counted 900,000 inhabitants. It was the first city in Europe to exceed a million population.

London's polity was relatively unchanged. In addition to the great offices of Lord

Mayor, the two Sheriffs, the Recorder, the Clerk, the Remembrancer and the Chamberlain (Rude 1971: 119) there were over 150 lesser posts and sinecures. The four important courts (Aldermen, Common Council, Common Hall and Wardmote) still functioned, though Wardmote declined as the municipality assumed former neighborhood functions. Common Council, made up mostly of successful tradesmen and craftsmen was able, by contrast, to enhance its power. At the parish level, the 18th century was the heydey of select vestries in London Churches. Their fading importance in the next century marked the diminishing of an aspect of grass roots democracy.

London suffered from a raging epidemic of crime which grew only worse as time went on. The City served a sort of buffer between the most seriously affected East End and the "polite" neighborhoods to the west. Gangs of a hundred or more members plagued some of the eastern parishes, rustling herds of cattle bound for Smithfield Market and descending en masse upon hapless commerical areas. A favorite trick was to save a particularly rambunctious bull from a purloined herd, with the raiders charging in the wake (Sheppard 1971: 33). Nowhere in the Metropolis was life and property adequately protected. The parish beadles and night watch, the constables, and other parts of the fragmented structure of London law enforcement, had been passed by with the growth of population and of the crime problem. A few specialized police units, a Thames detective band at Bow Street, had been created. But careful of their liberties, Englishmen were loathe to have a unified police force. Jealous of its prerogatives, the City was even moreso.

When the future Sir Robert Peel, Bart., became home secretary in 1822, he was dismayed at the spectacle of political and criminal disorder in London. Knowing the situation and being a skillful tactician, Peel approached the problem piecemeal and by so doing was able to slip through Parliament among routine bills first a study (1828) and then an authorization (1829) for the creation of a London Metropolitan Police Force. Its constables would be known as "Bobbies," in honor of Sir Robert. Peel excluded the City from the purview of the act on the pretext that law enforcement there was in a much better state than the rest of London. In fact, it was a concession to avoid the shipwreck of the entire act on the shoals of the City's power and wealth. Successive inquiries over the next decade urged the merger of the City's police into the Metropolitan Foce. But the City rallied every resource to protect its treasured autonomy, and in the end a bill was passed which gave the City a reorganized force under a commander appointed by the Corporation. The result in the judgment of experts at the time was improvement, but not to the level of the Metropolitan Force. However, both the City and the Metropolitan police proved remarkably successful both in controlling crime and quelling civil disorder without resort to the troops that had been required in the past.

The war years saw horrendous inflation of food prices, bread rising from 6 1/2 d a loaf to 1s 4d, and then 1s 5d. But London continued to prosper. Private investment financed the building of the London docks between 1810-1812, evidence of prosperity both past and future.

Overtly political issues produced two great tumults in London during the late Hanoverian period. The first revolved around parliamentarian, journalist and reformer John Wilkes, who was prosecuted by the government for libel after publishing criticisms of George III and Lord Bute in 1763. But Wilkes filed countersuit for false arrest and won. In a dizzying sequence of events Wilkes was expelled from Parliament, fled to the continent, and returned to win reelection to Commons. He became the darling of the City mob, for whom "Wilkes and Liberty!" became a popular chant. He was returned as Lord Mayor of London in 1774. Many London merchants supported his campaign for parliamentary reform, not unlike the measures which were finally enacted in 1832. He supported the rights of the American colonists in Parliament, and his court fights helped establish greater press freedom and abolish "general warrants," which permitted almost random searches. His popular appeal waned when he took a strong role in suppressing the Gordon riots of 1780, which were occasioned by a royal initiative to diminish Catholic disabilities.

Life in the City had improved through the years, with gas lighting on the streets and new iron water pipes under them. But the "polite neighborhoods" to the west beckoned and many of the more affluent citizens responded. This led to the decline of the economic level of some neighborhoods and to the gradual replacement of residential functions by businesses, warehouses and manufacturing in others. Aldermanbury parish was still a vital, mixed neighborhood at the end of the Hanoverian period. But in the course of the 19th century the demographic situation would change to the detriment of parish life. Still, the most significant event for the future development of the City and for the rest of the metropolis took place in 1833 when Parliament enacted a bill authorizing construction of the London and Birminghman railway. Sheppard (1971: 117) suggested it was the greatest human feat of engineering and construction up to that time, with the possible exception of the Great Wall of China. And in five years, it was done.

Aldermanbury under the Later Hanoverians (1760-1837)

The John Lawrence Era (1755-1790)

On 19 November, 1754, the Vestry was formally notified that the curate, Mr. Sandford had died. On 8 January, 1755, Mr. John Lawrence was chosen over eight candidates.

In 1755 the Churchwardens reported on a summons from the Commissioners of the Shores concerning pavement in front of the church. The Vestry agreed to attend to the manner "in a Workman like Manner." The next year the "Raker" reported great difficulty cleaning the Street and was given £5. On 19 November, the Vestry approved a plan to tear down several of the houses in the parish estate and build one or two new houses at a cost of £1000. The Vestry also heard that the expense for the poor was increasing.

On 1 March, 1757, the Vestry acted "to prosecute at the parish Expense Any Person that should Incroach Upon the Street and in this Parish by Loading or haveing Waggens or Carts or Shays Standing in the Streets." The growing commercial activity in the parish was becoming a more serious concern. However, it was not until 1 April, 1763, that the Vestry put into execution the order.

In 1758 it was reported that only two trustees of the parish estates still lived in the parish, reflecting the outward movement from the parish and the previously mentioned absence of any policy to elect new trustees. Eighteen trustees were added, creating a total of thirty-one. That same year marked the beginning of a listing of householders of the parish: when they came to the parish, their place of abode, and what parish offices they held (Ms 3563/1). The record was kept with varying degrees of thoroughness until 1830. The list began by recording that between 1706 and 1757 116 persons had entered the parish. Residences were listed on the following streets and courts: Addle Street, Bury Low, Bury Mid, Miller's, Bury Up, Dyers Court, Love Lane, Phillip Lane, Rose Court, and London Wall. In the next six years an average of about 13 persons entered the parish each year.

During 1760 the Parish spent over £722 to restore the church. The minutes only mention a new leading of the church. The same year the accounts speak of paying to get "security for a Bastard Child," but then more spent when the "Bastard [is] dropt and Baptized John Miller."

The first of the extant Visitation Returns of the Archbishop for the parish, now in the archives of Lambeth Palace Library, dates from 1762 (Osbaldeston 6, f. 115). In filling out the questionnaire Mr. Lawrence reported that he did not live in the parish because there was no parsonage. Lawrence also reported that he was also rector of a parish in Essex and preached alternatively at St. Botolph Bishopsgate. The curate was an unlicensed minister named Fran(cis) Leathes, who lived very near the church.

The next ten years were apparently fairly calm ones in the parish. The minutes reflect regular business and the accounts the ordinary expenditures for care of the poor and the church. For example, the Vestry authorized 10s6p in 1764 for a wooden leg for Sarah Surnam and 4s3p "to clearing ye Bone House."

Mr. Lawrence responded to an inquiry from the Bishop of 26 November, 1765, concerning "popish priests," saying he knew of none (LPL Terrick 20, fl. 101-102). He named only two widows who professed "Romish religion." He concluded the report by saying "As my parish is not very large, I am sure this is correct." Two years later he listed six people who were "Romish" (LPL Terrick 22, fl. 103-104).

On 14 January, 1767, the Vestry approved purchase of two of the "New Patent Stoves" for warming the Church on Sundays and Prayer Days" and at the same time 18 new fire buckets. It must have been a cold winter, for the next week the Vestry commented on the need to clear the frozen snow from the parish streets.

In 1770 a Mr. Finch was chosen as the new lecturer. On 4 December, 1772, there is the first mention in the minutes of a precinct meeting. £2 was allowed for the cost of the meeting.

An account of those confirmed in 1774 was dominated by girls, with 13 of the 15 listed (LPL Terrick 5 fl. 136).

On 20 July, 1775, at a special Vestry the churchwardens reported "the immediate want of money to defray the expenses of the Parish Poor." The parish was, they say, "deeply in debt" and this would continue "year after year so that the Parish may e're long be brought into an alarming Situation." The Vestry responded by creating a special committee to raise £500 by selling annuities. On 13 December a new Clerk was elected, with 9 women listed among the 71 voters.

The accounts for 1776 show 9s spent for a Fast Day (in response to the American colonies declaring independence?) and 1.8.6 for "cloathing M. Cross she being almost naked."

On 24 April, 1777, a new lecturer was elected. Rev. Prince was chosen over Rev. Ellis, by a vote of 62-14. At least 8 women voted for the winner, and none for the loser. Four days later the Vestry ordered the church shut at the first Sunday after Trinity for painting and whitewashing. The accounts include £10 "received of Robert Roolf for a Bastard child of Ann Taylor."

On the 3rd of June, 1777, an offer from Mr. Beverly to give to the church an organ was received. Two weeks later the Vestry voted 9-9 on a motion to receive this gift. The Churchwarden's deciding vote caused the offer to be declined.

On 18 June, 1777, a letter from a Mr. Whitechurch offered the painting of the Lord's Supper by Old Franks to be put up over the altar. The offer was accepted. On the same day the Churchwardens agreed to purchase two escutcheons of the royal arms with the garter with supporters the British and Hanoverian crowns, gilded with silver and painted on silk, to be placed in the church on the occasion of the death of his majesty, King George III. They would not be needed for another 43 years.

Eight days later the vestry received estimates on repairs of the church and agreed on 3 July to raise £400 to defray expenses through an annuity. Another £500 annuity was ordered to help pay the cost. Still another £250 annuity was approved on 29 June.

An issue of the Daily Advertiser in 1777 included the following advertisement (Lillywhite 1963: 106-107):

> Matrimony wanted, by a young Gentleman just beginning Housekeeping a Lady, between 18 and 25 years of Age, with a good Education, and a Fortune not less than 5000 pounds; sound Wind and Limb, Five Feet Four Inches without her Shoes; not fat; not yet too lean; a clear Skin; Sweet Breath, with a good set of Teeth; no Pride, nor Affectation; not very talkative, no one that is deemed to Scold ...; not over fond of Dress, though always decent and clean; that will entertain her Husband's friends with Affability and Cheerfulness and prefer his Company to Public diversions and gadding about; one who can keep Secrets ...
>
> Any Lady disposed to Matrimony answering this description is desired to direct for Y.2 at the Baptist's Head Coffee-House, Aldermanbury.

The Baptist's Head was at No. 2 Aldermanbury. It was also called the Aldermanbury Coffee-House at times. By the late 18th century it was said to be "situated in the vicinity of the wholesale tradesmen" much frequented by "country gentlemen and manufacturers" (Lillywhite 1963: 107).

On 16 December, 1778, the Vestry learned that Thomas Elliott and George Roach had been prosecuted for stealing lead out of a burial vault and Jonas Parker for buying the lead when he knew it was stolen. The Vestry refused to pay for the prosecution, deeming the bill from the attorneys to be too high. However, at the next Easter Vestry (9 April, 1779) the vote was reversed.

For the next eight years from 1780 through 1787 the Vestry met only for the Easter and Christmas vestries, to conduct parish and precinct elections. However, the accounts for 1782 include a number of entries related to "passes," which apparently were documents required for the parish poor to carry showing authorization for their activities or travel. A John Grice was apprehended at an expense of 1.18.6 for forging passes. To "2 casuals [a term for poor receiving funds on occasion, but not regularly] with a Travelling pass" 2s.

A 1784 advertisement for the Swan with Two Necks Inn on the southern border of the parish claimed that guarded mail coaches with four inside passengers left each day for Bath and Bristol, leaving at 8:00 p.m. and arriving in Bath before 10:00 a.m. the next morning and Bristol by noon. The fare was 20s each way, and no outside passengers were allowed. Fifty years later the mail coaches were still running. The Inn closed in 1859. (Lillywhite 1963: 562-563).

A 1787 survey of the City showed still listed 136 houses in the parish (Chancellor 1787: 36), with 784 houses in Cripplegate Within and 21,649 in the 26 wards of the city.

In 1788 the Treasurer and Churchwarden refused to pay any more out of pocket for parish expenses. A £300 annuity was authorized. In 1790 the Vestry instructed the Churchwardens and Overseers to visit the poor in the workhouse every quarter.

By the end of the 18th century the transition of the parish from residential to commercial was well underway. On the east side of Aldermanbury, glovers, haberdashers, and those engaged in the sale of other soft goods were in place (Goss 1944: 127).

The Charles Smith Era (1791-1802)

On 20 April, 1791, the Vestry was told that the Rev. John Lawrence had died. Three candidates were scheduled to preach. On 11 May, with at least 6 women voting, a general vestry of 100 parishoners voted 50-46 to hold the election on Wednesday, May 18, and by 50-48 to vote by ballot rather than by a poll. With 125 in attendance the Rev. Charles Smith was elected curate by a vote of 65-60, with 4 women voting.

On 13 April, 1792, the Vestry authorized two monuments on the side of the altar, one to Samuel Smith and another to his son, Captain John Smith, (see Ch. 6). On the 19th of April the Church was ordered shut up for three months after April 29 for white washing and the addition of new windows of "new Crown glass."

At least by 1795 the Industrial Revolution arrived in the parish. On 9 April the Vestry ordered a General Vestry to be held on the 23rd "for the purpose of taking into consideration the proper mode of removing a Steam Engine lately erected in this Parish." At that meeting the owner of the engine, Mr. Thompson, refused to remove it, so the Vestry ordered the advice of Counsel be sought. On 30 June Counsel recommended to a General Vestry that Mr. Thompson be taken to court, and the inhabitants accepted the advice. However, there is no word of the outcome of the case in the parish records. By the turn of the century, and in the first decades of the nineteenth, houses were being demolished, especially on the east side of Aldermanbury, for the erection of warehouses (See Figure 7.5). Private residences continued on the west side, but they too would be forced out by traders. (Goss 1944: 127).

The effect of the Napoleonic Wars on the parish is evident in the Vestry Minutes. On 2 January, 1797, at a meeting of the joint vestries of St. Mary Aldermanbury, St. Olave's Old Jewry, and St. Mary Staining, an act of Parliament of 11 November, 1796 was received, calling for the raising of four men for his Majesty's Army. The assessments to be drawn from each parish were listed as St. Mary Aldermanbury £3600, St. Olave £2590, and St. Mary Staining £1060. The Overseers of these parishes were ordered to advertise in the papers, place hand bills in public places, and consult with recruiting officers in order to raise the four men, at a bounty not to exceed £30 for each man.

On 21 April, 1797, the minutes reflected one of the clearest statements of the responsibilities of the most important parish offices. The two churchwardens were to collect the rents of the parish estates and the church rate, to receive the parish dues for burials, pay the annuitants, the clerk, the sextoness, and the Beadle, and all other necessary expenses and repairs of the church and churchyard. For all expenses of more than £2 for repairs of the church the churchwardens were to secure the approval of the Vestry. Those elected to serve as churchwardens who refuse were to pay a fine of £20.

The four overseers were appointed to collect the poor rate, pay the workhouse bills, pay the weekly pensioners, and all other business relating to the poor. The four auditors were responsible for auditing the accounts of the churchwardens and overseers once every six months, and reporting to the vestry.

On 25 April, the Vestry heard a complaint that smoke from a chimney on the south side of the church was inconveniencing the adjoining premises. At this meeting the minister, churchwardens, and parishoners were charged to go over the parish boundaries once every three years on Ascension Day.

On 15 May, the Vestry learned that the parishoners were liable for expenses related to the erection of "the gallery of the Singers" by the late Churchwarden William Reynolds, called by one contemporary observer "that wretched gallery" (Malcolm 1803: 117). The Vestry authorized voluntary contributions from the householders to save the parish from a tax to pay for this. Apparently the generosity of the inhabitants was not sufficient, for £200 was ordered borrowed on 11 July, on 4 September a £150 Life annuity was raised, and on 11 October a 1s church rate on the L was ordered for one year. At this same meeting £10 was approved for the Rev. Mr. Maidman who had been conducting worship services at the workhouse for 10 years.

On 22 March the minutes included the printed account of a meeting chaired by Rev. Smith called for the purpose of raising voluntary contributions for the defense of the country. The resolution, passed unanimously, read

> That in order to afford Persons of all Descriptions, resident
> in this Parish, an Opportunity of manifesting their love of
> their Country by contributing according to their Abilities
> toward its Defence against an Invation, threatened by an
> implacable and inveterate Enemy, whose avowed aim is to
> destroy its Existence as an independent Nation; a Committee
> be formed to receive the Voluntary Subscriptions of the In-
> habitants of this Parish for the above Purpose.

The book was to be left open until 5 April, and small donations were to be solicited. The account of the subscription shows gifts totalling £1473.17.6. Twenty-nine inhabitants and four businesses contributed, with one gift of £500 from a Mr. Atkinson.

For the first time at a regular meeting of the Vestry, on 28 March, 1799, the curate attended, although he was not identified as the minister in the roll. Later that year, on 20 November, a rate of 6d on the £ was ordered for six months to assist the Militia Men's Families.

One of the few remaining private residences in the parish was that of Dr. William Babington who resided in No. 17 Aldermanbury from 1800-1819.

In 1801 an assistant was appointed to help the churchwardens and overseers. The forementioned William Reynolds, Vestry Clerk, was named, at a salary of £20 yearly. In 1808 the accounts showed that Mr. Reynolds' (now deceased) account is over £225 in arrears.

The James Salisbury Era (1802-1843)

On 10 September, 1802, forty-nine parishoners attended the meeting at which a vacancy in the living was announced because of the death of Mr. Smith, who was known, according to Malcolm, as a "friend of the poor." From thirteen applicants, including the present curate, Richard Craddock, and nominees, the Rev. James T. Salisbury was chosen to replace Smith on 15 December at a meeting with 105 parishoners present.

In 1803 a new lecturer, the Rev. Mr. Japhson, was chosen at a meeting attended by 88 parishoners.

On 21 April, 1808, Mr. Thompson's steam engine again was the subject. A committee was appointed to consult with Mr. Thompson's landlord "to see if he intends to allow this nuisance to continue." On 4 May, Mr. Thompson offered to remove the nuisance outside the parish, no closer than 300 yards, if the parish would pay him £150. The Vestry deferred action.

Also during 1808 repairs of the Church were ordered, with a roof of slate to replace the lead roof and with funds to be raised by annuities and a rate of 2s. Four widows, including the widow Reynolds, were exempted from the rate. These repairs continued through 1810 and cost over £4000. During their repairs the meetings of the parish were held at various taverns and inns in the parish. Apparently the commercialization of the parish was bringing money into the parish, allowing for such extravagances.

On 7 June, 1809, at a meeting held at George Inn, the minutes recorded that "Mr. George Cooke was allowed and approved as deputy [Churchwarden} pursuant to the Act of 1st William and Mary relating to Dysenters." At the same meeting, a proposal to move the pulpit and reading desk to the middle of the aisle was referred to committee. The money raised for repairs not immediately needed was to be invested in India Bonds. On 31 August, the Vestry rejected a new gallery for the West end and approved seats to be erected for "charity children."

In 1810 the Vestry noted for the first time a violent crime in the parish. George Aldridge, son of the Ward beadle, had been injured in the defense of property in the parish, and the Vestry resolved to pay for his treatment. The parish Watch House during this period was located in a part of the churchyard, but in 1812 the Vestry complained to the Ward that this was a too confined location.

On 18 June, 1810, at the Kings Arm Tavern the Vestry minutes record that the "poor rate was changed from 4s4d to 3s." This was apparently the first mention of a new poor tax which continued until the Charities Commission assumed responsibility for relief of the poor.

Also in 1810 the Vestry acted to find out from Rev. Salisbury and Rev. Japhson if they intended to carry out their duties in person, because of the "extremely important privilege" of the parishoners in appointing clergymen and the extreme expense of repairing the church. In his response Salisbury said he would officiate if his health allowed and hoped that "the zeal expressed by those present at the Vestry will not abate upon our better acquaintance." Japhson's letter is indignant, saying that he submitted to the Bishop and to profess to the parish would be unnecessary and degrading. A unanimous resolution of the Vestry directed that the lecturer be informed that his letter is "not consistent with his duty to the Parishoners" and they considered it disrespectful.

An article in the 3 November, 1810 edition of <u>The Times</u> reported that "workmen employed to repair the Church of St. Mary, Aldermanbury, discovered a few days since the remains of the notorious Chancellor JEFFRIES (sic). A large flat stone was removed near the Communion table, and in a vault underneath men found a leaden coffin, containing the body. The coffin did not appear to have suffered much decay." The coffin was not opened, but it had a plate on it bearing Jeffreys' name. "After public curiosity had been gratified," the coffin was placed back in the vault and the stone refastened. (cited in Helms 1966).

In the Parish Poor Apprentice Book, required to be kept by an Act of Parliament, six boys, ranging in age from 9 to 19 were listed between 1810 and 1828. They were assigned to a weaver, a copper plate maker, a cabinet maker, a dairyman, and a shoemaker. (Ms. 3560).

The parish's list of householders for 1810 included 133 names (Ms. 3563/1), while on the Bishop's Visitation Return 104 housekeepers were counted. On the return Mr. Salisbury claimed that although many of the housekeepers were "opulent men of trade" they resided chiefly or entirely in the country. He reported that the Charity School had 50 boys and 25 girls. He also reported that neither he nor his curate lived in the parish, because the parishoners were letting the parsonage. He also said that for the last eighteen months the church had been under repair. He said that he served two cures himself and that because of his health he would not be able to live in the parish. (LPL Randolph 11 fl. 14).

On 19 April, 1811, lead pipe belonging to the Church was reported to have been cut. The Vestry agreed to join with St. Alban's Wood Street, in offering £10 each for the apprehension of offenders. During 1811 another £2050-2150 in annuities was authorized.

On 21 April, 1812, a letter was received asking that the commitment to the weekly poor be raised 6d per head because of an increase in the cost of bread. Other parishes had acceded to this request, and the Vestry agreed. At that same vestry the Sunday afternoon service was changed from 3:00 p.m. to 6:00 p.m. for a six month trial.

The Bishops Visitation return for 1812 named the curate as William Parker, a Fellow of Emmanuel College, Cambridge (LPL Randolph 14 fl. 57).

During this period the Vestry began to take action against parishoners who were in default on the church and the poor rate, listing them and the reasons for their failure to pay.

On 6 May, 1813, pursuant to an Act of Parliament the Vestry authorized purchase of an iron chest for the better regulating and preservation of parish registers. The Vestry also ordered that the Large Engine be sold.

In 1814 the front church yard was ordered closed to burials for an additional twelve months (beyond the past two years.) The Clerk, Mr. Bugg, complained that he was losing burial fees. In 1815 and 1817 the order was extended one more year, and burials in the churchyards or church were limited to lead coffins.

In 1815 Mr. Bean responded to an inquiry from the Bishop requesting answers to specific questions not completed on the Visitation Return. He listed the population of the parish as 743. He estimated that St. Mary's could hold about 330 persons and reported that there was no glebe house. (LPL Howley 50, ff. 23-24).

On 2 April, 1817, assessments for parish estates showed a total of £5200. On 8 April, 1817, the Vestry received word of a bill pending before parliament on the relief of the incumbents of certain livings in London. The Vestry expressed shock and dismay, in that the incumbent's stipend had been increased recently by 2/3 and neither he nor his curate had taken on increased responsibilities. The Vestry's resolution was ordered conveyed to Parliament and published in the Times and Morning Chronicle. Two years later, on 1 July, 1819, the Vestry approved £20 to help oppose this bill.

Another bill before parliament would force parishes to pay a certain salary to parish clerks. The Vestry on 8 April, 1819, expressed its opposition to this bill.

Also on 1 July, 1819, and again a year later, the Vestry circulated a list of persons receiving alms to neighboring parishes. Presumably, the Vestry felt that some of the parish poor may be "double dipping." On 29 June, 1820, the Vestry cautioned inhabitants against taking into their houses women to "lye in."

On 5 April, 1820, the Vestry was informed of a Bastard Child of which Ebenezer Radford was the reputed father. Mr. Bugg, the Vestry Clerk, told the Vestry that Mr. Radford had been confined to the King's Bench prison for debt. Mr. Radford's brother and attorney were present and explained that he was bankrupt. They offered £15 if the Vestry would drop all charges. The Vestry refused to accept this "inadequate sum" and ordered that the prosecution take its course.

At this same meeting the Vestry ordered escutcheons of the Royal Arms to be displayed on the occasion of the death of King George III.

During this period frequent shortfalls in the poor rate collection occurred. A number of people were granted exemptions, and some had permanent exclusions. On 4 July, 1820, the Vestry ordered that in the future no person occupying a house in the parish would be excused from the poor rate.

Also during this period Mr. Bugg was having financial difficulty. On 13 September, 1820, he said he would have to claim relief from the parish if he was not paid. His salary had been applied to his debts to the parish. However, a motion to pay him his £24 salary died for lack of a second. On 1 August, 1821, it was reported that Bugg owed the parish over £1315. The Vestry agreed to pay him 2/3 of his salary. Two months later it was reported he was in ill health, and his whole salary was paid.

On 28 March, 1821, the Vestry Clerk presented to the parish a statement of the charities under the management of the parish in response to a request from the Commissioners inquiring into Charities. This was the first step in the long process which led ultimately to the parish losing its property 65 years later. The request from Nicholas Carlisle, Secretary to the Commissioners, was dated 1 October, 1819, so it took the parish a year and a half to respond. The letter said, in part, "I am desired by the Commissioners to request that you will favour them with a list of all the Charities in your parish ... Stating by whom and when they were founded and for what purpose and likewise that you will mention what persons as Trustees or otherwise will be best able to give information with respect to each charity." The Vestry's response listed gifts of £100 in 1639 from Sir John Davy Knight and £60 from his executor. These funds were used to purchase "a Fee Farm Rent of £11 charged on the Rectory and Church ... and other premises which Rent was vested in Trustees." The trust was to pay £10 yearly to ten poor people and another 20s for a yearly memorial sermon. The only other gifts listed were Lady Gresham's 1670 gift, generating £3 a year for the poor, and a 1677 gift by Richard Wynne, resulting in gifts of 2s6p a year for four poor people.

The actual report of the Charity Commissioners on St. Mary Aldermanbury went into greater detail about how the bequests were being used for causes other than those originally intended (Vol. 4 1822:115-118). It claimed that Sir John Davy's £100 gift in 1639 had been designated for poor householders, but that of the £10 yearly distribution, the recipients were the parish clerk, sexton, and usually the beadle. The curate also received £1 for a sermon. Lady Gresham's 1560 will had provided for the distribution of 9.10.0 to poor householders in Aldermanbury and two other parishes, from rent of houses on Milk Street and Lad Lane. In 1566 the rent was just over £14, but by 1819 the yearly rent had increased to £902. Nevertheless, the Mercers Co. continued to pay St. Mary's just £3 yearly, which was given by the Overseer to poor persons at Christmas. The report concluded that although this was a proper construction of the will, had Lady Gresham foreseen the inflation in property value, she would have made "provision for extension of the charity." Richard Wynne's 1677 gift of £10 for four poor yearly had been discontinued after 1803. Thomas Benn's bequest of the rent from two houses had grown from £3 to about £40 yearly. A case was obviously being constructed for the removal of administration of these charities from parish control!

On 2 April, 1822, an offer to buy parish property on Maid Lane, Southwark, for £300 was accepted. The funds were invested in 4% annuities.

On 10 December, 1822, a petition was authorized to join with other parishes in opposing further money for the London Workhouse. The next week an act of Parliament requiring two fire engines was discussed. The larger engine was unfit for use and the smaller one was out of repair. The Vestry decided to purchase a new large engine and repair the smaller one.

In 1824 fifteen or sixteen houses which stood on the ground once owned by Sir John Swynnerton were pulled down to make room for warehouses by Mssrs. Bradbury Greatorex and Company (see Figure 7.5).

On 24 March, 1824, William Herbert, father of a Bastard Child, Rebecca Hammonds, asked to pay a lump sum in lieu of the weekly allowance he had been paying. He explained that he was only a servant and would soon be going abroad. The Vestry referred the matter to the churchwardens and overseers.

On 10 June, 1824, a committee was created to determine whether funds from the parish rents could be applied to the poor rate and used for the Church building. A year later, on 9 June, 1825, the committee reported that there was "a considerable annual surplus arising from the Rents of the Parish Estates." It sought opinion of Counsel, which was that application of the rents to the poor rate and alterations in the church (including erection of an organ) was legal. As a result an organ which cost £385.13.0 was built and placed in a loft in the west end of the church, where it remained until 1863, when it was taken down and the organ removed to the east end of the north aisle.

The committee also reported on the results of the poor rate in recent years. In 1821 a rate of 3s had generated about £739. In 1822, 2/6 resulted in about £606. In 1823 2s caused £481 and in 1824 brought £355. The average expense for the poor in the past four years had been £654, and £430 had been generated from the parish estates. The average total of other expenditures had been £174.

On 11 November the Vestry decided to hire an organist to play twice on Sunday and to instruct Ward School children in Psalmody an hour before services on Sunday. On 20 January, 1826, Miss Heather was hired as organist. An organ blower was also hired.

On 13 April, 1826, the Vestry was told that Mrs. Anne Streete and four children had come into the parish from St. Olave Silver Street, because she had been deserted by her husband. The Overseers were ordered to take necessary steps to apprehend

William Streete.

At the Easter Vestry, 1827, a special committee was created to investigate the expenditures of the parish in relation to the poor.

On 29 April, 1829, the curate, Mr. Bean, attended the Vestry and reported that on Good Friday at the conclusion of the collection before the Sacrament, he had been informed that Mr. Bugg was taking money from the plate. Mr. Bugg was present and confessed, saying that he had been driven to this act by his extreme poverty and distress. He was dismissed, but his salary was paid until Midsummer.

In 1830 a committee studied the repairs needed in the church. They reported on 1 July that the windows should be taken out and releaded and that ventilators should be installed. The repairs would cost about £500. They also recommended that the church be insured for £2000. The repairs were to be funded through £300 in the account and a special rate of 1s. The architect consulted also proposed further repairs in the church, the churchyard, and vaults.

On 14 April, 1831, Mr. Bean requested £2 yearly for Charity Children to encourage their singing. He reported that this parish was the only one in the Ward which did not have this practice.

On 25 April, 1832, after securing permission from the incumbent and the Bishop, William Jowett of St. John's College, Cambridge, was named Sunday evening lecturer (moving the lecture from the afternoon).

At the Easter Vestry, 1833, there was the first record of special donations to charities. £5.5 was given to the Cripplegate Ward School and £2.2 to the City Dispensary.

In 1834 Parliament passed a law establishing a poor rate for support of those in need throughout the metropolitan area. The law was resented by city parishes like Aldermanbury who thought they had been taking care of their own poor for centuries and could not understand why other metropolitan parishes could not do the same.

On 1 April, 1834, the Vestry heard a report of a special committee on the parish estates and other affairs. The Committee reported that parish rents were £650, from the houses at #12, 18, 19 Aldermanbury and next to the Church on Love Lane. £367 was being received from annuities. Annual expenditures beyond care of the poor and repairs were £225. The full, several page report was included in the minutes. The Weekly Poor Book of the same year (Ms. 3564/1) shows that an average of 50 poor were paid from £91-99 each quarter on a weekly basis. The workhouse bills and sundry expenses for "casual poor" totalled over £253. An interesting entry reports that £1.15 was spent for the prosecution of Sarah West for manslaughter at Old Bailey.

On 10 June, 1835, the Churchwardens reported that the sextoness, the widow of Mr. Bugg, and her second husband, were found dead in the Vestry Room after having been reported missing. No cause was mentioned, but the Bishop had ordered the church be shut up for three Sundays. At the same meeting a new sextoness was elected.

The expenses for the weekly care of the poor for the year prior to the Easter Vestry in 1835 totalled over £356 (Ms. 3564/1), with an additional £306 spent for the workhouse and sundry expenses. 18s was spent for sending a blind man, Thomas Boyle, back to Liverpool after he arrived in the parish. £1.4 went to keep Mrs. Bansfield's three children while she was in prison. During the year an average of 48 poor were given a weekly allowance.

On 22 March, 1836, the Vestry created a committee to examine raising the poor rate due to "the great Additions and Improvements in some of the Houses in the Parish." A very thorough report on one of the parish houses, at 19 Aldermanbury, received on 6 April, indicated that many of the rooms were being used as warehouses. Two years later further alterations "for the purpose of Trade" were authorized. The expenses for the weekly poor for the year were down to about £235, with and average of 35 paid per week, and the workhouse and other charges were about £300 (Ms. 3564/1).

On 19 January, 1837, the Vestry unanimously passed a resolution to pledge itself to "oppose by every means in its power the Introduction of the Poor Law Amendment Act into this parish." The resolution was to be published in the Times and Morning Chronicle. On 21 September, a Committee was created to make a new Assessment under the act to regulate parochial assessments. On 29 November, a letter was received explaining that the Board of Guardians had completed arrangements for taking management of the "In Door Poor" in London after 4 December, stating houses where the poor were to be taken. The Weekly Poor Book for the year reported that the number of weekly poor was down to about 30, costing the parish about £216, with £273 for the workhouse and £42 for bread (Ms. 3564/1). The accounts for 1837 showed over £37 spent for black cloth and hangings in the church on the death of King William IV.

On 14 December, 1838, an "Arnott's stove" was installed in the church, in response to complaints about the heating of the building. There were 31 poor receiving benefits from the parish on average each week, costing the parish about £231, with the poor house charge down to about £146.

Between 1830 and 1840 a quite thorough list of the occupations of officeholders in the parish was kept (Ms. 3563/3). It gives insight into the residents of the parish in a now quite commercialized parish, dominated by warehouses:

Warehousemen - 29

Hotel keepers (Axe Inn) - 5

Solicitor - 4

Tailor - 3

Plumber - 3

Flower manufacturer, Fender manufacturer, Grocer, Hosier - 2 each

Merchant, casemaker, cloth presser, carpet manufacturer, tavern keeper, broker, baker, coffeehouse keeper, hairdresser, printer, postman, shoemaker, carpenter, agent, gentleman - 1 each

The number of householders in the parish had reached its peak in 1830 with 141 listed (Ms. 3563/2), but by 1840 the number had dropped to 123 (Ms. 3563/3). Between 1791 and 1820 the number had fluctuated, with 101 in 1781, 133 in 1790, 122 in 1800, 133 in 1810, and 118 in 1820 (Ms. 3563/1).

In 1841 £2 was spent for a survey and map of the parish. They were not included in the Vestry Minutes.

On 29 March, 1842, the Vestry sent word to the Board of Guardians of the London Union asking them to consider "the enormous Expenses attending the Execution of the Poor Law in the Union." The Vestry also expressed concern about the absence of the Incumbent, Rev. Salisbury. On 14 August, a committee was established to investigate the list of poor receiving relief and whether an overseer to superintend the relief was necessary.

In preparation for Bishop Blomfield's October, 1842, visit to the parish, J. P. Bean, "officiating minister," submitted a report, dated 15 July (LPL Blomfield 72, f. 83). He reported the addition of two galleries used for Sunday school, providing an additional seating for about 50. Sunday School was held in the mornings from 9:30 to 10:00 and in the afternoon from 2:30 to 3:00, with and average of 110 attending. A Ward School (not in the parish) was held from 10:00 to 11:00 a.m. The number of congregants totalled about 120, he reported, but the number of communicants was only 15-20. In response to a question about whether he was careful not to solemnize marriage between parties not resident in the parish, he commented that when marriages could only be celebrated in the church, he was careful to investigate carefully before publishing Banns. Now, however, since marriage "has been degraded to a mere civil contact, I am glad to find Parties prefer the blessing of the Church to the entry of the Register," and he accepts their word unless he suspects one or the other is not of age.

Victoria and Her Great Ministers (1837-1894)

Young Queen Victoria had a mind of her own. She even arranged her own marriage in 1840 to her cousin, Prince Albert of Saxe-Coburg-Gotha. The marriage was apparently a genuine love match, and Victoria mourned Albert's untimely death in 1861 for the rest of her days. The royal couple produced nine children whose marriages ultimately made the Queen a relative of almost every remaining ruling house in Europe (a circumstance which did nothing to prevent World War I).

Albert had an interest in machines, technology, manufacturing and promoted the notion of what would today be called a "world's fair." The Great Exhibition of 1851 was a resounding success, drawing to London millions of visitors from all over Great Britain and from most other parts of the world. The symbol and centerpiece of the Exhibition was the Crystal Palace, a magnificent edifice of iron and glass. The flood tide of visitors produced a windfall for London map sellers. One of the most interesting products was the "Registered Exhibition Hand Guide to London," or "Glove Map" (Barker and Johnson 1990:119). The Exhibition and a second international exposition in 1861 (shadowed by Albert's death) helped reinforce perceptions of England's power and achievements.

A circle of German intimates who knew little and may have cared less about British constitutional arrangements advised Victoria early in her reign. Apparently they wished to make the Queen head of government as well as head of state. Fortunately for British democracy little came of it except that Victoria obliged her prime minister, the great Lord Palmerston, to advise her of all government actions and to change nothing after she approved it.

Victoria was fortunate to be served by some of the most able government ministers in British history. The resourceful Peel was among her early prime ministers (1841-

1846). Her "big three" prime ministers, however, were Lord Palmerston (1855-1858 and 1859-1865); Disraeli, later Lord Beaconsfield (1868, 1874-1880); and Gladstone (1868, 1880-1885, 1885-1886, and 1892-1894). The Marquis of Salisbury, descendant of the great Cecil family of Elizabethan and Jacobean times also led three governments for Victoria (1885-1886, 1886-1892, 1895-1902). But he was a much less colorful figure than the others.

The Whig party was on the wane by the mid-19th century, and in the process of being swallowed up by the new Liberal Party. The Liberal Party was the representative of the new economic classes, advocate of laissez faire, and more interested in personal morality than in social justice. The transition may be somewhat confusing since historians may differ in classifying a political figure as a Whig or a Liberal. Meanwhile, the Tories underwent one of their periodic Galifreyan regenerations and emerged under Disraeli as the party of progressive reform. The dominant social and economic classes had trembled before the popular Chartist movement during its flourishing years (1839-1848). The Chartist program was a six point platform of political reform. The movement was undercut by the repeal of the Corn Laws. The mass demonstrations and presentations of massive petitions died down. Then in an ironic political twist, most of the Chartist platform was enacted for their own reasons by the dominant classes under the leadership of Disraeli and Gladstone.

Palmerston, known affectionately as "Pam," was the compleat patriot, ever at pains to defend the honor of Britain and the British and to advance the British Empire.

Whereas some men seem to be worn out by political office, Pam thrived on it and served into his eighties. Historians regard him as one of the most popular and widely supported of all Britain's prime ministers. Though leader of the Whig/Liberal Party, he was a former Tory and wore his partisan hat somewhat lightly. His policy of supporting the Turkish Empire to keep Russia away from the British lake, the Mediterranean Sea, led to the highly dubious Crimean War. The only constructive outcomes were Florence Nightingale, and Tennyson's "Charge of the Light Brigade." He steered a careful course of neutrality during the U.S. Civil War. British entrepreneurs were less correct, building commerce raiders like the "Alabama" for the Confederate government and most of the fast shallow draft blockade runners, and selling freely to both blockade runners and the Confederate government. The United States blockade of Confederate ports hurt the British cotton textile industry. But the Evangelical mill owners and their Wesleyan workers preferred temporary recession to the support of human slavery. England's overall prosperity at home was such that she developed a new export—capital. Loans abroad brought interest earnings. British capital played a significant role, for example, in the construction of America's western railroads.

William Gladstone, Oxford-educated leader of the Liberal party (and another former liberal Tory) was less interested in imperial adventures than Palmerston and Disraeli. Though he and his Liberals were disinclined to interfere with "free market forces," and hence disinclined to pursue domestic social reforms, he was nonetheless a reformer at heart. His Irish policy was a case in point. His government disestablished the (Anglican) Church of Ireland and pushed land reform. He also advanced an Irish home rule bill, but was thwarted by the Tory, Salisbury. The historian must wonder how much anguish both Britain and Ireland might have been spared had Gladstone won on the issue of home rule! Gladstone was able to achieve government reforms. The Anglican monopoly on higher education was broken. (Many Liberals were Nonconformists.) The lower schools were extensively reformed. The civil service was reorganized and employment based on competitive examination. The military was also reformed and reorganized.

Gladstone opposed the building of the Suez Canal and broke with Palmerston's (and Disraeli's) policy by denouncing Turkish atrocities in the Balkans. And at the end of the day, he had eclipsed even the legendary Pam in political and physical longevity.

The edict of Edward I, expelling all Jewish people from England (1290), was never officially rescinded. Cromwell, with typically Calvinistic philojudaism and perhaps a touch of economic opportunism, sought an Act readmitting Jews to England. Parliament did not cooperate, so the Protector simply looked the other way while Jews from Holland began to settle in London. An Anglo-Jewish community thus began to be restored. British antisemitism tended and tends to be more snide and snobbish than to be violent and viscious in the continental fashion. The nineteenth century reform laws eventually enfranchised Catholics, Dissenters, and Jews, and Jews were for the first time admitted to the House of Commons. British tolerance was amply repaid in the political career of Benjamin Disraeli.

So dramatic was his persona and so significant were his political achievements that it is difficult to realize that "Dizzy" only served as prime minister for seven years, having been leader of the Tory party in the Commons for twenty-five. He sadly observed at seventy that power had come to him too late. His enemies would not agree. Benjamin Disraeli was the son of a Jewish writer and himself a failure in business but a success as a novelist. An apparently sincere Anglican and Tory, he exhibited a profound admiration for the landed aristocrats and in the end, as Lord Beaconsfield, he became one. His attitude toward the Queen might best be described as reverence. Such was his mastery of both the strategy and the tactics of politics, the grand scheme and the essential minutiae, that one might say Disraeli was to British politics as Marlborough or Wellington were to British arms. Many of the Tory squires in Parliament may have been a trifle dull of wit, but they quickly recognized in this most unlikely member, cynical in demeanor, flamboyant in dress and manners with a devastating wit and a rapier tongue, a leader of great promise. They were not mistaken.

Disraeli had a strong grasp of the great aristocratic virtue of noblesse, the obligation of the great and privileged to benefit the less fortunate. He was himself convinced that the landed aristocracy were the natural leaders of Britain and he believed the masses could also be convinced if the Tory party exhibited what he called "Tory democracy," "conservatism with a human face."

Gladstone had been undone by his own party in an attempt at electoral reform. As Tory leader of the house and deputy to the PM, Lord Derby, Disraeli riposted with a Tory electoral reform bill, broadly extending the franchise. Many Tory backbenchers may have swallowed hard, but they voted "yes." Disraeli came to head his first short-lived ministry (1868). The new voters turned out in large numbers at the next election to support Gladstone! So much for gratitude in politics.

On his return to power in 1874, Disraeli launched a reform program that included improvements in housing and working conditions, a food and drug law, a labor relations act giving trade unions great autonomy, sanitation laws and what would today be called "environmental laws." He executed one of the boldest diplomatic strokes in British history in 1875. The Suez Canal had opened in 1869, dramatically shortening the distance between Europe and the Orient. Britain was a prime benefactor with her interests in India, China, etc. The canal was built and owned by a private French company. About half the stock was owned by the ruler of Egypt, the Khedive. The Khedive was desperate for money and was willing to sell his Suez stock. Both speed and secrecy were essential. Disraeli prevailed upon the banker, Baron Rothschild, to arrange a loan of £4m, pledging the British government as security! He bought the shares (which turned out to be a very profitable investment, gave Britain greater influence over the "lifeline to India," and led to deeper British involvement in the valley of the Nile). Then he told the Queen that the shares were the property of the Crown. <u>Then</u> he told parliament, which fortunately upheld this rather irregular action. Disraeli also arranged for Victoria to be bestowed the title, "Empress of India." The Liberals thought this was a bit too grand, but Dizzy had his way.

The Queen was not overly fond of Mr. Gladstone. She said he addressed her as if she were a public meeting, and once referred to him as "that half-mad firebrand" who would ruin everything. But the Queen was genuinely fond of her devout devotee, Mr. Disraeli, who spared no effort to please his sovereign. No love was lost between the two heroic political advesaries, even less as they moved toward the showdown that would mark the end of Disraeli's political career. Both were masters of rhetoric and both strained the limits of polite parliamentary invective. Gladstone thought that Disraeli had turned the Queen's head with vulgar flattery, and that he resorted to cheap political tricks. But Gladstone's moralising opened him to a perhaps not entirely erroneous charge of hypocrisy. Dizzy reportedly observed that he did not mind it that Gladstone always had a fifth ace up his sleeve. What he objected to was Gladstone's assertion that the Almighty put it there.

The balance of power in Europe had been irrevocably shifted when Prussia, guided by the geopolitical genius of Bismarck, gave France a humiliating thrashing in the Franco-Prussian War and achieved the unification of "little Germany," the German states without Austria (1870-71). Henceforth, the German empire would take its place among the dominant powers of Europe and begin to challenge England and France in the imperial game as well. But as Europe moved through the 1870's, a more immediately vexing issue was Russia's design on the Balkans as she increasingly worked her will on the crumbling Turkish empire. The other powers would not tolerate this projection of Russia's power beyond her traditional sphere. Europe teetered on the brink of war when, in 1878, Bismarck hosted a European congress in Berlin. Disraeli attended as the fully empowered representative of the British empire and on this great international occasion gave a final exhibition of his political and diplomatic skills. Bismarck, the recognized master of <u>realpolitik</u>, grudgingly confessed that "the old Jew" got everything he wanted and Russia was pushed back a safe distance from Constantinople, and from Europe's back doorstep.

Two years later, declining domestic political fortunes felled Disraeli and his Tories before Gladstone and the Liberals. And in the following year he died. The Queen was reluctant to send for Gladstone after the 1880 election. But nobody else could form a government. And she would have to send twice more for him before he yielded his grasp on the Liberal leadership.

There was a strong and decided anti-imperial movement in Britain around the 1850's, despite Palmerston's enthusiasms, or perhaps because of some of them. The "Little England" group argued that, with the exception of India, the colonies were a burden that cost more to keep than they produced in income. They urged the course of spinning the colonies off as independent or semi-indepedent entities. (Canada was accorded dominion status in 1867.) But anti-imperial sentiment faded with Disraeli's years in office and the second half of the 19th century saw British imperial interests solidify and expand the hold on India, penetrate further into China and spread to new areas of southeast Asia and of Africa. The African expansion intensified as Germany began to compete with France and Britain on that continent. Some historians argue that the British Empire actually peaked during the days of Gladstone and Disraeli and despite some additional territorial acquisitions was in decline thereafter, though this was not evident at the time. Others see the decline setting in later, either prior to or as a result of World War I.

In any case, through the period covered by this chapter domestic growth and prosperity, interrupted by short periods of recession, and imperial growth, provided a firm basis for growth in Britain's mining and industrial areas and in her first city. Integral to these developments was the construction of a national railway network. Some writers speak of "railroad mania," for the construction was done on a highly speculative basis under the rule of laissez faire. Thus some lines failed, others were never completed, and there was unnecessary duplication. The canals, some of them quite newly built, were eclipsed in the freight trade. People could move rapidly all across the country, day and night. The frequent passenger trains, even into relatively small towns, made excellent mail service possible, with same day or next day delivery common. The great urban newspapers, particularly the London papers, could become national newspapers. The railroads needed the electric telegraph to carry their internal messages and safely coordinate their operations. But it was soon discovered that the telegraph could transmit all sorts of urgent messages between distant points. Thus a revolution in transportation and in communication became a reality.

The industrial revolution itself took another leap forward as the 19th century progressed. A technology was developed to generate and transmit electrical power. Steam had liberated factories from the streamside. Now they no longer need have a belching chimney to drive the machinery. Factories, particularly lighter industries, could be located some distance from the power generating facility. Thus it became possible to introduce plants with powered machinery into crowded urban areas. Into London, and into Aldermanbury!

The Victorian age saw the Church of England have its own internal revolution. The so-called "Broad Church" movement, inspired by the ideas of persons like Coleridge, regarded episcopacy as merely expedient and sought to make the established Church as comprehensive as possible. The counter-thrust was mounted originally from Oxford, by the "Tractarian" movement led by such thoughtful and scholarly figures as John Henry Newman and Edward B. Pusey. They believed the Church was menaced from without by demands of the state and from within by ignorance and by the loss of its very essence, which they saw in medievalism, ritualism and the sacraments, and the traditional episcopacy, the apostolic origins of which they did not doubt. Some of the leadership followed the logic of their position to its extreme conclusion and returned to Rome. Newman's journey was rewarded with a red hat. Others remained within the established Church, constituting themselves a High Church party, emphasizing episcopacy, tradition, and sacramentalism. Thus the term "High Church," formerly signifying loyalty to crown, bishops and prayer book, took on a new meaning, and the new High Church party gained a substantial following and considerable influence, though some of the first introductions of "ritualism" in London parishes touched off uproars and disorder. The catastrophic 1865 remodeling of St. Mary, Aldermanbury, and the subsequent creation of a "Lady Chapel" in the south aisle of Wren's overtly Protestant nave evince High Church influence. The medievalism of the High Church party was hand in glove with the general thrust of romanticism and helped give England (and the United States) a spate of architecture in the Gothic Revival mode, and not all of it in churches. Many tourists suppose that the Gothic houses of Parliament reflect medieval splendors, and that Tower Bridge (which they mistake for London Bridge) must be nearly as old. Both are, in fact, splendors of the Victorian Age!

The High Church did not, however, carry all before it. There was a counter to the counter as the Evangelicals constituted a "Low Church" party, deemphaszing ritual and tradition and placing a premium upon missions, the general advancement of the Gospel, and a variety of good works. Anthony Trollope's "Barchester" novels provide useful insights into the Church life of the period. The Archdeacon stands for the old High Church, or, as Trollope puts it "the high and dry Church." The Bishop's devious chaplain, Mr. Slope, is an Evangelical who in the end came to live up to his preaching. Mrs. Arabin, with the red rubrics in her prayer book, is high church.

Victorian London

Sheppard entitled his volume of <u>The History of London, London 1808-1870: The Infernal Wen</u>. And so many British folk perceived their capital city: a constantly spreading alien and parasitic boil on their social, economic and political life. The metropolis as a whole had grown to a population of 2,362,236 in 1851 (Sheppard 1971: 138). The City achieved its 19th century population peak in that year (129,128) and thereafter declined (Sheppard 1971:267), a trend notable in Aldermanbury.

London as a whole might strike awe, or fear, or jealousy by its very size and mass of people. But within metropolitan London, the City was in a class all by itself. Sheppard wrote of the centuries of bargaining between the City and the royal court, with "privileges and immunities being constantly exchanged for money and support, until at last, with the Revolution of 1688, nothing more was left for the City to acquire" (1971:19). Its wealth, power and influence were such that it was practically beyond the reach even of the national government. We have already seen how the City kept itself out of the jurisdiction of the Metropolitan Police. It was also able to win exclusion from the Municipal Corporations Act of 1835 which restructured all the rest. Radical reformer Francis Place had spoken of "our corrupt, rotting, robbing, infamous Corporation of London, a burlesque on the human understanding more contemptible than the most paltry farce played in a booth at Bartholomew's Fair, and more mischievous than any man living is prepared to believe" (Sheppard 1971:45). But even the City was not immune to change.

The great engines of change in mid-Victorian London were disease and the railroads (including the Underground). We noted in the previous chapter that civic improvements had led to lower death rates in London than in the past. But rates of disease and death in London exceeded those on its fringes. Arrangements for fresh water were most unsatisfactory. Better houses had cisterns which were filled by the periodic flow from water company pipes. Poorer accomodations depended on public taps, like the one at the corner of Aldermanbury and Love Lane. Often they were distant and inconvenient. The water companies drew their supplies from contaminated sources and failed to filter it properly if they filtered it at all. Such sewers as there were carried mostly surface runoff water. Waste water hookups were sometimes prohibited. Cesspits and pools and open dumps received most human wastes, the dumps also getting the product of pumped out cesspits.

Churchyards were far beyond their capacity for burials. A body would normally decompose in two years, given London soil and climate. But additional burials were made in the same plot much sooner. The poorer the neighborhood, the worse the conditions, complicated by the crowded, filthy and poorly ventilated housing of the poor. The stench was pervasive in some parts of east London. The germ theory of disease still lay in the future. Transmissions of disease, whether bacterial or viral, was poorly understood, though there was no shortage of explanations, each with its enthusiastic proponents. However, all but the dullest (or outright hypocritical—some, after all, were loathe to fund social change) noted a correlation between the filth of poorer neighborhoods and higher rates of disease and premature death. Then came cholera.

The first visitation of cholera came in the 1830's, orginating in Asia and migrating by way of Russia across Europe. Other epidemic diseases, including typhus, struck from time to time in London. But cholera, with its violent symptoms and 50% death rate, produced special terror. The disease is caused by the ingestion of a bacillus which can be transmitted by personal contact or by contaminated water.

The shock of the 1831-1832 epidemic prompted a flurry of activity nationwide. Two influential reports, which appeared in 1838, led to concrete action in London. Not until the Metropolitan Water board was created in 1902 was all London insured a generous supply of clean water. But a start was made (with some private water companies dodging the regulations to the detriment of their customers).

By 1848, there was a Metropolitan Board of Sewers in charge of construction and operation. Once more the City asserted its autonomy and got itself excluded from the Metropolitan authority and secured a separate act strengthening its Commission and creating the position of the Medical Officer of Health. This office was filled by the bright and energetic John Simon. When cholera struck again in 1849 his efforts had a mitigating effect. As time passed, Dr. Simon persuaded the Corporation to close the live cattle market at Smithfield, to close 65 churchyards to burials, and to establish a cemetery in Essex, while pursuing sewer and water supply improvements.

Cholera struck again in 1854, and for once the City's independent course benefitted all classes. Almost 11,000 people died in greater London, but just 200 of them were from the City. The creation of the Metropolitan Board of Works in 1855 (with three members elected by the Common Council) paved the way for a comprehensive solution to London's sewer problems. A masterful plan was devised to construct a west-east system of interceptor mains which would finally merge and carry the effluent far downstream from London. In summer the Thames frequently reeked like the open cesspool it was. Disraeli introduced a government bill in 1858 which set the project in motion. But the hard earned progress in sanitation of London and other cities was not universally heeded. Poorly maintained drains at Windsor are implicated in Prince Albert's death from typhoid in 1861. And sanitary violations by a water company instigated an 1866 outbreak of cholera in the East End.

Public construction was not limited to sewers. The Board of Works constructed a number of new streets to ease traffic flow, including Queen Victoria street in the City. The Corporation had built King William Street, Princes Street, and Moorgate in connection with the new London Bridge project. Later projects extended Cannon Street, built Blackfriar's Bridge and Holborn Viaduct, opened Farringdon Road, and built Billingsgate market and the Smithfield meat market. Thankfully, many medieval streets were preserved in the City, and can still be seen today.

However, private construction, specifically railroad construction, would have the more profound visible impact on the face of London. It was the poor who would feel the impact of this intrusion, for the railroads did not want to face the cost in money and bad public relations that would come from invading more comfortable neighborhoods.

The horse-drawn omnibus, a French import, had largely crowded out hackney carriages and short stage coaches as a metropolitan commuter vehicle. But they, along with passenger service by riverboat, would suffer in turn with the coming of the commuter railroad and the Underground. London's first railroad, the London and Greenwich, was what today would be regarded as a commuter line. But it would be a while before the railroad's full potential for urban commuting would be realized and commuter suburbs grow up along rail lines. The L&G terminal at London Bridge came to be shared with several trunk lines because of its easy access to the City, at least until railroad bridges across the Thames provided direct access to the north bank.

London was fortunate that chance, expense and occasional authority conspired to keep the terminals of the growing networks of trunk lines on the periphery of the then developed areas both in the City and to the west. A Royal Commission in 1846 prohibited railroad penetration of an arc defined by New Road, City Road, Finsbury Square and Bishopsgate Street (Sheppard 1971:129). Only Liverpool Street Station would prove to be an exception, located within the City, within walking distance of Aldermanbury.

By the early 1850's London would have well over half the main line stations still in use today, and much of the rail network rapidly interlacing England and Scotland. Euston Station with its hotel and monumental arch symbolized the wealth and splendor of the early rail age.

Schemes for a great single central terminal for all London rail traffic were floated from time to time, but none prospered. Where might such an installation have been practically located? It would have been a catastrophe for the urban landscape.

The Underground system to connect the main line stations and provide accesss to the City opened its first line in January, 1863. The Metropolitan Line was the world's first underground railway. Other lines followed, including the rival District Line. Public fears of underground travel soon gave way before speed and convenience. By 1864 the Metropolitan Line carried nearly twelve million people. The District Line joined with the Metropolitan Line and by 1884 the Circle Line opened. By the end of the century electric power became available and helped create the efficient (but often overburdened) system still in use today.

The railroads also changed urban demographics. It led to the depopulation of the city core. The affluent had long before gravitated to the "polite" neighborhoods toward the west. Now they could live even further away and still do business in the City or in Westminster. Workers formerly lived within walking distance of the workplace. Now working class suburbs grew up on the periphery, taking advantage of cheap rail and Underground fares. In between, the middle orders of society could also commute to their own comfortable and respectable suburbs. One can say that the railroads created a ghost town at night. The decline of Aldermanbury as a residential parish and the consequent decline in the St. Mary's congregation followed inevitably, if one may say so, in the train of the trains. The post-1878 version of the popular "Balloon View of London" (Barker and Jackson 1990:138-139) shows the Church of St. Mary and its neighbors surrounded by large buildings rather than residences.

London had from long since been the banking center of England and a significant hub of European banking. At the beginning of the Victorian age, much of the banking business was in the hands of privately held banks which rested on substantial family fortunes, such as the Barings and Rothschilds, or upon the resources of partnerships. These were increasingly overtaken by joint stock banks, some of which went on to become the great national clearing banks of modern times. The growth of other banks meant that the Bank of England no longer dominated the London financial scene as it once had, but it remained the essential balance wheel and ultimately the sole source of currency notes. The London stock market, operating from a rebuilt Royal Exchange, was challenged but never overtaken by the securities markets of the thriving industrial cities. Lloyd's coffee house, where underwriters assembled to do business, became synonymous with risk insurance, and London took a leading place in that industry as well. It is perhaps symbolic that the Bank of England, the Royal Exchange and Lloyd's stood together on Cornhill, which had also been the site of the Forum of Londinium.

Ironic it is that in the midst of its great prosperity, Victorian London was also host to a substantial population of impoverished and even pauperized persons. To some degree, the prosperity was bought at their expense, for they constituted a great reservoir of cheap labor for the building projects of the time, some of which (like the railroads) displaced many from their inadequate housing and crowded them into even more wretched lodgings. Such occupations as rag-pickers and sewer scavengers occupied the lowest rungs of the occupational ladder, but others were even crowded off the ladder altogether. Crime, drunkenness, prostitution and homelessness were epidemic as people scrambled to survive or reacted to the hopelessness of their situation. There was a Victorian tendency to blame poverty on the poor, and on their bad habits, especially drunkenness. The National Temperance League came forth about 1884 with a map of London showing public drinking places by red circles (Barker and Jackson 1990:140-141). Did anyone notice that the incidence of public drunkenness, as measured by police arrest statistics, dropped in better economic times? Henry Mayhew and Charles Booth offered detailed scholarly documentation for the agony portrayed in Charles Dickens' novels. Booth's multi-sheet map of London poverty published between 1889-1900 is a graphic presentation of the problem (cf. Barker and Jackson 1990:144-145).

If there was an aristocracy among the less advantaged in Victorian London, it was constituted of persons in domestic service. There were 250,000 domestic servants in London in 1851, and one out of six London women was a domestic (Sheppard 1971:368). Respectability was the hallmark of a proper domestic, and they tended to be respected "in their place." Persons entering domestic service essentially traded their personal freedom for much better living conditions and perhaps somewhat better pay than most persons of their social background might expect. But the pleasantness of their situation was very much a function of the household in which they worked and the personalities of their employers.

Oxford and Cambridge held a practical monopoly on higher education in England prior to the 19th century. London only got a university in 1836 when University and Kings colleges were brought together under the University of London. London had subsequently become England's third widely known university center.

It will be recalled that the fifty churches plan to provide Anglican parishes in the then new suburbs was never completed. London continued to grow, but neither Anglican church building, nor even the building of dissenter chapels, kept pace. A Church Building Commission was created in the early 19th century, but it got off to a slow start. There seemed to be an emphasis on a few large buildings which would add impressive numbers of seats, but that was not the need. Then, toward midcentury there was a spate of church building, the Commission completing 96 by 1856, and Dissenters contributing their own houses of worship, many in the same Gothic revival style popular among the Anglicans. The need for new parishes and parish Churches in outlying areas placed an unusual sort of pressure on declining urban parishes like St. Mary's. Diocesan officials reckoned that they could sell redundant City Churches which stood on potentially valuable commercial property for substantial sums and use the proceeds to construct needed new Churches in the suburbs. The reasoning has a certain attraction if one overlooks the crass commercialism and the cultural vandalism involved. The Wren Society Publications include the infamous "Black List of London Churches," Wren masterpieces that no longer existed when that work was done in the 1930's. Some had been destroyed by fire and not rebuilt. Others had been razed to make way for "civic progress" or simply sold for the cash return. The list would be longer today. Fortunately for lovers of beauty, the vestry and people of the parish of St. Mary, Aldermanbury, stood their ground until ultimately the survival of the Wren fabric was assured to the extent such things can be in this uncertain world.

Religious fervor seemed to be at a low ebb in the Metropolis. Just about a third of the population attended church in 1851 despite the strength of Dissenter groups, principally Wesleyans, Congregationalists, and Baptists (the Presbyterians remained a minority in their own camp). There were surprisingly few Catholics. Apparently Irish immigration was offset by Irish dropouts. And, saddest of all, there was almost no ministry to the poor. It would seem that the Established Church was too much identified with the government and the ruling class, and "Old Dissent" too smug in its middle class status. The Methodists and the Catholics were perhaps best situated to affect the issue. But Wesley's fears had been realized. Having gained upward mobility, his followers behaved much like Old Dissenters. And Catholicism faced the double handicap of continued prejudice against the faith in general and the Irish in particular, and of a serious clergy shortage. Anecdotal data discloses a number of cases of Victorian Londoners from the lower orders who professed never to have seen the inside of a Church. The popular historian's cliche is unfortunately true. The Churches did not lose the new urban underclass, because they never had them in the first place. It was such circumstances that drove General William Booth and his wife, Catherine Mumford, devout Methodist preachers, to establish the Salvation Army (1878).

Aldermanbury during the Victorian Age

The John Bean Era (1843-1854)

On 17 January, 1843, Rev. William Harrison was appointed as the Sunday evening lecturer. On 21 June, after the death of Rev. Salisbury, a resolution signed by 98 inhabitants recommended John Phillips Bean "now and for many years our respected Curate" be named incumbent. Bean had been "assistant curate" for 30 years. A copy of the recommendation was forwarded to the Bishop.

In response to an Act for relief of London incumbents on 27 July, 1843, the Vestry ordered a new assessment in lieu of tithes. On 28 September, 1843, the Vestry decided to dispense with the poor rate. However, by 4 January of the next year the poor rate was set at 8d. At the same meeting £244 was sent to the London Union. Also at this meeting a visit of the vicar, churchwardens, guardians of the poor, and Assistant Overseer to the parish poor at the workhouses at Stepney Pekcham and Norwood was reported.

On 11 April, 1844, a committee was set up to investigate repairs of the church.

At the next meeting, 9 May, the surveyor John Wallin reported. Wallin's lengthy report and the committee's response are included in the minutes. The repairs and alterations were carried out at a cost of about £1089, and the church was reopened for services on 27 October. The Vestry commended the committee (chaired by Rev. Bean) "on the very great and manifest improvement which the performance of these repairs has occasioned in the Church ... ." Among other things, Wren's broken pediment behind the altar was removed. Also, the location of the pulpit, reader's, and clerk's desk was changed and double pews in the middle aisle were moved. The reason, the report said, was that the present arrangement made it very difficult for many in the congregation to see and hear.

Throughout these years the Vestry frequently acted on requests from tenants of the parish houses, for new leases, permission to sub-lease, and authorization to make alterations to the property. As the years go on the process became more complex, with attorneys involved on the side of both the tenants and the parish. In discussion of a 25-year lease for #12 Aldermanbury on 13 December,1844 the point was made that "the neighborhood having much altered with respect to Trade purposes, ..."

On 12 February, 1846, Rev. William Harrison resigned as lecturer, and on 19 February the Rev. James Cohen, the only candidate, was elected.

On 16 April, 1846, the Fore Street Dispensary was added to the Ward School as a beneficiary of the annual gifts of the church. The next year the Society for Protection of Life from the Fire was added.

On 27 September, 1849, with Rev. Bean in the Chair for the first time, the Vestry heard a report from a committee on the poor recommending that some of the disposable property be applied directly to relief of the casual poor and house expenses at the Union poor houses rather than through Union Offices for Relief in order to save money. At the same meeting a letter was received from St. Dionys Backchurch (whose Vestry screens are now in the Church of St. Mary, Aldermanbury) requesting appointment of a committee from city parishes to discuss "a suitable place of interment for the City of London." A joint meeting was called for 23 October at London Tavern. The Vestry responded that since the government was giving attention to this matter, and the vaults and churchyards of St. Mary's did not require attention, they would not participate in the meeting.

Between October and December, 1849, the Vestry paid £37.1.0 to 12 poor, ages 33-89. Only two or three actually lived in the parish. About half were widows. (Ms.

3564/2).

On 21 February, 1850, a meeting was called at the request of "a large number of parishoners" to hear from representatives of the Metropolitan Parochial Water Supply Association who spoke of a plan to "obtain a constant supply on the principle of high pressure of pure water to every inhabitant of the Metropolitan District .... ." On a 4-2 vote the Vestry agreed to cooperate with the Association.

On 4 April, 1850, on a 8-3 vote, the previous year's auditors' report was ordered included in the minutes. The report held that too much was spent last year on repairs on the church, the £2000 insurance on the church was insufficient, the churchwardens gave to the poor more than the established charities, and an iron chest was needed for the parish deeds. As a result the Vestry ordered the insurance increased to £4000 and created a committee to investigate a new chest. On 9 May, on a 5-5 vote, broken by the chair, the Vestry voted to place the deeds in the strong room of a financial institution. The old Vestry and account books were placed in the Vestry safe.

In 1850 about an average of 15 poor per quarter received a total of £190 from parish funds (Ms. 3564/2).

On 13 March, 1851, the Vestry argued over the poor rate. A motion to set it at 6d on the £ was defeated 4-5; another motion to make it 1s was defeated; finally it was set at 8d on a 6-4 vote. Six months later a motion to use £250 in the treasury in lieu of the poor rate was turned back, on a 4-4 vote with the chairman voting. During the year about £180 went to an average of 17 poor per quarter (Ms. 3564/2).

At the 13 March meeting a letter was received from the Board of Health on claims for compensation due to loss of burial fees due to the cessation of intramural interments. The Vestry decided not to claim any. The Vestry also ordered the Vestry Clerk to classify the parish records into deeds, papers, and books and keep an inventory of them. They were to be made available to the parishoners.

On 30 October, 1851, a motion was made to use £250 in the parish treasury in lieu of the poor rate. An amendment stated that this was an undesirable precedent, but added that whether money in the treasury might be used in lieu of tithes should be studied. The amendment passed 4-4, with the chair voting. A poor rate of 6d passed 10-1.

On 20 November, 1851, a motion to pay Mr. Bean £250 out of the parish rents instead of a tithe to raise the funds passed 4-2, after an amendment to give the remainder to the parish poor was defeated 7-2. The practice of paying the curate out of the parish rents continued until the parish lost its property.

On 9 June, 1852, the Vestry received an application from Ellen Smith and two daughters that they be sent to Australia and referred it to the Committee appointed to advise the guardians with full power to decide and act. In 1852 the parish paid an average of 15 poor per quarter a total of about £162 (Ms 3564/2).

On 16 February, 1853, as part of the selection of a new Warden and Engine Keeper (also called Beadle) the duties of the office were listed as: attending all divine services to keep order and assist clergyman; attending all vestry, committee, and overseers meetings to carry out orders given; keeping watch over the parish property; assisting the Vestry Clerk in distributing notices; aiding in the reception and removal of the poor (casual or otherwise); sweeping up the church and yard, ridding the immediate neighborhood of "any nuisance;" and keeping the parish fire engine and fire escape ladders in working order.

On 2 June, 1853, the Vestry received a letter from the Undersecretary of State informing the parish that "for the protection of the public health" and by the order of Parliament burials in churchyards and vaults were to be discontinued. The Vestry agreed. The Vestry Clerk asked for compensation due to the loss of fees. On 10 November a formal order from the queen ending burials was entered into the minutes. On 21 February, 1856, the Vestry voted 3-2 to endorse a letter from the Burial Board setting fees for burials in the new London cemetery, Ilford. However, on 3 September, 1857, a letter from the City of London Burial Board of the Commissioners of Sewers informed the Vestry that parliament has disallowed fees for any parish officials for burials in the cemetery.

An average of eleven poor per quarter received a total of about £115 for the year. Only one of the eleven lived in the parish. (Ms. 3654/2).

On 6 February, 1854, a meeting of the inhabitants of the parish was held to consider a plan to alter or remove the Central London District School at Norwood because of the expansion of the Crystal Palace. Although the Vestry viewed this as not expedient, they agreed to its sale "if on very advantageous terms." They decided to send their views to the General Board of Guardians of the Poor.

The Charles Collins Era (1854-1917)

On 25 May, 1854, after the death of Mr. Bean and a vacancy in the Perpetual Curacy, the parishoners met to decide how to select a successor. On a 28-19 vote they decided not to have a screening committee but to have a preliminary vote to reduce the number of candidates to 12 (passed 30-21). They decided to have the 12 preach on Monday, Wednesdays, and Fridays following the nominations. However, on 2 June the Churchwarden reported the objection of the Bishop of London who said that they were "not to allow any Clergyman to preach in your Church during the vacancy of the Living except the licensed Curate who is charged with the duties of the Parish." 22 candidates had applied, so the parishoners decided to read their testimonials and reduce the number to 12. On 8 June, the Rev. Mr. Richard Whittington was elected, but a poll of the parishoners was called for. In a poll of 85 parishoners (with 4 women voting), the Rev. Mr. Charles Collins was elected over Whittington by a vote of 45-34, with the rest of the votes going to other candidates. Several votes were disallowed because the voters were not listed in the rate book. The votes of the Brewers Co. and the Lord Mayor for the Corporation were challenged, but apparently counted. Mr. Collins would serve as perpetual curate for over sixty years.

According to his friend Pierson Carter, the Rev. Mr. Collins, a graduate of Christ's College Cambridge, was a man of the "High Church school" who conducted himself with "quiet bearing and dignity" (Carter 1913: 57). The minutes reflect that he was considerably more active in parish governance than his predecessors. Previous to his tenure, the perpetual curate only infrequently attended vestry meetings. Collins not only attended most the of the Vestry meetings, he chaired them. Beginning in 1862 the parish showed its affection for Collins by giving him a £100 gratuity in addition to his £250 stipend. The gratuity was increased over the years to £200.

On 12 April, Collins requested that £10 be authorized for him to hire a choirmaster to teach the children to sing in order to improve the psalmody. Apparently, his intention was to create a choir, for on 9 August he complained to the Vestry that the organist refused to allow the choir to have access to the organ for practice, and on 1 November that the organist was refusing to practice with the choir. The organist resigned. The Vestry stipulated on 15 November that the new organist must be willing to train the choir and practice as much as twice a week. On 3 August, 1865, the Vestry chastized the Churchwarden for spending £68 for the choir when it had not been authorized.

At the Easter Vestry a committee was created to consider how the rents from the parish estates were being applied. This committee reported on 17 May that £742.1.8

was being received in annual rents from the parish property, 698.10.0 after payment of property taxes. During the past four years this money had been applied to the general expenses of the parish through the churchwardens, in advances to the committee charged with advising the Guardians with respect to the poor, and in payment of the annual stipend to the incumbent in lieu of a tithe assessment. The annual expenditure by the churchwardens had never been expressly limited by the Vestry. It had averaged over the past 12 years £401 (with £340 in salaries for parochial offers and £60 in repairs). The funds for the poor had ranged from £150 to £200 and the stipend for the incumbent £250. This had caused the treasury of the parish to drop from £500 in 1851 to £130 now. The Vestry acted to limit the Churchwardens' expenditures to £350 annually and the Committee on the Poor to £100.

During 1854 the poor received close to the £100 limit, as 10 poor per quarter received about £108 for the year. The next two years the same number of poor received about the same total amount. For the next eight years between 8 and 10 poor per quarter received about £100 per year. All had apparently lived at one time in the parish, but by 1861 none still resided there. (Ms. 3564/2).

In March of 1857 the Vestry, on the advice of Counsel, informed the London Union Guardians that it would refuse to pay assessments resulting from losses due to carelessness and illegalities rather than legitimate expenses for the poor. On 10 February, 1859, the Vestry was informed that a bill introduced in Parliament would impose a rate to pay for "the defalcations of Paul and Marini." The Vestry responded by sending a petition to Parliament stating that only the parishes which had hired these two as collectors should be held liable.

On 31 March, 1858, the Vestry endorsed a complex plan to trade some property with the Corporation of London at the back of #18-19 Aldermanbury because the parish boundary line passed obliquely through a building. The Vestry also authorized a new lease for these houses stipulating that the erection of 2 new houses "adapted for business purposes suited to the locality" be erected. However, the proposal had become "clogged with various stipulations by the city" a Vestry appointed committee reported on 6 August, 1858. On 13 January, 1859, the Vestry authorized construction of new warehouses on the site, at a rent of £430 (refusing the tenant's offer of £350).

On 8 April, 1858, the Vestry admitted a reporter to the Vestry meeting. With 26 parishoners present, Collins reported an application from the Bishop for information on "a Glebe House in the Parish and other matters connected therewith." The Vestry Clerk and Churchwardens had refused Collins' request to consult the parish deeds until the Vestry approved. The Vestry instructed the parish trustees to examine the deeds to insure that "appropriation of the Trust Funds is in accordance with the Deeds ... ." At a meeting on 3 June, the committee reported that the deeds clearly gave the trustees and their heirs control of funds forever for the use of the parish so long as a public Vestry gives them this right. They reported that the earliest deed bore the date 1 May, 1620.

In response to an attempt to impose a County rate to build a Pauper Lunatic Asylum, the Vestry passed a resolution on 18 November, 1858, stating that "the Lunatic Paupers of the City Parishes are already comfortably provided for" and such a new asylum was unnecessary. The Vestry asked the Alderman to call a Wardmote to ascertain the views of the inhabitants on the matter. They also voted to have their resolution published in the city press.

In the Bishop's Visitation Return for 1858 (LPL Tait 440/236) Mr. Collins complained that his £250 a year stipend was being paid out of rent from parish property rather than through the rate established by the act passed in the 44th year of George III. He cited a history of London to show that in 1620 the Vestry had agreed to raise funds for a parsonage by collecting a double portion of the poor rate, but that at present the parish was not providing a house for him. He said the population of the parish was now 500, and that 70 were attending morning services on average, with 25 communicants on average at the sacrament. In answer to the question why the attendance was not a better proportion of the parish population, he answered, "City people like to go out on the Sunday." He reported that he saw to distribution of offerings among the poor and bought clothes for school children. There were no church rates; rents from parish property paid all expenses. "The parish possesses (?)," Collins wrote, "a considerable income over which they claim absolute control." He reported that the charities included £6 yearly to the Society for the Propagation of the Gospel, £2 to the Mission to Seamen, £50 to St. Ann's Asylum, and £40 to the Ward School. Collins wrote that the church was in good repair and that the Lord's day was being observed "better than it was." The report included the following revealing comment:

> The non-residence of employers is very prejudicial to the moral
> welfare of the parish—numbers of young men are left almost

without care. The only remedy would be (in my opinion) a stirring appeal from the Bishop to the heads of firms calling on them to attend to their City parish churches and look after their dependents there.

In 1859 a parish institution, the Swan with Two Necks Inn, on the southern boundary of the parish, was demolished to make way for commercial development (Lillywhite 1963: 563-564).

The rents on the parish properties were going up rapidly as the value of the land rose. On 5 July, 1860, an offer to rent property on Love Lane for £590, after £1500 in repairs, was endorsed. At the same time, the membership of the trustees in charge of the property was still a matter of confusion and neglect. When William Payne received notice of a meeting of the trustees in 1859 he responded in surprise that he had not lived in the parish for 25 years and assumed he had been removed from the list of trustees. After much debate the number of trustees was limited to nine, and new trustees were elected on 17 March, 1859. They were to serve as trustees of parish buildings on the north side of Love Lane, adjoining the Church to the East, at #12 and #18-19 Aldermanbury, and also the Rectory and Church.

Plans to Merge St. Mary, Aldermanbury, with St. Michael, Bassishaw (1861-1872)

In 1860 Parliament passed the first Union of Benefices Act (23 &24 Victoria Cap 142). On 28 March, 1861, the Vestry received a letter from the Bishop of London, setting up a commission in accordance with an act of Parliament, which would produce a plan to unite the Perpetual Curacy of St. Mary, Aldermanbury, with the Rectory of St. Michael Bassishaw. The Vestry appointed a committee to "watch the proceedings."

On 16 May, 1861, the Churchwardens reported that at the Ascension Day perambulation many parish boundary markers were found to be missing. The Vestry appointed a committee to investigate.

On 9 January, 1862, 63 parishoners (including 1 woman) participated in the election of a new Beadle.

In preparation for the Bishop's 1862 visit Collins reported on 21 June, 1862 (LPL Tait 441/332) that in the four years since the last report the population had dropped from 500 to 444. He noted that he lived a mile and a quarter from the church at 9 Mecklenburgh Square, and had no other benefice. The average attendance was now about 40-50, not counting school children. The 40 boys of the Ward School attended Sunday services. About 25 communicants received the Lord's Supper. The greatest impediment to his ministry, he wrote, was still the absence of employers and the fact the churchwardens did not live in the parish. He also complained that goods were sometimes delivered to warehouses on Sundays and that a warehouse had been erected over a lay vault in part of the churchyard. In response to a question on the form, he said he did not hold services for the "labouring poor."

On 6 November, 1862, a letter from the Secretary to the Bishop requesting the parishoners' response to the previously mentioned commission's proposal to unite St. Mary's and St. Michael's was discussed. The seven page report of the commission, which included the Lord Mayor, three clergymen, and a layman, was included in the minutes. The report was dated 8 November, 1861, so apparently the parish had been delaying its response.

The report began with tables showing the decline in population in the two parishes. In 1801 there were 822 inhabitants in Aldermanbury and 747 in Bassishaw. By 1851 there were 687 in Aldermanbury and 616 in Bassishaw. The precipitous drop took place during the next decade, for in 1861 the population of Aldermanbury was 443 and Bassishaw 501.

The report went on to list the stipends for the two incumbents (both at about £250, though the incumbent at St. Michael's received an additional £25 for an unoccupied rectory in the parish). It also mentioned that the St. Mary's was in the Patronage of the Parishoners while St. Michael's was in the Patronage of the Dean and Chapter of St. Paul's. Neither incumbent resided in his parish.

The recommendation was that a united benefice, with a single incumbent to be called the Rector of the United Parishes of St. Mary, Aldermanbury, and St. Michael Bassishaw, be formed. The parish church would be St. Michael Bassishaw, with the parish of St. Mary having use of the church, Vestry Room, plate, etc. The plate of St. Mary's would be joined with that of St. Michael's, and the excess disposed of by the Bishop. The Church of St. Mary would be taken down and its materials and site sold. The proceeds were to be used to create an endowment to produce £350 annually for the new benefice. The two parishes were to pay for the Church and provide for worship in proportion to the total assessment of rateable property in each parish. The Dean and Chapter of St. Paul's were to give the Bishop the patronage of St. Michael's in exchange for the patronage of a different benefice. The United Benefice would be in the sole patronage of the patrons of St. Mary, Aldermanbury. Since that would increase the value of the patronage, the patrons would be asked to provide a suitable house for the rector. There was also an elaborate scheme for the protection of the two existing incumbents.

In response, the Vestry passed 17-0 the following resolution:
That in the Opinion of this Vestry no sanction should be given to any scheme for the Union of the Benefices which involves the removal of the Church of St. Mary the Virgin, Aldermanbury, but that the Fabric of such Church should be maintained and should in the event of such a junction of the Benefices as is proposed be the Church of the United Parishes.

On 20 November, 1862, with Collins in the chair, a proposal to hire a new organist with the same duties as those set forth on 15 November, 1855, was passed 8-7, with the chairman breaking a tie. However, a motion to grant £50 to improve the musical services was deferred. At the next meeting only £15 was allowed for this purpose. Apparently, Collins' enthusiasm for music in the church was not shared by everyone.

In 1863 the church was extensively repaired at a cost of £2400. A committee reported on 4 June that it had determined the following repairs were needed: removal of stucco outside the building, a new vestry room in the Churchyard on the north side of the church, opening an entrance from the street on the West side of the Church to this room, taking down the organ loft and gallery, remodelling and decorating the interior of the Church, and installing hot water heat. After receiving plans from three architects, the committee recommended Edmund Woodthorpe on a nearly unanimous vote. The Vestry approved the report. Woodthorpe's "remodelling" has been widely criticized as a desecration of the Church. For example, one contemporary critic noted, "Edmund Woodthorpe, prince of philistine restorers, despoiled [the church] of its woodwork, put in a 'Byzantine' stone reredos and font, and filled the windows with the bloated Venetian tracery which was his specialty" (Young 1956: 103). Another called the "modernization" a "terrible upheaval" (Bumpus 1924: 356). Woodthorpe's installation of stained glass "of poor design" (Birch 1896: 69) in the east window particularly offended those who considered Wren's clear glass essential to the design of the church. Birch called Woodthorpe's work "an awful example of what harm the modern innovator can work in these fine old seventeenth-century interiors" (69). Still another authority wrote that "the church has been excessively rearranged and modernized, and now presents anything but a venerable prospect" (Daniel 1907: 230). Drawings in the custody of the Royal Commission for Historical Monuments suggest that an even more castrophic outcome would have resulted had the architect's full intentions been executed.

According to one account, no trace of Judge George Jeffrey's coffin was found during the 1863 restoration (Cunningham 1927: 9).

The Building Committee was also asked to hire a new organist, and recommended that the offices of parish clerk and sexton not be filled. They suggested a new office, eventually to be called Church Attendant, be created to clean the church and that Beadle be given other responsibilities of the Sexton. However, the Parish Clerk refused to resign and insisted his full salary of £30 be paid. The office of Assistant Overseer of the Poor and Vestry Clerk were also merged during 1864.

On 28 February, 1866, the Charity Commissioners for England and Wales filed its thirteenth report for Parliament. In this report they pointed out that while the endowments of charities in London churches had enjoyed a "very large increase of value" the proper recipients for them "have greatly diminished or even ceased to exist." Many of the endowments were so large, they asserted, that they could not be legitimately used under their original trust. Therefore, reappropriation of these funds "to new charitable uses" was critical. (London Parochial Charities 1951: 10).

After receiving this report Parliament began to consider whether to abolish the maintenance of the poor by parishes and create a common fund for that purpose. On 15 March, 1866, the Vestry Clerk brought the proposed law to the attention of the Aldermanbury Vestry. He expressed concern as to the effect the new policy would have on the practice of paying "the more deserving poor some small weekly Sums." The Vestry decided to continue this practice "considering the claims which many of the poor people lately receiving assistance have on the Parish either arising from their long connection with it or their necessary circumstances." This practice had cost the parish only a little over £43 during the past year, with only 4-5 poor a week receiving stipends ranging from 15s to £1.5 (Ms. 3564/2). Given the high amount rents of parish property originally given to provide funds for the poor now drew, it is little wonder that the Vestry resisted relinquishing control.

By 1866 the parish had no further need of a fire engine and ordered it sold, if that was legal. However, the Vestry in 1867 decided to keep it "for general purposes" although they had the legal right to sell it.

On 5 September, 1867, the Vestry learned of a basis and standard for a County Rate and responded with a resolution that a County Rate in London was unnecessary. In addition, the proposed basis was unjust and unequal; the city parishes had been assessed higher due to the recent escalation in value of land in the city. The Vestry Clerk was instructed to advertise the resolution.

The crowding in of buildings on the church was made evident by two actions in 1868. In one the owners of 64 Aldermanbury requested permission for a second floor window overlooking the churchyard. In another, a company asked for an easement to allow the overhanging of an adjoining building into the churchyard.

On 7 January, 1869, the Vestry received a bill of £131 from the Guardians of the City of London Union under the provisions of the Metropolitan Common Poor Fund. After much discussion the Vestry passed a resolution expressing its view that the assessment was unequal. However, a 2d rate was established to pay the bill.

On 3 June, 1869, the Vestry discussed a proposal to unite the City of London Union with East and West London Unions, but after much discussion of the matter, took no action. In 1871 the Vestry expressed "great alarm" that the clerks of the East and West London Unions were being paid exorbitant compensation on the abolition of their offices by the Poor Law Board. The resolutions were sent to the Board and to the Press.

On 11 November, 1869, the Vestry received an unofficial draft of a revised version of the 1862 proposal to unite St. Mary, Aldermanbury, and St. Michael, Bassishaw. The Vestry took no action but expressed willingness to consider a formal proposal.

On 16 December, 1869, the Vestry was informed of an additional assessment for the Metropolitan Poor Fund of £147 due by January. A rate of 2d was ordered.

On 15 September, 1870, the Vestry received a report from a committee established to consider the state of the parish properties. The parish properties were yielding an annual rent of £1320, with annual expenditures of £835 (£480 in general, £250 for the incumbent's salary, and an annual gift to the incumbent of £105). Appended to the report were four schedules: a list of the parish property and to whom it was let, a list of the communion plate, a list of the deeds of the parish, and a list of the parish books. The committee also recommended that all parish records be kept in a fire proof safe in the Vestry.

On 30 March, 1871, a motion to seek counsel on application of parish funds to the poor rate was defeated. Instead, the Vestry acted to apply 1/3 of the surplus in parish revenue as a fund for church repair and 2/3 for aid of the poor rate. At the Easter Vestry that year (13 April) a motion to revise this action to designate £100 for the repair fund and £250 for aid of the poor rate yearly was tabled until the churchwardens' accounts were audited. This proposal was passed on 21 July, after efforts to designate £100 of this amount to the incumbent and reduce the amount for the poor by £105 was defeated 11-8.

On 4 May, 1871, the Vestry read a bill now before the Commons which amended the Charitable Trust Acts and gave the Charity Commissioners great additional powers. A resolution said the powers sought "an unjustifiable interference with the rights of the persons interested in the Property which is the subject of the Trust and an unwarranted attack upon the Trustees whose conduct in the discharge of their duties has been hitherto unimpeachable." The Vestry authorized the parish officials to take whatever steps they deemed desirable to put this resolution into effect.

On 21 July, 1871, a revised, preliminary proposal to unite St. Michael's and St. Mary's was formally reintroduced. The Vestry decided to circulate the proposal in the parish. On 26 October, a committee of eight was appointed to confer with the parish officers of St. Michael, Bassishaw, on the subject of the union, with the opinion of the Vestry expressed that the Union was desirable (but objecting to the payment of a £75 annuity).

On 23 November the Committee reported, saying that officials of Bassishaw refused to comment on the proposal because it was only a preliminary one. The committee also gave Rev. Collins an opportunity to comment on it, but he rejected the offer, saying he would wait until St. Michael's acted. Nevertheless, the committee offered its comments on the draft proposal.

The revised proposal pointed out that the population for Aldermanbury had declined to 308 by 1871 from 443 in 1861. No figures were given for Bassishaw. The proposal carefully outlined what the parishoners of St. Mary's, the Dean and Chapter of St. Paul's and the Bishop of London would relinquish and what they would receive as a result of the Union. The parishoners of St. Mary's would give up their patronage worth £250 and an annuity of £75. They would receive the patronage of the United Benefice at a value of £470 (with the possibility that from these funds a contribution would be made toward a parsonage house for the incumbent of the United Benefice).

The major change in the revised proposal was that under its terms the remaining

Church building would be St. Mary, Aldermanbury, not St. Michael, Bassishaw, which would be torn down and sold. According to Carter, (1913: 96) by this time the church of St. Michael had been condemned as unsanitary and unfit for worship. A new St. Michael's would be created in a new district, with half of the proceeds of the sale of the old St. Michael's going for a church in the new district. £2000 from the sale would go to a new parsonage for the new Benefice and £1500 for a parsonage for the new St. Michael's. St. Mary, Aldermanbury, would augment the parsonage for the United Benefice with an additional £2000. The rest of the revised proposal seemed to mirror the original proposal.

The Committee opposed the revised proposal at several points. It objected to the idea that St. Mary's should augment the funds for the residence of the Incumbent of the United Benefice. Secondly, the Committee asked that the union be called the United Benefice of St. Mary, the Virgin, Aldermanbury with St. Michael, Bassishaw not the United Benefice of St. Mary with St. Michael, Aldermanbury, as the revised proposal suggested. Thirdly, the committee wanted assurance that the parishoners of Aldermanbury not lose the right of presentment in any way. The committee was concerned that if the incumbent of St. Michael's left before the union became effective, the new rector appointed by the Dean and Chapter of St. Paul's, would, under the terms of the agreement, automatically become the minister of the United Benefice. Fourthly, there needed to be protection for each parish in the event that the other failed to provide for maintenance of the new church. Fifthly, the furnishings of the demolished Bassishaw church should first be offered to the Vestry of the United Benefice.

The discussions continued during 1872, with another revised proposal received on 11 January and further comments from the Vestry committee on 1 February. The committee was concerned whether an assurance that the Dean and Chapter of St. Paul's would respect the right of presentment of St. Mary's had "legal validity." The committee also still objected to St. Mary's unfair liability for the residence of the incumbent.

Still another draft from the Commission was received on 9 May (LPL Jackson) and circulated in the parish. On 6 June, the Committee reported and suggested several alterations. First, it should be made clear that in keeping with the tradition since 1620, the parish of St. Mary was the rector, so the minister should be called vicar not rector. Second, since there were no Parish Clerks and Sextons in Aldermanbury, the provisions of the proposal on parish clerks and sextons do not apply. Thirdly, £500 rather than £2000 should be the liability of St. Mary's for a parsonage. After considerable discussion on 12 June, the committee's report was adopted and the scheme was returned to the commissioners with the note that the sanction of the Charity Commissioners would be necessary before it could be implemented.

On 28 November, 1872, after hearing from the Commissioners that they intended to "carry out the wishes of this parish in their entirety," the scheme as amended was adopted by the Vestry "in its character of patrons of the Living of St. Mary, the Virgin, Aldermanbury." Apparently, the proposal failed to gain the support of St. Michael, Bassishaw, for it was never implemented, and St. Michael's was eventually united instead with St. Lawrence, Jewry (Carter 1913: 96).

The major rebuilding in the parish occurred during the period between 1860 and 1880. Towering warehouses had almost entirely replaced residences. (Goss 1944: 127).

Conflict with the Charities Commission (1874-1887)

By 8 January, 1874, only four poor persons received direct support from the parish. Only three were receiving weekly allowances, amounting to only 3-5s per week, with one receiving £1 at Christmas. Only two lived in the parish, so the Vestry advised them to call at the Vestry's Clerk's office rather than the church to receive their funds. At the Easter Vestry in 1874 Rev. Collins' gratuity from the parish rents was increased to £200 from 105.

On 21 October, 1875, the Vestry acted to acquire a new sword and mace rest for the Lord Mayor, on the Churchwardens' pew, since the old ones were not replaced after the 1863 renovation.

In 1875 Sion College divested itself of responsibility for care of the poor, setting up a new board to oversee a trust, with four members appointed by the College and four by the Charities Commission. The college moved out of its London Wall quarters because "the quarter of the city with which the College had so long been associated became more and more of a backwater, as far as the constituency of the College was concerned" (Pearce 1913: 335). In 1885 commercial developers purchased the college site for over £57,000 (339).

On 27 February, 1877, in its twenty-fourth report to Parliament, the Charity Commisioners documented the abuse of endowed parish trusts originally intended to benefit the poor. In one parish parochial charities produced £800 a year, but the population of the parish was now only 46, of whom only four or five actually slept in the parish. None were poor. They pointed out that while some of these large revenues were used for ward schools and to increase the stipend of the minister, large sums were being used to increase the salaries or testimonials given to churchwardens and other parish officers and for events "of a convivial nature, still more widely removed from the original objects of the foundation" (Trustees of the London Parochial Charities 1951: 11). The Commisioners further reported that some parishes (they would have included Aldermanbury had they been giving examples) were asserting the right to spend the money from their charities however they saw fit. They urged more Parliamentary action to insure that the charities income be directed as originally intended—to benefit the poor. (11-12).

On 5 April, 1877, in response to a communication from St. Augustine Watling Street, the Vestry passed a resolution expressing its "extreme dissatisfaction at the enormous and increasing amount of the annual expenditure upon the relief of the poor of the Metropolis." The Vestry did not object to providing for "the disabled, the Sick, and the imbecile poor," but the present administration of the law was "characterized by an absence of due regard both for the economy and for the necessary convenience of those for whom shelter has to be provided as well as in the selection of sites ... ." The Vestry ordered the resolution sent to the Times and other papers as well as the Poor Law Board.

On 11 October, 1877, the Vestry received a report of the Ascension Day perambulation of the parish. 69 markers were found, many in warehouses. Others were in such locations as the cupboard of a room in the George Tap and in a bedroom at #19 London Wall.

On 25 April, 1878, the Vestry responded to a request from the Educational Endowments Committee of the School Board for notice of any charities which had failed or become "disproportionate." The Vestry responded that it had none!

On 10 August, 1878, a Royal Commission was appointed to investigate the charities of the churches of London. The Commission was told that by 1876 the value of the parochial charities had increased to almost £105,000. (Trustees of the London Parochial Charities 1951: 13).

On 27 March, 1879, the Vestry Clerk submitted a letter reporting that the Attorney

General had been advised to take action against the Parish concerning the parish estates and charities. Although not recorded, the Vestry had apparently refused to cooperate with the Charities Commission's efforts to have control of parish property and charities transferred. At this meeting the Vestry Clerk reported that the Vicar, Churchwardens, and Vestry Clerk had been summoned by the Commission for an examination. The Vestry decided to send the clerk to say that given the possibility of legal proceedings, the Vestry did not think they should come for an examination. On 17 April, 1879, the Vestry Clerk reported that he had gone to the Commission and told them "no evidence could be given."

A 12 March, 1880, report of the Royal Commission appointed in 1878 to investigate the charities of the London churches portrayed the state of City parishes as follows (Trustees of the London Parochial Charities 1951: 13-14).

> Nearly one half of these parishes, each one containing a dense industrial and trading population whose religious and social institutions and feelings identified it with the locality, are now without inhabitants other than a few clerks and caretakers in charge of the great commercial buildings and warehouses, to make room for which the dwellings of the earlier population have been removed; for the same reason the churches erected by the piety of former ages are now in many instances almost, if not altogether, without congregations. The whole area of one parish is stated to have been absorbed by the Bank of England, and about three fourths of another by the General Post Office. Yet in all these parishes parochial machinery is still kept up, and in many large sums of money are spent on charitable gifts and doles, as well as for church purposes, including choir, organist, etc.

The report went on to point out that just in the last several years the value of property owned by the parishes had doubled, or even trebled. The report concluded that since the Poor Law Act of 1834 distributed a poor rate over the total metropolitan area and since it was now a "permanent tax," the continued local application of charitable funds by individual parishes was anachronistic. Instead, some of the funds were being used to pay the poor rate. This practice had the effect of excusing wealthier parishoners from paying their fair share of the rate. The report recommended that this practice be stopped. The Commission also concluded that "it is practically impossible to effect a satisfactory combination or re-arrangement of these Charities under the existing system" (16). The Royal Commission recommended that an Executive Commission be created and empowered to examine into the parish charities, classifying them as either eleemosynary or ecclesiastical (intended under the original bequest or through long tradition for church uses). From ecclesiastical charities a "City Church Fund" should be established, and from the eleemosynary charities a "Central Fund." From either or both funds should be set aside, unless in conflict with the original bequest, for the maintenance of the church fabric and services (17).

On 2 March, 1881, the Vestry discussed a plan for renovation of the church at an expense of £1250 by architect Frank Baggallay. The proposal called for the removal of the present glass in the windows and the stone traceries, which, according to Baggallay "entirely destroys the character of a building designed by an architect to whom in his particular style no one can now approach." Baggallay also intended to use two or three colors to relieve the "bare and cold" appearance of the walls and to open the parapet around the tower and south side, which had been added in 1864, which were, in his view, "a questionable improvement over the old plain one." The actual renovation included another stained glass window in the East End at an expense of £120.

On 23 June, 1881, the Churchwarden reported on a meeting of parish representatives held at the Cannon St. Hotel on 20 May to discuss the City Charities Bill. The group decided to try to alter the bill, letting the city parishes keep their charity monies if they could show they were still being used well, and appointing representatives from the city parishes to the body created in the bill. They also created subcommittees to try to influence the bill. The Vestry authorized £20 to support the effort. At a subsequent meeting more funds were authorized for this effort. The Vestry also instructed the Vestry Clerk to make separate accounts of charity funds and parish funds and to return to the Charities Commission only the account of the charity funds. They also hired someone to examine the old deeds and added a second lock to the parish safe.

On 6 October the Clerk reported that the London Union had billed the parish for £522 and £521 for October and January.

On 2 November, 1882, the Vestry heard a letter from the Charity Commissioners. It noted that for two years the parish had neglected to include parish estates in its accounts filed at the Commission and asked that they be forwarded "with the least further delay possible." The Vestry sent an account of the parish estates under protest "as one which the Trustees were not bound to send ... not as an Account of any Charity but as an Account of property which the parish claimed to deal with themselves."

In 1883 Parliament enacted the City of London Parochial Charities Act. Under the terms of this act the management of charitable endowments passed from the parishoners of Aldermanbury (and those of 106 other smaller parishes in London) to a body called the Trustees of the London Parochial Charities. The benefits of the charities were, by the Act, extended to the entire metropolitan area.

On 5 July, 1883, the Trustees reported that they had received from the Attorney General a draft of a proposed Statement of Claim against the parish by the Charity Commission. The Commission had asked the Chancery Court to rule that payments of the parish to oppose the Charities Bill on the administration of parish funds were illegal. Since the case of St. Mary, Aldermanbury, was strong, the Commission suggested that it be made a test case for other parishes. The Trustees proposed that if it was to be a test case, it be heard on the basis of the trust of St. Mary's alone. The Vestry concurred and allocated funds from the parish rent to cover the cost of the case, including counsel.

A Mr. Box visited the church on 19 February, 1882, as part of a study of church music in greater London. He reported a surpliced choir of fourteen, and an attendance of 40. His count of the population of the parish was 308. (Box 1884: 153).

On 20 June, 1883, Mr. Collins (now living on Gloucester Road, Teddington) submitted an ecclesiastical Visitation Return. He reported a population of 156 in the parish, with an average Sunday attendance of 40. The Sunday School program had been dropped. The main obstacle to his ministry was still, he wrote, "the absence of chief parishoners." (LPL Jackson 2/374).

On 9 April, 1885, the Vestry authorized £150 to decipher the old Vestry Books and Accounts as requested by the Trustees. The result was a summary of Vestry records now in the Guildhall Library (Ms. 3570A). At this meeting the Vestry granted a lease to Sir H. E. Knight, Alderman, for a portion of #11 and 12 Love Lane for 21 years.

In 1885, on the site of the now demolished Sion College, Aldermanbury Avenue was created. It ran west out of Aldermanbury at No. 47 to Phillip Lane. (Harben 1918: 6)

On 13 January, 1886, the Vestry authorized the purchase of a new organ, to be built by Bishop and Son at a cost of £780 (less £100 for the old organ). The also elected new parish trustees for the final time. Only Alderman Knight expressed willingness to continue as a trustee, so six new trustees were selected.

On 1 October, 1887, in accordance with the City of London Parochial Charities Act of 1883, the Commissioners classified the Rectory Church, Advowson, and Parish Estates of St. Mary, Aldermanbury, as Ecclesiastical Charities. In a petition dated November, 1887, the trustees of the parish "and all the other parishoners of St. Mary, the Virgin, Aldermanbury," asked the Chancery Court to declare that the above not be declared charity property at all.

The parties were called before Mr. Justice Kay of the Chancery Court on 10 December, 1887. On 26 November, 1887, Counsel for the parish presented a petition for Sir Henry Knight, Alderman; John Warren, Merchant (18 Aldermanbury); Frederick Lloyd, Merchant (14 London Wall); Henry Gardiner, Merchant (4 Aldermanbury); William Gibson, Merchant (20 Aldermanbury); William Braham, Gentleman (9 Aldermanbury) on their behalf and the parishoners of Aldermanbury (GL Pamphlet 11360). He presented in evidence the deeds, which showed that the rectory, advowson, and the parish estates were all deeded in perpetuity to the parishoners, beginning with the purchase of the church and advowson in 1621.

The petition pointed out that in 1664 the curate had agreed to accept a stipend in lieu of a house, and that since 1666 only from time to time had a house been provided. In recent years, the trustees of the parish had provided from £105 to £210 yearly to the curate, above the £250 annual stipend. Therefore, they claimed, the parish had no obligation to provide a parsonage.

They further argued that the rectory church and advowson should not be classified as charities, nor should the parish estates. They listed the parish estates and current rent as 12 Aldermanbury (£300), 18 and 19 Aldermanbury (£430), 9-12 Love Lane (£590), and other (£437). Half of the income (£660) was reserved for ecclesiastical uses of the parish.

The ruling of the Court was against the parishoners. The Court ruled that the Church building and parish estates were to be transferred to the London Parochial Charities Commission. Only the advowson was left in the hands of the parishoners.

Conclusion

The Chancery Court's decision was a terrible blow to the Aldermanbury parishoners. Not only was it financially devastating, it crippled their ability to manage parish affairs. The changed circumstances in London would have made it increasingly difficult for the parish to retain its autonomy, so the 1887 decision was an ecclesiastical coup de grace. It was inevitable, but no less difficult for the proud parishoners to swallow.

In this chapter we have witnessed the decline of the Aldermanbury parish in population and autonomy, as the industrial age brought sweeping changes to London and its churches. The parishoners could have easily given up at this point and closed the church doors. However, as the next chapter will illustrate, the parishoners of St. Mary, Aldermanbury, were determined to keep the church open and their heritage alive.

Bibliography

Barker, Felix and Peter Jackson
 1990 The History of London in Maps. London: Barrie and Jenkins.

Birch, George
 1896 London Churches of the xviith and xviiith centuries. London: Batsford.

Bumpus, Thomas Francis
 1924 Ancient London Churches. rev. ed. London.

Chancery Court Petition
 1887 "Petition of the Parishoners to the Chancery Court in the matter of the Rectory Church and the City of London Parochial Charities Act of 1883," 26 November, 1887 (GL Pamphlet 113360).

Charities Commissioners
 1822 Further Report of the Commissioners Appointed in Pursuance of Two Several Acts of Parliament concerning Charities in England, for the Education of the the Poor. London. Report on Aldermanbury in Vol. 4, pp. 115-118.

Cunningham, George
    1927   London: Comprehensive Survey of History, etc. London: J. M Dent and Sons.

Daniel, A. E.
    1907   London City Churches, 2nd ed. London: Archibald Constabe & Co.

Goss, Charles
    1944   "A History of The Parish of St. Mary the Virgin, Aldermanbury," Transactions of the London and Middlesex Archaeological Society. 9 (1944-47), 113-164.

Harben, Henry A.
    1918   A Dictionary of London. London: Jenkins.

Helm, Peter
    1966   Jeffreys. London: Robert Hale.

Hyde, Ralph
    1975   Printed Maps of Victorian London. Folkstone, Kent: William Dawson, Ltd.

    1987   The A to Z of Victorian London. London: The London Topographical Society (publication no. 136), 1987.

Lillywhite, Bryant
    1963   London Coffeehouses. London: George Allen and Unwin, Ltd.

Olsen, Donald
    1979   The Growth of Victorian London. Harmondsworth: Penguin.

Pearce, E. H.
    1913   Sion College and Library. Cambridge: University Press.

Reeder, David A., ed.
   1984   Charles Booth's Descriptive Map of London Poverty.
           London: London Topographical Society (publication no. 130).

Sheppard, Francis
   1971   History of London, 1808-1870: The Infernal Wen. London: Secker and Warburg.

Trustees of the London Parochial Charities
   1951   A History of the City Parochial Foundation, 1851-1951. London: C. F. Rowarth.

Young, Wayland and Elizabeth
   1956   Old London Churches. London.

CHAPTER EIGHT: THE STRUGGLE FOR SURVIVAL (1887-1940)

Introduction

After the loss of control over the parish properties and responsibility for the parish poor, culminating in the Chancery Court's ruling in 1887, the activities of the Vestry were more limited. Despite these limitations and the continuing decline in the parish's population, the parishoners continued to work to make the church a vibrant institution. They responded to the changing neighborhood by instituting weekday services on Wednesdays, and later on Fridays, and opening the church and churchyard as a place of rest for people working in the neighborhood. The parishoners also had to resist several plans to demolish the church building. We have already witnessed diocesan plans to amalgamate St. Mary, Aldermanbury with St. Michael, Bassishaw. Other plans to link St. Mary with other parishes would be advanced, discussed, then die, until union with St. Alphage, London Wall, was achieved in 1917.

In this chapter we will witness a parish struggling to survive, committed all the while to preserving its historic building, its rectorial rights, and its ministry. The parishoners proved themselves able to resist the growing pressures of a church bureaucracy intent on destroying the parish and church. It would ultimately take the German Luftwaffe to bring down (in London) the Church of St. Mary, Aldermanbury. This story will be told in the context of the world shattering events which began to unfold as the new century progressed.

The End of Eras (1887-1914)

Queen Victoria celebrated the golden jubilee of her reign in 1887 and in 1897 her diamond jubilee. The kingdom and the empire joined. The British have long excelled at what military folk call "drill and ceremony." The rituals were worthy of the splendors of her sixty year reign, even worthy of the stately cadences of Sir Edgar Elgar's "Pomp and Circumstance" march which many associate with the diamond jubilee, even though it was not written until five years later. Rudyard Kipling, the great balladeer of imperialism, sensing a hollow materialism in the ostentatious display of wealth and power, penned his "Recessional," which was to prove all too prophetic over the next half century. The elderly queen supported her government in the vigorous prosecution of the Boer War and the Commonwealth Bill for Australia (1900). Victoria is credited with doing much to restore both the respectability and the popularity of the monarchy after the escapades of George IV (though surely gruff old William IV had begun the process).

Edward Albert, Prince of Wales, had experienced in full measure the ambivalent situation of the heir of a long-lived monarch. But despite an occasionl indiscretion, it must be said that both in character and in public image, he weathered the long wait much better than the Prince Regent. Excluded from state business by his stern mother, he was nonetheless delegated by her to assume many ceremonial duties which she shunned during her long mourning, exposing him frequently to his future subjects who responded warmly. A sportsman and a horseman, he and his wife, Princess Alexandra of Denmark, were a popular royal couple. He ascended the throne on Victoria's death in 1901 and as **Edward VII** became perhaps Britain's most popular sovereign since the Merry Monarch himself. He also showed a talent for statecraft, above all for diplomacy. He always took a ranking foreign office representative on his diplomatic ventures so there was never any question of royal indiscretion or constitutional infringement. Some writers dubbed him "the peacemaker" for his efforts, especially the ground-work for several treaties of friendship. Perhaps most important was his role in reapproachment with France as the dubious behavior of cousin Wilhelm II of Germany erroded Victoria's philogermanic tilt, largely accepted by her governments. Edward was near sixty and a grandfather when he began his reign, making his death in 1910 no great surprise.

Barbara Tuchman used Edward's funeral as a metaphor of the last hurrah of a dying order (1962:1-14). The high royalty of Europe, including nine kings, many of them kin thanks to Victoria's fecundity, rode in the funeral procession. They, or at any rate their nations, would soon be at each others' throats. Some of them and some of their thrones would not survive the coming war and its aftermath. The Emperor of Austria-Hungary was represented by his nephew, whose death would touch off the avalanche, while the emperor would die even as the empire crumbled. The Czar, the "little father of all the Russians," would be deposed in a revolution and murdered with his family by the Bolsheviks. The Kaiser would abdicate in defeat and devote his remaining days to such exciting hobbies as chopping wood. Only Edward's heir, **George V**, would experience anything like a really happy future.

George V was titular head of an empire in full flower, whether or not it was still at full vitality. His sovereignty extended over 400 million subjects, a quarter of Earth's population and a quarter of its land area. The sun indeed never set on the British empire (because, as the joke had it, even God could not trust the British in the dark!). The outcome of the impending war would confer some former Turkish and German territories as "League of Nations mandates," but the Empire in its own right was essentially complete.

Victoria's last years, the reign of Edward VII, and George V's early years saw developments of great significance for the future of Britain and of the world. The Franco-Prussian War had signalled an irrevocable change in the continental power balance. Germany had displaced France as the foremost power. Kaiser Wilhelm II's arbitrary dismissal of Bismarck signalled an era of dangerously personal leadership by that unstable monarch. Germany had entered vigorously into colonial competition with England and France, especially in Africa and the Pacific. More disquieting yet, Germany entered into competition with the Royal Navy for superiority in capital ships. This challenge Britain readily met both in design and armaments, and in keel-layings and launchings. Finally, both Germany and the United States were overtaking Britain in international trade. About half of American exports were agricultural produce, some bound for Britain and in any case no worry. But Germany competed directly with British manfacturers, often with cheaper but attractive products and efficient selling techniques. Japan was a less pressing rival, but her potential was ever more evident.

Kitchner had avenged excesses at Khartoum (including the killing of General "Chinese" Gordon) in a battle against the Mahdi and his followers at Omdurman in 1898. There young Winston Churchill took part in one of the last British lancer charges (firing a pistol) and later writing a book about the "River War." Britain's hold on Egypt and the Sudan and much to the south was enhanced. The American war against Spain was fought in the same year. The American action was unpopular on the continent. But Britain supported the United States. The full extent of support has never been documented, but Royal Navy units backed the American forces after the Battle of Manila Bay when they were challenged by a stronger German squadron. It appears that the Anglo-American "special relationship" was in place, with much of the early initiative from the British side. It would pay handsome dividends to both over the long haul.

Britain had her own unpopular war, against the Boers of South Africa (1899-1902). The strong showing the outnumbered Boers made against the British army did little to enhance its credit. Mr. Churchill, now a war correspondent, escaped a POW compound and with a price on his head made his way to freedom and then into Parliament. Lord Salisbury retired from office in 1902 and in proper aristocratic fashion bequeathed the Tory leadership (and the Prime Ministry) to his nephew, Arthur Balfour. Wags began to call No. 10 Downing Street the "Hotel Cecil." But the Tory majority had melted away by 1905 and a Liberal ministry took over Hotel Cecil, further strengthening its majority in the next election. The Liberal majority was supported on some issues by a growing delegation of the new Labour Party, and by the Irish Nationalists. The stage was set for a new surge of reform legislation. A Workman's Compensation law and the Trades Disputes Act, which exempted unions from harassing and burdensome damage suits, were passed in 1906, and an old age pension bill in 1908. Finally, health and unemployment insurance were incorporated in the National Insurance bill of 1911.

Meanwhile, constitutional crisis had reared its head. The Lords blocked the so-called "Lloyd George Budget" in 1909-1910. The power of the unelected and predominantly conservative Lords to veto legislation passed by the Commons had long rankled. Now the outcry grew. Edward VII had been deeply concerned by the matter, but took no action. His son, George V, broke the logjam in 1911. The Commons advanced the Parliament Bill under which the Lords might delay legislation for two years but not veto it outright. The Lords were opposed. The king, like William IV in 1832, let it be known that he would create enough peers to pass the bill if that was what it took. The Lords swallowed hard and passed the bill by 17 votes, with numerous abstentions. The new law also set the term for parliamentary elections at five years, which still stands.

Events half a world away signalled yet another shift in the balance of power.

Japan had thrashed the tottering Chinese empire in the Sino-Japanese war of 1892-95. Europe took urgent note that this nation only jarred out of the Middle Ages by American gunboats less than fifty years before should have made such strides into industrial and military modernity. But a greater shock awaited. Japan not only defeated Russia in the Russo-Japanese War (1904-05), the victory was decisive. Australia took little comfort. The home ports of the Japanese navy were much closer than the home ports of the Royal Navy! President Theodore Roosevelt's Nobel-prize-winning role in securing the peace settlement and the world cruise of his Great White Fleet gave an even clearer signal than the Spanish war that yet another world power was upon the stage.

Despite the reform legislation so recently adopted, Britain found herself awash in strife during 1911-1912. The "Suffragettes," radical campaigners for the right of women to vote, resorted to tactics of disruption and vandalism. Some even chained themselves in the gallery of the Commons. And there was a mounting wave of labour unrest. Such was the level of turmoil that some continental observers wondered if England would, or even could, take part in a war in Europe, should one come.

Aldermanbury during the End of Eras

<u>*The Charles Collins Era (1854-1917) (continued)*</u>

More Plans to Merge St. Mary', Aldermanbury with other Parishes (1887-1907)

Although the parishoners no longer owned the church, they continued to provide for its repair. On 6 April, 1888, a committee was established to determine what renovations were necessary. Their report, approved on 25 June, called for £400 in repairs, focusing on adding decorations at the east end. Also in 1888 new lead was added to the spire and a lightning conductor was added.

Even though the parish had lost its property and its responsibility for the parish poor, the Vestry was still being billed by the Metropolitan Board under the Poor Rate Law of 1834. For example, in 1889 the parish was charged for £795. In 1888 the poor rate was 8d, but by 1906 (the last time a poor rate is listed) it had risen to 2s5d to pay an assessment of about £3000.

A letter dated 4 July, 1889, from the Charities Commission notified the parish that a representative of the Commission would soon survey the church and interview the churchwardens concerning funds spent on repairs on the church during the past 20 years.

On 19 September, 1889, the Churchwardens reported the theft of the communion plate from the church safe. A report in the Western Daily Press, Bristol, on 22 August, 1889, said that it consisted of several silver flagons and pierced silver chalices, one of which bore the name of a benefactor, "Mr. A. Brookby, Merchant, 1658." It was last used on 7 July, and was found missing on 4 August when it was to be used again. The press report cited no forced entry, and the Churchwardens strongly suspected the Beadle, the Church Attendant, and a man hired by the Beadle. The Beadle, the Churchwardens reported, was a heavy drinker, was heavily indebted, admitted to having taken a coin from the poor box once, and to having sent for, received, and consumed gin during a church service. The Church Attendant admitted to drinking during services. And the third man was described by the police as a "bad character." On the basis of this evidence, the Beadle and Attendant were dismissed on a 5-2 vote. Since no parish could be found willing to sell old plate, new plate was purchased for £100. It was the plate in the safe the night the church was bombed in 1940, and is now on display at the Churchill Memorial, showing the effects of the fire.

On 24 October, 1889, the scheme of the Charities Commission was still not implemented, as the trustees' opinion with proposals for change was received by the Vestry (but not included in the minutes). On 8 April, 1891, the Vestry petitioned the Charities Commission to use the balance still in the parish accounts from parish estates to clear up liabilities to the parish through 25 March, 1890.

During 1890 the Churchyard was renovated and opened on 25 September for use as a public park. Ward Deputy Robert H. Rogers donated a drinking fountain, on the condition the Vestry maintain it. A design supplied by the Metropolitan Drinking Fountain Association was rejected in favor of one more in keeping with the vicar's wishes. The drinking fountain, still to be found in working order on the corner of Aldermanbury and Love Lane, stands near the site of the 15th century conduit, which was one of the first to bring fresh water into the City. (See Ch. 2).

On 30 March, 1894, hydraulic power was added to the organ at a cost of £78. On 31 July, 1895, a letter was received from C. C. Walker of Lilleshall Old Hall, Shropshire, offering to build a monument to John Heminge and Henry Condell (see Ch. 3). According to Mr. Walker, he was dismayed that their role as editors of the first folio of Shakespeare's plays was not widely appreciated. Therefore, he proposed to put up a monument to them in the Aldermanbury churchyard at his own expense. Although others urged him to put it up at Blackfriars or Southwark, where the plays were first produced, he had decided on the parish where they so long lived and were buried. The monument was to include an open book, representative of the first folio, and a bust of Shakespeare (the only public one in London, as far as Mr. Walker knew). The inscriptions on the four sides of the pedestal would give a concise account of how the first folio came to be, Heminge and Condell's own words from the preface, and a brief statement of their residence in the parish.

The monument, endorsed enthusiastically by the vicar, was approved by the Vestry and set up in the churchyard. It survived the World War II bombing and remains a part of the Churchyard. The inscription includes the following:

To the memory of John Heminge and Henry Condell, fellow actors
and personal friends of Shakespeare. They lived many years in
this parish and are buried here. To their disinterested affection the world owes all that it calls Shakespeare. They alone
collected his dramatic writings regardless of pecuniary loss,
and without hope of any profit, gave them to the world. They
thus merited the gratitude of the world.

On 6 February, 1896, the Vestry expressed outrage that the assessment of property in the city was greatly in excess of that in the outlying areas.

On 28 April, 1897, the Vicar reported that application had been made to the Charities Commission for £250 to supplement the £250 the Churchwardens had in order to repair the church. (The change in designation of the Rev. C. Collins from curate to vicar was in keeping with a recent Act of Parliament.)

On 29 April, 1897, the Estates Committee of the Ecclesiastical Commissioners for England endorsed the Bishop of London's request that a grant of £250 be made to St. Mary, Aldermanbury out of the City Parochial Charities Fund for repairs to cost £500. (CC No. 833/1845, File No. 67141).

On 21 July, 1897, on a vote of 7-6 the Vestry resolved that "the time has now arrived when the Benefice of this Parish should be united to that of an adjoining Parish." In a letter to the Vestry dated 4 August, 1897, Churchwarden J.A.S. Lovatt expressed opposition to "the suggested demolition of our fine old church." His fellow Churchwarden and the Vicar also strongly opposed the proposal. It came, Lovatt said, from Mr. Rogers of Addle Street who was intent on joining St. Mary, Aldermanbury with St. Lawrence Jewry. He urged that a poll of those who have lived in the parish, even if they are not rate payers, be taken and submitted to the Ecclesiastical Commissioners. (Ms. 3558: 5).

A poll of the parish was demanded, and one was taken on 19 October, defeating the resolution 87-39. An article in the City Press (Clarke 1898: 337-338) reported on the poll. It claimed that a considerable number in the parish had come to the conclusion that "the cost of keeping up the church in Aldermanbury might be utilised to better advantage in some poorer neighborhood of London." They wanted the church sold, leaving the tower and the churchyard. They pointed out that the sale of the church site would create an endowment of £500, which together with the current expenditures for upkeep and stipends of £750 would create £1250 or £83 a head for the average of 15 worshippers. Opponents said that the fact the church was built by Sir Christopher Wren and had links to Milton and Shakespeare was sufficient to preserve it. They also pointed out that the stipend for the Vicar would have to be paid anyway. Despite their defeat advocates of union claimed that it was only a matter of time until their side prevailed, and they planned to keep pressing the case.

On 15 December, 1897, Mr. Lovatt and the Vicar, now living at 50 Grand Parade, Eastbourne, wrote the Commissioners, asking whether the parish was obliged to pay for upkeep of the fabric of the church from money allotted for services (Ms. 3558). Letters in the same collection suggest repair of the church during 1898 and 1899.

H. W. Clarke's study of the city churches, published in 1898, is a valuable source of information on the status of the parish at the close of the 19th century and gives us insight into the argument of those who wished to close the church (Clarke 1898: 332-339).

Clarke began his analysis by stating that the parish was 4.4 acres, with only 13 occupied houses in 1891. The population had declined from 168 in 1881 to 102 in 1891 and 97 in 1896.

The author then cited the fact that since 1621 the parishoners had been the rector, by virtue of the purchase of the rectory and advowson. He wrote that "after maturely weighing and considering the desirability of making the parishoners the patrons of the living, I have come to the conclusion that the system is open to grave objections. ... the parishoners of the City parishes take but little interest in parochial matters, and are indifferent as to the clergyman appointed to the living" (332).

The article continued by stating that the total amount of parish charities was

£1,335 a year, all but £14 coming from the parish properties. The properties consisted of 12, Aldermanbury Street (rent of £300); 18 and 19 (£430); 9-12, Love-lane (£590); and Consols (£15). £1,321 was expended on the fabric, salaries, and divine service, with the vicar receiving £461. Only £14 a year went to the poor. The trustees gave £415 to repair the fabric of the church and only 10.8 a year for life to one poor woman!

The author complained in the article that by paying the vicar's stipend of £250 (£200 more than his legal income) out of the charities rather than from a tithe assessed on the parishoners, the City Parochial Charities Commission was allowing the Aldermanbury parishoners to be "in the glorious position of being tithe free." £250 was the amount specified by the Charities Commission to be paid the vicar. The present incumbent, Rev. Collins, received a total of £461, but his successor would get only the £250.

Clarke chastized the Vestry for failing to respond when called before a Royal Commission to give evidence about their charities. He went on to say that the practice of paying the minister out of parish rents rather than by a tithe-rate was done initially "to relieve the conscientious scruples of Quakers and other Dissenters who were ratepayers and occupiers in the parish."

Clarke also pointed out that for the 43 years of his curacy, the Rev. Collins had never actually lived in the parish, residing instead at Teddington, Middlesex. His curate lived near Regent's Park.

The author further stated that the church had recently been opened on a trial basis from 12:45 to 1:45 p.m. weekdays, after having been open during the week only from one to two p.m. on Wednesdays for divine service for the past 13 years. The author had visited the church in recent months and found the average attendance at services on Sunday morning 13 and 9 on Sunday evening. For example, on Sunday morning, 25 April, 1896 (?), the congregation consisted of 3 men, 7 women, 14 in the paid choir, 2 clergymen, and 2 officials; in the evening there were 5 men, 7 women, 10 in the choir, 2 clergy, and 2 officials. On average 20 attended the Wednesday afternoon service. They were mostly young women between the ages of 15 and 20 who worked in the neighborhood.

Clarke argued that there should be more weekday services and the churches should be open from at least 11:00 a.m. until 5:00 p.m. weekdays. He also concluded that "the parochial system in the City of London has completely broken down," the city churches having become "comfortable retired sinecures for young as well as old clergymen."

Clarke emphasized the proximity of St. Mary, Aldermanbury to other churches (337).

> It may be of public interest to state that the Church of St. Mary, Aldermanbury, is 133 yards from St. Lawrence Jewry; 40 yards from St. Alban's, Wood-street; 233 yards from St.Anne and St. Agnes; and 283 yards from St. Vedast, Foster-lane.
>
> Here is an object lesson for the City Church Preservation Society. This church is, as I said, 40 yards from St. Alban's; the income of the two incumbents is £1,019; and £574 is allowed for fabric and domus.

In a sarcastic note, Mr. Clarke suggested that it would be futile for St. Mary, Aldermanbury, and other city parishes to try to attract more parishioners "unless the sleepy paper sermons are pitched into the Thames, and unless the people get good, practical, and short extemporaneous discourses which they can remember" (337). Clarke laid the blame for the decline of the city churches on the shoulders of the incumbents, many of whom did not come to their parishes except on Sundays, when they were virtually empty. He challenged them to be seen on weekdays in their parishes. It was the clergy, not the laity, who needed awakening, he urged.

In 1900 the Churchwardens reported to the Charity Commissioners that the accounts of the church consisted of 150.18.10 in the Bank of England and 7.3.6 in petty cash (Ms. 3558/102).

In the Visitation Return submitted in 1900 (LPL Creighton 1/40) Mr. Collins reported that the average number of adults at Sunday worship was 22.2 in the morning and 18.3 for evensong. If the choir and officials were counted the total was 78 for both services together. On average 15 received Holy Communion. There were no children and no schools in the parish. In responding to the question of whether the parish had any organizations, societies, or guilds, Mr. Collins responded, "I have tried various methods for the young men; I found that without constant novelties one's labour goes for nothing." He also noted that "my Dissenting parishoners are among my best helpers." The greatest problem was still, he said, the non-residence of parishoners. He concluded by saying "an occasional visit by the Bishop himself would be encouraging." Collins' discouragement about the declining fortunes of his parish is painfully obvious.

When on 9 April, 1902, the Vestry received a request for funds for a celebration for inmates of the City Union, the Vestry Clerk was instructed to respond, "the Parish property having been taken over by the City Parochial Charities Trustees, the Vestry regret that they have no fund from which they can further the object for which the appeal was made."

On 20 April, 1904, at a meeting presided over by Rev. Collins, and attended by 33 parishoners and several reporters, a letter from the Bishop of London, dated 11 March, was read. It was a proposal to unite St. Mary, Aldermanbury, with St. Michael, Bassishaw and St. Lawrence, Jewry. The meeting was fully reported in The City Press, Saturday, 23 April, 1904, under the headlines "The Threatened City Church" and "Strong Speech by the Rector." A full roster of those in attendance was included.

After the letter requesting the parishoners' cooperation with a commission to study the matter was read, Mr. E. Sidgwick proposed "that the parishoners of St. Mary-the-Virgin, Aldermanbury, being patrons of the living, having fully considered the above letter, do not consider it expedient to facilitate the passing of any scheme which would prejudicially affect the benefice or church of this parish."

Mr. Joseph Hicks reminded the parishoners that seven years earlier he had brought forward a similar scheme, which was soundly defeated. He said that although he had decided not to sponsor another such proposal "while the rector remained" he felt duty bound to support the Bishop's plan. He said that the Church of St. Mary and several others nearby were "absolutely unnecessary." He said that if the church could be taken to the suburbs it would do a great deal more good than in its present location. He said the opposition to taking down the church seemed to come from a group of parishoners with premises overlooking the churchyard, who were more concerned with preserving their view than they were in "spreading religion in the suburbs."

Deputy Sir Robert Rogers supported Mr. Hicks and added that from a business point of view the amount spent on St. Mary, Aldermanbury; St. Alban's, Wood Street; and St. Alphage's, London Wall was a "wicked waste." He said that at least two of these churches should be destroyed, and the three parishes united into one.

Pierson Carter then spoke of the utility of the church, saying that during the week it was a refuge for many city workers. He said it was regrettable that the gentlemen the Bishop had consulted about this matter were those who had a personal stake in seeing the church taken down.

Mr. Hicks then pointed out that the value of the site of the church, not including the tower and churchyard, was £20,000, an amount quite sufficient to endow a church in the suburbs with an income of £250 a year. They could also support a "hard working clergyman in the East End." He moved an amendment saying that the Vestry intended to give the Bishop all information requested in the event of an inquiry. Sir Robert Rogers seconded.

Then Rev. Collins spoke, stating that the Bishop already knew what there was to know. He reminded the parishoners that his position and income were secure, and that he had no personal stake in the closing of the church.

An unidentified "Nonconformist" parishoner then took the floor, saying that he hoped the church would remain, claiming that he really appreciated the type of services held in the church. The amendment failed 2-29.

Mr. Collins then took the floor to deliver prepared remarks. He pointed out that this was the fourth time the proposal had come before the Vestry. It had been before them in 1862, 1871, and 1897. He said that the Vestry had previously wisely decided to reject the proposal. He reminded them that the Church belonged to God, not the Bishop; that numbers of worshippers are not a fair criterion to use in judging the worth of a church; that a church was a "noble landmark;" that the Bishop (an "exuberant young man") had given no reasons for the scheme; that it reminded him of the story of Naboth's Vineyard in the Bible, when King Ahab wanted for no good reason the ancestral property of one of his citizens; that selling a church site for the money was a "desecration;" that if people were that concerned about the East End they could donate to the societies already doing work there; that 53 City churches had already been abolished in the last century; that a benefactor would not have put up a monument to Shakespeare had he thought the church would be pulled down; and finally that the Church of St. Mary, Aldermanbury was doing a great spiritual work. After the Vicar's impassioned plea the motion passed, 29-2, according to the article. The Vestry Minutes record the vote as 30-2, apparently adding Mr. Collins'.

A postscript to the article reported that Alderman Sir Henry Knight had written to the Vestry, saying that only Mr. Collins and he had fought destruction of the church for 40 years. A letter from Henry Pollard also supported the Vestry's decision, claiming that many workers in the city warehouses cut their dinner hour short in order to attend the Wednesday services and that the church is "architecturally beautiful." The plan apparently died in the face of such strong objection.

An article in the Daily Graphic on Thursday, 28 April, congratulated the parishoners for resisting the scheme, calling the church a "fair specimen of Wren's style" to be associated with "our great national right—representative municipal government."

On 8 June, 1904, Mr. Collins presented an alms-dish to the parish in commemoration of the completion of fifty years as Incumbent of the parish.

On 4 April, 1907, the Vestry tried to protest a marker which had been set up in memory of Judge George Jeffreys, but Rev. Collins ruled that it was not in their power to overrule the erection. The power of the Vestry had clearly eroded over the years. Until the mid-19th Century the incumbent did not even attend Vestry meetings. Now he was telling the Vestry what they could and could not do!

A 24 June, 1907, letter from the Church Commissioners reminded the Vestry that the parishoners should pay the stipend of the vicar and that it should not come from other sources. (CC File 67141).

The Great War and its Aftermath (1914-1920)
Two major alliances had emerged in Europe. One combined Germany, Austria and Italy. But Italy was a shaky partner and when war came she hung back, finally putting in on the other side, with Turkey joining the "Central Powers." In the Pacific, Japan again asserted her great power status and joined the allies. But for rebuffs by the Kaiser, England might have been closely allied with Germany also, whether or not this would have preempted the Anglo-French entente cordiale. Nobody wanted a war. At least, few admitted that they did. But Europe was an armed camp. France spoiled to avenge her humiliation by Bismarck, and Germany was unlikely to wait for France to strike first. The continental powers had all adopted the Prussian system (originally devised to circumvent Napoleonic treaty limits) of conscripting young men in a particular age group, subjecting them to intensive army training, mustering them into the reserve, and calling up the next class for training. In this way a large cadre of trained soldiers was developed and maintained by periodic refresher camps, with the military obligation extending into middle age. A sytematic national mobilization plan told each reservist where to report when called. Substantial standing armies were also in being. Russia had 1,200,000 in her standing army and 3,800,000 in the reserves; Germany 800,000 and 4,000,000, respectively; and France 800,000 and 2,300,000. Austria and Italy mustered less than half the German total.

A German prince was cited as observing that you could do lots of things with bayonets, but you couldn't sit on one, which rather summed things up. France and Germany were needed for a general European war, otherwise the combination of the two with England could intimidate a lesser combination into composing their differences. When war was joined, Russia turned out to be a hollow giant. Russian soldiers were brave, but poorly led and poorly equipped.

Things were quite different in England. England's democratic traditions were inimical to militarism. The first Duke of Marlborough had observed that Englishmen smelled a tyrant under every uniform, probably a reference to Cromwell. The navy was the first line of defense. About half of the 200,000 man regular army was in India or otherwise securing the Empire, and there were only 100,000 reservists. Bismarck is supposed to have remarked that if the British army landed in Europe he would have the police arrest them. Sheltered by two wide oceans the United States reversed the British figures: 100,000 regulars and 200,000 reservists. The English speaking democracies were obviously not spoiling for a big land war in Europe.

War was not inevitable, though the ambiguity of the system of alliances made a war, through what has been called "the domino effect," a danger. As late as the Balkan wars of 1912-13, Germany and England cooperated to achieve peace. When war did come, it was ignited in the Balkans, "the tinder box of Europe." Archduke Ferdinand of Austro-Hungary and his wife were murdered by Serbian extremists at Sarajevo, Bosnia, in June, 1914, and the old Russo-Austrian rivalry in the Balkans boiled over. Austria leaned hard on Serbia. Russia began to mobilize in support of Serbia. Germany issued an ultimatum to Russia. Russia continued to mobilize. Germany declared war on 1 August. France came in on the side of Russia. British efforts had been aimed at preventing war. Her diplomacy had been skillful but tentative. Whether even a Disraeli could have leashed the dogs of war in late July, 1914, is dubious. But it was a war that Englad did not have to enter, a war in which no British vital interest was at stake but for German strategic arrogance.

The German strategic plan against France had been the work of the late chief of staff, Count von Schlieffen. It called for a wide flank attack through neutral Belgium, sweeping to the Channel and enveloping Paris from the rear. The plan had several advantages. It would not require the reduction of the strong French fortifications opposite Germany. And it offered the promise of a quick victory, before the Russians could invade East Prussia. It almost worked.

France herself was not averse to attacking through Belgium either, but apparently meant to let the Germans sin first. And sin they did. Germany issued an ultimatum to the Belgians to stand aside and let them march through to France. Britain, ever sensitive concerning the Low Countries, issued an ultimatum to Germany, but German troops were already on the move. On 4 August, England declared war and a British Expeditionary Force was dispatched to support France and defend the Low Countries. (England had previously assured France that the Fleet would protect French ports since most of the French fleet was in the Mediterranean under an earlier Anglo-French naval agreement.)

The Belgians offered heroic but futile resistance to the German horde. The small British regular force was also unequal to the task, but they were tough professionals and fought well despite hesitant top command. Still, British and French forces were pushed back deep into France. Then the Germans made the error which cost them quick victory, stalemated the war, and ultimately produced German defeat. The Schlieffen plan called for the German army to sweep west of Paris. (Already the French government had fled the capital.) Instead, they turned east of Paris, not only exposing their flank, but also opening a gap in their forces. The French, with the slow and reluctant help of the British command, pressed a counterattack in what became the first battle of the Marne. The German advance was halted and the Germans forced into a thirty mile retreat. Denied Paris and a quick victory, the Germans began "the race to the sea," an attempt to seize the Channel ports and flank the Allies to the north. Four-fifths of the officers and men of the original BEF perished in the decisive battle of Yrpes which stopped this second German quest for decisive victory. During the dark early days of World War Two, when England struggled with a shortage of competent flag grade officers, Mr. Churchill mused aloud about the whereabouts of the bright, able majors and colonels, ripe for promotion to flag rank. Old General Ironside replied, "They died in Flanders, sir."

The trench war on the western front, along lines established in the first weeks of fighting, became a war of attrition. Heavy artillery pounding and rolling barrages from field guns led infantry "over the top," into barbed wire and the teeth of machine guns, and all for a few yards of scorched and blasted ground—if that much. The carnage on both sides was staggering. Military deaths reached ten million, a million from Britain and her empire, before it was over. Yet England managed to support its effort with a volunteer army for two years, and when conscription came in 1916, it was in part to equalize the burdens and to get at the "slackers." The lot of survivors was often tragic, too, maimed in body or mind ("shell shocked"), or suffering the after effects of poison gas.

A liberal government under Asquith led Britain into the war. It became a coalition to reflect national unity, still under Asquith, in 1915. Then, in December, 1916, a stronger coalition was formed under the energetic David Lloyd George. Constitutional adjustments were made to advance the war effort. A small War Cabinet was created under the Prime Minister to direct the war. Its members were excused from most regular duties. There was a larger Imperial War Cabinet which included representatives of the Empire. Harsh wartime restrictions were imposed, contravening many ancient citizen rights, but most seemed to agree that such was justified by the emergency.

The war, however, was not going well. The western front remained in a stalemate. The Dardanelles campaign to take Turkey out of the war in 1915 was a bloody fiasco (for which Churchill was unjustly scapegoated). The Germans got some bad press in the U.S. for sinking the Cunard liner, Lusitania. But the disaster was prophetic of the menace to Britain posed by the U-boat in both world wars.

Nor could it be said that 1916 was much better. The Good Friday rising in Ireland, though handily suppressed, pointed to future as well as past grief. The Battle of Jutland at the end of May was a qualified success, after which the Germans did not again challenge the Royal Navy. In the ground war, England lost 171,000 men to gain 2 1/2 miles in the Battle of the Somme. But thanks to the innovative mind of Mr. Churchill, a weapon was now in hand that might weaken the mastery of the machine gun, the tank.

Adroit British propaganda and German ineptitude finally brought the United States into the war on the Allied side, no small achievement considering the large German-American population of the midwest. The U.S. declared war in April, 1917. Despite British successes against the Turks in Iraq and Palestine, the allies almost lost the war before the Americans could arrive in force. The Italian army collapsed and required allied reinforcements to stabilize its front. Large parts of the French army mutinied. Germany smuggled Lenin into Russia to lead the Bolsheviks against the new liberal government. When the Bolsheviks took power Russia dropped out of the war. British and American support for counterrevolutionary forces served to heighten the antiwesternism of Russia's new ruling elite. Britain alone of the

European powers weathered the test of world war without cracking.

German forces introduced poison gas into the armory of warfare. Soon both sides were using it. The mustard and chlorine gasses were not very effective against troops prepared to deal with them, but few weapons in the history of warfare have struck greater terror.

The aeroplane introduced a signficiant new element into warfare. Used at first as a scouting vehicle, technology quickly improved, allowing bombing of sites on the ground and aerial combat. The air war reached as far as London. Long range "Gotha" bombers paid occasional daytime calls. The greatest property damage of any single strike was caused by a 300 kilo bomb dropped from an aeroplane in Warrington Crescent. More fearsome for the civilian population were the Zeppelin raids. The Zeppelins came at night, and they were relatively silent. These rigid, lighter-than-air craft could lift heavier bomb loads and had a longer range than existing bomber aircraft. There were seven Zeppelin raids on London between May, 1915 and October, 1917, with thirteen aircraft in one attack. Defensive measures were lacking at first, but tracer bullets turned out to be very effective against the hydrogen filled lift bags of the airships. British authorities censored reports of the raids to deny intelligence to the enemy. Consequently, press reports of the Zeppelin bomb which caused slight damage at St. Mary, Aldermanbury, are more than a trifle vague. There was a spate of "now it can be told" stories after the war. Several maps were published showing the places hit, casualties, etc. Germany mounted 51 Zeppelin and 57 aeroplane raids against Britain in the course of the war. Just over a thousand civilians were killed, nearly three thousand injured. The death toll in London was 587 (Barker and Jackson 1990: 154-155). The losses were minor in the great picture of the war. But they were also prophetic of the vicious air war of 1939-45, in which more than 190,000 Londoners perished.

Much deadlier for the civilian population was the terrible worldwide epidemic of Spanish influenza, which also wreaked havoc among the armies. It was probably the most virulent strain of the disease on record and death rates were high, particularly since there were no effective drugs to combat complications like pneumonia.

With Russia out of the war, Germany could shift troops formerly pinned down on the eastern front to France. These additional forces permitted the Germans to launch their 1918 offensives, but with increasing desperation. American troops were now arriving in substantial numbers and contributed to the final great allied push. The army "doughboys" and "devil dogs" (as the Germans called the U.S. marines) quickly proved their mettle. Despite equipment shortages they marched into battle singing. A joint Franco-American push in late July and a British offensive in early August turned the tide. The German fleet mutinied, and the Kaiser abdicated and fled. The German people had had enough. At the eleventh hour of the eleventh day of the eleventh month, the guns fell silent on the western front. The Allies had won the war to end all wars and to make the world safe for democracy. Then they made the peace that caused the next war.

Germany negotiated the armistice of 11 November on the basis of the "14 points," a draft peace plan issued earlier by the American president, Woodrow Wilson. There was an annex in which Germany agreed to pay reparations for damage actually done by its invading armies. The 14 Points foresaw a non-punitive settlement which sought to prevent war by removing many of its causes. Such was not to be the case.

The peace conference that was to conclude the business of the Great War assembled in Paris in January, 1919. History has bestowed the names "Versailles Conference" and "Treaty of Versailles," though only part of the activity centered there. Separate settlements were arrived at in different places with each of the Central Powers. What transpired in Paris was a rather unusual peace conference. Unlike the Congress of Vienna which concluded the Napoleonic Wars and led to a century of relative stability (except for the Franco-Prussian War) the defeated powers were excluded from the conference. The business was conducted as personal diplomacy among the heads of the three major allied governments: Clemenceau of France, Lloyd George of Great Britain, and Woodrow Wilson of the United States. Clemenceau was dominant, intent on weakening Germany as much as possible while gaining the maximum for France. Lloyd George came to the conference constrained by domestic political considerations. He had no alternative but to join in the demand for heavy German reparations. Wilson was ready to compromise for the sake of support for his League of Nations plan.

Making the losers pay for the war was an old European custom, and in a sense Germany may have been fortunate in not being docked more terriroty than she was. Still, the German representatives were shocked when given the final treaty, which went far beyond what they had agreed to in the armistice including substantial reparations. But the allies had continued the debilitating blockade, and there was the treat of military occupation, leaving little choice but to sign.

The treaty deprived Germany of some territory and substantial iron and coal reserves. The Rhineland was demilitarized, and the German army was limited to 100,000 troops, with no tanks, heavy guns or aircraft. The demanded reparations were 33 million dollars. The Austro-Hungarian Empire was dismantled (as was the Ottoman Empire). Poland attained autonomy as did Czechoslovakia (where a German minority was ill-treated, setting the stage for Hitler's later seizing of the Sudentenland). Yugoslavia was created out of a number of ethnic groups with long memories and deep hatreds. Britain and France divided the Near East into spheres of influence legitimized as League of Nations' mandates, despite promises to the Arabs who had risen against Turkey, and to the Jews in the Balfour Declaration. Back in Europe, French and Belgian troops occupied the Ruhr when Germany fell behind in reparations payments.

Europeans came rather soon to suspect that the Versailles treaty was a failure. British economist John Maynard Keynes gave articulate voice to this suspicion in an economic critique that spoke of Clemeanceau's "Carthegenian peace." In the United States, Americans were not ready to assume the obligations of world power. The Senate had become Republican and was in no mood to cooperate with Wilson, a Democrat, in his efforts to win support for the League of Nations. The Senate voted to reject both the Versailles Treaty (with its provisions for the League) and a separate Franco-American mutual security pact.

The League of Nations was a collective security arrangement between sovereign states, not a world federation or a super government. It had a professional secretariat, an Assembly in which all member states could vote, and a Council where most of the power resided. The Council was to have consisted of the wartime Big Five (France, Great Britain, Italy, the United States, Japan). Without the United States the organization was hopelessly crippled. Added to this was the fact that two members of the Council, Japan and Italy, became in due course major disturbers of world peace.

Union with St.Alphage, London Wall (1907-1917)

In 1907 Parliament passed an act (61 & 62 Victoria Cap 23) mandating the union of parishes. A commission was created to inquire into the "expediency of uniting the Parishes of St. Alphage London Wall and St. Mary the Virgin Aldermanbury." The members were Rev. Ernest Pearce, Vicar of Christ Church Newgate St., with St. Leonard Foster; the Rev. Henry Danvers Macnamara, rector of St. James Garlickhithe;

Sir Robert Rogers, Knight, of 11 Addle Street; and William Thomas of 18 Ironmonger Lane. On 2 July, 1907, the Commission reported to the Bishop of London that after holding two meetings in the respective parishes and receiving petitions signed by numerous occupiers of the parishes, they urged the Bishop to agree to the union. (CC 11210 2/3).

A letter from the Bishop suggesting amalgamation of St. Mary, Aldermanbury, and St. Alphage, London Wall, was read at the Vestry on 30 March, 1908. No action was taken. On 21 April a scheme (not included) was approved subject to several modifications: that the stipend for the incumbent be at least £700 since no house was provided, and the patronage of the Church and other Benefices pass to the Bishop; that there be a parish house whether by preservation of St. Alphage, London Wall or otherwise; and that there be increased provisions for services in the church. The matter was discussed further on 5 May, 1909, but without action.

On 16 December, 1909, we find the first record of a precinct meeting in the Vestry Minutes since 1853. (It seems that the minutes of precinct meetings must have been separated from the Vestry minutes at that point. The minutes from 1904 through 1917 are in rough form, never having been recopied.) Eight were nominated to the Wardmote to represent the parish in the Common Council.

Gifts to an organ fund totalled £302 in 1909 (with £100 from the Rev. C. Collins). The fund included £11 received at a church collection on 22 October, 1909. This is presumably the first indication of the tradition of holding an annual Harvest Festival. That tradition was reinstituted in the Church in 1988.

On 2 April, 1913, the church and its furnishings were valued at £12,500 for the purpose of a fire insurance policy. At the same meeting £150 was approved for a parish map.

In 1913 Pierson Cathrick Carter, who had served as Churchwarden at St. Mary's since 1900, published <u>The History of the Church and Parish of St. Mary the Virgin, Aldermanbury</u>. It was less a history of the church than a collection of excerpts from the Vestry Minutes, Churchwardens' Accounts, and Deeds, from the safe of the Church, organized according to subject. It was published by 76 subscribers, including many in the parish. According to Carter he collected this material in order to "stimulate a desire on the part of the parishoners, present and future, to retain and preserve their parish church, with its Incumbent's stipend intact, realising that it is in every sense their own property which they are called upon to guard ... ." As our frequent references to it have indicated, Carter's compilation of the records has been a valuable resource for this history.

On 14 May, 1914, at a meeting of parishoners called by the churchwardens, the issue was raised of how best to celebrate the 60th anniversary of the Rev. C. Collins' tenure as incumbent. It was decided to raise a monetary gift, and all present pledged £1.1 each.

On the night of 8 September, 1915, several windows in the church were shattered as the result of one of the rare German zeppelin raids over London during the First World War, as mentioned above. They were the last of the clear glass windows in the style of Wren. In the raid several adjacent buildings were destroyed completely (Goss 1944:155-156). No direct mention was made of the bombing in the Vestry minutes or in the contemporary press. However, on a list of those who served the parish during World War I (listing 338 names) mention was made of the church being closed for repairs from August 1916 through January 1917 (Ms 3569). And the Churchwarden accounts recorded receipt of an insurance payment of £237 for damage to the churchyard railings and the clearing of rubbish from the trees.

Also on this list are some notes about church attendance during the period 1912-1917. In 1912 at the Sunday morning service the congregation numbered 5-10 (17 on Easter), with the choir numbering 15-20, and "officials" 4 or 5. At the evening service there were 10-20 in the congregation, 15-20 in the choir, and 4 officials. On the Wednesday services the congregation averaged 5-10, with 4 officials. By 1915 the size of the congregation had dropped, but the choir remained the same. During 1916 and 1917 there was no evening service and the attendance at the morning service ranged from 2-14, with 13-15 in the choir. Special services included a Brahms requiem on 30 November, 1913, which drew 90 and the Harvest Festival on 4 October, 1914 which drew 62. A performance of Handel's Messiah on 28 April, 1915, attracted 32.

A record of the proceedings related to the scheme to merge the parish with St. Alphage was entered in the minute book by order of the Vestry on 18 April, 1917 as a permanent record to show that the parishoners "maintain all rectorial rights other than presentment of the living, now vested in the Bishop." It reflected the mark of Pierson Carter.

The chronicle began with five points. First, the parishoners have been the rectors and freeholders of the rectory and its rights for 350 years. Second, although the church and parish estates were "taken from them" under the Charities act, they did not lose the rectorial rights. Third, by terms of the amalgamation with St. Alphage, London Wall, the parishoners have of their own free will placed the right of presentation into the hands of the Bishop. Fourth, no other rights rectorial or otherwise have been forfeited. Fifth, any question of levying tithes under the Fire Acts is disposed of. As alluded to above, the Fire Rate had set up a tax (called the tithe or tithe rate) to provide stipends for incumbents after the Great Fire. As also mentioned previously, since St. Mary's had property of considerable value, it had paid the stipend from the rents and had cancelled the rate altogether in 1851. The parishoners of St. Mary's considered it the Charities Commission's responsibility to provide the stipend since they now have the property and continued to resist any levying of a church tithe.

The scheme to unite St. Mary and St. Alphage was formally approved by the parishoners of St. Mary's on 24 May, 1916, with the stipulation that the parishoners be removed from the rate "permanently." During the Summer of 1916 there was an exchange of correspondence on this issue. Solicitors for the Bishop of London refused to guarantee exemption from the Fire Tax rate. The Vestry withdrew the condition, but insisted that its interpretation was correct. A 15 January, 1917, letter from H. A. Mason to the Church Commissioners urged that the Union be settled because the two Vestries were becoming impatient and further delay "endangers friendly relations" between them (CC File 67141). The scheme was approved by the parishoners as patrons on 14 February, 1917.

The scheme was then approved by His Majesty in Council on 13 June, 1917, and published in the London Gazette (CC 767141) two days later. It obligated the Ecclesiastical Commissioners to continue to pay C. C. Collins' annual stipend of £460 as long as he lived (or remained a member of the Church of England). It also established a yearly grant of £120 to provide for the care and maintenance of the churchyards of the two parishes and the vestry and porch of St. Alphage. The plan included the stipulation that the Porch and Tower of the old Priory Church of Elsynge Spital, now the Vestry, be left standing when St. Alphage was torn down. It should be noted that by this time St. Alphage was in very poor repair. The Incumbent of the United Benefice was to be Henry Alfred Mason, the Rev. Prebendary of St. Paul's and rector of St. Alphage for the past two years. His stipend was to be £250. A new church was to be built out of the proceeds of the sale of the site of St. Alphage either in the

Metropolis or within its vicinity. The church eventually built was St. Alphage, Hendon.

Mason was a wealthy man, who earned his money selling a cough nostrum called "Mason's Lung Syrup." He wore a bowler and gaiters to church, and is remembered by Fred Turnbull, a member of the boy's choir during the 1930's, as decidedly "old school."

After over fifty years of efforts, a plan to unite St. Mary, Aldermanbury, with another parish finally went into effect. All the papers relating to the union were gathered by Pierson Carter, with the note that "these papers should be kept in case an attempt is made to levy a rate in the future" (Ms. 3599).

The Great Depression and the "Gathering Storm" (1920-1939)

Under the head of "unfinished business," Parliament enacted a "fourth reform bill" in 1918, further extending the franchise. Perhaps in recognition of women's contributions to the war effort, women over the age of 30 were permitted to vote! (The "fifth reform bill" of 1928 lowered the female voting age to 21, as for men.)

There was yet another Irish rising in 1919. This one finally led to dominion status and then independence for the greater part of the country, with its Catholic majoirty. In the north, Ulster, with a Protestant majority, retained its connection with Britan. Deep social and sectarian bitterness insured that this compromise would not mark a peaceful end to the "Irish problem."

The war had rent the social fabric of Europe, including its economic skein. Germany was, as we shall note, a very big loser. But the winners suffered, too. Britain's national debt increased twelvefold despite high war taxes. Britain never regained the overseas markets lost during the war. Germany was too broke to trade. The Japanese and Americans were proving tough competitors.

On the domestic scene, an effort had been made to hold the wartime coalition together, but it fell part amidst a Liberal schism, "Asquith" liberals against David Lloyd George and his faction. The Tories won the the 1922 election and Labour emerged for the first time as His Majesty's Loyal Opposition. The divided Liberals fell to what would prove to be a declining third place among Brititish parties. Labour in fact won elections and organized governments in 1924 and in 1929-31. Labour had a small radical Marxist wing, but so intent were these Labour ministries in proving that they were "safe" that their social and economic policies differed little from the

Tories.

The postwar governments, unlike their continental counterparts, pursued deflationary monetary policies and practiced stern government economies. With Churchill (a Tory turned Liberal turned coalitionist and now a Tory again!) at the Exchequer, Britain returned to the gold standard in 1925. The result was a very strong pound sterling, perhaps too strong, making British exports increasingly costly in inflated foreign currencies. Through the 1920's unemployment was never below 10%, fluctuating between 1 and 2 million. Labour unrest became endemic, especially in sectors controlled by Marxist unions. The great crisis came in 1926 with a 9 day general strike, which began in the coal industry. The public at large did not support the strike. Volunteers pitched in to sustain vital services. The government showed restraint and there was no widespread violence. The strike played out, but 1927 saw legislation restricting union activity.

World production and trade had returned to prewar levels by 1925, but 1929's "Black Friday" in the United States signalled an international depression. The Bank of England almost failed in 1931, requiring loans from American banks to keep it afloat. A "national" government replaced the second Labour ministry in the time of crisis. Ramsay MacDonald (Labour) remained as prime minister, but Tories held the majority of cabinet posts, and England was treated to an election in which the Labour leader fought on the Tory side against Labour and the Liberals. Unemployment reached 3 million in 1933. (In the previous year, 22% of the world's industrial labour force was unemployed. German unemployment stood at 6 million.)

The aftermath of the war to make the world safe for democracy proved an unhappy time for democratic forces in Europe. First Lenin, then Stalin, in the Soviet Union pointed the way to the totalitarian police state under a dictator with a political cabal, styled a "party," constituting a sort of state within the state. Italy, Germany, Spain, and much of the rest of Europe adopted this model to various degrees as liberal democratic institutions floundered in the face of the world economic crisis. The rise to power of Hitler and the Nazi (National Socialist) party in Germany (1933) proved to be the crux. Hitler was quite open about his goals. He regarded Germany's pre-1914 borders as too restrictive, let alone the Versailles boundaries! And his murderous antisemitism was a foundation of Nazi doctrine. The Weimar Republic had begun with hope under the Social Democrats and the Catholic Center Party. But the center was eroded by the ruinous inflation of 1923 (a mark exchanged at 65 to the dollar in 1921 dropped to 4.2 trillion to the dollar!), and by pressure from left and right. Germany had been admitted to the League, but Hitler took it out and renounced the Versailles treaty. (Japan also left the League and began the conquest of China.) There had been hope that the Locarno Treaty of 1925 had solved Europe's postwar security problems. The hope was vain.

As early as 1935, confronted by Germany's rearmament program Britain increased defense estimates by 40%. Defense estimates were raised in succeeding years but still came only to about 25% of the German armaments budget. Providentially, much of the new British expenditure went to the development and production of advanced fighter aircraft, so that by 1940, 608 of the superb Hawker Hurricanes and Supermarine Spitfires were in service. Some of the army equipment included tanks that were too slow and lightly armed and armored to face the German models. The Navy was better served, but some of the admirals failed to appreciate the danger from the air (not a uniquely British failing!).

Historians note that the European powers frequently acted in concert during the 1920's to secure the peace. But during the 1930's this cooperative spirit began to flag, and particularly the dictatorships began to engage in overtly hostile and provocative acts. It is sometimes said that leaders in the democracies did not recognize the danger posed by Hitler, and some did not. It might be more accurate to say that the danger was recognized but either leaders were not sure what to do, or they were unable to coordinate their actions. Scarred by the Great War, who among them had the stomach for a challenge that might touch off another general European conflagration? Yet when Austrian Nazis attempted a coup in 1934, murdering Chancellor Dollfuss, France and England warned against German intervention. Mussolini supported them by mobilizing along the Austro-Italian frontier. Hitler held his public peace and Anschluss was postponed. But a year later when Mussolini made unprovoked war on Ethiopia and Britain took strong measures, France abstained. The League of Nations failed to act and from that moment was morally if not physically dead. Then when Hitler defied the Versailles agreements and moved troops into the neutralized Rhineland, Britain was luke-warm to French appeals. The German forces apparently had orders to withdraw if militarily opposed. The hard lesson is that Hitler might have been stopped and peace preserved by resolute action in time. There were powerful quarters in Germany, especially in the military, who were at best dubious of Hitler. But their doubts were disarmed if not dissipated as the little Austrian's charismatic intuition proved itself time and time again. The balance of history shifted progressively against peace and against the democracies.

Britain enjoyed the respite of a royal celebration, a royal funeral and a royal crisis before the impending storm broke. King Geroge V celebrated his silver jubilee in 1935. The economy was on an upturn and the National Government took advantage of good spirits to call and win an early election. This time a Tory, Stanley Baldwin, organized the government, for MacDonald was ill. But it was still called a "National" government. Then in January, 1936, King George died and his eldest son ascended the throne as Edward VIII.

Edward had been a popular Prince of Wales in Britain, in the Commonwealth and Empire, and much of the world at large. But the prince had lost his heart to Mrs. Wallis Warfield Simpson, an American lady who was not once but twice divorced. The Church of England had not been notoriously moralistic for quite a long time, particularly where royal morals were concerned. But it drew the line at remarriage after divorce, particularly where a future queen was concerned. A preponderance of the national leadership (Prime Minister Baldwin adamantly so) and a good proportion of the public shared this view. Only Mr. Churchill among prominent national leaders supported the king, an act of loyalty that did not enhance his popularity during those "wilderness years." (Churchill had been promised but never given cabinet posts since the end of his tenure at the Exchequer, where many regarded his performance as lacking. He was still dogged by the ghosts of Gallipoli, and his increasingly outspoken warnings about the dangers of Hitler's Germany caused some to regard him as a warmonger.) The reign that began with such high hopes in January ended in December with an abdication speech broadcast by radio to the nation. King Edward VIII became the Duke of Windsor and Mrs. Simpson his duchess. His shy younger brother, the Duke of York, became George VI. Historians and biographers offer differing judgments concerning the sort of king Edward might have been, and what sort of queen the Duchess, particularly during wartime. The truth is that no one can know. We can only know what in fact happened. George shouldered every burden, faced every challenge that duty pressed upon him, proving a stalwart wartime sovereign. He was accompanied to the throne and sustained upon it by a splendid Queen, later the beloved "Queen Mum," Elizabeth. With George safely crowned, Baldwin retired and Neville Chamberlain assumed leadership.

England's interlude of domestic crisis did not interrupt the world slide toward chaos. 1936-37 saw the Axis alliance between Germany, Italy and Japan emerge, initially as an anti-Bolshevik coalition. The Spanish civil war broke out in 1936, and soon Italy and Germany were assisting Franco's fascists, utilizing the conflict as a proving ground for their military equipment. Japan launched her undeclared war on China in 1937 and in 1938 Hitler initiated a series of moves that enhanced his advantage when war came. First he achieved <u>Anschluss</u> (union) with Austria by the simple expedient of military occupation, an act welcomed by Austria's large Nazi movement. The Western powers were docile. Then Hitler demanded that Czecholslovakia hand over to Germany the Sudentenland with its large ethnic German population—and the mountains which constituted central and eastern Euorope's natural bulwark against the southern invasion route. Russia and France were guarantors of Czech security. But when Britain, France, Italy and Germany met to negotiate in Munich, neither Russia nor the Czechs were invited. Hitler claimed that if he got the Sudentenland he wanted nothing more, and he got it. So "Munich" becamed the crowning symbol of the policy of appeasement, of buying peace by feeding Hitler's insatiable imperial appetite. Chamberlain came home to a hero's welcome, claiming "peace with honour," and "peace in our time." Then in March, 1939, the German army gobbled up what was left of Czechoslovakia.

Western flaccidity and the changed strategic situation convinced the Soviet Union that their best hope lay in an accomodation with Hitler. The Molotov-Ribbentrop pact was concluded in August, 1939, clearing the last obstacle to Hitler's designs on Poland. It included a secret agreement to partition Poland. It also included an arrangement under which Russia sold substantial quantitites of raw materials to Germany, which helped undergird the invasion of France and still later, Hitler's invasion of Russia.

The H. A. Mason Era (1917-1940)

The first meeting of the United Parishes was held on 7 November, 1917, with Mr. Mason in the chair. The Rev. C. C. Collins had retired from the incumbency of St. Mary, Aldermanbury, on 15 August, 1917, after 63 years of service to the parish. He died on 30 December, 1917.

The Rev. W. Kingston who had served as curate for 18 months by arrangement with Collins claimed compensation for loss of employment, but the Vestry claimed no power to act. The Vicar reported that he and the churchwardens had the matter of "encroachment" upon the churchyard on the north side "in hand."

On 31 August, 1918, a plan to refurbish the church, delayed "due to the Kaiser," was submitted by architect W. D. Caroe. It included leveling the floors; moving the pews from St. Alphage; and fitting the chapel for private prayer with a screen, sixteen chairs and the reredos from St. Alphage. The estimated expense was £1887 (CC File 67141:23234 6/8). On 25 November, 1918, Mr. Mason submitted a request to the Church Commissioners for a grant of £1,000 to repair the church. He pointed out that St. Mary, Aldermanbury, was one of Wren's finest parish churches and that it could become "a great centre for Church life in the very heart of the City." The request of £1,000 was based on the fact that the Commissioners held property in the parish which once had belonged to the church, from which they received large sums.

A "Church Statistics" report prepared by Mr. Mason for the 1918 calendar year claimed that 252 services had been held in the church, with 2007 in attendance at morning services and 6650 at evening services (including 5067 at the Friday weekly service and organ recital). Collections were 180.18.0. Weekday visitors totalled 8221, with 19,548 visitors to the churchyard at dinner hour.

At a meeting on 24 April, 1919, church collections of £252.3.10 between April 1918 and April 1919, were reported. This compares to offerings of £19 in 1916, 51 in 1917, and 74 in 1918. Expenditures were to the Hospital Sunday fund and other charities and for communion wine.

In February, 1919, a letter was sent from Mr. Mason, the churchwardens, and a series of businesses in the parish to solicit support for a scheme to restore the Church of the United Benefices as a Memorial for those fallen in the Late War. The plan (now estimated to cost £3000) would include a chapel with a memorial tablet for men connected with the businesses in the parish who had lost their lives in the Great War. It also noted that the Ecclesiastical Commissioners had promised £500 if the parishoners could raise £2500. The listed businesses included Bradbury Greatorex and Co.; Horrockses, Crewdsen and Co.; Stapley & Smith; W. F. Lucas & Co.; Rylands and Sons, Ltd.; Foster, Porter & Co, Ltd.; and Biddle, Thorne, Welsford & Gait. The letter included a list of subscriptions already totalling £1,492. On 22 May, 1919 Mr. Mason wrote the Church Commissioners to say that funds should be in hand for the refurbishing of the church by the end of the year, despite "strikes and counter strikes" which were delaying the effort. He also noted that his quarterly payment from Parochial Charities had been delayed in coming the last two quarters. (CC 6741).

By April 1921 nearly £5000 had been spent on the project, and £4500 raised. On 30 March, 1921, Pierson Carter resigned after 21 years of service as churchwarden.

Although it was not mentioned in the minutes an effort was mounted in 1920 by the London Churches Commission to demolish nineteen churches, including St. Mary's. A storm of public protest caused the Privy Council to intervene and stop implementation of the plan. In accord with the Plan of Union, St. Alphage, London Wall, was taken down in 1920 (according to Goss 1944: 164) leaving only the vestry room and 14th century tower, as a memorial to the Elsying Spittal hospital (see Ch. 2).

A note in the minutes of the 8 March, 1923, meeting indicated the Vestry had sent a protest to the National Assembly of the Church of England, the Bishop of London, the City Corporation and the press over a plan to close 9 city churches.

An article on St. Mary, Aldermanbury, by Walter G. Bell appeared in The Daily during this period, sixth in a series of articles on "Threatened City Churches." Bell called the Aldermanbury churchyard "a quiet, restful spot, almost a dead end, where there comes only a whispered message of London's ceaseless traffic." He stressed the association of the church with Shakespeare through John Heminge and Henry Condell (see Ch. 3), and also with John Milton (see Ch. 4) and Judge George Jeffreys (see Ch. 6). Although deploring innovators who "replaced almost everything that was movable," he said that St. Mary's still showed the Wren style. "It should be preserved," he said, "because it is a good type." In the current renovation, he reported, wainscoting had been brought from the demolished St. Alphage and the chancel was being restored to more of a Wren-style.

During 1921 receipts totalled £406.10.1. Attendance at morning services totalled 1,782 and at evening 10,074 (8355 of which were participants in a Friday evening dinner hour). In addition, over 14,000 persons visited the church and over 43,000 the gardens. The next year receipts were down £100, attendance at 220 services was 1,560 in the morning and 8,845 in the evening (7,223 at the Friday dinner and organ recital). Weekday visitations numbered 7700 and 59,275 visited the gardens.

On 1 May 1922, the final record of the Church Restoration and Chapel Memorial Fund was given. £4,869 had been raised from donations and £550 from the Ecclesiastical Commission. During 1922 attendance at 157 services was 1,032 in the morning and 6,350 in the evenings (4,945 at the Friday Dinner Hour), with 6,004 weekday visitors and 43,461 to the gardens.

A service held on 21 April, 1923, attended by the Archbishop of Canterbury, the Lord Mayor, Sheriffs, the Dean of St. Paul's, and the American ambassador, commemorated the 300th anniversary of the First Shakespeare folio.

On 22 July, 1923, the Vestry Clerk reported that although most of the parish deeds had been transferred to the Guildhall Library, many of the old Vestry records were in the safe in the church. Fortunately for us, because of the risk of fire or burglary, the Vestry agreed to return them to the Guildhall Library.

During 1923 attendance at 179 services was 2,045 at morning services and 6,457 at evening (5,264 on Fridays) with 8,196 visitors to the church and 49,806 to the churchyard.

During 1924 a "Light and Air" Committee was created to consider sale of the St. Alphage, London Wall, site, to Higgs and Hill, Ltd. with a guarantee that the height of any buildings to be erected would not cause too many problems. Also in 1924 a new survey of parish bounds was completed and a perambulation ordered.

The Vestry Room at St. Alphage, London Wall, was now being used as a rest room during the dinner hour for young women employed in the city as "a little bit of social work," the minutes suggested on 8 April, 1924. At this meeting Rev. Mason reported on yet another threat to close churches and the need for a piano for the choir and a screen for the chancel.

On 31 March, 1925, the Vestry complained that the allocation from the Charities Commission to St. Mary for church expenses and the fabric fund was "wholly insufficient" due to the increase in expenses in the last 30 years. The Rector and Churchwardens were instructed to approach the Trustees of the Commission to ask for an increase. At the same meeting the Vestry voted £62 for the St. Paul's restoration fund.

During 1924 £288.15.5 was collected. Attendance at 168 services was 1683 in the mornings and 5,682 in the evenings (3,583 on Fridays). There were 8176 visitors to the church during the week and 51,763 to the churchyard. The 29 May, 1924 Ascension Day perambulation found 71 boundary markers for Aldermanbury, 46 inside buildings and 25 outside. One was in the Guildhall over the Judge's seat. Another was in a lavatory, and a third was fixed on a basement ceiling.

On 16 March, 1926 a 250th Anniversary Service for the Wren fabric of St. Mary, Aldermanbury, was discussed. It was also reported that the clock, which had worked since 1808, had been repaired. A strip of land from the church property had been designated for the widening of Aldermanbury, the Ecclesiastical Commission reported. Collections for 1925 were at £343, and attendance for 148 services at 1,396 mornings and 5695 evenings (3,742 Fridays). Visitors numbered 7,683 to the church and 51,244 to the gardens.

On 31 March, 1927, it was reported that 200 people attended the 250th Anniversary Service. A formal resolution was adopted stating that "the time has long since arrived when an increase in existing grants for maintenance and fabric funds should be made" and was forwarded to the Charities Commission. A 1926 collection of £306, and attendance of 1,581 and 5,081 (3,446 Fridays) was reported. Visitors numbered 8,218 to the church and 57,375 to the gardens. In his "annual statement" Rev. Mason called the general strike "folly" and laid it on the coal miners especially. He praised the actions of the House of Commons to reject a plan to close churches.

On 23 March, 1928, the rector reported that the Ecclesiastical Commission claimed not to be in a position to increase the grant to St. Mary's. He said he would apply directly to the Bishop. The 1927 report showed a collection of £328, attendance of 1945 at morning services and 6,010 evenings (2,911 Fridays). There had been 10,271 daily visitors and 66,328 to the Gardens. The next year collections dipped below £300 and attendance was 2,043 mornings and 4,539 evenings (2,879 Fridays), with vistors at 10,617 and 68,998. In his annual statement in 1929 Mason explained a Vestry decision to reduce donations to the diocesan fund in light of the inability of the Ecclesiastical Commission to increase the grants.

On 21 March, 1930, the Vestry learned that Piersen Carter had died during the previous year. Rev. Mason also reported progress in the efforts to raise the allowance. Collections were back up to £319, and attendance to 2,159 mornings and 4,134 evenings (with 2,598 on Fridays). There were 8,499 and 57,229 visitors. The next year collections fell to £274, and attendance was at 2,499 mornings and 3,858 evenings (2,346 Fridays), with 9,629 and 75,641 visitors.

In his pastoral letter for 1931 Mr. Mason noted that 1930 was one of the most disheartening years ever for London. He suggested that "if England itself could be rid of slums, overcrowding, gambling and drink and kindred evils it would be in a stronger position to give a lead to the world ... ." He expressed gratitude for his recovery from a long and serious illness and the hope that he would be able to add to his 57 years as a clergyman and 17 as a City Rector. In 1931 1,011 attended morning services and 3,700 evening (including 1819 at the Friday dinner hour). 9,483 used the church on weekdays and 52,805 visited the gardens. Receipts from services totalled £242.

In a study of churches in the South London borough of Lambeth between 1870 and 1930, Jeffrey Cox has made some observations which apply equally to Aldermanbury. Until the mid-19th century the Church of England and the nonconformist communions were deeply engaged in ministry to the poor and working classes. They had created a "vast parochial and philanthropic network which provided the sacraments and social services to the working classes and the poor" (Cox 1982: 6). The churches were the best hope of bridging the gap between classes. The real decline in churchgoing and associated piety appears to have begun in the 1880's and accelerated at the turn of the century. Government and private agencies were providing the social services, leaving churches with little to do and less to say (273). The churches participated in their dismantling because they realized that others could provide the services better than they. However, the result was a terribly weakened church, increasingly turned inward, focusing on denominational structure and church union (275-276).

During 1932 Rev. Mason suffered another long illness, and the Vestry praised Mrs. Mason for carrying on in his place. Improvements to the Vestry Room were noted. Receipts were down to £242. Attendance at services was 1,011 mornings and 3,700 evenings (1,819 Fridays), with 9,483 and 52,805 weekday visitors.

At the 24 March, 1933, meeting two representatives of the Parochial Church Council were present and 17 representatives to the Parochial Church Council were elected. Receipts had fallen further to £218 and attendance was 1,162 in the morning and 3,673 in the evening (2,009 Fridays), with 8,734 and 43,100 weekday visitors.

Excursus: The Inns of Aldermanbury

In 1932 or 1933 the Axe Inn of Aldermanbury closed its doors for the last time. Thus ended a 500 year tradition of such establishments in the parish. As we have noted throughout the narrative, the Axe and other Aldermanbury inns, taverns, and coffeehouses were often the places for parish meetings and celebrations. Several of the establishments associated with Aldermanbury were on the boundaries of the parish: the Swan with two Necks Coaching Inn (see Figures 6.3 and 6.4) and Baptisthead or Aldermanbury Coffeehouse on the southwest, and Ye Old Cheshire Cheese Hotel to the west. However, two inns were in the heart of the parish. This seems an appropriate point for a retrospective on these two long-lived parish institutions.

Axe Inn. The oldest of the Aldermanbury inns was the Axe. It was located on east side of Aldermanbury, with an entrance from the street between what was to become No. 20 and 21 after the Great Fire. The first documented references to it come in a 1359 in a reference to a sale of the Inn of Aldermanbury and a chantry in St. Mary's (see Ch. 2).

The first reference to the sign of the axe came in a note from the Brewers Company accounts which refers to the "Ax yn Aldermannebury" (cited in Goss 1944: 134). The derivation of the Axe sign is unknown, although it may relate to the arms of the Cooper's Company, two crossed axes.

The Axe Inn served travelers, functioning as a place of lodging and departure for travelers on their way to or from the north, particularly Liverpool. A 1584 deed lists "roomes, buildings, yardes, barnes, stables and hayloftes" (Goss 1944: 135). In its heyday it was a galleried inn, similar to the present George Inn, the only remaining such structure (located south of the Thames, near London Bridge Station, and now a part of the National Historic Trust). It had an "arched entrance, leading to a courtyard, around which the rooms and offices formed the four sides of the square" (Goss 1944: 135). Warehouses for goods and stables for horses, coaches, and wagons completed the complex.

Perhaps John Heminges and Henry Condell brought their friend William Shakespeare to the Axe while Shakespeare lived in the neighborhood between about 1598 and 1614 (see Ch. 3).

The first regular wagon service to Liverpool was established from the Axe Inn in 1630 (Goss 1944: 135).

One legendary traveler who apparently frequented the Inn was "Dapper Dick" Brathwaite (also known as "Drunken Barnabee"). However, Dick must have worn out his welcome at the Axe. In Barnabee's Journal the following rhyme is found (Goss 1944: 136):

Country left, I in a fury
To the Axe in Aldermanbury
First arriv'd, that place slighted
I at the Rose in Holborn lighted.

In the years before the Great Fire the Axe was one of the most popular coaching inns in the City. It was rebuilt after the Fire, apparently in 1670, before the first stones were laid for the Church. By 1681 it was capable of holding well over a hundred guests.

With the growth of the soft goods trade in the parish the Inn became "an important meeting place for wool merchants" (Goss 1944: 137). The Axe continued as an Inn until 1844, when the site became too valuable to continue to serve as a tavern. The once large coaching inn was reduced to a public house, inhabiting a corner of the original property, in Three Nun Court. The rest was turned into warehouse and showroom space. The sign of the Axe, twenty-one miniature axes and a large diagonal axe on a dark red field, with the motto "In hoc signo spes mea" was finally removed with the closing of the pub in 1932.

The Chartered Insurance Institute was opened on the site of the once thriving inn on 28 June, 1934. The shape of the building's outline was almost identical to the plan of the Inn after the Great Fire.

George Inn was located (according to the Ogilby and Morgan map of 1677) to the north of Axe Inn, behind nos. 22-24 Aldermanbury, with an entrance off George Yard, just south of no. 22. The Inn had originally been called Bassett's Inn, named after the owners of the property in the 13th Century. Like the Axe Inn, Bassett's was apparently a converted mansion house (Goss 1944: 138). According to a 1591 entry in the court books of the Merchant Taylor's Company it belonged to the Company, which held ownership until 1661 (139). After its destruction in the Great Fire, Bassett's Inn was caught up in litigation and was not rebuilt until at least 1677. By 1720 it had become known as the George Inn, probably in recognition of the first Hanoverian king, George I. It passed again to the Merchant Taylor's Company who apparently owned it until its demise in the late 19th century.

This old George Inn figured in the life of the parish. The Churchwarden Accounts reflect meetings there, the saddest of which was an inquest into the death of Samuel and Frances Holden, who were found with their throats slit in the Vestry in 1835.

After 1834 the establishment was known as George Inn and Hotel. In 1862 it was called simply the George Hotel. In the mid 1800's it was used by carriers for conveying goods to and from the railways. A tap was put in the hotel in 1840, and the then proprietress acquired part of the Axe Inn property for the purpose. The George Hotel was finally closed in 1892, another victim of the declining residential population in the parish.

The H. A. Mason Era (continued)

At the 1934 meeting attendance at services was reported as 1,291 mornings and 3,595 evenings (1,214 on Fridays). Visitors numbered 9,243 and 57,375. A note showed that the St. Alphage Vestry Room was still being used as a dinner hour rest room for women. An extant bulletin (see Figure 8.4) identifies the Dinner Hour Service on Friday, May 18th, 1934, from 1:15 to 1:45 p.m. as the 753rd such program. The service included prayers framing a series of solos and organ pieces. Notes on the borders of the bulletin note that the church is open daily between 11:00 a.m. and 2:30 p.m. for prayer, rest, and meditation, with books provided for reading. "Try and come in sometimes," it says; "It will help you!" Those in attendance are asked to ask other people to come to our "happy Service" that the church may be full. A donation of 20/- is suggested as "very acceptable.

According to Noel Mander, during the 1930's the church was open on weekdays from 7:00 a.m. so that workers who had come into the City early to take advantage of cheaper fares would have a place to stay until their places of work opened.

From 1934-37 Fred Turnbull was a member of the boy's choir, which sang for services (Turnbull 1992). He was eleven when he joined the choir. The boys came from Thomas Street School in East London. Turnbull reports that at most services the choir and the clergy and officers of the church were the only people present. He said a policeman might sometimes venture in or a tourist or two, but there was no congregation in the parish left. No services at all were held for six weeks during the Summer, and Evensong was suspended from Autumn until Lent. The highlight of the year, according to Turnbull, was the Harvest Festival, held on a Wednesday in the Fall. A large loaf was placed on the altar during the service and Turnbull often took it home after the Festival. Turnbull also remembers walking through Guildhall to "beat the bounds" of the parish on Ascension Day.

On 12 April, 1935, Mrs. Grace May Mason was present as a representative of the Parochial Church Council. She was also elected Churchwarden, the first woman to be elected to this office in the history of the Church. Collections of £239 were reported and attendance at services for 1934 was 1,243 mornings and 3,346 evenings (1,140 Fridays), with 9,369 and 54,562 visitors. The next year receipts were down to £154 and attendance to 1,665 mornings and 2,657 evenings (1,311 Fridays). There were still 7,947 and 58,011 visitors. For 1936 services the collection was £203, but attendance was 1,319 mornings and 3036 evenings (1,070 Fridays). Vistors were 10,779 and 44,390.

The last entry in the minute books was 8 April, 1938. A note in another manuscript (3750a/1) dated 5 November, 1941, says that the minutes for 1939 and 1940 were removed for copying. Apparently, they were never replaced.

On 24 October, 1938, the City Parochial Charities awarded the church a grant of £150 toward £160 in repairs. Mr. Mason had appealed that "the parish is in such a way financially it's absolutely impossible to ask for help." On 14 February, 1939, another £30 was awarded toward what was now a total of £250 in repairs.

On 4 September, 1939, Mr. Mason, who had served as Vicar of the United Benefices of St. Mary, Aldermanbury, and St. Alphage, London Wall, since the union in 1917, died. G. F. Saymell was appointed to succeed Mason. However, in a letter now in the Church Commissioners files (CC 67141) Mr. Saymell said that when he had accepted the appointment of the Lord Chancellor to the United Benefices he did not realize that the stipend had been reduced by £400 (£150 from the income of St. Alphage for St. Alphage, Hendon and the £250 grant from Parochial Charities) and that he would have to reconsider. He apparently withdrew.

A note in the City Press, dated 26 January, 1940, entitled "A Famous City Parish: The Story of St. Mary, Aldermanbury" recounted the illustrious history of the church and announced that on 8 February, the Rev. Phillip Davenport Ellis (curate of St. Botolph's Bishopgate) would become the Vicar of St. Mary Aldermanbury as part of his appointment to the United Benefices. His stipend was to be £990, less the £150 for St. Alphage, Hendon. The continuation of the £250 which had been paid to Mason in lieu of the stipend from parish properties continued as a source of dispute (CC 67141).

World War II (1939-1945)

World War II began for Europe on 1 September, 1939. After years of appeasement when every advantage was frittered away, Britain and France began in the Spring of 1939 to offer assurances to Poland and to other states threatened by Germany and Italy. Now German forces rolled into Poland, and England and France took their stand. Hitler was told to withdraw or face the consequences. The Panzers pushed deeper into Poland. Chamberlain, the former arch appeaser, went on the radio to tell the British people they were at war on 3 September, and France followed suit.

In the east, Germany introduced the world to Blitzkrieg. Tactical aircraft struck both military and civilian targets while columns of tanks and motorized infantry broke through static defenses and exploited their penetration in depth. Poland's hope of a stand in the east was crushed on 17 September when Soviet forces swept in to claim their share of a dismembered nation. Hitler made some peace overtures to Britain, but they came too late. Nothing much happened in the west through the winter. Wags spoke of the "phoney war" and "Sitzkrieg." France and Britain stood on the defensive, conceding the initiative to Hitler. In the east, the Soviets fought a dishonorable war with tiny Finland and occupied the Baltic states of Lithuania, Estonia, and Latvia.

Germany invaded Denmark in April 1940, and beat the British in a race to occupy Norway. Public and parliamentary sentiment had turned heavily against Chamberlain. He was seen both as a symbol of appeasement and as inept in organizing the war effort. Winston Churchill had been brought into the government at his old World War I post of First Lord of the Admiralty with war impending. On 10 May, Churchill answered the call to Buckingham palace and replaced Chamberlain. Churchill was able to bring Labour and the Liberals into a genuine war coalition. John Churchill, Duke of Marlborough, had been Britain's greatest soldier. In Winston Churchill the country gained its greatest civilian war leader. And none too soon! German forces slashed into the Low Countries on the day Churchill became prime minister.

The German attack, as in 1914, avoided a direct assault on the fortified Franco-German frontier, defended on the French side by the formidable Maginot Line. But the 1940 plan was no mere replay of 1914. The initial thrust was designed to draw allied forces northward while the main blow struck through the Ardennes and into the heart of France. Both attacks went well. Holland collapsed. Rotterdam, an "open city," was pulverized by merciless air attacks. Tactical air units were turned upon columns of civilian refugees creating carnage and chaos. The main attack swept aside inadequate French defenses. Once more there was a race to the sea which the Germans won in record time—five days. Then the Blitzkrieg turned north to trap and eliminate the British Expeditionary Force. The British fought their way to the beach at Dunkerque where one of the greatest rescues in the history of warfare was executed. The Royal Air Force was able for the first time to establish air superiority while 200 Royal Navy vessels and a curious assortment of volunteer craft picked 338,000 British and French troops off the beach and ferried them safely to England. But all equipment had to be abandoned. For a perilous period the army had little more to defend against a threatened German invasion than empty beer bottles. At this juncture, the United States made available most of its inventory of World War I rifles, machine guns and artillery pieces. These began to reach Britain in quantity during July, and were rapidly distributed. This major breach of American neutrality, which Germany prudently ignored, would be followed by the sale of fifty old destroyers which Britain desperately needed for convoy escorts, the Lend-Lease program (which obviated the debt problem of 1914-18), and more energetic American naval activity in the western Atlantic. But the American congress and people were not prepared to actually go to war. The U. S. military conscription program barely survived a congressional vote as late as the autumn of 1941. The collapse and surrender of France had left Britain to face the mighty Nazi war machine alone. The Hitler regime floated peace feelers, but the Churchill government stood firm.

German armies were arrayed along the French coast. Long range German artillery could fire across the straits of Dover. German aircraft could fly the short route from French bases, while RAF Bomber Command had to fly a much greater distance against Germany. The emergency American arms shipments made Britain look less naked to invasion, but Operation Sea Lion (as the planned invasion was called) was more than just a gleam in Hitler's eye. British schemes to repel the attack went forward as Germany set the stage for the assault. The key to the whole matter was in the air. The Luftwaffe had to gain control of the sky over Britain, above all to crush RAF Fighter Command, for an invasion to succeed. 8 August, 1940, is generally given for the onset of the Battle of Britain, the aerial struggle that could lead to either a German victory or the prolongation of the war and perchance an eventual German defeat. German attacks were directed against British communications and defenses and, above all, RAF fighter bases. Britain had resisted desparate French appeals to expend her Hurricanes and Spitfires after all was lost on the continent. The wisdom of that course was demonstrated as, day after day, outnumbered British squadrons rose against the German bombers and their Messerschmitt 109 escorts. Clearly, the Hurricanes and Spitfires were making a good account of themselves. The RAF thought that they had a 3-1 kill ratio, and some historians have reported so. But Churchill (1949:339) notes that Luftwaffe records showed 1,733 aircraft losses (against British claims of 2,693), while 915 RAF planes were lost or damaged beyond repair between 10 July and 31 October, 1940. The most desperate day was 15

September. Every unit in Fighter Command was engaged against massive German attacks. There was no reserve left, not even to fly cover when planes landed to refuel and rearm. British losses were under 40 at the end of the day, German losses 56 (with 183 claimed). Bomber Command struck back at potential invasion port facilities. Churchill wrote that 15 September was the turning point (1949:337). Two days later, Hitler put Sea Lion on indefinite hold and in the spring of 1942 it was finally cancelled. Some military experts believe that if the Luftwaffe had concentrated its full resources against Fighter Command and continued the pressure longer, Germany might have won the Battle of Britain. But at the end of October the daylight raids and with them the aerial war of attrition ended.

The Battle of Britain gave way to the Blitz. The air war itself was far from over. For the civilian population of Britain, and later that of Germany, it had only begun. The Luftwaffe turned to night raids, making the task of defense more difficult. City after city felt the lash of the German aerial juggernaut. British civilian air raid deaths totalled 23,767 in 1940 and 20,881 in 1941. Raids diminished to a relative trickle after Hitler invaded Russia and improved British antiaircraft and night fighter capability took an ever larger toll of raiders. Deaths fell to 3,236 in 1942 and 2,367 in 1943. Things might have been even worse but for what Mr. Churchill called the "Wizard War." British scientific intelligence and technical development managed to thwart German radio navigation to the point that perhaps only 20% of German bombs struck their intended targets. British cryptographers also cracked the German codes so that in due course British intelligence was reading all enemy mail, including Luftwaffe radio communications.

St. Mary, Aldermanbury and the Second Great Fire of London (29 December, 1940)

Greater London was a frequent target of the nighttime raids, especially the East End, with its strategic docks. Nor was the historic square mile City of London to be spared. On the evening of Sunday, 29 December, 1940, the Luftwaffe's attempt to undermine British morale through firebombing raids on civilian targets in London began. The raid was in retaliation for British raids on German cities, including Berlin, on 20 December, and was planned with demonic thoroughness. The Thames was at record lows and the attack was timed to coincide with low tide so pumping from the river to fight fires would be difficult. Special high explosive devices designed to fracture water mains were dropped early in the raid. Elite pathfinders struck first, igniting fires to guide the main waves of bombers. The attack was to be a two-stage affair. First came a massive fire raid, raining 20,000 incendiary bombs on the City. There was to be a second assault with high explosive bombs, targeted on the fires. Fortunately for the City worsening weather caused the German command to cancel the second phase of the attack.

What happened was bad enough. Massive fires raged around Cheapside, near St. Paul's, and in the Barbican. A shortage of water, men, and equipment forced the difficult decision to let the Barbican burn and concentrate efforts to the south where something might be saved. At about 6:45 p.m. the Church of St. Mary, the Virgin, Aldermanbury exploded in fire as the result of a direct hit from a German incendiary bomb. Thanks to the heroic efforts of fire watchers, St. Paul's Cathedral was spared (though it was hit), but the neighborhood around Aldermanbury was totally devastated. There were no fire spotters assigned to the City churches because of a shortage of manpower. In a few hours thirteen Wren churches, including St. Mary, Aldermanbury and the neighboring St. Alban, Wood Street, St. Lawrence Jewry, and Saint Vedast alias Foster were destroyed. The old Gothic St. Giles Cripplegate had escaped the Great Fire of 1666, but this time its luck ran out. The wood roofs of the old churches made them fire traps waiting to be sprung. Although the small incendiary bombs which landed on the ground could be easily extinguished with sand, when they hit the churches' roofs they caused the structures to burst almost immediately into flame. 163 people had been killed in the raid and over 500 injured.

The next morning only the gutted and blackened shell of the Church of St. Mary, Aldermanbury, and its columns stood. All the furnishings had been destroyed, including the rare 17th century church chest and an elegant pair of chancel chairs. The wine in the communion vessels was crystalized by the intense heat. The tower was intact except for the turret and vane. The charred stubs of a few oak beams balanced grotesquely atop Wren's elegant interior columns.

A young soldier named Noel Mander, home on leave, had volunteered as a fire warden on that fateful night. He described his experience that night in this way (Mander 1982):

> I spent the night in Gresham St. in the city. We couldn't do
> anything because the water mains had all been fractured,
> and the river was so low, record low, they couldn't suck
> water up from there. They could do little, very little.

> Unfortunately, the churches were all locked, so we couldn't get into them and I saw that night St. Mary, Aldermanbury; St. Vedast-alias-Foster, my own church - I saw them all burn, and it was a sensation that I will never forget - hearing the bells fall down the tower, hearing the organs burn, because the hot air blowing through the organ pipes almost sounded as if the poor old organs were shrieking in agony in their destruction.

The rest of the parish was in total ruins. Only about ten business houses and the newly-erected Chartered Insurance Institute remained, and they were badly gutted (Goss 1944: 127). Cecil Brown's "balloon view", Devastated London, is a cumulative picture of war damage in the City (Hyde 1990). But most of the ruin traces to that single dreadful night, properly remembered as "The Second Great Fire of London."

Conclusion

This chapter has covered the period between the St. Mary's parishoners' loss of control of their parish property in 1887 and the destruction of the church building in a German bombing raid on 29 December, 1940. Even though the increasing centralization of church bureaucracy and the changing nature of the Aldermanbury neighborhood took its toll on the parishoners, they refused to accept what many considered inevitable: the destruction of the Wren building. They fought to survive and to maintain a viable ministry for the parish, and impartial observers would judge their efforts successful. Because of its historical significance and architectural beauty, Vicar C. C. Collins and the vast majority of St. Mary's parishoners resisted any plan for a merger of parishes in which the Church of St. Mary would be destroyed. When an Act of Parliament mandated the union of London parishes, the parishoners accepted a plan for merger with St. Alphage, London Wall, which allowed for the Aldermanbury building to survive. The merger took place in 1917. The united parishes continued to hold regular Sunday worship services and conducted innovative weekday programs for city workers. When the church was left in ruins by a Nazi incendiary bomb, a new incumbent had just been selected and the parishoners were looking to the future. However, the events of 29 December, 1940, sealed the fate of St. Mary, Aldermanbury, as a parish church in London.

The fabric of the Church of St. Mary, the Virgin, Aldermanbury, continued to stand in London for another twenty-seven years while church and civic authorities tried to decide the fate of the blitzed Wren churches. Before any decisions could be made, however, there was, of course, a war to be fought and won. We will turn in the next chapter to the story of the rest of the War and its aftermath, after the destruction of St. Mary, Aldermanbury, and the intriguing tale of how the Phoenix of Aldermanbury once more rose from the ashes.

Bibliography

Barker, Felix and Peter Jackson
    1990   The History of London in Maps. London: Barrie and Jenkins.

Carter, Pierson Cathrick
    1913   History of the Church and Parish of St. Mary the Virgin, Aldermanbury. London: W. H. and L. Collinbridge.

Churchill, Winston S.
    1948-53   The Second World War. Boston: Houghton Mifflin.

City Press
    1904   "The Threatened City Church. St. Mary the Virgin, Aldermanbury. Strong Speech by the Rector," The City Press (April 23).

Clarke, H. W.
    1898   The City Churches. London: Simpkin Marshall.

Cox, Jeffrey
    1982   The English Churches in a Secular Society, Lambeth, 1870-1930. New York: Oxford.

Goss, Charles
    1944   "A History of The Parish of St. Mary the Virgin, Aldermanbury," Transactions of the London and Middlesex Archaeological Society. 9 (1944-47), 113-164.

Hyde, Ralph, ed.
    1990   Devastated London: The Bombed City as Seen from a Barrage Balloon. London: The London Topographical Society. Publication #142.

Johnson, David
    1980   The City Ablaze. The Second Great Fire of London-29th December, 1940. London: William Kimber.

London Topographical Society
   no date   City of London, showing Parish Boundaries prior to the Union of Parishes Act, 1907.

Laxton, Paul, ed.
    1985   The A to Z of Regency London. Lympne Castle, Kent: Harry Margary (in association with Guildhall Library, London).

Mander, Noel
    1982   Interview with Warren Hollrah. Winston Churchill Memorial. Fulton, Missouri. September, 1982.

Stevenson, John, ed.
    1977   London in the Age of Reform (1850-1950). Oxford: Blackwell.

Tuchman, Barbara W.
    1962   The Guns of August. New York: Macmillan.

Turnbull, Fred
    1992   Interview with the authors. 4 April.

CHAPTER NINE: FROM THE ASHES AGAIN (1941 -)

Introduction

After the destruction of the Church of St. Mary, Aldermanbury, by a German incendiary bomb early in World War II, the ruins of the church remained untouched for over a quarter century (see Figure 9.4). The construction in the area after the War focused on the Guildhall and other buildings of the Corporation of London, and the redeveloped Barbican. By the mid-1960's, a tree growing inside the church had attained a height of thirty feet. The Parish of Aldermanbury was combined with a dozen other ancient parishes into the United Parishes of London, with services held in the Church of St. Vedast, Foster lane. There was no plan to rebuild the church. It was designated a "chapel of ease" of the United Parish for the benefit of those who might want to meditate or pray in a Wren Church open to the sky. Meanwhile, the elements worked their will upon the elegant 17th and 18th century marble monuments in the Church. Their whereabouts today remain a mystery.

Less than a year after the end of the War, Sir Winston Churchill, no longer Prime Minister of Great Britain, responded positively to an invitation extended by Westminster College President Franc "Bullett" McCluer to deliver a lecture at the College in the Green Foundation Lecture Series. A Westminster College alumnus, General Harry Vaughan, was serving as President Harry S Truman's military aide. General Vaughan approached the President with the invitation, and Truman added a handwritten postscript to the letter saying that if Churchill accepted the invitation he would come to Fulton to introduce him.

On 5 March, 1946, Churchill spoke in the Westminster College gymnasium on the topic "The Sinews of Peace" (see Figures 9.1 and 9.2). Churchill urged a scheme for peace through collective security in which the Soviet Union might share if they would. But the basic thrust of the speech was a call for Anglo-American cooperation in order to keep strong the Temple of Peace the two nations had sacrificed to build. In one line in the speech, Churchill vividly described the "iron curtain" descending over Eastern Europe as a result of Soviet domination. He warned of the danger of Soviet expansionism and urged that this recent ally be approached with utmost caution. The speech has been remembered as the "Iron Curtain" address, and during the Cold War was considered as prophetic as Churchill's earlier warnings about the threat posed by Nazi Germany.

This chapter begins with an account of the rest of World War II. We will then survey the life of the Church of St. Mary, Aldermanbury, between the destruction of the building in 1940 until 1960. It then tells the story of how the search by Westminster College leaders for an appropriate memorial to Churchill led them to what Churchill called the "imaginative concept" of restoring the war-damaged Church of St. Mary, Aldermanbury on the Westminster College campus. Once again, the Phoenix of Aldermanbury would arise from the ashes, this time to begin a new life in a new land and become one of the most faithful restorations of Christopher Wren's work anywhere in the world. We will also briefly describe the life of the Church in its new collegiate setting.

War Goes On

New Year's, 1941, brought Britain to the halfway point of its lonely struggle, when, under Winston Churchill's leadership, the United Kingdom held the barricades of humane civilization against Nazi barbarism. Of course, Britain was not <u>entirely</u> alone. The Dominions—Canada, Australia, New Zealand, and South Africa—had proved loyal. The Indian nationalists used Britain's dilemma in an effort to advance their own cause, but Indian troops served well on many fronts. DeGaulle's Free French, refugee Poles, and others were part of the effort. Young American volunteers crossed into Canada to join the Eagle Squadrons. American aid, despite the Neutrality Acts, reached the point of "war in all but name" as American naval patrols with "shoot" orders policed the western Atlantic and American troops moved into Iceland. But the United States did not enter the war officially or fully. And when all qualifications have been stated, Britain bore the brunt.

Few, particularly outside Britain, have realized the price the Churchill government paid for that dogged defense of democracy. The cost in deaths, injuries, lives blighted, is the tragic human side of the story. The economic cost would weigh heavily on Britain's postwar fortunes. British overseas investments were estimated at £3.6 billion ("thousand million") in 1939. Most of this investment was liquidated and used to pay the costs of war, and debt took its place. (A great deal of what was left went to pay the cost of food imports during the difficult years of postwar "austerity.") Gold reserves, foreign exchange reserves and foreign currency holdings were likewise sacrificed. It can be argued that Britain has never fully recovered from this devastating loss of capital, willingly expended in a good cause.

August, 1941, saw Mr. Churchill and the American president, Mr. Roosevelt, meet in a shipboard conference off Newfoundland. They issued the Atlantic Charter with its Five Freedoms, which supplied a noble war platform and admirable postwar objectives. But the United States was still not in the war.

Quite unexpectedly, England got her first effective war ally on 22 June, 1941, when Hitler invaded the Soviet Union. German forces struck to the suburbs of Moscow, but a potential quick victory was botched by dubious tactical moves. Once again the Russian tactic of trading land for time and the severe Russian winter took their toll on an invader. The struggle became known in the Soviet Union as "The Great Patriotic War," as the peoples of Russia, Ukraine, and the other Soviet republics waged a nationalistic crusade for a holy homeland, desecrated by foreign invaders. The eastern front stabilized in the winter of 1942, but the turning point came only in February, 1943, when the German forces at Stalingrad were surrounded and captured. Hitler had refused to admit defeat and forbidden a retreat. From that point onward, the Russian counteroffensive ground westward until Soviet forces met Anglo-American units in 1945. Invading the Soviet Union before settling his accounts in the west must be put down as Hitler's greatest blunder. One may wonder if, without Soviet participation, the western powers could have successfully invaded the continent and brought Germany to terms. Mr. Churchill accurately observed that it was the Russians who "tore the guts" out of the German army.

England got a second major ally on 7 December, 1941, when Japan attacked Pearl Harbor and the U.S. declared war on the Axis powers. Churchill was soon in Washington and a "Europe First" strategy was agreed upon. The first U.S. "Flying Fortress" squadron was in England before the New Year. But the war was going dreadfully. Japanese forces swept the British out of southeast Asia and moved through Burma toward India. The Dutch East Indies fell. U.S. and Philippine forces put up a stubborn but futile fight. Australia was menaced. Yet by late spring the Pacific situation was stabilized. The Japanese were stopped by U.S. carrier forces in the Battle of the Coral Sea in May, 1942. In June the Japanese navy was defeated and turned back with ruinous carrier losses at the Battle of Midway. American forces invaded the Solomon Islands in August. A largely American air, naval, and amphibious war which would bring Japan itself under destructive air and naval attacks and end after the detonation of the first (and hopefully last) two nuclear devices used in warfare. Britain faced a difficult defense of India right down into 1944, and conducted a dramatic operation to recapture Burma in 1945.

Britain and the U.S. created a unified command structure early in the war which facilitated operations. A Combined Chiefs of Staff met in Washington, safely out of reach of German bombers. In each theatre of operations a British or an American officer was named supreme commander, with a deputy from the other nation. National rivalries, personality conflicts and differing strategic and tactical doctrines were not eliminated, but they were kept under control.

RAF Bomber Command launched the strategic air war against Germany in late 1941. Cologne was the first city to be hit by a raiding force of 1,000 aircraft, each carrying an average of three tons of bombs, in a night saturation attack. It would not be the last. By 1943, American heavy bombers were plying their specialty of daylight precision bombing, so that Germany was under "round the clock" aerial assault. Postwar studies indicate that the strategic bombing offensive did not cripple the German war effort to the extent of early estimates. But it did devastate many German cities and reduce many factories to rubble, with heavy civilian casualties. It may also have produced anger and a stronger will to fight, as German air raids had in Britain.

The western front in World War II extended all the way down into the desert of northern Africa, where fleets of tanks could maneuver like ships at sea, and control of the air was even more essential than over non-desert terrain. British forces were initially pitted against the Italians and had very much the better of it. Then the Germans came in led by Rommel, the "desert fox." Particularly when the desert army was depleted in a doomed effort to aid Greece, British forces sank to a low ebb and Rommel pushed into Egypt, threatening Alexandria. In these straits, Britain found her most successful general of the war, Montgomery. In October, 1942, his Eighth

Army hurled Rommel's forces back at El Alamein, the battle which Churchill regarded as "the hinge of fate," the turning point of the war. Then to the west, in November, American and British forces mounted the first of a number of decisive amphibious operations, landing in French North Africa. The Eighth Army and the units of Operation Torch would finally link up and end Italo-German presence in North Africa. July 1943 saw Anglo-American forces invade Sicily, and, that objective secured, proceed in September to the invasion of Italy. Italy surrendered, but the Germans continued to fight stubbornly. Allied forces inched their way arduously up the mountainous spine of Italy, slow and bitter going. Germans may have outnumbered the allies on the Italian front after substantial forces were drawn off for the invasion of France. But the slow allied advance continued to the end of the war.

The Beveridge plan was made public in Britain in February, 1943. This was a scheme of social insurance to guarantee all British people a decent quality of life. One of its most notable features was a National Health Program ("socialized medicine"), under which the government would assume responsibility for providing free medical care to all. Labour wanted to proceed with implementation, but Churchill balked and temporized. It was clear that the wartime coalition government would not long outlast the war.

"D-Day," the allied invasion of France, came on 6 June, 1944. The Channel crossing had been a given of allied strategy from the start. Stalin had been urging this "second front" to mitigate German pressure on Soviet forces. But Anglo-American planners did not want to proceed until they were certain they had the resources to succeed. "Operation Overlord," led by American General Dwight Eisenhower, involved a masterful deception to convince German defenders that the invasion would take the short route, the Dover to Calais crossing. Instead the allied forces landed in Normandy, secured their beachheads, extended their perimeters, and, after bitter fighting, broke out into the open countryside. The allies proved they had learned well the business of Blitzkrieg. Allied mechanized units rolled to the liberation of Paris, the honor going to a French armored division.

June 1944 had also seen the appearance of Hitler's "V weapons." First came the V-1 "buzz bomb" or "doodlebug." Today it would be called a cruise missile, a pilotless jet powered flying bomb. Soon it was joined by the V-2, a true ballistic missile. Both were capable of inflicting great damage. Fighter aircraft and antiaircraft fire could cope with the V-1. But there was no defense against the V-2. Had the V weapons come earlier and in larger numbers they would have constituted a major difficulty for Britain. As it was, their range was limited and when allied forces overran their launch sites the problem was solved. Many fell on London, but the ruins of St. Mary, Aldermanbury, undisturbed since 29 December, 1940, were not hit by either of the V weapons. If they had, there would have been no fabric left, and the church's fate would have been sealed.

Allied armies pressed on to the Rhine. A daring but overly elaborate plan to strike through Holland with a combined airborne and mechanized force and secure a Rhine bridgehead failed. The overall advance was slowed by the lack of adequate port facilities. Still, winter found the western allies investing Germany's borders while Russian forces ground in from the east. In December, the German army launched a desperate counteroffensive against American forces in the Ardennes. This "Battle of the Bulge" potentially threatened allied port facilities and supply lines. However, American troops held at key points, including the road junction of Bastogne. The U.S. Third Army in a remarkable maneuver moved through the rear of other American forces to strike at the neck of the "Bulge." A similar move from the north would have trapped the attacking Germans. As it was, they had to withdraw. The German army was now on the defensive, and Spring saw the western forces across the Rhine and fanning out through Germany while the Russians fought their way into Berlin. British and American units linked up with the Russians. 7 May, 1945, was Victory in Europe (VE) Day. Germany surrendered and the war in Europe was over. Weary, battered, depleted, Britain had survived her greatest danger and earned the jubilation displayed in the moment of victory. Victory in Japan (VJ) Day came on 1 September.

Most historians give Winston Churchill considerable personal credit for mobilizing his fellow Britons to stand firm in the face of seemingly overwhelming aggression. Churchill himself said, "The British people provided the lion's heart, I only supplied the roar!" However, as the war ended, the support for Tory leadership faded and Churchill was to pay the price.

Labour grew increasingly restive in the coalition government during the last stages of the European war, unhappy with their perception of the prospects for reform and postwar reconstruction. The government had been formed for the duration of the war, but the Pacific war seemed remote and to a large degree an American show. So parliament was dissolved and an election called in late May. It should be noted that this parliament had sat for ten years, twice its normal term, due to the wartime emergency. It should also be noted that it was not simply the parliament that Churchill had led to victory in war. It was also the parliament of Baldwin and Chamberlain, the parliament of Munich and appeasement, the parliament which had prepared so inadequately for war (excepting the providential Hurricanes and Spitfires!). Finally, it was a parliament that had simply worn out its welcome. Thus, the Tory electoral debacle in 1945 should not be understood as a personal repudiation of Mr. Churchill, though he initially saw it so himself and contemplated retirement. He was in fact returned to his old seat in the house and assumed the role of the opposition leader. Labour, with 390 seats had gained an independent majority and could form a government without Liberal support.

President Roosevelt died in 1945. The Potsdam Conference between President Truman, Stalin, and Churchill was meeting when the denouement of the British election became clear. Prime Minister Clement Atlee, the Labour leader and Deputy PM in the coalition government, assumed the British seat at the conference. Was this lesson in the ways of democracy lost on Stalin? Or did it simply fortify his resolve to avoid such embarrassing events in the Soviet Union?

Persons of speculative bent may dispute how or whether a Tory victory in 1945 might have affected the course of history for Britain, her Commonwealth and her Empire. But this is very clear. The fact that the Tory party lost in 1945 enabled Mr. Churchill to make a visit to the United States in 1946, and, freed from the political constraints of office, make one of the most prophetic and important speeches of his career. And that speech had a most profound impact on the future of Westminster College and the Church of St. Mary, Aldermanbury.

After the War

The history of St. Mary, Aldermanbury, as a parish church in the City of London was effectively terminated (as we have observed) by the events of 29 December, 1940. The parish itself, though without residents, continued a sort of technical existence as part of the United Parish. But its future history, if one may speak of such, would be intertwined with the Church of St. Vedast, Foster Lane. Still, it seems appropriate to continue our contextual narrative down to the point that St. Mary's Wren fabric departed to its new home at Westminster College in the United States.

Austerity

"Austerity" became the watchword once victory celebrations subsided. Britain was battered, exhausted and financially drained as a result of the war. Annual interest on overseas debt ran to £112 million, well in excess of the earnings on shrinking foreign investments. Britons realized that they had to conserve on everything, use as little as possible, curb imports as much as possible, rebuild or reconvert industries, and try to recapture lost export markets; this in a world economy desolated by war. Wartime rationing was continued, in some cases even more stringently than before. Bread went on the rationing list in 1947. Britain had come closer to agricultural self-sufficiency during and after World War II than in World War I, but a gap remained that had to be closed by imports. Things did not go well. The trade deficit was a moderate £353 million in 1950, but rose to £1,208 million the next year. The fate of the Pound Sterling may supply the most graphic symbol of Britain's economic plight. The historic value of the pound against U.S. currency was $4.87. It was trading around $4.09 in 1949 when the Labour exchequer devalued it to $2.80. Canadian and U.S. loans barely kept Britain afloat in the immediate postwar years. 1947 had seen the birth of the American Marshall plan to aid in the reconstruction of Europe. There was hope and promise, but it would be a while in realization. Today, American graduate students study in universities of the United Kingdom on Marshall Scholarships provided by the British government as continuing expression of gratitude for Marshall Plan aid.

The World Outside

Britain was quite unable to play her accustomed international role in her depleted and straitened circumstances. Some of her burdens devolved on the U.S., others on the United Nations, the newly formed international organization. Britain occupied a permanent seat on the U.N. Security Council, as did the U.S., the Soviet Union, China, and France as major victors in World War II.

Mr. Churchill had spoken brave words about not presiding over "the liquidation of empire." It is dubious that any British government could have halted the process of dissolution, though Labour could probably manage the matter with more grace and less grief than a Tory administration. The creation of India and Pakistan out of the former "jewel in the crown" in 1947 may stand for the process that saw most of the empire slide away, and ties to the Commonwealth loosened. One side effect of decolonization was the migration to England by persons of Indian ancestry who were squeezed out of their homes in former African colonies by unfriendly ruling majorities. Additional persons of colour migrated from other parts of the Commonwealth, creating the potential for racial disharmony in Britain.

Britain did not, however, become an international cypher. She shared in the creation of the NATO alliance in 1947 to shield Europe from the threat of Soviet imperialism. Britain and the U.S. stood together from June 1948 through May 1949, mounting the Berlin airlift which broke a Soviet blockade and saved free West Berlin. Britain also supported the U.S. prompted U.N. "police action" in Korea, preserving non-communist South Korea from an invasion by communist North Korea, and then an invasion by China. European integration had moved forward to the formation of the European Economic Community (EEC), or Common Market, in 1957. But it would be some years before Britain was ready to join.

Anglo-American relations reached a nadir in 1956 when Egypt nationalized the Suez Canal. Egypt had also announced a blockade of Israel's outlet to the Red Sea. Britain and France abetted Israel's inevitable effort to neutralize the blockade and then used the ensuing war as a pretext to invade Suez, supposedly to protect the canal from hostile action. But the competence of the Israeli army was underestimated and the Anglo-French operation itself clumsily managed. The Israelis were peacefully camped by an undamaged canal before France and England could get there. Thus the hollow pretext of the operation was exposed. Under the circumstances, the U.S. could hardly be expected to support France and England in the U.N., where the matter ended up. There was blame enough to go around among the old allies in the developments that led to the crisis and in their failure to adequately communicate among themselves as events moved toward an avoidable catastrophe. But it is difficult to escape the impression that the Eisenhower administration heaped excessive humiliation on its old and loyal allies in an outburst of diplomatic moralism. Certainly Mr. Churchill saw it so. His valedictory on the situation was, "This would never have happened if Eisenhower had been alive" (Gilbert 1991: 950). But the hurts of Suez were forgotten in 1961, when Britain and France supported the Kennedy administration during the Cuban missile crisis. It was also Kennedy who signed the joint action of the U.S. Senate and House of Representatives conferring honorary American citizenship on Winston Churchill (April, 1963).

Domestic Politics

The Labour government moved to keep its election promises by nationalizing parts of the transport system and much of basic industry, and implementing the Beveridge plan. The crowing achievement was the creation of the National Health scheme, which was realized in 1948, culminating the process of social reform begun over a century earlier. No government since has been able to seriously contemplate its abolition.

Labour's majority was substantially reduced in the 1950 elections. Then divisions in the Labour party forced new elections in 1951. The Tories won a slender majority and Churchill returned to organize his second government at age 77. The Tories would hold power for nearly a decade and a half with increasing parliamentary majorities in successive elections. Eden (his ministry cut short by the failure of the Suez adventure), Macmillan and Douglas-Home would organize Tory governments before Labour turned the tables in late 1964, ushering in the first Wilson government.

King George VI died in 1952 and was succeeded by his daughter, Princess Elizabeth. She was crowned in 1953 as Elizabeth II.

London

Garside (1990: 471) argues that London was historically characterized by a stability based on its very dynamism, "... driven by physical and economic growth." But after 1950, he held, "... changed economic and political conditions accentuated the fragility of London." While we would recognize such to be the case in parts of the metropolis, we would suggest that such was seldom the case for the City. While there have indeed been brief periods of stagnation and economic slowdown, the City has successively reinvented itself (not always in an aesthetically satisfying fashion) during the postwar years, ultimately emerging as the banking and financial capital of Europe. In sum, dynamic stability based on economic and physical growth has persisted in the City. And since it could not grow out, it has grown up (utterly spoiling the Wren skyline, once the loveliest in Europe). We are of course dealing with developments which extended far beyond 1965. But already the process was afoot.

The Aldermanbury parish and neighborhood offered a microcosm of extensive City change. The Industrial Revolution and its aftermath had created a neighborhood of warehouses and light industry. Postwar reconstruction would see Aldermanbury annexed to the financial district. A large bank building, ultimately replaced by a larger bank building, arose where Aldermanbury Tenement once stood, north of the Church on Aldermanbury. Aldermanbury Square, a small park-like enclave, replaced the eastern end of Addle Street. London Wall, displaced to the south and no longer a mere street but a major carriageway, expedited traffic across the northwest part of the City. Beyond London Wall would rise the Barbican development, combining centres for the arts, theatre, education and music with an assortment of businesses (including some hospitable pubs!), office blocks and apartment towers in an adventuresome approach to urban planning. The incomparable Museum of London would eventually join the complex. Nestled beneath the Barbican Highwalk and London wall, on the edge of a carpark, stood the remnants of the old tower of St. Alphage, London Wall, itself the medieval remainder of Elsyng Spittal (see Ch. 2). At various points the old City Wall is visible, with markers pointing out the location of the St. Alphage churchyard. None of the residential development fell within the boundaries of the Aldermanbury parish. Rather, business and office structures and a parallel to the Barbican Highwalk rose on the south side of London Wall (with pedestrian bridges at several points). The southernmost extension of the highwalk in fact debouched into the northwest corner of the St. Mary's Churchyard.

The needs of the City Corporation claimed much of the parish east of Aldermanbury, though the delightful Charter Insurance building continued to hold its place opposite the Saxon Palace/tenement. Space to the south of this land would eventually be filled by the new Guildhall Library, with its remarkable collections of maps, prints and manuscripts and its competent and helpful staff. The remainder west of Aldermanbury went to private commercial development.

With the general context set, let us now return to the period after 29 December 1940, to see in greater detail what happened to the Church of St. Mary, Aldermanbury.

The Post-War Fate of the Church of St. Mary, Aldermanbury in London (1941-1961)

The 1941 Easter Vestry was held on 26 March, 1941, at the offices of Bradbury, Greatorex and Co., Ltd. (4 1/2 Church Passage, Guildhall). The minutes (Ms. 23,917) record that the Rector (still P. D. Ellis), Churchwardens F. H. Gilbert and Owen Hunt, and the Vestry Clerk were present. The Rector reported that Mr. Sidney Tatchell had agreed to serve as architect to carry out any work necessary to protect the interests of St. Mary, Aldermanbury. The Vestry Clerk reported that because of enemy action on 29 December, 1940, both churches of the United Parishes were practically destroyed, but that almost all the registers and papers of St. Mary Aldermanbury were in good order and stored at the offices of Bradbury, Greatorex, and Co.

A 11 December, 1941, note in the Church Commissioners files (CC 67141) indicated that the Commissioners would be unable to resume payment of the £250 annual stipend which had been given to Mr. Mason in lieu of the payment from parish properties formerly awarded the curate.

For the next several years Easter Vestries were held, with the same in attendance (including Mrs. Ellis from 1942), but, according to the minutes, no substantial business occurred. There is no extant record of vestries held after 1944.

On 25 September, 1945, the Rev. A. J. Macdonald of St. Dunstan's, Fleet Street, was made sequestrator, with responsibility for the affairs of the Aldermanbury parish during the "vacancy." On 6 January, 1946, he returned to the Commissioners two checks in the amount of 18s4d which had been the Commissioners' payment for the income from the Aldermanbury benefice. He claimed it was hardly worth it to open an account with such a sum. This amount, a dividend payment, was now the sole income of the parish. (CC 67141).

In a 2 December, 1947, letter the Bishop of London suggested that the Ecclesiastical Commissioners pay £150 yearly to St. Alphage, Hendon and £500 to St. George in the East in lieu of the tithe now absent from St. Alphage (CC 67141).

In 1944 Parliament passed a Reorganization Measures Act which called for a linking of London parishes, including St. Mary, Aldermanbury. On 12 December, 1946, the Ecclesiastical Commissioners ordered that such a reorganization be carried out. Similar orders were issued on 10 January, 1952 and 15 August, 1952. However, it was not until 29 January, 1954 that a plan affecting St. Mary, Aldermanbury, was adopted by the Commissioners. The plan was published in the London Gazette on 2 February, 1954. (CC R.2 3/H/4, Part 1).

The plan called for the formation of a new benefice and parish of St. Giles Cripplegate with St. Bartholomew, Moor Lane and St. Alphage London Wall with St. Mary, Aldermanbury (8). The plan included the assignment of the Aldermanbury church to the new benefice (9), with the church restored "as soon as practicable" (31) along with 39 other London parish churches. The Commission acknowledged holding endowments for St. Mary, Aldermanbury, with St. Alphage of £3,344.

An undated note in the same Church Commissioners file recommended varying the above proposal to join St. Mary Aldermanbury with St. Vedast instead of St. Giles, with the proviso that "the east wall of the Church of St. Mary, Aldermanbury shall be preserved in situ or shall be taken down, preserved and re-erected by the Board in some appropriate place."

A handwritten addendum to this note pointed out that the 1944 Reorganization Scheme had assigned St. Mary, Aldermanbury, in one clause to St. Giles (7[2]) and in another to St. Vedast, Foster Lane (8[2]) and said, "we had better get the Church Commissioners to rectify this." The addendum also recommended vesting the site of the demolished Church of St. Mary, Aldermanbury, and its burial ground, in the Diocesan Board of Finance. This change in the Reorganization scheme was made on 2 February, 1954.

Five years went by before the Bishop of London approved on 6 February, 1959, and forwarded to the Church Commissioners, the draft reorganization scheme which joined St. Mary, Aldermanbury and nine other parishes, with St. Vedast, Foster Lane. The other parishes were St. Michael-le-Querne; St. Matthew, Friday St.; St. Peter, Cheap; St. Alban, Wood Street; St. Olave, Silver St.; St. Michael, Wood St.; St. Mary, Staining; St. John Zachary, Gresham St; and St. Anne and St. Agnes. Canon C. B. Mortlock of 45 Warwick Square was named rector of what became the United Parishes of St. Vedast alias Foster.

On 16 February, 1959, the published draft scheme included the plan to demolish the Church of St. Mary, Aldermanbury and sell the site, provided the East Wall was either preserved in situ, incorporated into another building on the site, or taken down and re-erected under the supervision of the Diocesan Board of Finance. This suggestion had come from the Royal Fine Arts Commission and the Central Council for the Care of Churches. The secretary of the Council, Judith Scott, reported to the Commissioners in a 23 February, 1959, letter that the proposal was "warmly welcomed" by the Council, who hoped that the work would soon be done.

However, the Ministry of Housing and Local Government objected in a 16 March, 1959 letter that if the East Wall was preserved in situ, the nave would also have to be preserved as an open space. The Ministry of Works weighed into the discussion with an objection against destroying the church at all, saying preserving the East Wall was only second best.

On 22 April, 1959, the Archdeacon of London called the Commissioners to say that the diocese must receive the site value from St. Mary, Aldermanbury, in order to proceed with restoration of "more important City churches." He considered the

Ministry of Works proposal to preserve the church "quite unrealistic." He said he thought the best idea was to leave the East End in situ and turn the nave into an open space. A month later he called again to say that the retention of the St. Mary's site as an open space, with the East End preserved, fit in with the Corporation of London's plans.

In the meantime the Church Commissioners had urged the Royal Fine Arts Commission to intervene with the Ministry of Works to make clear that realizing the site value of St. Mary, Aldermanbury, was critical to the success of the overall plan to restore city churches "of greater importance." In response the Commission said that it really wanted to preserve the Aldermanbury church and had gone along with the Central Commission's plan to preserve only the East End reluctantly. It refused to intervene with the Ministry of Works.

The various agencies continued their internecine debate, sending mixed signals to those interested in the old church. Some wanted to preserve the entire Church; others wanted to save only the east wall, which displayed the most evidence of Wren's artistry; some were willing to see the church totally demolished to make way for the modern City. However, no one wanted to take responsibility for pronouncing the death warrant on the old church.

On 3 June, 1959, the Administrative Committee of the Church Commissioners authorized preparation of a scheme to demolish the remains of St. Mary, Aldermanbury, preserving the East wall. A 16 June, 1959, surveyor's report indicated that the City Corporation had already acquired property on the western boundary of the churchyard (for construction of a police station) and that no evidence of crypts or burials in the passageway north of the church had been found.

On 4 August the Commissioners expanded the scheme to allow for movement of the East wall to another site satisfactory to the Board of Finance. (Letters and papers to this point are from CC R.2 3/H/4, Part One. Subsequent correspondence and papers are from Parts Two and Three of the same file.)

A 28 September letter from the Archdeacon expressed concern that the plan seemed to imply liability for re-erecting the Wall fell on the purchaser of the site, which would diminish the value of the site. He indicated that the Diocesan Fund was reluctant about preserving the East Wall because it complicated the sale of the site, but that he was hopeful the Corporation would agree to the terms. On 20 October the Administrative Committee of the Church Commissioners agreed to take responsibility for preserving the East Wall. However, a 29 October letter from the Corporation pointed out that retention of the East wall "would involve the construction of supporting buttresses, which would be aesthetically undesireable." The Corporation, therefore, could not agree to the retention of the wall, but would have no objections if it were taken down and re-erected elsewhere at the expense of the Diocesan Board.

A 10 April, 1960, article in The Observer, by Ian Cairn, entitled "Who Will Defend the Wall?," objected that "enough worthwhile buildings have to come down through serious incompatibility with the twentieth century without adding to them gratuitously." He argued that Wren would have propped up the East wall "with great scrolls on lion's paws." "... the least we can do," he concluded, "is to pass on what we can until a generation comes along with a less dithery and more comprehensive set of values." He urged people to write the London Planning Office to register their opinion.

On 3 May, 1960 the Church Commissioners received a letter from the Royal Fine Arts Commission and Central Council for the Care of Churches reporting on a meeting held at the St. Mary, Aldermanbury ruins on 18 February, 1960, with representatives of these two groups, the Archdeacon, the diocesan surveyor, the City Planning Officer and a representative of the London County Council. The following proposal for the Aldermanbury site and the East wall had been developed:

1) the east wall be "cut down to the top of the blocking course below the east window and to the bottom of this course on either side, the pediments above the doors being retained."
2) the doorways be opened up as secondary entrances to the new public garden.
3) the wall between the doorways form the back of a simple shelter in the garden.
4) the centre of the upper part, including the east window opening with the scrolls on either side, and the pediment above be taken down and re-erected on a low plinth on the north side of the garden, to mask, the flank of the building behind and to form an end to the view across the garden from the southern part of Aldermanbury.
5) the old window be treated as a niche in this new position with suitable backing, to form a secondary shelter in the garden.

Those present felt that this would "not only preserve some of the more interesting remains of the church for posterity, but would in fact enhance the value of the site as a public open square."

It is somewhat difficult to envision precisely how such an arrangement would have looked (no drawing is included with the letter), but like many compromise solutions it was hardly satisfactory.

Apparently officials of the Corporation objected to this proposal, because a letter dated 18 October, 1960, from the Diocesan Fund to the Church Commissioners said no progress had occurred.

A year later (20 October, 1961) the Church Commissioners wrote to the Diocesan Fund to point out that two years had passed since the scheme to demolish St. Mary, Aldermanbury, and sell the site had been issued. The response (24 October, 1961) was simply that "Several interesting and difficult points have arisen." The veiled allusion was to inquiries, now well underway, as to the possibility of Westminster College acquiring the fabric of the church. Why the Church Commissioners were being kept in the dark about this proposal is not clear.

Whether by reason of bureaucratic ineptitude or providential intervention, the plan to tear down St. Mary, Aldermanbury had been delayed just long enough for the fabric to still be available when the Churchill Memorial project began. The clearly inadequate proposal to cut the east wall in two in order to preserve it created the context in which a proposal to remove the church fabric and restore it elsewhere would be well-received.

The Selection and Securing of the Church of St. Mary as the Churchill Memorial (1961-1964)

(Note: We are indebted in this section to Westminster College alumnus James H. Williams, who gave us permission to utilize his unpublished senior history thesis, "An Imaginative Concept: The Winston Churchill Memorial and Library Project." Mr. Williams sifted through the extensive archive of the Churchill Memorial, including correspondence files, in his work, which deserves independent publication. In addition, we draw upon our own experience. Prof. Hauer supported the Churchill Memorial/ St. Mary's project as a member of the Westminster College faculty from its inception and was acquainted with many of the principals mentioned below. Prof. Hauer was a member of the first group named Fellows of the Winston Churchill

Memorial and Library in the U.S.A. He has remained active in the work of the Memorial. Prof. Young, also a Fellow of the Churchill Memorial, has been active on behalf of the Memorial since he joined the faculty of Westminster College in 1975 and has become acquainted with the survivors among the original principals. Other information has been drawn from the files of the Church Commissioners of the Church of England and remarks by Professor Patrick Horsbrugh delivered at the Wren Symposium [1989] and conversations with Dr. Robert L.D. Davidson [1990]).

On 5 June, 1961, Robert L.D. Davidson, President of Westminster College, held a meeting in his office, prompted by the interest of members of the English Speaking Union, to discuss an appropriate memorial for the 1946 visit of Sir Winston Churchill to the College. Present at the meeting were landscape architects Ruth Layton; her husband, architect Emmet Layton; and Patrick Horsbrugh, then Professor of Architecture at the University of Nebraska. When Horsburgh asked President Davidson what the College most needed, he responded that the greatest need was for a new chapel.

Discussion turned to a Life magazine article by photographer Mark Kaufmann, entitled "The Realm of Christopher Wren." The photographic essay showed Wren parish churches of London, some of which were to be left in ruins or demolished. The idea emerged from this conversation that one of the redundant Wren buildings might be brought to Westminster. Horsbrugh (1989: 9-10) writes that he then offered to look into the possibility when visiting London that summer.

Without Davidson's vision and persuasive abilities and Horsbrugh's imagination, knowledge, and determination, the project would probably never have been realized. These two stand out among many as the principal persons responsible for saving St. Mary, Aldermanbury, from destruction and restoring the Church in Fulton. Davidson has graciously said that "if anybody deserves credit for this building, it's Patrick Horsbrugh" (Davidson 1984-2: 3, 8-9).

Horsbrugh immediately began correspondence with contacts in England. By mid-July the Church of St. Mary, Aldermanbury had been recommended by the Earl of Rosse, Lawrence Parsons, Chairman of the Georgian Group (Horsbrugh 1989:14) and accepted as the first and best choice. During July and August, 1961 Horsbrugh visited 21 redundant churches of Wren and other architects in the London area and made the necessary contacts with church and civic officials. Other churches seriously considered for removal to Fulton were St. Alban, Wood Street; St. Michael,

Paternoster Royal; and St. Anne and St. Agnes, Gresham Street. He also briefly considered the possibility of building, from Wren's plans, St. Mary's, Lincoln's Inn Fields, a church which Wren had never had the opportunity to build (Horsbrugh 1989: 19-20). His site visits confirmed the choice of St. Mary, Aldermanbury, because of its size, design quality, and the fact that it would fit well into the open surroundings in which it would be placed in Fulton (Horsbrugh 1989: 15-18). Horsbrugh had as his criteria of selection: suitability of size, extent of remaining fabric, simplicity of plan, architectural character, historic relevance to the American scene, the quality of the interior, lack of viable parish, lack of disruption to site left after removal, and appropriateness when moved to a rural setting (Horsbrugh 1989: 14-17, 32).

Horsbrugh has identified 112 persons in Great Britain who were involved in the negotiations concerning the choice, removal, rebuilding, and rededication of St. Mary, Aldermanbury, and other matters (Horsbrugh 1989: 34-43). Space allows us to name only a few here. Miss Judith Scott, Secretary of the Central Council for the Care of Churches, was particularly instrumental in helping secure the release of the Church by the necessary officials in the Church of England. Indeed, in Horsbrugh's opinion, she probably suggested that Lord Rosse recommend it (Horsbrugh 1989: 22). As it turned out, church authorities were very cooperative in deeding the church fabric to Westminster College. As we have seen, the removal of St. Mary, Aldermanbury, helped them resolve the problem of how to preserve it but also make available the site for other purposes. Also instrumental in the success of the project in Great Britain were Canon C. B. Mortlock, rector of the United Parishes, and Noel Mander, MBE, FSA, Churchwarden of St. Vedast (see Figure 10.8), who had been present on 29 December,1940 when the Church was bombed (see Ch. 8) and who would build the organ for the restored structure and be instrumental in securing many of its furnishings.

On the American side, the Westminster College trustee appointed to chair the Board of Trustees committee responsible for the project, Neal Wood, was also a key player. According to Davidson, Wood had responded enthusiastically when first approached about the idea of bringing a Wren church to the campus, saying "Let's do it!" Davidson has said that without Wood's support the project would never have gotten off the ground (Davidson 1984-2: 4, 9-10). Wood was joined on the Committee by Layton Mauze, pastor of the Central Presbyterian Church of St. Louis, and Richard Amberg, Publisher of the St. Louis Globe-Democrat, and several others.

The St. Louis and Kansas City chapters of the English Speaking Union were also involved in gaining support for the project.

While in London Horsbrugh also made contacts with the Churchill family and began the process of securing Sir Winston's endorsement. Meanwhile, President Davidson contacted former President Truman who graciously agreed to write Churchill an informal letter asking for his endorsement of the project. By 28 September word had been received indicating that Churchill was honored by the concept. Initially the project was to commemorate the famous speech, but all understood it would one day be a memorial to Churchill himself.

Chosen to supervise the dismantling of the Church, when it was ready to be moved, and to plan its restoration, was Marshall Sisson, renowned reconstruction architect. He had been involved in helping Horsbrugh select St. Mary's as the right church for removal and had a great deal of experience in church reconstruction. St. Louis architect Frederick Sternberg was later selected to supervise the actual rebuilding of the church in Fulton. Sisson and Sternberg consulted on a number of occasions, and their ability to work cooperatively was also crucial for the success of the project. Sisson's commitment, supported by Horsbrugh, to follow Wren's 17th century design as nearly as possible and Sternberg's willingness to follow through on this sometimes difficult criterion combined to make the reconstructed building one of the most authentic Christopher Wren churches in existence.

Difficulties in raising money to fund the project caused delays which became worrisome. Could the College find enough sponsors to get removal of the Church underway before the pressure of commercial development in London caused church authorities to sell the site? At this point the estimated cost of the project was $1,500,000 (Stinson 1971: 72). If commercial interests purchased the land they might not be willing to postpone plans for use of the site until the church was dismantled for reconstruction.

In January, 1962, President Davidson journeyed to London, met with many of the dignitaries whom Horsbrugh had consulted, and visited the site of St. Mary Aldermanbury with reconstruction architect Marshall Sisson (see Figure 9.3). His meeting with City Corporation officials at the Guildhall may very well have sealed the issue. He also went to the Parliamentary Committee with oversight for the care of churches. (Davidson 1984: 2).

In March, 1962, an exchange of letters between the Church Commissioners and the Diocesan Fund indicated that they were still not being informed as to the Westminster proposal. On 9 November, 1962, Sovereign Securities, Ltd., who were in charge of construction of the building to the north, asked about the status of disposal of the church, because it was impeding the lighting of the building and access to the basement car park.

The Church Commissioners had been notified by 23 November, 1962, of the proposal to move the church to Westminster College, because a letter from the Royal Fine Arts Commission said that in a meeting of 14 November, the Commission had agreed that the proposed restoration in Fulton was much preferable to the plan to dismember the wall.

A key turning point was the 26 November, 1962, letter of Churchill to President Davidson, in which the Prime Minister said:

> I am honored that Westminster College should wish to commemorate the speech I made at Fulton on March 5, 1946. The removal of a ruined Christopher Wren church, largely destroyed by enemy action on London in 1941, and its reconstruction and re-dedication at Fulton, is an imaginative concept. It may symbolise in the eyes of the English-speaking peoples the ideals of Anglo-American association on which rest, now as before, so many of our hopes for peace and the future of mankind.

The letter was actually written by President Davidson and sent to Churchill as a suggested draft. Churchill used Davidson's draft verbatim.

The same day the story broke in the London press, with brief articles in the Daily Telegraph and Times. The Times article said the London Diocesan Reorganization Committee had agreed to an offer from "Fulton University in Missouri."

The next day the London Diocesan Reorganization Committee officially notified the Church Commissioners, asking them to amend the Reorganization proposal to meet the London Corporation's objections and to allow the demolished remains to be forwarded to "Fulton University." They pointed out that the rector, Canon Mortlock, was on the Reorganization Committee and approved the proposal. The Committee noted that they were consulting the City of London Corporation, the London County Council, the Ministry of Housing, and the Ministry of Works on the project.

An undated article from The Times in the Church Commissioners' files reported that the London Diocesan Fund would promote a bill in Parliament to secure permission for removal of the Church. It quoted the Archdeacon as saying that all ecclesiastical authorities concerned had given their consent. The article also quoted President Davidson, who said the project would require £70,000 to transport the church to Fulton and £1,700,000 to rebuild it on the campus. He said the church would be used at Westminster College as a chapel to house 650 students, and that a proposal for exchange scholarships for British and American students was also being considered.

On 3 December, 1962, the Board of Trustees of the College officially approved the project. According to President Davidson (1990), the Committee of the Board responsible for the Memorial (Neal Wood [chairman], Richard Amberg, Layton Mauze, and Missouri Governor John Dalton among them) was instrumental in convincing the Board to proceed with the project. At this time the cost of bringing the church building to Fulton and reconstructing it was estimated at $1.2 million, with an additional $800,000 necessary to endow operations. President Davidson assigned David Stinson, Westminster's Vice-President for Development, the responsibility of managing the day-to-day aspects of the project for the College.

About the same time there was the first public opposition to the project in England, and, interestingly, in the Soviet Union in an article in the Communist party newspaper, Pravda. The latter proved helpful in gaining support for the project in the United States.

A 4 February, 1963 letter from the Diocesan Fund to the Church Commissioners said that the way was now clear to amend the Reorganization scheme. On 24 February, 1963 the Church Commissioners Administration Committee gave approval to the revisions, stipulating that "no demolition shall take place until the Bishop of London shall certify to the Church Commissioners that satisfactory arrangements have been made for the transfer of the remains of the said church, or such of them as the Board may direct, to the U. S. of A. for re-erection at Fulton University (sic) in the state of Missouri." By the end of March all the concerned agencies had agreed, with the Ministry of Works urging that the Heminge and Condell monument be retained in the churchyard and not sent to America.

On 4 April, 1963, the Secretary to the Commissioners noted that the reference in the draft proposal to Fulton University should be changed to Westminster College. On the next day the Commissioners agreed that the whole church should be sent, but not the Heminge and Condell monument.

On 18 October, 1963, the scheme was officially sealed, having secured the approval of all concerned. It was laid before the Houses of Parliament on 4 December and confirmed on 19 December. The order was published in the London Gazette on 14 January, 1964.

The Reconstruction of the Church Of St. Mary, Aldermanbury, on the Westminster College Campus (1964-1969)

After a year dedicated to raising the funds necessary to bring the church to Fulton, ground was broken on the Westminster campus on April 19, 1964. By this time three former U.S. Presidents had signed on as honorary chairmen of the project: Truman, Eisenhower, and, before his death, Kennedy. Just prior to the groundbreaking ceremony (April 5) President Lyndon Johnson had endorsed the project in the White House. In his formal statement, President Johnson said the project demonstrated "in an unmistakable way the deep affection and esteem and respect which this great man has in this country." By this time Missouri Governor and Westminster College trustee John Dalton had become directly involved in promoting the project, citing its advantages for the state. He agreed to serve as Chairman of the project. Neal Wood served as the chairman of the Trustees committee and was involved, with Stinson and Davidson, in the management of the project.

At the groundbreaking ceremony British Ambassador Lord Harlech, President Harry Truman, General Vaughan, and many other members of the 1946 platform party were present. Truman turned the first, ceremonial spade before a crowd of 2,500 (see Figure 9.7).

During 1964 over $500,000 was raised under the leadership of the Memorial's campaign chairman, Henry Luce, Ambassador Averell Harriman, and Industrial Chairman, Dr. Charles Allen of Monsanto. The death of Churchill on 24 January, 1965, resulted in a flood of gifts for the project. (Stinson 1973: 72).

In the Fall of 1964 Sisson began the tedious work of measuring and marking the stones of the church in preparation for their dismantling. Prof. Edgar Thompson of University College, London, used photogrammetry to measure the church, to help guide the reconstruction plans. Because Wren had utilized the irregular 1437 foundations in his design, nothing in the church was parallel. Sisson therefore faced considerable problems converting the specifications to the simple rectangle required for the Fulton site. The lead cupola, totally consumed by fire, was redrawn on the basis of photogrammetric studies of old photographs. In March of the following year Sisson visited Fulton for the first time to acquaint himself with the site and meet Sternberg and others who would be involved in the reconstruction.

The John Epple Construction Company was selected as contractor for the reconstruction phase of the work. Like Sternberg, Epple accepted no fee for the project. Appropriately, Emmet and Ruth Laydon would later be chosen to act as landscape architects for the project.

On 15 May, 1965, the Bishop of London officially certified to the Church Commissioners that satisfactory arrangements had been made for the transfer of the remains of St. Mary, Aldermanbury, and their re-erection "exactly as designed by Sir Christopher Wren." The Bishop also said that during dismantling a watch would be kept to look for "any interesting medieval worked stones." He also noted that "the incongruous pierced parapets and window tracery added to Wren's design in 1865 will not be preserved or re-used." The burial vaults would not be destroyed nor would the Shakespeare Memorial. He cited Marshall Sisson's intent to restore the interior furnishings in conformity with Wren detail, but with the insertion of an organ gallery in the western end of the church.

The first stones were actually removed and cleaned on July 7, 1965, and dismantling was nearly completed before the end of the year. The cost of taking down the structure totalled nearly $100,000, not counting architectural fees. Sisson's meticulous drawings were used by workmen, who chiseled the corresponding number on to each stone. Sisson based his drawings of the roof, ceiling, and interior on 19th century drawings and photographs taken before the war. Craftsmen cut new stones to replace missing or broken ones, from the same Portland quarry used by Wren in the 17th Century. Other stone came from the Wren Church of St. Swithun London Stone which was being demolished at the same time. Stones from St. Swithun's were added to provide some spare stonework should it be needed.

With the walls, columns, and tower taken down, only the foundations and bases of the columns remained to mark the site. These have been preserved by the Corporation of London in a park much used by city workers at noon, even as the churchyard had been earlier in the century (see Figure 9.5). On the foundation of the tower is a plaque, placed by Westminster College (see Figure 9.6), which says:

THE SITE OF THE CHURCH OF ST. MARY ALDERMANBURY

**FIRST MENTIONED IN 1181, DESTROYED BY THE
GREAT FIRE OF 1666. REBUILT BY WREN.
DESTROYED BY BOMBING IN 1940. THE REMAINING
FABRIC REMOVED TO WESTMINSTER COLLEGE, FULTON,
MISSOURI, U.S.A. IN 1966 AND RESTORED AS A MEMORIAL
TO SIR WINSTON CHURCHILL**

*

THIS PLACQUE PLACED BY WESTMINSTER COLLEGE

The park was formally opened by the Lord Mayor on 16 April, 1970. In 1984 U. S. Ambassador to Britain Charles Price planted a tree in the park.

The U. S. Shipping Board graciously arranged to have the stones travel as ballast on supply ships returning empty from England to the United States. In England Neal Wood arranged for the stones to be shipped in the order they would be needed at the Fulton site. However, problems arose. Instead of being placed in two shipments, as originally planned, the stones had to be divided into six 100 ton shipments. This disrupted the order of the stones, which were packed without regard to the part of the building from which they had come.

When the stones arrived in Norfolk, Virginia, the stevedores reduced their charges for unloading in deference to the nature of the project. The stones were held up for a time when the U.S. Department of Agriculture insisted on inspecting the "straw" between the stones to make certain it did not contain hoof and mouth disease. When they discovered the "straw" was plastic fiber, the Department of Commerce became involved to insure the fiber did not have traces of poisonous residue! (Davidson 1984-2: 12). The Norfolk and Western Railroad transported the stones by rail to Mexico, Missouri without charge. They began to arrive in Fulton in mid-March, 1966. When Eris Lytle, master stonemason for the project (see Figure 9.8), began to unpack them he found stones from the north wall placed next to stones from the south wall. The stones were spread out across a field next to the site, and the piecing together of what the *Times* of London called the biggest jigsaw puzzle in architectural history began (see Figure 9.9). Further confusion and anxiety occurred when a load of the stones was sidetracked at Mattoon, Illinois, for several weeks.

Before the stones had arrived, the basement foundation and a tunnel to connect the Churchill Memorial to Champ Auditorium on the West had been completed. The basement would create a 16,500 square foot undercroft which would house the museum, library and offices for the Memorial. At this point Fred Sternberg estimated that the reconstruction would take until May, 1967 to complete. The last stone was actually laid in August, 1967.

The foundation stone for the reconstructed Church of St. Mary, Aldermanbury, was laid by the Lord Bishop of London, Robert Stopford, on 6 October, 1966, three hundred years after the Great Fire of London had necessitated the first Wren rebuilding. At the ceremony Governor Averill Harriman spoke of his fifty year association with Churchill. The following Monday Stopford and Davidson appeared on the Today Show and were interviewed by Hugh Downs about the project.

By March, 1967, the outer walls and tower of the church had been raised. The church measured 84 by 54.5 feet, and the tower rose 106 feet. The shell looked virtually the same as Wren's 17th century design, with one significant exception. Sisson chose to place a Wren-style window in the tower to provide natural light for the staircase to the undercroft of the memorial. In London the west front was against neighboring buildings, so a window there would have been useless. In Fulton it enhanced the structure; Wren would have undoubtedly agreed with Sisson's decision. Sisson and Mander arranged to have as the keystone in this window a stone from another Wren parish church which was not being restored, St. Swithun's, London Stone, on Cannon Street. The stone was left uncleaned to show the state of all the stones before they had been cleaned when the church was dismantled.

The craftsmen who assembled the church certainly deserve special recognition. Space allows that only two be singled out. The Epple Construction Superintendent, Rienzo Palmer, and the master stonemason, Eris Lytle, proved that 20th century craftsmen have the same pride and skill as their 17th century predecessors. In the northwest corner Lytle placed a sealed metal box with the workers' log book, Kennedy half dollars, a Fulton newspaper, and several kinds of grain. He said that perhaps they would be found "when the church is torn down again in another three hundred years."

Another person critical to the success of the project was Westminster College Vice-President David Stinson, whom Davidson credits with "unsurpassed leadership" in the raising of funds for the project (1990).

Finishing the interior of the church proved nearly as complex as the exterior. Most of 1968, into the Spring of 1969, was spent on this phase of the project. Davidson refused to allow several of the capitals on the columns to be cleaned, to call attention to the burning of the church. The 1940 bombing had left none of the furnishings intact, so Sisson had to base his interior design on pre-war photographs and drawings. He worked with English woodcarver, the late Arthur Ayres, who brilliantly produced carving in the style and to the quality of Wren's famous carver, Grinling Gibbons. Ayres made carvings of flowers and cherubim for the wood reredoes as well as carvings for the pulpit, baptismal font and balcony. The carvings on the Vestry room screens are actual seventeenth century work in the Gibbons' style, perhaps even from Gibbons' shop. They came from another Wren church, St. Dionis, Backchurch. Horsbrugh had taken the risk of reserving them in his name early in the project. Unable to find a British craftsman to produce the handblown clear (cathedral) glass windows prescribed by Wren, the builders located a West Virginia firm able to fabricate the panes.

Through the efforts of Canon Mortlock the College received a double set of 17th century communion silver from the Church of St. Anne and St. Agnes. Dr. Mander, at this time Churchwarden of the United Parishes of St. Vedast alias Foster, was again instrumental in arranging the transfer. He went to Canon Mortlock, pointing out that St. Vedast had some eighty pieces of silver from the thirteen parishes in the United Parishes. Canon Mortlock agreed to give one set to St. Mary, Aldermanbury, and the Parish Council readily agreed. Three pieces were chosen from a set of six, but the Diocese committee which had to give its approval ruled that the set must not be broken. Dr. Mander took this as a tacit permission that all six should be sent. So he delivered all six pieces to Neal Wood, then in London, and a week later the set of six was in Fulton. The vessels have been placed in the Churchill Memorial museum as a memorial to Canon Mortlock.

The Roman Catholic Westminster Cathedral graciously provided candlesticks for the altar. Again Dr. Mander was the intermediary. He had gone to St. Paul's Cathedral and asked whether the Cathedral Chapter might have candlesticks to give to St. Mary, Aldermanbury. The Chapter declined. Dr. Mander then approached Westminster Abbey and received a similar response. However, Canon Bartlett, treasurer of Westminster Cathedral, invited Dr. Mander to choose from among about thirty pairs of candlesticks which he had laid out for him to examine. Dr. Mander selected those now on display in the Memorial museum. They are placed on the altar only for very special services of worship.

The Mander tracker organ would be placed in an organ case built using a portion of the case built for the 1741 organ at the parish church in Woolwich, Kent. Later a gilded crown and Bishop's mitres, rescued by Mander from another Wren church, St. Michael, Paternoster Royal, were added to the organ case, as had been done after the Restoration of the monarchy and episcopacy in 1660. Mander's organ company would later construct a communion table for the church modelled after the 17th century table in All Hallows, Bread Street, now in the north chapel of St. Vedast, Foster Lane. During World War II Mander had rescued that table from the ruins of the church where it had been placed after All Hallows Bread Street was demolished in 1877.

Five new bronze bells were cast for the tower by the 300-year old foundry, Petit and Fritzen of Holland (Stinson 1973: 75). The bells and tower were a gift of Amy McNutt, a memorial to her husband.

In January, 1968, former Fulton newspaper editor Virgil Johnston, Jr. was hired as the first Director of Affairs for the Churchill Memorial. He participated in the final stages of the project and administered the Memorial during the first crucial years of its existence. The governing authority for the Memorial resides in the College's Board of Trustees and a Board of Governors selected by the Trustees.

By April, 1969, a rush was on to complete the reconstruction before the scheduled dedication on May 7th. Mander took charge of shipping not only the tracker organ his firm had built but also the pulpit and lectern. These were sent on a TWA flight, which arrived on April 20. That gave Mander and three assistants a very short time to assemble and test the organ. Mr. Mander also suprevised the gilded inscription of the Ten Commandments on the reredos, a traditional feature of 17th century English churches (see Figure 10.1).

On 7 May, 1969, the Church of St. Mary, the Virgin, Aldermanbury was rehallowed by the Bishop of Dover as a place for ecumenical worship. The Bishop knocked symbolically three times on the door, and President Davidson welcomed him with the words, "Come into American's oldest and newest church." Appropriately, a Roman Catholic Bishop, American Episcopal Bishops, a Reform Jewish Rabbi and clergy of the Presbyterian Church joined in the reconsecration.

Dr. William Huntley, Westminster College Chaplain, was now, in effect, the "perpetual curate" of St. Mary, Aldermanbury. The advowson had passed into the hands of the Trustees of Westminster College, and the "college was the parson." The church was dedicated as the "Churchill Memorial Chapel," but its original name has proven more popular. Early in the project, Prof. Horsbrugh had remarked that it would be inappropriate to rename a historic church after a modern person, however prominent. Outside the Church a crowd estimated at 10,000 gathered for the dedication ceremony, featuring an address by the Earl Mountbatten of Burma, the Queen's representative at the event (see Figure 9.12). Sir Winston Churchill's daughter, Lady Mary Soames and her son Nicholas, represented the Churchill family. A number of other dignitaries, including Governor Harriman, were present as American representatives in this affirmation of Anglo-American cooperation and friendship. The crowd which gathered in Fulton for the rededication of St. Mary's, was twice as big as the population of the historic City of London, which by 1970 had declined to 5,000!

The reconstruction of the Church of St. Mary the Virgin, Aldermanbury, was made possible by gifts from hundreds of donors on both sides of the Atlantic. Perhaps the most unusual was a Confederate ten dollar bill sent by a British veteran who had been wounded in the Battle of Gallipoli in World War I, the ill-fated mission for which Churchill was blamed (see Ch. 8). The old soldier said he could just not bring himself to forgive Churchill for that military blunder. (Davidson 1984-2: 14).

St. Mary, Aldermanbury as the Churchill Memorial (1969-

Since its rehallowing, St. Mary, Aldermanbury has served several purposes. As the Winston Churchill Memorial Museum and Library in the United States it attracts thousands of visitors yearly who come to marvel at Wren's architectural genius and tour the undercroft museum. In the museum they see an introductory slide show made possible by donations from the Friends of the Churchill Memorial. They tour the Memorial's regular exhibits, which tell the story of Sir Winston's life, his visit to Westminster, his literary achievements, and his pastimes (including several of his paintings). They also see exhibits on Sir Christopher Wren, the rebuilding of the church, and the history of the Church while it was in London. One gallery is set aside for display of articles related to the church, including the beautiful Phoenix vestments and paraments.

The church also serves as a beautiful setting for concerts, lectures, and other cultural and educational events. In recent years the Church has hosted lectures in the Crosby Kemper Series on Churchill and Anglo-American relations, one by Churchill's biographer, Martin Gilbert, another by his daughter, Lady Mary Soames, and others by close associates of Churchill. The Church was also the site for a Green Foundation lecture by renowned philosopher, Paul Ricoeur. In April, 1986, the Memorial hosted a Churchill Symposium, directed by Prof. Russell Jones of the Westminster History Department, featuring internationally recognized experts on the Churchill era. In April, 1989, the Memorial held an International Symposium on Christopher Wren, directed by Prof. Hauer. Scholars from England and the United States spoke on Wren's work after the Great Fire, his philosophy of church architecture, his engineering achievements, and his scientific work. During the Symposium, Christopher Dearnley, organist at St. Paul's Cathedral, offered a recital on the Mander organ and directed a concert of music from the age of Wren.

Every two years since 1985, the Church has been the site for a meeting of the Robbinett Family Association, a group composed of descendants of Allen and Margaret Robbinett, whose marriage on 29 September, 1653, is recorded in the registers of St. Mary, Aldermanbury (see Ch. 4).

On November 9, 1990, the end of the Cold War and the first anniversary of the lifting of the "Iron Curtain," symbolized by the penetration of the Berlin Wall, were celebrated. Former President Ronald Reagan dedicated a sculpture created out of sections of the Berlin Wall on the Churchill Plaza, near the Church of St. Mary, Aldermanbury (see Figure 9.13). The sculpture, by Churchill's granddaughter, artist Edwina Sandys, is called "Breakthrough." Ms. Sandys went to East Berlin, shortly after the breaching of the Wall in November, 1989, and secured the sections. She had cut from the walls the outline of a female and male figure to symbolize the penetration of the wall, from oppression to freedom.

On May 6, 1992, former President of the Soviet Union, and General Secretary of the Communist Party, Mikhail Gorbachev, delivered the forty-sixth Green Lecture in front of the Breakthrough Sculpture and in the shadow of Franta Belksy's larger-than-life statue of Churchill and the Church of St. Mary, Aldermanbury, before a crowd estimated at 20,000 (see Figure 9.14). President Gorbachev symbolically marked the end of the Cold War and the beginning of the peaceful cooperation which Churchill had called for in "The Sinews of Peace" forty-six years earlier.

St. Mary, the Virgin, Aldermanbury is first and foremost a living church, serving as the Westminster College chapel. Ecumenical services for students and others in the College community, and visitors to the memorial, have been held during the academic year ever since the church was rehallowed. A mass, sponsored by the Newman Club, has been celebrated each Sunday in term. In 1975 Dr. William Young succeeded Dr. Huntley as chaplain of the College and "perpetual curate." In 1991 Ms. Gina Tollini became coordinator of religious life at the College, the first woman to serve as a minister of the Church of St. Mary, Aldermanbury, in the 800 year history of the church. Special services are held frequently in the church: weddings, baptisms, and Presbyterian and other church gatherings. A series of three festivals is held each year: a Harvest Festival, a Festival of Nine Lessons and Carols, and a Spring Festival held on Palm Sunday. When the Board of Governors and Fellows of the Memorial gather for their annual meeting and to induct new Churchill Fellows, an honorary society of those who have made special contributions to the memorial, special services based on the 1662 Book of Common Prayer are held. This would have been the type of service celebrated in the Wren church throughout its years in England.

The Churchill Memorial has given Westminster College a special place in the Anglo-American "special relationship." The annual Robertson Visiting Lectureship in British History brings an outstanding, younger British historian, selected by the Fulbright Commission, to the College. This scholar teaches a general course in British history and a course in her or his own specialty at the college, and delivers special lectures at other locations in collaboration with the Churchill Memorial's outreach program. The first Robertson visiting professor was Dr. John Charmley, Lecturer in British History at the University of East Anglia, Norwich. Dr. Charmley was in residence during the 1992-93 academic year.

Since St. Mary, Aldermanbury, was a London City Church, many common interests exist with the City of London. Two Bishops of London have paid three visits between them to the Church. The Museum of London and the City's Guildhall Library have been particularly helpful in the development of permanent and temporary exhibits for the Memorial Museum, in work on research projects (including this book!), and in supplying actual materials for major exhibits. The British Library, the Royal Society, the Royal College of Surgeons and the Sir Hans Soanes Museum in London, and the Codrington Library, All Souls College, Oxford, also have assisted with exhibits. The Lord Mayor of Stratford Upon Avon visited Westminster in the Spring of 1992 in connection with the presentation of a bust of William Shakespeare, a replica of the one which adorns his tomb at Trinity Church in Stratford (see Ch. 3 on Shakespeare's connection with Aldermanbury).

The proper furnishings for a City Church include a Lord Mayor's Sword Stand. The great ceremonial sword, a symbol of authority, is carried in procession before the Lord Mayor on official visits and installed in the stand. Dr. Noel Mander led a campaign in England to obtain a sword stand for reconstructed St. Mary's. Appropriately, since St. Mary, Aldermanbury, was the guild Church of the Worshipful Company of Haberdashers, the largest gift was made by the Haberdashers. We shall discuss the fabrication of this artistic piece of metalwork in the next chapter. It is a replica of a seventeeth century stand in Haberdashers Hall. On the occasion of its official installation, the Worshipful Company of Barbers presented a handsome certificate of recognition concerning the work of restoration and preservation of St. Mary, Aldermanbury.

A sword stand requires a sword, and in the autumn of 1991, a refurbished antique sword from City stores was presented through the good offices of the City Corporation and the Worshipful Company of Cutlers. It was accompanied by an act of Common Council, ordaining its display in the Church on appropriate days. At other times it occupies an honored place in the Musuem.

Conclusion: St. Mary's "Westminster" Connection

One of the more interesting ironies of the story of the Church of St. Mary, Aldermanbury, revolves around the name "Westminster." As we have seen in Ch. 4, in the 17th century the perpetual curate of St. Mary's, the Presbyterian leader Edmund Calamy, played a prominent role in the Westminster Assembly which bequeathed the name Westminster to Presbyterianism. A number of Presbyterian institutions were given the name "Westminster" to memorialize the historic Assembly and the Confession of Faith and Catechisms which were its principal legacies. One was a College begun in 1851 in Fulton, Missouri, under the leadership of Presbyterian minister W. F. Robertson and the First Presbyterian Church of Fulton. The college had first been named "Fulton College," but received the name Westminster when it was adopted by the Presbyterian Synod of Missouri. The original mission of the college was to train Presbyterian ministers. A century later another Englishman with another kind of Westminster connection, Winston Churchill, made an historic visit to Westminster college, inspiring the search for a memorial a decade and a half later. The memorial chosen was St. Mary, Aldermanbury, saved from destruction in the 17th century by the graduate of another school called Westminster, Christopher

Wren. In a strange turn of fate, or perhaps by the hand of providence, the Church which had been involved through its most famous minister in linking Presbyterianism and the name Westminster was saved from 20th century destruction by a Presbyterian-related college called Westminster.

Whether the Church of St. Mary has been saved time and time again from destruction by chance or providence is a decision for readers to make themselves. From our perspective as historians, it is clear that the story of St. Mary, Aldermanbury, is a tale of vision and determination of people famous and not so famous. We think of the mysterious royal or noble figure responsible for the first St. Mary's in the 11th or early 12th century; the great preacher and leader, Edmund Calamy, who stood by his principles and paid the price; the 17th century parishoners who struggled to restore the church after its destruction in the Great Fire of 1666 and the great architect who redesigned it; the 19th and 20th century church leaders who resisted efforts to destroy St. Mary's; and those whose story we have told in this chapter, who persevered in the challenging task of bringing the church across the Atlantic, and restoring it to its 17th century grandeur as a memorial to the greatest Englishman of this century.

The history of St. Mary, Aldermanbury, is a microcosm of the human story: noble ideals threatened by tragedy, selfishness, and sometimes simple inertia and the passage of time, kept alive by people unwilling to let them die. We feel fortunate indeed to be associated with St. Mary, Aldermanbury, and honored to have had the opportunity to tell its remarkable story.

Bibliography

Churchill, Winston S.
    1948-53   The Second World War. Boston: Houghton Mifflin.

Davidson, R. L. D.
    1984   "The Winston Churchill Memorial and Library at Westminster College," A History of Callaway County. Fulton, MO: The Kingdom of Callaway Historical Society, 97-100.

    1984   "An Imaginative Concept Becomes a Reality." Unpublished lectures presented to the Mid-Missouri Friends of the Churchill Memorial, April-

June.

Garside, P. L.
    1990   "London and the Home Counties," The Cambridge Social History of Britain, vol 1, 471-539.

Gilbert, Martin
    1990   Churchill: A Life. New York: Henry Holt.

Horsbrugh, Patrick
    1964   "A Wren Church for the United States: Problems of Choice, Transportation, Siting and Reconstruction," unpublished address to the Iowa Chapter of the American Institute of Architects.

    1989   "Sinews of Peace-Sinews of History: Wren and Symbolism (the rationale establishing the choice of the Church of St. Mary Aldermanbury to provide the focus for the Winston Churchill Memorial in these United States)," unpublished address delivered at The Christopher Wren Symposium.

Kauffman, Mark
    1961   "The Realm of Christopher Wren," Life (June 2, 1961), 103-109.

Nairn, Ian
    1960   "Who Will Defend the Wall?" The Observer. April 10.

Parrish, William
    1971   Westminster College: An Informal History, 1851-1969. Fulton, MO: Westminster College.

Stinson, David
    1973   "The Winston Churchill Memorial and Library in the U.S.," Journal of Library History, Philosophy and Librarianship.

8 (April, 1973), 72-77.

Thompson, F. L. M., ed.
    1990   The Cambridge Social History of Britain, 1750-1950, 2 vols. Cambridge: Cambridge University Press.

Williams, James
    1986   "An Imaginative Concept:" The Winston Churchill Memorial and Library Project, 1961-1969. Unpublished Westminster College Senior History Thesis.

CHAPTER TEN:
THE TREASURES OF
ST. MARY, ALDERMANBURY

Introduction

The Church of St. Mary the Virgin, Aldermanbury, has been the recipient of many treasures, formerly at home in other churches or institutions. While in London the process had already begun, but it accelerated when the church was restored at Westminster College. These gifts are tangible symbols of the common faith, values, and friendship shared by the people of Great Britain with the people of the United States. As Sir Winston Churchill said in his "Iron Curtain" Speech in 1946, the Anglo-American friendship is fundamental to the future peace, freedom and security of the world.

In this final chapter we will catalogue the rich treasures which St. Mary, Aldermanbury, has inherited. The reader will be aware that sentiment and symbolism may count for more than intrinsic value in defining a treasure.

Before the Great Fire

As acknowledged above, we know little of the contents of the various St. Mary, Aldermanbury buildings prior to the Great Fire of 1666. Dean Ralph de Diceto's Inquisition (1181) has no indication of what the earliest Church of St. Mary, Aldermanbury, contained. The survey of the Church's property in 1538 (see Ch. 3) lists holdings without identifying their source. Stow's Survey of London (1598, 1603) describes the Church and cloisters and describes a large human bone on display (see Ch. 3). However, it does not constitute a "treasure."

Professor Grimes' excavation of the site of the Church in 1969, after the removal of the fabric to Westminster College, gives us the first indication of the passing along of what deserves to be called a treasure. In this case, it was the Church building itself. Grimes confirmed the literary tradition of <u>Parentalia</u> that Sir Christopher Wren utilized the foundations of the Gothic building of 1437, as well as the stub of the medieval tower, in his reconstruction. That Wren could execute an English renaissance church on Gothic foundations is a tribute to his architectural ingenuity. Thus, the outline of the 1437 structure is preserved to this day, in the basic shape and dimensions of the ground plan of the church as it has been restored at Westminster, and in the Aldermanbury churchyard park in London.

There has been some dispute whether the small spiral staircase, which now rises from the balcony into the bell tower, was a relic of the Gothic Church, or was a Wren contribution. The plan published in 1929 by the Royal Commission on Historical Monuments clearly shows that the staircase was part of the tower structure which the Commission had consigned to a 15th century date. Professor Grimes' findings seem to reinforce this conclusion.

Wren's Rebuilding

We have documented in Ch. 5 that Sir Christopher used Kentish ragstone from the walls of the Church of St. Mary Magadalene, Milk Street, in the reconstruction of St. Mary, Aldermanbury. The stone was used as the rubble core of the new Portland limestone walls. Although not a treasure by aesthetic standards, the St. Mary Magdalene stone would have been an economic boon, saving considerable money in the rebuilding. However, it would not have been economical to transport this rubble across the Atlantic, so it is not a part of the present structure. In any event, Marshall Sisson and Frederick Sternberg had agreed to use modern building techniques on the parts of the building not seen, meaning the rubble core was not to be used.

It may have been that rubble from the old St. Paul's, a few blocks from Aldermanbury, was used in Wren's rebuilding. Such was Wren's practice in the building of parish churches, although it is not specifically documented in the case of St. Mary, Aldermanbury.

After the Union with St. Alphage, London Wall

When St. Mary, Aldermanbury, joined with St. Alphage, London Wall, the latter church building was destroyed and many of the furnishings were transferred to St. Mary's. The costly oak reredos, pulpit and pews were moved and can be seen in all extant pre-Blitz photographs of the interior.

The large church chest also probably originated outside the Church, though it was there prior to 1885. The Royal Commission on Historical Monuments Report of 1929 dated the chest to about 1660, but other antiquarian authorities suggest that it was in fact a bridal chest of the 15th century or earlier, to which ecclesiastical decorations were added. The decorations on the chest are the *Magen David* (Star of David), perhaps in recognition that St. Mary's, like its neighbor the Guildhall Church of St. Lawrence Jewry, stood within the old Jewish quarter of London. The Church also had processional staffs bearing the *Magen David*, which presumably perished in the Blitz. However, the *Magen David* is also used as a trinitarian symbol in Christian iconography.

The 19th century communion plate which replaced the stolen 17th century plate, mentioned above, was in the Church safe on the night of 29 December, 1940. The heat of the conflagration severely damaged the surface finish of all the vessels. President Robert L. D. Davidson instructed that the set not be cleaned or replated so it might serve as a reminder of the horror of the Blitz. The plate in the set is inscribed: "This plate was purchased by the parish to replace a set of plate presented by Walter Brockley and Walter Pell in 1658 and stolen from the church in July 1889."

The church chest, discussed above, was probably destroyed by the fire of 29 December, along with two fine 17th century chancel chairs deemed worthy of inclusion in the 1929 report of the Royal Commission on Historical Monuments. Knowledgeable persons have lodged inquires in the City, and found nothing to suggest that either the chairs or the chest were rescued. Professors Hauer and Young ran an inquiry in <u>Church Times</u> (1988) which also failed to locate any of the missing artifacts.

The monuments within the Church remained inside the roofless nave following the Blitz. It was decided on two grounds that they should not be transported to Westminster. First, they were British monuments and should properly remain in England, although one commemorated a young naval officer lost off the American coast. Second, the Churchill Memorial plan envisioned the restoration of the Church to Wren's original conception, and the monuments were all later additions. But rather than being conserved and properly catalogued, the monuments were apparently mislaid or discarded. Inquiries lodged by the representative of the Churchill Memorial in England, Dr. Noel Mander, and Professor Hauer produced no information concerning their fate. The Royal Commission on Historical Monuments Report of 1929 had singled out the double monument to the Chandler Brothers as a particularly fine example of 17th century monumental marble work. Whether any of them should belatedly be brought to the Churchill Memorial Museum must therefore be a purely hypothetical question. In the meantime, we are left with the surveys of the monuments such as the one preserved in the Guildhall Manuscript Collection (Ms. 2480: Monumental Inscriptions [compiled in 1913] and published in Carter's history of the church [Carter 1913: 78-81, with illustrations]). The monuments Carter includes, with the date(s) of death, are:

Robert Aske (1688)
George Barren Jeffreys (1690)
Richard Chandler (1691) and his brother John (1686)
Mrs. Mary Hack (1704)
Samuel Lambert (1727)
Joseph Bagnall (1728) and his wife Margaret (1703)
Timothy Betton (1731) and his wife Anne (1713)
Joseph Letherland (1764)
Lieutenant John Smith (1782)
Samuel Smith (1789) and his wife Elizabeth (1782)
John Fryer (1796)
Thomas Taylor (1815)
William Rust (1826) and his wife Dorothy (1832)
James Holt (1827)
Rev. John Willott (1846) and his wife Sarah (1838)
Rev. John Philipps Bean (1854)

After the Restoration on the Campus of Westminster College

Treasures from other churches and institutions were added to St. Mary's when the church was reconstructed as the Winston Churchill Memorial. They include several items from other Wren churches in London, which reflect the ecumenical support for the church, and gifts from livery companies of the City of London as well as the City Corporation.

One of these treasures is on the exterior of the church. It is the keystone of the window on the west side, in the base of the tower. So long as St. Mary's stood on its original London site, the west wall of the tower was hard against either a house or a commercial or public building. Thus Wren designed no window into the lowest courses of the west tower wall. It is a tribute to Wren's integrity as an architect that he nevertheless lavished great care on the west front of the Church. The gifted reconstruction architect, Marshall Sisson, reasoned that Wren, given his love of light, would have put a window in the lower west tower wall had the London churchyard offered the open exposure of the Westminster site. Many of his churches have such a window. Consequently, Mr. Sisson designed a Wren window for that wall. But the remains of St. Mary's lacked a keystone for the additional window. An authentic Wren substitute was located at the Church of St. Swithun, London Stone, on Cannon Street, which was being dismantled at the same time as St. Mary's. It is a charming piece, composed of double gargoyles. It still bears the grime of old time London fogs and the soot left by the dreadful fire caused by the German air raid on 29 December, 1940. The "London stone" itself, now known to be a gatepost from the Roman governor's palace, has been set into the alcove of a wall of a bank building opposite Cannon Street Station in London. Actually, St. Swithun was one of the London churches Westminster might have obtained, but St. Mary's was judged more appropriate. Still, viewers of St. Mary's west front must applaud not only Wren's elegant overall conception, but as well the Wren-Sisson collaboration on the west tower window.

The vestry doors and screens now incorporated in St. Mary's are reputed to have been produced in the 17th century workshop of Wren's woodcarver, Grinling Gibbons. However, no documentation exists to support this conjecture. The doors and screens stood originally in the Wren-designed Church of St. Dionis Backchurch. They had been put in storage when St. Dionys Backchurch was dismantled in the 19th century, and were used in the construction of the present vestries in St. Mary, Aldermanbury. Motifs of cherubim and various fruit and leaves, characteristic of the Gibbons style, were used as models for the skillful woodcarvings of Arthur Ayres in the rest of the reconstructed St. Mary's (see Figures 10.3 and 10.4).

On 4 August, 1968, a double set of 17th century communion silver was presented for use in the Church of St. Mary (see Figures 10.1 and 10.6). The circumstances surrounding this gift have been discussed in Ch. 9. The six items of plate came from a Wren church located very near Aldermanbury, St. Anne and St. Agnes (John Milton's parish). When this church was incorporated into the United Parishes, their treasury came under the control of St. Vedast, Foster Lane. Two 10 inch, 36 ounce flagons dated 1636 came originally from St. John Zachary, as did two patens dated 1638. St. John Zachary was among the City churches not rebuilt after the Great Fire of 1666. It stood directly across Noble Street from St. Anne and St. Agnes at the point Noble Street intersects Gresham Street. Presumably, part of its plate was transferred to St. Anne and St. Agnes after the Great Fire. St. John Zachary was a favorite burial place for members of the Goldsmiths Company. The patens, about 8 inches in diameter, were the gift of Alexander Jackson, Saymaster of Goldsmith's Hall, to the Parish Church of St. John Zachary. They carry the date of 1638. The chalices, both 9 inches high with 4 1/2 inch bowls, weighing 19 ounces, were each inscribed "St. Anne and St. Agnes Parish 1633."

Portions of the beautiful case for the organ, built for the Church of St. Mary, Aldermanbury, by the St. Peter's Organ Works of London, under the supervision of Dr. Noel Mander, MBE, FSA, came from the Woolwich Parish Church, Kent. The original case had been built in 1741.

The Mander organ is a treasure in its own right (see Figure 10.2). English Baroque organs were usually small and generally lacked a pedal rank (though German organs had them). The pedal rank, however, is essential to play most of the modern organ repertoire. So Dr. Mander created an instrument which achieves a rewarding synthesis between the late English baroque instrument and the demands of contemporary organ music. It retains the direct mechanical "tracker" action of an earlier age. The four foot pipe on the Swell (Stopt Diapason) and the eight foot pipe on the Great (Chimney Flute) in the St. Mary's organ were made by George England in 1770. England had built the first known organ in St. Mary's about that time. Some renowned organists have pronounced it the finest baroque organ in the United States. It is built in the highest traditions of the craft, made to last not decades but centuries.

The organ case is surmounted by decorative crown and mitres, symbolic of the restoration of the English monarchy in 1660 (see Figure 10.2), and the subsequent reestablishment of the episcopacy in the Church of England, with the monarch as Head of the Church. Dr. Mander was responsible for the rescue and restoration of this set which formerly stood in the Wren Church of St. Michael Paternoster Royal. They had originally been atop the organ in the Wren Church of All Hallows the Great,

Lower Thames Street, which had been demolished in 1876. That organ was transferred to St. Michael. When St. Michael's was badly damaged during the Blitz, the architect who restored the church did not leave enough room above the organ for the crown and mitres. Dr. Mander secured permission for them to be tranferred to St. Mary, Aldermanbury, and supervised their restoration. St. Michael was the parish church of Dick Whittington, famous medieval Lord Mayor of London. Given the role played by St. Mary Aldermanbury's perpetual curate Edmund Calamy in the restoration of the monarchy, but also his rejection of appointment as a bishop and his loss of his living because of his conscientious reservations about episcopacy as such (see Ch. 4), the placement of these treasures in Calamy's church is both appropriate and ironic.

As we have noted in Ch. 9, the altar table in St. Mary's is not an original 17th century piece, but a splendid reproduction executed by Mr. Tom Hooper of St. Peter's Organ Works. Mr. Hooper modelled the table, presented to the Churchill Memorial in 1983, as a memorial to Neal S. and Josephine Wood by the Wood family, after the Wren communion table fashioned for the Church of All Hallows, Bread Street. That table is now in the north chapel of the Church of St. Vedast, Foster Lane. A similar table is found in the Lady Chapel of St. Paul's Cathedral. It had been the original "high altar" in Wren's design of St. Paul's. The elegant but simple table reflects the Puritan de-emphasis on the altar in worship.

As previously stated, the silver candlesticks, now on display in the ecclesiastical gallery of the Memorial museum, are a gift of the Bishop of Westminster, the Roman Catholic primate of England (see Figure 10.6). They formerly stood in a side chapel of Westminster Cathedral, London. They are tangible symbols of the ecumenical heritage and present mission of the Church of St. Mary, Aldermanbury. They are used in the church only on very special occasions, and are otherwise kept in the Undercroft's Ecclesiastical Gallery. The cross, which accompanies the candlesticks, was secured in the United States by Mr. Wood, whose contributions to the acquiring of many of the "treasures of St. Mary's" and, as we have made clear in Ch. 9, the church itself were extensive.

The Churchwarden's (or Beadle's) Staff is surmounted by a small bust of a woman, presumably a representation of the patron of the Church, the Virgin Mary. It dates to 1756, and was one of St. Mary's own treasures not destroyed in the Blitz. The bust was restored and mounted on its present handle under the direction of Dr.

Mander.

The processional cross is of 17th century provenance, and came from the Church of St. James, the Great, Bethnal Green. St. James, now redundant, was known as "the red Church" because of its red brick construction. It was also known as "the marrying Church." A former vicar, noting that poor young couples were cohabiting without a formal marriage because they could not afford church fees, endowed a fund to pay wedding costs for the indigent. The cross was turned into a crucifix during the 19th century. The corpus was later removed, but restoration was unable to remove all traces of damage to the surface. The cross was obtained for St. Mary's through the good offices of Dr. Noel Mander.

Lovely needlepointed ecclesiastical paraments in the colors of the liturgical year, designed by local artist Jean Berry, a Fellow of the Memorial, adorn the pulpit and standing Bible.

The stand for the Lord's Mayor ceremonial sword, and the sword to go in it, are the most spectacular recent additions to St. Mary's (see Figure 10.7). All City Churches required a sword stand for official visits by the Lord Mayor. The great City ceremonial sword, symbol of mayoral authority, is carried before the Lord Mayor, and deposited in the stand during the Church service. Dr. Mander particularly felt the lack of a stand in restored St. Mary's, and took the lead in obtaining one for the Church.

St. Mary's had been the guild Church of the Worshipful Company of Haberdashers, and so the Haberdashers played a major role in the project, as did the Corporation of London. Additional livery companies joined in, as did other persons and institutions in Britain. Livery companies contributing were the Haberdashers, the Mercers, the Merchant Taylors, the Pewterers, the Barbers, the Tallow Chandlers, the Armourers and Braziers, the Saddlers, the Innholders, the Blacksmiths, the Musicians, the Farriers, the Shipwrights, and the Parish Clerks. Other contributors were Sir Ralph Perring (Lord Mayor, 1962, and Parish Clerk of St. Michael Wood Street); Sir Francis Dashwood; Sir John Plumb; Alderman Graham; A. B. Wilson; A. G. W. Scott; Lord Dunleath; St. Paul's Cathedral; Westminster Cathedral; Portsmouth Cathedral; St. Lawrence, Jewry; Barclays Bank; the Council of Christians and Jews; Bevis Mark Synagogue; Chartered Insurance Institute; Southeby's; and Frederick's Place. The stand bears the crown of the Sovereign and the arms of the Haberdashers and of the City. Medallions bearing the arms of the other donors are mounted on flanking bars. The gift was made "to the Church of St. Mary, Aldermanbury by Liverymen and Citizens of the City of London," 24 April, 1988. The gift memorializes Robert Aske, the great 17th century master of the Haberdashers company, philanthropist, and benefactor of his parish Church, St. Mary, Aldermanbury (see Ch. 6), on the 300th anniversary of his death. It also commemorates the 540th year since King Henry VI granted letters patent to the Haberdashers.

The stand is a precise replica of one made by Robert Bird in 1687 for the City Church of St. Michael Wood Street, now in Haberdashers Hall. The commission was executed by Mr. Hector Moore of Brandeston Forge, Suffolk, one of England's most renowned smiths, and by his wife, Mrs. Mary Moore. Mrs. Moore, an artist, photographs works to be duplicated and draws actual size plans. When Mr. Moore has done the metalwork, she adds required gilding and enameling. During the work, Mr. Moore pointed out that the vine tendrils on the Bird stand were tapered. Modern works frequently use untapered tendrils. He was delighted when Dr. Mander informed him that the donors would prefer to follow the costly path of authenticity.

Many persons associated with the Churchill Memorial project assumed that the St. Mary's sword stand would remain empty unless or until a Lord Mayor of London paid a formal visit. But this was not to be the case. An appropriate sword, fabricated ca. 1720, was found in City stores and restored by the Wilkinson company, with splendid results. The sword was presented to St. Mary, Aldermanbury by the Corporation of the City of London, and by the Worshipful Company of Cutlers in the autumn of 1991. It was accompanied by an ordinance from Common Council, proclaiming days on which the sword may be displayed in the stand even if the Lord Mayor is not present (one being the feast of St. Michael and All Angels—29 September—, election day in the City). The sword resides at other times in a special display case in the Churchill Memorial Museum.

The sword stand is affixed to the west wall of the south vestry so that it is in full view, but does not (as in some London Churches) obscure the views of the pulpit or chancel for any worshipper, a consideration we believe Dr. Wren would have approved.

The west wall of the north vestry bears a scroll presented by the Worshipful Company of Barbers, recognizing the important work of the Churchill Memorial in restoring and preserving the Church of St. Mary, Aldermanbury.

A bust of William Shakespeare stands at the west end of the nave. It is a replica of the bust on Shakespeare's tomb in Holy Trinity Church, Stratford-Upon-Avon, and was presented by the Stratford town council. Also on display at the west end of the nave is a cast metal 19th century parish boundary marker, bearing the initials StMVAB. Another is on display in the museum. Such markers greatly simplified the annual task of "beating the boundaries" of the parish.

The newest addition to the Church is a memorial to the Eagle Squadrons, the young Americans who volunteered in the cause of freedom and enlisted in the Royal Air Force before the United States entered World War II. The memorial consists of framed paintings of the squadron badges which were approved by King George VI. The paintings of the three squadron badges were done by the College of Arms and are a gift of the RAF. They were dedicated on the 50th anniversary of the transfer of the Eagle Squadrons from a British to American command (26 September, 1942). The memorial is a particularly poignant reminder of that Anglo-American friendship and shared stock of values and convictions to which Sir Winston Churchill so frequently referred.

The lectern Bible in St. Mary's is an especially fine copy of the Oxford Lectern Bible in two volumes. It is number 193 in a limited edition of 200 copies, printed on hand made paper. The text is the Authorized Version of 1611, the approved translation of the Bible for the Church of England during most of the years that the Wren Church stood in London. The St. Mary's Bible was custom bound by Mr. Frank Langham. Mr. Langham noted that a lectern Bible of Wren's time would have been bound by boards, and recalled a source from which boards salvaged out of the old Houses of Parliament (which were destroyed by fire in 1835) might be obtained. He fashioned the covers from some of this wood, creating yet another "Westminster connection" for St. Mary's. (Panels recovered from the blitzed modern House of Commons are also on display in the Museum.) The Bible is a memorial to Charles Bethune Horsbrugh and Marion Rose Horsbrugh, and a symbol of their great admiration for Sir Winston Churchill.

Mrs. Joseph A. Bascom of St. Louis chaired the American Tapestries Committee, which coordinated the work of over 400 women (and a few skillful men as well!) from 38 American states and some foreign countries who executed the nine needlepoint designs. The designs for the kneelers, by Mr. Francis Stephens, ARCA, display symbols of Wren motifs in the Church of St. Mary, the City, and the Spencer-Churchill arms.

Mrs. Derek A. Lee, an Englishwoman resident in New York, chaired the British Embroideries Committee, which supplied needlepoint seats for the chancel chairs and the seven large kneelers at the communion rail. The communion kneelers display symbols related to Winston Churchill's life and career. The designs were by Mr. Stephen A. Lee of the Arthur H. Lee tapestry works, Birkenhead, Cheshire, and by Mrs. Derek A. Lee. They were executed in <u>petit point</u> by Miss Mona Smith, a retired artisan from the tapestry works.

We have already noted that some treasures of St. Mary's are displayed in the Museum rather than the Church proper. We shall conclude by cataloguing additional items in the Museum, including a display on the history of the Church, on the Blitz and reconstruction, on Sir Christopher Wren, and on "A Living Memorial"—St. Mary's as a functioning Church today, all at the west end of the main gallery.

The display on the history of the Church includes three decorated floor titles found in the excavations conducted by Professor W. F. Grimes (see Chapter Two). The tiles are on extended loan from the Museum of London. Experts at the Museum of London date them to the 14th century and one of Professor Grimes' available excavation photographs shows that they were in the nave of the original church building, probably replacing more humble flooring material during a period of affluence. Whether they were reused in the 1437 building is not clear at present. Miss Anna Hauer found a box of the tiles in Museum storage during a 1987 summer student internship. She informed Professor Hauer, who arranged a loan of three representative examples with Museum authorities.

The Wren display includes a replica of the Edward Pierce bust of Wren (see figure 5.1), executed in 1673. Pierce was a noted 17th century sculptor who worked with Wren at St. Paul's. The marble original is in the Ashmolean Museum, Oxford. Also in the Wren display is a reduced size color reproduction of the Wren "presidential portrait" from the Royal Society. The secretary of the Royal Society presented a quality print of the portrait to Professor Hauer during preparations for the Wren Symposium, and the Royal Society gave permission for its use by the Churchill Memorial. Most of the items included in the Symposium museum exhibit, "Christopher Wren's London," are either the property of, or on extended loan to, the Memorial. Not ordinarily displayed, these items may nonetheless be made available for inspection by scholars and other qualified parties through advanced arrangement.

The Queen Mother Elizabeth presented the Memorial with a large sized copy of the Book of Common Prayer of the Church of England. This personal touch, typical of the beloved "Queen Mum," makes the book a favorite of visitors to the Church and Museum. It is displayed in the Ecclesiastical Gallery alongside the Westminster Cathedral cross and candlesticks and the St. Anne and St. Agnes plate. Also in the Ecclesiastical Gallery are additional works of the British Embroideries Committee. There are two sets (one red, one white) of magnificent modern frontals, burses and veils, with matching stoles and chasubles. There is also a blue set consisting of burse, stole and veil. The white set bears a spectacular rendition of the Phoenix symbol which has become identified with St. Mary, Aldermanbury. The Churchill Memorial has published a detailed catalogue entitled "The Churchill Memorial Tapestries," citing the numerous gifted British designers and craftspersons who contributed to the works of the British Committee, as well as more details on the work of the American Committee. Also catalogued is a pulpit fall designed by Mr. Leslie Tilletts of New York commemorating the honorary American citizenship bestowed on Sir Winston Churchill.

The Phoenix is also the central symbol of a modern illuminated stained glass panel, displayed beside the entrance to the Memorial theater. It was executed by artists Judith Cato and Deborah Boatner.

The west wall of the ecclesiastical gallery is covered by a large tapestry depicting an array of cosmic symbolism. It was executed by Ms. Georgia K. Tewell and presented by the Gamble family as a memorial to Mr. Clark R. Gamble, a fellow of the Memorial, and to the artist, who was his granddaughter.

Also displayed in the ecclesiastical gallery are several historic Bibles and Prayer Books, including a 17th century lectern Bible from the English Church in Riga, Latvia, which made its way back to England, and thence to Westminster College. A number of other smaller items are also displayed in the Ecclesiastical Gallery.

The communion plate from the Mount Olivet Presbyterian Church of north Callaway County, Missouri, is not on permanent display in the museum, but is sometimes used in services in the Church of St. Mary. When the Mt. Olivet Church was rendered redundant by the depopulation of its community, the surviving members conferred the set on St. Mary's. The gift was an appropriate one, since through much of its history the pulpit of the Church was supplied by faculty members and students from Westminster College.

Finally, from Westminster Abbey, the Memorial was presented with the chair used by Captain Henry Gatteridge during the coronation of Queen Elizabeth II. The Memorial has been the recipient of a large number of other items of great interest which are of secular rather than ecclesiastical importance and hence are not catalogued here.

The Church of St. Mary the Virgin, Aldermanbury, itself remains the greatest treasure for its religious meaning, its historic significance and its aesthetic excellence. Persons expert in architectural history recognize it as one of the finest, if not the finest, restorations of a Wren Church. Even where circumstances suggested a departure from strict adherence to Wren's original plan (and these are few!), the departure was itself pure Wren. We discussed above the Wren-Sisson west tower window. Another case in point is the Wren-Sisson staircase. St. Mary's sat on ground level in London with no undercroft, only small unconnected burial vaults. But at Westminster the Church was to stand above an undercroft museum, and direct access between Church and museum was essential. The use of modern construction techniques permitted Mr. Sisson to open the tower base into a small narthex, illuminated by the west window. Wren had done the same in several of his City churches, but at St. Mary's, the bulky medieval tower stub and the location against other buildings ruled out such a possibility. Then Mr. Sisson provided a Wren staircase between the narthex and museum, inspired by the cantilevered spiral tower staircase in St. Paul's Cathedral.

Conclusion

Readers of this work are aware that the conservation of a monument like St. Mary, Aldermanbury, is a costly endeavor. Hardly had Dr. Wren completed his work than the vestry began to face the need for repairs and upkeep, and this continued throughout its London history. The removal of the Church to the United States unfortunately complicated the ongoing task of maintaining the building. The extremes of summer solar radiation, heat and humidity, and winter cold with very low humidity are a far remove from the milder climate of London. One architect likened buildings to organisms which adapt to their environments. St. Mary's is a 300 year building now adapting to a new environment that Wren could not have foreseen, presenting severe stresses to both the interior and the exterior of the Church. The Board of Trustees of Westminster College, the Board of Governors and the Society of Fellows of the Winston Churchill Memorial and Library in the U.S.A., and members of the Friends of the Churchill Memorial, have assumed a firm resolve to preserve St. Mary Aldermanbury, in the form of Wren's inspired vision.

We have told St. Mary's story because of our love for the Church and above all for that which it symbolizes. If our words bring others to share this love and to encourage and share this resolve, our work as authors will be well rewarded. And, in the end, *Soli Deo Gloria*.

APPENDIX: THE CLERGY OF ST. MARY, ALDERMANBURY

Dates	Name
1540	John Morris (?)
1544	John Webbe (?)
1569	Christopher Bateman
1570	Mr. Rose or Rese, M.A. (lecturer?)
1574	William Trevor
1575	Robert Bliethman
	Mr. Gilpin
1576	Christopher Blythman (brother of Robert)
1576	Christopher Salford
1588 (?)	Michael Salford (lecturer then curate)
1591-1617	Robert Harland
1617-24	Thomas Downing
1624-26	Robert Harris
1626-32	Dr. Thomas Taylor
1632-39	Dr. John Staughton
1639-62	Dr. Edmund Calamy
1643-48	Matthew Newcomen (lecturer)
1651	Simeon Ashe (lecturer)
1663	Richard Martyn
1664-65	Dr. Anthony Walker
1665	John Pechell (lecturer-?)
1670-77	Dr. Simon Ford
1677-83	Benjamin Calamy
1678-	Mr. Steven (lecturer)
1681-83	Dr. Francis Bridge (lecturer)
1683-89	Nicholas Stratford
1684-1702	Richard Bird (lecturer)
1689	Ezekiel Hopkins
1690-1717	Lilley Butler
1705-22	Nathaniel Marshall (lecturer)

Dates	Name
1717-31	Joshua Smith
1731-1755	Dr. William Sandford
1731-	Henry Bund (lecturer)
-1750	Dr. Nichols (lecturer)
1750-	Mr. Ellison (lecturer)
1755-91	John Laurence
1762-	Fran(cis) Leathes (unlicensed curate)
1770-	Mr. Finch (lecturer)
1777-	Mr. Prince (lecturer)
1791-1802	Charles Smith
?	Richard Craddock (curate)
1802-43	James Salisbury
1803-	Mr. Japhson (lecturer)
1812-	William Parker (curate)
1832-	William Jowett (lecturer)
?	John Phillips Bean (curate-?)
1843-54	John Phillips Bean
1843-	William Harrison (lecturer)
1846-	James Cohen (lecturer)
1854-1917	Charles Collins
1915-	W. Kingston (curate)
1917-39	Henry Alford Mason
1939	G. F. Saymell
1940	Phillip Davenport Ellis
1945-	A. J. Macdonald (Sequestrator)
1969-74	Dr. William Huntley (Chaplain of Westminster College)
1974-75	Mr. Ed Phillips (Chaplain)
1975-	Dr. William Young (Chaplain)
1991-92	Gina Tollini (Coordinator of Religious Life)

Note: As part of the United Parishes of London, St. Mary, Aldermanbury, can also be considered part of the charge of the incumbent serving St. Vedast, Foster Lane, seat of the United Parishes. St. Mary, Aldermanbury, still appears on the list of churches in the United Parishes displayed in the narthex of St. Vedast, Foster Lane.

GENERAL BIBLIOGRAPHY

Note: This General Bibliography contains data on all the manuscripts noted throughout the narrative, and other general works related to more than one chapter. Works related to individual chapters are noted in the bibliographies found at the end of each chapter.

MANUSCRIPTS

Note: Manuscripts from the Guildhall Library Manuscript Collection are abbreviated GM. Pamphlets from the Guildhall Library are abbreviated GP.

Records of and relating to the Church of St. Mary the Virgin, Aldermanbury in the Guildhall Library, London

Vestry Minutes
Ms 3570: Vestry Minutes
  Vol. 1, 1569-1609
  Vol. 2, 1610-1763
  Vol. 3, 1763-1815
  Vol. 4, 1815-1849
  Vol. 5, 1849-1870
  Vol. 6, 1870-1903

Ms. 3570A: Vestry Minutes and Account Book Extracts (a summary prepared in 1885)
  Vol. 1, Vestry Minutes (1569-1737)
  Vol. 2, Vestry Minutes (1737-1885)
  Vol. 3, Accounts (1569-1665)

Ms. 3571: Vestry Minutes (Rough Draft)
  Vol. 1, May, 1872 through December, 1886
  Vol. 2, April 1887 through April, 1917

Ms. 4852: Minute Book of United Benefices of St. Mary, Aldermanbury and St. Alphage, London Wall (1917-1938), including boundary lists (1925)

Ms. 23,917: Easter Vestry Minutes, 1941-44

Parish Registers

Ms. 3572: Parish Registers (Baptisms, Marriages, Burials)
  Vol. 1, Baptisms (1538-1722), Marriages (1538-1721),
      Burials (1538-1722)
  Vol. 2, Baptisms (1722-1812), Marriages (1722-1754),
      Burials (1722-1812)
  Vol. 3, Baptisms (1813-1940), Marriages (1813-1837),
      Burials (1813-1859)

Ms. 3573: Marriages (1754-1791) and Banns (1754- 1804)

Ms. 3574: Marriages
  Vol. 1, 1791-1812
  Vol. 2, 1837- 1940

Ms. 3575: Banns (1804-1854)

Ms. 3576: Banns (1852-1940)

Ms. 3576A: Banns, Correspondence, etc. (1928-1939)

Ms. 3593: Marriage licenses (1837-1928)

Note: Parish Registers published by the Harleian Society, ed. W. Bruce Bannerman (vols. 61, 62, 65 [1538-1859]).

Financial Records

Ms. 23,737, vols. 81-85: Deeds related to Parochial Charity Estates (1308-1889).

Ms. 23,737A: Calendar of deeds relating to London Parish Estates (1308-1889). Published by the Trustees of the London Parochial Charities. 1924-1925.

Ms. 3556: Church Warden Accounts
  Vol. 1, 1570-1592
  Vol. 2, 1631-1677
  Vol. 3, 1676-1737
  Vol. 4, 1737-1790 (includes disbursements for poor)
  Vol. 5, 1790-1800 (includes disbursements for poor and general accounts [1796-1829])
  Vol. 6, 1828-1869
  Vol. 7, 1869-1891
  Vol. 8, 1897-1920

Ms. 2500A: Churchwardens Account Rolls, with parson's tithes, clerk's wages, and inhabitants' names (1577, 1591, 1593-1596)

Ms. 3590: Tithe Notebooks (1671, 1674, 1804)

Ms. 9801: Parish tithe assessments (1671-1685)

Ms. 3561: Yearly Rates for Poor
  Vol. 1, 1706-1792
  Vol. 2, 1793-1809

Ms. 3557: Rental of Parish Estates (1733-1797)

Ms. 3592: Parish fees (1790 and 1834)

Ms. 3565: Overseers Book of Receipts and Payments
  Vol. 1, 1828-1837
  Vol. 2, 1837-1848
  Vol. 3, 1848-1867

Vol. 4, 1867-1886

Ms. 3564: Weekly Poor Book
  Vol. 1, 1833-1838
  Vol. 2, 1849-1865

Ms. 2047: Poor Notebooks, 120 vols. (1838-1899)

Ms. 3567: Account books of Committee to Advise the Guardians regarding the poor (1880-1891)

Ms. 3598: Parish papers, including estate papers and charities (1883-1918)

Ms. 2368: Overseers Receipts and Payments (1887-1908)

Ms. 3566: Collections Monthly Deposits, 4 vols. (1887-1908)

Ms. 3594: Cash Book (1890-1891)

Ms. 3568: Collecting and Depository Book, 5 vols. (1898-1908)

Ms. 2369: Poor Notebooks, 12 vols. (1900-1907)

Ms. 3562: Rate Book, 4 vols. (1901-1902)

Ms. 4855: Accounts (1908-1938)

Ms. 23,921: Cash Book (1938-1950)

Ms. 2368: Overseers Receipts and Payments (date uncertain)

Ms. 19,225, vol. 49: Parish papers and deeds (chiefly 19th and 20th centuries)

The Wren Rebuilding after the Great Fire (1666)

Ms. 25,540: Copies of orders from the Committee for rebuilding City Churches (1670-1685) (also coded as St. Paul's WE 16 f. 156).

Ms. 25,535 (?): Warrants for payment to Sir Christopher Wren of money from the coal tax
 Vol. 1, 1670-1688
 Vol. 2, 1688-1717

Ms. 25,536: Audited expenditures for City Churches, 14 vols. (1670-1694)

Ms. 25,537: Draft accounts of expenditures, 3 vols. (1670-1694) (See also Mss. 25,538 and 25,541-25,547)

Ms. 25,539: Charges in Rebuilding the Church of St. Mary, Aldermanbury (1672-1677).

Ms. 25,548: Salaries paid to Sir Christopher Wren and others engaged in rebuilding the city churches

Ms. 25,549: Annual abstracts of money paid from the coal tax
 Vol. 1, 1688-1700
 Vol. 2, 1700-1705

Ms. 25,550: Abstract of the Bills paid for all Parochial Churches (1671-1694)

Other

Ms. A54-34 Chapter Building Account, St. Paul's Cathedral (1532)

Ms. 5445/20 Minutes of the Worshipful Company of Brewers (1671)

Ms. 3563: List of housekeeps within the parish
 Vol. 1, 1758-1830

Vol. 2, 1831-1844
Vol. 3, 1812-1882

Ms. 3560: Parish poor apprentice book (1810-1828)

Ms. 3600: Papers related to repairs to organ and church fabric (1814-1920)

Ms. 3559: List of clergy occasionally officiating (1827-1848)

Ms. 3735: Confirmations (1855-1933)

Ms. 3599: Parish papers concerning the amalgamation of St. Mary, Aldermanbury and St. Alphage, London Wall (1893-1918)

Ms. 3558: Churchwarden's Letter Book (1897-1908)

Ms. 3569: List of those serving in World War I, numbers in attendance at services, and collections (1912-1917)

Ms. 2480: Monumental Inscriptions (compiled in 1913)

Ms. 3591: Address on the history of the church given by Alec Raven Briggs on November 28, 1936

Ms. 22,287: Surveys and Plans for proposed layouts of Churchyards, etc. (including the St. Mary Aldermanbury Park) (1939-1958)

Manuscripts related to the Church of St. Mary, Aldermanbury in the Lambeth Palace Library (abbreviated as LPL)

Fulham Papers (Visitation Returns in preparation for the Bishop of London's visit or responses to inquiries)
Osbaldseston 6, f. 115 (1762)

Terrick 20, f. 101-102 (1765)
Randolph 11, f. 14 (1810)
Randolph 14, f. 57 (1812)
Blomfield 72, f. 83 (1842)
Tait 440/236 (1858)
Tait 441/332 (1862)
Jackson 2/374 (1883)
Creighton 1/40 (1900)

Other

Howley 50, f. 23-24 (1815)
Jackson (1872)

Manuscripts relating to the Church of St. Mary, Aldermanbury in the Archives of the Church Commissioners of the Church of England (abbreviated CC)

File No. 67141 (selected)
  Estate Committee Minutes (29 April, 1897)
  Letter to Vestry (24 June, 1907)
  Letter from Rev. Mason (15 January, 1917)
  Proposal from architect (31 August, 1918)
  Application for grant for repairs (25 November, 1918)
  Letter to CC from H. A. Mason (22 May, 1919)
  Grants for repairs (24 October, 1938; 16 February, 1939)
  Certification of Mr. Ellis as curate (4 September, 1939)
  Letter from G. F. Saymell (22 November, 1939)
  Refusal to restore stipend (11 December, 1941)
  Appointment of Rev. Macdonald as sequestrator (22 September, 1945)
  Return of two checks by Rev. Macdonald (6 January, 1946)
  Letter from Bishop (2 December, 1947)
Ms. 11210 2/3. Report to Bishop of Commission on Union of St. Mary Aldermanbury and St. Alphage.
Ms. R.2 3/H/4 (Parts 1-3). Proposed Supplementary Schemes, Diocese of London Area No. 8 for Reorganization of Parishes, papers and letters.

Sermons preached and pamphlets published by the ministers of the Church of St. Mary the Virgin, Aldermanbury or at the Church by others

Harris, Robert (1624-1626)

"God's Goodnes and Mercie," preached at Paul's Crosse in 1622. London, 1626.

"Hezekiah's Recovery," 1630. GP S pam.21 or 9110.

"The Way to True Blessedness," London, 1635.

"Sermon preached to Commons at a Public Fast on 25 May, 1642.

Taylor, Thomas (1626-1632)

"A Commentary on the Epistle of St. Paul to Titus," London, 1612.

"David's Learning, or the Way to True Happinesse," London: 1618.

"The Progresse of Saints to Full Holinesse," London, 1631.

"Christ's Victorie over the dragon, or Satan's down Fall. A Plaine and Pithy Exposition of Rev. 12," London: Dawlman, 1633.

"The Principles of Christian Practice," London, 1635.

Calamy, Edmund (1639-1662)

"God's Free-Mercy to England," preached before the House of Commons on 23 February, 1641.

"Groanes for Liberty, presented to Parliament, by reasons of the prelates tyranny," (1641). Published under the acronym *Smectymnuus*, standing for Stephen Marshall, Edmund Calamy, Thomas Young, Matthew Newcomen, William Spurstowe.

"England's looking-glasse," preached before the House of Commons on 12 December, 1641.

"The Noble Man's Pattern of True and Real Thankfulnesse," preached before the House of Lords on 15 June, 1643.

"A Speech delivered at Guildhall on the occasion of desiring assistance from our brethren in Scotland in this warre," 16 October, 1643.

"England's Antidote; Against the Plague of Civil Warre," preached before the House of Commons on 22 October, 1644.

"An Indictment Against England because of her Self-Murdering Divisions," preached before the House of Lords on 25 December, 1644.

"The Door of Truth Opened," in response to Henry Burton's "Truth Shut out of Doors," London, 1645.

"The Monster of Self-Seeking, Anatomized," preached at St. Paul's on 10 December, 1654.

"<u>Jus divinum ministerii evangelici</u>, or the divine right of the Gospel-ministry," London, 1654.

"The Saint's Transfiguration," preached at the funeral of Dr. Samuel Bolton, Master of Christ's College Cambridge at St. Martin's, Ludgate on 19 October, 1654.

"Precepts for Christian Practice," London, 1655.

"A Patterne for all, especially for Noble and Honourable Persons, To teach them how to die Nobly and Honourable," preached at the interment of the Right Honourable Robert Rich, Earl of Warwick. 1 May, 1658.

"Farewell Sermon," preached at St. Mary, Aldermanbury on 17 August,1662.

"Eli Trembling before the Ark," preached at St. Mary, Aldermanbury on 28 December, 1662. In response to this sermon and Calamy's subsequent imprisonment the following pamphlets appeared:
—Womock, Laurence. "Aronbimnucha; or, an Antidote to cure Calamites of their trembling fear of the Ark, with other oddities."
—Udall, D. "Perez uzza, or, A Serious letter sent to E. Calamy, 17 January 1663 touching his sermon at Aldermanbury."
—Wild, R. "A poem upon the imprisonment of Mr. Calamy in Newgate."
—"Anti-Boreale. An Answer to that Seditious and Lewd piece of Poetry, upon Master Calamy's late confinement," London, 1663.

The Art of Divine Meditation. London: Tho. Parkehurst,1680.

Burton, Henry (lecturer, 1645)
"Truth Still Truth, Though Shut out of Doors," London, 1645.

Jenkins, William (guest preacher, 1651)
"A Sermon Preached at St. Mary, Aldermanbury on the 5th Day of November, 1651, Being a Day Set Apart in Remembrance of that Great Deliverance from the Gunpowder Treason," London, 1652.

Calamy, Benjamin (1677-1683)
"Sermon before the Lord Mayor at Bow Church," 29 May, 1682. GP 4566.

"A Discourse about a Scrupulous Conscience, 1683

"A Sermon preached before the Lord Mayor at Guildhall Chappell," 30 September, 1683. GP 2371.

"Sermon before the Lord Mayor at le Bow ," 2 September, 1684 (the anniversary of the Great Fire)," GP 5091.

"A Narrative of the Sufferings of Thomas Delaune, for writing, printing, and publishing A Plea for Nonconformists, 1684. GP A.4.4.no.60.

Nicolaus Stratford (1683-1689)
The Lay-Christian's Obligation to read the Holy Scriptures. London: Richard Chitwell, 1687.

Butler, Lilley (1690-1717)
"Sermon Preached at le Bow before the Lord Mayor," 26 June, 1696. GP 699.

"Funeral Sermon," 27 March, 1694. GP 10214.

"A Discourse, Proving that the Faith and Practice of some Christians are not just a matter of Shame and Reproach," eight sermons preached at St. Paul's in 1709 (Boyle Lectures).

"Sermon Preached at St. Paul's before the Lord Mayor," 5 November, 1710.

Marshall, Nathaniel, lecturer (1705-1722)
"A Farewell Sermon," delivered on 24 June, 1722. GP 3764.

Collins, Charles Creaghe (1854-1917)
"Youth and its Responsibilities," 26 November 1882. GP 3676.

"Christ Present, a Reality and Light," Preached at St. Paul's, 14 January 1883. GP 3678.

"The Hope Laid up in Heaven," 29 August, 1886. GP 3681.

"Man Dependent upon God," preached at St. Lawrence Jewry, 1883. GP 3679.

"The Christian's Usefulness after Death," 19 July 1896 (on the unveiling of the monument to Heminges and Condell). GP 3677.

BOOKS and ARTICLES

The Church and Parish of St. Mary, Aldermanbury

Carter, Pierson Cathrick.
    1913   <u>History of the Church and Parish of St. Mary the Virgin, Aldermanbury</u>. London: W. H. and L. Collinbridge.

Dyson, Tony.
    no date   "Aldermanbury," an unpublished manuscript.

Goss, Charles.
    1944   "A History of The Parish of St. Mary the Virgin, Aldermanbury," <u>Transactions of the London and Middlesex Archaeological Society</u>. 9 (1944-47), 113-164.

Oliver, Dame Beryl.
    no date   "The Church of St. Mary the Virgin, Aldermanbury, re-erected at Fulton, Missouri," (Pamphlet 11277 in the Guildhall Library Collection).

    1969   <u>The Winston Churchill Memorial and the Church of St. Mary the Virgin, Aldermanbury: A Brief History</u>. London: The Faith Press.

Royal Commission on Historical Monuments.
    1929   "The Church of St. Mary Aldermanbury," <u>The Monuments of London (City)</u>. London: The Royal Commission, pp. 91-92.

London City Churches

Birch, George.
   1896   London Churches of the xviith and xviiith centuries. London: Batsford.

Bumpus, Thomas Francis.
   1924   Ancient London Churches. rev. ed. London.

Capes, Alfred and John Moore Capes.
   1880   The Old and New Churches of London. London.

Clarke, Basil F. L.
   1966   Parish Churches of London. London.

Clarke, Charles.
   1820   Architectura ecclesiastica Londini. London: Booth.

Clarke, H. W.
   1898   The City Churches. London: Simpkin Marshall.

Clayton, John.
   1848-49   The Dimensions, Elevations, and Sections of the Parochial Churches of Sir Christopher Wren, erected in the cities of London and Westminster. London.

Cobb, Gerald.
   1977   London City Churches. rev. ed. London: B. J. Batsford.

Cox, Jeffrey.
   1982   The English Churches in a Secular Society: Lambeth, 1870-1930. New York: Oxford University Press.

Daniell, A. E.
  1907   London City Churches of the 17th and 18th Centuries. 2nd ed.
          London: Archibald Constable and Co., Ltd.

Freshfield, Edwin, Jr.
  1894   The Communion Plate of the Churches in the City of London.
          London: Rixon and Arnold.

Godwin, George.
  no date The Churches of London: A History and Description of the
           Ecclesiastical Edifices in the Metropolis. London.

Hennessy, George.
  1898   Novum Repertorium. London: Swan Sonneschein.

Jenkinson, Wilberforce.
  1917   London Churches before the Great Fire. London.

Morgan, Dewi.
  1973   Phoenix of Fleet Street: 2000 Years of St. Bride's. London:
          Charles Knight and Co.

Norman, Philip.
  1923   The London City Churches. London: The London Society, 1923.

Peusner, Sir Nicholas.
  1957   The Buildings of England. 12. London I. The Cities
          of London and Westminster. Baltimore: London.

St. Auby-Brisbane, F.
  1929   If Stones Could Speak: The Old City of London Churches.
          London: Alexander-Ouseley, Ltd.

Young, Wayland and Elizabeth.
    1956   Old London Churches. London.

Histories of England

Dictionary of National Biography.
    1973   Revised edition. Oxford: Oxford University Press.

Churchill, Winston
    1956-58   A History of the English Speaking Peoples. 4 vols. London.

Hall, Walter Phelps and Robert Albion, with Hennie Barnes Pope.
    1953   A History of England and the British Empire. 3rd ed. Boston: Ginn and Co.

Histories of London

Allen, Thomas.
    1827-28   History and Antiquities of London. 4 vols. London.

Barker, Felix and Peter Jackson.
    1974   London: 2,000 Years of a City and Its People. New York: Macmillan.

Beaver, A. B.
    1908-13   The Alderman of the City of London. 2 vols. London.

Bozer, Mary Cathcart.
    1977   The City of London: A History. London: Constable.

Chancellor, William.
    1787   Account of the Several Wards, Precincts and Parishes of the City of London from 1660 to the Present. London: G. Kearsley.

Cunningham, George.
    1927   London: Comprehensive Survey of History, etc. London: J. M. Dent and Sons.

Delaune, Thomas.
    1690   Angliae metropolis: or the present stere of London. London: Harris.

Entick, John.
    1775   The History of London ... continued to the year 1771. London: Wilkie.

Gordon, Caroline and Wilfrid Dewhurst.
    1985   The Ward of Cripplegate in the City of London. Oxford: University Press, 1985.

Gray, Robert.
    1978   A History of London. London: Hutchinson.

Hatton, Edward.
    1708   A New View of London. 2 vols. London: R. Chiswell.

Henry, Thomas.
    1828   The Wards of London. London: Gifford.

Hibbert, Christopher.
    1980   London: the Biography of a City. rev. ed. Harmondsworth: Penguin.

Howell, James.
    1657   Londionopolis. London: Twiford.

Hunter, Henry.
    1811   The History of London and its environs. London: Stockdale.

Keene, Derek.
   1987   Historical Gazetteer of London before the Great Fire: Cheapside. Cambridge: Chadwyck-Healey. 57 microfiches.

Lillywhite, Bryant.
   1963   London Coffeehouses. London: George Allen and Unwin, Ltd.

Maitland, William.
   1775   The History of London. London: Wilkie.

Malcolm, J. Peller.
   1803   Londinium Redivivum: An Ancient History and Modern Description. 2 vols. London: John Nichols and Son.

Noorthouck, John.
   1773   A New History of London. London: Baldwin.

Pearce, E. H.
   1913   Sion College and Library. Cambridge: University Press.

Pennant, Thomas.
   1825   The Antiquities of London. 3rd ed. London: Coxhead.

Schofield, John.
   1984   The Building of London from the Conquest to the Great Fire. London: Collonade, 1984.

Smart, John.
   1741   A Short Account of the Several Wards, Precinct, and Parishes in London. London.

Stow, John.
   1598   A Survay of London by John Stow, Citizen of London. London:

John Windet, 1598 (1603).

Timbs, John.
    1855   Curiosities of London. London: Bogue.

London Archaeology

Biccle, Martin and Daphne Hudson.
    1973   The Future of London's Past. Worcester: Rescue.

Grimes, W. F.
    1968   The Excavation of Roman and Medieval London. London: Routledge and Kegan Paul.

    1969   "London: Church of St. Mary, Aldermanbury," Medieval Archaeology. 13, p. 251.

    1984   "Interview with Prof. William A. Young on the Site of the Church of St. Mary, Aldermanbury," Unpublished.

    1988   "Interview with Prof. Chris Hauer, Jr. and Mr. Noel Mander at Prof. Grimes' home in Swansea, Wales," Unpublished.

Hill, Charles, Martin Millett, and Tomas Blagg.
    1980   "The Roman Riverside Wall and the Monumental Arch in London," Excavations at Bayard's Castle, Upper Thames Street, ed. Tony Dyson. Special Paper no. 3. London: London and Middlesex Archaeological Society.

Marsh, Geoff and Barbara West.
    1981   "Skullduggery in Roman London," Transactions of the London and Middlesex Archaeological Society. 32, pp. 86-102.

Schofield, John and Tony Dyson.
    1980   The Archaeology of the City of London. London: The Museum of

London.

London Topography and Demography

Cunningham, Peter.
    1891   London: Past and Present. 2nd ed. London: John Murray.

Darlington, Ida and James Howegego.
    1964   Printed Maps of London circa 1553-1850. London: George Philip and Son.

Ekwall, Eilert.
    1954   Street Names of London. Oxford: Oxford University Press.

    1987   The Concise Oxford Dictionary of English Place Names. Oxford: Clarendon.

Habben, F. H.
    1896   London Street Names. London: Unwin.

Harben, Henry A.
    1918   A Dictionary of London. London: Jenkins.

Kent, William.
    1970   An Encyclopedia of London. 3rd ed. rev. by G. Thompson. London: Dent.

Malcolm, C. Salaman.
    1916   London: Past and Present. London: Studio Ltd.

Zetterstan, Louis.
    1926   City Street Names. 3rd. ed. London: Selwyn and Blount.

INDEX

Advowson 24,33,36,38,79,89,311,395
Act of Uniformity 208
Aldermanbury
    Church of St. Mary, the Virgin,3,7,8, 9,12,14 *et passim*
    Conduit 41-2
    Court of 106,107-8,245,262
    Manor 14,37-8
    The name 10-12
    Parish of 9,35-44,
    Saxon Palace in 8,9,56
    Street 5,8,10 *et passim*
    Tenement 9,12
Aldermen 10,11,12,14,28
    Court of 11,58,189
Alfred the Great 8
All Hallow's, Bread Street, 399
Anne, Queen 200,206,219,2217,236,260 307,344
Aske, Robert 184,218,396
Axe Inn 37-8,57,76,177,209, 346-8

Baptist Head Tavern 176,230, 241,266-7
Battle of Britain 352-3
Bean, John 292-5
Bloody Assizes 210,212
Book of Common Prayer 53,58,63
Brewers Hall 32,175,177,186
Brooke, Sir Christopher 10,20, 24,28,30
Burgh 10
Butler, Lilley 227-32

Calamy, Benjamin 199,207-8, 213 ,6, 247,248
Calamy, Edmund 199,208,390
Calamy, Edmund (the younger) 229, 239,248
Calvin, John 65,206
Catholic, Roman 169,202-3,205 ,211, 236 ,337,384
Cavaliers 120-1
Cambridge University 100, 101,208, 217,272,291,296
Carter, Pierson Cathrick xxii, 296,325,334-5,337,343,345
Chantry 26,32-3,57
Charity Commissioners 274, 302,304, 306-12,319,320,323-4,344-5
Charles I 83,86,102-5,108-9, 115,117,119-23,133
Charles II 134,145-6,148-50, 157,168- 71,167-9,199, 210,214, 216
Cheapside 7,32
Church Commissioners 370-4, 377-9
Churchill, John (First Duke of Marlborough) 148,201-5,210,219, 222-4,328
Churchill, Sarah (First Duchess of Marlborough) 202,219, 222,224
Churchill, Sir Winston 317-8,32930,338, 351,353,359-65,366- 8, 386,389,402
Churchwarden 25
    Lower 217

Upper 217
City, the (see London, City of)
Civil War, English 119-33
Collins, Charles 212,295-311, 319 27, 341
Colonies, American 83,113
Common Council, Court of 106,107, 120,146,209,214,262,389,401
Common Councilman 106,261
Common Hall 106
Commonwealth 133-4,214
Commons, House of 114,124, 126,153, 225,232,281
Condell, Henry 49,76,78-81,320-1,343, 347,379
Cripplegate 4
    Roman Fort 3,9,12,14
    Ward 9,41,43
Cromwell, Oliver 109,112,121,132,133-5,143-4,145,149
Cromwell, Richard 135,144
Cromwell, Thomas 54-5
Curate, Perpetual 89,90-1, 227-8,242, 270,295

Davidson, Dr. Robert L.D. xxiv,375-9, 383,385,390,395
DeLaune, Thomas 215-6,249
Department of Urban Archaeology, Museum of London (now Museum of London Archaeological Service) 4
Disraeli, Benjamin 280,281-4
Downing, Thomas 88-90
Dubois, John 176,184,187, 189,191,213, 229
Dyson, Tony xxiii,8,10,11

Eagle Squadrons 360,402 Economics 32-44,263,284, 290-1,338,366
Edward the Confessor 11,14
Edward VI 55
Edward VII 316-7
Edward VIII 340
Elizabeth I 26,55,56-9,62-4,81
Elysyng Spital (also Elsing Spittal, Elsynge Spittal) 26,33,38-9
Epple, John 381
Estfield, William 40-1

First Folio (of Shakespeare's Plays) 78-81
Folkmoot 23,106
Ford, Simon 184-5

George I 232-4,235,348
George II 234-8
George III 238,254-6,266
George IV 256
George V 317
George Inn 177,271,307,347-8
Gibbons, Grinling 186-7,384, 397
Gladstone, William 280-4
Glorious Revolution 199,204-7, 212
Gorbachev, Mikhail 387
Goss, Charles W. F. xxii,27,42, 187
Great Fire of London, First (September, 1666) 150,157,167,173-4
Great Fire of London, Second (29

December, 1940) 353-5,365,369,397
Greaves, Richard 100
Grimes, W. F.xxiv,3,4,12,13,42,193,211, 394,403
Guildhall, The 5,11,12,22,30
Guildhall Library, The xxii,5, 310,344, 388
Guilds 30-2,58
Gunpowder Plot 86

Haberdashers, Worshipful Company of 31,218,389,400-1
Hagas (Haws) 27-8
Hanoverians 226,232-8,254-64
Harris, Robert 90-1
Harley, Sir Robert 92
Heminges, John 49,76,77-81,320-1,343, 347,379
Henry VII 51-2
Henry VIII 26,52-5
Henry, Prince of Wales 102
Hooke, Robert 178,182-90
Hopkins, Ezekiel 227
Horsbrugh, Patrick 375-7, 386,391
Husting, Court of 23,108

Independents 65,122,127,129,140
Industrial Revolution 199,247, 253,256-8, 268,285,368

James I/VI 64,81-8
James II/VII 199-204,210-1,227
Jeffreys, George 177,199,204-5,207-12, 247,250-1,271,302,327

Jones, Inigo 50

Laud, Archbishop William 103-4,127
Lawrence, John 264-7
Lectureship 69,71,99,216-7
Liu, Tai 100
Livery companies (see Guilds)
Londinium 1-4
London, City of 3,5,8 *et passim*
Lord Mayor 22,29,58,60-2,107, 108,146, 173,189,213,261-3,296
Lords, House of 111,124,126, 232,318

McCluer, Franc 359
Mander, Dr. Noel P. xxiv,349, 354-5, 376,384-5,389,396,398-400
Marshall, Stephen 116,136
Mary I (Mary Tudor) 53, 60
Mary II 199-200,219-21
Mary Queen of Scots 63-4
Mason, H. A. 341-6,349-50
Methodism 65
Militia, London 109,120
Milton, John 135,141-3,322, 343,398
Monck, George 145-7,150,205
Monmouth's Rebellion 200-1, 210
Mortlock, Canon C. B. 371,376, 384
Museum of London 369,388,403

New England 85,92,123
Newcomen, Matthew 123,125
Nonconformists 208,215,225,239,281, 326
Normans 20,22

Organ (St. Mary, Aldermanbury) 275, 311,320,334,385,398
Overseers, Parish 269,275,292
Oxford 120,203,216,227,291

Parentalia 192
Parish 23-27, 58
Parliament 52,54,84-5,102-106,117,121, 128,168-69,200,202,205-6,232,258, 263,302,337,380
Pearl, Valerie 105-6,108-10
Phoenix
Plague 35
Plague, The (1665) 150,167, 171-3
Plaisterer's Hall 32,189
Poor, Care of 57-8,70-1,73, 139-40,199, 217,228,231,239-40,242-7,261,265, 269,272,275-6,278,293-7,303,306
Poor Laws, Elizabethan 63
Presbyterian 65,104,109,1112,1212,136, 147,149,152-3,215,219,220,226,229, 292,385,389
Protectorate 133-45
Puritan 64-6,86,109
Pym, John 105,111,119-20

Quaker 145,214

Rate, Poor 273,275-7,292,294, 303,308, 319
Reagan, Ronald 387
Restoration, The (1660) 145-8,213
Rich, Sir Robert (Earl of Warwick) 101, 112-3
Robinett, Allen and Margaret 137-8,387
Roosevelt, Franklin 361,365
Roundheads 236

St. Anne and St. Agnes 183,324,371, 376,384,398,404
St. Alban's, Wood Street 7,13,241,324, 325,354,375
St. Alphage, London Wall 39, 315,325, 333 -7,344,350,369,394-5
St. Augustine, Watling St. 307
St. Dionys Backchurch 293,384, 397
St. Giles, Cripplegate 453,370-1
St. Lawrence Jewry 5,217,322, 324,325, 354,395
St. Mary le Bow 214,238
St. Mary Magdalen, Milk Street 394
St. Mary Staining 181,371
St. Mary, the Virgin, Aldermanbury (see Aldermanbury)
St. Michael Bassishaw 228,254, 299- 306,315,325
St. Michael Paternoster Royal 376,398-9
St. Olave, Silver Street 371
St. Paul's Cathedral 7,33,35,36, 181,354, 394,399
St. Swithun, London Stone 397
St. Vedast, Foster Lane 183, 324,354, 359,365,370-1,384-5,399
Salisbury, James 270-9
Saxons 6,8,13,20,22
Schofield, John xxiii
Shakespeare, William 49,64,76-81,320-

2,326,343,347,388,401-2
Sheriff 29,108,262
Sion College 39,90,147,306,310
Sisson, Marshall 377,380-3,397,405
Smectymnuus 111,141
Soke 9,27-8,36
Solemn League and Covenant 121
South Seas Annuities 234,241
Staughton, John 92
Sternberg, Frederick 377,383
Stow, John 11,73,215,393
Stratford, Nicholas 216-9
Stuarts 64,82,101,199-207, 222,232-3
Swan with Two Necks Inn 267,299
Sword, Lord Mayor's 218,306,389,400

Taylor, Thomas 91-2,108-9
Tory Party 168,202,221,224,232,254, 260,280-1,318,364-5,368
Tower of London 21,211
Trained Bands (see Militia, London)
Truman, Harry 359,380
Trustees, Parish 264,304,311
Tudors 51-81
Tyndale, William 53,65

Victoria 279-86,315-6
Vestry 23, 107,114,117,175-7,190,207, 213
    Easter 243-4,246,267, 276-7, 296,304,369
    General 23,207,214,216, 227
    Select 23,107,207
Visitation Returns 265,272, 273,278-9, 298,299-300,310,324

Ward 28-30,58,228,231,244
Wardmote 106-7,214,262
Wesley, John 258
Westminster Abbey 2,404-5
Westminster Assembly 124, 125,127, 130,132
Westminster, Borough of 210,289
Westminster Cathedral 399, 404
Westminster Confession 131
Westminster College (Fulton, Missouri, USA) 218,365, 381-5,389
Whigs 65,168,200-3, 205, 221,224-5, 232,238,254,255,260,280
William of Orange 199-200, 204-7,219-21,255
William the Conqueror 20,21
Wood, Neal S. 376,379,380,382,384,399
Woodcock, Katherine 147-8
Woodthorpe, Edmund 301-2
Wren, Sir Christopher 1,13,178-82,183-93,200,216,232-3,235,291, 322,344, 359,380,381,386,390,394,403
Wren, Bishop Matthew 101,103, 180
Wycliffe, John 53,55,56